Teaching Music through Performance in Choir
Volume 2

Also available from GIA Publications, Inc:

Teaching Music through Performance in Band, Volume 1

Teaching Music through Performance in Band, Volume 2

Teaching Music through Performance in Band, Volume 3

Teaching Music through Performance in Band, Volume 4

Teaching Music through Performance in Band, Volume 5

Teaching Music through Performance in Band, Volume 6

Teaching Music through Performance in Beginning Band

Teaching Music through Performing Marches

Teaching Music through Performance in Orchestra, Volume 1

Teaching Music through Performance in Orchestra, Volume 2

Teaching Music through Performance in Choir, Volume 1

G-7100

Teaching Music through Performance in Choir

Volume 2

Jerry Blackstone
Heather J. Buchanan
Janet Galván
Ann Howard Jones
James Jordan
Libby Larsen

Compiled and Edited by Heather J. Buchanan
and Matthew W. Mehaffey

GIA Publications, Inc.
Chicago

Dedication

To our daughters, Paige Elise Buchanan Stewart
and Veda Jane Mehaffey.

For a complete searchable index of works covered in the Teaching Music Series, as well as audio clips of more than 900 pieces, visit the Web site TeachingMusic.org.

Teaching Music through Performance in Choir, Volume 2
Jerry Blackstone, Heather J. Buchanan, Janet Galván, Ann Howard Jones, James Jordan, and Libby Larsen
Compiled and edited by Heather J. Buchanan and Matthew W. Mehaffey
www.TeachingMusic.org

7404 S. Mason Ave., Chicago, IL 60638
www.giamusic.com
Book layout: Robert Sacha
Dust jacket design: Robert Sacha
Images from Katherine Bolcar,
featuring Montclair State University Chamber Singers

Printed in the United States of America
G-7100
ISBN: 978-1-57999-663-5

Table of Contents

PART II: The Choral Conductor as Music Teacher Repertoire Resource Guides

ACKNOWLEDGMENTS

The following research associates are gratefully acknowledged for their scholarly contributions to the "Repertoire Resource Guides":

Ken Berg
Music Director
Birmingham Boys Choir • Birmingham, Alabama

Heather J. Buchanan
Director of Choral Activities
Montclair State University • Upper Montclair, New Jersey

James Bowyer
Conductor
Dorian Singers and University Chorale • University of Puget Sound

Matthew Culloton
Artistic Director
The Singers, Minnesota Choral Artists • Minneapolis, Minnesota

Tom Cunningham
Artistic Director
Manhattan Choral Ensemble
Associate Conductor
Masterwork Chorus • New York, New York

Eduardo Garcia-Novelli
Director of Choral Activities
Lamar University • Beaumont, Texas

Wayne Glass
Conductor
Sydney, Australia

William Hammer
Director of Choral Music
Blair Academy • Blairstown, New Jersey

Jennifer Haywood
Assistant Professor of Music
Ithaca College School of Music • Ithaca, New York

Christopher Jackson
Director of Choral Activities
Adams State College • Alamosa, Colorado

Brandon Johnson
Director of Choral Activities
Greatbatch School of Music, Houghton College • Houghton, New York

Lani Johnson
Director of Music and Liturgy
St Stephen the Witness Catholic Student Center • Cedar Falls, Iowa

Lani Knutson
Director of Choirs
Valley View and Centennial Middle Schools • Snohomish, Washington

Matthew J. LaPine
Assistant Conductor
Williamson Voices, Westminster Choir College, Princeton, New Jersey

G. Mikael Lindström
Director of Choral Activities
University of the Ozarks • Clarksville, Arkansas

Michael Lippert
Director of Academy Choirs
Punahou School • Honolulu, Hawaii

Matthew W. Mehaffey
Associate Director of Choral Activities
The University of Minnesota • Minneapolis, Minnesota

Marcela Molina
Doctoral Candidate
University of Arizona • Tucson, Arizona

Amelia Nagoski
Conductor and Music Editor
Naugatuck, Connecticut

Lee Nelson
Director of Choral Activities
St. Cloud State University • St. Cloud, Minnesota

Russell Nelson
Director of Music
Central United Methodist Church • Asheville, North Carolina

John Perkins
Doctoral Candidate
University of Arizona • Tucson, Arizona

Paul Rardin
Associate Director of Choirs
University of Michigan • Ann Arbor, Michigan

David Scholz
Director of Choral Activities
The University of Texas at Tyler • Tyler, Texas

Joshua Shank
Composer
Minneapolis, Minnesota

Philip E. Silvey
Composer and Assistant Professor of Choral Music Education
The University of Maryland, College Park • College Park, Maryland

Elizabeth K. Swanson
Doctoral Candidate
Northwestern University • Evanston, Illinois

Emilie Sweet
Doctoral Candidate
The University of Minnesota • Minneapolis, Minnesota

Rae Jean Teeter
Director of Vocal Music
Guilderland High School • Guilderland Center, New York

The following choral directors and music educators are gratefully acknowledged for their repertoire suggestions for the "Repertoire Resource Guides":

Jerry Blackstone
Director of Choirs and Chair of the Conducting Department
University of Michigan • Ann Arbor, Michigan

Heather J. Buchanan
Director of Choral Activities
Montclair State University • Upper Montclair, New Jersey

Bruce Chamberlain
Director of Choral Activities
University of Arizona • Tucson, Arizona

Allen Crowell
Heyward Professor of Choral Music
University of Georgia • Athens, Georgia

Matthew Culloton
Artistic Director
The Singers—Minnesota Choral Artists • Minneapolis, Minnesota

Janet Galván
Professor of Music
Ithaca College • Ithaca, New York

Eduardo Garcia-Novelli
Director of Choral Activities
Lamar University • Beaumont, Texas

William Hammer
Director of Choral Music
Blair Academy • Blairstown, New Jersey

Ann Howard Jones
Director of Choral Activities
Boston University • Boston, Massachusetts

James Jordan
Associate Professor of Conducting
Westminster Choir College of Rider University • Princeton, New Jersey

Laurie Lausi
Director of Choral Activities
Cherry Hill East High School • Cherry Hill, New Jersey

Jerry McCoy
Director of Choral Activities
University of North Texas • Denton, Texas

Matthew W. Mehaffey
Assistant Director of Choral Activities
University of Minnesota • Minneapolis, Minnesota

Amelia Nagoski
Conductor and Music Editor
Naugatuck, Connecticut

Paul Rardin
Associate Director of Choirs
University of Michigan • Ann Arbor, Michigan

Kathy Romey
Director of Choral Activities
University of Minnesota • Minneapolis, Minnesota

David Scholz
Director of Choral Activities
The University of Texas at Tyler • Tyler, Texas

Joshua Shank
Composer
Minneapolis, Minnesota

Philip E. Silvey
Composer and Assistant Professor of Choral Music Education
The University of Maryland • College Park, Maryland

Rae Jean Teeter
Director of Vocal Music
Guilderland High School • Guilderland Center, New York

Introduction

Heather J. Buchanan

The response to *Teaching Music through Performance in Choir, Volume 1* has been tremendous, and we continue to receive positive feedback from many people in the choral profession who are effectively using both the book and the companion CDs. In addition to the high school choral directors for whom that volume was specifically targeted, college and university directors, students studying choral methods, and community choir directors have all found Volume 1 to be a valuable resource. Building on the overwhelming success and lessons learned from Volume 1, it is with great pride that we enthusiastically present Volume 2 to the choral world.

As with its predecessor, Volume 2 was written primarily with the needs of high school choral directors in mind, and the selection and rating of the repertoire specifically reflect that. This is a book that is intended to be used often—it is a practical, multifaceted companion for your artistic journey. This volume can be used as a reference or guide for the selection and teaching of repertoire and also to investigate topics of interest and in doing so confirm or challenge your choices. Either way, the information herein will support and facilitate the continuing education and development of choral directors worldwide. We also know that this book will be of great interest to conductors in other forums and sincerely hope that it will continue to be used for the teaching of choral methods classes in colleges and universities.

The structure of this book is similar to Volume 1; it is divided into two parts. Part I features six chapters written by people who are highly visible in the choral field, and Part II includes the Repertoire Resource Guides, which include historical, biographical, and analytical information about 102 choral pieces for mixed voice, women's, and male-voice ensembles. My coeditor and compiler, Matthew W. Mehaffey, gives a comprehensive explanation of the Repertoire Resource Guides in his introduction to Part II.

Janet Galván's chapter, "Does It Communicate? Finding Musical Nuance and Inspiration through Score Study" provides a thematic bridge from the

Volume 1 chapters "Does It Sing?" and "Does It Dance?" Her writing eloquently conveys the means by which conductors can teach their choirs to sing with heart, enthusiasm, skill, and understanding—by thinking like a composer! Galván's chapter is a comprehensive guide to this journey, accompanied by numerous musical examples that brilliantly illustrate every point. In addition to score study, she also takes the opportunity to relate each point to the rehearsal process, and in doing so provides many valuable tools to add to the repertoire of rehearsal techniques.

James Jordan's chapter, "The Literate Choir," challenges us to reconsider traditional approaches and beliefs about teaching sight-reading. He advocates Harmonic Immersion Solfege, a new pedagogical tool for teaching choirs to "hear" in order to teach them to "read." Jordan's research is grounded in the work of American music researcher and educator Edwin E. Gordon, and the practical information Jordan provides for developing aural literacy in choirs is both illuminating and compelling.

Ann Howard Jones shares a wealth of information gathered over her extensive career and cherished years with the late Robert Shaw in her chapter "Preparing the Chorus for Performance with Orchestral Accompaniment." Many choral directors find themselves in the position of rehearsing their choir for an orchestral collaboration, and all too often they are ill prepared for the experience of turning their choir over to the orchestral conductor. Jones's chapter abounds with clear, practical advice guaranteed to produce excellent results. In addition to sharing the wealth of her own experience, she also puts the legacy and teaching of Robert Shaw into clear perspective for us.

"The Conductor's Dream: Score-Based Imagination, Improvisation, and Inspiration" by Jerry Blackstone gives us clear insight into his approach to the rehearsal process and the related activities that come with the job. His description of the imagination, improvisation, and inspiration that link the process of selecting repertoire with planning rehearsals and presenting final performances is guided by the acronym LISTEN: **L**–earn the score; **I**–magine the finished artistic product—formulate the dream; **S**–how the dream through gesture; **T**–ransform the initial sound into the dream; and **EN**–spire the performance—take the next step toward artistry.

Libby Larsen is the first composer to write a chapter for this series, and she is an appropriate choice because of her stature as a composer of choral works and her commitment to music education. Janet Galván's chapter asked us to "think like a composer"; Larsen's chapter, "Composing, Words, Music," introduces us to the composer's perspective and what she expects from the conductor and choir in the process of bringing the score to life. She begins with the inseparable relationship between words and music, the basis for musical meaning. For those of you who have ever wondered what the composer hoped for, wonder no more.

Larsen's chapter unravels the mystery beautifully with narrative descriptions and musical examples from her composition *The Settling Years*.

My chapter, "Enhancing Musical Performance through Somatic Pedagogy: An Introduction to Body Mapping for Choral Conductors" presents vital information about the importance of movement for choral conductors and singers. Quality of movement is critical for musicians because it underlies all forms of musical communication and expression. The complete choral experience begins with accurate mind-body awareness, and this chapter presents specific information clarifying the myriad of movement misunderstandings that plague conductors and their choirs and contribute to technical problems, musical frustrations, and music performance related injuries. The "urban myths" of breathing are also exposed and replaced with clear information. This highly practical chapter provides information to assist you in evaluating the effectiveness of your own gesture and also to teach your choir to perform with ease.

Volume 2 has been a team effort, and we give special thanks to each of the authors and researchers who worked with us to complete this book in record time. We also appreciate the commitment from the team at GIA Publications, in particular GIA President Alec Harris and our copy editor, Elizabeth Bentley. We are also delighted that James Jordan and Jerry McCoy are involved in the companion CD recordings, and their choirs will again provide excellent role models of much of the repertoire we present.

As we put the finishing touches to the book, all of us involved in this project have a very special feeling about Volume 2. The depth and breadth of the information are tremendous, and we hope you will take time to immerse yourself in its pages. We are absolutely sure that you will emerge from your reading with renewed enthusiasm and vigor for this very special "thing" that we choral conductors do: finding the human impulse behind the music and breathing life into it—enriching, enlightening, and inspiring the countless lives and souls of the singers who honor us with their voices and the audiences who appreciate our music.

PART I

THE TEACHING OF MUSIC

CHAPTER 1

Does It Communicate?

Finding Musical Nuance and Inspiration through Score Study

Janet Galván

On Wednesday night Susan came in at 8:45 to audition for a school choral group. The directors were tired toward the end of the second full day of auditions. Susan began singing a piece from a genre detested by the directors. Her voice was nice, but certainly not exceptional. However, as she sang, the directors found themselves drawn in and touched, and by the end of the song, one director was wiping tears from her eyes. In spite of the fact that they were hearing a song that they didn't care for by a voice that was not one of the best of the day, Susan's performance captured the directors in a way that others had not. Susan had absorbed the composer's intent. She did not allow her vocalism to get in the way of the music or the text. She used her voice as a means of expression, conveying the heart of the music that she sang. It was clear that she was singing to share music. She communicated.

Before the reader assumes that all one has to do is sing with a great deal of heart and enthusiasm, it is important to realize that heart does not communicate without skills and understanding. Without technique, we cannot express even our most treasured musical ideas. Most musicians can remember a time when they had great musical intentions but were not able to meet the technical demands required of the piece they wanted to perform. Great frustration occurs when musicians know what they want to do with the music but simply cannot do it. Robert Shaw expressed this clearly with humor when he said, "The dove doesn't descend until the cage is clean." However, performing with technique divorced from conveying the musical whole does not move an audience.

Ultimately, we want to communicate with the audience. We want to communicate the essence of the music. We want to communicate the notes, rhythms, text, and specific instructions from the composer. We want to realize the score for the audience. What is it that takes one performance out of the realm of simply singing notes and rhythms and words to an extraordinary performance? What is it that makes performances stale even though they are technically close to perfection? What is it that creates an exquisite communication from performers to audience and from performer to performer?

There is no magic pill or technique. However, the following ideas can set the stage for communication. Think like a composer, conduct like a singer, present like an actor, coach like a voice teacher, direct like a creative spirit, imagine like a child, move like a dancer, read like a poet, and respond like an audience member. This chapter can only serve as a springboard toward addressing these goals because each topic is worthy of an entire book. Although this chapter provides ideas for each of the topics, the organizing idea is "thinking like a composer." Gunther Schuller states so eloquently:

> The compleat conductor must possess a whole range of diverse talents and acquire a broad and deep knowledge of the literature that goes far beyond that required for any other type of performing artist—instrumentalist, pianist, singer, whatever. But all these talents must be encompassed in one all-embracing basic attitude: a deep humility before the art of music that contains in it a profound love for and unswerving commitment to serving that art, a humility that considers it a privilege, an honor, to bring to life the masterworks of our musical heritage, and to communicate through them to our fellow human beings. With such an unostentatious approach, the many other talents a conductor needs to possess will evolve in proper perspective.[1]

Therefore, thinking like a composer becomes the main highway of the journey through this chapter. Just as on an actual trip on a highway we sometimes find ourselves on a road that is both Highway 95 and 81, the main road of this chapter will run simultaneously with other roads of thought, including additional ideas so necessary to the communicative performance. If we begin with score study and thinking like a composer, we can discover the musical nuance in the music and work with the chorus to create the nuance in the performance.

Think Like a Composer: The Work of the Mind

> Yes, it takes intellect to reach the heart.
>
> —William Schuman

In order to be a conduit for the composer, the conductor cannot skip the work of the mind. The work of the mind is score study. Stephen Hatfield[2] encourages conductors to "think like a composer" when studying a score. Score study is the key that unlocks many mysteries. Without really knowing the score, one cannot communicate the score.

Lee Kesselman[3] encourages his conducting students to know the score as well as if they had composed it. What does that mean? For this author, it means studying the score for every subtlety. Take in all that there is to see on the musical page and understand how the piece is organized. How is it put together? Obviously, one must study and know all the pitches and rhythms. Because of the frequency of printing mistakes, this sometimes means questioning the score. For example, is that interval really supposed to be a seventh or an octave? What are the clues in the score that lead one to the answer? Are there clues from other compositions by this composer? There are many resources for score study, and the purpose of this chapter is not to repeat the many good instructions that are given but to link those instructions to thinking like a composer and to connect the score study to vital rehearsals and performances.

What does one do when the score study is complete? Elizabeth Green wrote that the goal of the conductor and chorus is to "bring the music to full fruition—to breathe life into the symbols on the printed page...a conductor and his musicians work cooperatively together toward one ultimate goal: the finest possible musical realization of the score."[4] However, thinking like a composer is a unique twist to score study. This idea of studying from the viewpoint of a composer helps stimulate one's imagination.

To begin the task of realizing the score, we need to first study the music without sound—without recordings. Avoid choosing specific phrasing simply because someone else did it. If you heard great musicians do it, go to the score to try to figure out why they made that choice. After studying the score, you might come to a different conclusion. Be sure that you see the phrasing in the score rather than imposing it on the score. Analyze the score from a theoretical standpoint. Composers tend to think in large forms first—the overall picture. Therefore, one can begin by looking at the big picture.

Think Like a Composer: Text (Read Like a Poet)

Read the text—what does it mean? Many composers write choral works because they were inspired by a specific text. This is where the instruction to read like a poet comes in. What is the meaning of the poem? Does the composer paint the text in musical ideas? How is this done? How can this be shared with the audience?

Study the poet's background. What does that tell you about the poetry? Fine composers tend to read the poem for deeper meaning. Therefore, in order to understand the musical setting, the conductor needs to do the same. A look at the musical ideas James Mulholland used to express the poetry of "Heart We Will Forget Him" provides an example of how one might go about looking at a poem, a poet, and the marriage of text and music. In demonstrating his setting of this poem, many musical ideas that are discussed with other musical examples later in the chapter will be covered. All of these musical ideas are tied to the idea of the text. The poetry by Emily Dickinson is as follows:

> Heart! We will forget him!
> You and I—tonight!
> You may forget the warmth he gave—
> I will forget the light!
> When you have done, pray tell me
> That I may straight begin!
> Haste! Lest while you're lagging
> I remember him!

TEXT, HARMONIC FUNCTION, AND MUSICAL PACE

This is a powerful poem written by a woman who chose to live most of her life as a recluse. That knowledge sheds light on the idea that she is talking to herself (her heart). The first four lines clearly go together, and Mulholland sets those four lines in a very slow tempo in mm. 5–10. He also uses dissonant tones (e.g., the tritone above the root in m. 1) that resolve to consonance.

FIGURE 1. "Heart We Will Forget Him," m. 1

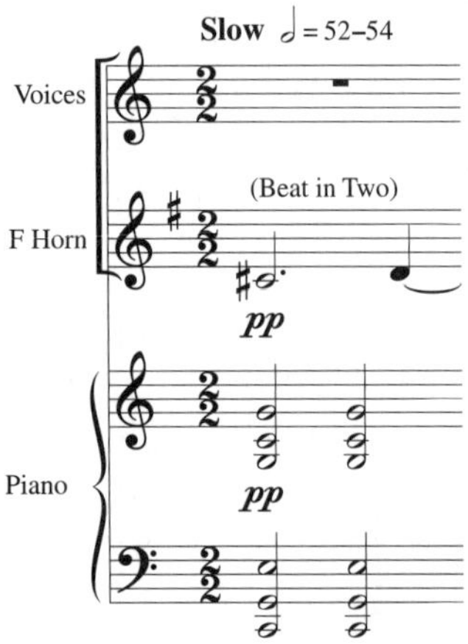

This is beautiful word painting for the torment before the resolve. The fact that the dissonance resolves upward makes it sound like a sigh. When the poet writes "tonight," as though this is the time we will forget him, in m. 11, the singers settle on the C, which has been the underlying chord throughout the first two lines. Meanwhile, the accompaniment moves to an F chord with a ninth, a seventh, and a sixth before finally resolving to a B-flat chord in m. 13, introducing a new thought—what the heart will forget and what the speaker will forget. The speaker is speaking to the heart as if a person—convincing the heart to allow her to forget. Therefore, those F chords, which move to the B-flat chord, have to influence the way the singers hold the C in mm. 11 and 12—it seems that intellect and heart are resolved, but in fact, they really are not. The C must be sung with a sense of motion. Thinking like a composer takes harmonic analysis away from an intellectual or musical exercise and moves it toward using the harmonic information as a tool of expression.

FIGURE 2. "Heart We Will Forget Him," mm. 33–47

Mulholland chooses to set the first four lines a second time in mm. 21–36; this time the tempo moves forward. In essence, the pulse is quickening as the speaker thinks of what she will have to forget. The dissonance is still there, but the accompaniment is more active. Whereas the opening is mostly in unison, the second statement is more two-part voicing—perhaps showing the division of the heart from the brain. Finally, piano, voices, and horn resolve to a firm C chord in m. 35. Immediately after the fermata on the C chord, the piece moves to a G chord (m. 36), and, through contrary motion, the voices (now in three parts) move to D in m. 37. The general harmonic movement in mm. 38–47 goes through an F-sharp chord with a seventh and a ninth moving to C-sharp major, F-sharp minor with added notes, E major, B minor, G^7 with an added ninth, C/G, Dm^7/G, G^7, and finally returning to C. This rapid harmonic movement is for the last four lines of the poem, which speak of haste.

The second setting of the last four lines (mm. 49–62) goes back to the initial tempo. Even though the speaker is asking the heart to tell her when it is done, the pace is much slower. It is almost as if the speaker is trying to regain resolve and composure. An interesting dilemma takes place in the second setting. Mulholland separates "that I may straight begin" (mm. 53–54) from the preceding, "When you have done, please tell me" (mm. 49–52). The conductor has to decide how to handle the rest in the vocal line. Does the singer connect those two phrases and sing "that I may straight begin" as a continuation of the preceding phrase, or does the conductor allow the singer to fall into the halting way of speech?

From reading the poem, the continuation seems to be a good choice. Even though the utterance of the thought is broken by time, it is one thought. Mulholland confirmed this choice in an interview about this composition. By making this decision, the conductor must then rehearse the singers to make the connection between the two phrases and sing the second phrase not as a beginning but as a continuation. Finally, Mulholland brings in the absolute torment of forgetting one's lover as he moves the dynamics, the pace, and the pitches louder, faster, and higher in mm. 57–73. Mulholland is very specific in writing in accents and ritards for the accompaniment, but the conductor must decide how much ritard to take. Mulholland expresses his thoughts: "The two representing tools that allow individual conductors interpretation are tempos and dynamics. They are the frame that surround the painting."[5]

If one considers the poetry, the changes in tempo become a vehicle for dramatically presenting the words of Emily Dickinson. At the end, the utterance becomes so slow and so soft that one thinks the speaker is truly speaking to the heart as something inside herself rather than as a different character. This is reinforced by the fact that the horn, which could be interpreted as the heart responding, now echoes the exact pitches of the voices. This idea of the use of the horn as the voice of the heart is reinforced by looking at where Mulholland decided to keep the horn silent. The heart simply listens during much of the first statement of the last four lines. After the singer speaks about the heart lagging, the horn literally lags in the slower tempo.

Because the setting is so dramatic, the piece will reach many audiences even if one only follows the directions on the page. However, if conductors read like poets and observe how the composer represents every nuance of the poem, they can come to a presentation that reflects a more thorough understanding of the marriage of the text and the music, one that is much more communicative.

Richard Cox[6] said in a rehearsal of "Choose Something Like a Star" that when a choir sings great poetry, the first thing that should strike the audience is what a great poem they are hearing. Secondly, they should think what a great musical setting it is. Finally, the response should be how well the choir sings. If we truly want to communicate, we put our egos out of the way of the art. Just as the composer works to enhance the poem, the truly communicative choir has the same goal in mind.

Text and Instrumentation

In thinking like a composer, one should also look at the instrumentation. Why was the instrumentation chosen? For example, James Mulholland loves the sound of the French horn with treble voices because he thinks the color of the French horn, with its minimal vibrato, complements the purity of the treble voice. He wrote the piano and horn parts to function as leitmotifs that serve as the subliminal ideas of the poem. Mulholland states that "the accompaniment should not be used only to support the voices in pitch and dynamics but should be used for an emotional addition to the composition."[6] They are a part of the framework. He uses the horn as a character, another voice—a voice without words. In other cases, one can ask how the color of that instrument is used. How does the composer vary the voicing? What are the reasons? Why is one section unison? What happens in the accompaniment? How is it varied? Does it bring out details of the text? How should the accompaniment be shaped? The conductor must include the accompaniment in the preparation of the score, and the conductor must have an ideal in his or her head for how the instrumental lines are to be played.

Text and Dynamics

In "The Little Land," from *Four Heartfelt Anthems*, David Del Tredici uses word painting when he carefully marks a D pedal tone softer than the harmonized melody in measures 5–9.

The pedal tone is traded between the top part (Treble I) and the bottom part (Treble III). Because the pedal is in different octaves, there is a back and forth motion reflective of sailing far away as indicated in the text by Robert Louis Stevenson. One can simply follow the dynamics, or one can "think like a composer" and grasp the imagination so important to the child in the text and the composer. This will lead to a difference in sound.

FIGURE 3. "The Little Land," mm. 5–9

TEXT AND MELODIC IDEAS

Del Tredici also makes subtle changes in the melody at the beginning of the text before all the imaginative ideas are described (mm. 5, 14, 145, and 153).

FIGURE 4. "The Little Land," mm. 5, 14, 145, and 153

A discussion of why these changes take place not only helps the singers see how the composer set the text but also allows the singers to understand the text and learn the subtle changes.

There is also a delightful moment in mm. 59–61 when Del Tredici sets the text "and the round sun rolling by" with a rolling of pitches part to part.

FIGURE 5. "The Little Land," mm. 59–61

This text setting leads naturally to using movement to help singers understand the musical enhancement of the text. For example, singers can use a "wave effect" of rolling motion to illustrate the text. Have the group that is singing the part make a circular motion and "hand off" the circle to the next group that has the idea. Once they have put this idea into a physical motion, this method of teaching will help students of various learning styles. Those who are kinesthetic have done it. Those who are visual have seen it. Those who learn aurally have heard it.

Think Like a Composer: Present Like an Actor

The discussion of "Heart We Will Forget Him" began with the text. The first step was to examine what the composer did to enhance the text. The next step must come from the singers and the conductor. The chorus needs to relate to the audience like actors.

Some of the people with the most beautiful voices have a difficult time showing expression. This is a skill that requires practice. Videotaping rehearsals is sometimes horrifying but revealing to the singers. Another activity to help encourage acting as part of the presentation is to have students work in groups and "act out" the piece. This can be used for a small section or an entire piece. The director can also give brief stage directions for rehearsals that lead students to a livelier place. In Randall Thompson's "Alleluia" from *Place of the Blest*, there is only one word—"Alleluia." The piece begins very softly and builds. To get singers to think like actors, one idea to enhance meaning is to have the singers decide what each "alleluia" means. In past experiences using this method, the results written in the scores varied from alleluias for chocolate to alleluias for a mother surviving breast cancer. However, the result was that the alleluia became more than a written word, and the audience saw more than blank expressions or a one-face-fits-all singing expression.

Knowledge of the meaning of the text is central to communication. Having students contribute ideas of what they think the text means is also stimulating and leads singers to independent thinking and initiative. For example, the conductor can occasionally ask questions throughout the rehearsal process. This makes the process more collaborative and invites the singers to commit to the poetry and the music. Again, this allows the singers to relate more personally to the text and invites them into the process of fully preparing a score.

Think Like a Composer: Structure and the Role of Dynamics

> Practice in minute detail until every note is imbued with internal life and has taken its place in the overall design.
>
> —Pablo Casals

The conductor needs a clear idea of how the parts fit together. In the Mulholland piece, the singers must listen and respond to the other parts to make the piece work artistically. At the end of the composition, when the sopranos are singing high Gs and As, the other parts must sing with the same drama in order to give the first sopranos the support they need.

FIGURE 6. "Heart We Will Forget Him," mm. 69–70

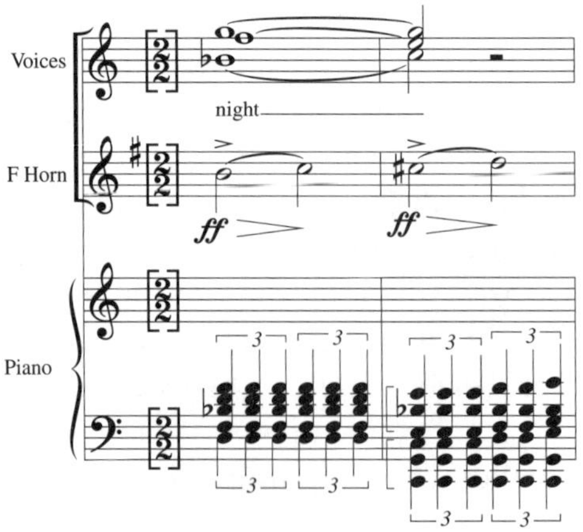

The first sopranos need to hear the lower parts in order to sing with nuance. When they are singing the G, they must listen to hear when the second sopranos move from dissonance to consonance. If they listen to the movement of the horn and piano, it will help them maintain the flow of breath and keep the note alive rather than allowing it to become static, pinched, shrill, and overbearing.

In working for balance, we can use humor to make the point. I have often used the analogy "One part is Gladys Knight. The others are the Pips."[7] The Pips are there to enhance Gladys, not to cover her. However, if Gladys never listens to the Pips, her performance will suffer. (Younger singers have to learn the identity of Gladys Knight and the Pips. Once they know this is a singer and back-up group, you have a shortcut direction. "Listen! You're not Gladys. You're a Pip!")

Every choir really needs to function like a large chamber group with each member listening carefully both within the section and across sections. For this reason, changing formations in rehearsals is a great idea. We can build sectional unity by having each section rehearse in a circle so that each voice within the section can listen to every other voice. This also helps singers get over the fear of being heard. If circles are impossible because of space limitations, the first row can face the second row, and the third row can face the fourth row. To help singers hear across sections, the entire group can be in a huge two-row circle. The conductor can also place risers in four corners of the room by sections. Each section stands in its normal formation, but each section can hear all other sections clearly.

When composers go to great lengths to pass around an idea from voice to voice, conductors need to be aware of that technique and allow it to be heard rather than allowing the same part to dominate throughout or for all parts to sing equally throughout. This clarification of form does not happen if we are going note to note, part to part. It happens when we teach the music from a compositional standpoint.

FIGURE 7. "Gloria," mm. 8, 14, 20, and 28

Copyright © 1975 by Boosey & Hawkes, Inc.

In passing around thematic ideas from part to part, dynamics play a part as well. How loud is *forte*? Are there degrees of *forte*? For example, in Dominick Argento's "Gloria" from *The Masque of Angels* the altos make the first choral entrance in m. 8 with a melodic theme that is eventually introduced in each voice. That is marked *forte*.

When the altos move to the next melodic figure in m. 14 and the basses enter with the first theme, the basses are marked *forte*. There is an articulation marking for the altos (marcato), but there is no dynamic marking. Therefore, the altos are in the range of *forte*, but along with the marcato marking and new thematic idea, the altos can pull back slightly in volume in order to enhance the original theme in the bass voices. As the texture thickens with the addition of new ideas and the passing of each idea to other voices, the voices not singing the original theme must sing in a manner that allows the original theme to be heard.

"Gloria" will come across differently if the singers understand how the music is constructed. In rehearsals, for example, one could teach this piece by thematic idea, beginning with all voices singing the opening alto part. Singing with movable Do also aids in making the structure clear. For example, begin with D as Do in the alto part. Me, Te, and Le are included in the line. Then, sing in A when the basses enter, again using Te, Me, and Le.

Sing the original theme in E when the tenors enter in m. 20, and finally in G when the sopranos enter in m. 28. Then add the second idea, tracing it from alto to bass to tenor. (The tenors have a slight deviation from the statement in the other voices.) This awareness of the other parts helps the choristers sing in a manner that allows the audience to hear how the various parts interact. The singers understand the gradual build to the end as the first theme is turned upside down, altered, put in canon, and ultimately leads into a grandiose burst of praise.

This idea of making the form clear for the audience can also be seen in Mozart's "Laudate pueri" from *Vesperae solennes de confessore*, K. 339. In many chorus rehearsals, the first sing-through results in all singers on all parts singing full voice with little or no regard for the other voices, for who has the main idea, or for how the part they are singing fits into the whole. In one rehearsal after a particularly loud reading, Robert Shaw said to one section of the chorus, "I think if you sing less and listen more, we'll hear more Bach." In the Mozart, if everyone sings full volume and is unaware of the structure of the piece, then it sounds like a big "mess" of loud singing.

It becomes our duty to make sense of the music for the audience. If everyone sings all parts at the same volume level, we do not hear the compositional genius. One way to make singers aware of who has the part that should be in the foreground is to have the section members stand when they have the most important idea. The results can be quite comical but also quite instructive. In a painting, the artist provides a distinction between foreground and background through various techniques. In the same way, the performer must be aware of the techniques needed to show foreground and background in the musical composition.

Think Like a Composer: Illumination of Information to Facilitate Learning the Piece

Although the original meaning and root of the word rehearsal is not "rehear," the idea of using "re-hear" is a good way to guide rehearsals for energy and to keep interest. If a goal for the conductor is to allow singers to hear something new in the composition (i.e., "re-hear") during every rehearsal, the compositional ideas can be brought out over time. Then rehearsals become engaging and informative rather than seemingly endless repetitions, and the understanding of the composition as discussed previously will guide them. Formation, movement, solfege, count-singing—when to use each technique becomes clearer with analysis. This leads to the idea of responding like an audience. What is important for the audience to see and to hear? Your answer could influence the formation of your choir, from sections to mixed, from formal to informal, from standing still to movement.

Dana Wilson's "I Love My Love" is based on the octatonic scale, alternating half and whole steps. Once the singers understand that, the pitches become easier because each half step and whole step is not being learned in isolation, but as a pattern, as a harmonic language. Each passage in which the octatonic scale is used is not a new set of patterns but something familiar set slightly differently. Knowing this saves rehearsal time. At the beginning of the piece, in mm. 1–3, the conductor needs to hear all three parts as one composite pattern. The outer two parts form a rhythmic duet linked by the steady movement of the middle part. At m. 4, the first soprano enters with the first line of text by Samuel Taylor Coleridge. Although there is no indication for a change in articulation, the change in writing style and lack of any staccato markings let the conductor know the text needs to be sung in a more legato fashion.

FIGURE 8. "I Love My Love," mm. 1–4

It is also helpful to know that the octatonic scale beginning on C can "lock in" to the C major triad so that it can be practical: C (D-flat, E-flat) E, (F-sharp) G. This is helpful in the transition from m. 43 to m. 44.

FIGURE 9. "I Love My Love," mm. 43–44

Think Like a Composer: Choice of Tempi

> A great work of art is made out of a combination of obedience and liberty.
>
> —Nadia Boulanger

How seriously does a conductor take metronome markings? First of all, one should know whether the marking is that of the composer or an editor. If it is an editor, it is simply the opinion of one musician, not a direction from the composer. Beethoven was the first major composer to use metronome marks. Although he was said to have been very careful in selecting those markings, he was also known to perform his works at tempi different from the markings.

Sometimes knowledge of the composer is helpful. I know, for example, that James Mulholland is meticulous about choosing metronome markings. However, I have worked with other composers who simply want the composition within a range of the marking. A good rule is to begin with what is indicated. Try it. For example, in "This Is the Day," Gerald Smith marks the chorus entrance at quarter note = 76. Taken at the composer's intended tempo, the music takes on a very different feel than it does at a faster tempo that is frequently chosen by conductors. It's a great piece and will certainly sound good at the faster tempo. However, Smith really did intend to have the piece taken more slowly.

Sometimes the initial reaction to a composer's marking is that it is wrong, and the natural instinct is to take it much faster or slower. However, after living with the piece, we discover that certain parts of the music are highlighted more with the original marking, and it is worth the effort to fight the natural instinct. That being said, there have been many occasions in working with composers in which I have followed their metronome markings seriously in preparation for their hearing my group, but I really felt that the music needed to be at a different tempo. When the composers have arrived on the scene, I have presented my dilemma to them and gotten responses such as, "Oh, yes, I think you're right" or "I was really being rushed to put a specific marking down, but it's too fast." However, when taking liberties with the metronome, following the instructions such as *allegro vigoroso* or other clues on the page will help to find the tempo that works.

There are other considerations in varying from a prescribed metronome marking. Some pieces call for a specific tempo, but if moving a bit faster allows your group to sing with more sense of line, more energy, or more in tune, it is appropriate to consider those factors in making a decision. Factors influencing tempo change include the size, age, and vocal abilities of the ensemble. The performance space also makes a difference. Is the room very reverberant? Is there a sound delay? If so, a slower tempo should be considered. Some tempi that work beautifully in cathedrals do not have the same effect in a school auditorium. Taping rehearsals and listening objectively when you are not in front of the group can also help. When listening as an outside observer, problems in tempo become obvious. Listening objectively while you are actively involved in the performance takes time.

Other questions to ask in preparing a piece include how much accelerando you want, or how fast *presto* or any other marking really is. Many of these answers are dependent upon the musical context, which means we must also understand musical practices in relation to period and style. What is the style of the piece? How much do you know about that style? What instructions does the composer provide in the score? All of these questions can be answered through careful study, but it is the questioning and seeking of answers through score study that lead us to nuance.

Think Like a Composer: Rhythmic Structure and Movement

In Stephen Hatfield's "Las Amarillas," the key to keeping the piece together is having singers know when they are on the beat and when they are off the beat and finding the duets within the piece.

FIGURE 10. "Las Amarillas," mm. 29–31

At m. 29, the Treble IIs have the melody. A typical mistake in m. 31occurs when the Treble IIs rush when they hear offbeats around them. However, if they have a strong sense of being on the beat and know where the beat is, they will wait for the fourth beat of m. 31. This sense of feeling the beat also helps in feeling the offbeat. In order to feel the offbeat, one has to feel the beat.

Likewise, beginning in m. 30, the Treble Is and the Treble IIIs trade rhythms. That is to say that the Treble I begins with a four-note figure beginning on the second half of one. The Treble IIIs have the same figure beginning on the offbeat of four. Having the singers feel this physically

FIGURE 11. "Las Amarillas," mm. 41–45

through stepping the beat together allows the singers to internalize the rhythm. They focus on keeping the beat steady as they watch the conductor (who really functions like a dance band leader in this piece) to be sure that they are all moving as a unit.

The conductor should not try to "do the rhythms for the singers" but teach the singers the secrets of singing on and off the beat so that they can be independent. This same idea can be applied to mm. 41–45 where the outer two parts trade rhythms of onbeats and offbeats while the inner part is in a different rhythmic feel and must focus on being on the beat on beats one, two, four, and five and on offbeats after three and six. If the singers are led to this independence, they can find their way back even if they get into trouble. They become more independent musicians.

Think Like a Composer: Style, Cultural Context, and Movement

Once the conductor has studied the score of "Las Amarillas" and read the notes from the composer, the secret to teaching this difficult piece becomes clear. This piece also leads to a topic mentioned earlier—style. Hatfield gives many hints as to the style he wants. His notes make it clear that this is not a piece in which singers stand still with their hands by their sides as is done in a Western European classical tradition. The music must be memorized in order to execute the hand clapping and body percussion. How do dancers from Mexican culture move to this type of music? This music comes from a tradition in which the audience listens actively—with movement. Therefore, learning the music through a process of movement and freedom is crucial to understanding the cultural context.

When preparing to conduct "Las Amarillas" with this freedom of movement, the conductor needs to practice moving in a way representative of the culture. The conductor must feel the rhythmic underpinning, which is from a tradition other than classical music. When we approach music from a culture other than our own, understanding the cultural context is important. For example, many cultures do not dress in formal black attire and stand still on risers separated from the audience reaction until the ending applause. If you have the opportunity to attend a World Symposium on Choral Music or another venue with choirs from many cultures, you will see choirs standing in varied formations, moving, playing instruments, and wearing colorful outfits representative of their culture.

In today's world, there is a wide array of resources to help us see authentic performers and gain some knowledge of the cultural context. One can purchase CDs and DVDs or search the Internet. There are also many choirs throughout the world touring and performing at various conferences in the United States. Learning any style, from Baroque to West African singing, dancing, and drumming, requires learning a set of practices within a cultural context. If dance is at the heart of the tradition, one must dance. Besides embracing dance for the cultural context, conductors need to move like dancers because conductors who move easily are able to convey more styles and show phrasing so much more musically.

The conductor's body is his or her instrument. Therefore, conductors need to be expressive with their bodies. There are many ways to become less rigid looking. Taking courses in various cultural styles of dance will help in the study and performance of music from various countries. Any activity that helps with releasing the body, such as certain types of yoga, Tai Chi, Body Mapping, Feldenkrais, or The Alexander Technique can help conductors become more comfortable in their own bodies. This will be beneficial in releasing inhibitions about moving.

Think Like a Composer: Coach Like a Voice Teacher

> I'm not interested in having an orchestra sound like itself. I want it to sound like the composer.
>
> —Leonard Bernstein

Technique, Language, and Vocal Color

As we think like composers, we also need to consider the vocal sound that the composer is requesting or indicating. One of the most striking things I learned from growing up in North Carolina was that the human voice is capable of many colors and that color is heavily influenced by vowel production. Even within my small church, there was one vocal color used by choir members when singing classical music and another color used when singing the country hymns on Sunday night in the basement of the church or during revival week. This color was stretched even further when performing spirituals in the school choir. Because the local speech had a bit of a Southern drawl that tended to produce a spread sound and the director wanted a sound like that of the Tuskegee Choral Institute,[8] students learned immediately that the repertoire had an influence on vocal color. The conductor wanted to recreate the spirituals in a way that Anton Armstrong refers to as "respectful and successful interpretation with integrity."[9]

Because the ease of hearing sounds from throughout the world has opened our ears to a wider palette of vocal color, we must question which vocal color is appropriate. This is true of various cultures, styles, and periods. We cannot know for certain the preferences of composers who are no longer living, but there is an abundance of research to guide decisions of color, weight, and timbre. Sometimes one has to guess, but the guess can be educated.

When performing "Chinese Mountain Songs" by Chen Yi, there are no directions for vocal color. However, when working with choirs Chen Yi instructs groups to use a very percussive, bright quality. Many singers are hesitant to do this because it seems as though they are mimicking a different culture and that the imitation could come across as disrespectful. However, one can emulate the color of a specific choir without being disrespectful. In the case of the Chen Yi folk songs, the effect of singing the pieces with an American lyrical tone really makes the pieces sound like very different compositions. In an interview, Chen Yi said she had a specific vocal color in mind. To ignore this is to ignore timbre as much as someone would who substitutes a trombone for a cello.

Technique, Language, and Word Stress

Along with vocal color, we need to consider word stress in all languages. Is the stress pattern for the language different from English? Has the composer set the text in a way that allows the natural stresses to be present? In order to think like a composer when singing other languages, we need word-for-word translations. We could miss much of the word painting without such a translation. Also, it is important to understand the way the language sounds. Does the language have distinguishing timbre, rhythm, vowels, or consonants? Consider Camille Saint-Saëns's "Salut au chevalier printemps."

Figure 12. "Salut au chevalier printemps," mm. 7, 12, 16, 34, and 105

He set the text so there is a tension release on the word "ride," which ends in the mute <e> in m. 7. In singing (as opposed to speaking), the mute <e> is sounded if that syllable is set on a different note. In speech, however, the mute <e> would either be silent, sounded only as the hint of a schwa, or in poetry reading, sounded, if necessary, for a syllable count. Although the French stress appears only on the final syllable of a single utterance in spoken French,[10] most authorities would agree that pulling back in volume on the schwas absent in spoken French makes the singers sound more like native French singers.

In this composition by a French composer, the musical setting supports this idea. All uttered final schwas are in places involving musical stress release (m. 7), where the final note gives way to a new idea (m. 12 in the alto part), where the final note is lower in pitch (m. 16), where the final note is of lesser rhythmic value (m. 105 in all parts), or where the final note is set on a weaker beat (m. 34). Knowing that final schwas follow the stressed sound in the spoken language allows the delightful musical phrasing to come through to the listener. If one sings the mute <e> with equal weight to the main vowel in the stressed syllable, the sound of Saint-Saëns's phrasing is lost.

One way to convey word stress in foreign languages to American singers is to say a sentence in English with equal word stress on all syllables or to emphasize the wrong syllable (e.g., I AM goING shopPING TOday.).

Sound Technique for Maximum Expression

As one works with any composition, one must teach and guard vocal technique. Therefore, in analyzing the score, the conductor links thinking like a composer to preparing to guide singers to meet the technical demands of the score. In many school situations, the choir teacher is the only teacher of fundamental skills of vocal technique. Fundamentals lead to freedom in performance. The best way to have fun on the stage is to be prepared both technically and musically. If one is struggling with technique, it is hard to communicate. Therefore, some rehearsal time needs to be spent on building technique and skills. We need to build muscle memory of sound vocal technique. Students have to have more experience doing things correctly than doing them incorrectly. To accomplish this, the choral conductor needs a clear understanding of the vocal mechanism and the characteristics of healthy singing.

Good body alignment is essential for the singer. One thing conductors can do to encourage good posture is to demonstrate it as we conduct. A well-grounded posture demonstrates strength. If you as a conductor are wandering all over the podium, your students will not feel a firm foundation for their sound. If you stand with your feet locked together, that tends to give a sense of tense energy centered higher in the body. As singers, we need to be connected to and energized from the lower body. If you stand with that connection, your singers will find it easier to connect to the breath. Where is your conducting plane? If it is too high, it will raise your shoulders—not an ideal position for singers.

One of the aspects of singing frequently overlooked in choral rehearsals is breath. In singing, as in life, breath is a cornerstone. We can relax our singers and ourselves by breathing deeply. An exercise to engage the breath for the conductor is to imagine that the arms will not move without being started by breath. Move your arm without breathing. Then move your arm as a result of the breath—as though the breath moved the arm. The feeling and the appearance are totally different. Try this with singers. Start phrases with and without breath. This helps singers memorize the feeling of what it is like to begin the sound on the breath. Allow your preparatory beats to be drawn from a place that seems as if you are drawing from the breath. This will encourage breath from your singers and will remind them of their vocal training in breath management skills.

Another important part of technique for singers in a choir is vowel formation. Vowels are the backbone of tone. The conductor must have a thorough understanding of vowel formation. Combined with good breath management, good vowel production leads to a resonant tone. While warm-ups are a great place to work on uniform, round vowels, this work needs to be continued into the repertoire. The conductor must make decisions about how each word is to be pronounced before the first rehearsal. Much technique can be taught through good vowel work. The corners of the mouth should not be spread sideways for any vowels. A good expression to use is "long, tall vowels." Much technique can be taught through good vowel work. It is important for the conductor to know exactly how to pronounce each vowel, including diphthongs and triphthongs. Singers of any age can understand and sing good vowels.

Think Like a Composer: Pitfalls on the Road to Phrasing

> The heart of a melody can never be put down on paper.
>
> —Pablo Casals

Performance of many musical genres generally involves going to a point of a phrase, reaching a point, or coming from that point. Phrasing takes us from a note-to-note approach to shaping an idea. This can come about in a number of ways. In general we want a sense of movement toward the point of the phrase. Phrasing is also achieved through the natural rise and fall of syllabic stress created through articulation, dynamics, and slight tempo shifts. There are several pitfalls to legato phrasing. Leaps upward tend to sound louder. Unless one wants the higher note emphasized, singers need to sing that higher note more softly in order for it to sound as though it is part of the phrase. Another pitfall is encountered when singing a series of notes of equal value. Whenever that occurs, the singers have to work hard to create forward movement from one note to the next.

Yet another obstruction to creating phrases occurs when singers give in to the "tyranny of the barline." Even though the barline is only there to help organize the music, too many times singers are affected by the barline and put undue emphasis on the downbeat or think of a break at the barline. One very famous example of this is at the end of Benjamin Britten's "This Little Babe" from *A Ceremony of Carols*. I have heard performances in which there is a break between mm. 63 and 64, between mm. 65 and 66, or between mm. 68 and 69.

FIGURE 13. "The Little Babe," mm. 63–70

If one looks at the text and Britten's instructions, it seems that those breaks would not be taken. The text is "If thou wilt foil thy foes with joy, then flit not from this heavenly Boy." The only logical place for a lift or a breath is in m. 65, after the word "joy." Britten gives us hints by placing a *crescendo* leading to the downbeats of mm. 64 and 66. He also provides the instruction *sostenuto*. The harmonic underpinning shows a clear movement to the downbeat. In m. 63, there is a D chord on the third beat leading to a G chord on the downbeat of m. 64. Likewise, in m. 65, there is an F chord on the last beat leading to a B-flat chord on the downbeat of m. 65. As for the connection from mm. 69–70, one has to decide whether saying "boy" should become an event separated from the rest of the text or simply the exciting ending to the phrase.

The conductor also needs to remember that commas in the text are not instructions for breaths, but marks of punctuation. There are times when a comma does indicate a lift or a breath, but it does not always do so. Sometimes, like the barline, the punctuation simply organizes the poetry into lines. Another common problem with phrasing is that singers will take a breath before a final big chord. One has to guide the singers to realize that this is not always appropriate. Should that final chord be separated from what has come before?

Good phrasing goes back to listening across the chorus. What is the interplay between parts in reference to stress, release, dynamics, and movement? If one note is held and there are moving notes in the other parts, where are the stress and release? Those singing the held note need to listen to the moving parts in order to shape the held note. Those singing the moving notes need to be aware of how those moving notes relate to what else is happening. Are there other moving parts? Is some sort of duet going on? Are the moving notes moving with dissonance and consonance to the held notes? All of these details lead to shaping each line to create the whole effect set by the composer. The composer cannot write every nuance of shaping. This must be determined and carried out by the performer.

Movement is an effective way to deal with teaching phrases. Having students move in a way in which they are stepping the notation but allowing their upper bodies to show the phrasing creates awareness and a thoughtful process to discovering phrasing. One can also do simpler movement activities such as having students push their hands forward for stress and back for release or having two singers work together by pushing one palm to the palm of another singer for stress and releasing for the release. Helping students become aware that there is always motion in music paves the way for better phrasing. I once heard a pianist say that it was not the notes that he played that made the artistry but what he did between the notes; in other words, how he moved from one note to the next had a great effect on the resulting sound.

Finally, another pitfall of phrasing relates to the earlier discussion of the Mulholland—missing the big picture of the text and its relationship to the music.

In "Yet Gentle Will the Griffen Be" Francisco J. Núñez paints an incredible picture of the mythical creature.

FIGURE 14. "Yet Gentle Will the Griffen Be," mm. 25–29, 34–35

Núñez, moved by the visual images of the poetry of Vachel Lindsay, created an aural image to enhance the visual. The piano accompaniment becomes the griffen in its larger-than-life, flamboyant nature. The listener hears the griffen "creep across the sky" in the scalar passages of the piano. In mm. 26–29, Núñez creates laughter by having the pitches become faster and faster until the voices transform into laughter. That is a big hint for the phrasing in mm. 34 and 35. If one stresses the first note of each measure and pulls back on the others, the voices sound as if they are crying as they sing the word "cry." The message is there from the composer, but one has to understand the visual images and understand the child's imagination to communicate this piece with the energy so clearly notated on the page. It is necessary for the conductor to speak with the drama and energy of the text and to find a colorful vocabulary for description.

Think Like a Composer: Direct Like a Creative Spirit

> Notation, the writing out of compositions, is primarily an ingenious expedient for catching an inspiration with the purpose of exploiting it later. But notation is to improvisation as the portrait to the living model. It is up to the interpreter to resolve the rigidity of the signs into the emotion.
>
> —Pablo Casals

In the end, studying the score determines the rehearsal plan. If one truly teaches the score, the students perform with more understanding. Ultimately, the understanding leads to communication. Studying every detail of a score helps the conductor find musical nuances that are otherwise missed. The nuance takes the chorus to elevated communication. It is obvious if students have learned only their parts and really do not have an understanding of the whole work. It would be like having someone learn only their lines to a play and when to say the lines without understanding how their character fits into the play or what the play is about. Lines out of context have no more meaning for choral singing than for acting.

For the teacher, musical understanding is also important educationally. It is unacceptable for a student to be in chorus for four years and have his or her accumulated knowledge be the ability to sing the tenor part to forty-five songs. We need to teach musical understanding and musical independence. In this way, students become musical apprentices and are able to make music on their own after the schooling is completed. However, the motivating reason for musical understanding is that it changes the way one performs a piece of music and, in turn, what the singers and the audience get out of the performance.

As one undertakes the work of thinking like a composer, the general question becomes "Why did the composer do this?" This sparks imaginative thought. It can be very helpful to include ensemble members in this questioning. If something seems odd or unexpected, first try to decide why the decision was made through score study and research on the composer, the period, the style, or the text. If we can find a good reason for the composition to go the way it does, then we can communicate it with more conviction. It is hard to communicate effectively when you are not convinced. Many great actors say that they must find a motivation for their character to take the actions they take. This is particularly true for roles in which they portray less-than-desirable actions. The actor must believe in the character to portray the character, just as the musician must believe in the music.

People sometimes ask, "What if your reasoning is not what the composer had in mind?" Obviously, we do not want to impose external ideas on the music that take it away from the composer's intentions. However, if we are getting our clues from appropriate research and score study, we generally will not wander too far from the composer's intentions. This is a fine line. However, if the composer has put down what he or she wants on the page and we study this with musical integrity, we will come closer to a desired performance rather than further away. Several composers have said that the conductor who really digs into the score will often find ideas that were not conscious choices but had to be somewhere in their minds. In other words, the person who is trying to bring the work to life can often find things in the creation that the creator has yet to see.

One very important part of thinking like a composer is to take every opportunity to meet, study with, and collaborate with composers. If there is any way to commission a work from a composer with whom you can work closely, not only do you and your choir get to premiere a new work, but also you will learn so much during the process. There are incredible opportunities to work with composers at conventions, at workshops, and at colleges and universities. These are also places to meet more experienced conductors who have worked with many composers or who have expertise in a certain type of music.

Finally, thinking like a composer compels us to study every detail of the score before we begin the process that is called interpretation. Gunther Schuller prefers the term "realization," a term he got from Ravel, who said that one should not interpret his music, but realize it. Schuller contends that most conductors do not heed quite a bit of what is in the scores for them to see. When conductors consider the fact that they are the voices of the composers, realizing a work of art becomes an awesome responsibility.

One of the goals of conductors is to have singers in any ensemble they direct rejoice in the gratification that comes from working hard toward a goal and realizing the immense satisfaction that comes from making the music come alive. We try to set an atmosphere at concerts that says "We love singing and would sing together whether you, the audience, were present or not. However, since you're here, let us share this music with you." Share the music! That is the goal.

By thinking like a composer, one can grasp the details of a score that can lead to nuance. By fully digesting the score, the conductor can lead the singers in a choral ensemble to a performance with a variety of shadings, intelligence, drama, and energy. The process will also be more interesting and challenging. All of the conducting and singing skills should be employed with the goal of communicating the music to the audience. This does not diminish the need for technique. However, without the guiding score, what is the point of technique?

Béla Bartók described it in the following manner: "In a performance setting, there can be no monologues. Every note, every breath, each moment sends messages between musician and listener. To ignore this two-way flow of feeling and meaning is to relinquish artistry for ego-gratification."

The composer is always our team teacher. The composers and repertoire that we choose to perform define the chorus and the performances. Our ability to study the score determines whether we have truly shared the music with the singers and the audience. In thinking like a composer, we can get closer to communicating on a higher level. Complete study of the score allows inspiration to enter.

In discovering the inspiration of the composers, we become inspired. If we are inspired, we will find a way to communicate. Thorough knowledge of the score unleashes ideas that might otherwise not be considered and allows conductors to readily understand the composition and get to the essence of the music. When conductors combine intelligence with intuition and thorough knowledge of the score, we find creative and practical solutions to the challenges in the music. Then we understand more fully what the challenges are, why they are challenges, and how to rehearse the ensemble to meet those challenges. Rehearsals and performances become vital and energetic. The chorus and the conductor become one expressive vehicle that can elevate the audience to a better place for that moment in time.

Just as working with voices is a sacred trust, taking someone's creation and bringing it to life is a sacred trust. We are presenting a work of art. To do so with anything less than our most intense effort is unacceptable.

Yes, it will communicate!

Notes

1. Gunther Schuller, *The Compleat Conductor* (Oxford: Oxford University Press, 1997).
2. Stephen Hatfield is noted for his exciting arrangements of world music and for his original works weaving influences from diverse cultures into a fresh and distinctive idiom. His choirs have earned gold medals at national festivals, and he has received various awards for his work in education, music, and poetry, including the Governor General's Gold

Medal. He is often featured as a guest conductor and workshop leader throughout the world

3. Lee Kesselman is director of choral activities at the College of DuPage. He is known for his original works, folksong arrangements, editions, and awareness of historical and international styles. Kesselman is founder and director of the New Classic Singers, a professional choral ensemble, and has been a member of the faculty of the CME Institute for Teacher Training since its inception in 1986.
4. Elizabeth A. H. Green and Niccolai Malko, *The Conductor and His Score* (Englewood Cliffs, NJ: Prentice-Hall, 1975).
5. From a conversation with James Mulholland, August 2005. Mulholland is a much published and performed composer and arranger. His compositions have appeared as required repertoire on more than forty state high school choral lists. In addition, they are performed regularly by universities and choral associations throughout the United States, Canada, and Europe. Mulholland has written commissioned works for many choirs throughout the world, including the Los Angeles Children's Choir, the International Children's Choir Festival, and the American Choral Directors Association.
6. Richard Cox was director of choral activities and professor of voice at the University of North Carolina at Greensboro for many years.
7. I use the name of this particular popular singing group because the name is so colorful. Some of my singers have to be told who Gladys Knight is, but the image still works. Any pop group with back-up singers would work.
8. William Dawson founded the Tuskegee Institute of Music in 1930 and, over the following twenty-five years, led its choir to international renown. His most famous work, the *Negro Folk Symphony*, had its world premiere in 1934 with the Philadelphia Orchestra, under the direction of Leopold Stokowski. Dawson's arrangements of spirituals now represent part of the canon for choral societies throughout the world.
9. Heather J. Buchanan and Matthew W. Mehaffey, ed., *Teaching Music through Performance in Choir, Volume 1* (Chicago: GIA Publications, 2005).
10. "Introduction à la phonétique corrective"—Pierre et Monique Léon (Hachette/Larousse, 1976); Jane Kaplan, Ithaca College, professor of French language and literature.

Compositions discussed in this chapter:

Argento, Dominick. "Gloria," *Masque of Angels*. New York: Boosey & Hawkes, 1975.

Britten, Benjamin. "This Little Babe," *A Ceremony of Carols* (treble). New York: Boosey & Hawkes, 1943.

Chen Yi. *Chinese Folk Songs*. King of Prussia, PA: Theodore Presser, 1998.

Del Tredici, David. "Little Land," *Four Heartfelt Anthems* (treble). New York: Boosey & Hawkes, 2003.

Hatfield, Stephen. "Las Amarillas." New York: Boosey & Hawkes, 1995.

Mozart, W. A. "Laudate pueri," *Vesperae solennes de confessore*. WB Music Corp., 1996.

Mulholland, James. "Heart We Will Forget Him" (*colla voce*, treble). Tustin, CA: National Music Publishers International, 1985.

Núñez, Francisco. "Yet Gentle Will the Griffen Be," *What Grandpa Told the Children* (treble). New York: Boosey & Hawkes, 1997

Saint-Saëns, Camille. "Salut au chevalier printemps" (treble). Dayton, OH: Lorenz/Roger Dean, 2002.

Thompson, Randall. "Alleluia," *Place of the Blest*. Boston: E. C. Schirmer Music Co., 1971.

Wilson, Dana. "I Love My Love" (treble). New York: Hendon Music/Boosey & Hawkes, 1997.

References

Buchanan, Heather, and Matthew W. Mehaffey. *Teaching Music through Performance in Choir, Volume 1*. Chicago: GIA Publications, 2005.

Elliot, David J. *Music Matters: A New Philosophy of Music Education*. New York: Oxford University Press, 1995.

Green, Elizabeth A. H., and Niccolai Malko. *The Conductor and His Score*. Englewood Cliffs, NY: Prentice-Hall, 1975.

Schuller, Gunther. *The Compleat Conductor*. New York: Oxford University Press, 1997.

Recommended Resources

Advanced Training in French Pronunciation. Middlebury, VT: The College Store, 1949.

Bartle, Jean Ashworth. *Lifeline for Children's Choir Directors*. Toronto: Gordon V. Thompson Music, 1988.

———. *Sound Advice: Becoming a Better Children's Choir Conductor*. New York: Oxford University Press, 2003.

Carduner, Sylvie. *D'Accord: La Prononciation du Français International, Acquisition et Perfectionnement.* New York: John Wiley, 1982.

Castel, Nico. *A Singer's Manual of Spanish Lyric Diction.* Foreword by Plácido Domingo. New York: Excalibur Pub., 1994.

Colorni, Evelina. *Singer's Italian: A Manual of Diction and Phoenetics.* New York: G. Schirmer, 1970.

Cox, Richard G. *The Singer's Manual of German and French Diction.* New York: G. Schirmer, 1970.

———. *Singing in English: A Manual of English Diction for Singers and Choral Directors.* Lawton, OK: American Choral Directors Association, 1990.

Dansereau, Diane M. *Savoir Dire: Cours De Phonétique et de Prononciation.* Lexington, MA: D.C. Heath, 1990.

Decker, Harold A., and Colleen J. Kirk. *Choral Conducting: Focus on Communication.* Englewood Cliffs, NY: Prentice-Hall, 1988.

Glenn, Carole, and Howard Swan. *In Quest of Answers: Interviews with American Choral Conductors.* Chapel Hill, NC: Hinshaw Music, 1991.

Haasemenn, Frauke, and James Jordan. *Group Vocal Technique.* Chapel Hill, NC: Hinshaw Music, 1991.

Jeffers, Ron. *Translations and Annotations of Choral Repertoire: Volume I, Sacred Latin Texts.* Corvallis, OR: Earthsongs, 1988.

Leon, Pierre R. *Phonetisme et Prononciations du Francais: Avec des Travaux Pratiques D'application et Leurs Corriges.* Paris: Editions Fernand Nathan: 1997.

McKinney, James. *The Diagnosis and Correction of Vocal Faults.* Nashville: Broadman Press, 1982.

Miller, Richard. *The Structure of Singing: System and Art in Vocal Technique.* New York: Schirmer Books, 1986.

Neuen, Donald. *Choral Concepts.* Belmont, CA: Schirmer/Thomson Learning, 2002.

Rao, Doreen, and Bill Pierson. *Circle of Sound Voice Education.* Boosey & Hawkes/Alfred Publishing, 2005.

Robinson, Ray, and Allen Winold. *The Choral Experience: Literature, Materials, and Methods.* Long Grove, IL: Waveland Press, 1992.

Uris, Dorothy. *To Sing in English: A Guide to Improved Diction.* New York: Boosey & Hawkes, 1971.

Willetts, Sandra. *Beyond the Downbeat: Choral Rehearsal Skills and Techniques.* Nashville: Abingdon Press, 2000.

Janet Galván, professor of music at Ithaca College, conducts the Ithaca College Women's Chorale and the Ithaca College Chorus and is artistic director for the Ithaca Children's Choir. In great demand as a guest conductor, Galván has conducted all-state and larger regional honor choral festivals throughout the United States. She was the sixth national honor choir conductor in the over forty-year history of ACDA. Galván is also the conductor of the North American Children's Chorale that performs annually in Carnegie Hall. In 2002 she conducted the Mormon Tabernacle Choir.

Her own choral groups have been chosen to perform at national, regional, and state music conferences, invitational choral festivals, and in concerts in the United Kingdom and Europe. Galván has also served as master teacher and clinician at national, regional, and state conferences of the American Choral Directors Association (ACDA) and the Music Educators National Conference (MENC). She has been featured at workshops in Brazil, the United Kingdom, Belgium, and Canada and at the 2002 World Symposium on Choral Music. Galván's expertise in treble repertoire led to an association with Roger Dean Publishing Company and the publication of two choral series. She is also the series advisor to Latin Accents with Boosey & Hawkes. Galván was a member of the Grammy Award–winning Robert Shaw Festival Singers during Shaw's final years.

CHAPTER 2

The Literate Choir

James Jordan

Introduction

Choral music education has been, perhaps correctly, focused on providing choirs with sight-reading skills. Many states have adjudication standards for sight-reading. However, for some reason, we have taken our eyes off of the correct "pedagogical ball." It is my goal to convince you of the value of teaching hearing rather than reading. I will also try to make the case that, if hearing is taught via the choral ensemble, music reading occurs as a convenient by-product of choral rehearsal pedagogy.

The Language Parallel

The method of teaching both music and language should be parallel, but in many ways, they are not. When we learn language, we learn how to speak individual words, and then we learn to speak those words in short phrases. When we speak in those short phrases, many times the grammar is not quite right because, as young communicators, we have not yet deciphered the system. After a while, we begin to communicate in sentences. When we attend school, we learn how to read. What is important here is that reading is the last step in the process. Reading occurs only after the sound of the language is familiar to our ears. When we come with "language in our ears," we can learn to read. Reading then becomes a simple act of association. That is, we associate written signs with sounds we already have heard and used in daily conversation.

Lowell Mason, in his handbook for the teachers of the Boston Public Schools in the beginning of the nineteenth century, asked teachers to teach the ear before the eye. Classroom teachers who use and adapt the teachings of Zoltán Kodály understand this basic tenet of teaching. But, for some reason, the same procedures for learning language have become a bit mired within the confines of the choral rehearsal. Teaching choirs to read notation before they have significant instruction in how to hear is a futile, if not hopeless, task.

What Is Literacy?

There seems to be confusion concerning what qualifies as literacy in the world of the choral ensemble. In fact, this confusion abounds when speaking of the training of musicians in general. It is generally believed that for a musician to be classified as "literate" they must be able to read. This rather broad definition skips over the many subcategories under the heading of literacy: reading literacy, writing literacy, improvisational literacy, and timbral literacy. An inability or deficiency in one or more does not qualify someone as illiterate. The question that begs answering from a pedagogical perspective is which one is most important to becoming a musician. In fact, the question may be: which is most essential and central to the development of musicianship?

Good Rote versus Bad Rote: Essentials of Music Understanding

The work of American music researcher and educator Edwin Gordon has provided both theory and experimental evidence to help the cause of understanding the music learning process. Because of his work and the work of those who have followed him there is now a clear pedagogical roadmap for music learning that deserves our attention, care, and heed.[1]

The problem, as I see it, begins with the actual rehearsal process and specific procedures employed to teach a choir a piece of music. Rehearsals that focus only upon music reading do not advance the cause of hearing within the choral ensemble. Rehearsals that begin with introducing a piece of music with text, I believe, confound the music learning process for the singers. The pedagogical process must allow for ample time for singers to aurally acquire the music without the complications of text.

The ability to hear is the key for all other music learning to take place. It also seems that educators need to be given necessary pedagogical tools to facilitate choirs to hear sounds in the correct musical context if those pieces are to have both musical meaning and understanding. Without sounds heard first without text, which are then associated with music symbols after they

1. The writings and research of Edwin E. Gordon form the foundation for the pedagogical procedures and philosophies presented in this chapter. Readers who desire further detail and clarification of these underlying principles should consult Gordon's writings listed in the bibliography of this chapter. The volume *Learning Sequences in Music: Skill, Content, and Patterns* was the germinating text for much of my thought.

have been firmly planted in one's hearing (audiation),[2] choirs will never understand what they are hearing. Stated in another way, sounds sung without being heard and understood will never be retained or be able to carry any human content.

What Is Essential to Begin the Music Listening Process?

There are basic ground rules concerning music listening within an ensemble. It dawned on me several years ago that choral ensembles are not taught to hear in the same way that instrumental ensembles are taught to hear. As a clarinetist, I was always taught two important facts: 1) I needed to listen to everyone else except myself when playing in the ensemble and 2) if I did hear myself, I was either overblowing my instrument, or I was out of tune.

If one thinks about how choral singers view their roles and responsibilities regarding choral ensemble singing, the exact opposite is usually true. Choral ensembles are not taught to listen across the ensemble. In most choirs, singers believe it is their job to hear *only* themselves! Translated into a choral rehearsal, the rules for instrumentalists work well for choral musicians.

1. *Develop a heightened aural awareness in every rehearsal so that you listen to everything else musical except yourself. Listen harder and with the greatest awareness of sound possible!* By doing this, several complex objectives are accomplished with little effort. Listening now becomes a matter of broad aural awareness rather than an issue of focusing on a single or a few aspects of music.
2. *Listening to everything else except yourself includes listening to the accompanist and the accompaniment. Listening to all other voice parts and also listening to the accompanist will contribute to ongoing and progressive developments both as ensemble singers and musicians.*
3. *Develop aware listening that acknowledges the presence of the harmonic structure one is singing at all times rather than only having awareness of isolated melodic material. Keeping a choir in a continual state of aural awareness of the harmonic structure reaps many musical rewards. Intonation improves because of such vigilant and constant awareness. Aural music literacy grows by leaps and bounds when musical language is*

2. The concept of "audiation" is central to all the ideas presented in this chapter. This word, coined by Edwin Gordon, is an umbrella term to describe the complex act of hearing. Audiation is the ability to hear musical sounds without those sounds being physically present. The focus of all aural literacy teaching for any ensemble should be audiation rather than music reading. Music reading will occur as an associative act after the sounds of the music have been acquired with meaning through a defined teaching method and a body of teaching procedures.

acquired within a harmonic context. The melody or their individual parts are always learned within the context and syntax of the harmonic structure.

Remember that listening to only one part actually masks and retards musical growth because "the part" is learned devoid of the harmonic structure that defines the function and expressiveness of individual parts. *Harmonic context is everything in developing literacy in a choral ensemble.* The harmonic structure clarifies and defines mode, the momentum of musical line, the human content of the music, and the color and texture of the piece. Given its important function, it seems that harmonic structure and the hearing of that structure through an increased, almost an acute and omnipresent aural awareness, is the key to the musical growth and flourishing of the literate choir.

The New Role of the Choral Accompanist

If one believes in the pivotal role that harmonic awareness has in the development of the literate choir, then it follows that the role of the accompanist needs to evolve. Accompanists, when empowered by the conductor, can play a central role in the rapid evolution of the literate choir, providing the conductor observes some important pedagogical ground rules.

The choir should "input" every choral piece through the use of solfege syllables. During the learning process, all choral parts should always sound, so as to keep the choir constantly immersed in its harmonic "sea." Without the presence of harmonic surroundings, individual vocal lines have limited musical meaning. Harmonic structure defines each part. An analogy would be to consider a choral rehearsal similar to building a puzzle. Assembling a puzzle without the completed picture of the puzzle as a guide is the same as learning a piece without the harmonies always being sounded. The moment one reduces the rehearsal to the singing of a single part, musical growth comes to an abrupt halt. Consequently, the accompanist must, instead of merely doubling the parts, be empowered by the conductor to provide other aural cues to accelerate the literacy growth of the ensemble. What are those aural cues, and which can act as catalysts for the ensemble's musical growth?

The Accompanist's Aural Cues: Wordless Clues to the Harmonic Structure

If the conductor remains constantly vigilant about reminding the choir to listen to everything except themselves, then the stage is set for individual singers to hear other musical information that may be transmitted nonverbally by the accompanist. That information acts, in a way, like a harmonic road map for the choir. After careful analysis of the music by the conductor and the accompanist,[3] areas of changing modal structure can be identified. In medieval music, this has been labeled as modal modulation. That is, while transitions between modes are achieved harmonically through chromatic chord structure, shifts between and among modes are what singers aurally recognize.

Choral singers, for the most part, do not hear harmonic relationships. In their ears, I believe they hear music as quick, sometimes aurally abrupt shifts, similar to changes in the texture and color in a patchwork quilt. These shifts, if identified and acknowledged by the conductor through analysis, provide the aural context and parameters for listening and, hence, aural literacy development. Remember this important fact: while trained and aurally experienced musicians can hear using the knowledge of music theory, younger or musically inexperienced choirs simply become aurally confused when theoretical harmonic structures and relationships are used as the only vehicle for musical learning. In an aural sense, while those relationships exist in a theoretical world, they rarely, if ever, exist in the aural world of the choral singer. It takes a fairly sophisticated and experienced musician to wed the intellectual elements of music theory to one's ear.

To be able to hear music moving to another key area is one thing, but to remember the original key and mode area that began the piece and then relate all that comes after it and then tune new passages to the original tonic or resting tone of the piece is virtually impossible for everyone except a highly experienced ensemble of schooled and theoretically savvy musicians. While you as the conductor may be able to hear in that way, the choir that sits in front of you, in all likelihood, probably cannot. Students with high tonal aptitude[4] within your ensemble will most certainly be able to hear as

3. It is important that the analysis by the conductor and the accompanist *not* focus solely on harmonic structure but on the modal structure of the work. Harmonic analysis has little relevance in the development of aural ensemble literacy. The harmonic structure, as defined by mode in most choral music, is the key to literate aural development. This system of analysis is detailed in the text *Choral Ensemble Intonation: Method, Procedures, and Exercises* (Jordan and Mehaffey, GIA Publications). Practical applications can be seen and studied in the solfege editions of the Evoking Sound Choral Series (GIA Publications). Pieces in the series include: "Amazing Grace," "Love's Gift," "She Moved through the Faire," *Geistliches Lied*, "Pange lingua," "Elegy," "O God of Light," "Alleluia, Alleluia, Hearts and Voices Heavenward Raise," "Come, Labor On," "He Gave Them Hailstones," "Love Is Life," "When Spring Is Born at Last," "Psalm 100," "I Wonder as I Wander," "Come, Soft Slumber," "I Close My Eyes and Dream," "The Coventry Carol," "Nobody Knows the Trouble I've Seen," "God Rest Ye Merry, Gentlemen," and "Venite exultemus Domino."

4. The concepts of both developmental and stabilized music aptitude as measured by the standardized tests PMMA, IMMA, and AMMA are discussed in the chapter concerning music aptitude in the text *The Choral Ensemble Warm-Up* (Jordan, GIA Publications, 2005).

experienced and sophisticated musicians and be able, in most cases, to wed music theory with the music they sing. But it is the other 95 percent of your choir that may need some additional aural direction and help. The accompanist can provide that help.

Once the piece has been analyzed for aural function,[5] the accompanist can depart from merely doubling notes of the choral score. In fact, he or she should abandon as much of this doubling role as possible. The accompanist, listening to the choir at all times, should provide dominant ostinatos in alternating octaves above the tessitura of the choir. The providing of the dominant function for the mode that the choir is currently immersed in provides the most valuable context for establishing meaningful aural points of reference. When the dominant is clearly sounded as an ostinato in alternating octaves above the tessitura of the choir, the choir can and does infer (quite remarkably) the tonic or resting tone of the mode they are in and on.[6] When those modal parameters are established in their ears, intonation immediately improves, and the choir is able to "learn" the music because it has been entered into their hearing (audiation) in a musically meaningful way.[7]

While it may seem that the providing of this very simple device may not be effective, once used, its results are astounding, even for the most inexperienced choirs. So "listening to everyone except yourself" acquires new importance. Not only should choirs be kept in constant aural awareness of all parts other than their own, but their listening frontiers should be expanded to include *always* listening to the aural information provided by the accompanist.

"In a Mode or Key" versus "On a Mode or Key"

Perhaps this is a semantic play of words, but the difference between "in" versus "on" is central to understanding the aural world of the literate choir. When one is "in" a mode, one is able to aurally relate that mode to all modes

5. The basics of this analysis approach for performance can be studied in *Choral Ensemble Intonation: Method, Procedures, and Exercises* (Jordan and Mehaffey, GIA Publications) and can be seen in performance editions in the Evoking Sound Choral Series listed at the end of this chapter.
6. One can study this concept in published accompaniments by Marilyn Shenenberger. The reader is referred to the *Ear Training Immersion Exercises for Choirs: Choral Exercises in All the Modes* and *The Choral Warm-Up: Core Vocal Exercises* (both GIA Publications).
7. Examples of this technique can be seen and heard on the *Choral Ensemble Intonation* Video (Jordan and Mehaffey, GIA Publications). This technique for choral accompaniment can be seen and studied in *Listen! Introductory Harmonic Immersion Solfege for Individuals and Choirs* (Shenenberger), *Modal Warm-up Exercises for Choir* and *Accompanied Canons for Choir* (Ames, Shenenberger, and Jordan), and in the *Ear Training Immersion Exercises for Choirs* (Jordan and Shenenberger), all published by GIA Publications.

(and key relationships) that have come before it. Few choral singers can do this without there being serious damage done to intonation. I believe that choral singers exist in an aural world in which they are "on" a mode or key. That is, they hear every new mode or key area as a separate and unrelated musical event!

For many years I attempted to "help" the choir by explaining via music theory the nature of the key/mode relationships in the futile hope that intonation and reading would improve. They never did. I have long since acknowledged that most singers hear in a "musical quilt" sort of way. That is, each new mode or key, in their ears, is a new and separate musical event, unrelated to anything except where they are at that moment. Moreover, I am convinced beyond a doubt that singers, for the most part, only hear in major. And, when confronted with a mode that is not major, they will make reading mistakes in an attempt to morph their parts toward a major tune.

In order for a choir to become aurally literate, the battle of harmonic relationships and interdependency should not be waged. Solfege should be used to organize their vocal parts in relation to major.[8] If parts are then sung with the harmonic structure present, it sounds as though, almost by accident, that the singers possess an understanding of complex harmonic relationships that usually takes years of study and musical experience to develop!

What Is Essential to Become Musically Literate?

Music literacy exists in various forms. There is reading literacy, hearing literacy, improvisational literacy, compositional literacy, and style literacy. The list can go on and on. Of everything on the list, hearing literacy is the most important because none of the other literacies can happen with any degree of true meaning or understanding without hearing. In short just as we cannot learn language unless we can remember it, we cannot learn music unless we can remember what we have heard. When we remember what we have heard, we can bring those sounds to notation and give it meaning. In that way, true musical understanding via meaning begins to take hold.

The essentials of what it takes to begin this process are stupendously simple. The basic elements of choral ensemble music learning are twofold: consistent tempo and resting tone. For one to learn and make sense of the

8. These teaching procedures are detailed in two publications, *Choral Ensemble Intonation* (Jordan and Mehaffey) and *Ear Training Immersion Exercises for Choirs* (Jordan and Shenenberger), both published by GIA. The first volume details the theory of using solfege within the choral rehearsal. The second volume is an ear training method for choirs that uses Harmonic Immersion Solfege exercises that prepare the choir's ears for what will be heard within the choral rehearsal. The methods involved with the dominant ostinatos are detailed in the *Ear Training Immersion* volume.

structure of rhythm in a musical way, all rhythm must be learned within the confines of consistent tempo. That is, when a piece is read with a choir, the conductor must ensure in some pedagogical way that a consistent tempo is being both aurally and kinesthetically reinforced. That reinforcement, I believe, must be from an aural, external source such as a metronome.

It is important that as a choir hears a piece for the first time, they hear it at a consistent tempo. This way, they can then understand, or rather, intuitively perceive and then understand, the structure of the rhythm. However, without an omnipresent and overriding sense of consistent tempo, it is impossible for rhythm to be perceived and then organized in any logical way in one's hearing. What is important to understand about rhythm learning is that it is the kinesthetic, or the feeling, of "being" in a tempo that both hastens and anchors rhythmic understanding. Without an overriding sense of consistent tempo at all times, there can be no, or at least only a very limited sense, of rhythm. The use of overriding and omnipresent consistent tempo promotes accelerated rhythm understanding, and, hence, retention.

Thought of in another way, choirs will never perform in a consistent tempo unless all rhythms are aurally received via a consistent tempo. Choirs that are allowed to read pieces and "learn" pieces awash in a sea of inconsistent tempo are hearing every piece in unusual meter! Consistent tempo is the vehicle by which sounds are organized and retained in a musician's ear.

Regarding the pitch aspects of music, the parameters are somewhat similar. All parts must be sounded at all times. Harmonic context is everything for reasons I will detail in the following section. Parts should never be sung alone and should always be sung first with a neutral syllable and then immediately following using a system of solfege that organizes the pitches one is hearing almost like file cards. The accompanist should provide dominant ostinatos in alternating octaves above the tessitura of the choir. If one ponders how instrumental ensembles learn pieces, whether the group is an orchestra or a jazz ensemble, pieces are read and rehearsed always while all parts are being sounded. Parts are very rarely rehearsed out of their harmonic surroundings. When parts are rehearsed separately, it is usually done to fix specific technical problems. Choral ensembles will make more significant musical advances if conductors can read choral works with all parts sounding because this improves the intensity and awareness of ensemble listening skills.

The Human Dilemma of Listening

Before any degree of musical hearing can take place, choral ensembles must understand that the hearing ears that they bring into the choral rehearsal each day are woefully inadequate. Simply stated, choral singers bring into rehearsal the ears that they use in daily life. The world we live in dulls our hearing and protects us, in a way, from the things we would rather not hear in the world. Choral singers must be constantly reminded to heighten their hearing awareness by simply listening harder and listening to everyone except themselves. Listening and, consequently, hearing involve being in a constant state of awareness. Vigilance on the part of the conductor on this single element will solve many intonation problems. Aware hearing should be the overriding factor of any choral ensemble rehearsal.

To Text or Not to Text: That Is the Question

Actually, the use of text when learning a piece should not be a question. To read with text severely inhibits the musical growth of an ensemble. In fact, it stops any aural development of the choir. In any human, language is a powerful force. Much of our thinking occurs using language. The portion of the brain that houses language is *not* the portion that houses music. When one uses language to read a piece of music, one lives in the side of their brain where language resides, not music! Inexperienced or young choirs cannot hear the tonal or rhythmic aspects of the music when language is vying for their brain function. It is impossible to build a musically literate choir with the use of text. They hear music as a "bundle" of information, both sound and text, and are never able to separate the two. Moreover, the use of text hopelessly confounds the music learning process and the developing musician. Text should only be added after the music has been learned with either a neutral syllable or a system of movable-Do solfege.

Resting Tone

Just as important as consistent tempo is to the understanding and performance of rhythm, resting tone has equal importance to the tonal understanding world of the singer. In reality, one is able to sing in tune because one is able to "understand" or "hear" what anchors any tonality, the resting tone of that mode and the dominant function of that mode. Without these two aural markers, one will remain adrift in a harmonic sea of sorts. Choral ensemble intonation suffers in most choral ensembles because the choir cannot track both the initial resting tone and dominant, and then they are unable to shift their hearing when a new dominant and resting tone appear. Repeated rehearsal does not help the singer out of this aural confusion, and, hence, the ensemble never really sings in tune. The conductor must correctly analyze the music to determine shifting resting tones with respect to mode, not harmonic structure! And singers must be guided to use a system of solfege that will organize the modal structure in their ears.

Harmonic versus Melodic Hearing

Central to understanding the choral rehearsal dynamic, is an understanding of how choirs learn their parts. Many of us have been educated using principles of what I call "interval replication solfege." That is, we learn to sing tunes based upon their inherent intervallic structure, i.e., singing by intervals. We are taught to learn the sound of a major third, a perfect fifth, a perfect fourth, and so on. However, that system is severely problematic. That system works flawlessly as long as those intervals appear in the confines of major. Taken out of major and placed in various modes, a simple major third may transform itself into a very difficult interval based upon its harmonic surroundings or harmonic context.

Consider the following example. If I sing the descending minor third Sol–Mi, a descending minor third, many would agree that it is the most common interval found in music. Also, many would agree that it is an "easy" interval to sing. Well, in major, that may be true. But if I take that same interval and label it Do–La in minor, it becomes more difficult to both recognize and sing. Why? Because of its harmonic context!

A minor third can appear in many different harmonic contexts, bringing either an increase or decrease in difficulty. The same interval, depending upon its harmonic surroundings, can become more difficult than it is in major. Taken one step further, depending upon the mode (major, minor, Dorian, Phrygian) and the harmonic surroundings, some simple intervals in major become more difficult to *hear* in other harmonic contexts. Solfege is the only way by which the conductor can teach to the increasing difficulty of the same interval in different harmonic contexts. Systems of melodic interval recognition have little long-term learning validity because intervals learned in major do not transfer to other modes. Singing a sixth to the tune, "My Bonnie Lies over the Ocean" works for the tonality of "My Bonnie." But take that interval into Phrygian, and it assumes another character. Training people to recognize intervals devoid of harmonic surroundings has little pedagogical value outside of major.

The Dilemma and Challenge of the "Major" Ear

One of the casualties of such interval recognition training is that, like it or not, choral directors might more seriously adopt a more stringent pedagogy toward choral ear training when they simply acknowledge that choirs only hear in major. If you think about your most recent choral rehearsal, you may realize that every note error made, especially in the first reading of a piece, resulted when the choir tried to make the piece in major. Moreover, that situation is compounded by the fact that during the warm-up process nothing is done to prepare the choir's ear for the mode or modes they are about to hear.

The choral conductor must understand that, when left unattended, the default of every choir is to hear only in major. When preparing or reading a new piece, left pedagogically abandoned, they will try to fit that new piece into their major world. So the choral conductor must attack this problem on two fronts: 1) prepare the "ears" of the choir for what they about to hear (major, minor, Dorian, etc.) and 2) analyze the music with respect to its melodic structure to prescribe a system of solfege that will operate from the strength of major. While harmonic analyses of pieces are important in later stages of music ensemble learning, I have found that melodic analysis that reduces parts to the closest version of their "major ears" reaps the most immediate benefits both for musical recall and choral intonation.[9]

For an ensemble to improve its hearing skills and, consequently, its literacy, an approach to rehearsal that involves always sounding the entire harmonic structure of a piece becomes a necessity. Thought of in another way, no part should be sounded devoid of its harmonic surroundings. Without the harmonic surroundings, a choir will not be able to place the scale construction within its appropriate mode or its appropriate musical context. When that occurs, intonation will become highly unstable because choirs lose track of where the resting tone and dominant function are. Without the resting tone and dominant function, music understanding will be limited. Moreover, choirs that fail to understand the harmonic context (in an aural way) of what they are singing will never be able to read with any degree of understanding and will certainly be unable to retain much of what they read. So, instead of using the term "sight-singing" to refer to the reading process, perhaps we should use a term that more accurately reflects the process, "sight-hearing."

The Acoustic Environment of the Choir— The Alto-in-Front Seating Arrangement: Maximizing Your Choir's Sound and Hearing Potential

The rehearsal acoustic of the choir can either help or hinder the aural literacy development of the singers in that ensemble. In fact, the way your choir sits in rehearsals can either rapidly improve their musical hearing skills or pose an insurmountable pedagogical barrier to their aural development. This seating arrangement works regardless of the acoustics of your rehearsal space. A

9. To assist the choral conductor, I have has created a series of solfege editions using this approach, known as Harmonic Immersion Solfege. These editions, labeled clearly as Solfege Editions, are available in the Evoking Sound Choral Series published by GIA.

resonant acoustic is obviously more desirable than a dry or dead space, but this seating arrangement works in both situations.[10]

Several years ago, I rediscovered this seating arrangement and have never returned to a traditional block arrangement for rehearsals or concerts. Weston Noble introduced me to this concept of choral seating. Consider the following seating arrangement for an SATB choir, using a *curved* formation. The singers marked in boldface mark the beginning of the section as determined when an acoustical standing is done.[11]

FIGURE 1. Alto-in-Front Seating Arrangement

←————————————→

B1 B1 B1 B1 B1 **B1 B2** B2 B2 B2 B2 B2
T1 T1 T1 T1 T1 **T1 T2** T2 T2 T2 T2 T2
S1 S1 S1 S1 S1 **S1 S2** S2 S2 S2 S2 S2
A1 A1 A1 A1 A1 **A1 A2** A2 A2 A2 A2 A2

Conductor

Regardless of the numbers of singers in each section, four rows and only four rows should be used. Double rows should not be employed. If one examines this set-up, several things become apparent. First, most conductors will agree that it is important for the alto section to be able to hear pitch within the ensemble to remain stable. Placing them in the front row assigns the altos to the prime hearing and listening location. Second, this set-up actually creates a quartet standing arrangement, vertically from front to back. Third, all sections of the choir can hear the bass section because the sound of the bass section comes over the "top" of the choir. Fourth, choral blend is enhanced because the use of acoustical space is maximized. This arrangement disburses choral sound much more equitably than traditional block arrangements.

Fifth, because of the physical spaciousness of this arrangement, choral sound, or rather the overtones within sections, does not get "jammed" or backed up. In this arrangement, overtones mix more easily using a more spacious acoustic. Sixth, all sections will hear better, especially in polyphonic music. Seventh, the larger voices within your choir will find it easier to sing without tension because they are free to make sound in this arrangement and should not need to lessen their sound or be shushed by the conductor. And

10. This seating procedure and a procedure for determining standing positions for individual singers are detailed in the chapter on Standing Position in *Evoking Sound: The Choral Warm-Up* (Jordan) and can be seen in the DVD by Weston Noble, *Achieving Choral Blend through Standing Position* (both GIA Publications).

11. This procedure can be found in *Evoking Sound: The Choral Warm-Up* (Jordan, GIA).

eighth, and perhaps most important, this arrangement lessens or eliminates what I refer to as the choral grunt. I have found that when choirs sit sectionally, due to the abundance of like overtones surrounding them, the vocal mechanism becomes tired and stressed because the environment requires them to "make" sound. Also, because of the restricted resonant space around them, they do not accurately perceive their sound and, hence, rely less on the sensation of singing correctly and more on the sound that overcomes them.

Larger voices tend to become tired, and smaller voiced tend to push because of the massive amount of sound around them. Regardless of the acoustic of the rehearsal or performance room, this arrangement is one of the most musically and acoustically efficient I have used. Choirs that sit in this arrangement never want to return to more traditional ways of seating. However, for very large symphonic choirs, this arrangement is impractical because of space and stage considerations. And, in the case of large choirs, the "striped" or vertical sectional arrangements work best.[12]

Venturing into Solfege

After some thought and reading, many conductors become intrigued with the solfege ideas I have presented. Their next concern is how to begin using solfege with their choirs. While it is hard to believe, the transition to the use of solfege is remarkably easy and effortless if the choir has had sufficient prior exposure to music via listening. Solfege syllables used within a La-based minor system provide an almost immediate intuitive aural logic to even the most inexperienced singers *as long as syllables are always used with the entire harmonic structure being sounded at all times around them.* I have found that the use of solfege using melody devoid of harmony teaches little to singers because without the harmonies surrounding them, they are free to sing intervals with whatever harmonic context they can imagine in their mind's ear.

If the choir has never used solfege, then it is recommended that two sets of instructional materials be used in the warm-up to familiarize them with syllable usage. As an introduction, I suggest *Listen! Introductory Harmonic Immersion Solfege for Individuals and Choirs* (Shenenberger/Jordan, GIA Publications, 2007) and *Ear Training Immersion Exercises for Choirs: Choral Exercises in All the Modes* (Jordan/Shenenberger, GIA Publications, 2004). These drills are able to provide a solid foundation for teaching beginning choral ensemble solfege skills.

---

12. Adaptations of this seating arrangement for other sizes of choirs and other voicings can be found in *Evoking Sound: The Choral Ensemble Warm-Up* (Jordan, GIA).

Choral Ensemble Pronunciation of Solfege Syllables

To ensure accurate intonation, some adaptations must be implemented to allow the solfege syllables to "sing in tune." If these changes are not made, despite the fact that the choir sings the correct syllable, the choir will sound out of tune because of vowel issues. Basically, the conductor must close vowels to ensure more pitch core and fundamental in the sound, remove all diphthongs, and, finally, for syllables Fa and La, make certain the sounds are high and forward. See the pronunciation guide below:

FIGURE 2. Solfege Syllable Pronunciation Guide

ACTUAL WRITTEN SYLLABLE	SUNG AS
Do	DOO
Re	REE With lips rounded in "oo" shape, wrap lips around the vowel.
Mi	MEE With lips rounded in "oo" shape, wrap lips around the vowel.
Fa	FAH This vowel is very problematic for amateur choral singers. The American "ah" is generally not high and forward enough. This vowel should be sung as a bright Italian "ah."
So (or Sol)	SOO Wrap lips around the vowel.
La	LAH This syllable has the same vowel problem as Fa. The "ah" vowel should be sung similarly to the bright Italian "ah." An additional problem is the American pronunciation of "l." Choirs must be taught to execute the "l" with the tip of the tongue. If not executed properly, the "l" is generally swallowed, causing a back placement of the vowel and poor intonation.
Ti	TEE Wrap lips around the vowel.
Do	DOO

Use of Solfege in Reading and Learning Choral Literature

It is easiest to understand the concepts advocated in this article by examining three excerpts of choral literature with the solfege analysis completed. First examine the excerpt below.

FIGURE 3. Felix Mendelssohn: "Psalm 100: Jauchzet dem Herrn, alle Welt." Evoking Sound Choral Series, GIA Publications, Inc., G-5929, mm. 32–36

The system of solfege advocated in this article places a priority on what is really heard by the singers rather than solfege assigned on the basis of harmonic function. In this system, there is an attempt to make the solfege adhere as closely to major as possible. In looking at the example above, one could solfege the entire page in F major. That would indeed work for mm. 32–34. However, if one enters into m. 35 in F, with the chromatic syllables Fi and Ri, one quickly discovers that either the choral singers cannot sing the correct intervals within the chord, or, if the notes are sung, they are out of tune. If one assigns solfege based upon what is aurally occurring in the singer's ears, the passage tunes. It is my belief that while it is easy for many of us to hear the harmonic relationship between F major and C major, inexperienced singers are not able to hold the first tonality in their ears while they sing the new area. I am convinced that singers hear the C major as new and not related to anything except itself. Simply by identifying a new Do as C and singing syllables in C major allows the choir both to *sing the music* and *sing it in tune*.

A more dramatic example of this solfege procedure can be seen below:

FIGURE 4. Roger Ames: "She Moved through the Faire." Evoking Sound Choral Series, GIA Publications, Inc., G-6507, mm. 1–5

In other systems of solfege, one would assume that the above work is in D major. However, the work is in D Mixolydian. If something is not adjusted in the learning process, the choir will always try to change the piece into D major. Not only is the piece in D Mixolydian, but it can be seen that within this Mixolydian harmonic framework the choral parts appear to be clearly in G major. Because of the harmonic surroundings of D Mixolydian, for ease of reading one should sing the vocal parts with G as Do. This allows the choir to stay in their comfort zone of major where they can negotiate the C-naturals with considerable ease and also with beautiful intonation.[13]

FIGURE 5. Johannes Brahms: *Geistliches Leid*, Op. 30. Evoking Sound Choral Series, GIA Publications, Inc., G-6480, mm. 29–32

This system works extremely well when dealing with modulating or highly chromatic passages. If one examines the passage above, it would be difficult to negotiate the passage if one's ears remained locked in E-flat major. However, one

13. To encourage accurate intonation, it is necessary to sing solfege syllables with closed vowels and to avoid the singing of all diphthongs. Also, remember to keep the syllables Fa and La high and forward because of their tendency to flat.

will find that if the sopranos solfege in C major, altos in F major, tenors in B-flat major, and basses in E-flat major, the choir sings the passage with unbelievable ease and accurate intonation. Remember, the reason for the success of this system is that the individual melodic lines, while in different keys, assume context because the harmonies are always sounded while they are singing.

Harmonic relationship, then, is inferred by surroundings. The solfege becomes a tool for accurate interval navigation. If the parts are sung individually without the others sounding, the choir will *not* be able to sing their parts. I am sure that all of us as schooled musicians would admit that we hear on various levels. Young musicians are able to hear *both* their melodic line within a harmonic structure and give the intonation meaning. This is a miraculous aural occurrence. Solfege should be used for interval replication within the harmonic structure that gives it meaning and, thereby, become the arbiter of accurate intonation, providing that singers are listening to everything except themselves.

Perhaps the most dramatic example of how this choral ensemble solfege system can be useful is seen in the following example.

FIGURE 6. Morten Lauridsen: Movement 1: "Lament for Pasiphaë" *Mid-Winter Songs*, mm. 1–3 (Opus Music/Peer Music)

If one examines the example above, reading it with any choir might prove to be very problematic. The accidentals in each vocal part would create havoc in most choral ensembles. However, if one assigns solfege based upon what the choir really hears, the problems with reading this piece disappear. The soprano and alto parts are in D-flat major. Have those parts sing D-flat as Do. The tenor and bass parts are in A-flat major. Have those parts solfege with A-flat as Do. When doing so, even though there are two key areas for solfege of the melodic material, it is the harmonic structure that gives a larger meaning to the singer's ears. Melodically, the singers will be able to negotiate their individual lines with great accuracy as long as all the harmonies are always sounded as they read their parts. Perhaps it is more appropriate to say that they will be better able to hear their parts as long as all the harmonies are sounded as they sing.

If you continue to examine the music score from m. 4, the tenor part is in A-flat major, and the bass part appears to be in E-flat. So, ask the tenors to set A-flat as Do. Ask the basses to solfege in E-flat. If you perform this simple experiment with your choir on these three measures of music, you will see that they will most likely read it without errors! Remember that the premise of Harmonic Immersion Solfege™ is that the sounding of the harmonies supplies powerful harmonic context. The overriding principle for this system is that it is an "intonational" system, not a system of melodic literacy. Melodically analyzed solfege allows the singers to negotiate their individual parts within the harmonic structure. For each succeeding phrase, do an independent melodic analysis of each part, and assign solfege accordingly. Remember, assign solfege based upon how the part actually appears, not according to the key signature.

Pursue Rhythm and Pitch Issues from Different Pedagogical Approaches

Many of the problems in achieving a literate choir have their roots in the confounding of issues of pitch and rhythm. In general, choral pedagogy has advocated an approach that attempts to remedy pitch and rhythm issues as they present themselves as problems within the choral rehearsal. This chapter advocates that rhythm and pitch literacy be approached as separate pedagogical issues in the choral rehearsal. Consistent tempo must be constantly reinforced throughout the rehearsal process if rhythm learning is to be meaningful. Pitch issues should be approached through the use of Harmonic Immersion Solfege if the choir is to acquire pitch aural literacy.

Understanding the Kinesthetic Structure of Rhythm: Teach Within a Consistent Tempo at All Times

Building rhythm skills within a choral ensemble requires patient, diligent, and consistent pedagogical efforts on the part of the conductor. Surely a choir's rhythmic ability is directly related to their inherent music aptitude as measured with a standardized test. However, regardless of that aptitude level, rhythm performance skills can be maximized through a logical approach to the teaching of the concept of consistent tempo. Consistent tempo is the grammar of rhythm. Without consistent tempo, the choir will be unable to process and organize the rhythm they hear and feel.

Most conductors attempt to teach and correct rhythm problems by simply having students echo or repeat the rhythm back after the conductor's example. This is imitation. Imitation is imitation. The choir will imitate the rhythm without any understanding. Clapping a rhythm, likewise, is a futile effort because it is an exercise in imitation. Simple clapping and simple verbal repetition should never be used as devices for correcting or teaching any aspect of rhythm. What is central to the learning and consequent understanding of rhythm as a performance tool is the teaching of rhythm using the layered structure in which we hear and organize rhythm.

All music that is rehearsed must be sung in consistent tempo. Consistent tempo is central to rhythmic, energized breathing. Rhythmic pulse is established and initiated with breath that, in and of itself, is rhythmic. Once a breath is taken within the structure of a tempo, it is the responsibility of the singer to maintain that consistent tempo. I frequently refer to Robert Shaw's often-used admonition to many choirs: "I am out of the tempo business...that is *your* responsibility."

So how does one build such a skill within the choir? Through a consistent way of inputting the three distinct layers of rhythm simultaneously! One should never allow warm-up exercises to be sung with a fluctuating tempo. If fluctuating tempo is allowed in the warm-up, then it most certainly will creep into the performance literature. Once the problem is manifest in the performance literature, it is more problematic to correct and wastes valuable rehearsal time. The teaching of consistent tempo is best accomplished during the warm-up period.

Rhythm teaching is hierarchical. That is, one must be coordinated before one can organize and feel the structure of rhythm. If a choir cannot maintain a consistent tempo, the ability to perform simple coordinated movements should be examined. Those coordinated muscle movements, once taught and drilled, will allow for a higher level of music learning to take place. Remember that, ultimately, all rhythm is learned kinesthetically. Without the ability to organize the large beats of music through the feeling of body movement, the learning of rhythm becomes a mathematical exercise. Rhythm that is thought is never learned. Only rhythm that is felt and experienced will be retained and used.

Singing at a consistent tempo is a kinesthetic state and must be taught as such. Ensembles must learn to feel what it is like to sing in a consistent tempo. The choir must establish a communal tempo for rhythm to have an exciting life of its own. The ability to recognize and perform at a consistent tempo is a prerequisite to musical performance. This ability is based upon one's ability to simultaneously hear a larger beat structure with its subdivisions. An inability to recognize and perform at a consistent tempo is rooted in one's inability to move in a coordinated manner to music. Before one learns about the larger beat structure with its subdivisions, fine muscle coordination of the body must be achieved.

Muscle Coordination Development

This fine muscle coordination is developed separately from music listening abilities, which help aurally identify larger beats and their subdivisions. Muscle coordination is usually developed using an external music stimulus, such as a recording. After the necessary coordination has been developed, a music learning process, which internalizes rhythm pulse, becomes necessary. The following coordination sequence is based upon the work of Phyllis S. Weikart (1989).

Coordination instruction moves through the following consecutive levels. Level One must be achieved before Level Two can be attempted, and so on.

Movement Coordination Sequence

1. Single Coordinated Motion of the Arms—the movement of both arms together.
2. Single Coordinated Motion of the Legs—the movement of both legs together.
3. Alternating Single Motion of the Arms—the movement of the arms alternately.
4. Alternating Single Motion of the Legs—the movement of the legs alternately.
5. Single Coordinated Motion of the Arms and Legs—the movement of both arms together and both legs together.
6. Alternating Single Motion of the Arms and Legs Together—the movement of the arms alternately and the legs alternately.

When performing the coordination sequence above, observe the following:

1. Perform the various levels of the coordination sequence seated.
2. Until you have executed a level of the sequence accurately, no external beat should be supplied.
3. After mastering a level as evidenced by a number of successful executions, then perform that level with music. Perform each level at a different tempo.

Rhythmic Response to External Music versus Internal Musical Impulse

Many people believe anyone who can move to music has demonstrated a certain rhythmic competency. Movement to music may be an indicator of a musical rhythmic understanding. It may also be an indicator that one is able to coordinate one's movements quickly to the music that he or she hears with little or no musical understanding. Ultimately, until one demonstrates in solo, without external music, one can never be sure of the origin or depth of one's rhythm responses. Traditional prescriptive rhythm exercises such as clapping the beat or clapping the rhythm may or may not indicate the extent to which someone hears rhythm.

How, then, can one be sure that one hears rhythms internally? Many rhythm pedagogies make the error of *not* having a consistent "input" strategy ensuring that one "hears" all the component parts of the rhythm structure. The choir is bombarded with many teaching "techniques" that are well meaning, but hopelessly confuse the choir and destroy their logic for the understanding of rhythm. The following approach attempts to do this.

The Structure of Rhythm and Its Relation to Choral Rhythm Pedagogy

> While most persons would agree on the importance of teaching and reinforcing rhythm skills, perhaps no aspect of music pedagogy has been subject to such confusion. Many attempts have been made to develop pedagogy for the teaching of rhythm, but that pedagogy lags behind the pedagogy for the teaching of tonal skills. Most music curricula limit rhythm content to relatively few patterns in duple and triple meters, and even then there is confusion about whether to teach those rhythm patterns using numbers, e.g., "1–e–and–a" (for four

> sixteenth notes), or using mnemonic devices, e.g., "Mississippi," for the same pattern. Whatever system is used, terminology is inconsistent, leaving a chasm of illogic for conductors between what is heard and what is written. While advanced musicians have suffered through and eventually reconciled those inconsistencies of rhythm notation, children and adults who have limited experiences with music are hopelessly confused by those same inconsistencies.
>
> —James Jordan
> *Evoking Sound: Fundamentals of Choral Conducting and Rehearsing*, p. 49

Natural Body Response to Rhythm: The Foundation for Understanding Rhythm

Between birth and age three, children learn without bias (and without notation). Their bodies move and respond to rhythm in a natural way. They play and experience rhythm and movement without inhibition. As adults, it is helpful if we try to learn as a child learns music.

The core of rhythm learning must be based in movement. Consider the following controversial example. Audiate (hear the sound without it being physically present) "My Country 'Tis of Thee." A music theorist might describe the tune as being in 3/4 time, three beats in a measure and a quarter note representing one beat. That is visually correct. However, there is a conflict between the measure signature and how the music is heard, or audiated. Silently hear (audiate) "My Country 'Tis of Thee" again, but this time move to music. Do you move on each quarter note? You probably do not. Do you step or move once each measure? You probably do. Is it amusical to step to each quarter note? Yes. Would children step to each quarter note? They most likely would not.

The learning of rhythm must be organized and based upon the body's response to audiated rhythm and free of notation. Rhythm learning should be rooted not in music theory, but in audiation. While the theory of music is important to the explanation of the common practice of a given period, it is not necessary for the learning of rhythm. In the same way reading individual letters and knowing the principles of grammar are not necessary for speaking or reading a language, the knowledge of note values and of the theory of meter signatures does not directly bear upon the beginning stages of rhythm learning. However, a body that responds naturally to rhythm is a necessary prerequisite for the learning of rhythm and for the establishment of a consistent tempo.

Layers of Rhythm Audiation

Rhythm, when audiated with understanding, is heard at three different levels concurrently. For the purpose of this explanation, consider the three levels as layers of audiation—that is, rhythm is audiated in relation to three separate elements. To audiate rhythm, one must organize rhythm patterns either consciously or unconsciously, but organization must take place at some level. For very talented students, the organization at more basic levels takes place unconsciously. The three elements of rhythm are pictured in Figure 5. The *macrobeat,* the largest unit of pulse to which the body can move comfortably, is at the bottom of the chart, indicating that it is fundamental to rhythm audiation. *Microbeats* are the principal subdivisions of the macrobeat; the macrobeat is divisible into either two or three microbeats (except in the rare case of an intact macrobeat). While the macrobeat is fundamental to rhythm audiation, a consistent tempo cannot be established without the concurrent audiation of macro- and microbeats. The macrobeats and the microbeats must be audiated separately and then combined in audiation. If macrobeats and microbeats are not audiated separately before being combined, both lose their fundamental character and relationship to the other; hence, an inconsistent tempo is the result.

Melodic rhythm is the third layer of rhythm audiation. Melodic rhythm cannot be audiated with meaning and with consistency of tempo unless the previous two layers of rhythm are audiated concurrently. Melodic rhythm is superimposed over the microbeat layer, which in turn is superimposed over the macrobeat layer. Melodic rhythms can be categorized according to one or a combination of two or more of the following descriptive terms: divisions, elongations, rests, ties, and upbeats. Combinations of those functions constitute the rhythm of the melody, which are then superimposed over the audiation of macrobeats and microbeats. Rhythm audiation is, therefore, a threefold hearing process. Of the three layers of rhythm "hearing," the most crucial, if not the most fundamental, is the middle layer. Without the ability to accurately place microbeats, one will know only unusual meter and will never experience the feeling of a consistent tempo.

What is the practical application toward the development of rhythm skills in the choral ensemble? Consider the performance of the following rhythm pattern within a sequence of rhythm patterns: two eighths, two eighths, four sixteenths, and two eighths. You perform the rhythm but rush the sixteenth notes. Now consider the previously suggested threefold layering of rhythm audiation. How should the rushing be corrected? First, you should move your body to macrobeats at a consistent tempo while chanting microbeats (eighth notes), emphasizing an equal subdivision of the beat. You should continue that procedure until you sense a consistent tempo.

FIGURE 5. The Fundamental Elements of Rhythm Audiation: Layering of the Elements of Rhythm (Melodic Rhythm) (From *Evoking Sound*, p. 51.)

Layer 2	Establishment of Consistent Tempo **MICROBEATS**
Layer 1	**MACROBEATS** (through body movement)
	AUDIATION
	Simple

When the consistent tempo has been established, the third layer of rhythm, the melodic rhythm, may be added. Remember that the strongest indicator of correct rhythm audiation is a person's sense of consistent tempo. If a consistent tempo is not present, you must remove each layer of rhythm audiation, beginning with melodic rhythm, until the problem is solved. You can then rebuild the layers back through melodic rhythm, so long as consistency of tempo is maintained. The strength of this approach to rhythm is that it separates the audiation of rhythm into three distinct layers and reveals that melodic rhythm is superimposed over two more fundamental rhythm elements, which together provide a foundation for consistent tempo.

The Role of Consistent Tempo in Music Performance and Music Learning

One of the problems when initially learning a new work is that we are not persistent enough to maintain a consistent tempo. Consequently, in subsequent study sessions of the work, the tempo is more subject to flux based upon the lack of a rhythmic anchor, a consistent tempo that comes from within us. In the initial stages of learning a piece, follow the guide below:

1. *Walk the room to step and rhythmically chant the piece or exercise to find the macrobeat.* Walk about the room and step the rhythmic example while you chant it on a neutral syllable such as "bum," "doo," "pah," etc. The pulse you most naturally step to (regardless of the meter signature) is the macrobeat, or largest rhythmic unit of the work. Remember that the unit of pulse you step to may not be the unit of pulse signified by the meter signature. Always rely on what you hear, not what you see on the printed page. If you have any difficulty

doing this, perform the movement coordination sequence discussed previously in this chapter.

2. *Locate the microbeat in your hands while concurrently tapping the macrobeat in your feet.* After walking the exercise, be seated. Tap the beat that you just stepped in your feet. While chanting the exercise, determine whether the beat in your feet can be divided into twos or threes by lightly tapping your index and middle fingers of your right hand lightly onto your upturned left palm. The division of the macrobeat into the next smaller subdivisions is known as the microbeat.
3. *Chant through the exercise, breathing for each entrance.* Continue tapping the macrobeat in your feet and the microbeat in your hands. Rhythmically chant the entire exercise on a neutral syllable, taking care to breathe for each entrance. The nonrhythmic breathing of singers most often causes inconsistent tempo problems. Rhythmic breathing, key to a choir's consistent tempo, grows out of the consistent inner tempo of the conductor, rooted in the concurrent macro- and microbeat.
4. *Chant through the exercise without tapping.* Remove the tapping of the macrobeats in the feet and the microbeats in the hands and rhythmically chant the piece, while still breathing for each entrance. This will determine whether the consistent tempo of the piece is anchored within your audiation. If you have difficulty doing this, repeat steps one through three until the tempo stabilizes.

The Use of a Metronome to Establish Communal Kinesthetic Tempo

A metronome is an invaluable tool for allowing the choir to experience the feeling of consistent tempo. Many of the problems associated with rushing and slowing have to do with the inability of the choir to be aware of the kinesthetic that is felt and perceived when one sings in consistent tempo. Many believe that the way to accomplish this is to teach music theory. However, teaching the reading of rhythm has very little effect on a person's ability to perceive, feel, and organize the rhythm he or she hears. What one needs to teach and reinforce is the feeling that accompanies the state of consistent tempo.

The process to accomplish this is relatively simple. As the choir sings or reads a piece, simply turn on an aural metronome. (I prefer to use the TAMA Rhythm Watch, A-100.) Have the metronome click both the macrobeats and the first subdivision, the microbeat. After the metronome is sounding, have the choir sing with the metronome. You will find that this procedure allows them to experience the feeling of a consistent tempo. As soon as the ensemble begins to rush, stop them, and ask them to listen again to the metronome. Repeat this procedure until the tempo is consistent and stable. Remember that maintenance of a consistent tempo is the responsibility of each individual choir member. Always correct tempo problems in the same way each time they occur. The use of the metronome forces rhythmic responsibility upon the ensemble, plus it awakens the choir to the kinesthetic of consistent tempo. Once consistent tempo is established and the three layers of rhythm are audiated, true rhythmic learning and understanding can take place.

How Does Music Reading Evolve?

Music reading should be the last literacy skill taught to any choir. In fact, if you do your teaching from an aural perspective as advocated in this chapter, music reading happens just as it does in language: by a simple associative act. If singers have a vocabulary of musical sounds in their ears input via solfege in a harmonic, not melodic, context, then the singers simply and efficiently associate the sound in their cars to the musical signs on the page. In this way, the singer brings meaning to the notation rather than trying to constantly take meaning from the notation or decipher notation. Trying to take meaning from notation without a library of heard and acquired sounds appropriately filed with solfege will severely retard or totally inhibit the aural and musical development of any ensemble. Reading should be (and perhaps must be) a by-product of careful aural education that emphasizes the ear before the eye. While such an approach may be initially difficult for any choir, that period of difficulty vanishes once the choir begins to rely on the ears instead of the eyes.

Building Modal Aural Familiarity Skills

A choir will only sing in tune to the extent that that they are familiar with the inherent sound characteristics of each mode. It is my belief that the best way to achieve such familiarity within a choral situation is to have the choir throughout the year make their way through all of the *Ear Training Immersion Exercises for Choirs*. A regular aural diet of these exercises at the conclusion of each choral warm-up is an efficient way to provide this necessary training.

Summary

1. Teach through the ear at all times; teach only what is aurally significant to your singers. Avoid all things that have only visual significance.
2. Teach the way your choir hears, not how you hear.

3. Redirect the choir's hearing and awareness to a heightened level of listening and awareness.
4. Use the choir's seating arrangement to enhance their ability to hear.
5. Avoid developing music-reading skills or even focusing on music-reading skills until sufficient aural experience is achieved.
6. Rehearse choral ensembles with all parts sounding at all times. Avoid single part rehearsal without sufficient harmonic surroundings. Avoid sectional rehearsals.
7. Use a La-based minor system. Avoid Do-based minor, numbers, and all other systems that are unable to clearly identify new resting tones in each mode.
8. Never introduce or read a piece with text.
9. The accompanist should be empowered to provide dominant function notes to provide harmonic context and to anchor intonation.
10. All choral rehearsals should be conducted in a state of consistent tempo developed through persistent use of the metronome to reinforce the kinesthetic of consistent tempo.
11. Music reading develops as an associative process. When sounds are firmly in the ear, those sounds can then, and only then, be associated to the notation with musical meaning.

Bibliography

Ames, Roger, Marilyn Shenenberger, and James Jordan. *Modal Warm-up Exercises for Choir* and *Accompanied Canons for Choir*. Chicago: GIA Publications, in preparation.

Gordon, Edwin E. *Advanced Measures of Music Audiation*. Chicago: GIA Publications, 1989.

———. *Intermediate Measures of Music Audiation*. Chicago: GIA Publications, 1982.

———. *Iowa Tests of Music Literacy*. Chicago: GIA Publications, 1991.

———. *Learning Sequences in Music: Skill, Content, and Patterns—A Music Learning Theory*. Chicago: GIA Publications, 2003.

———. *Preparatory Audiation, Audiation, and Music Learning Theory: A Handbook of a Comprehensive Music Learning Sequence*. Chicago: GIA Publications, 2001.

Jordan, James. *Evoking Sound: The Choral Warm-Up: Core Vocal Exercises*. With Marilyn Shenenberger. Chicago: GIA Publications, 2004.

———. *Evoking Sound: The Choral Conductor's Aural Tutor: Training the Ear to Diagnose Vocal Problems*. Chicago: GIA Publications, 2006.

Jordan, James, and Matthew Mehaffey. *Choral Ensemble Intonation: Methods, Procedures, and Exercises*. Chicago: GIA Publications, 2001.

Jordan, James, and Marilyn Shenenberger. *Ear Training Immersion Exercises for Choirs*. Chicago: GIA Publications, 2004.
Lauridsen, Morton. *Mid-Winter Songs*. Evanston, IL: Opus Music Publishers, 1983.
Shafir, Rebecca Z. *The Zen of Listening*. Wheaton, IL: Quest Books, 2003.
Shenenberger, Marilyn, and James Jordan. *Listen! Introductory Harmonic Immersion Solfege for Choral Ensemble Singers at All Levels*. Chicago: GIA Publications, 2007.
Shuter-Dyson, Rosamund, and Clive Gabriel. *The Psychology of Musical Ability*. London: Methuen, 1981.
Tomatis, Alfred. *The Conscious Ear: My Life of Transformation through Listening*. Barrytown, NY: Station Hill Press, 1991.
———. *The Ear and the Voice*. Translated by Roberta Prada and Pierre Sollier. Freely adapted by Roberta Prada and Francis Keeping. Lanham, MD: Scarecrow Press, 2005.
Weikart, Phyllis. *Movement for Confined Spaces*. Chicago: GIA Publications, in preparation.

Video/DVD

Jordan, James, and Matthew Mehaffey. *Choral Ensemble Intonation* (Video) Chicago: GIA Publications, 2001. This video demonstrates all of the teaching principles espoused in this chapter.
Noble, Weston. *Achieving Choral Blend through Standing Position*. Chicago: GIA Publications, 2005. This DVD details the procedures for seating a choir to achieve improved intonation and ensemble timbre. It is highly recommended.

Further Study Resource Materials for This Chapter

Solfege Editions in the *Evoking Sound Choral Series* (GIA Publications)
The performance solfege editions below apply the solfege principles advocated in this chapter. All editions contain pedagogical notes concerning solfege decisions by the author who completed the solfege analysis, Marilyn Shenenberger. Each edition also includes historical notes, texts, and translations in addition to rehearsal suggestions.

Ames, Roger, arr. "She Moved through the Faire." Traditional Irish song (SSATB) (G-6507).
———. "The Riddle Song" In *Three Appalachian Folk Songs*. (SATB/piano) (G-6488)

Brahms, Johannes. *Geistliches Lied, Op. 30: Lass dich nur nichts nicht dauren.* Edited by James Jordan (SATB, organ) (G-6480).

Bruckner, Anton. "Pange lingua." Edited by James Jordan. (SATB) (G-6481).

Custer, Gerald. "Elegy." (SSAATTBB/piano) (G-6479).

Hill, Jackson. "Love Is Life." (SATB divisi) (G-6369).

Mendelssohn, Felix. "Psalm 100: Jauchzet dem Herrn, alle Welt." Edited by James Jordan. (SSAATTBB) (G-5929).

———. "Richte mich, Gott." Edited by James Jordan. (SSAATTBB) (G-6482).

Phillips, Joel. "Come, Soft Slumber." (SATB) (G-6368).

Shenenberger, Marilyn, arr. "God Rest Ye Merry, Gentlemen." (Jazz arrangement, SATB) (G-6486).

James Jordan is recognized and praised from many quarters in the musical world as one of the nation's preeminent conductors, writers, and innovators in choral music. He has been called a "visionary" by *The Choral Journal.* His career and publications have been devoted to innovative educational changes in the choral art that have been embraced around the world. A master teacher, Jordan's pioneering writing and research concerning the use of Laban Movement Analysis for the teaching of conducting and movement to children has dramatically changed teaching in both of these disciplines.

One of the country's most prolific writers on the subjects of the philosophy of music making and choral teaching, he has produced ten major textbooks and several choral series bearing his name as well as contributing to four other textbooks. His latest text for conductors, *The Conductor's Aural Tutor: Training the Ear to Diagnose Vocal Problems* (GIA Publications), is the first text of its kind designed to train conductors to hear and diagnose vocal issues within a choir. Jordan also serves as Executive Editor of the Evoking Sound Choral Series published by GIA. This series presents choral literature at the highest levels for high school and college choirs. Jordan teaches and conducts at *Westminster Choir College of Rider University* in Princeton, New Jersey, where he is an associate professor of conducting and senior conductor. For twelve years he served as conductor of the Westminster Chapel Choir, and in fall 2004 he became the founding conductor of Westminster's premier chamber choir, the Westminster Williamson Voices.

CHAPTER 3

Preparing the Chorus for Performance with Orchestral Accompaniment

Ann Howard Jones

Introduction

The purpose of this chapter is to examine the conductor's responsibilities in the preparation of choral music accompanied by orchestra. At the outset, I must say that these ideas and issues are found in every rehearsal prior to any performance, regardless of the music to be sung or whether the work is accompanied. Some of the conclusions are mine, but they have been shaped and influenced considerably by mentors and professors, most notably Robert Shaw, Daniel Moe, Don V Moses, and Herald Stark as well as by countless colleagues and students who have discussed, debated, and shaped these ideas with me over the years.

Coming out of my experiences with Robert Shaw, who was without equal in the preparation and performance of the repertoire for chorus and orchestra, I learned that he believed there could be no successful performance without appropriate preparation and score study, thorough knowledge of the score, and effective training of the musicians. All of this occurred at a level few could comprehend without being in his presence. Shaw's charisma, personal commitment, passionate intensity, and dynamic leadership notwithstanding, the stature he achieved was the result of hard work and constant problem solving as he attempted to find ways to make the great works in the repertoire communicate. His tireless efforts enhanced the music; his ideas about how a chorus might work better influenced countless numbers of singers and choral conductors.

I still feel the impact of those experiences daily and never more strongly than when I step onto the podium to prepare or conduct a performance of the Verdi Requiem, the Brahms Requiem, the Britten *War Requiem*, a Bach Passion, the Haydn *Creation*, a Beethoven Mass, or a choral score of any size or genre. Shaw taught all of us that attention to the details presented in this chapter provides the foundation by which a performance can be more communicative, expressive, powerful, and, most important, give voice to the composer's intentions.

Preparing for Another Conductor

As Shaw's assistant with the Atlanta Symphony's choruses, I performed in and rehearsed ensembles he conducted. It is not unusual for choral conductors to be asked to prepare a chorus for a performance that will be conducted by someone else. This is an opportunity for you to explore literature you and your chorus might not normally sing, and it can give you the opportunity to study, observe, rehearse, and engage in an effort for which someone else will have the ultimate responsibility, There are some other advantages: you will be fully engaged in the process, the chorus will reflect your hard work, and you will have the chance to step back from your own choral work and listen. This will often result in an important new perspective for you. Make no mistake; the observation and involvement in the process are important parts in readying yourself for the day when you will step onto the podium for a choral/orchestral performance you will lead. If you have already had the experience of conducting a choral/orchestral performance you undoubtedly know that each opportunity has its own challenges and chances for growth.

A considerable amount of the work is simply practical. This takes place long before the first rehearsal and involves important decisions. None is more important than the choice of the musical work to be performed. Weighing all the factors in the choice is sometimes daunting, but one of the most important is that you must love the piece and want to conduct it. Once the work has been chosen, securing a date is high on the list of things to be done, and so is contracting performance and rehearsal space. Sometimes a decision about a work to be performed depends, of course, on the availability of the right hall or church. For example, one probably should not think about performing a work that requires an organ in a hall without an organ.

Early on, you select a suitable (and available) edition, gather the choral and orchestral materials, contract the orchestra and the soloists, and get the publicity machine rolling. Hopefully you have a contractor with whom you work comfortably who will put the orchestra together if you are not performing with an existing orchestra. If not, try to find someone and let him or her find players who will be excited to play a performance with you and the chorus. A good group of volunteers or a good board can help you with publicity and all the details such a performance presents. Organizations like Chorus America specialize in helping community choruses with organizational details. Join and let them help you with the multitude of non-musical tasks that affect the performance. You might supervise, but I would advise that you find responsible people to assemble the lists of names, lay out the program, design the cover, or line up the ushers and all the things others who are competent can do for you. What you need time to do is to study the score, prepare the choral and orchestral parts, and begin to plan the rehearsals.

Once you have been contracted, and early in the process—ideally before the first chorus rehearsal—you will want to be in touch with the conductor of the performance to introduce yourself and to ask if there is anything in particular the conductor would like to have you do to make your preparation most effective and his or her work the most productive.

First to discuss are matters of tempo. With Robert Shaw, his tempos, even if they varied only slightly from those suggested in the score, were always marked. He knew within just a few points on the metronome the tempo he intended, and, as the preparer of the chorus, I had to know that, too. It was rarely necessary for us to converse about this. Other conductors are not so specific, and, in cases in which the composer has been particularly confounding, (e.g., Beethoven's tempo indication at the beginning of the Mass in C) tempos can vary considerably from one conductor to another.

For many (Shaw is the notable exception among those with whom I have worked), tempo is an evolving and flexible thing, not an absolute from which the conductor makes a conscious decision to depart. In those cases, the preparer arrives at a working tempo based upon a number of things: one might listen to a variety of recordings by several conductors with a tempo watch firmly in hand; one might try to have a conversation with the conductor of the performance to ask for a metronome marking, or one might prepare the chorus with a variety of tempos and advise them to watch carefully and adjust as needed. With Mr. Shaw, I always had a tempo watch and metronome at hand so that I knew exactly what speed he wanted and at what speed we were going.

If the conductor for whom you are preparing has recorded the work in question, by all means listen to it carefully. I have found that it is not always a perfect guide, however, so try to ask the conductor ahead of time if there is a recording to which you might listen. Prior to a recent preparation for Charles Dutoit for a Carnegie Hall performance of French choral music, Dutoit's recording of the Fauré Requiem was recommended to me by his agent. I found it very helpful, but if there was any uncertainty on my part about where a particular consonant should be placed, or where a sound ended, I simply made a decision, hoped for the best, and prepared the chorus for the possibility of a change. What I have learned is that when working with a well-trained, well-disciplined chorus any decisions made about places where the score is unclear generally are accepted by the conductor without question. If a chorus is uncertain and tentative, strong intervention will be required from the performance conductor, and valuable time will be spent, often necessarily, clarifying and setting tempo.

In early discussions with the conductor, you might ask about articulation, dynamics, tone color, and any other aspects of the work that concern you. This conversation tends to be more productive after you have done a considerable amount of score preparation yourself. Some conductors know exactly what they want to hear, and they can articulate that in advance. Most will leave all of that to you and then listen to what you and the chorus have prepared and adjust as needed.

It is wise to tell the inexperienced chorus that the preparation will have been completely adequate if, at the first rehearsal, the conductor listens to them, smiles broadly, thanks them sincerely, and sends them on their way, having said very little. This happened to a chorus of high school singers I was asked to prepare for the composer/conductor John Williams for a performance at Tanglewood. The young singers were asked to sing with the Boston Symphony at a concert regularly attended by 15,000 concertgoers. The evening, called "Film Night," is a celebration of music composed for the movies. Naturally it was important that the chorus arrive at the first rehearsal well prepared. With such young singers, I knew that they needed a warning about what to expect from Mr. Williams, if I could guess. I told them that we should be pleased if our portion of the concert required very little attention or correction from him. Imagine our delight when he heard the chorus with the orchestra, cautioned the chorus about one complicated quarter note triplet, smiled broadly, thanked them, and sent them on their way. The singers beamed, having been tipped off that if he were pleased he would require very little time of us.

I had also trained that same chorus to figure out their starting pitch for the "Olympic Hymn" for the same concert from tuning pitches given by the orchestra. This meant that no starting pitch for the chorus was needed to open the work. This is an impressive thing to do for music that begins with no orchestral introduction (e.g., the opening pitch of the Beethoven Mass in C, the beginning of the Mozart Vespers, K. 339, or the start of the Barber *Prayers of Kierkegaard*). If it doesn't assume too much risk, it is also a nice touch for the chorus to take the opening pitches among themselves from a pitch pipe during the applause as the conductor enters the stage. The audience can rarely hear that taking place, and the chorus can then begin the work without a chord or a note before the music begins. Everyone must be confident that the pitch is secure in order for these techniques to work well, however.

When the performance conductor meets the chorus for the first time, hopefully in a separate rehearsal before the orchestral rehearsal, you may be asked to conduct while he or she listens and observes. This can be unnerving, to say the least, especially if you are not prepared for this to happen! I have observed this with James Levine and the Tanglewood Festival Chorus conducted by John Oliver, with Robert Shaw and the many choruses he conducted around the country, and many others. Sometimes you may be asked to conduct the entire work from start to finish without a word from the conductor. Other times, there will be some stopping and starting with suggestions from the guest. It is best to alert the chorus to the possibility of this happening, even if you don't know for certain that it will. This, of course, might be able to be clarified ahead of time in your conversations with the conductor.

At some stage in the preparation, someone has to think about standing and sitting cues for the chorus and soloists. Some conductors have strong ideas about this, and others will leave it entirely to you. Mr. Shaw would often ask for suggestions and then make the final decision. It was Shaw's belief that giving the chorus musical cues for standing or sitting was preferable to having the cue come from the conductor. Simply put, the conductor is not always the most reliable or dependable source for such an important cue.

I remember singing a performance of *Elijah* where the conductor had taken upon himself the responsibility for asking the chorus to stand at the beginning. He forgot, and we had no other option worked out, so there was a frantic rising up before the first choral entry, and the singing was less powerful as a result. To avoid all of this I ask the chorus to stand at the start of a concert, as I step onto the podium. Or, if there is a lot of music before the chorus sings, the chorus would stand on a musical cue. In a long work like *Messiah*, valuable time can be saved if the chorus stands or sits with the music—for example, on beat one, on the downbeat of m. 35, on the final chord of a movement, three measures from the end on beat one, and so on. It is the same for the soloists. They need time to get themselves prepared to sing, but they, too, can stand and sit as part of the music. These cues are worked out in rehearsals and in the solo coachings and given to the singers for insertion in the scores and rehearsed as part of the preparation.

As a general rule in rehearsals with "guest" conductors, you should be prepared to remind the conductor that the chorus may need to sit occasionally during a long orchestral rehearsal. Some conductors think of this, and some do not. In works that have limited choral involvement, the conductor will often rehearse the chorus movements first, and then let the chorus go early or call the chorus late, just as one would be considerate of trumpeters and timpanists who play very little in a long work like *Messiah*. In Mahler's Symphony No. 2 or Beethoven's Symphony No. 9, for example, it is generally not required for the chorus to sit through the entire work until the final dress rehearsal. If the conductor doesn't think of that in scheduling the rehearsals for the chorus, you might be prepared to make the suggestion.

Some inexperienced choruses need further reminders about stage etiquette. Someone will always ask if the chorus should applaud for the orchestra, the soloists, or the conductor (generally not a good idea), about turning pages with the soloists (no), or about general demeanor on stage. Even walking in and out can be a real challenge for some choruses.

The guiding principle is that the group appears as professional as possible. You might want to practice some of these things. In the end it is all worth it when the chorus enters the stage with everyone's music in the same hand, when the chorus raises the music as the conductor steps onto the podium, when all stand and sit together, when the tuning of the orchestra is not accompanied by the chorus chatting, and when the final bows go smoothly. The conductor of the performance will likely invite you to the stage for a bow when the concert has ended. Dress appropriately, acknowledge the chorus for its excellent work, and follow the conductor's lead about getting on and off the stage gracefully.

Finally, it is of vital importance to think about the acoustical environment in which the chorus will be asked to sing in the final rehearsals before the performance. For me, it is necessary to have the chorus warm up on the stage before both the dress rehearsal and the concert. This might mean that the chorus has to arrive an hour ahead of the call time for the orchestra, but it is well worth it to have them in the acoustic in which they will sing and not in some far away rehearsal hall with very different sound properties.

On concert nights in Atlanta, the chorus would appear with Mr. Shaw on stage at 7:00 p.m for an 8:00 p.m. performance. There, we would work totally undisturbed for thirty minutes, after which the house would open, the audience would enter, and the orchestra would assemble. In those thirty minutes, an enormous amount of detail was covered, and the chorus sang much better when it could sing in the acoustic in which it was about to perform. In many concert halls, this time must be requested. In Boston, when the Boston University choruses sing in Symphony Hall, sometimes we only get fifteen or twenty minutes for that warm-up on stage; but I always ask for it, and the chorus needs it. Be certain to start and stop on time. Union rules may affect these times and dictate when you may call the chorus ahead of the announced rehearsal start. Be well informed about the regulations as they concern the chorus.

Whatever your role is in the final performance, the work of readying the chorus is in many ways the same as the kind of work you would do for an *a cappella* performance or for a performance with other instruments, including piano. When my good friend and colleague from the University of Georgia School of Music, Mary Leglar, and I were discussing these ideas, she said, "There really isn't anything different about the work we do to prepare a chorus for the orchestral performance; it is just a question of emphasis." In many ways, she is right.

Preparing the Chorus for Your Own Performance

If you are preparing the work and conducting the performance yourself, there are additional considerations that require your attention. It is my observation, based on conversations with singers (and singer-conductors like Craig Jessop, Joseph Flummerfelt, Christopher Cock, Norman Mackenzie, Charles Bruffy, Jerry McCoy, James Morrow, Pamela Elrod, Jean Ashworth Bartle, Janet Galván, Hilary Apfelstadt, William Thomas, Bingham Vick, Maurice Casey, and a host of others who participated in Shaw ensembles) who sang and participated in Shaw ensembles and workshops, my own experience and training, and teaching of graduate students, as well as after hours and hours of rehearsal, reflection, and study, that the following constitutes a list of issues every choral director must resolve effectively in order to be thorough and well prepared.

The list omits two significant aspects of the choral rehearsal: tone quality and musical style. In some choruses, the vocal sound is a consequence of the singer's vocal training apart from the choral rehearsal. In other choruses, perhaps the majority, it is the responsibility of the conductor to build the vocal sound or tone of the singers in the choir. In this instance, every rehearsal includes a significant amount of time and work on matters of clarity of vowel, appropriate resonance, range extension, breath management and control, and all the other aspects of building tone that a singer requires. Vocal tone can be dealt with separately from a discussion of pitch, but we all know that good pitch depends on good singing in the first place. This discussion focuses on the sound that results from well-trained singers singing together. The question of musical style is a complex one and has been dealt with by other writers in this series. In the context of this discussion, I believe that the appropriate musical style for every composition will result from the correct treatment of rhythm, dynamics, phrasing, line, and articulation.

The order is important; no one issue can be ignored at the expense of any other, but you might choose to emphasize some that would be of particular importance to your group and the level of your singers.

Rhythm
Pitch
Dynamics
Text
Phrasing
Line
Color
Articulation
Balance

These elements are isolated and rehearsed in a well-ordered and efficient sequence that leads to the performance being well prepared. Every conductor has techniques for approaching these issues, and while all of us could undoubtedly sharpen our skills in any number of significant ways, the point of this chapter is not to discuss rehearsal techniques but to discuss specific techniques that might help you better prepare your chorus for performance with an orchestra.

Dealing with all of the above elements requires, first and foremost, the conductor's comprehensive knowledge of the score itself. Others have dealt extensively with the ideas of score preparation. (For a clear example, see Chamberlain, Mehaffey, and Reeves in "Masterwork," *Teaching Music through Performance in Choir, Vol. 1*, published by GIA Publications, 2005.) For purposes of this discussion, I assume that the conductor has absorbed the structure (form) and harmony of the music to be prepared. The items in my list are then built upon the construct of formal and harmonic analysis that it is essential for the conductor to know before proceeding to the specific elements I have identified as essential for the readying of the chorus for the orchestra.

The list begins, appropriately, with *rhythm*. In all the years during which I observed Robert Shaw, this one element stands out above all the rest. We rehearsed for rhythmic clarity from the first moment of work on a composition. In fact, the idea of count-singing was employed as a sight-reading tool; we were encouraged to learn the rhythms of a work first.

Rhythmic subdivision has been around forever, and many have suggested ways of dividing beats rhythmically. I can remember as a young piano student learning that one counted eighth notes by saying "1 and 2 and," sixteenth notes by saying "1 ee and uh 2 ee and uh," and triplets by saying "1 and uh 2 and uh." Many have refined the techniques for counting rhythms, most notably those professional music educators who have devised complex systems for dividing beats (e.g., Edwin E. Gordon and Kodály). Robert Shaw, more than anyone I know, made this part of choral rehearsals. He divided every pulse into its divisions or subdivisions and counted rhythmically on the pitches written by the composer. Pitch was also rehearsed in this way, but rhythm was the emphasis. Dynamics and text were completely eliminated from this early part of the process.

I do not know that Robert Shaw invented count-singing. I do know, however, that no one employed it more tenaciously, believed in it more vigorously, espoused it with more different kinds of ensembles, or used it more effectively. He found it helpful in works as different as the B Minor Mass of Bach with its relatively regular rhythms and the *Harmonium* of John Adams with its complicated and irregular rhythms and in textures both homophonic and contrapuntal. He found ways to break rhythms down into their divisions and subdivisions to clarify them and to make them reliable no matter what the circumstances. He used it when the tempo was completely and reliably steady, and he used it when the tempo was full of rubato. He used it to fix problems of ensemble, of course, and he used it to deal with problems of intonation. (See number two below.)

Mr. Shaw's premises were few:

1. In rehearsals, create as little opportunity for error as possible (the piano almost always played along).
2. The right note at the wrong time is the wrong note.
3. A chorus is a "gluey" ensemble, and so everything possible has to be done to make the rhythm clear and the pitches line up vertically.
4. Listen more, sing less, and sing everything "off the voice," especially in the early stages of rehearsal, not only to save "vocal gold" but to *hear* better. (He used to talk about Julius Herford, the distinguished

German musicologist, visiting a rehearsal of a Bach motet with the Robert Shaw Chorale. When the rehearsal had finished, Herford said he thought there would be more Bach if there were less singing and more listening. This experience guided Shaw during all the years I worked with him.)

5. Use octave transpositions at every opportunity if they would help to save the voice and avoid vocal strain.

There is little doubt that some singers are quicker at learning to count in a choral rehearsal than others, but it was always clear that every ensemble, no matter how experienced, profited from this kind of work on rhythm in a rehearsal. Very particularized counting helps the most. The legato is negated, to be sure, but the clarity is immediately evident. Pitches have centers because of the precision, and because the singers are extremely conscious of rhythm the ensemble is much cleaner. There is no question that count-singing helps contrapuntal music, but it is effective in homophonic music as well. The beginning of the Brahms Requiem, with its block chords, is more beautiful and haunting when it is first of all absolutely unanimously together rhythmically.

In a Shaw chorus, everything that could be "rhythmicized" was: *crescendo* and *diminuendo* were rehearsed over a certain number of beats to achieve control and smoothness; pitches were raised and lowered (intentionally!) over sixteen pulses to refine intonation and to remind singers that any duration at all provides the opportunity for the improvement of the pitch; and final consonants were placed rhythmically and rehearsed while count-singing. Shaw built final consonants into the counting, e.g., "1 and 2 and tee and 4 [t]" with [t] being the final consonant of a word. (This is especially useful with the ubiquitous [s] at the ends of words because it places the [s] precisely and limits its duration. The syllable "tee" is substituted in counting to avoid the possible delay in the arrival of the vowel on the beat if the "thr" combination at the beginning of the word "three" is used. Similarly, "sev" can be used for "seven.")

In extreme cases, and based on the proven success of count-singing, I have taught a work first on a neutral syllable—[du] or [do] or [po]—and then gone back to count-singing once the singers are familiar with the pitches. They catch on quickly, but for some the task of counting everything the first time through is so daunting that it interferes with their ability to sing proper pitches at all. I have even used count-singing after the fact, in a piece that the singers already know well, to demonstrate the count-singing technique. Singers can be resistant to this at first, but I have no doubt of its effectiveness and have found that with people who don't understand rhythm this is the beginning of a method by which they can learn to take responsibility for the rhythmic clarity of their voice parts. People who can sing proper rhythm benefit from the increased precision afforded by count-singing.

While count-singing works for any kind of choral singing, it is particularly effective in the preparation of accompanied singing, and it is most helpful in preparing to sing with an orchestra. In every instance with an orchestra, attacks must have rhythmic precision. A tone must start on time. The governing principle is that the vowel must sound on the beat. Any consonant that precedes a vowel has to come just before it, and the consonants have to be executed quickly and with a great deal of energy in order for the text to penetrate the sonority of the orchestra and in order for the vowel to be heard on time. This takes a lot of work, finely tuned coordination between the breath and the onset of the tone, crisp and precise diction, and well-placed vowels.

It is my goal in preparing the chorus that neither I nor a guest conductor has to say, "Chorus, you are behind." I spend a great deal of time rehearsing rhythm and tempo. The conductor sets the tempo, attempts to maintain it, and changes it when appropriate but is at the mercy of the chorus and the orchestra to meet the demands. The musicians realize the tempo, not the conductor, after all. The chorus must have its own integrity in terms of rhythm and tempo. (This, incidentally, is why it is so important to rehearse in a carefully chosen tempo that does not fluctuate unintentionally.)

Pitch is second on the list and is no less important than rhythm. With a good orchestra, excellent pitch is a given, so the chorus must strive to sing beautifully in tune. It is easy to instruct singers to listen to the orchestra for assistance in producing in-tune pitches, but it is obviously more reliable to teach the chorus from the first rehearsal onward to sing well in tune on its own.

Conductors generally agree that the way the chorus is "seated" directly affects intonation and tone quality. I would add that it is a good idea to seat the chorus so that the section is in close proximity to the instrument it is doubling. For me, this is especially true in contrapuntal music. I like to hear the material that is played by the violins and sung by the sopranos coming from the same place on the stage. This helps with intonation, I find, and, as an added benefit, can assist with balance. There is no substitute for a chorus secure in its own pitch, but its spatial relationship with specific sections of the orchestra can align and steady the pitch even more.

A chorus capable of manipulating pitch is usually more secure in singing well in tune than a chorus that starts with pitch considerations as secondary to the delivery of beautiful tone, perfect diction, or exciting dynamics. Every sound that comes out of the mouth of every individual in the chorus must first of all be well in tune. Shaw effectively used the exercise of raising the pitch by one half step incrementally over sixteen pulses to increase pitch awareness in the singers and to make each singer aware of his or her capacity to change pitch for the better while sustaining a tone.

The chorus must be especially attentive to sing well in tune when the orchestra enters following an *a cappella* section (e.g., the Sanctus of the Beethoven Mass in C). The chorus sings a long section, and then the orchestra comes in. If the accurate pitch of the section for chorus has not been maintained, the orchestral entrance will sound like it is establishing a new key center. There are examples all through the Brahms Requiem as well where the chorus sings just a measure or two *a cappella* and then the orchestra reenters.

I rehearse those spots separately and carefully from a list made during score study. These spots must be rehearsed again and again until the chorus can manage the demands of maintaining excellent pitch. The Berlioz Requiem has the notorious "Quaerens me" *a cappella* for the chorus. I remember count-singing that for weeks with the Atlanta Symphony Chorus. Shaw was always hopeful that the opening interval from A to C-sharp would somehow right itself! We count-sang that movement for weeks with the admonition from Shaw that every division of the beat we articulated gave us an opportunity to listen more and to improve its pitch. When we finally added the text, new problems arose as the singers strove to unify vowels. (He did not take into account the singers' issues with negotiating a natural lift in the voice with vocal skill. He expected the singer to manage those issues competently from the start—something you might not be able to do with your chorus.) The chorus needs to understand and execute intervals carefully and sing and improve every note it sustains with an ear toward more accurate pitch.

The range of *dynamics* that must be available to a chorus when singing with an orchestra is, of necessity, both softer and louder. The extremes of *forte* and the extremes of *piano* are to be explored, controlled, and enjoyed. One of the exercises that can be used to help a chorus experience a range of dynamics that includes everything from ***ffff*** to ***pppp*** is one I learned from Shaw. The chorus begins on the pitches F-sharp (bass and alto) and A (soprano and tenor). Any syllable will do, but I usually choose "naw" because it is open enough for both dynamic extremes. Beginning at *mezzo piano*, sing those two pitches, take a breath, and then move up one half step and sing *mezzo forte*, changing dynamics with each new set of pitches. Arrive at *tutta forza*, and then go back to the original pitches and descend by half steps until ***pppp*** is reached. If this exercise is done at the beginning of every rehearsal as a referent for the dynamic range available to that group of singers in that room at that time, I can always go back to it and remind the singers of how softly they might sing, or how loudly for that matter.

Crescendo and *diminuendo* can also be rehearsed abstractly. On any given pitch, *crescendo* for four beats, or eight beats, or sixteen beats, and then *diminuendo* in the same way. Combine *crescendo* and *diminuendo* in an exercise over twelve beats. Limit the peak of the *crescendo* to *forte* or to *mezzo piano*—whatever the music requires. Give the singers a chance to practice getting louder and getting softer under control and within every dynamic marking. This can be coupled with exercises in articulation, which I will discuss later, because, though our instincts are the opposite, when singing in *piano* it is often necessary to sing slightly more detached to improve the rhythmic clarity and audibility when singing with an orchestra.

Dynamics and *balance* are closely related matters, and one must keep a careful ear to the issue of balance at all dynamic levels. Balances can be worked out so that the tenors in the highest part of the voice at the loudest dynamic will not overbalance every other part. Sopranos can be taught not to automatically sing loudly at the top of the staff and above. Singers can be asked to sing louder and to sing softer without changing tone color. This is especially important and a valuable skill.

Tone color can also be manipulated so that the tone is not automatically dark and diffuse when soft and bright and pointed when loud. One exercise that can help singers understand their responsibility for contributing to the balance of the chorus is to assign the whole tone scale degrees E, F-sharp, G-sharp, and A-sharp to alto II, alto I, soprano II, and soprano I and the same pitches to the bass II, bass I, tenor II, and tenor I parts. On a neutral syllable ("naw" or "noh"), the chorus sings the assigned pitches at a set dynamic level. Each part, listening to the others, adjusts for balance. The object of this exercise is to achieve a desired balance among the sections of the chorus and to establish the chorus sonority at a variety of dynamic levels.

There is little question but that the orchestra can overpower the chorus at any dynamic. When the orchestra is playing at the loudest end of its dynamic range, the rhythmic precision, the brightness of the vowels, and the articulation of the text may be more significant choral issues than simply dynamics. Just to be safe, tend carefully to those things in the choral rehearsal, and reduce the dynamic markings in the orchestra parts where the character of the music will not be compromised unacceptably. I have found that it is better to anticipate those places and to mark the orchestral parts accordingly, especially the brass, rather than constantly saying to the orchestra that they must play softer. Warn players by marking their parts ahead of time or insert into their parts *accompagnato* or some such word to let them know to listen for the chorus. The opposite is true, too, of course. When the orchestra is playing without the chorus, I sometimes mark *soli* in their part to let them know that they can play with less concern for balance with the chorus.

If an instrumental part is doubling a voice part, the instrumentalists must always be sensitive to the ability of the voice to be heard. Think of the trombones doubling the voices in the fugue of the Mozart Requiem's Kyrie. The trombones must be cautioned to avoid covering the voices because of the need to hear the text, and the singers must be prepared to articulate the text and the pitches with clarity. In any Bach chorale, as another example, the instrumental doublings must never obscure the text. In music where the chorus and the orchestra have independent parts, the text must be heard. Orchestras can be encouraged to listen for the voices and the text, but it helps to point out the places where voices and text are apt to be obscured during the orchestral rehearsals. Remember, too, that this can all change with any variation in acoustics. That is one reason why I think it is important to give the chorus as much time as possible in the acoustic of the performance. They need to experience the room in order to adjust to what the space requires.

The question of delivery of the *text* is vital to the success of any choral/orchestral work. In any performance where there is instrumental accompaniment, issues of text must be carefully addressed. First, there is the matter of the delivery of the vowel on the beat. Think of the beginning of the Poulenc Gloria, for example. In order for the first word of the text to be heard in its proper place rhythmically, the "g" and the "l" have to precede the beat so that the "aw" is heard on the beat. Sometimes it is necessary to rehearse such a place as if the consonant were actually a grace note rhythmically ahead of the beat and fast in order to get the vowel on the beat and for the consonants to be heard.

Final consonants separate into two large categories for our purposes: those that have pitch and those that do not. For those consonants with pitch (*b, d, g, j, l, m, n, r, v, w, z*), it is necessary for the location of that pitched or voiced consonant to be rhythmically precise. The final "d" of the word "God," for example, should have the same pitch as the preceding vowel and be placed rhythmically. For audibility and finality, especially when the orchestra plays, the final voiced consonant should also have an "ih" sound at its end on the pitch of the preceding vowel. Avoid the use of the *schwa* here because it can cause the pitch to dip: ("deadih" not "deaduh").

Final consonants that do not have pitch (*f, k, p, s, t, x*) also need precision as to placement and duration. Sometimes it is useful to precede a final unvoiced consonant with the tiniest *decrescendo* (decay) and the shortest possible rest (space) to better allow it to be placed unanimously by the chorus.

Clarity of text requires attention to interior consonants and vowels, too. Singers are often taught to avoid glottalization of interior vowels, but there is no way one can be articulate without some use of the soft glottal stroke. I can remember as a young singer learning to sing "it is" as if it were one word—"i-tis." Now we think that better diction requires that the second "ih" should be sung with a slight separation from the previous "t"—a light glottal stop: "it:is." The same situation exists with a combination like "and I." Once we were content to hear "an-dI." Now we know that it is better to slightly glottalize the word "I." Singers can do this carefully and well, and the language is the better for it. (Certainly in German this is an essential part of the delivery of the text.) With an orchestral accompaniment, the issue for the chorus is rhythmic accuracy. The vowels must be on time.

Interior consonants often require a shadow vowel to make them heard. Late in Shaw's career, he was occupied almost exclusively with the articulation and pronunciation of the English language. We added shadow vowels all over the place, but especially between two voiced consonants. "And the" as in "And the glory of the Lord," for example, would become "Anduhthe." The neutral syllable would happen on the pitch of the previous consonant and be slipped in right before the next word. "For unto us" would be "For:unto:us:a child-uh:iz-uh-born-uh." Looks like gibberish but sounds fabulous! I marked my text with apostrophes whenever the *schwa* was asked for remembering that it was an unaccented neutral vowel. (Remember that "uh" really works better if it moves toward "ih" to avoid a drop in pitch when "uh" is pronounced.)

All of these devices and many others assist the chorus to achieve rhythmic clarity and energy in the delivery of the text. Arguably, this will help create better ensemble with the orchestra and help the chorus to penetrate the orchestral sonority.

In the matter of *phrasing*, the biggest problem confronting most choirs when they sing with an orchestra (or with any accompaniment, for that matter) is that the breath can add time, and it is not thought of as a rhythmic event. Breath can interfere with the pulse. It is extremely important that breathing places be worked out in the rhythm of the music. As a guiding principle, the breath must be taken from the phrase preceding it and not taken from the phrase that is to come. The breath can be assigned a rhythmical value, and as such it can be rehearsed into the music at the same time the chorus is count-singing.

So, for example, if there is to be a breath at the end of beat three before beat one of the next measure, a decision is made about the duration of the breath, and then it is rehearsed when the music is counted. For example, "1 and 2 and T" with silence for the breath where the "and" following "T" would have been, demonstrates a breath on the "and of three." If it is desirable to have a full quarter note breath (e.g., in a very fast tempo), the breath would occupy all of beat three and the counting would be "1 and 2 and" in the counting with silence for the space of both "T" and "and." Always the point is to keep the rhythmical subdivision or division going in the singers' minds while the breath is being taken.

The shaping of a phrase of music with text is almost always text driven. The best players in an instrumental ensemble want to know the text to assist them in providing accompaniment that is sensitive to the words. This is especially true if you are stressing a syllable or creating a strong/weak grouping in the choral parts in a section in which they are doubling the chorus. Once in a rehearsal of Bach motets with one string on a part, the string player who doubled the choral part sat in the middle of a circle of that voice part. All the carefully worked out nuances in the choral parts were immediately audible to the player. Wonderfully sensitive playing resulted. (It should be noted that the players were all members of the famous Preucil family—sophisticated and talented musicians!) Orchestral parts may be marked with indications of shaping, but it is much faster to actually have the players hear what the singers are doing so that they can play their parts with understanding that is informed by the singers' phrasing.

Musical *line*, the relationship of one pitch to another in the context of a phrase, is often in jeopardy when accompaniment is added to the sonority. Singers tend to be overwhelmed when hearing the orchestra for the first time, for example, and all the inflection and musical refinement that have been so carefully worked into the choral rehearsals are lost as the singers try to hold their own against the sound of the orchestral material. Some of the problem can come from the fact that the chorus may be singing too linearly, in too legato a manner. Let us hasten to add that it is often the case that the orchestra is playing too loudly, but the chorus must be encouraged to sing very rhythmically and often, in order to cut through the orchestral sonority, they must sing less legato, with less line.

Shaw had a particular turn of phrase that has become more and more meaningful to me as I try to help choruses when they sing with orchestras. He would say that musical sound is not like water pouring out of a hose but like beads on a string. Every note has a shape, every syllable has integrity, and every sound of every syllable must be sung...and on time. This image has helped me to think of the legato, and therefore the breath, as the string holding the beads of a necklace together, but the individual sounds of a musical line are the beads themselves. If the chorus is prepared in this way, there is much more definition to the musical line and not simply a long, connected, indecipherable sound in an unrelenting legato articulation.

The concepts of *articulation* and *color* help to determine the character and *style* of music. In the case of articulation, this is one more concept we can use to help clarify and define the chorus in complex textures. It helps me to think of articulation as descriptive of the duration of notes. If a note is marked with a staccato articulation, that note is shortened. If a note is marked with a tenuto articulation, it is lengthened, all within the rhythmic pulse, of course. Accents and *forte-piano* can be considered articulation marks because they almost always require a slight space around the notes that are marked. One of the necessary articulations in choral singing is that which is required in the performance of melismatic music. It is the *martellato*, or "hammered" articulation that pianists know and that singers use to articulate the separate notes in a melisma. This specific articulation requires refined control of the breathing mechanism. Each note in a melisma receives a slight intensification of breath to define it and to separate it from those around it.

The most elegant treatment of melismatic singing I have ever heard is that of Peter Schreier, the famous and eloquent singer who recently conducted a performance of Bach's B Minor Mass at Carnegie Hall. He could not understand why we sang melismatic passages so heavily when his performance made each note sound like the most perfect pearl. Every note was perfectly sung and perfectly clean and clear with no extraneous sounds intruding in-between. How many singers can do such elegant singing? Very few. How many try? All who strive mightily to deliver all those choruses in Handel's *Messiah*.

Some conductors tell singers simply to rearticulate the vowel on every note of a melisma. Others ask for a consonant to be inserted between each note. In the latter case, it is best to avoid the use of the aspirate "h" for articulation on each note. It is far better to use voiced "d" because it does not interrupt the tone with a small spurt of air, and it can carry the pitch of the notes being sung. In some cases, I ask only some singers to insert the consonant. Others can deliver the line with a *martellato* approach to the breath, and the result is usually satisfactory. A few singers adding the consonant will help clarify the line and make it more rhythmically controlled, especially if the orchestra is doubling.

It has often been said that a chorus is a monochromatic instrument. I couldn't disagree more, but one has to work very hard to get singers to explore the *colors* of the voice. We can do this with tone quality itself, of course, asking for breathier sounds or straight tone or exceptionally bright vowels, and I think we should do all of these things as we look for opportunities to expand the color palette of the chorus.

The beginning of the chorus part of Mahler's Symphony No. 2, comes to mind. There are few works requiring a more ethereal sonority, and a special kind of tone is asked for from the chorus: barely audible, exceptionally awe-inspired, and enormously different from anything the listener has heard in the work up to that point. Then think of the Verdi Requiem's opening "Requiem." It is more a breathy plea than anything and requires a very special tone. The Britten *War Requiem* has the remarkable opening, too, and the *a cappella* sections first on "Kyrie eleison," second on "Pie Jesu," and finally on "Requiem aeternam" all require enormous control of a very soft dynamic, precise movement of every syllable, and wonderful unanimity of vowel and tone, but also a quality of sound that takes the breath of the audience away. Or think of a Beethoven *Missa solemnis*. There are moments when one can just feel Beethoven pounding on the table or the nails being pounded into the hands and feet on the cross of the crucified Christ.

In each of these works, the chorus must strive for a sound that conveys the musical event. Often there will be a clue in the orchestral writing. Accents, staccato markings, or *forte-piano* marks will be present for the chorus to duplicate, but there are times when dynamics are simply not enough, and the tone color itself has to change. Taste must govern all such decisions, of course, but to think of the chorus as having only one color is to deny all the expressive possibilities of the voice when it delivers text. In fact, such coloration is an aspect of expression that instrumentalists have been trying to copy for centuries.

All questions of *balance* are dependent on individual circumstances, of course, but the ideal balance is often impossible to achieve because of the number of available singers in a particular section or acoustical anomalies in the performance hall. As long as we have performances where the chorus is behind the orchestra and the singers are on the level of the stage on risers, we will struggle with issues of balance. In the chorus itself, my preference is for a pyramid-like structure. Ideally, I would prefer to have more basses and fewer tenors—and that is not too unlikely—and more altos than sopranos—and that is quite unlikely.

If balances can be worked out in the process of selecting the members of the chorus, fine. If they have to be worked out in the music itself, then a system of voicing the chorus so that some voices "float" or "rove" from one section to another as needed works well. To this end, it is usually better to have the chorus stand in an SATB configuration across the stage from the conductor's left to the conductor's right. Then the lowest soprano and the highest alto stand side by side and can interchange their voice parts when needed, and so on across the entire chorus. This is especially important at the low end of the alto section and the top end of the tenor and at the top of the bass section and the low end of the tenor.

Often the singers in these strategic places sing many notes of another section's part in any given performance. The reasons for this are myriad. I have often asked four or five low altos in a 180–200 voice chorus to join with the first tenors in passages that lie high in the tenor range. I don't want to hear the alto quality; I simply want the highest tenors to have some reinforcement, especially if the part is long and demanding. (I am very careful not to ask altos to sing tenor as a rule, and I try to be certain that the notes in the tenor part that I am asking an alto occasionally to sing lie comfortably for the alto voice.) The same can be said for high altos singing soprano when the soprano part dips into the lowest range of the soprano voice. It works well to shift singers from any voice part to another that can help in easing problems of quality and range. One must be careful not to ask inflexible and insecure singers to do a lot of changing, but a few well chosen voices used for reinforcement here and there can do wonders for problems of balance.

Some conductors prefer to have the chorus sing arranged in quartets and then moving individual voices from one part to another to assist in balance is perhaps less troublesome. I prefer to have the chorus in sections, especially for contrapuntal music, but I will sometimes adjust the arrangement of the sections differently from the SATB formation recommended above. If the number of tenors and basses is significantly smaller than those of the sopranos and altos, I like to center the men in the chorus. Sometimes we stand SBTA. This keeps the basses and tenors next to one another for matters of reinforcement and the tenors next to the altos should the low altos be needed for the highest tenor notes. Sometimes we have stood SBTAS to dilute the volume of soprano in a chorus that is overloaded with the highest voice.

What doesn't work in solving matters of balance is to find yourself constantly saying, "sopranos, sing softer; basses, sing louder." It is usually better to find a way to add and subtract voices from a section to affect balance rather than resorting to stifling some and constantly begging for more from others.

Some final considerations: I think that the most important thing we can do for the chorus in preparing them to sing with an orchestra is to help them sing more rhythmically. They will be greatly aided, and the orchestra will find its task easier if the gesture you use in conducting is clear, concise, and free of idiosyncrasies. Because it is often the case that the orchestra has very little time to prepare the work, the more you can do to help them, the better, even if it means leaving the chorus to sing without you from time to time. The orchestra needs to see a clear downbeat in every measure and important cues from you—a first entry, an entrance after several measures of rest, a pitch change in a part after it has played a large number of measures of a repeated ostinato, a cue of encouragement for a solo line, etc.—but they need clear instructions, and they need to know that you have the score firmly in your mind and ear.

It is important to give the players well-marked parts. You have checked ahead of time for rehearsal letters and measure numbers, you know that the chorus has letters and/or numbers that are the same as those in the orchestra parts, and you have paced the rehearsal carefully so that you can begin on time and end on time, having covered all the necessary music. You are confident that you have rehearsed the difficult spots for both the chorus and the orchestra. You have rehearsed the seams in the music so that everyone is comfortable, and you have the tempos clearly in mind. The only thing left is to enjoy the performance!

Ann Howard Jones is professor of music and director of choral activities at Boston University, where she conducts the Symphonic and Chamber Choruses, teaches graduate choral conducting, and administers the MM and DMA programs in Choral Conducting. In summer 2007, Jones will begin her twelfth season as conductor of the BU Tanglewood Institute Young Artists' Chorus, an auditioned ensemble of eighty high school singers who rehearse and perform at Tanglewood, the summer home of the Boston Symphony. Recognized as a distinguished clinician, adjudicator, teacher, and conductor, she has received a Fulbright Professorship to Brazil, and she has conducted choruses, workshops, and master classes in the U.S., Europe, South America, Canada, and Asia.

From 1984–98, Jones worked with Robert Shaw and the Atlanta Symphony choruses. She was assistant conductor for choruses, sang in the alto section, assisted with the Robert Shaw Chamber Singers, and was one of the organizers of the Robert Shaw Institute. She worked with the Festival Singers both in France and in the U.S. Jones was invited to conduct the Robert Shaw Tribute Singers in performance at the ACDA National Convention in San Antonio in 2002. Choruses at Boston University have been invited to appear at conventions of ACDA in Boston and New York City. In 2004 Jones was awarded the coveted Metcalf Award for Excellence in Teaching from Boston University. She earned the bachelor of music, master of music, and doctor of musical arts degrees from the University of Iowa.

CHAPTER 4

The Conductor's Dream:

Score-Based Imagination, Improvisation, and Inspiration

Jerry Blackstone

What guides the rehearsal process? Why do some performances seem completely natural and inevitable while others feel contrived? What is it that makes rehearsal time seem to fly by? Is it really, after all, only about personality? What is the role of the composer in creating exciting and moving performances? With all the time and energy it takes just to learn the notes, how is it possible to create lasting beauty in the limited time between concerts? Does gesture really matter, given the limited musical sophistication of some of the singers?

Who, on occasion, has not asked at least a few of these questions? The conductor's mission is to create beauty out of raw resources—to take the composer's and the author's limited suggestions and transform them into sounds capable of transforming musical lives for a lifetime. While daunting, this remarkable privilege is ours every time we step onto the podium. Even more important, however, is what happens before we meet with the ensemble. Ask yourself: Have I allowed myself the luxury of being engaged by the poet and the composer? Do I have a strong and valid musical/emotional/intellectual perspective informed by what the composer has given me? Have I chosen repertoire that is challenging and rewarding for everyone?

The process—from repertoire choice to final performance—involves *imagination*, *improvisation*, and *inspiration*. I am firmly convinced that what we do as conductors—how we shape rehearsals, what we stress in rehearsals, the pacing of our rehearsals, the specific tools we use to transform the ensemble from beginners to artists, and the gestural language we use to rapidly communicate this information—emanates from our score-based imagination. Our *dream* guides us through the intricacies of sound, vowel shape, rhythmic vitality, dynamic variation, and the myriad of other choices that come our way. The Book of Proverbs says, "Where there is no vision, the people perish." (Proverbs 29:18). Conductors without a *dream* lead choirs in sluggish rehearsals and "democratically informed" performances, where every singer's vowel color, rhythmic intention or lack thereof, and individualized articulations and dynamics are allowed to flourish.

The successful artistic process, from study through performance, involves *learning* the score, *imagining* the finished artistic product, *showing* the conductor's musical imagination through gestural language, *transforming* the initial sound into the conductor's *dream*, and *en-spiration*—taking the next step toward artistry that makes the music come alive in a personal and communicative manner. This process of imagination, improvisation, and inspiration may conveniently be thought of as LISTEN.

L–earn the score.
I–magine the finished artistic product; formulate the *dream*.
S–how the *dream* through gesture.
T–ransform the initial sound into the *dream*.
EN–spire the performance; take the next step toward artistry.

Learn the Score

Of all the activities in a conductor's life, this step is most often shortchanged. The pressures of e-mail, administration, student interaction, family—in short, life!—tend to get in the way of our spending time with the composer's gift to us. What does "learning the score" really mean? Isn't it enough to play it through at the piano, to listen to a good recording, and to mark where the breaths should be taken? There are as many ways to learn a score as there are scores to be learned and conductors to learn them. There are, however, common elements in every score that deserve our attention if a creative and appropriate *dream* is to be realized.

From Big to Little

Just as one plans a cross-country road trip by starting with a country map, then a state map, then a city map, then a tour of the residence, and finally finding a spot for your toothbrush, the same is true in approaching a score. The possibilities for "big picture" viewing are many: play the work completely through at the piano, visually/aurally hear it in your head, or listen to several excellent recordings. Whatever it takes, the conductor needs to look at the forest or see the mountain range before beginning the painstaking process of delving into the minutiae. Once the big picture has been experienced, determining the work's overall structure is the next step. Questions to ask include: 1) How does the text influence the structure of the piece? 2) What is the structure of the work? Is it in a standardized form (e.g., ABA), or did the composer feel compelled by the nature of the text and his or her musical reaction to it to devise a nonstandard formal structure?

After determining the overall structural, tonal, and textual components (detailed harmonic analysis may be helpful but is not imperative for the conductor's purposes), it is time to purposefully step into the forest and begin to look at both the trail and the trees along that trail. Questions for this step include: 1) If the first section is rather lengthy, are there subsections of shorter durations? 2) If so, how long are they? 3) Is there a reason for these lengths? Might the lengths of these sections influence my pacing of the composition in performances? 4) In each of these subsections, what is the length of each individual phrase?

It is important to realize that there are few right or wrong answers in making the above determinations. One conductor will see a four-bar phrase where another sees an eight-bar phrase and another a twenty-four bar phrase! The important point is that the conductor has looked deeply enough at the music to make a strong and valid judgment from his or her perspective. Having begun with the big picture and then proceeded to examine the smallest details, make sure to note in each part where mistakes, such as awkward intervals and tricky rhythms or entrances are likely to occur, and begin to devise creative solutions to remedy them.

Marking the Score

There are countless ways to successfully mark a score. It is even possible to successfully prepare and conduct a work with no markings whatsoever, although doing so is dangerous and may, except in the case of the most brilliant conductors, produce slipshod performances. Marking a choral score typically involves 1) numbering the measures, 2) editing each vocal line for consonant and breath placements, 3) reinforcing dynamic markings with colored pencils (it is very hard to ignore a bright red *fortissimo* in the tenor line, for example), 4) marking macro and micro structural elements, from big-picture sections to the smallest phrase, 5) noting the various vocal entrances, 6) marking articulations, 7) underlining stressed syllables, particularly in foreign languages, and 8) writing in translations, both word for word and poetic.

Who? Why? When? Where? How?

An informed *dream* brings with it background information on both the composer of the music and the author of the text. Why was the work composed, and for whom was it written? If the work is from a past era, who sang the first performance, and how many performers were involved? Do the location and date of the first performance provide us with significant information regarding placement of the singers and/or instrumentalists? Understanding this information will certainly influence elements of phrasing, dynamic variation, and articulation. Now that the conductor has studied the score, it is time to develop the *dream*, to *imagine* the ideal performance.

Imagining the Dream

Conductors who approach a rehearsal without a dream realize their level of aspiration immediately. If I just want food, it is pretty easy to find a meal. If, however, I imagine a gourmet meal, including appetizer, main course, and dessert (of course!), that will take a good deal more time to plan and execute. A run-of-the-mill rehearsal and an average performance are not difficult to accomplish, but an artistically compelling performance requires a dream that informs the entire process, from the preparatory beat of the first rehearsal, right through to the release of the final note in the performance.

Building Your Dream Account

Dreams are built on past experiences. Listening to evocative and artistic performances by other ensembles adds principal to one's dream account. If one is to become an artistic conductor, it is important to listen to great choral and instrumental ensembles rehearse and perform great music. Stand in the back of the room during rehearsals of fine orchestras and bands, and analyze why they sound so beautiful or dramatic. Watch other conductors, and analyze why the music sounds the way it does for them. Several years ago, the five living former conductors of the University of Michigan Men's Glee Club were invited back to campus to each lead a piece with the ensemble during one of the concerts. I was immediately struck by the remarkably different sounds the group made for each of the conductors. Not one of them said, "I'd like you to sound _____." They simply rehearsed and conducted their pieces, yet the ensemble sounded different for each conductor.

Sing in a great choir led by a fine conductor, and personally experience what it feels like to be led by someone else. Continually ask yourself, "Why? Why did he or she make that choice of gesture, or tone color, or vowel sound? What effect did it have on my ability to sing freely and communicatively? How would I have done it differently? Why was I inspired to go beyond the notes in that performance?"

The Score-Based Dream

Artistic dreams are often the result of careful analysis of the interplay of text and music. How does the music amplify the words? What do I think the author is saying, and how does the music paint it, clarify it, or, perhaps, distort it? Nearly every phrase of text has a "color" word or thought, such as "*deep* peace," "*crying*," "*amazing* day," or "*sweetly* sang." It would be hard to imagine performing Haydn's *Creation* without consciously attempting to paint the "*ponderous* beast" or the "*light* and *flaky* snow." To avoid the obvious opportunity to vocally embody these ideas is to accept black and white instead of full color.

The musical score often includes dynamic, tempo, and articulation indications. These "givens" should most often be just that—the starting points from which the dream is developed. To change a composer's specific markings is dangerous and can be presumptuous. We are all aware of exceptions in which a slightly different tempo can make the difference between success and disaster, but by and large we must adhere to the composer's specific suggestions. Merely aurally reproducing the printed score, however, is not enough. The compelling *dream*, one that is convincing and deeply felt, will have a conductor's well-reasoned and intuitive perspective. "I can't imagine it any other way" is most often the guiding principle behind an artistic conductor's rehearsal process. Coming to the first rehearsal with a specific musical dream allows the conductor to proceed with energy, engagement, confidence, and forward vision.

Will the dream change during the rehearsal process? Absolutely! Every ensemble is unique, bringing with it its own individual singers' strengths and weaknesses. Each singer's artistic abilities will also influence the possibilities available to the conductor. It is, for example, artistically valid and exciting to conduct *Messiah* with either 180 singers or with 20, and each ensemble will affect the conductor's dream to a remarkable extent.

A score-based dream enables the conductor to energetically lead rehearsals from a big-picture perspective. "I've been there, and you are going to love it" is quite different from "I'm riding the bus with you and am wondering where we're headed." This is particularly important when rehearsing new and stylistically unfamiliar repertoire with singers.

Show the Choir Your Dream

Don't tell them—*show them*! When the dream has been deeply informed and shaped by the score, it is possible for every gesture to flow from that perspective. If the conductor imagines a passage to be *gently piano*, then an appropriate *gently piano* gesture will more naturally occur. If the ensemble is to efficiently realize the conductor's dream, then every gesture must reflect that dream. Problems occur when conductors 1) mirror what is coming back to them instead of providing the visual solution, 2) think no one is watching and thus provide very little gestural information for those who *are* watching, or 3) work too hard, thus clothing the gestural dream in static and irrelevancies.

If we reflect what we hear instead of what we dream, we allow the ensemble to get in the way of the efficient realization of the dream. "It's too loud!" spoken or yelled while conducting in a large or generic manner *sounds* ridiculous, but, in point of fact, this is often done. Extra loops, jerks, swoops, sweeps, and hitches are more often the conductor's reaction to a lethargic or musically untrained ensemble than a direct visual interpretation of his or her dream. If a dish has too much salt in it, will the chef add more? Conductors, however, often overconduct in an effort to instill overt musical ideas in a seemingly less-than-responsive ensemble. The conductor is the keeper/sharer of the dream, which means sharing it in a gesturally viable manner, beginning with the preparation for the first note of the warm-up of the first rehearsal. If, as Paul Vermel used to remind us, "conducting is the communication of music information through pantomime," then the pantomime needs to match the dream as much of the time as possible.

"But no one is watching! They're only reading, you know." While few may be looking directly at the conductor, they are *all* watching. The conductor influences the ensemble simply by how he or she says "good morning," by his or her personal appearance, and by how tidy the room is. Every gesture, every facial movement, every spoken and sung sound made by the conductor influences the ensemble. While the singers may not observe 100 percent of the conductor's gestures during the reading stages of a new piece, they are observing and storing artistic ideas.

It is crucial, therefore, that the conductor's gestures match his or her dream from the very beginning. It is even more crucial that *musical expression* and *shape* be expected from the ensemble beginning with the first note of the learning process. If the conductor waits until all of the notes are learned and all of the text is immaculate, then blandness becomes the ingrained norm. There should never be "note banging" sessions. If the music is worth singing, then it is worth our musical souls from the moment we start the process. Why allow ourselves and our singers to be less than spectacularly musical in every rehearsal? Our colleagues who teach voice expect vocal and musical excellence at all times, and so should choral conductors.

"But I need to work really hard to get them to sing a pulled, legato line. I'm earning all of this money; I really should look like I'm working hard." Conductors who work too hard by clothing their gestures in extra loops, hooks, swoops, and hiccups engender singers who routinely think, "He/she doesn't really mean I'm supposed to sing that phrase with jerks and hiccups; he really means I should sing it in a legato manner." The more we gesturally say exactly what we mean, the more quickly the rehearsal process will proceed and the more we will hear from ensemble members, "He/she is easy to sing for. I feel vocally free when I sing in that ensemble."

Transform What Comes Back

It would be wonderful—and extraordinary—if the conductor's dream-based gestures automatically corrected all vocal faults and instantly connected with every singer in the ensemble. If that were the case, conductors' gestures would improve quite dramatically! But since there will always be issues of pitch, timbre, vocal color, articulation, dynamics, etc. that must be corrected, we are forced to be creative in the manner in which we address them. We must transform what we *hear* into what we would *like to hear*; in other words, we must make it into our dream.

Almost anything is fair game during rehearsals. This may include jumping, standing, sitting, using falsetto, running, dancing, snapping, counting, touching, poking, throwing, and imagining. Whatever it takes to match the dream is fair game. Settling for *normal* or *okay* is not an option. Waiting until the notes are learned before heading for the dream is not an option. Confusing mediocrity with lack of skill is not an option. Selling the ensemble short is not an option. If the conductor can imagine it and can teach it, the ensemble will, in nearly all cases, be able to accomplish it.

Great, transforming rehearsals are improvisational and based on a deep and passionate knowledge of the score. They are not solely based on a conductor's personality, although personality shapes everything conductors do. We are, most often, true to ourselves, and we seldom act in ways contrary to our personalities. Great, transforming rehearsals are successful, however, when the conductor is constantly thinking ahead of the ensemble, analyzing what is working and what is not, and coming up with three or four possible solutions for each problem. Boring and unproductive rehearsals are often based on a logical, prearranged plan. "Plan-less" rehearsals can be just as pointless, but improvisational rehearsals, where the score-based dream infuses every engaging gesture and rehearsal device, are exciting, invigorating, and often mentally and physically exhausting for the conductor and singers alike.

Transforming rehearsals, while seemingly spontaneous, are the result of thoughtful planning. Warm-ups that focus the choir, address the ensemble's vocal and musical issues, and build the ensemble's musicianship skills, help set the vocal stage for a stimulating and productive rehearsal. The alternation of fast and slow tempi, new and familiar pieces, and vocally demanding and vocally restful pieces will help keep the ensemble engaged. Rehearsals tend to be most productive and inspiring when they are viewed as performances, in the best sense of that word.

Great improvisers do not become proficient simply by improvising. They begin by listening and by observing, then by practicing, by trying. Great jazz musicians practice scales, transcribe recordings, sit next to master improvisers, listen to a wide variety of recordings, and take chances. They go for it! Their remarkable ability to make performances new and engaging every time is based on their past experiences, both personal and observed.

The same is true for conductors who lead exciting, improvisational rehearsals. They simply cannot imagine the music being less than spectacular, so they wrack their brains to come up with several possible ideas to make things work better. They adjust their game plan on the fly by carefully watching the ensemble and intently listening to what is coming back. They think: If the pitch is awry, what can I do—or better yet, what can *they* do—to improve it? Will my verbal instructions correct it? Is my gesture enough? Could a gesture or movement from the ensemble correct what I've been talking about for far too long? If I lifted my hand or had the singers lift one of their hands, would this improve intonation? Would a more horizontal gesture improve the linear quality of that phrase? Conductors who approach the rehearsal process with a dream and a bank account full of seemingly spontaneous, corrective ideas will encounter willing, engaged, creative, and artistic ensembles. A compelling performance is but a short step away.

En (In)-Spiration

Defining inspiration in the choral rehearsal and performance process is nearly impossible. A compelling performance causes us to hear the music in a new way, as if for the first time. Compelling performances often appear to be effortless, natural, and inevitable, as if someone were telling a deep and heartfelt story and we were the privileged listeners. We also know that one's perspective dramatically affects how a performance is perceived. For example, the experience of *singing* the Duruflé Requiem may be quite different from *hearing* the Duruflé as an audience member. Conducting the Requiem will provide a third perspective. We also know that the very same performance may be completely compelling for one listener and a dreadful bore for the listener's friend. How, then, is it possible for the conductor, with a score-informed dream, to inspire the singers toward a compelling performance? While there are myriad possibilities, let me suggest a few key ideas.

Internalizing the Text

Has rehearsal time been allotted for not only pronouncing and enunciating the text clearly and evocatively by the ensemble, but also for ingesting the meaning behind the words? It is one thing to sing a requiem text and another to sing the same text having recently lost a loved one. While a death in the family is not necessary for a singer to project a profoundly moving requiem movement, it is exceedingly important for singers to "make the text their own," to sing thoughts rather than syllables. Is it necessary to actually believe a text before one can present a compelling performance? Of course not. Similarly, one need not be a thief to portray a thief on stage. One has to, however, *imagine* how the thief might feel and act, in short, develop a motivation for the action. The same is true when singing. "Why?" and "How?" are viable questions for every singer to ask, particularly in the final stages of preparation for a performance.

In addition to creating, understanding, and owning the story behind the words, it is important for the singers to understand the interplay between words and music. While it is helpful, on occasion, verbally to point this out to the singers in the ensemble, it is often just as effective to allow the music to make its own case.

Composers begin with the text, which most often generates the musical impulse. Looking backwards, then, can be very informative and inspirational. "Why was the music written as it was?" is a question that can have a great impact on the performance. There are as many possible answers to this question as there are personalities and abilities in the ensemble. Allowing the performers to come to their own conclusions can be helpful. But it may also be advantageous, and perhaps even imperative, to unify a group's image of certain passages. Each great work presents different opportunities for textual/musical relationships, and it is up to the conductor and the ensemble to decipher how these relationships will influence, even infect, the performance. It is not good enough to just sing beautifully. We must sing and conduct from a perspective of intimate familiarity with both text and music.

Is It Fabulous?

Normal is boring. Beige is bland. Good is only okay. While there is a time and place for everything (having one's body temperature noted to be "normal" is preferable to the alternative), normal, beige, or good choral singing is less than optimal. Many times, a simple reminder to be as "beautiful" or "terrific" or "expressive" or "elegant" as possible (the list is endless) will aid in achieving a compelling performance.

I remember a vocal master class I attended that left a lasting impression on me. A young singer had just given a lovely performance, and it was time for the master teacher, the late Arlene Auger, one of America's great singers, to share her wisdom. Expectations in the room were high because Ms. Auger had presented a magnificent recital the evening before, and we were, of course, hopeful that she would share insights into how she sang so elegantly and expressively. Ms. Auger responded to the performer with a gentle, "Would you sing that again even more beautifully?" The singer responded with an even lovelier performance than the first. This time, Ms. Auger responded to the singer, whose name was Barbara, with "Is that the most beautifully Barbara can sing it?" The third time Barbara sang the song, it was absolutely magical. Everyone in the room knew immediately that we had witnessed something very special. Ms. Auger could have offered hints about dynamic variation, vowel color, textual/musical relationships, physical gestures, eye contact, or dramatic intent. Instead, she simply encouraged Barbara to perform as only Barbara could, expecting her to project her deepest emotions through her very beautiful voice.

I have often stood in the back of the rehearsal hall of the University of Michigan School of Music, Theatre, and Dance and listened to H. Robert Reynolds rehearse the symphony band. In sustained, elegant passages the sound was absolutely golden and burnished. I would leave those rehearsals imagining how I could engender that same lushness in the choirs I was conducting. I finally asked one of the players why the symphony band always sounded so beautiful when Professor Reynolds was conducting. He replied, "He simply expects us to play our very best all the time."

Inspiring and compelling performances will not be far away if singers are expected to sing their very best at every minute of every rehearsal. Every aspect of the process will be affected, from the gesture to the sound, from the first note of the first rehearsal right through to the final release of the performance. Compelling performances stem from a deep and profound knowledge of the score that influences every aspect of the rehearsal and performance process. Every gesture, every rehearsal device, every vowel color, every articulation, every dynamic nuance, every communicative phrase is informed by the conductor's score-based dream.

Dream in full color!

Acknowledgments:

To every conductor whom I have observed and admired and with whom I have made music.

To Sandra Snow, choral conductor/teacher and former colleague at the University of Michigan, whose ideas about score study and rehearsal improvisation continue to be exceedingly helpful.

To Dody Blackstone, my editor-in-residence and dearest friend.

Jerry Blackstone is director of choirs and chair of the Conducting Department at the University of Michigan School of Music, Theatre, and Dance, where he conducts the Chamber Choir, teaches conducting at the graduate and undergraduate levels, and administers a choral program of eleven choirs. In February 2006 he won two Grammy Awards (Best Choral Performance and Best Classical Album) as chorus master for the critically acclaimed Naxos recording of William Bolcom's monumental *Songs of Innocence and of Experience*. Professor Blackstone is considered one of the country's leading conducting teachers, and his students have received first place awards and been finalists in both the graduate and undergraduate divisions of the ACDA Biennial National Choral Conducting Awards competition. *U.S. News and World Report* ranks the graduate conducting programs at the University of Michigan first in the nation.

Professor Blackstone has appeared as festival guest conductor and workshop presenter in twenty-eight states as well as Hong Kong and Australia. Choirs prepared by Blackstone have appeared under the batons of Neeme Järvi, Nicholas McGegan, Raphael Frübeck de Burgos, James Conlon, and Yitzak Perlman. As a strong advocate for the training of young musicians, Professor

Blackstone serves as director of the University of Michigan's Summer Programs for High School Students and Adults, which includes MPulse Ann Arbor, a series of music and performing arts camps for high school students from around the world held on the Ann Arbor campus. Professor Blackstone serves as director of the University of Michigan's summer programs for high school students and adults, and he leads the Michigan Youth Ensembles program.

CHAPTER 5

Composing, Words, Music

Libby Larsen

In 1956 I was five years old, in first grade, and enthralled with the idea of learning. So enthralled, in fact, that I couldn't contain myself and would excitedly chatter on loudly to no one in particular. This behavior quickly earned me the corner seat by the window in the back of the classroom, where I could respond spontaneously (which meant talking out loud, humming, and getting up out of my seat to respond and dance about) without disturbing my classmates. This seat assignment turned out to be a brilliant move on the part of my teacher, Sister Helen Marie, who recognized a passionate communicator when she saw one.

On the desktop of my assigned seat were two No. 2 pencils, a box of Crayolas, a small stack of ruled paper, and three books: a workbook entitled *Think and Do*, a Grade One basal reader, and a Grade One music textbook. We were set up to tackle the basic elements of an educated mind—numbers, letters, colors, and the symbols of music. The game afoot, we regularly practiced writing twenty-six letters, ten numbers, and seven musical tones using pencils or one of three basic color crayons. Then things got really interesting. Numbers went from zero to nine. After nine, you started combining them to make other numbers. Letters went from A to Z. After Z you started combining them to make words.

There were three colors—red, yellow, and blue—which you could combine to make other colors. Musical tones ascended A, B, C, D, E, F, and G. They had another set of names too—Do, Re, Mi, Fa, Sol, La, and Ti—and you could arrange these tones to make intervals.

We learned that A was a letter of the alphabet and that it occupied a place among other letters to make a word. At the same time, we learned that A was a tone in music and it occupied a place among other tones to make a melody. Yes, this A was an exciting and interesting symbol to us! You could use it to make a word, and when you did this it had two sounds, short A and long A. Each sounded different depending on the letters surrounding it. A was also a musical tone that occupied a place among other notes to make up a musical scale. You could use this A to create a melody, and, like the letter A in a word, it also had a different sound depending on the other tones around it.

By sounding out each vowel, figuring out each numeric answer, and creating melodies as we went, we were soon writing simple words, simple equations, and simple music. We became masters of the "four languages" by fifth grade: arithmetic, reading and writing, drawing and painting, and reading and writing music. For us, words, music, mathematical proportion, and color existed in the same creative universe, and each was a part of the other's specialized investigations. I believe this is the point at which I started to compose. It's from this perspective that I view the composer's approach to the relationship between words and music.

Words Are Music/Music Is Words

"Which comes first, the music or the words?" I'm often asked this question in social situations. I can tell by the expectant look on my questioner's face that a tidy but informative answer is anticipated. So I usually respond with something like, "It depends on the composer. Some compose the music first and then put in words. Some find words first and then create the music. Others do both at the same time." In social situations, this answer is usually enough to satisfy the moment. As easy an answer as this is, it is *no* answer at all.

The fact is that words and music are not only inseparable; they are one and the same. Their combination holds the *meaning* of the music. A word has meaning and in the company of other words, it has complex meaning, suggested by context. Music deepens the context by providing an abstract order of sound in time and space, which allows the listener to dwell in emotion—private and unique as that emotion may be.

Take, for instance, the Gregorian chant on the following page.

Each Latin word has its meaning. Put together, the words suggest a complex meaning. Combined with the tones of church Mode 1, the downward sequence of the interval of a third· and the variation in the motive (Mi–Sol–(Mi)–Do/Re–Te–Do–Do), the context becomes much deeper. When you sing or listen to the words and music combined you dwell in an emotion—in this case, one that is ominous and inevitable. This musical phrase from the "Dies irae" is so potent that it evokes this specific emotion whenever and wherever you hear it.

FIGURE 1. Sequence—"Dies irae"

Working for Musical Meaning with a Choir

Composer Dominick Argento, my teacher, considers singing to be the first art. He often suggests that perhaps primitive humans sang *before* they spoke—humming a child to sleep, wailing over the wounded body of a loved one, moaning in prayer to whatever makes the world what it is, or crying out in excitement over a joyous moment. These were the primal beginnings of the lullaby, the hymn, and the glee. Perhaps we composers start here as well, taking the word backwards, before it sounds as a word, searching for ways to heighten the voice to singing, to bring this heightened voice to the poem, and to enhance the poem through song.

Can you imagine a classroom of eleven-year-olds learning to sing the "Subvenite," "Dies irae," and "In paradisum"? In my grade school there were practical reasons for learning to read and write music, just as there were practical reasons to learn to read and write words and numbers. From fifth through eighth grade, we were pressed into service to sing Gregorian chant at church services, including high and low masses, weddings, holy feasts, and funerals. We learned how to pronounce church Latin as well as being taught general translations of the words. While we could look up the words "Day of judgment, day of wrath!" we had no experience in recognizing what these words meant other than a few minor scrapes, such as spilling Kool-Aid on the carpet or dropping a toy cowboy down the sink drain. Yet we, the choir, were charged with carrying the meaning of the "Dies irae" during a funeral mass through our singing.

The Sisters of St. Joseph of Carondelet had to find a way to penetrate our innocence with mysticism. We needed to understand that when we sang "Kyrie eleison" we voiced a supplicant's utterance, a plea for mercy. When we sang "Dies irae" we voiced resolute knowledge of mortality and atonement.

At levels we could understand, the nuns would teach us about the Latin text. Word by word, we learned the history and meaning of each word along with its meaning in the liturgy. The hope was that when we sang "Dies irae, dies illa"("Day of judgment, day of wrath!"), we would naturally color the music with our understanding of the words. This, combined with our youthful age and voices, must have given the meaning of the chant an extraordinary depth.

"You've Got Music and I Can Feel It"

In 2002 at the Sixth World Symposium on Choral Music, the late Moses Hogan and I shared a session in which we discussed how we worked with texts, voices, and choirs. Hogan gave one of the best descriptions I've heard on how a composer works with a choir to find meaning in the words and music of a piece. Rather than paraphrase his message, I thought it best to quote him from the transcripts of that session.

On August 8, 2002, Moses Hogan commented on his session preparing students to sing his new work, "Music Down in My Soul": "I talked to the kids about it ["Music Down in My Soul"] and I said, 'You know, you've got music, and I can feel it. It is that expression that makes the song come alive.' "

In the same session, he commented on singing in an unfamiliar language:

> With young people it is important, I have found, that in singing a song in a foreign language, or when you are doing one of these spirituals, to talk about what this text means to you [the singer]. We had a session, and I said, "I want to hear from you what you feel, what you have received from the text of this song. What do you feel is the message? There is no right or wrong answer. Many times, kids look to us to tell them the answer, and then they respond, "Yes, that's what I feel." But that's not always the case. You have to have an open session, I believe, to find out what the song means to you. Once you do that, you open the door to have them deliver the song, and that's the most important thing...because the singer sings the message... you've got to know that is what you are singing about. I heard a choir sing a composition in a foreign language and they had only learned it from the phonetic side. Not a clue what they were singing about. So there was no passion, there was no facial expression. Sadly, that's not music. And so, once we did that, I believe that enabled the song to go to the next level.

Moses Hogan was right. Going to the next level, that level beyond singing in tune, singing in time, and singing with good diction, is absolutely necessary if a choir intends to communicate the *meaning* of the text to an audience. Words are what inspire composers to write music for choir. We work in layers of great detail with the text in order to compose the music that goes on the page. We count on you and your choir to go to the next musical level with as much curiosity and energy as you can give.

Words Signify More than Their Definitions

When I work with a text, I work in layers. First, I spend a significant amount of time thinking about what the words mean. Then, I spend a great deal of time understanding what the words *signify* beyond their immediate meaning. It's from this understanding that I compose the music. Let me take you through my compositional process by examining a work of mine, the second movement from my piece *The Settling Years*, "Beneath These Alien Stars."

Beneath These Alien Stars

Beneath these alien stars
In darkness I have stood alone.
More than mountains
Come between me and my home.

The desert wind has waved my hair.
Desert sands have etched my face
And the courage of the mountains
Has bound me to this place.

And something of its peace I've won.
I have stood with only God
Between me and the sun.
—Vesta Pierce Crawford

At first reading, Vesta Pierce Crawford's poem expresses the thoughts of someone separated from home by both physical and psychological distance. The words suggest that this person has endured harsh, life-changing, and even life-threatening, conditions. Without actually using the words trip, voyage, or travel, Crawford makes it clear that this person has been on a journey and is now living in a strange new place. Though nothing looks or feels like "home," the person takes comfort in and attains a sense of peace from the surrounding mountains. The poem is an eloquent statement of courage, endurance, peace of mind, and faith. The words are uncomplicated.

I found this poem in the book *Best Loved Poems of the American West*, which caused me to assume that Crawford lived in the Western United States during our pioneer years. Research confirmed this, and, as a result, it might seem obvious that I would choose to compose the music to echo and resonate with "western" musical themes. This would provide a tidy and recognizable situational context for the words and an easy way for the singers to relate to them.

But the poem *signifies* a great deal more than its situational context. Its message is universal and timeless. It resonates with the mythological journeys of Achilles, Ulysses, and the Swiss Family Robinson. Its empathetic touchstone is the ultimate aloneness of the human condition. Its affirmation of faith in a Greater Being is unmistakable. Hasn't each one of us at a pivotal moment in our lives metaphorically "stood with only God between [us] and the sun"?

Three Audiences: Conductor, Attending Audience, and Choir

Creative delight—that's what I'm offered with such a poem. My work is to combine the words with music that will allow the singers to understand what the poem *signifies*. As they perform, I want them to actually *feel* adrift yet grounded, distanced yet home, apprehensive yet confident, bound to a key area in ways alien to their traditional ear training, and, finally, peaceful. *The singers, after all, make up the third audience for the music.* The first audience is you, the conductor. The second is made up of the people who come to hear us sing. The third, and to my way of thinking, the most important, is the choir—an audience who viscerally and spiritually experiences the words and music through performing.

Composing with Musical Tools in Order to Suggest Meaning

Within arm's reach of my composing space is a shelf. It's my "cigar box" of little inspirations, I suppose. On it are a few agates I've found, some feathers, three arrowheads, an antique lamp, an inkwell given to me by one of my dearest friends, an antique folk puppet, a stamp box, a model wooden rowboat with oars, and a small, leather-bound journal. I keep this journal to write down precious quotes, poems, and words.

In one of my favorite quotes, Robert Shaw reminds us, without fanfare, that we must always work deeply and in detail: "I am amazed again and again how the mastery of successive minute details releases floods of spiritual understanding" (Mussulman 242). When I compose for the voice my compositional tools include pitch, harmony, rhythm, meter, the sound of the words, vocal range, color, and breath. These are my "minute details." I expect and assume that you, my conductor and first audience, are also inspired by Robert Shaw and that you will find your way into a new piece of music by discovering and mastering its layers of minute compositional details before you apply the successive, minute details of performance technique.

Pitch

"Beneath these alien stars in darkness I have stood alone."

FIGURE 2. "Beneath These Alien Stars," mm. 7–12

I decided to work with this group of pitches to set the words: Sol–Do–Re–Te–Do–La–Sol–Te–Do–La–Fa–Sol. In numbered scale tones, this is: 5–1–2–flat7–1–6–5–flat7–1–6–4–5, or Dorian mode.

As a conductor, you might approach the pitches of this opening passage using functional harmony, in which case the tonic is D. For the first notes of the singers' lines I chose the melodic interval of a perfect fifth, Sol–Do, or 5–1, to give the singers complete confidence and a feeling that they know where they are going. How many familiar melodies begin this way? A countless number! I added a minute rhythmic detail here though, a quarter rest on the first beat, to weaken the 5–1 relationship just a bit.

It's the arrangement of the next ten notes that gives the singers the visceral experience of "journey," in this case a journey of tonal relationships. In Gregorian chant, pitches relate to each other by intervals and in reference to the tonus. Our Western ears are trained to relate pitches to the tonic differently, using a three-chord framework (I–IV–V). In the above example, the tonic D is embedded linearly, within the vocal line, asking the ear to relate to it as modal chant.

When you prepare the score, you have an interesting choice of journeys in regard to tuning the line. If you tune the line in equal temperament, using the piano as your guide, both Re and Te will need attention. In this line, there is no Mi, which means that tuning the line relies on Sol—making the most important intervals Te–Do, Re–Te, and Sol–Do. Excluding Mi from the line removes the ability of the ear to use the third member of the scale in order to tune Do–Sol or 1–5.

I believe it is most useful for the choir to warm up on modes, *a cappella*, so that they can practice tuning their ears to the subtle differences among the modes in seconds, thirds, fourths, and fifths. To master the difference between tuning the Dorian mode in equal temperament by singing *with a piano* and tuning the Dorian mode *a cappella* is a minute detail. But this specific detail is one that elicits vocal color that unlocks the spirit of the words and reveals yet another meaning for "beneath these alien stars."

Harmony

> "And something of its peace I've won. I have stood with only God between me and the sun."

When Vesta Pierce Crawford chose the words "alien stars" for her poem, was she referring to maritime navigation? Perhaps. Maybe she was thinking of the three wise men following the Star of Bethlehem. Or maybe she had just read J. M. Barrie's *Peter Pan* and was captured by the idea of following the stars to find Neverland. Regardless of her inspiration, when she names the stars as "alien," she provides a profound poetic metaphor: navigation by unknown stars. If you are forced to find your way in a strange place and all you have to guide you are landmarks that you recognize but do not know by experience, how do you do it? Instinct? Sense? Luck? Adaptability?

More creative delight for me! This metaphor is rife with compositional possibilities. How do I provide you (the conductor), the singers, and the audience with a musical experience akin to alien star navigation?

One compositional layer of my solution to this question of providing a musical experience akin to alien star navigation is to work with harmony. For this passage, I decided to use pitches that belong together in an E-flat Lydian scale but are never sung as this scale during the passage. (See Figure 3.)

The pitches are all part of a stacked-third E-flat13 chord: E-flat–G–B-flat–D–F–A–C. The tonic of the chord is E-flat. I composed the bass line so that its points of arrival are on E-flat, G, or B-flat (except on the penultimate measure). This gives the singer's ear the sense, though not necessarily the feel, of being grounded in E-flat throughout this phrase (musical meaning: are we "home" or are we distant from "home"?).

The pitches in the soprano, alto, and tenor are all members of the thirteenth chord, but I've composed each part so that the singer's ear must trust the intervallic tuning by relating pitches linearly, not vertically. Taken alone, the soprano line could be in G minor, the alto line could be in D minor (until m. 92, where it outlines E-flat–G–B-flat), and the tenor could be in C minor (until m. 90, where it could be in B-flat major but actually circles and outlines the seventh, ninth, and eleventh of the E-flat13 chord). Given that E-flat is the root of the chord, the result is that each voice relates by ear to

FIGURE 3. "Beneath These Alien Stars," mm. 83–92

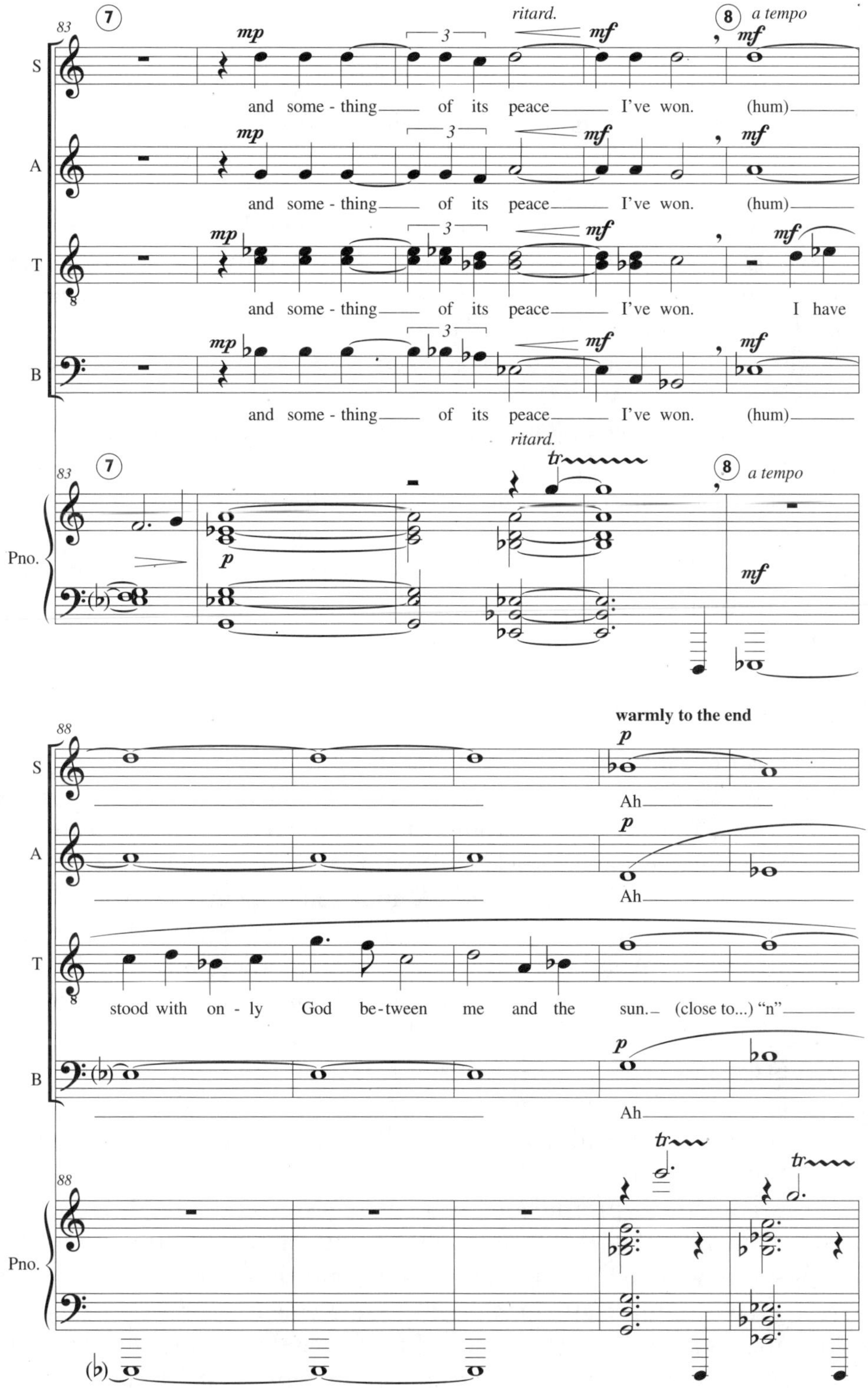

E-flat but not necessarily to the other parts. Each part is *adrift yet grounded, distanced yet home.*

RHYTHM

> "The desert wind has waved my hair. Desert sands have etched my face."

I've been keeping private tabs on how many times I've heard this passage in rehearsals and made the same comment: "The line is too metric, too 'notey.' Could you give it more rhythm and flow and *less* beat and meter? I want you to *sing* the relentless desert wind and endless waves of sand. I want you to *sing* the rhythm of the meaning of the words, not the beats of the notes you see on the page!" (See Figure 4.)

This said, I just can't stop myself from climbing onto a small soapbox and writing a few words about pulse, beat, and rhythm. I suggest you get out your metronome to help illustrate what I'm about to discuss. Set your metronome for any tempo you like. Tempo matters, but not any specific tempo. You have to choose your own. Start your metronome. This is how I think about pulse, beat, and rhythm. Read on.

What is Pulse? Beat? Rhythm?

Pulse is regular reoccurrence—strokes, vibrations, or undulations. You have pulse. Everyday speech has pulse. The Earth has a pulse. All these pulses have different tempi. You have just set your metronome at a tempo and you are now hearing pulse. Does it have stress? No. It's just pulse. If you demonstrate pulse using a metronome for your choir, ask individual members to take their pulses. Then match their pulses to their natural tempi. One singer's pulse tempo might be 72. Another's might be 80. Still another's might be 57. The singers connect immediately to the concept of pulse and can now move to understanding the difference between pulse and beat.

Beat is the imposition of meter and stress on pulse. Beat anchors the music through its precise placement. Beat is not pulse. Beat is not rhythm.

Is your metronome still going? Good. What's the meter? There is none. Not until you assign it.

Go ahead and assign a meter to the pulse. Now you have beat. You've placed a numeric value that defines increments of time to the pulse. You could, if someone asked you, use math to explain those increments of time. You're now practicing math in motion. One element of music is math in motion. You can explain your choice of meter aurally by assigning stress to further define your choice of meter and its servant, beat. If you use your

Figure 4. "Beneath These Alien Stars," mm. 48–52

metronome to illustrate this to the singers, pretty soon they'll be assigning all kinds of simple and complex meters, stresses, and beats to the pulse.

Rhythm is what happens in between and around the beat. Is beat rhythm? Absolutely. If you divide a whole note in half, resulting in two half notes, and continue on, dividing two half notes each in half, resulting in four quarter notes, is this rhythm? No! It's math. It is precise duple subdivision of beat. We might think this is rhythm, and call it rhythm, but it is not rhythm unless (take note!) the style of music *needs* precise duple subdivision as rhythm in order to define the music's style, such as a march, or a Schottische, or "Grandfather's Clock," or "The Geographical Fugue." The fact is that two is two, four is four, and eight is eight—that's all. These are mathematical groupings. *Context* defines what kind of twos, fours, and eights the music needs. And context leads to rhythm.

The best definition of rhythm I've heard occurred in a conversation I had recently with Thelonious Monk, Jr., at Carnegie Mellon University. Five of us were discussing the general confusion among music educators about pulse/beat/rhythm. You can imagine that this discussion, which included two jazz musicians, two composers of notated and electronic music, and a music educator (three of whom were directors of Schools of Music) was, shall we say, lively. Finally, Thelonious Monk, Jr., said (and I paraphrase) that rhythm is *feel* and it happens around and in between the beat. It pulls, it stretches, it smoothes, it soothes, it's what makes music human. After this statement, we all nodded, settled down, and went to dinner.

Is your metronome still going? Practice giving *rhythm* to the pulse to which you've assigned meter, beat, and stress. Have your singers do the same, and see what happens to their musicality and how they communicate the meaning of the music they sing. Rhythm is *feel*. It happens around and in between beats. It's what makes the music human.

Turn off your metronome. I'm climbing off of my soapbox and getting back to successive minute details in "Beneath the Alien Stars."

Vocal Range

> "And the courage of the mountains has bound me to this place."

When writing for the voice, I am extremely careful about using vocal range to help color the words and reveal their meaning and significance. For instance, in this passage you can easily see that I placed the basses in their middle range on the pitches D, E, F, and C. (See Figure 5.) These pitches are supported by the piano in its mid to low range, which reinforces the overtones in the bass part. The combination of the two gives the impression that the basses are singing a texture much richer than it actually is, and this gives musical

FIGURE 5. "Beneath These Alien Stars," mm. 55–59

meaning to the words "has bound me to this place." The basses are bound to G without actually singing it. The upper voices, moving in parallel motion, are bound to the basses.

"I have stood with only God between me and the sun."

For this passage, I placed the tessitura of the soprano, alto, and bass in the mid range in order to focus attention on the tessitura of the tenor, and the leap from C to G, across the break of the voice. High G is approached by a leap rather than by step to give the tenors a moment, small but meaningful, to establish the ideas of wonder and hope and to allow them to believe they will all land together in tune and on pitch. *Musical meaning: A leap of faith.*

You might notice that the words "I" and "me" are placed on the pitch D and the word "God" is placed on the pitch G. "Sun" is placed on F, below G. Yes, this is on purpose, again to suggest meaning—more "minute" details for me to delight in as the composer and for you to discover as the conductor.

BREATH AND BREATHING

In mm. 87–92 (see Figure 3), I assume staggered breathing in the soprano, alto, and bass for two reasons: to focus attention on the words through the efforts of the tenors while they sing "I have stood with only God between me and the sun" and to create a completely vulnerable musical moment (accomplished by the tenors). *Musical meaning: apprehensive yet confident.*

While the soprano, alto, and bass use staggered breathing, the tenors must sing their line in one uninterrupted breath. This is hard to do. For some, it's impossible. Sometimes the section isn't able to sing the line, and so it is assigned to a solo voice.

I would suggest in warming up the choir for this piece that special attention be given to breath support for long phrases like this one. Breath, the placement of breath, and the psychological affect of breath on the words and music are all part of my thinking when I compose.

When all of the above are combined (pitch, harmony, vocal tessitura, and breathing) these ten measures carry musical meaning that transcends the situational meaning of the poem. If the choir accomplishes these ten measures successfully, the singers will indeed experience a musical journey in an alien land (in relationship to their traditional musical journeys). They will feel bound to the new, yet strange, harmonic place, and they will attain a sense of peace in their sonic surroundings. The music they produce will, I hope, take each member of the audience on a similar, though unique and private, journey.

A Word about Warming Up to Rehearse a New Work

I love choral warm-up exercises. Whenever I am invited to work with a choir on one of my pieces, I always warm up with them. Sometimes I get right into the soprano section and fire up my voice.

However, usually I stand off to the side inconspicuously and study the choir as I warm up. Then I wait for the choir to warm up on musical exercises that prepare them to sing my piece. This rarely happens. And I think to myself, "Why would you warm up a baseball team for a tough game by having them kick a soccer ball around a field?" Why not prepare exercises for your choir that pertain to the piece at hand? If the piece warrants it, warm up with melodic intervals such as tritones and sevenths. Try singing modes, practicing impossibly long phrases in one breath, singing with your eyes closed to effect chanting in unison, or playing intricate rhythm games. *Then* get down to rehearsing the piece at hand. I've often thought that the warm-up period of a rehearsal session could be fertile ground for developing instructive, productive, and exciting ways to get at mastering the details of a new work. Creating customized warm-ups for each piece to be rehearsed would warm the hearts of composers, both in and out of the grave.

You may be surprised that I've devoted so much space to text and meaning. Many composers work long and hard to understand the significance of the text *before* they decide on the details of the music: pitch, meter, tempo, texture, vocal ranges, and rhythm. The truth is, this is what happens. And I assume (and hope!), as do my colleagues, that the conductor's exploration of the score begins in the same way. If you work to discover the layers of minute detail any composer worth his or her salt puts into the music, then you will discover all the musical meaning the composer has brought to the page in combining the words and the music. All I expect is that you, the conductor, study my music, in fact *any* composer's music, by remembering Robert Shaw's words: "I am amazed again and again how the mastery of successive minute details releases floods of spiritual understanding."

References

Crawford, Vesta Pierce. "Beneath These Alien Stars." In *Best Loved Poems of the American West*. Compiled by John J. Gregg and Barbara T. Gregg. Garden City, NY: Doubleday, 1980.

Larsen, Libby. "Beneath These Alien Stars," *The Settling Years*. Boston: ECS Music (#4286).

Montani, Nicola A., ed. *The St. Gregory Hymnal and Catholic Choir Book*. Rev. ed. with supplement. Philadelphia: The St. Gregory Guild, Inc., 1940.

Mussulman, Joseph A. *Dear People…Robert Shaw: A Biography.* Bloomington, IN: Indiana University Press, 1979.

Libby Larsen is one of America's most performed living composers. She has created a catalogue of more than 220 works spanning virtually every genre, from intimate vocal and chamber music to massive orchestral and choral scores. The Grammy Award–winning composer is widely recorded, and more than fifty CDs feature her work. She is sought after for commissions and premieres by major artists, ensembles, and orchestras from around the world and has established a permanent place for her works in the concert repertoire.

As a vigorous, articulate advocate for the music and musicians of our time, in 1973 Larsen cofounded the Minnesota Composers Forum, now the American Composer's Forum, which has become an invaluable aid for composers in a transitional time for American arts. The former holder of the Papamarkou Chair at John W. Kluge Center of the Library of Congress, Larsen has also held residencies with the Minnesota Orchestra, the Charlotte Symphony, and the Colorado Symphony. She is currently completing a book, *The Concert Hall That Fell Asleep and Woke Up as a Car Radio* and her next major opera work, *Every Man Jack.*

CHAPTER 6

Enhancing Musical Performance through Somatic Pedagogy

An Introduction to Body Mapping for Choral Conductors[1]

Heather J. Buchanan

> The singer uses his body both to sustain life and to cultivate his art. He can never escape from himself, for his physical life either furthers or hinders his artistic life.
>
> —Wilhelm Ehmann
> *Choral Directing*

Introduction

The quality of movement is critical for musicians because it is movement that underlies all forms of musical communication and expression. Choral conductors have a dual responsibility to secure the quality of their own movement and that of their singers. We know that singers are profoundly influenced by what they see us doing on the podium, so it behooves us to cultivate freedom and poise in our gestures so we can communicate a full range of musical intentions and simultaneously promote good body usage in our singers. Musical sound is directly affected by the type of movement that produces it. For example, a conductor whose posture is characterized by the head being pulled down and forward will compress the sound of the choir. Similarly, the conductor who fails to gesture with a correctly aligned arm structure will be severely limited in his or her ability to move gracefully and safely and will, consequently, operate within a confined musical range and always with the specter of injury close by.

In the opening chapter of his book *Directing the Choral Music Program*, Kenneth H. Phillips writes, "Every choral conductor automatically assumes the role of teacher. There is no escaping the responsibility of imparting knowledge in the choral art." In my experience, the knowledge we are obliged to impart must begin with the body, the instrument with which we, as conductors, perform. I work with the sequence MIND–BODY–SPIRIT–MUSIC because the mind-body connection is the vital foundation for music-making and facilitates the spirit-music relationship. Musicians who fail to honor the mind-body relationship suffer no matter how musical their imaginations or well intentioned their expressive ideas.

During my student years at Westminster Choir College of Rider University, I often heard the words of the late Frauke Haasemann quoted to the conducting students: "There are no bad choirs, only bad conductors." This blunt statement underscores the conductor's vital leadership responsibility for the *complete* choral experience—which must include mind-body awareness.

Body Mapping

A new discipline rooted in the somatic (mind-body) tradition established by The Alexander Technique, Body Mapping achieves freedom of movement through accuracy of the body map, one's physical self-representation in the brain. Body Mapping is a valuable means by which choral directors may secure quality in their own movements and also effectively teach the movement of singing to their choristers. It is important to emphasize that injury prevention and promoting technical facility are the two primary purposes of Body Mapping. By cultivating "inclusive awareness," the combination of inner awareness (kinesthetic, tactile, and emotional) with auditory and visual information, the conductor and singers experience heightened musical awareness and complete freedom of expression through poised, dynamic, musical movement.

FIGURE 1. Definitions

Somatics:	The study of the body in movement, derived from the Greek root *soma* meaning "body." F. Matthias Alexander was a pioneer in the field of somatics, along with Moshe Feldenkrais, Mabel Todd, and Irmgard Bartenieff. Today's pioneers are neurophysiologists who study how the brain creates movement.

FIGURE 1. Definitions (continued)

Body map: A scientific term that first appeared approximately one hundred years ago. Body map means "physical self-representation" and is used interchangeably by scientists with the terms "body scheme," "body model," "neuronal representation," and "internal representation." We literally map our own bodies with our brains, and our body maps are very specific. The brain maps our structure, our function in whole and in part, and our size.

Body Mapping: "The conscious correcting and refining of one's body map to produce efficient, graceful, coordinated, and effective movement."[2] It is a self-inquiry method for correcting one's body map that was originally discovered by William Conable in the early 1970s and is being further developed today by Barbara Conable and the members of Andover Educators. Founded by Barbara Conable in 1987, Andover Educators (www.bodymap.org) is a growing network of teachers dedicated to "saving, securing, and enhancing musical careers with accurate information about the body in movement."[3]

The Alexander Technique: "A simple and practical method for improving ease and freedom of movement, balance, support, flexibility, and coordination. Practice of the technique refines and heightens kinesthetic sensitivity, offering the performer a control that is fluid and lively rather than rigid. It provides a means whereby the use of a part—a voice or an arm or a leg—is improved by improving the use of the whole body, indeed, the whole self."[4]

Why Body Mapping?

For generations, music teachers have had to teach without an effective way of conveying accurate information about the most significant of all instruments—the body. Most taught movement intuitively (often with inbuilt patterns of misuse) and with imagery. The result is that musicians the world over are suffering from pain and limitation in their performing, many to the point of losing their careers. Research findings from numerous sources, including the International Conference of Symphony and Opera Musicians, students at Catholic University's Benjamin T. Rome School of Music, the American Symphony Orchestra League, and the Orthopedic Research Institute in Muenster, Germany, cite unacceptably high statistics of injury in the music profession.[5]

The range and severity of musicians' injuries are astounding and include (but are not confined to) conditions such as thoracic outlet syndrome, tendonitis, carpal tunnel syndrome, focal dystonia, temporomandibular joint disorder, and rotator cuff tendonitis. Music medicine is, of course, the appropriate first step for any musician suffering from pain and the most appropriate means of treating a medical condition. Unfortunately, music medicine has only been successful in treating conditions that have a medical cause. When body misuse is the cause of the problem, the situation needs to be addressed with movement retraining based on correcting and refining the musician's faulty body map.

Musicians Move for a Living!

Musical performance is incredibly demanding! In fact, musicians make demands on their bodies similar to those of top-level athletes and dancers, though typically for longer periods of time. In addition, musicians are engaged in actions that are more highly repetitive and require fine-motor control of the delicate musculature of the upper body extremities, whereas athletes and dancers work with predominantly large muscle movements. Finally, unlike musicians, athletes and dancers are trained to think of themselves as movers, so body awareness and good form are integral parts of their technique from the outset. Unfortunately, the majority of musicians are largely ignorant of their bodies, and until they make the radical paradigm shift to think of themselves as movers, they are at risk of developing problems ranging from performance limitations at the lesser end of the spectrum to debilitating injuries in the worst cases. It is a simple fact: bodies that are out of balance are susceptible to pain and injury.

Body Map Errors

Body Mapping cultivates an accurate and adequate body map, trains movement, trains the relevant senses, and trains attention. In the body map, *structure* is our anatomy, primarily the neuromusculoskeletal system, with organs such as the lungs also included; *function* refers to physiology, the way anatomical structures interact in movement; and *size* refers to the dimensions one has mapped for the various body parts and the whole of oneself. For example, a conductor who has accurately mapped his or her spine—its structure, its function, and its size—will have core support for gestures and will evoke a sound from the choir that reflects the ease and grace of his or her movements.

There are various types of common errors in a body map, which result in movement that is either awkward or potentially injury producing for conductors. Size errors are among the most widespread mapping inaccuracies. For example, size mis-mapping is evident in conductors who habitually stoop or compress their bodies to fit their psychological self-concept that they are in fact shorter in height than they really are. Stooping will cause many problems for a conductor, including poor breathing, restricted arm movement, and possibly neck pain.

One structure that is often mis-mapped is the arm. For example, the conductor who believes the arms begin at the shoulder joints instead of the sternoclavicular joints will have limited range of motion of the arms. Attempting to rotate the lower arm at the wrist instead of the elbow and using the wrist like a hinge are both examples of functional mis-mappings. Vagueness, blankness, or absence of a body part in the body map is also a mapping error. Conductors *must* carefully consider the effects of their movements on the choir too; all mis-mapping is detrimental to the singers and the choral sound.

Training the Senses

Students of Body Mapping are trained to use and coordinate four of the six senses: visual (sight), aural (sound), tactile (touch), and kinesthetic (movement). The common absence of kinesthesia in the training of the senses accounts for much of the ignorance of the relationship of this sense to the others, in particular the kinesthetic-aural connection, which is paramount for musicians.

Training Movement

The easiest way to retrain a tense or inefficient gesture is to correct and refine the body map governing the movement. This is analogous to correcting the score from which the musician reads rather than constantly fixing the wrong note he or she is playing. Modeling good movement is also powerful—the conductor who does this is a valuable visual role model for his or her choristers.

Training Attention

Body Mapping often uses the analogy of playing in tune to teach musicians how to apply sensitivity, discernment, and responsiveness to their kinesthesia. As musicians we use our auditory sense to hear a pitch, discern if it is in or out of tune, and correct accordingly. We are also capable of similarly training our kinesthetic sense to be able to feel our bodies as we sing and conduct, discern if our movement is correct, and respond by adjusting the movement so we either come back to balance or free ourselves to move more effectively.

Figure 2 summarizes this analogy. In this figure, the key elements (sensory awareness, sensitivity, discernment, and responsiveness) are initially presented in the analogy to the auditory sense that is familiar and readily understood by musicians. The introduction of the kinesthetic sense is presented in terms that are parallel to the language and experience of musicians, thereby enhancing their comprehension of these concepts and how they are experienced.

FIGURE 2. Sensitivity–Discernment–Responsiveness

Sense	Sensitivity	Discernment	Responsiveness
Auditory	I hear the note I'm playing.	I sense the note is sharp.	I bring the note back in tune.
Kinesthetic	I feel my body as I perform.	I sense I'm off balance.	I bring myself back to balance.

"Attention" is the scientific term used by Andover Educators on the recommendation of T. Richard Nichols, PhD (science advisor for Andover Educators and a neurophysiologist at Emory University) because the word "attention" connotes what musicians do. Synonymous with attention are awareness, consciousness, and mindfulness—all terms that describe the completeness of sensory information and experience necessary for musicians who must cultivate the ability to be simultaneously self-perceiving and world-perceiving.

The good news is that an inaccurate body map can be replaced over time with an accurate body map through the conscious process of remapping because human beings are born with the innate ability to map their bodies. Our body maps are naturally amenable to change because our bodies experience physical changes throughout the lifecycle, e.g., when we grow as infants, children, and adolescents; lose or gain weight; experience pregnancy; and as we age. The adequacy and the accuracy of our body maps ultimately determine the quality of our movements. For musicians engaged in the precise art of musical performance, the body by extension becomes a precision instrument. A fundamental Body Mapping principle therefore applies: the integrity of any movement is dependent upon the integrity of the body map that governs it.

Consider the ease and grace of your musical movements. Can you find balance? Are you poised? Is your body a dynamic, responsive instrument that readily serves the demands of your performing? Do you experience freedom in your music-making? If the answer to these questions is an unequivocal "yes," then congratulations! You are safe from pain and injury and will know no physical limitations in your technique. However, if the answer to these questions is "no," "maybe," or "sometimes," then consider how Body Mapping can help you enhance your musical performance ability.

The Core of the Body

The human body is built around the spine, which functions as the core structure for our balance. Whenever we sing, conduct, or play, we should perform with our entire body, which is supported and organized centrally around our spinal core. Visualize the core of a well-formed apple that provides the central structure for the surrounding flesh of the fruit. This metaphor translates to the location of the weight-bearing (forward) part of the spine in the human body. Do you have an accurate body map of the structure, function, and size of your spine? Experience has shown that people who have accurately mapped the spine and understand its true size will experience an increased sense of strength and stability in their curvy vertebral column.

FIGURE 3. The Spine in Context

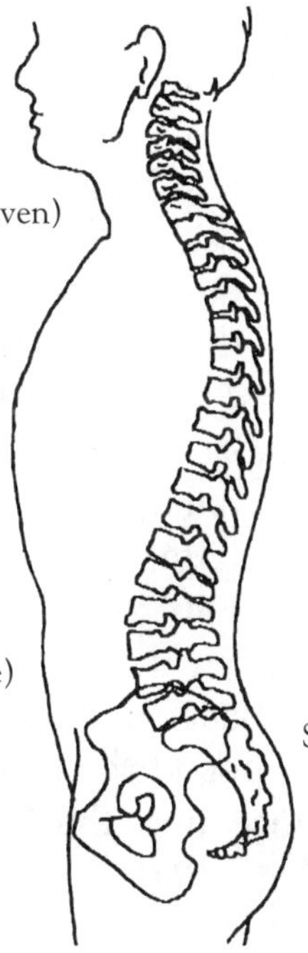

Illustration by David Gorman

- **Structure.** The spine is comprised of five divisions—seven cervical vertebrae, twelve thoracic vertebrae, five lumbar vertebrae, the sacrum, and the coccyx. The size and shape of the vertebrae vary according to their function. The spine is segmented and has four natural curvatures—cervical, thoracic, lumbar, and sacral. There is also space to house the spinal cord.
- **Function.** The spine is our massive internal support. The four curvatures help to maintain balance, absorb shocks, increase strength, and protect from fracture during movement. Two important functions of the spine are weight bearing and weight delivery (front half) and nerve protection (back half). Look again at a picture or a model of the spine, and you will clearly see how this is possible. The spine's flexibility is due to its ingenious structure, which allows conductors to be very mobile, bending and twisting the torso as needed to gesture. Most important is the "gathering and lengthening" movement that occurs during breathing.
- **Size.** The spine is a massive structure providing support for the body and all its movement. The shape and size of the vertebrae correspond to the function and the amount of weight they bear. For example, each vertebra is bigger than the one above because it has to bear and deliver more weight.

The Places of Balance

In order to teach musicians how to stand and sit easily, Body Mapping teaches six places of balance: the atlantooccipital (A-O) joint, lumbar spine, hip joints, knees, arches of the feet, and arm structure (see Figure 4).

These particular locations are taught first because they are the places where balance can be discerned most easily, although we ultimately use almost all places in our body (except for organs) to find balance. Achieving balance, standing or seated, is thwarted by the twin evils of "posture" or "relaxing." For example, the cultural virus of "good posture" is perpetuated by well-intentioned conductors whose instructions to "sit up straight" or "pull your shoulders back" or "elevate your chest" result in an unnatural posture and tension detrimental to effective body usage. By contrast, attempts to coax choristers out of a "stiff" or "wooden" posture with instructions to "relax" while they sing often results in slumping or some kind of drooping in the body alignment. Both of these cultural viruses result from mis-mapping the core of the body. Teaching our singers to find balance or poise around the core, and to discern the places of balance in relation to core balance, frees them to develop dynamic and poised body usage.

FIGURE 4. The Places of Balance

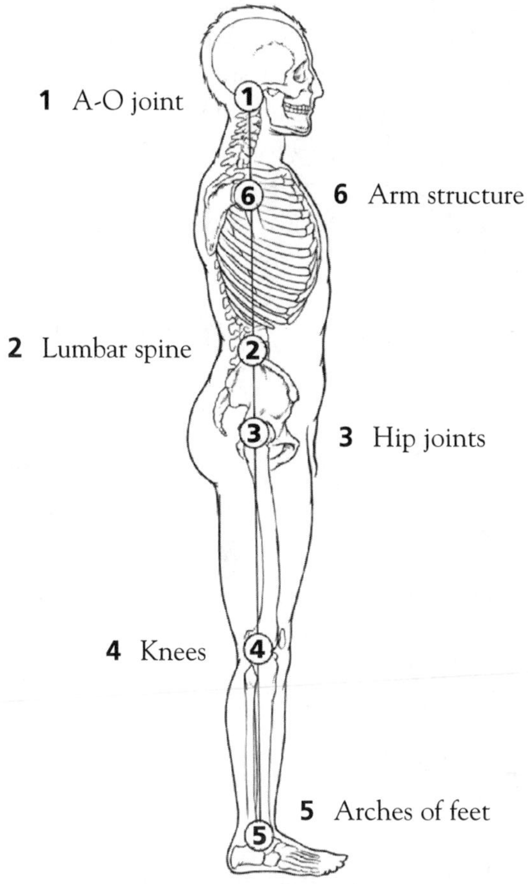

Illustration by Benjamin Conable.

The effects of misalignment on sound will vary according to the distortion of balance. As you read through the descriptions of each of the six places of balance, experiment with the effects of going on and off balance on your conducting gesture or your voice. You will know when you have found balance—it is the place where your body is at ease and movement in any direction is facile.

The places of balance are not positions we remain fixed in once we've found them. Rather, we will need to move in and out of balance as we conduct and sing. The importance of the places of balance is their role in organizing our body movement. Balance is the place where we begin and end and the place we will return to frequently during performances. Because it is the place of "no work," balance naturally facilitates the cultivation of muscle recovery required when the body is working, and this contributes to the overall ease of movement required to perform. The following are further explanations of the points labeled in Figure 4.

1. **A-O joint:** the place where the top vertebra (atlas) meets the base of the skull (occiput); this is where the skull balances on the spine. You can locate the A-O joint by finding the intersection of an imaginary line from right between the ears at the sides, the base of your nose at front, and the base of the occipital bone at the back/base of your skull. You will need to locate the A-O joint using your kinesthesia. We free the A-O joint by intention, in the same way we think and sing a pitch. Learn to free the A-O joint so your head balances beautifully at its center on the spine.

FIGURE 5A. The A-O Joint

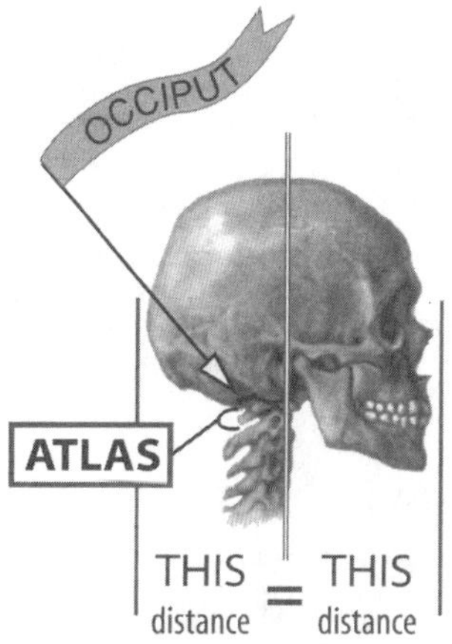

FIGURE 5B. The A-O Joint

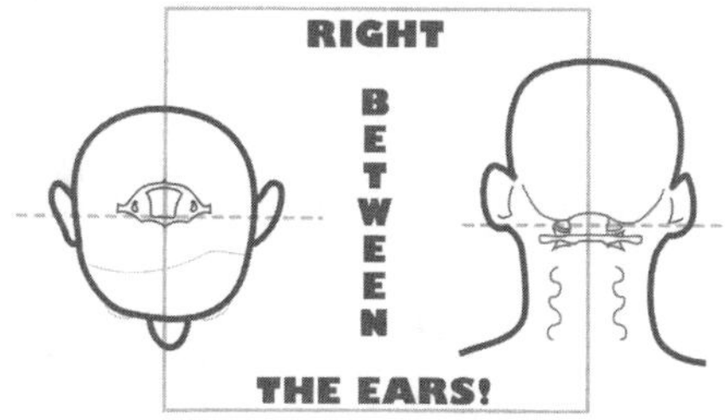

Illustrations this page by Benjamin Conable.

2. **Lumbar spine:** the place where we balance our thorax on our lumbar vertebrae.

FIGURE 6. The Lumbar Spine

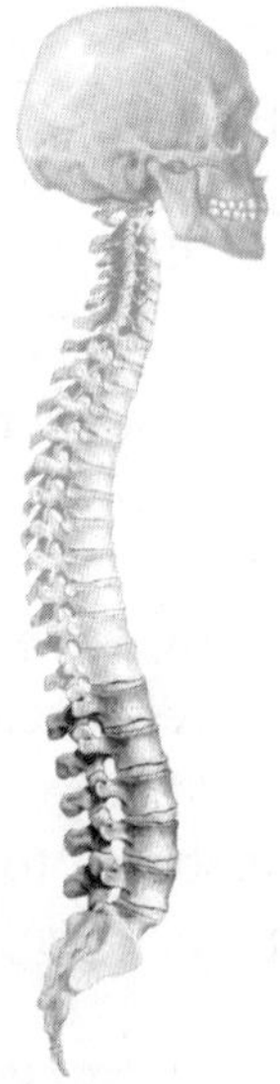

The five lumbar vertebrae are the largest vertebrae and are designed to bear the weight of the thoracic area and above. Explore the effects of balancing your thorax, along with your head, neck, and arm structure, on your lumbar vertebrae. You can locate the lumbar core via the sides of your body where you feel the pelvic crest. From this position, trace your hands to the center of your body, front and back. This places you at approximately vertebra number three, the middle of the five lumbar vertebrae, and the center of your lumbar spine. It is also the center of your lumbar vertebrae from front to back. Study Figure 3 again to see the central location of the lumbar vertebrae.

3. **Hip joints:** the exact halfway point top to bottom in human beings, not the waist. The pelvic rockers constitute our base for sitting, i.e., upper body weight is transferred through the lumbar spine into the pelvic rockers; and when standing, weight is delivered by the pelvic arch out to the center of the thigh bone (femur) downward to the knees.

FIGURE 7. Hip Joints and Pelvis

- When seated, the pelvic arch delivers weight into sitting bones.
- When standing, weight is delivered by pelvic arch out to the center of the thigh bone (femur) downward to the knee.

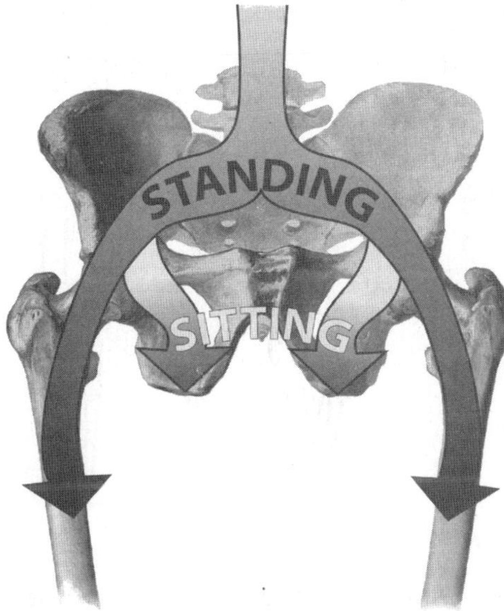

Illustration by Benjamin Conable.

Experiment with the balance of the pelvis when seated and standing. Notice that when you are seated with core balance you don't sit on your legs at all because your legs are external to your pelvis. You get stability when seated by delivering the weight of your upper body through the weight-bearing spine and ensuring your balance is centered over the hip joints and pelvic rockers.

FIGURE 8. Seated Balance

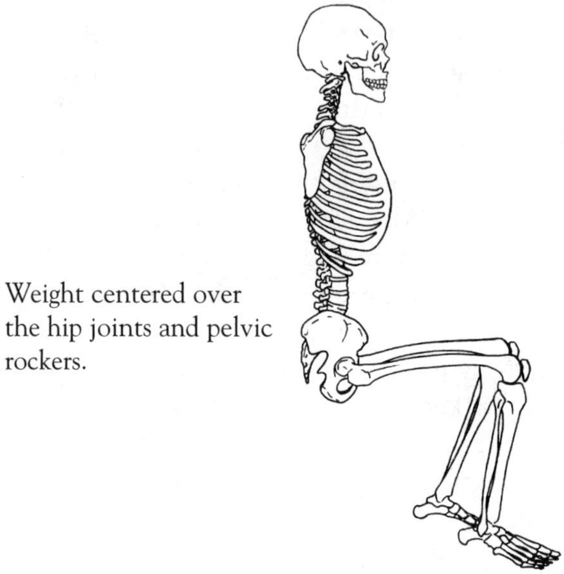

Illustrations this page by Benjamin Conable.

4. **Knees:** upper body weight distributes through the knees to the ankles when standing. There are three positions or conditions of the knees: locked, balanced, and bent.

FIGURE 9. Three Positions of the Knees

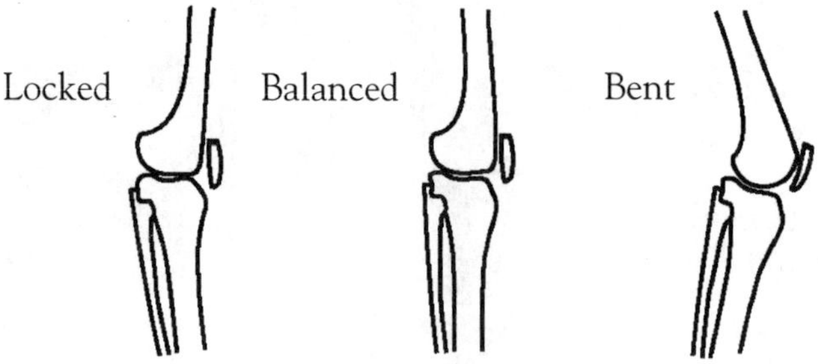

Balanced is the preferred state; however, the knees will need to be locked as compensation to stabilize the body and protect the lumbar spine when you are not aligned and your body weight is thrown back onto the lower back. This is nature's protective mechanism for the lumbar disks.

5. **Arches of feet:** the arch of the foot is formed from the heel at back to the ball of the foot at front, but the toes are not included.

FIGURE 10. The Arch of the Foot

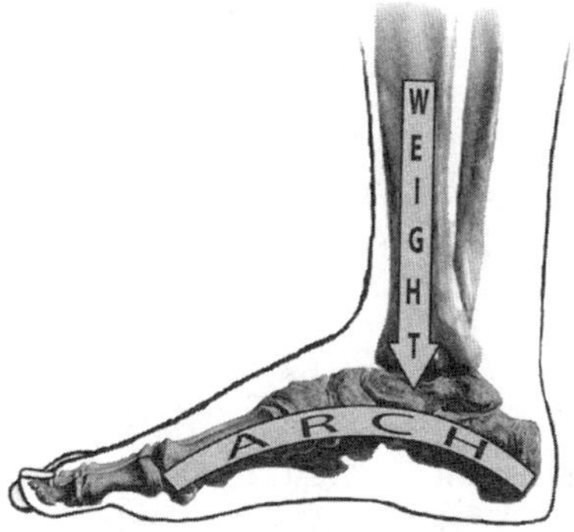

Illustrations this page by Benjamin Conable.

The arches of the feet receive the weight of the body when standing, and weight is delivered into the arches when balanced. Experiment with the fifth place of balance and the effect it has on the rest of your body. For example, observe how imbalance in your feet generates tension elsewhere in your body, such as your legs, back, and neck. Also notice what is happening to your breathing. The effects of misalignment and tension are profound because of the interconnectivity of the body structures.

6. **Arm structure:** the complete arm structure includes the collarbone (front), shoulder blade (back), humerus (upper arm), radius and ulna (lower arm), carpal bones (wrist), and metacarpals and phalanges (hand).

FIGURE 11. Arm Structure

Includes collarbone (front), shoulder blade (back), upper arm, lower arm, wrist, and hand.

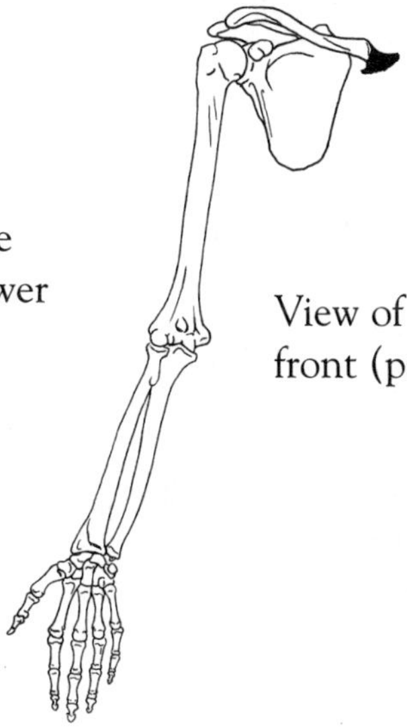

View of right arm from front (palm facing front).

> There are four joints in the arm structure: sternoclavicular (where the sternum/breastbone meets the clavicle/collarbone), humero-scapula[6] (where the humerus/upper arm meets the scapula/shoulder blade), elbow, and wrist. To find the balance of your arms, the collarbones and shoulder blades should be elegantly suspended over the ribs—not pulled up, pulled back military style, pulled down, or dropped forward in a slump.

Everything in your body is connected. Tension in one area will translate to other areas, impeding quality of movement and resultant musical sound. As you remap those areas of your body that are mapped inaccurately or inadequately and, as a result, find balance, you will notice how much you can recover ease of movement and reduce tension and distortion in your body. This should be evident in your everyday living as well as in your musical performance because the body in which you live is the body with which you perform.

Breathing

How accurately can you describe the process of breathing? Over time many distorted images and descriptions of breathing have evolved as choral conductors and singers have tried to explain breathing to their students. Unfortunately, these images have often been misconstrued or are just plain wrong. Because much of the movement of breathing is concealed from our eyes and is experienced internally, an accurate and clear understanding of the structures and movement of breathing is the simplest and fastest way to correct breathing problems and improve technique.

Balanced breathing produces a wavelike motion from top to bottom on inhalation and exhalation. In a body that is free of tension, breathing feels like a single movement, sequential and coordinated, top to bottom. Once you have accurately located the structures of breathing (nose and mouth, nasal, oral, and laryngeal pharynx, trachea, bronchi, lungs, ribs, diaphragm, abdominal wall (front, sides, and back), inner pelvic muscles, pelvic floor, and spine (see Figure 12), seek clarity about the way they function to produce tension-free breathing that is sequential and coordinated.

The breathing process is summarized in Figure 13. Note that while the stages of the sequence are listed in numerical order, when the movement of breathing is tension-free and well coordinated it feels like a single movement. Also note that the movement of the ribs and diaphragm on inhalation is simultaneous—one does not occur without the other, but they are compromised in a body that is not free and balanced.

FIGURE 12. The Relationship of the Spine and Breathing Structures

- The action of the spine is important for breathing—map structures in relation to it.
- Breathing structures along the entire length of the weight-bearing spine:
  - nasal, oral, and laryngeal pharynx
  - trachea
  - bronchi and lungs
  - ribs
  - diaphragm
  - abdominal wall
  - inner pelvic muscles
  - pelvic floor

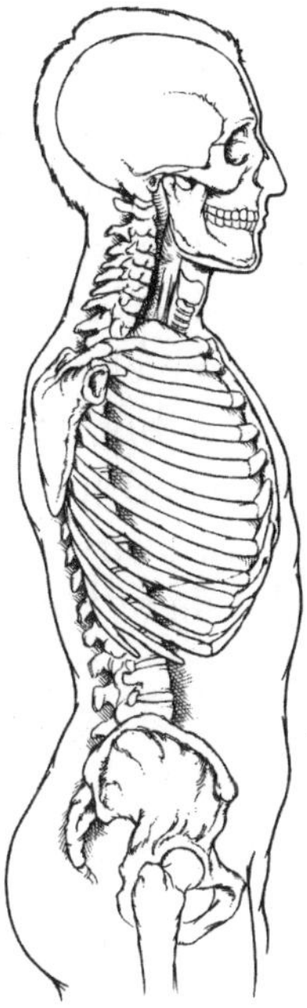

FIGURE 13. Balanced Breathing[7]

Inhalation
1. The ribs swing up and out.
2. The diaphragm descends from its highly domed position to a less domed position.
3. The abdominal and pelvic viscera are moved outward and downward by the powerful descending diaphragm.
4. The pelvic floor is pushed downward by the pressure of the displaced viscera.

Exhalation
1. The ribs swing down and in.
2. The diaphragm ascends back to its highly domed position.
3. The abdominal and pelvic viscera flow inward and upward as the diaphragm ascends, and the cylinder of abdominal musculature springs back inward as pressure from viscera is gradually reduced.
4. The pelvic floor muscles likewise spring back to rest.

Gathering and Lengthening

As you work on your breathing, you may also notice the gathering and lengthening movement of the spine (see Figure 14). If we are free enough, on inhalation the spine gathers as the ribs swing up and out and the diaphragm contracts to its less domed position, partly as a result of our becoming bigger around the abdomen. The curves of the spine deepen, and the vertebrae move closer together, but only if we are free enough. On exhalation, the spine lengthens reflexively as the ribs swing down and in, and the diaphragm relaxes to its highly domed position. The lengthening phase is led by the famous up-and-over movement of the head that singing teachers have taught for hundreds of years and which F. M. Alexander called "forward and up" because of the slight but significant rocking of the head on the top vertebra in very free singing.

FIGURE 14. Gathering and Lengthening of the Spine

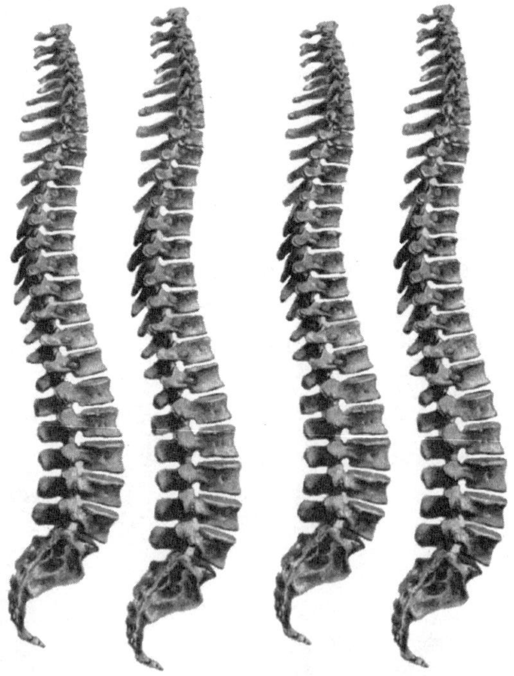

Inhale Exhale Inhale Exhale

Illustration by Benjamin Conable.

Gathering and lengthening are involuntary movements of the spine, and the lengthening is a marvelous primary source of support for the choral sound for conductors and choristers who cooperate with it. Remember, the spine is the core of all body movement, including breathing, singing, and conducting. You will regain the spine's natural gathering and lengthening movement by avoiding conditions that inhibit freedom of movement, e.g., tightening your neck muscles, chronically shortening yourself, and mistakenly seeking a straight spine. To cultivate excellent breathing, there must be freedom from tension throughout the body, lively, ongoing body awareness, and an accurate body map of the structures and movement of breathing.

Breath Support

What do we really mean by "breath support"? Can you clearly explain it? Chances are it's a term you use often, and it's also likely there are singers in your choir who still find it confusing. Explaining the concept of breath support is done more easily and effectively when singers begin with a clear understanding of the structures and movement of breathing. Once this is clear, teaching them how to regulate the air pressure from the lungs that sets the closed vocal folds into vibration is the essence of breath support.

Voice teacher and Andover Educator Melissa Malde explains it thus: "*Assuming proper alignment, support in singing is the act of maintaining dynamic equilibrium between the expiratory breath flow, which originates with elastic recoil in the abdominals and pelvic floor and the resistance to that breath flow from the diaphragm, external intercostals, and vocal folds*." "Dynamic equilibrium" in this context is defined as opposing muscles working in tandem, i.e., one releases as the other contracts. A simpler way to say this to your choir is "*support is the dynamic equilibrium between the muscles of expiration and inspiration*."[8] You should choose the definition that makes the most sense to your students. What is certain is that your singers will be relieved to have a definition that makes sense to them and allows them to effectively develop their breath support skills.

A Valuable Pedagogical Tool

Body Mapping is not a substitute for music lessons. It is a valuable pedagogical tool that can be used as an adjunct to musical instruction in studios, classrooms, or ensemble settings. Body Mapping can assist in the music teaching process if one remembers that the easiest and fastest way to train free, efficient, effective, beautiful movement is to help students cultivate an absolutely adequate[9] and accurate body map. Remember that students naturally develop, refine, and correct their body maps as they practice and perform if they maintain a lively, integrated awareness of their movement. For that reason, you should teach body awareness, and you should absolutely model it.

Mind–Body–Spirit–Music

In conclusion, we return to MIND–BODY–SPIRIT–MUSIC. Remember that with full body awareness, you experience yourself as one whole being, not merely a collection of parts. Wholeness of musical experience means unrestricted access to all parts of MIND–BODY–SPIRIT–MUSIC. Ultimately, we decide how our minds and bodies will respond. If we are physically balanced and grounded, then we have a powerful means by which our musical voice, our spirit, and our musical imagination can be unleashed. Without this, our musical potential is trapped in a body that is ill equipped to express the passion and emotion of the music. Through Body Mapping, musicians recover the ability to be truly free in their music-making.

Bibliography

Alcamo, I. Edward. *The Princeton Review Anatomy Coloring Workbook*. New York: Random House, Inc., 1997.

Andover Educators 2003, *What Every Musician Needs to Know About the Body*. http://www.bodymap.org (accessed August 24, 2003).

Conable, Barbara. *The Scientific Basis of Body Mapping*. Portland, OR: Andover Educators, 2004.

———. *The Scientific Evidence for the Body Map*. Portland, OR: Andover Educators, 2004.

———. *The Structures and Movement of Breathing: A Primer for Choirs and Choruses*. Chicago: GIA Publications, Inc., 2000.

———. "Ways to use Body Mapping in Your Alexander Technique Teaching." Paper presented to Alexander Technique teachers. Oregon, July 2003.

———. *What Every Musician Needs to Know about the Body: The Practical Application of Body Mapping to Making Music*. Rev. ed. Portland, OR: Andover Press, 2000. (Illustrations for Figures 4, 5, 6, 7, 8, 9, 10, 11, and 14 courtesy of Benjamin Conable.)

Conable, Barbara, and William Conable. *How to Learn the Alexander Technique: A Manual for Students*. 3rd ed. Columbus: Andover Press, 1992.

Conable, William. *NASM 2002 Presentation*. Portland, OR: Andover Educators, 2004.

———. "Origins and Theory of Mapping." In *How to Learn the Alexander Technique: A Manual for Students*. 3rd ed. Columbus: Andover Road Press, 1992.

Damasio, Antonio R. *The Feeling of What Happens: Body and Emotion in the Making of Consciousness*. New York: Harcourt Brace, 1999.

Dawson, William J. "Playing without Pain: Strategies for the Developing Instrumentalist." *Music Educators Journal* 93, no. 2 (November 2006), 36–41.

Ehmann, William. *Choral Directing*. Translated by George D. Weibe. Minneapolis: Augsburg Publishing House, 1968.

Gelb, Michael J. *Body Learning: An Introduction to the Alexander Technique*. 2nd ed. New York: Henry Holt & Co., 1995.

Gilmore, Robin. *What Every Dancer Needs to Know about the Body: A Workbook of Body Mapping and the Alexander Technique*. Portland, OR: Andover Press.

Horvath, Janet. *Playing (Less) Hurt: An Injury Prevention Guide for Musicians*. Kearney, NE: Morris Pub., 2002.

Jordan, James, and Heather Buchanan. *Evoking Sound: Body Mapping Principles and Basic Conducting Technique*. Video/DVD. Chicago: GIA Publications, Inc., 2004.

Likar, Amy. *Amy Likar—Body Mapping*. http://www.amylikar.com/bodymap.html (accessed August 23, 2003).

Mark, Thomas. *What Every Pianist Needs to Know about the Body*. Chicago: GIA Publications, Inc., 2003.

Mencimer, S. "Tuba Lips, Guitar Nipples, and Other Musical Maladies." *Washington Post*, March 25, 2003, HE01.

Mills, K. "Cellist Strikes Chord against Pain: Personal Plight Spurs Research." *Telegram & Gazette*, July 17, 2003, C5.

Musicians and Injuries. http://eeshop.unl.edu/music.html (accessed August 24, 2003).

Nesmith, D. "What Every Musician Needs to Know About the Body." *The Horn Call* 4 (1999): 71–74.

———. "How Body Mapping and the Alexander Technique Will Improve Your Playing." *International Musician* 6 (2001): 11–12.

Nichols, T. R. *Scientific Basis of Body Mapping*. http://www.bodymap.org (accessed November 26, 2004).

Norris, R. "Seating Problems of Vocalists." In *Choral Pedagogy* by Brenda Smith and Robert Thayler Sataloff. San Diego: Singular, 2000.

Pearson, Lea. *Body Mapping for Flutists: What Every Flute Teacher Needs to Know about the Body*. 4th ed. Chicago: GIA Publications, Inc., 2006.

Phillips, Kenneth H. *Directing the Choral Music Program*. New York: Oxford University Press, 2004.

Smith, Brenda, and Robert Thayler Sataloff. *Choral Pedagogy*. San Diego: Singular, 2000.

Notes

1. The information in this chapter is based on Barbara Conable's book *What Every Musician Needs to Know About the Body*, my study of Body Mapping to receive certification as an Andover Educator, my PhD research, and firsthand experience of the power of this information through work with the numerous choirs, choral conductors, and musicians who have allowed me the privilege of sharing and working with them.
2. Barbara Conable, *What Every Musician Needs to Know about the Body: The Practical Application of Body Mapping and the Alexander Technique to Making Music*, rev. ed. (Portland, OR: Andover Press, 2000).
3. Andover Educators: http://www.bodymap.org.
4. Conable, *What Every Musician Needs to Know about the Body*.
5. Statistics for playing-related injuries in musicians:
   American Symphony Orchestra League: 40 percent of musicians play in pain and require medication; 10 percent of professional musicians are out of work due to playing related injuries.
   International Conference of Symphony and Opera Musicians, 1986 survey: 76 percent of professional instrumentalists reported music-related playing injuries.
   National Rehabilitation Hospital, Washington, DC, 1993 survey of Catholic University/Benjamin T. Rome School of Music students: 76 percent of students suffered music-related injuries severe enough to keep them from playing for more than two weeks.
   Orthopedic Research Institute Study, Muenster, Germany, 2001: 70 percent of musicians have spinal problems; string players are at the highest risk; classical musicians are twice as likely to suffer serious backaches as other professionals; professional musicians frequently suffer pain and limited movements in the shoulder and neck regions.
6. The term "humero-scapula" is used to describe the shoulder joint relationship between the humerus and scapula (shoulder blade). It is not an official anatomical designation. Author Thomas Mark identifies the shoulder joint as the glenohumeral joint due to the articulation of the ball end of the humerus with the glenoid fossa on the shoulder blade, the small, basin-shaped surface that forms the outer end of the shoulder blade. Humeroscapular rhythm is an official anatomical designation used by anatomists and neurophysiologists to designate the phenomenon of correct, whole-arm movement.
7. Barbara Conable, *The Structures and Movement of Breathing: A Primer for Choirs and Choruses* (Chicago: GIA Publications, Inc., 2000).
8. Melissa Malde, DMA, assistant professor of voice and vocal pedagogy, University of Northern Colorado, Friday, September 15, 2006, Andover Educators list-serve discussion.

9. The use of the word "adequate" in this context is positive and means sufficient for the demands of the musical activity.

Heather J. Buchanan is director of choral activities at the John J. Cali School of Music at Montclair State University, New Jersey, where she conducts the 144-voice Chorale and 48-voice auditioned University Singers and teaches choral methods and Body Mapping. Prior to her position at Montclair, she was on the conducting faculty at Westminster Choir College of Rider University. A certified Andover Educator, Buchanan specializes in the teaching of Body Mapping and somatic pedagogy for musicians and is a PhD candidate with the University of New England (Australia) researching the impact of Body Mapping on student musicians. She is also a certified Johrei Reike practitioner.

Australian born, Buchanan earned a bachelor of music from the Queensland Conservatorium of Music (Australia) and a master of music degree with distinction from Westminster with a double major in choral conducting and music education. Her publications include coediting and compiling the GIA *Teaching Music through Performance in Choir* series, the Video-DVD *Evoking Sound: Body Mapping Principles and Basic Conducting Techniques*, and several GIA choral octavos coedited with Matthew Mehaffey. A vibrant musician and dynamic pedagogue, Buchanan is in demand as a guest conductor, clinician, and adjudicator in the U.S. and her native Australia. Recent performance highlights include preparing the Montclair State University Chorale for performances of Beethoven's Symphony No. 9 with the New Jersey Symphony Orchestra under the baton of Maestro Neeme Järvi, completing a ten-day Central European tour culminating in a performance at the Ferenc Liszt Zeneakadémia in Budapest, conducting the World Premiere performances of *Madison's Descent* by celebrated Irish composer Mícheál ÓSúílleabháin, conducting the inaugural Australian National Seniors' Choral Festival in Newcastle, Australia, and performing with renowned American composer Merideth Monk and Company in her first college choir collaboration, a historical first for the University Singers and Monk.

PART II

THE CHORAL CONDUCTOR AS MUSIC TEACHER

Repertoire Resource Guides

Introduction to the Repertoire Resource Guides

Matthew W. Mehaffey

Working on the second volume of *Teaching Music through Performance in Choir* has truly been a labor of love. Arriving at a list of 100 pieces of music that will thrill all readers is no easy task. For this reason, my coeditor Heather Buchanan and I polled dozens of music educators from across the globe for their insights into repertoire suitable for the high school chorus. Through endless revisions and consultations across the profession, we arrived at the list presented to you in this book.

This volume does not include a piece by every great composer who has ever lived; however, you will find familiar titles and new titles, sacred titles and secular titles, *a cappella* and accompanied titles, ancient music and modern music, and English language selections and foreign language selections. There is something in this list for everyone, and we guarantee that it is all of the highest musical quality. While every piece in this volume may not be appropriate for the choir you conduct, we hope this list will broaden your repertoire knowledge and inspire you to lead your choir to the next level of repertoire.

For each piece in the **Repertoire Resource Guides**, we have provided you with historical, biographical, and analytical information helpful in score preparation and useful fodder for teaching. These resource guides are not meant to be complete studies of each piece but places to begin your musical journey.

To complete these resource guides, we enlisted the help of professors, teachers, and graduate students from across the country. These authors have graduated from and teach at institutions with some of the richest choral traditions in our country. Because of the great richness of background among our contributors, they were encouraged to write the resource guides from their own perspectives instead of sticking to a prefabricated style or form. We hope that as you read each resource guide you will discover rehearsal techniques you can apply across your teaching and in other repertoire.

A new feature of this volume is that many composers and arrangers were asked to write the resource guides for their own music. We are so excited about the perspective this will offer you and your students. Unlike the last volume, this one does not contain an extensive analysis of a major work; however, this volume does include larger pieces like Eric Whitacre's *Five Hebrew Love Songs*, Emma Lou Diemer's *Three Madrigals*, and Ronaldo Miranda's *Suite Nordestina*.

We have continued using the new choral rating system we developed for Volume 1. We have received many positive comments about the accuracy of this rating system; it is proving to be very helpful when deciding whether a piece is indeed appropriate for one's choir. The rating system employs a five-point scale with Level 5 being the most difficult.

Each piece is assigned an **Overall** difficulty rating, which gives the conductor a quick reference point. In an effort to give teachers and conductors more information, we provide two additional ratings: **Vocal** and **Tonal/Rhythm.** The vocal rating assesses the vocal difficulty of each piece by considering the range, tessitura, dynamics, and diction issues: the higher the number, the more advanced the required technique. Pieces with a higher number will be more likely to contain passages with extreme ranges, long vocal lines, extended vocal techniques, challenging diction, and stylistic issues.

The tonal rating assesses how difficult this piece will be to teach/learn from an aural perspective: the higher the number, the more complex the composer's harmonic, melodic, and rhythmic language. Pieces with a higher tonal rating will be more likely to have chromatic and/or modal passages outside of the major/minor tonalities, instances of mixed meter, and difficult rhythms.

The **Overall** rating is essentially an average of the **Vocal and Tonal/Rhythm** ratings; therefore, to have a complete understanding of the difficulty, please consult the additional ratings when choosing repertoire. (The number of vocal parts, divisi, length of composition, and intangible musical elements were taken into consideration but were not weighted as heavily as the aforementioned criteria.) We have calibrated our ratings to the ability of the average high school choir; the average high school choir should be able to perform, without great difficulty, anything with a rating of three or lower.

The chart below summarizes possible characteristics of the music in each level. However, because the repertoire in this volume is very diverse, not all pieces in each level contain all of the qualities/criteria listed in the chart, and it should be noted that this list is not exhaustive. Each higher level assumes all the criteria of the previous levels.

Level	Vocal	Tonal/Rhythm
1	• Short, simple vocal lines with limited ranges • Conjunct vocal lines prevail • Comfortable vocal range • Manageable tessitura	• Major or minor tonality with little to no chromaticism • No modulations to other keys or tonalities • Straightforward rhythms within simple or compound meter
2	• Phrases of moderately challenging length • Slightly disjunct vocal lines • Brief, yet negotiable forays into extreme ranges • Basic dynamic range • Basic diction challenges in languages commonly encountered in choral music (e.g., English, Latin, German)	• Major or minor tonality with brief, obvious chromaticism • Brief modulations are obvious and move to closely related tonalities • Modal passages • Dissonances are approached and resolved by step • Short passages of challenging rhythm within simple or compound metric structure
3	• Short passages requiring advanced vocal technique • Short passages of challenging tessitura • Long phrases requiring good breath control • Vocal melismas of moderate length requiring martellato technique • Wide dynamic range • Extended *crescendos* and *decrescendos* • Wide range of languages encountered	• Major/minor/modal tonality • Concrete or implied modulations to different tonalities or modalities • Dissonance approached by leap • Added-note harmonies • Imitative and nonimitative counterpoint • Difficult rhythms may occur, but are usually repetitive • Simply constructed mixed meter
4	• Long phrases requiring excellent breath control • Extreme ranges • Vocal lines requiring subtlety of shape, dynamics, and expressivity • Long vocal melismas • Alternative vocal techniques (i.e., non-Western techniques) • Refined diction required as stylistic vehicle	• Extended modal passages • Passages in non-diatonic harmony • Frequent chromaticism • Challenging rhythmic passages may be extended and non-repetitive • Full compositions in mixed meter

LEVEL	VOCAL	TONAL/RHYTHM
5	• Vocal maturity required • Extreme ranges and tessituras • Repertoire at this level will provide numerous challenges for the experienced choral ensemble	• Atonal passages or passages of extreme dissonance • Unprepared/unresolved dissonant harmonies • Very complex rhythmic/metric structure • Repertoire at this level will provide numerous challenges for the experienced choral ensemble

We encourage you to read this book in many different ways: to learn more about old repertoire, to learn about new repertoire, and to refresh your perspective when you feel rehearsals have become stale. We hope you find these resource guides to be helpful in all levels of your music making and inspire you to venture into choral repertoire with renewed dedication to the choral art.

Level One

Mixed voices:

Treble voices:

Men's voices:

Teacher Resource Guide

I'm Going Home on a Cloud
arr. Seán Deibler

Unison or SATB
Ascolta
Overall: 1
Vocal: 1
Tonal/Rhythm: 1

Composer

Seán Deibler studied clarinet and voice at Susquehanna University and went on to study conducting and chamber music to his studies at the Franz Liszt Academy in Budapest, Hungary. Deibler established the Music Group of Philadelphia in 1978, a mixed vocal chamber ensemble dedicated to performing great choral repertoire from all musical periods with special emphasis on new, seldom performed, and virtuoso works. In addition to this ensemble, he founded the Choral Arts Society of Philadelphia, which has recorded with the Philadelphia Symphony Orchestra. He has been a guest conductor and lecturer throughout America as well as in England and Hungary.

Deibler's awards include the Hungarian Medal Pro Arbitus and an honorary doctorate of fine arts from Susquehanna University. Deibler conducts, sings, and plays clarinet throughout Europe and the United States.

Composition and Historical Perspective

"I'm Going Home on a Cloud" is a spiritual of which there are many arrangements. The accompaniment in this arrangement is almost in the gospel style, with grand, rhythmically repeated chords. With four independent vocal lines, the tune can be repeated in unison or with up to three lines of harmony at any dynamic.

Technical Considerations and Musical Elements

This piece is versatile and therefore incredibly useful. It can be sung by any choir—men's, women's, or mixed—of any age or ability level. The range is moderate. It can be sung in unison or in up to four parts, *a cappella* or accompanied. The piece can be as long or as short as need be, depending on the number of repetitions and the dynamic contrast can vary. The adaptability and multitude of possibilities make "I'm Going Home on a Cloud" a piece you could perform at any time, with any choir.

One important point is that, though the piece is by no means intended for treble choir only, all four lines are written in treble clef. This presents an opportunity to discuss clefs, reading in different clefs (which the basses have to do), the nature of octaves, and even the reason for unison/parallel octave singing and the difference between female voices and changed male voices.

Another interesting musical element is the presence of flatted sevenths, which pass by as blue notes rather than suggesting a nonmajor modality.

In my experience the piece works better accompanied in acoustically dry spaces and *a cappella* in very ringy spaces. Accompanied, it sounds more easy-going, self-assured, and gospel-like and works best sung mostly *forte* and louder. *A cappella*, it can be subtler with longer musical lines and possibilities for understated emotional development to the end of the piece. For example, starting soft and in unison and growing to *forte* in four parts, changing from a hopeful sort of sound to a celebratory one, works best without the strictly *maestoso* piano part. One possibility for making the accompaniment softer and creating some contrast throughout the piece is to have the accompanist roll chords gently in a verse or two. Also:

- Possibilities are listed by the composer on the first page.
- Omit the third line, which is the lowest, if you need to focus on head-voice singing and want to avoid the temptation of moving into chest voice
- To shorten the piece choose just two lines—sing one, then the other, then both together once or twice.
- To increase the piece's duration, use the "two-line" approach twice: sing one (most likely the melody, the top line, then another, and then the two together. Then sing a third line by itself. Next, sing it with the melody. Sing the fourth line alone, and then add the melody. Then sing the third and fourth lines together. Next add three and four with the melody. Then sing all four lines.

As you can see, the possibilities are nearly unlimited. There will never be a "definitive performance" of Seán Deibler's "I'm Going Home on a Cloud," and that allows the students to make suggestions for performance options. For example, if students suggest singing it *piano*, then *forte*, this reinforces their familiarity with those terms. The same is true of suggestions to sing the piece unison, *a cappella*, *marcato*, legato, etc.

So much music lays out detailed instructions and restricts choirs to appropriate performance practice that this piece is a treasure in its flexibility. Students can decide how the writer seems to feel about the subject, which is basically death, and select tempos, dynamics, and textures that express it further. Have each section come up with a plan for singing and have those plans available during rehearsals. Try singing it "the tenor's way," "the alto's way," etc.

Another option I have used relates to the "alleluia" section, which is harder to sing than the rest of the piece and has a much more complicated accompaniment. If you need a big, dramatic ending, it's fabulous. But I have sometimes been interested in a folk song–like simplicity and have just left it off. Not doing the "alleluia" results in the last note being a unison D, which has a strength of its own and works especially well if approached with a dramatic ritard.

Stylistic Considerations

Because this piece can be adapted for so many contexts and interpreted in any way, stylistic interpretations are not restricted. This song can be sung in just about any style, but base your decisions for technical aspects on stylistic considerations. For example, if you choose to use the piano accompaniment, a very refined, precise style of singing won't work as well as freer, folk-style of singing. However, if the choir sings *a cappella*, there is a wider variety of stylistic approaches that can work.

Form and Structure

If you choose to use the piano accompaniment, there are two measures of introduction.

There is an eight-measure melody and three harmony lines in the vocal parts, though only the melody (the top line) is necessary. The passage can be repeated and sung in as many parts as desired.

Finally, there is a three-measure optional "alleluia."

Text

One of these fine mornings, at break of day,
I'm going home on a cloud.
King Death goin' find me here at my play,
I'm going home on a cloud.

Ev'ry morning ev'ry day,
Close my eyes and I begin to pray.
Thank the Lord for all His ways,
Close my eyes and pray.

Spread my wings and fly away,
Fly up to heaven on a big white cloud.
I'm goin' fly
High upon a white cloud.

Alleluia, sing to the Lord,
A song of love and joy!
Alleluia, sing His name.
Sing of love and joy!

Additional References and Resources

Deibler, Seán, arr. "I'm Going Home on a Cloud." Ascolta. (Contact: P.O. Box 162, 3990 DD Houten, the Netherlands, 31-(0)30-6374237, fax: 31-(0)30-6373956.

Web site:
Music Group of Philadelphia: www.mgphila.org (accessed November 10, 2006)

Contributed by:

Amelia Nagoski

Teacher Resource Guide

O Music

Lowell Mason
(1792–1872)

arr. Doreen Rao

Unison with piano/two- or three-part canon, a cappella
Boosey & Hawkes: OCTB6352
Overall: 1
Vocal: 1
Tonal/Rhythm: 1

Composer

Commonly known as the "father of music education," Lowell Mason was born to parents actively involved in their Medfield, Massachusetts, church choir. As a child, Mason attended a singing school, studied composition, and learned to play several instruments. At the young age of sixteen, he became his church's choir director.

In 1812, Lowell Mason moved to Savannah, Georgia, where he worked as a bank clerk but pursued his love for music and opened the first Sunday school for African American children in all of North America. While in Savannah, he led singing schools and concerts, taking the position of choir director and organist of Independent Presbyterian Church. His work in Savannah became known to church leaders in Boston; from their contact, Mason was contracted to supervise music in three Congressional churches, leading to his move to Boston.

In Boston, Mason revitalized the Boston Handel and Haydn Society, and in 1833 Mason and George James Webb founded the Boston Academy of

Music to raise the standards of church music and to promote music education to the public. In 1834 Mason published *The Manual of the Boston Academy of Music*; this publication was incredibly influential on local music teachers. Also in 1834, Mason and his followers held conventions for music teacher training that lasted a week to ten days. These conventions later incorporated choral festivals for students from surrounding states. This group experimented with teaching music in the Boston public schools. At the time, Mason volunteered at a grammar school, implementing a music curriculum that secured music's place in that school. From 1827–45, Mason became the music superintendent of the Boston Public School System, thus spreading a music curriculum to districts outside of Boston.

Besides introducing music to the public school curriculum, Mason brought European classical music to an area that was familiar with the fuguing tunes and *Sacred Harp* tradition used in churches since colonial times. Traditionally "American" composers and teachers such as William Billings were being replaced by proponents of the European tradition and singing schools of the type preferred by Mason. Some of Mason's numerous musical collections include *The Boston Academy's Collection of Choruses*, *The Hymnist*, *The Hallelujah*, and *The Boston Chorus Book* and children's collections, such as *Juvenile Psalmist*, *The Song-Book of the School-Room*, *The Primary School Song Book*, *Little Songs for Little Singers*, and *Musical Exercises for Singing Schools*.

Arranger Doreen Rao is known in the choral world for her extensive work with children's choirs. She is the founder of the Choral Music Experience, a series of choral editions that focuses on "distinctive, diverse, multicultural choral repertoire in which students can experience the joy of learning through singing. An invaluable resource for conductors, teachers, and student teachers."

Composition and Historical Perspective

"O Music" was written by Lowell Mason as an exercise for use in his singing school. The text encourages children to sing for enjoyment and the love of music. It is an appropriate song for beginning singers to be used in performances and rehearsals (ear training, sight-reading, etc.). "O Music" could be programmed nicely with a set of rounds and canons that are written in two or three parts.

Technical and Stylistic Considerations and Musical Elements

"O Music," as arranged by Doreen Rao, is in two different versions. The first version is the tune sung in unison with a basic piano accompaniment. The second version is a three-part canon of the tune. Both versions are in G major.

Version 1

This version opens with a two-measure piano introduction establishing the G major tonality in a chorale style. The melody highlights the G major scale with stepwise motion at the top with fourth-space E (treble clef) and descends as far as B below the staff, giving this melody a range of an eleventh. The melody first ascends on Do, Re, Mi.

Although the motion of the melody is mostly step-wise, there are a few large skips, such as G down to B (minor sixth) found in m. 13 (the end of the melody). The other major skip in the piece is from Do down to Sol in m. 5 and mm. 11–14. When teaching this, educators must ensure that the pitch stays just, especially in the places where there are skips (e.g., the skip from Do down to Sol in m. 5).

Common causes for pitch problems in a piece with such a wide range for young children are 1) they do not listen and monitor themselves and 2) they move out of head voice. Pay extra attention to students pushing their voices on the upward scalar passages and switching into a pseudo-chest voice when singing the downward leaps. It would be helpful to practice singing the line on the neutral syllable "noo." The "oo" vowel will help focus the sound and keep it in the head voice.

The accompaniment in this version is easy for most teachers with only a limited amount of keyboard instruction and experience; however, the accompaniment provides plenty of harmonic and rhythmic support for the singers and sounds much richer and more difficult than it is. For educators with limited keyboard experience, this would be a good beginning piece for your children's choir to help you learn to accompany them.

VERSION 2

The melody and text of Version 2 is exactly the same as in Version 1. The difference is that Version 2 is an unaccompanied canon in two or three parts (depending on the size and skill of the ensemble). To begin this version, all voices state the theme in unison. Then the canon begins with the first voice, followed by the second voice four measures later and the third voice four measures after that.

When the second voice enters, the first two voices are in thirds for two and a half measures, after which the voices move in contrary motion. When rehearsing this canon, the teacher should take the time to help the singers become aware of the motion in thirds to make sure it constantly tunes. If the students are aware that they are singing in thirds and told to listen carefully to the other voices, the music will be in tune.

When singing a canon, students must be aware that voices often cross. For example, in m. 21 of "O Music," the third voice enters on the third of the chord, the second voice sings the fifth, and the first voice (the top voice) has the root of the chord (and the lowest note). Again, a simple explanation of the workings of a canon would be helpful to the singers before they begin one.

Lowell Mason wanted this piece not only to help children become excited about singing but to help teach students how to sing properly. Teachers must keep vocal technique in mind when teaching such a simple piece of music. Although the music will be easy for the director to teach and for students to learn, the vocal technique and singing principles needed to properly sing this piece will take time to develop. Be patient and allow this to happen; do not stop working on "O Music" once the notes are learned. Make sure that students understand their voices and how to use them.

Form and Structure

"O Music" is written in 4/4 with a phrase structure of three four-measure phrases. Version 1 is stated plainly in this structure. Version 2 is a two- or three-part canon, with a new part entering in each new phrase (every four measures).

Text

O music, sweet music
Thy praises we will sing;
We will tell of the pleasures and happiness you bring.
Music, music, let the chorus sing.

Contributed by:

Matthew J. LaPine

Teacher Resource Guide

Ose Shalom
(The One Who Makes Peace)

John Leavitt
(b. 1956)

SATB, TTBB, SAB, two-part/accompanied
Hal Leonard: 8703341
Overall: 1
Vocal: 1
Tonal/Rhythm: 2

Composer

John Leavitt was born and raised in Leavenworth, Kansas. He completed his undergraduate education at Emporia State University (Kansas) and earned a master's degree from Wichita State University and a doctorate of musical arts from the Conservatory of Music at the University of Missouri-Kansas City.

Leavitt was the recipient of the W. A. Young Award for teaching excellence in recognition of his career at Friends University in the fields of music theory and choral and church music. He also served briefly on the faculties of Concordia College in Edmonton, Alberta (Canada) and Concordia University in River Forest, Illinois. Leavitt resides near Wichita, Kansas, where he has held the position of music director at Immanuel Lutheran Church and Cantor at Reformation Lutheran Church. He also conducted the Master Arts Chorale and Youth Chorale during their twelve-year tenure. In March of 2003, he received the Kansas Artist Fellowship Award from the Kansas Arts Commission for his contribution to music composition. He most recently completed a tenure as director of music at Newman University in Wichita.

Leavitt continues to teach, lecture, and guest conduct numerous workshops, festivals, and symposia. His compositions are represented in nearly every major music catalog, including Augsburg Fortress, Concordia, Hal Leonard, MorningStar, GIA Publications, Hope, Shawnee Press, and Alfred. He has numerous publications for choir, piano, organ, handbells, and string orchestra and is coauthor of the widely used choral music method textbook series Essential Elements for Choir. His music has been performed in more than thirty countries across the globe, and his music is frequently performed on the radio.

His discography includes *A Sonic Spectacular* (organ, 1997), *A Little Night Music* (piano, 1998), *Handel's Messiah* (choral, 1998), *Sweet Songs of Christmas* (piano, 2000), *Adoration* (piano, 2000), *How Sweet the Sound* (piano, 2000), *Requiem* (choral, 2001), *What Child Is This*, (choral, 2002), *Silent Night, Wondrous Light* (piano, 2002), *Wonder, Love, and Praise* (orchestra, 2003), *Shall We Gather at the River* (orchestra, 2005), and *Jubilee* (choral, 2005).

Composition and Historical Perspective

Ose Shalom is the concluding verse of the Kaddish, a traditional Jewish prayer recited for remembrance of the dead. It is the only verse of the prayer in Hebrew; the preceding verses of the Kaddish are in Aramaic. Although it is commonly considered a mourner's prayer, variations of the Kaddish are often recited for purposes other than commemorating the dead or mourning. In the 1960s and 1970s pop musicians began to excerpt this text and set it in a folk/popular fashion as a call for peace. This brought about numerous settings and popularized the text.

Leavitt's impassioned setting of the *Ose Shalom* text beautifully conveys a simple message of peace, making it appropriate for a variety of concerts. The work is best described as a twenty-first-century setting of a Jewish prayer.

Leavitt has composed and published a tremendous amount of music during the past thirty years. This work, published in 2002, is considered a later work in his extensive compositional career.

Technical Considerations and Musical Elements

"Ose Shalom" is not technically difficult and can be easily approached by a variety of choirs. The lyrical, soaring melodies are wonderful studies in legato singing and provide many opportunities for artistic phrasing. Younger singers may find it difficult to negotiate the moderately long phrases and may insert multiple unnecessary breaths that interrupt the beautiful melodic line. The importance of breath support and control will need to be stressed early in the learning process to ensure that the melody remains fluid. Encourage singers to think of the subdivided arpeggios in the accompaniment as reminders to sing through the long notes.

The tessitura is very comfortable for all voices. The ranges are:

Soprano: B3–F-sharp5 (F-sharp only occurs twice, both times as a brief quarter note and they are approached stepwise)

Alto: B3–E5 (E5 occurs only once and is doubled by sopranos)

Tenor: F-sharp3–F-sharp4

Bass: B2–E4 (E4 is always doubled by tenors)

Leavitt's straightforward approach to the formal structure makes this work easy to teach. Nearly every phrase is eight measures divided into two four-measure phraselets. The work is divided into two similar sections that both state the entire *Ose Shalom* text (see the formal analysis in Form and Structure below). In the A section (mm. 14–30), the text is mostly set for two- or three-part choir. The only true four-part writing occurs in the final two measures of the A section (mm. 29–30).

In the A´ section (mm. 38–53), the sopranos continue to sing the melody while the alto, tenor, and bass voices provide a new homophonic motive that beautifully underpins the melody. Leavitt further accentuates this by also changing the piano texture from the fluid stream of arpeggios to a *forte*, homophonic accompaniment. The homophonic texture provides a secure foundation for the second reiteration of the *Ose Shalom* text. Rehearsing the ATB parts separately allows the singers to hear how their parts fit together harmonically. A common mistake singers make is shortening the half note on "lom" (*sha-lom*), which creates a sense of rushing and weakens the *forte* character. To avoid this, encourage the choir to sing through the half note and use an active cutoff on the following eighth rest. This will ensure that the next entrance will be together rhythmically and in the same character of the previous measures.

Every voice part has clear-cut voice leading and engaging part writing that will keep the interest of the singers. Leavitt creatively reuses many of the choral parts in various sections of the work. In fact, once the men have learned mm. 7–14 and 23–30, they will have learned all but nine measures of the piece, and those nine measures are set in unison. The sopranos basically sing the melody throughout the work. The altos have the most music to learn, but much of it doubles one of the other voice parts.

One challenging aspect of this work is the modal harmonic language indicative of the Jewish/klezmer music tradition. For example, in m. 18, the melody includes a descending augmented second (D sharp to C natural). This will require special attention in rehearsal because the previous measure incorporates a C sharp in the melody. Fortunately, Leavitt provides a supportive accompaniment that doubles the C natural, providing security for the singers.

"Ose Shalom" also provides the opportunity to feature a soloist or small group of singers (mm. 14–18). This section, which includes the augmented second, is a wonderful "first solo" for more inexperienced singers as it is only four measures long and the range is comfortable for most voices (B3–B4). The work also provides opportunities to showcase the men of the choir (mm. 22–26, mm. 45–49).

Several different arrangements of this work are available, and a wide variety of choirs should be able to perform it. The list includes: SATB choir and piano, SAB choir and piano, two-part choir and piano, TTBB choir and piano, and string orchestra arrangement

All of the choral arrangements have the option of using the klezmer instrumentation, which includes clarinet, violin, cello and contrabass. The use of any or all of the extra instruments is highly encouraged. The instrumental parts provide a rich timbre that is characteristic of the klezmer tradition and add warmth to the voice parts. The instrumental parts are not overly difficult and can easily be played by competent high school students. There is also opportunity to showcase a strong violinist on the short cadenza that closes the piece. A simple cadenza is written, but a creative student could easily embellish it to provide further interest.

Stylistic Considerations

Even though it is an original composition, "Ose Shalom" draws upon the inherent lyricism found in the Jewish vocal tradition. It should be sung with a full, rich sound that conveys an underlying emotion of peace. Leavitt provides ample instructions for phrasing and articulation. However, the conductor may also find it helpful to listen to authentic recordings of klezmer music to further understand the intricacies of this rich Jewish tradition. This will help guide and inform stylistic decisions.

Form and Structure

Section	Measure	Event and Scoring
Introduction	1–6	Instrumental introduction
	7–14	(4 + 4), choral and instrumental introduction
A Section		First setting of the entire text
	15–22	Two phrases (4 + 4), optional solo, melody and choir
	23–30	Two phrases (4 + 4)
Interlude	30–37	Piano interlude
A′ Section		Repetition of the entire text
	38–45	Two phrases (4 + 4), similar to mm. 15–22
	46–53	Two phrases (4 + 4), TB parts are exactly the same as mm. 23–30 (SA parts are different)
Coda	54–61	(4 + 4), all voice parts are exactly the same as mm. 7–12
	62–65	

Text and Translation

The short Hebrew text is easy to learn, and a pronunciation guide is provided in the score to aid in the teaching process.

Ose shalom bimromav,	The one who makes peace in the heavens,
Hu ya'ase shalom aleynu,	May he make peace for us,
Veh'al kol Yisrael,	And for all Israel,
Veh'imru, imru Amen.	And let us say, let us say Amen.

Additional References and Resources

Web site:

John Leavitt: www.johnleavittmusic.com/conductor.html

Contributed by:

Lee Nelson

Teacher Resource Guide

The Path to the Moon

Eric Thiman

(1900–1975)

Unison and piano
Boosey & Hawkes: 48003957
Overall: 1
Vocal: 1
Tonal/Rhythm: 1

Composer

Twentieth-century British composer Eric Thiman began learning music mostly on his own, later earning a doctor of music from London University. He had a distinguished career as an educator with the Royal Academy of Music and London University, serving from 1956–62 as LU's dean of the music faculty. He toured England, South Africa, Australia, New Zealand, and Hong Kong as an organ recitalist and an examiner for the Royal Schools of Music. He was appointed director of music at London's City Temple in 1957.

Although Thiman is best known for chorus, organ, and solo voice pieces, he also wrote orchestral, chamber, and piano works, sometimes based upon folk melodies. His large-scale choral-orchestral works on sacred and secular themes often set the texts of great poets. According to *The New Grove Dictionary of Music and Musicians Online*, Thiman's work is characterized by:

> A neat, textbook craftsmanship and easy melodic flow, and a firm grasp of what is practical and effective for the amateur. He was a prolific composer in the best Kapellmeister tradition, writing sacred and secular cantatas, anthems and services, unison songs and part-songs, and piano

and organ music, all of which have proved enormously popular with less ambitious school and amateur musicians.

Among his extended choral works are *The Last Supper* (1930), *The Parables* (1931), *The High Tide on the Coast of Lincolnshire* (1932), and *The Temptations of Christ* (1952).

Composition and Historical Perspective

This melodic two-stanza poem setting with gentle words in a gentle mood typifies Thiman's short choral works in its simple two-part form, liquid melody, and logical layout. It displays little of his contrapuntal prowess, since piano and voices flow together in similar manner throughout. One sees only the occasional sequential measures, the temporary switches from a steady eighth-note pattern—painting the silvery sailing path on the nighttime ocean—to quarter-eighth or other combinations. Thiman emphasizes the final cadence with a single measure in 3/4 before resolving for the last time to the tonic of A-flat major.

The work is organized in two sections, the first setting the four lines of the first poetic stanza, the second setting the final stanza, which is again of four poetic lines, but also carries as a "tail" the last line of the first stanza. Thiman used the same melody for each stanza, pausing between them to replay the first four introductory piano measures. At the end of the second stanza, after a two-measure bridge, he constructs the "tail," which does not seem to be a coda, since the poetic text is not complete until this line has been repeated—from mm. 20–22 and mm. 13–16—adding an extension derivative from prior accompanimental material and a closing arpeggio.

Technical Considerations and Musical Elements

This is a perfect teaching piece for tone, resonance, and phrasing because its engaging and not entirely predictable melody bears repetition. It will bring a peaceful closing to one section of a concert or ease an audience (and choir) into the first program of the academic year.

The harmony is simple, using a few secondary dominants; the melody is diatonic; and the 6 | 8 rhythm exudes peace. The piano accompaniment is well within an average player's ability. Many will successfully sight-read it. A teacher may help a high school pianist express the languor of the setting with artful sensitivity. Observe the elasticity of tempo in mm. 20 and 38–40. Consider adding a touch of rubato to the accompaniment in mm. 4 and 30 and maybe in selected other places when voices are present. M. 12 suggests itself as a possibility; it separates the text line which will be repeated from its internal repetition in the musical setting, while allowing singers to catch a breath for the end-of-stanza emotion.

There are only two difficulties: phrasing, including expressive shaping, and breath. Fully half of the first stanza (two lines of poetry, four bars of music at dotted quarter note = ca. 48) should be sung without taking a breath, especially at the junction of the two poetic lines. A conductor can help his or her choir "tank up" during the four-measure cantabile introduction by modeling the breath and by opening the mouth in the shape of a resonant "ah" for the anacrusic "I long," which covers an upward octave leap on an E-flat. This leap may require warm-up exercises at the beginning of each class to teach and initiate tall vowels, resonance, loose jaws, and effective abdominal support. The E-flat octave is no voice part's inbuilt beautiful interval, and requires each of the four types to master this difficulty. Thiman asks singers to perform this leap at *mezzo piano* with a tenuto over the second (top) pitch. From there, thankfully, the melody goes no higher, although it repeats the E-flat from time to time. Presumably English choirboys are at home in this area. The low E-flat completes the melodic compass of this utterly beautiful piece, which has only an octave range.

After the choir's first two notes, the challenge is to continue the phrase's building intensity from the first words, "I long," to the high point, "night." Again, there is no breath in m. 6. Do not allow singers to relax until the peak of the phrase in m. 7. Then they should fall evenly back to their first breath, m. 8, after "cool." Notice that the "no breath between lines one and two" prohibition does not apply to the second stanza (m. 22). Take one there.

The dotted-eighth-sixteenth followed by two tied eighth notes (mm. 13–15) is the next phrasing challenge. Allow the audience to hear the figure climbing. Be sure to seize the opportunity to teach singers about sequential melody sections and their role in intensifying an emotion, so they may better express the line "to carry, carry, carry me over the sea." This area of repeated text builds dynamically from *piano* to *forte* and falls back in its last measure (m. 16), making another nicely arched phrase. Each "carry" should *carry* its own flavor, one tripping after the next to bear the listener "over the sea."

Form and Structure

Measure	Event and Scoring
1–4	Introduction, piano and anacrusis of initial octave leap: be prepared
5–16	Three phrases (4 + 4 + 4)
17–20	Piano interlude
21–28	Two phrases (4 + 4)
29–30	Bridge
31–37	One phrase: "tail"
38–41	Ending

Text

I long to sail the path to the moon
On a deep blue night, when the wind is cool:
A glist'ning path, that runs out to sea,
Silver the sails to carry me over the sea.
So will I sail, on a starry night
On the path to the Moon, a seabird's flight;
Skimming the waves, where the fishes play,
Traveling on, for many a day;
Silver the sails to carry me over the sea.
—Madeline C. Thomas

Additional References and Resources

Barnett, Rob, ed. *Classical Music on the Web*, s.v. "English Composers for Amateurs: No. 2 – Eric Thiman." http://www.musicweb-international.com/amateurs/Thiman.html (accessed May 13, 2005).

Macy, L., ed. *The Grove Dictionary of Music and Musicians*, s.v. "Thiman, Eric." (by Michael Hurd) http://www.grovemusic.com (accessed May 13, 2005).

Contributed by:

Lani Johnson

Teacher Resource Guide

The Turtle Dove

arr. Linda Steen Spevacek

SATB with piano and flute
Hal Leonard: 43725024
Overall: 1
Vocal: 1
Tonal/Rhythm: 1

Composer

Linda Steen Spevacek (b. 1945) is a composer, arranger, clinician, adjudicator, choral conductor, and voice teacher. Her more than seven hundred published works have sold over seven million combined copies. Recently, her publications have been performed in the 2003 PBS broadcast of MENC World's Largest Concert, which includes the song "M. T.'s Sage Advice" in 2003. She has won several awards in composition from American Society of Composers, Authors, and Publishers (ASCAP). She has received commissions from large choirs throughout the United States, and many of these have become signature pieces for the commissioning choir. In addition to her choral compositions, Linda Spevacek has complied dozens of collections, six collections of vocal music and five books of music for piano.

Spevacek has written various texts and videos about choirs and singing. Her most recent book, *The Choral Director's Guide to Sanity…and Success!*, coauthored by Randy Pagel, is designed to help choral directors and teachers have successful rehearsals. She produced a video titled *The Choral Director as Voice Teacher*, which aims to bring out the very best in each voice in the choir.[1]

Composition and Historical Perspective

"The Turtle Dove" is a British folk song adapted by people living in the Appalachians. The text of this song is a journey about saying farewell to a love. When programming Linda Spevacek's arrangement of "The Turtle Dove," one should look for other folk song arrangements to compliment this piece.

Technical and Stylistic Considerations and Musical Elements

Although this arrangement of "The Turtle Dove" is strophic, each verse is arranged quite differently and has its own set of technical challenges. Thus it will be best to examine each verse as a separate entity.

Overall Diction Suggestions

Because the text is British, closed vowels and quick consonants should be employed. To help achieve this sound, closed vowels with spacious and forward resonance should be used throughout.

Introduction

When performing this introduction, the accompanist must make sure that the melody is present with appropriate contour. If the line is missing or poorly played, it will be difficult for the choir to sing the musical line.

Verse 1

One of the most challenging aspects of this verse, other than sustaining the long phrases and understanding the contour of the melody, is beginning the tune appropriately. The introduction is quite long and lilting; it is easy for the choir to lose focus. Also, the last two measures before the choir enters have a syncopated bass line. All of these little things will easily catch even an upper-level choir off guard. In order to prepare the choir for this entrance, it would be wise to count the introduction aloud. The choir should count steady eighth notes (one and two and three and four and) for each measure. The counting should be short and separated (also, it is wise to say the syllable "ti" rather than "three," as a choir will get stuck and loose rhythmic integrity on the "thr" sound). On the beat before the entrance, the choir should breathe for the length of the beat.

At the end of the verse, make sure that the sound is sustained for the written duration on the word "miles." The "s" of the word should come right on the rest on the fourth beat.

Verse 2

This verse begins with the men and women in unison. On the downbeat of m. 22, the men sing a third below the women. Pay careful attention so the B-flat in the men's part doesn't drop in pitch; the men are singing on a break, so pitch control may be difficult. It may help to ask the men to think higher on that B-flat than the one right before it. The women drop a minor sixth (from B-flat to D). Make sure that the D on the downbeat of m. 22 does not enter chest voice. If it does, it will be difficult for the women to get back into their head voices. This jump from B-flat down to D happens often in this melody. Make sure that the women are aware of what their voices are doing when they sing these pitches. A way to fix this is to sing the line on the neutral syllable "noo." The "oo" vowel will help focus the sound and keep it in the women's head voice.

VERSE 3

The piano accompaniment gets strong in mm. 33–39, and although the men enter at a marked *forte*, they must be cautious to maintain a supported tone in the upper register. It may be wise to ask the men to change the dynamic to ***mf***. In the pickup to m. 40, the sound should be nearly transparent. The choir should not be too quiet, as the dynamic has not changed at all, but there needs to be an entirely new color after the caesura.

VERSE 4

The color of the fourth verse must be a continuation of the color found at the end of verse three as the melody is passed from women to men. When the women have the melody, be careful in handling the downward skips (as mentioned above), and when the men have the melody, make sure that the line arches over and beyond the high Ds. When the verse moves to four parts, those with sustained notes must constantly tune with the moving notes around them. To help with this, listening exercises that force singers to listen critically while singing can be included in the warm-up. The general principles learned in these exercises can and should be applied to all pieces of music.

CODA

This is not a real verse; m. 60 to the end acts as a coda. Be mindful of the sustained notes, as discussed earlier. Since this is the very end of the piece, it is important that the tuning be impeccable. Sing with the same color and feel used for the first verse. This will help the singers because the first verse began the motion of the entire piece, and reminding the singers of the beginning will help to bring that motion to this final section. If motion is lost at the end, it will sound dead; make sure that the air continues spinning through the final cutoff. This will help both the intonation and the color consistency of the coda section.

GENERAL REMINDERS

- Make sure the women do not use chest voice on the descending leaps (especially all of the melodic leaps from B-flat down to D).
- The men should maintain a supported sound without vocal pressure (especially in the high Ds in m. 35). They must move the line through to the end.

- Allow for new tone colors for each verse.
- Beware of the syncopation in the accompaniment; count-singing will help.

This folk song arrangement lends itself to long vocal lines. It is important that the singers pay extra care to not allowing the lines to die or decay as they run out of breath. When conducting this piece, strive for color changes between verses. Many of these changes already are written into the arrangement; thus it is crucial that these changes are heard in performance.

Form and Structure

This arrangement of "The Turtle Dove" is strophic with each verse arranged differently.

SECTION	MEASURE	EVENT AND SCORING
Introduction	1–7	Piano (or harp) and flute
Verse 1	8–18	Piano/harp, unison chorus, flute
Interlude	19–20	Piano/harp
Verse 2	21–31	Piano/harp, four-part chorus
Interlude	32–33	Piano/harp
Verse 3	34–43	Piano/harp, four-part chorus
Interlude	44–47	Piano/harp, flute
Verse 4	48–59	Piano/harp, three-part chorus (divided men), flute
Coda	60–75	Piano/harp, two-part chorus

Text

Fare you well, my dear, I must be gone
And leave you for a while.
If I roam away I'll come back again,
Tho' I roam ten thousand miles, my dear,
Tho' I roam ten thousand miles.

So fair thou art, my bonny lad,
So deep in love am I,
But never will prove false to the bonny lad I love,
Till the stars fall from the sky, my dear,
Till the stars fall from the sky.

The sea will never run dry, my dear,
Nor the rocks ever melt with the sun,
But I never will prove false to the bonny lad I love,
Till the stars fall from the sky, my dear,
Till the stars fall from the sky.

O yonder sits that little turtle dove,
He doth sit on yonder high tree,
A making a moan for the loss of his love
As I will do for thee, my dear,
As I will do for thee.

Fare you well, my dear, farewell.

Contributed by:

Matthew J. LaPine

---

1 Linda Spevacek: http://www.softwaredynamix.com/music/bio.shtml.

Teacher Resource Guide

This Little Light of Mine

arr. Ken Berg

Unison voice, piano, and cello
Colla voce: 20-96460
Overall: 1
Vocal: 1
Tonal/Rhythm: 1

Composer

A native of the Virginia/North Carolina area, Ken Berg (b. 1956) graduated from Samford University in Birmingham, Alabama, with a bachelor of musical arts in 1977 and a master of music education in 1981. For twenty-eight years he was the director of choirs and fine arts chairman at John Carroll High School in Birmingham before retiring in 2005 to become the music minister and resident composer at Mountain Brook Baptist Church.

In 1978 Ken and Susan Berg were appointed music directors of the Birmingham Boys Choir (www.birminghamboyschoir.com), a position they still hold. They are the parents of two sons, Michael and David, both fine musicians in their own right.

Ken has served as a state and division officer with the American Choral Directors Association (ACDA) and has also been on the Training Courses Committee of the Royal School of Church Music in America. In addition to touring extensively throughout Europe and North America, his choirs have sung at ACDA, OAKE, and MENC state, division, and national conventions.

Ken often serves as a clinician and adjudicator throughout the U.S. His music is published with Carl Fischer, Chorister's Guild, Colla Voce, Emerson

Music, Hal Leonard, National Music Publishers, Pavane Music, Santa Barbara Music Publishers, and Walton Music.

Composition and Historical Perspective

"This Little Light of Mine" is technically an American folk song, although it could easily fall into the category of spiritual, lullaby, or even hymn anthem. There are two very different tunes associated with this text; one generally fast and rhythmic, with an ascending melody, which is often given a rock-and-roll treatment, the other sweet and slow with a descending triadic melody, generally more contemplative and personal. This particular setting clearly falls into the latter category.

"This Little Light of Mine" was written because the choristers of the Birmingham Boys Choir were working on a different setting of the piece that just wasn't coming together well. Almost in desperation, Ken Berg instructed all the boys to "just sing the melody," and with some "seat of the pants" improvisation, it just happened.

Technical Considerations and Musical Elements

As is often the case with folksong literature, this anthem provides some excellent teaching tools in the areas of music reading, vocal technique, and musicianship.

There are ample opportunities for students to "be good detectives" and find phrases in the score that are similar. "Where does this happen again?" is always a great questions for young singers in that it requires them to "see" a musical statement on the staff and find the same or similar statement in another place on the staff. Some other questions you might want to try are: "How is this phrase different from the one we just did?" and "Is this a scale or an arpeggio?" More great learning opportunities!

Regarding vocal technique, the consistent use of four-measure phrases is great for teaching how to take a full breath and manage breath control in the musical phrases. Also, the diphthong in the words "light" and "mine" and "shine" provides an excellent opportunity to address vowel formation and uniformity in the lower and upper registers. In the third verse, the "ah" in "all" and the "oo" in "thru" again provide multiple opportunities to reinforce good vowel formation and usage.

The optional solo in verse two can be very useful for discovering hidden talents and musicianship within the choir. When a director finds a chorister who really sings this verse well, it has the potential to positively reinforce good tone production and work ethic and to increase support for fellow singers throughout the choir. Also, the use of the B-flat in the ending phrase provides an unexpected blues influence that can be very intriguing for the choir and the listeners. The use of the piano/cello combination with unison voices can be very engaging for the singers and the audience.

Stylistic Considerations

While "This Little Light of Mine" is very lyrical, it should not be sung too slowly. Each phrase should have a very natural rise and fall in both dynamics and tempo. The beauty is in the simplicity of the tune and the elegance of the singing. A good cellist with a nice full tone can have a very profound impact on the presentation by the choir, modeling sonority and intensity of dynamic and phrasing.

Form and Structure

There are three repetitive verses in this song.

Section	Measure	Event and Scoring
Verse 1		
Phrase 1	6–9	Basically a descending major triad with only one "visiting Fa"
Phrase 2	10–13	Ascending first half and descending scale in the second half
Phrase 3	14–20	The long phrase at the end; more step/skip combinations as well as the same descending tonic triad, but followed by the "ending" of the phrase with the "bluesy" B-flat, setting up the descending scale to Do; some teachers may prefer to break this third phrase into two shorter phrases, mm. 14–17a and mm. 17b–20, which is fine
Verse 2		Verse 2 follows the same form as verse one with the exception that phrase 2 (mm. 28–31) has the harmonically lowered seventh and sixth just to show off what the soloist can do
Verse 3		Verse 3 is almost the same as verses 1 and 2 with just a little bit more of everything; more dynamic contrast; the softs are softer and the louds are louder; phrase 3 has the only dotted quarter-eighth combination in the piece; phrase 3 also has the "augmented" notes to create the finality of the ending; this allows the discussion of how a coda brings things to finality

Contributed by:

Ken Berg

Teacher Resource Guide

Verleih uns Frieden

Felix Mendelssohn

(1809–1847)

SATB with keyboard or orchestra
Oxford University Press: 3418150
Overall: 1
Vocal: 1
Tonal/Rhythm: 2

Composer

Felix Mendelssohn was an extraordinarily gifted child. He came from a distinguished Jewish family. His father was the head of a major Berlin banking firm, and his grandfather was a famous Jewish philosopher. Mendelssohn's elaborate private education was organized by his mother and included a daily regime of music, languages, literature, drawing, and many other skills. He was a natural at everything he did, including music, and would have been successful in anything to which he turned his attention. His talents in music were also quite diverse. He was one of the finest pianists, conductors, and organists of his day. In fact, some say that he could have been one of the great violinists.

Mendelssohn's music was always skillful but conservative and polite in some ways. When compared to his contemporaries such as Richard Wagner and Giuseppe Verdi, his Romanticism was very subdued. His harmonic language was largely diatonic and his music clearly organized. He was the most classical and balanced of the early Romantics.

Mendelssohn's awareness of music's past was also responsible for one of the greatest musical resurrections in history when he conducted J. S. Bach's *St.*

Matthew Passion on March 11, 1829. One cannot blame him for being conservative as he grew up in a home that taught him to be polite and avoid offense. His masterpieces include the oratorio *Elijah*, A *Midsummer Night's Dream* Overture, Octet in E-flat Major for Strings, and his *Songs without Words* for piano.

Composition and Historical Perspective

Mendelssohn composed "Verleih uns Frieden" after receiving a copy of the Lutheran Hymnal from Franz Hauser, a Bach enthusiast. Inspired by the words and music of this book, Mendelssohn composed six chorale-cantatas, two motets, and this setting. The text for this piece is Martin Luther's, but the music is entirely composed by Mendelssohn. Mendelssohn wrote to Hauser that he intended to "set the little song 'Verleih uns Frieden' as a canon with cello and bass." The canonic opening of the work end up being for divided cellos, and its theme recalls the second subject of the *Hebrides* overture of 1830. Mendelssohn completed "Verleih uns Frieden" in 1831; however, it did not receive a performance until 1839 and was not included in his compositional catalog until after his death. He composed "Verleih uns Frieden" in Rome, one of the destinations on his multi-national tour.

Stylistic Considerations

Tempo

It is easy for performances of this piece to be slow and plodding. Note that the tempo is marked andante, which means at a walking tempo. This is neither too fast nor too slow. The ability of your singers to sustain a legato line will be the determining factor of your tempo. Choose a tempo that makes it easy for your singers to complete the lines in one breath. As this is Romantic music, a tasteful amount of rubato should be employed throughout the work.

Language

Originally composed in German, it is possible to find commercially available editions of this melody with a Latin text, *Da nobis pacem*. If your choir has never attempted German before, this is a wonderful piece to use as a primer, as many of the sounds of the language are found in this short text. The two biggest challenges are the several occurrences of umlauted vowels. These are most efficiently taught in the warm-up. Try doing warm-ups on mixed vowels and warm-ups that juxtapose mixed vowels with non-mixed vowels for several rehearsals before introducing the language of this piece. If taught properly, your choir will not have much difficulty with this concept.

The second challenge, which is more difficult to master, is the unaccented final syllables of the German words. The best rule of thumb is to remember that any unstressed syllable can be sung as a schwa (an unaccented neutral vowel). A schwa is performed by rounding the lips, which mutes the vowel. I often ask my singers to "wrap their lips around the vowel." Doing this mutes the vowel and aids in performing the syllable without an accent. This must happen on the final syllable of all of the following words, *Frieden*, *unsern*, *Zeiten*, *andrer*, *könnte*, *streiten*, *unsrer*, and *alleine*. Failure to use schwa will result in the final syllable being accented, especially if the syllable comes on a metrically strong beat (e.g., the final syllable of *alleine*.)

TONE

The tone employed for this work should have a spacious, high, and forward placement. It should be neither too dark nor too bright. The line should be as legato as possible. This is a wonderful piece with which to work on choral tone, as the ranges are not extreme and the notes and rhythms are simple. This piece works very well with young and mature voices.

PHRASING

The phrasing of "Verleih uns Frieden" is predictable. The phrases should be shaped to the high point of each phrase and then tapered to the end. A slower tempo and tranquil mood might cause the singers to lack energy in their breath, which would yield a dull phrase. Using movement or count-singing during rehearsals can help combat this problem.

Musical Elements

"Verleih uns Frieden" is a simple motet composed in a hymn-like style. There are few vocal challenges in this piece if the choir sings with good technique from the beginning of each verse. You will note that most of the phrases in this piece begin with a leap; a choir that does not think ahead can end up reaching for these higher pitches and singing them out of tune. Amateur singers often worry about producing a note once they get there instead of preparing the voice before leaping. The first phrase of the melody, for example, contains two leaps, one of a major third and the other of a perfect fifth. This phrase must be sung on one breath. The singer starts on an E-flat, which is relatively low in the voice for all parts. On the eighth beat of the phrase the singer must still have enough air to leap up to a B-flat. This will be quite easy if the singer prepares the space for the B-flat on the initial breath for the phrase. Not breathing with enough space for the higher pitches of the phrase will yield a sound that is pressed and is most likely out of tune. Such leaps occur over and over again in this work. This concept of preparing leaps can be presented with the melodic material of the music in a carefully structured warm-up. Because this melody is simple, it lends itself well to rote teaching.

Tonally, this music is very simple; in fact, only one phrase of the melody contains any chromaticism at all. This short two-measure phrase first appears at m. 28. This descending melody is essentially an A-flat Phrygian scale (with B-flat omitted). This melody can be taught easily with solfege (moveable Do,

A-flat = Do) or simply by rote. It would be wise to present this melody in the warm-up as a sort of game. This way the singers will be familiar with the melodic context when they read the music from the score.

The first verse is marked for basses only. It is perfectly acceptable, and perhaps even desirable, to have the tenors join them in this section. The second verse is scored for alto and bass. Again, it would be wise to ask the sopranos to join the altos and the tenors to join the basses. The third verse is scored for four parts.

Do not underestimate the difficulty of the bass's countermelody in the second verse. While by no means difficult, it will take a few times through to perfect, as the way in which this countermelody weaves with the alto melody can cause the men to miscount and get lost, particularly in or around m. 53.

Form and Structure

"Verleih uns Frieden" is a hymn setting set three times. The text remains the same in each verse.

Verse 1: basses only on hymn tune (may add tenors)
Verse 2: alto on hymntune melody (may add sopranos), basses on counter-melody (may add tenors)
Verse 3: four-part hymn setting with final four part coda

Text and Translation

Verleih uns Frieden gnädiglich,	Grant us peace, mercifully,
Herr Gott, zu unsern Zeiten!	Lord God, at our times
Es ist doch ja kein andrer nicht,	There is indeed no other
Der für uns könnte streiten,	Who for us could fight
Denn du, unsrer Gott alleine.	Than you, our God, alone.

Contributed by:

Matthew W. Mehaffey

Teacher Resource Guide

A New Year Carol from Friday Afternoons, Op. 7

Benjamin Britten
(1913–1976)

SSA/piano
Boosey & Hawkes: 48003743
Overall: 1
Vocal: 1
Tonal/Rhythm: 1

Composer

Benjamin Britten was born in Lowestoft, Suffolk, in 1913. The youngest of four children, he was strongly influenced by his mother, a pianist and singer herself. His musical training started with piano lessons at an early age and then viola lessons at age ten. At the age fourteen he had already composed one hundred pieces. In the 1920s he traveled to London to study composition with Frank Bridge and years later entered the Royal College of Music, where he won several competitions and awards.

In 1935 Britten composed the first of his several documentary film soundtracks. That same year his friendship with W. H. Auden began to blossom, and it later become both a collaborative and creative partnership. Britten often set Auden's poetry to music. In 1939, motivated by Auden's departure to America and because of the difficulties World War II presented to Britten's pacifist political bent, he moved to the United States, along with his partner, tenor Peter Pears. Britten's antiwar feelings are evident in many of his works, but are especially obvious in the *War Requiem*, which he completed in 1961.

In 1942 he returned to England and set Auden's texts for *Hymn to Saint Cecilia* and *Ceremony of Carols*. By 1945 he finished one of his well-known operas, *Peter Grimes*, which was performed with great success. With this opera he wanted to "restore the musical setting of the English language [to] a brilliance, freedom, and vitality that have been curiously rare since the death of Purcell."

Britten's stylistic perception and musical language expanded in the 1950s as he researched dodecaphony and Far Eastern cultures. His diverse output includes operas, choral and orchestral works, and music for films, radio, and stage. One of the most successful English composers, he employed a unique harmonic language. Britten is a key figure in the development of the twentieth-century British musical tradition.

Composition and Historical Perspective

Friday Afternoons, a set of twelve songs composed from 1933 to 1935 and dedicated to his brother, was Britten's first attempt at or experiment in writing for children, whose voices fascinated him. The text comes from *Tom Tiddler's Ground: A Book of Poetry for the Junior and Middle Schools*, an anthology compiled and edited by Walter de la Mare.

Writer Walter de la Mare (1873–1956) was born in Charlton, Kent, England. A writer of stories, novels, poetry, critiques and compilation of anthologies, De la Mare received numerous awards and honors. The song was originally a Marian carol with many references to the imagery of light and water. In "A New Year Carol" the "Fair Maid" refers to the Virgin Mary, an appellation more common in historical times. The carol is proper to the Feast of Annunciation of the Blessed Virgin Mary, also known as Lady Day, which is celebrated on March 25. There is some disagreement on where and when the carol originated. One view is that the Feast of Annunciation began in medieval England, while other scholars suggest that the tradition originated in seventeenth-century Wales. The tradition from Wales relates the custom on New Year's morning when, before dawn, boys carried around a container of fresh water and branches of evergreens. The boys sprinkled the faces, hands, and rooms in the houses of people. If not allowed to enter a house, they still sprinkled its doors to bring good luck in the New Year. Villagers gave their visitors coins in return. While walking around and sprinkling water, the boys would sing carols, including this one.

Technical Considerations and Musical Elements

Benjamin Britten demonstrated a special ability to write for children, providing them musical enjoyment in pieces suited to their abilities. "A New Year Carol" is a simple but beautiful piece. The uncomplicated, melodic refrain, its tune all three times sung by soprano I, is the basis of the whole piece. The melody is first stated in unison in all voices, next split between sopranos I and II, and finally divided among soprano I, soprano II, and altos. The interrelationship of the three voices is triadic, with several voice crossings. A good way to start the piece would be to introduce the tune to the whole choir with all voices singing in unison on a neutral syllable. Teach the phrases and shape as singers learn notes and rhythms. The choir should know (particularly soprano II) that some parts are occasionally above soprano I, so they do not follow the soprano I tune. The third and last statement of the tune is stated first by the soprano I, and the refrain ("Sing levy dew, the water and the wine; the seven bright gold wires and the bugles that do shine") is stated by the soprano II as the soprano I floats over the two other voices.

The tune is scalar within an octave, uses repeated notes and descending sequences, and is easy to sing. The piano accompaniment harmonically supports the tune.

The harmony, alternates between E-flat (I) and F minor (ii), with a regular E-flat pedal until the final phrase. The third statement of the refrain contains G minor (iii) and A-flat major (IV). The piano is basically used to accompany the choir but complements the calm imagery of water from the poetry. However, since a four-measure piano introduction starts the piece, it should set the mood. The conductor must make sure the pianist follows the indications of pedaling and dynamics, all of which enhance the poetic atmosphere. The piece is soft throughout. Choirs may be tempted to slow down every time they have an even softer dynamic, as in m. 49. The *rallentando molto* does not begin until m. 52, and the conductor must ensure that the choir does not slow down prematurely. It is imperative that the conductor and choristers understand the poem because it is rich in metaphors.

Stylistic Considerations

It is important to insist on and work for a choral sound that is bright and forward. Consonants should be crisp and light and vowels tall and narrow. The conductor should encourage the choir to sing with a British accent as a way for accomplishing this tall and narrow sound. It is important to examine Britten's dynamics carefully to guarantee the shape of the phrases and the mood of the piece. The conductor should coach the pianist so both choir and piano are "in tune" with the color, phrasing, and atmosphere of the music.

Form and Structure

The tune of this piece is stated three times with some rearranging for voicing at the end.

SECTION	MEASURE	EVENT AND SCORING
Section I	1–22	
	1–4	Piano introduction
	5–22	Unison (4 + 4 + (4 + 4–refrain) +2)
Section II	23–40	
	23–40	SS (4 + 4 + (4 + 4–refrain) + 2); tune in soprano I; soprano II accompanying (voice crossing)
Section III	41–56	SSA (4 + 4 + 4 + 4–refrain); tune in soprano I; pick-up to m. 39 soprano II with the refrain

Text

Here we bring new water from the well so clear,
For to worship God with, this happy New Year
Sing levy dew, sing levy dew, the water and the wine;
The seven bright gold wires and the bugles that do shine.

Sing reign of Fair Maid, with gold upon her toe,
Open you the West Door, and turn the Old Year go.
Sing levy dew, sing levy dew, the water and the wine;
The seven bright gold wires and the bugles that do shine.

Sing reign of Fair Maid, with gold upon her chin,
Open you the East Door, and let the New Year in.
Sing levy dew, sing levy dew, the water and the wine;
The seven bright gold wires and the bugles that do shine.

Additional References and Resources

Buchanan, Heather, and Matthew W. Mehaffey, eds. *Teaching Music through Performance in Choir, Volume 1*. Chicago: GIA Publications, 2005.

Cooke, Mervin, ed. *The Cambridge Companion to Benjamin Britten*. Cambridge: Cambridge University Press, 1999.

Evans, Peter. *The Music of Benjamin Britten*. London: J. M. Dent & Sons, 1979.

Macdonnell, Frances. "Letters: What Does 'Levy Dew' Mean?" *The American Organist 21* (1987): 12–13.

Palmer, Christopher, ed. *The Britten Companion*. London: Faber & Faber Ltd., 1984.

Thurman, Elinor H. "Letters: What Does 'Levy Dew' Mean?" *The American Organist 20* (1986): 10–12.

Contributed by:

Marcela Molina

Teacher Resource Guide

Hello, Girls
arr. Lloyd Pfautsch

SSA/piano
Lawton-Gould Music Publishers/Alfred Publishing Co.
Overall: 1
Vocal: 1
Tonal/Rhythm: 2

Composer

Lloyd Pfautsch (1929–2003) was a native of Washington, Missouri. He received a bachelor of arts degree from Elmhurst College and a master of divinity and master of sacred music from Union Theological Seminary in New York City. He received honorary doctorates from Elmhurst College, Illinois Wesleyan University, and West Virginia Wesleyan College. In 1992 he retired from the faculty of the Meadows School of the Arts at Southern Methodist University in Dallas, Texas, where he had been professor of sacred music and director of choral activities since 1958. Pfautsch wrote more than three hundred and fifty choral compositions, arrangements, and editions published by eighteen different music publishers.

Composition

This piece is a traditional American folk song.

Technical Considerations and Musical Elements

This piece presents a number of challenges. The tempo is marked "perky," and the half note = ca. 84 or 88. Singers must feel the piece in two for it to have rhythmic grounding. This can be achieved by having them do a "toss-clap." This involves their clapping lightly and then rotating the clapping hand in a circular motion as if throwing around pizza dough. Be certain that their toss-claps always involve the right dynamic (size of clap) and articulation (weight of clap) for each section. Have them experiment with various combinations of size and weight to experience the correct and incorrect versions. Feeling the rhythmic structure of the piece will keep it from running away from you.

Fast pieces can cause singers to lose their sense of a low breath. Ask singers to breathe a full half note before entrances to seat the breath. Quick releases (quarter and eighth rests) may cause their larynxes to lift. Ask them to "reset the mechanism" to its low position on those releases. These releases can also be made quite accurate by having them snap where they are supposed to put the consonant. If they snap together, they will release together.

The "fa la la" refrains present a number of diction issues. The first challenge is attaining a true "ah" vowel for "fa la la." There will be a tendency to sing "uh" instead of "ah" because of the speed. Ask singers to sing use a true "ah" vowel on each and every syllable. Getting the first "fah" to be pure will help make subsequent vowels correct. Ask them to drop their jaws a little bit after each consonant. Their jaws must stay loose to articulate these words quickly. The running eighth notes of these refrains must also be light and playful. The "l" of "la" can cause rhythmic sluggishness and may pull the tone too far back. Ask singers to sing the "l" on the tip of the tongue. They can practice by singing them as "fa da da" first. Put the "l" in later so they have the muscle memory of singing a quick "d" on the tip of the tongue.

Articulation and attention to musical details are vital. Singers must differentiate tenuto from staccato in m. 13, for example. "Fa" is also accented many times during the refrains. They must sing m. 25 differently than the first entrance because of the slurs. Ask students to come up with physical motions for each type of articulation and to "choreograph" a phrase. Get them involved in noticing where the articulations occur.

When learning the piece, start on a the neutral syllable "doo" at a slower tempo. Keep the dynamic level down if you feel that a louder dynamic will invite too much chest tone initially. If they do sing it softly at first, ask them to sing it with immense energy and focus in the sound. The "d" of "doo" will also help make the rhythm clear from the beginning.

This is a piece to be performed and enjoyed by everyone. It is not meant to be serious by any means. Encourage singers to have fun and to act as much as they sing. Ask them to speak the text as a poem to find the natural stresses of each word and to enjoy such silly words as "good-for-nothing" and "sassafras tea." The more the singers enjoy the piece, the more the audience will enjoy it.

Stylistic Considerations

A really outstanding performance of this piece requires some acting and possible pantomiming. The extent will vary based on the type of group performing the piece and available rehearsal time. An example of this would be pantomiming shaking one's finger in a motherly way in m. 7 when the text states "Don't you ever marry no good-for-nothing boys." Another prime example would be pantomiming having empty pockets in m. 30. At the very minimum, something special must occur in m. 55. During the third verse, the texts talks about the sweet names men call their girlfriends at the beginning of a relationship. It goes on to say that after he's married there is "no such thing." Emphasizing this line would really add life and fun to the piece.

While these types of additions may be out of the comfort zone for some of us, they will certainly add value and authenticity to the spirit of the piece. These motions also help younger singers to really perform the piece instead of just singing it. However, these little additions should be carefully selected to enhance the performance.

Form and Structure

Each major section begins with virtually the same four measures in the piano. The only changes are the slight variations in right hand chords. The left hand is exactly the same all three times. Each section is similar in structure, consisting of a verse and a "fa la la" refrain. These refrains are marked *piano* during the first two verses. However, the refrain differs in the third verse. The refrain begins *piano* but becomes *forte* in m. 66, then subito *piano* in m. 67, and subito *forte* in m. 69. These dynamic shifts create a very playful and enjoyable ending.

Mm. 1–20 (4 + 2 + 2 + 4 + 2 + 2 + 2 + 2)
Mm. 21–40 (4 + 2 + 2 + 2 + 2 + 2 + 2 + 2 + 2)
Mm. 41–72 (4 + 4 + 4 + 4 + 2 + 2 + 2 + 2 + 2 + 2 + 2 + 2)

Text

Hello girls, listen to my voice,
Don't you ever marry no good-for-nothing boys.
If you do your doom shall be
Hoecake, hominy, and sassafras tea.
Fa, la, la . . .

Young boys walking down the street,
Young girls think they look mighty sweet.
Hands in their pockets, not a dime do they find.
Oh how tickled, poor girls mine.
Fa, la, la . . .

When a young man falls in love,
First it's honey and then turtledove.
After he's married, no such thing.
"Get up and get my breakfast, you good-for-nothing thing."
Fa la la . . .

Contributed by:

William Hammer

Teacher Resource Guide

Song for the Mira

Allister MacGillivray

(b. 1948)

arr. Stuart Calvert

Cabot Trail Music/Gordon V. Thompson Music: VG326-W
SSA, TTB, or SATB/piano and flute
Overall: 1
Vocal: 1
Tonal/Rhythm: 2

Composer

Composer Allister MacGillivray was born in the coal mining and fishing town of Glace Bay, Nova Scotia. MacGillivray's family embraced their Cape Breton–Celtic heritage by continuing to speak the Gaelic language throughout his childhood. They also encouraged his early musical talent. As an adolescent MacGillivray performed throughout Cape Breton and Nova Scotia with several variety shows.

After graduating with a bachelor's degree from St. Francis Xavier University in 1969, MacGillivray focused his musical energies on performing and composing traditional Celtic and folk music of Cape Breton, Nova Scotia. During the 1970s, he collaborated with several notable Canadian musicians including John Allen Cameron, Anne Murray, and the trio *Ryan's Fancy*. In 1980 MacGillivray settled in rural Cape Breton with his wife and two children to continue documenting the culture of the region in song.

MacGillivray has published several collections of folk repertoire celebrating maritime Canada including *The Cape Breton Song Collection* and *The Nova Scotia Song Collection*. He composed "Song for the Mira" in 1973, and it was arranged by Canadian composer Stuart Calvert for chorus and piano for the Elmer Iseler Choral Series in 1985.

Composition and Historical Perspective

Allister MacGillivray's "Song for the Mira" was written in 1973 as a folkloric expression of the culture of Cape Breton, specifically the geography that follows the Mira River. It has evolved into something of a patriotic anthem for the province of Nova Scotia and, to a lesser extent, Canada as a whole.

The maritime province of Nova Scotia, as its name suggests, has a heritage of Scottish immigrants, and the culture of Cape Breton has embraced this lineage in many aspects of modern life. In fact, the Gaelic language is still alive in this community. As you prepare this work, you will soon discover how the geography and rich cultural history of this region are inextricably linked to the music—from the textual references to geographical landmarks such as Marion Bridge to the choice of instrumentation by the arranger to depict the flavor of the area.

Technical Considerations

There are several technical issues that may arise as you prepare this arrangement. Because the six verses to this text are set in similar ways, it may be a challenge to provide variety in rehearsal and performances of this piece. You might consider using more than one soloist or perhaps even small ensembles to contrast the full unison chorus. Also, some variety can be provided by attending diligently to the true dynamics suggested by the arranger.

Another challenge one might encounter with the choir is achieving true legato. There are several places where a singer might feel inclined to breathe, dividing the line into eight two-measure phrases per verse. Both issues can be addressed by encouraging your singers to imagine a flow of energy through a subdivision of pulse.

Imagining (and even feeling) the subdivision of the pulse is also an excellent way to prevent an unwanted slowing of the tempo. I often encourage singers to tap the eighth or sixteenth note subdivisions of the pulse on their sternums to combat slowing.

Stylistic Considerations

Although folk arrangements for chorus may not yet be a formal musicological genre, a savvy choral conductor can employ several performance practices to create an authentic interpretation. Perhaps the most important generalization a conductor should recall is that folk music is an expression of a group of people often unified by a cultural or linguistic history, gender identity, or common political struggle. This is not an expression of an elite group, and characteristics of the genre reflect that (using lyrical melodies, diatonic or modal harmonies, and simple rhythms).

There are two easy ways to improve the authenticity of the performance of this genre—diction and tone production. Simplicity is key here. In terms of diction, while it is unnecessary to try to replicate the dialect of the Cape Breton region, you may choose to encourage your singers to avoid overly rounded vowels and to soften consonants to create a more universal effect. Again, I recommend simple tone production as well. This does not mean unsupported sound but a color and placement closest to speech, unencumbered by excessive vibrato and artificial darkening.

Musical Elements

Melody

Stuart Calvert's arrangement of MacGillivray's folk anthem holds true to the melodic source. It is predominantly a syllabic setting of the text illuminating MacGillivray's simple, lyrical melody. Phrases are regular (four measures) and periodic, grouped by the rhyme scheme.

Harmony

Calvert sustains a D major tonality throughout the arrangement. Harmonies are diatonic with occasional secondary dominants.

Accompaniment

Calvert approximates the folklike sound of an acoustic guitar with simple chordal figuration in the right hand of the piano, while outlining harmonic structure with single sustained pitches in the left hand. The obbligato oboe or flute used for several of the verses aurally depicts the flowing Mira River.

Rhythm

Allister MacGillivray depicts Cape Breton's Mira River with a lilting triple meter. In the spirit of folk music, the rhythm of the vocal line only subdivides to the eighth note, creating an arrangement suitable for all ages. However, Stuart Calvert gives the obbligato instrument sixteenth and quintuplet subdivisions of the pulse, which is significantly more difficult.

Texture

The texture of this arrangement is homophonic. The choir sings in unison with the accompaniment and has accompanimental figures during the solos.

OTHER: DYNAMICS/ARTICULATION/TEMPO/RANGE
Dynamics: ***ppp–mf***
Articulation: tenuto as indicated, all others *a piacere*
Tempo: quarter note = 120–125, some slowing at structural pillars
Range: G-sharp3 to F-sharp5

Form and Structure

This setting of a Cape Breton folk anthem is organized into ternary form; its six verses are divided into three sections by two settings of a bridge-like refrain. The texture of the setting corresponds to its structure. Sections one and three are sung by a soloist, while section two is sung by the choir. The use of obbligato oboe on particular verses does not seem to be related to structural design. The six verses and the refrain have four phrases each. There is a ten-measure instrumental introduction to this work, as well as a four-measure tag at the end.

SECTION	MEASURE	EVENT AND SCORING
Introduction	1–10	Obbligato oboe
Verse 1	11–26	Solo
Verse 2	27–42	Solo with choral hum, obbligato oboe
Refrain	43–58	Unison chorus
Verse 3	59–74	Unison chorus, obbligato oboe
Verse 4	75–90	Unison chorus
Refrain	91–106	Divisi chorus (SSAA split)
Verse 5	107–122	Solo with choral hum, obbligato oboe
Verse 6	123–141	Solo, obbligato oboe
Tag	141–144	Choral hum, obbligato oboe

Text

Out on the Mira on warm afternoons
Old men go fishin' with black line and spoons
And if they catch nothin' they never complain.
I wish I was with them again.

As boys in their boats call to girls on the shore,
Teasin' the ones that they dearly adore,
And into the evening the courting begins.
I wish I was with them again.

Refrain
Can you imagine a piece of the universe
More fit for princes and kings?
I'll trade you ten of your cities for Marion Bridge*
And the pleasure it brings. . . .

*Marion Bridge is a town on the Mira River.

Suggested Recordings

Here are two recordings of the Calvert arrangement of "Song for the Mira" and one version of the original MacGillivray folk song:

Arrangement: *My Heart Soars: A Canadian Celebration of Life, Laughter, Love and Praise*, Toronto Children's Choir, Jean Ashworth Bartle, conductor, Marquis Music, 1997.

Original: *Now & Forever*, Anne Murray, SBK Records, 1995.

Contributed by:

Emilie Sweet

Teacher Resource Guide

Hard Times Come Again No More

Stephen Foster
(1826–1864)

arr. Donald Moore

TTBB with optional string bass
Warner Bros./Alfred Publishing Co.: SV8938
Overall: 1
Vocal: 1
Tonal/Rhythm: 1

Composer

Stephen Foster's songs are among the most widely known in American music. Almost anyone can hum a few measures of "Oh! Susanna" or "Old Folks at Home." Songs such as these have become so common in American culture that they are more like folk songs than composed material because of their popularity, widespread performance, and numerous arrangements and variations.

Stephen Collins Foster was born in Lawrenceville, Pennsylvania (now Pittsburgh) on July 4, 1826. He was a mostly self-taught musician; however, it is believed that he studied with Henry Kleber, a German immigrant who was known to be an accomplished musician and performer. As a child, Foster was not encouraged by his family to pursue a career in music, as it was not considered to be fitting of a young man. At the age of twenty, he moved to Cincinnati to work as an accountant for his brother, all the while exploring his love for songwriting. His first major success was the publication of "Oh! Susanna" in 1848, which helped convince him that there were great possibilities for him as a composer. In 1850 he decided to give up his accounting career and return to Pittsburgh to write songs full-time. His career saw many ups and downs yet despite his successes, poor decision making ultimately led to his demise. He relocated to New York in 1860, where he died nearly four years later, alone and penniless.

Out of his approximately two hundred songs, twenty-eight were written for the minstrel show stage (a popular form of entertainment at the time), and many of his others, although not specifically for the stage, were in that same style. In contrast, a large number of his compositions are considered to be "parlor songs," which have a sentimental or nostalgic sensitivity and are usually on subjects of "hearth and home." The genteel tradition was prominent in his family circle, and, as a result, he was not immediately excited about the growing popularity of the minstrelsy.[1]

Composition and Historical Perspective

During the mid-1850s, the blackface minstrel show became popular as a form of dramatic musical entertainment. Foster wrote a number of songs for such a stage, often using Negro dialect in his texts, which he referred to as "Ethiopian" songs. However, he later decided to "reform" the minstrel style by merging it with that of the genteel parlor songs.[2] The similarities to a slave work song, for example, in "Hard Times Come Again No More" are apparent, in that it speaks of yearning for a better, easier life. Yet its simple melody and lighthearted sound make it seem natural to be sung in the home parlor.

Like most of Foster's songs, there are various arrangements of "Hard Times Come Again No More," with a variety of voicings and instrumentations. In the Firth, Pond, and Company publication (one of Foster's original publishers), it appears for solo voice and a simple accompaniment with a choral setting of the refrain at the end.

Technical Considerations and Musical Elements

One major consideration in the performance of the work is proper balancing of the parts so that the melody is not obscured. As noted in Form and Structure, the melody alternates between the parts, appearing sometimes in the tenor and sometimes in the baritone. The singers should always be aware of where the tune lies in the texture so they can listen for it and adjust their dynamics accordingly.

Since the piece is *a cappella* (other than the optional string bass), the singers who do not carry the tune must realize their role as accompanists and tackle the vocal and rhythmic issues therein. For example, the basses are required to execute consecutive leaps, such as the arpeggio in m. 11. It is a common error for singers to approximate pitches when the motion is not stepwise, making the distance between the intervals inaccurate. This can cause a host of problems, the most troublesome of which is the lack of harmonic clarity and intonation. The singers must first learn their notes in a slow tempo, allowing their voices to "settle" into the pitches comfortably. Singing on a neutral syllable or on the text are equally effective in this case. Then if the pitches are still inaccurate, each note can be sustained out of rhythm and tuned to the harmony of the other parts. If sliding occurs, staccato singing (again with a neutral syllable or the text) will encourage the singers to find the pitches accurately, removing any sustained time between notes during which a change of pitch could take place.

Since the accompaniment helps drive the rhythm of the piece, it is important that singers on those parts be very consistent in their counting. There are some cases in which the accompaniment parts enter on the "and" of a beat while the melody does not (mm. 20 and 32, for example). The key to accuracy on these entrances is the preceding breath. The chorus may need to be reminded that rhythmic breathing is imperative; if a choir breathes on time, it will sing on time. In the case of mm. 20 and 32, an eighth note breath on beat one will set the rhythm. If the chorus has difficulty timing the breath, count-singing (with no counting on the rests) may also prove helpful.

Stylistic Considerations

"Hard Times Come Again No More" is a minstrel-style song. The arranger notes that it "reflects Foster's childhood days when he would often accompany the household maid to church where [he] would listen intently to the strains of the black choir." It should be sung with a rich tone quality and rhythmic fervor.

Since variation is common with Foster's songs, it is certainly appropriate, if desired, to take some liberties in the presentation of this music. For example, there are optional finger snaps that can be performed throughout, intermittently, or not at all. The same is true of the optional string bass. Instead of finger snaps, wooden rhythm sticks or some other simple percussion instrument could be used or interchanged with the snaps. There are also many ways to be expressive with the text, such as a tenuto (or even a fermata) sometimes on the word "oh," particularly when it is a reiteration. Depending on the venue, creating a few simple motions or adding dramatic staging could make the piece more enjoyable for the audience as well as the chorus, and doing so is in keeping with the tradition of stage drama from which this song came.

The quality of the performance does not hinge on these stylistic suggestions, because this arrangement is outstanding on its own. In the final analysis, whether the conductor interprets the score very literally or takes liberties, the performance need not seem pristine or rigid.

Form and Structure

Section	Measure	Event and Scoring
Stanza 1	1–9	Unison chorus in mm. 1–5; TTB in mm. 6–9, melody in second tenor
Refrain	10–19	TTBB; melody in the tenor (usually second tenor in the divisi)
Stanza 2	20–27	TTBB; melody mostly in the baritone
Refrain	28–36	TTBB; melody exchanges between baritone and second tenor (and first tenor in m. 30)
Coda	37–38	TTBB

Text

Let us pause in life's pleasures and count its many tears
While we all sup sorrow with the poor.
There's a song that will linger forever in ours ears,
Oh! Hard times, come again no more.

Refrain
'Tis the song, the sigh of the weary;
Hard times, hard times come again no more.
Many days you have lingered around my cabin door.
Oh! Hard times come again no more.

While we seek mirth and beauty and music light and gay,
There are frail forms fainting at the door,
Though their voices are silent, their pleading looks will say,
Oh! Hard times come again no more.

Additional References and Resources

Chase, Gilbert. *America's Music: From Pilgrims to the Present*. 3rd ed. Urbana and Chicago: University of Illinois Press, 1987.

Web site:
University of Pittsburgh Center for American Music, Stephen Collins Foster: www.pitt.edu/~amerimus/foster.htm (accessed January 22, 2006)

Contributed by:

Russell Nelson

1 Gilbert Chase. *America's Music: From Pilgrims to the Present*. 3rd ed. (Urbana and Chicago: University of Illinois Press, 1987), 249.

2 University of Pittsburgh. Center for American Music: Stephen Collins Foster. http://www.pitt.edu/~amerimus/foster.htm (accessed January 22, 2006).

Teacher Resource Guide

Sea Shanties
arr. Ron Jeffers

TTBB a cappella
earthsongs: S-131
Overall: 1
Vocal: 1
Tonal/Rhythm: 1

Composer

Ron Jeffers is professor emeritus at Oregon State University. His two-volume *Translations and Annotations of Choral Repertoire* has become invaluable to conductors around the world. Jeffers is an active composer and the owner of earthsongs, an Oregon-based music publisher specializing in multicultural music.

Composition and Historical Perspective

This piece was written for the Rex Putnam High School Men's Choir in 1999. Jeffers has frequently been commissioned by men's choruses of all levels.

Technical Considerations and Musical Elements

These pieces are quite simple and fun. They have quite a bit of unison and two-part singing. The pitches are all diatonic, and the ranges should not pose problems for choirs of any level. In fact, the tenor parts, if anything, are on the low side, and the singers may be inclined to bring too much weight into the sound, as most of it sits under their break. The rhythms are the only substantial challenge of these pieces. The rhythm and the text work in tandem, so it will be useful to rehearse the piece slowly at first by speaking the text (the second may be the only exception). When having the choir speak the text, ask them to speak it in a high, spacious voice like Mrs. Doubtfire. This will allow them to experience the proper interior spaciousness and bring more of their upper voice down.

The first piece is in a faster tempo and presents distinct problems. Be sure that the choir articulates without diminishing the length of the vowels. Ask for articulation with legato breath. This will allow the larynx to stay low as they sing these faster sections. It is also important that pick-ups be articulated cleanly so that they are clearly heard. Depending on how fast the tempo is, the choir may have to almost accent the pick-ups for them to be heard in front. It is helpful for the choir to sing fast passages of text with a very loose jaw. The choir should also be sure to maintain a consistent tempo.

The first and third pieces also present potential vocal problems with descending lines. For example, the opening line of "Whistlin' Shanty" could potentially become quite heavy on the words "Portland Street." A useful rehearsal technique would be to have them bounce lightly on their toes in order to remove the weight from the sound. This will also assist in the articulation and energy of the piece. Singing the first fourteen measures up an octave will also bring lift and easiness into the sound. If the singers add weight on the descending octave in m. 11, they could try singing those last two notes in the same octave and transfer that feeling into the lower octave. This holds true for every reoccurrence of this leap. Singers must not associate descending octave leaps with a change in palate position. They must almost feel that the palate lifts on the descending leap in order for gravity not to take over! Ask them to keep the sound bright on the bottom and to let it be softer than the upper note if need be.

Inexperienced singers add weight to the bottom notes because they try to sing them just as loudly as the upper ones. They can incorporate a physical movement to remember this concept. For their first attempt they can push their hands down on the lower octaves as though dribbling a deflated basketball with each hand (palms down). Obviously, the sound will become heavy and out of tune. For the second time, have them brush their hands in little circles upward on those two lower notes (palms up, forehead level). This will bring more head tone into the sound, especially if they do it with their hands high enough. This piece also involves some short passages of whistling the tune. This may require some rehearsing, or you may just have a few singers on this part.

The second song of the set is slower and will require a more legato articulation. The most important issue in this piece is the shape and accentuation of the words like "Tommy" and "Singapore." It is vitally important to decide how the words "Tommy" and "gone" will be sung. Will there be more "ah" or "aw" in the first syllable of both words? How much "t" would you like to hear at the beginning of "Tommy"? How long will singers stay on the initial vowel before going to the "m" of "Tommy"? The words "Tom" or "Tommy" are sung more than twenty times in these forty-five measures, so choose wisely! Be sure to put the textual emphasis on the correct syllables. Singers may underline the stressed syllables to create a visual reminder of the syllabification. You may also want to ask a singer from the group to read the text out of rhythm, while paying close attention to syllabic stress and punctuation (commas, exclamation marks). It is also useful to lightly snap on the stressed syllables. Singers will soon find that they are usually snapping on the beat and will gain insight into how the composer set the text.

"Johnny, Come Down to Hilo" presents challenges similar to the first piece's in regard to rushing and high-larynx singing. The opening, repeating bass motive already provides the chance for pitch problems. Repeating notes have a tendency to sag and this tendency is strengthened by the "l" of second syllable. American speakers typically allow the consonant "l" to fall back, so it will need to be sung on the tip of the tongue to counteract pitch inaccuracy and rhythmic sluggishness. You may also want to ask the basses to make the second syllable of the word slightly more closed in order to focus the pitch.

The pickup notes for tenors are often E-naturals, which is potentially problematic. To maintain lightness and an "up and over" feeling on those notes, have the men toss those notes like a tennis ball (*not* a bowling ball) in a light and easy way. Make sure that they toss with arc and don't throw downward as if they are aiming for a point ten feet in front of them. This should incorporate more head tone into the sound and also cause them to engage their bodies more in the sound. When rehearsing this piece on a neutral syllable, sixteenth notes can be sung on "doo-bee," while other notes can be sung on "doo." It is vital to the success of this piece for the text to come alive. The singers can practice speaking the text very softly in heightened speech to feel the intensity of articulation. Modeling for them can literally "speak volumes" for these activities if they follow along in their music while you model. This allows them to hear what you want while seeing it on the page. Be particularly specific about the length of vowels when speaking.

Stylistic Considerations

Since these pieces are sea shanties, the conductor must think about how the text is presented. Should the vowels be as proper and tall as usual? Should the singing be very vocal or have places with a quality more like speech? The other key to these pieces working is the attitude the choir brings to the piece. These pieces could be extremely enjoyable to the audience if the choir sings as a bunch of sailors would. They could even have small costume additions (e.g., a sailor hat) to get them more involved in the performance. The personality and dynamic of the group will factor into how far one will go in portraying the piece. One must also consider how much time will be taken between each piece. Will you take the same time between each? Will you pause longer before "Tommy's Gone" and less before "Johnny, Come Down to Hilo"? These are all important considerations.

Form and Structure

These pieces are strophic with slight changes between verses. The first piece is in B major, the second in A major, and the third in E major. The relationship between the final notes of one song to the first note of the next is always a perfect fourth.

Text

"A Whistlin' Shanty"

I met a gal in Portland Street,
This gal I met in Portland Street was the sweetest gal I ever did meet.
Sez me, "Me gal, 'ow do ye do?"
Sez she, "The worst for seein' you."
"Now miss," sez I, "I like yer style."
Sez she, "Young man, just wait a while."

"Tommy's Gone"

Tommy's gone, what shall I do?
Tommy's gone to Hilo town, away you, where all them gals do gather 'roun',
Tom's gone to Hilo!
Tommy's gone to Callyo, away you, he won't come back from there I know,
Tom's gone to Hilo!
Tommy's gone to Singapore, away you,
Tommy's gone forevermore,
Tom's gone to Hilo!
Oh, haul away, me bully boys, oh haul away, kick up some noise,
Tom's gone to Hilo!

"Johnny, Come Down to Hilo"

I love a little gal acrosst the sea,
She's a 'Badian beauty an' she sez to me,
"Oh Johnny, come down to Hilo, you poor old man!"
Oh wake her, oh shake her,
Oh wake that gal wid the blue dress on when Johnny comes down to Hilo,
Oh poor old man.

Oh wuz ye never down in Mobile Bay, ascrewin' cotton for a dollar a day?
Oh wake her, oh shake her,
Oh wake that gal wid the blue dress on when Johnny comes down to Hilo,
Oh poor old man.
"Oh Johnny, come down to Hilo, you poor old man!"
Oh wake her, oh shake her,

Oh did you ever see the ol' plantation boss,
An' his long-tailed filly, an' his big black hoss?
"Oh Johnny, come down to Hilo, you poor old man!"
Oh wake her, oh shake her,
Oh wake that gal wid the blue dress on when Johnny comes down to Hilo,

Oh Sally in the garden, pickin' peas,
An' the hair of her head hangin' down to her knees.
"Oh Johnny, come down to Hilo, you poor old man."

Contributed by:

William Hammer

Teacher Resource Guide

Steal Away

arr. Brazeal W. Dennard

TTBB
Shawnee Press: C-279
Overall: 1
Vocal: 2
Tonal/Rhythm: 1

Composer

Brazeal Dennard has been active as a musician in the greater Detroit community since his public school and private musical studies as a young man. In addition to his work as an arranger, Dennard has served as guest conductor, clinician, lecturer, and church choirmaster. Dennard earned his master of music education degree from Wayne State University and began his conducting career in the public schools as Fine Arts Department Head at Northwestern High School. Dennard's choirs at Northwestern High earned superior ratings in state final competitions and appeared before the national MENC.

Throughout his career, Dennard has been active in numerous professional organizations, including the National Endowment of the Arts and the Department of Cultural Affairs for the city of Detroit. He has been president of the National Association of Negro Musicians, Inc. Dennard was presented with the Maynard Klein Award by the Michigan Chapter of the American Choral Directors Association in recognition of artistic excellence in the field of choral music

In 1972 Dennard founded the Brazeal Dennard Chorale, a group of professional singers dedicated to developing the choral art at its highest level. The chorale performs throughout greater Metropolitan Detroit as well as throughout the United States at choral workshops and concerts for universities, churches, and choral conventions. In 1985, Dennard added the Brazeal Dennard Community Chorus as an outreach program by the Brazeal Dennard Chorale to encourage participation of community members and to provide them with vocal training and professional performance opportunities. Dennard also works with the Brazeal Dennard Youth Chorale, which is comprised of singers ages thirteen to twenty-two. This Youth Chorale functions to provide the opportunity for the serious study and performance of challenging choral literature. Dennard serves as adjunct faculty at Wayne State University.

Composition and Historical Perspective

The Brazeal Dennard Chorale is dedicated to remembering, rediscovering, and preserving the roots of African American choral heritage. "Steal Away" is one of many spirituals performed by the Brazeal Dennard Chorale and was arranged by Brazeal Dennard for men's voices (TTBB). Anton Armstrong, in the first volume of *Teaching Music through Performance in Choir,* lists "Steal Away" under the specific category of "escape spirituals." The message of the lyrics of these particular spirituals indicates a plan for escape to freedom. The joy of the sacred text shares the joy of the Holy Spirit in the life to come as well as the joy of the freedom to be experienced after escape. The notes to the CD *Remembering, Discovering, Preserving—Songs of African American History* describe spirituals as follows: "The songs expressed profound religious beliefs, an unshakable faith, relief from the suffering of slavery, and the optimism for a better world to come. In truth they were a major contributing tributary to the musical stream which diverged into gospel and blues."

Technical and Stylistic Considerations and Musical Elements

This arrangement includes very specific stylistic and musical considerations for the conductor and performers. Dennard clearly and beautifully shapes the flow of give and take within each phrase through the diligent use of dynamic markings. The use of the fermata in m. 15, beat three and the ritard and slower tempo indicated in the final five measures (mm. 26–30) is significant and poignant.

The authentic performance practice notes indicate a call for singing the opening refrain (mm. 1–9) two times, followed by all three verses consecutively, and concluding with the final refrain, mm. 18–30. Dennard indicates that a more modern interpretation of alternating refrain, verse, refrain, verse, etc., concluding with the final refrain (mm. 18–30) is also an option.

The tessitura of this arrangement of "Steal Away" lies so musically in men's voices. Careful attention should be paid to round, rich, resonant vowels throughout while diligently maintaining healthy intonation. Unaccented syllables should be especially de-emphasized, particularly final syllables and final consonants. Again, pay particular attention to the indicated dynamics and tempo markings as they shape the journey and expression of the piece. Dennard summarizes the musical intent of the piece with his one-word opening direction indicating that the piece should be sung "reflectively."

Form and Structure

Measure	Event and Scoring
1–9	*Piano* refrain
10–17	Subito *forte* verse 1, "My Lord calls me"; subito *forte* verse 2, "Green trees abending"; subito *forte* verse 3, "My Lord calls me"
18–25	*Piano* refrain as in mm. 1–9 without the initial swell indicated in m. 3–4 and with ritard in m. 25
26–30	Extension of the refrain repeating the text "Steal away" three times throughout a *diminuendo* and slower tempo, concluding with a full, uplifted final F major chord on the word "home"

Text

Refrain
Steal away, steal away, steal away to Jesus.
Steal away, steal away, steal away home,
I ain't got long to stay here.

Verses
My Lord calls me. He calls me by the thunder.
The trumpet sounds withina my soul.
I ain't got long to stay here.

Green trees abending. Poor sinner stands atrembling.
The trumpet sounds withina my soul.
I ain't got long to stay here.

My Lord calls me. He calls me by the lightning.
The trumpet sounds withina my soul.
I ain't got long to stay here.

Suggested Listening

Brazeal Dennard:

Hush: Somebody's Calling My Name. Brazeal Dennard Chorale. Brazeal Dennard, conductor. Brazeal Dennard Chorale CD.

Interpreting Spiritual Songs. Brazeal Dennard Chorale. Brazeal Dennard, conductor. Mark Custom Recording. ACDA89MC-15.

Remembering, Discovering, Preserving—Songs of African American History. Brazeal Dennard Chorale. Brazeal Dennard, conductor. Brazeal Dennard Chorale CD.

Measure for Measure, *Celebration in Song*. Leonard Ricciento and Scott Larson, conductors. Mark Custom Recording. 2747 MCD.

Contributed by:

Jennifer Haywood

Level Two

Teacher Resource Guide

April Is in My Mistress' Face

Thomas Morley
(1557/58–1602)

SATB a cappella
E. C. Schirmer Music Company: 1612
Overall: 2
Vocal: 2
Tonal/Rhythm: 2

Composer

Thomas Morley was born in Norwich, England. He studied with the well-known English composer William Byrd, to whom he dedicated his treatise *A Plaine and Easie Introduction to Practicall Musicke* in 1597. This treatise was a significant source of information on notation, counterpoint, musical form, and English music in the late Renaissance.

The period in which he studied with Byrd formed and influenced Morley's tendencies of composition as evidenced in his Latin motets and Anglican Church music. By 1588 Morley earned his bachelor of music degree at Oxford University and was appointed organist at St. Paul's Cathedral a year later. His interest on Italian madrigal tradition was encouraged by Edward Paston, a musically knowledgeable landowner who owned many books and music collections, including a large collection of Italian madrigals. Influenced by the Italian vocal style, Morley implemented it in his madrigals, which show Morley was not only a composer but an editor, translator, and arranger.

Because of his musical excellence and service in the Catholic Church, Morley was named Gentleman of the Chapel Royal in 1592. After resigning from the Chapel Royal in 1602 due to health issues, Morley focused his energy on publishing. His publications reached the height of their popularity during the first eight years of publication (1593-1601). Morley contributed to *The Triumphes of Oriana* (1601), a collection of madrigals by twenty-three English composers modeled after the Italian *Il trionfo di dori*. The collection was intended as an entertainment to honor the queen, and it enhanced the madrigal performance and its contribution to the repertoire. Morley connected and adapted to the Italian madrigal tradition with the English tradition, enriching English music and influencing the next generation of composers.

Composition and Historical Perspective

The etymology of the word madrigal comes from *mandrialis* (flock), *materialis* (secular as opposed to spiritual), and *matricalis* (from mother tongue). Madrigals were poetic forms, mainly secular verses, set to music and very popular in Italy during fourteenth and sixteenth centuries. "April Is in My Mistress' Face" belongs to Morley's *Madrigals for Four Voices* collection written in 1594 and is one of his most loved madrigals.

English madrigals of 1580s and 1590s are characterized by material borrowed from Italy. Manuscripts of Italian madrigals came to England around 1530 however, manuscripts appeared around 1590s.

The decade of 1590s was productive literary period in England, and this carried over into the madrigal tradition. Translations of the texts and settings of this to music were collected in anthologies such as *Musica transalpina* (*Music from across the Alps*, 1588). Morley published several books, including *Canzonets or Little Short Songs for Three Voices* and *ballets*, which are transcriptions into English of the *balletos* of Gastoldi and other composers (strophic texts with homophonic texture characterized by sections of nonsense syllables such as "fa la la"). Some of Morley's best-known *balletos* are "Now Is the Month of Maying" and "Sing We and Chant It." Morley expanded the repertoire of madrigals widely in England and "Englished" Italian sounds so masterfully that his influence can still be heard in subsequent generations of English composers.

Technical Considerations and Musical Elements

Morley's music is characterized by textural clarity, and "April Is in My Mistress' Face" bears that out. The text is set homophonically most the time and in a variety of textures (two, three, and four voices). Usually Morley separates women's and men's lines in thirds and joins them in homophonic texture. The conductor should isolate these duets or trios and rehearse them separately. This will enable the choir to understand who sings with whom.

The homophonic parts may tend to get heavy. Introducing the piece on a neutral syllable may help to generate the light feeling of the madrigal. His use of counterpoint in this piece, as in many, is not elaborate or lengthy but pleasing to the ear. An example is m. 11 where the basses start their motive on "and with July in her eyes hath place." Harmonically, the motive is modulating toward B-flat major, and the effective counterpoint helps the voices get there smoothly. Even though there is no exact repetition of the motive in all voices, the text and melodic idea are the same. The conductor should demonstrate the phrasing and articulation, isolate one voice, and ask the whole choir to sing it in unison. Be sure to point out the accidentals in advance because the change comes quite quickly.

Near m. 23, the contrapuntal writing is more evident and longer. The conductor should apply the same concept to teach this section. Mm. 25–30 are exactly the same as mm. 33–38. The conductor can save rehearsal time by teaching those two sections back to back because their only differences are color and mood. The repetition of the final section is one of Morley's madrigal compositional hallmarks.

Harmonically "April Is in My Mistress' Face" is diatonic with very little chromaticism. Because this madrigal is *a cappella*, the aid from the piano during rehearsals is valuable. However, the choir should not depend on it, and the conductor should gradually remove the support of the piano and start rehearsing sections *a cappella* from the first rehearsal. The choir will keep their intonation by being aware of breath support and vowel delivery. The conductor can check intonation at arrival points by holding those chords when all voices arrive together and ask the piano to play the written chord.

Stylistic Considerations

To choose the appropriate tempo, the conductor should consider factors such as the mood and content of the text, the contrapuntal writing, and harmonic rhythm. This madrigal should be performed with a small ensemble. The text of this madrigal refers to the seasons and the fickle nature of a man's mistress as time passes. For example, Morley captures the longing and desire for a lover's embrace, among other moods. The conductor should capture each atmosphere.

The mood of the text will define the dynamics of the piece. Because this madrigal contains repeated music and text, the conductor should decide what to do differently in the repeated areas so it does not sound uninteresting.

Modern editions contain barlines but this was not so in editions of Morley's time. Therefore, ignore the metered stress pattern, and articulate the music according to text stresses. Chant the text and rhythm of the phrases with proper text stresses and phrasing, and ask the choir to do the same before singing on pitch. Ask for narrow and tall vowels. Having the choir sing with more of an English accent than an American one is okay.

The points of imitation should be performed with identical emphasis to help balance and tuning. Morley had the opportunity to work with boy and male choirs through his position at the Chapel Royal. Since this sound was the one he had in mind, the conductor could ask the female voices to use a boy-like sound. This will help them diminish their vibratos and lighten some voices.

Form and Structure

MEASURES	EVENT AND SCORING
1–9	First line of the poem; (3 + 3 + 3)
9–15	Line two; (2 + 4)
15–23	Line three; (2 + 6)
23–38	Line four; (7 + 8)

Text

April is in my mistress' face,
And July in her eyes hath place.
Within her bosom is September,
But in her heart, a cold December.

Additional References and Resources

Salotti, Daniel. "The Madrigals of Thomas Morley." *American Choral Review* 19 (1977): 3–6.

Taylor, David. "Thomas Morley's First Book of Ballets to Five Voices: An Introduction for Conductors." *Choral Journal* 23 (1983): 5–20.

Contributed by:

Marcela Molina

Teacher Resource Guide

Black Is the Color of My True Love's Hair

arr. Stuart Churchill

SATB with piano
Shawnee Press: A01000
Overall: 2
Vocal: 2
Tonal/Rhythm: 2

Composer

Born in Long Island, Kansas, Stuart Churchill (1907–2000) left studies at the University of Michigan to join Fred Waring's Pennsylvanians, for which he sang tenor and played trumpet, saxophone, bassoon, and drum set. Except during World War II and during a stint as a single soloist, he worked with Fred Waring's Pennsylvanians from 1929 through 1951. During his tenure, he penned 145 arrangements for the Pennsylvanians, many of which are published by Shawnee Press.

In 1951 Churchill attended Columbia University and received bachelor's and master's degrees in music education and then took a position at the Central Washington College of Education in Ellensburg, Washington. In 1959 he became the director of the music department at the Lewis-Clark State College in Lewiston, Idaho. He formed and directed the Lewiston Symphony Orchestra, a Civic Chorale, and church choirs.

He retired to nearby Clarkston, Washington, in 1971 but continued to teach, write, and arrange music up to the time of his death. He arranged Helen Davis's (1905–92) "Washington My Home," which became the state song of Washington.

Composition and Historical Perspective

"Black Is the Color of My True Love's Hair" is an Appalachian folk song, and like much folk music it has varying lyrics, several melodic variations, and a vague past. Those who hear a Scots-Irish cast to the melody may be right: a variant exists in Scotland, and many Celtic songs traveled to Appalachia in the nineteenth century, where they evolved into American music. An eighteenth-century English tune with different lyrics, "Black Is the Color of My True Love's Eyes," and another with similar lyrics but a different tune, "Dark Is the Color of my True Love's Eyes" exist as well.

Those who remember "Black Is the Color of My True Love's Hair" as written by composer, collector, and balladeer John Jacob Niles (1892–1980) may know the most authentic version. It was his habit—in addition to collecting songs—to use song fragments in his own compositions. By 1940 he had published "Black," perhaps built from a fragment of collected tune and text, as was his very popular "Go 'Way from My Window."

An anecdote links Niles to this song. By the 1930s he regularly appeared on radio broadcasts for the landmark Listening Center Network, which eventually reached eighty-four remote locations in Eastern Kentucky. One day first lady Eleanor Roosevelt, who was slated to speak on the network, was kept waiting while Niles sang each of the seemingly countless verses of "Black Is the Color of My True Love's Hair."

Stuart Churchill arranged the song, selecting verses to include for Fred Waring's Pennsylvanians. His arrangement regularly appears on choral festival programs and repertoire lists.

Technical Considerations and Musical Elements

The melody of this rhapsodic love song, while in minor mode (F minor in this setting), matches perfectly with a profoundly poetic text. Sung *a cappella* by a soloist, "Black Is the Color" grip listeners. Stuart Churchill has added musical elements but successfully captured the emotion and crafted a new approach to a historic song.

Intensity is built into the rising triad of the first three long notes, and the choir must take the natural breaks of the text repetitions ("bla-k, bla-k, bla-kiz-thuh kuh-luh . . .") as the editor's tone syllables and the text's commas illustrate. The high point of each verse—Churchill sets two of the many available in folk tradition—is at the beginning of the third phrase.

The key is consistently F minor. The meter accommodates the text with a temporary change from 4/4 to 2/4. The accompaniment imitates a well-played guitar with prevailingly sixteenth note motion interrupted with a few slower and different patterns. A very brief *a cappella* section begins the piece and another is placed just before the end.

In general, the setting is homophonic, although there are places with staggered entries and very short canons (see alto and soprano "oo" canon, mm. 20–23). The main technical challenges are to achieve a smooth but intense legato sound throughout and to maintain an uninterrupted closing for the final five measures (six measures for tenors). Staggered breathing will accomplish the latter. To maintain a smooth line, begin and end legato and use the consonants. See, for instance, mm. 3–4, where the percussive "k" sound can point out the overarching legato nature of the initial phrase. See also m. 11, in which the top three voices should hold "hands" for two full beats and place the "ndz" sound on beat three, where basses introduce the next phrase with a glottal-aided "i," pronounced "ah" and only slightly admitting the diphthong "ee" at the very end.

Another tricky cutoff is at m. 20, where the second sound of the "knows" diphthong and the word's terminal "z" sound should line up on beat two with the second note in the altos' "oo." Clearing the air in beat three of the measure will point out the tenors' reentry on beat four. The conductor may also choose to shorten note durations is in m. 21. Tenors should shorten "goes" to a quarter note, placing the "z" sound on beat three, take a good breath, and reenter. Basses also should end on beat three, matching the tenors. Altos should shorten the last beat of their "oo" section to an eighth note, so they may take a breath and coordinate the ATB entry on beat four. There are other similar situations in which singers should cut off a beat or a half beat early, thereby coordinating cutoffs and the initiations of sound and unifying what the audience hears.

Take the arranger's neutral syllable specifications ("hum," "oo") as suggestions, bearing in mind that the piece was composed for the professional Fred Waring Pennsylvanians, and assign vowels that suit the nature of your ensemble. Be sure to exploit the possibilities in these sections: they, too, should be expressively phrased.

Churchill gives an abundance of expressive markings that convey his sense of the composition. Perhaps this piece need not be performed in exactly the same way each time.

Stylistic Considerations

There is no need to over dramatize the expression and performance of "Black Is the Color of My True Love's Hair." How to interpret the single tempo marking "moderately slow" depends upon the group's ability to produce a light but resonant sound in the space in which they sing and is among the conductor's choices. The dynamics are on the soft side. The piece rises only to ***mf*** and ends ***ppp***. This will be a worthwhile challenge to young voices or large ensembles.

Form and Structure

SECTION	MEASURE	EVENT AND SCORING
Introduction	1–2	TB, unison, hum the consequent of phrase 1; piano confirms the key of F minor in a tonic arpeggio
Verse 1, phrase 1	3–6	
Phrase 2	7–8	
Phrase 2	9–11	M. 10 in 2/4
Phrase 4	12–13	
Verse 1	14–17	Extension, neutral syllable "oo" built on the melody, m. 16 in 2/4
Verse 2	18–29	Set differently from Verse 1, still in F minor
	30–33	Rounding the form, repeats "Black is the color of my true love's hair"

Text

Black, black, black is the color of my true love's hair.
Her lips are something wond'rous fair;
The purest eyes and the daintiest hands.
I love the grass on where she stands.
I love my love and well she knows.
I love the grass on where she goes.
If she on earth no more I'd see,
My life would quickly fade away.

Additional References and Resources

Information on Stuart Churchill courtesy of Peter T. Kiefer, coordinator, Fred Waring's America Collection, The Pennsylvania State University, 313 Pattee Library, University Park, PA 16802-1800

Suggested Listening

Folk Songs, Westminster Choir, Joseph Flummerfelt, conductor, Gothic Records #38130, ASIN # B000003J87, 1994.

The following recording seems to contain Churchill's arrangement but does not. The artistic approach, however, is acceptable for a folk song sung chorally.

Blue Wheat, Dale Warland Singers, American Choral 122, ASIN # B000003M4T, 1996.

Contributed by:

Lani Johnson

Teacher Resource Guide

Bullerengue
José Antonio Rincón

SATB a cappella
Third Planet Music
Overall: 2
Vocal: 2
Tonal/Rhythm: 3

Composer

José Antonio Rincón currently lives in Puebla, Mexico, and has composed many choral pieces are well known throughout Latin America.

Composition and Historical Perspective

Bullerengue is a dance rhythm of Afro-Colombian heritage, having evolved from the mixing of African slaves imported to South America (in this case, Colombia) with the native population. Women have an important place in its history—their role in both the dance and the poetry. The music is traditionally sung by women and accompanied only by drums. This has changed in modern practice, and now men and instruments are included in performances of *bullerengues*. Rincón suggests some of the old heritage in his compositional style with the percussive, rhythmically complex accompaniment lines that mimic the sounds of drums.

As a piece of music based on traditional dance music, it would be useful to compare "Bullerengue" with dance music from other cultures and eras. The basic pattern is in the bass, but the other lines move quite independently—often two against three—making for a distinctively complex rhythmic texture.

Other dance music students have performed probably does not do this—often dance music has simplicity and clarity of rhythm—so have them compare other dance music they know to "Bullerengue."

Another interesting comparison to make is with jazz. The histories of *bullerengue* and jazz are parallel, beginning with the introduction of Africans to the New World and their assimilation of new musical ideas. Students can discuss the similarities between the two (their histories, rhythmic complexity, syllabic text setting) and their differences (such as jazz's chromaticism, swung rhythms, and tied-note syncopations).

Technical Considerations and Musical Elements

The use of diatonic pitches in the key of E minor make this piece easy to learn. There is much stepwise motion and triadic outlining, which are both useful for sight-singing. The piece is strictly in four parts until the end, when the women divide and a tenor solo begins, but then the women literally only sing three different notes. There is also a great deal of repetition, which contributes to making the piece easy to learn.

The rhythms are the challenge in "Bullerengue." Without being very syncopated, the composer divides a measure of 2/4 in almost every possible way. The best preparation you can give your students is exercises in which they divide half notes into quarters, quarter note triplets, eighths, eighth note triples, and sixteenths. At first, pair quarter notes and quarter note triplets. Separately, work on eighth notes and eighth note triplets. Then add sixteenth notes at the end of that drill. When they can do the quarter note set and the eighth note set consistently apart successfully, combine them into one long exercise. Show them the notation, teach them by rote, and practice this long before you give them the music for "Bullerengue." This preparation, combined with the simplicity of the pitches, makes teaching the piece a breeze. Have them read the rhythms on a neutral syllable like "ta," keeping the quarter note beat by tapping their feet or patting their knees. Counting-singing with similar parts grouped together will also be helpful.

Rincón does not indicate a tempo. Of course, the tempo you choose will depend on the usual factors of the size of the choir, acoustical properties of the performance space, etc., but "Bullerengue" should never sound rushed. Remember that the text must be clear and crisp, even on groups of sixteenth notes. Start around quarter note = 88 and adjust up or down as suits your group and their situation.

While accurate and percussive rhythmicity is important, the phrases must still grow and taper. Prevent singers from smacking the last note of a phrase by hissing a *crescendo* and *decrescendo* while clapping the rhythm of their line, demonstrating that every note has a different dynamic and is either becoming louder or softer. In particular, dotted eighth notes should fade away, gently separating from the following sixteenth note.

The dynamics are marked *mezzo forte* in the beginning with no changes until the *fortissimo* at the end. You'll probably want to make adjustments to this, including assigning a louder dynamic level to the various voices that take over the melody throughout, changing the dynamic when music is repeated, defining separate sections, or reflecting the text. For example, the introduction could be very soft, and then when that music returns as a transition it could be very soft again. I have suggested dynamic changes under Form and Structure below. Better still, have the students suggest changes in dynamics, giving reasons in the music and the text for their ideas.

Stylistic Considerations

Any size choir can perform this piece, from twelve to two hundred, as long as the rhythm is precise and the language is bright and delicate. There are no special requirements for the tone of the choir—the piece should simply be sung well. You may consider asking the women to sing with a chest-rich blend in the very lowest parts, such as mm. 40–44, for flavor and an energy boost.

Form and Structure

SECTION	MEASURE	EVENT AND SCORING
Introduction	1–8	*Piano* but intense, like a secret they can't wait to share
First stanza (beginning)	9–12/13	Homophonic, sung twice (first time ***mp***, then ***mf*** for a little more intensity)
First stanza (end)	14–17/18	Melody in tenor, polyphonic accompaniment lines, sung twice (first time ***mp***, then ***mf*** to reflect the previous phrase)
Second stanza	19–26	Sung in two-measure pattern repeated four times (each two-measure pattern starts soft, *crescendos* to the second measure, then fades away; each repetition starting at a slightly louder dynamic)
Transition	27–30	Identical to mm. 5–8 (***p***, like the introduction)
Third stanza	38/39	Mostly homophonic, sung twice (first time ***mp***, then ***mf*** like the opening phrases, building in intensity towards the end)
Fourth stanza	40–47	Duet between men (in thirds) and women (in unison), first ending (***pp*** but percussive—like the text says, "if I were a small drum, I would beat very softly for you")

SECTION	MEASURE	EVENT AND SCORING (continued)
Fourth stanza (second ending)	40–46, 48–51	*Pianissimo* until the second ending, then very gradually *crescendoing* to ***mf***
Tenor solo	52–57	Ad lib with sustained chords in other voices (***p*** to balance with soloist)
	58–63	A tempo, bass same as intro with sustained chords in other voices (*crescendo* constantly and quickly to ***ff***)

Text

The text is original poetry by Jorge Artel, the pseudonym of a Colombian lawyer, journalist, and poet born in 1909. Much of his writing is political in nature, but the text Rincón uses for "Bullerengue" has a romantic character. Here is an excerpt of the translation provided by the publisher:

> If I were a drum, my dear one
> I would sound only for you
> For no one but you

Spanish diction requires dental [d] and [t]—pronounced without aspiration—as well as a bright [a] and flipped [r]. These basic principles will provide the necessary color for the language and aid appropriate articulation of the music.

The text is frequently set with the rhythmic stress on the unstressed syllables. Remember that the percussiveness is the important factor, and the composer is using the words for their sound, not their meaning. Because the accompanying lines are emulating the sounds of drums, the diction helps with the instrumental sound. Consonants need to be clear and precise.

Bibliography and Suggested Resources

Web site:

Third Planet Music: www.thirdplanetmusic.com (accessed May 30, 2006)

Suggested Listening

José A. Rincón, "Bullerengue" on *Choral Songs of Latin America*, Chamber Choir of the National Symphony Orchestra of Costa Rica, Marco Dusi, Washington, D.C., Inter-American Musical Editions, 1980.

Contributed by:

Amelia Nagoski

Teacher Resource Guide

Christ lag in Todesbanden No. 7 from Opella nova I

Johann Hermann Schein
(1586–1630)

Two high voices and one low voice (chorus or soli) with instrumental bass ad libitum and continuo
Alexander Broude, Inc.: 225-10
Overall: 2
Vocal: 2
Tonal/Rhythm: 2

Composer

Johann Hermann Schein served as cantor at St. Thomas's Church in Leipzig from 1615 until his death, preceding Johann Sebastian Bach's tenure at this very post. In 1618 Schein published Part I of *Opella nova* ("The New Work"), a collection of thirty *Geistliche concerten*, or "sacred concertos." These concertos were intended for three to five vocal and instrumental parts, based mostly on German chorale melodies and well-known German and Latin texts. The success of Part I allowed Schein to publish *Opella nova II*, which consists of thirty-two concertos for three to six parts.

Composition and Historical Perspective

The term "concerto" first appeared in the works of the Gabrielis, the famous family of sixteenth-century Venetian composers, who applied the term to distinguish vocal compositions with instrumental accompaniment from unaccompanied music. Before the concerto morphed into its present-day form, it produced several well-defined subgenres, among them the sacred concerto. As exemplified by Schein's output, this type of concerto flourished in the seventeenth century, usually featuring the interplay of contrasting bodies of sound—instruments and voices or solo voice and chorus. This stylistic use of the term persisted through Bach's lifetime (several of his cantatas bear the designation "concerti").

Both the *cantus firmus* and the text of Schein's "Christ lag in Todesbanden" ("Christ lay in death's strong bonds") were created by Martin Luther (1483–1546), the eminent German theologian and leader of the Lutheran movement. It is likely that this particular hymn was originally performed in unaccompanied unison. If treated in a polyphonic context, the hymn was often used in spiritual motets and printed in collections of polyphonic settings.

Technical Considerations and Musical Elements

Schein's setting of *Christ lag in Todesbanden* is well-suited for choral ensembles in which the treble or soprano and alto voices outnumber the lower voices. Alternatively, it is an excellent performance opportunity for three solo voices. The range of each voice sits well within their respective tessituras: the range of soprano (High Voice I) spans C4 to G5 while the alto (High Voice II) sings C-sharp4 to E5. The range of the tenor (Low Voice) barely exceeds one octave (D3 to E4). The least active of the three, this part outlines the *cantus firmus* verbatim and is therefore suitable either for tenors or high baritones.

From a technical perspective, the challenges for either of the treble voices are few. Although Schein's setting does contain a few difficult leaps, modulations, and melismatic passages, this is not of concern if proper rehearsal time is allocated for the treble voices. (For the sake of time, consider rehearsing the upper two parts separately from the tenor). It is important that the *cantus firmus* be balanced with the treble voices. For this reason, the upper two voices should not only be aware of the *cantus firmus* but also be consistently sensitive to its presence in polyphonic passages that engage all three voices.

Stylistic Considerations

According to Kurt Stone's performance remarks:

> [T]he vocal parts permit great flexibility of choice—children's and/or women's voices for the upper parts, soli, or chorus. Concerning the accompaniment, Schein states in his prefatory remarks for *Opella nova I* that the instrumental bass part may be performed on the trombone, bassoon, double bass (*viola grossa*), or similar instrument. The part may, however, be omitted altogether. The continuo is best played on an organ or harpsichord (Schein also mentions *Tiorba*). Its bass line should be doubled by a suitable instrument, either on pitch or in the lower octave. In the present edition, the instrumental and continuo

> bass lines have been combined, even though the original provides separate part books. The bass of the continuo represents both bass lines wherever they are identical; where they differ, horizontal brackets and small notes and rests show the instrumental bass. (No separate part for the instrumental bass has been issued.)[1]

While preserving the original pitches and note values, this edition adds barlines and changes voice designations (Schein's *Canto I and II* and *Tenore* become "High Voices I and II" and "Low Voice(s)," respectively). All clefs are modernized, and interpretive markings are added as well.

Form and Structure

Schein's chosen texture of the sacred concerto is polyphonic throughout. The tenor (Low Voice), while considerably less involved than the high voices, articulates the *cantus firmus*. The treble voices elaborate on the *cantus firmus* by relying extensively on points of imitation and emphasizing rhythmic freedom. The instrumental bass and the continuo provide harmonic support.

The large form of this work (four larger sections in total) follows the structure of the *cantus firmus*. Section A is divided into two identical halves, each setting two lines of text: A1 "Christ lag in Todesbanden/Für unsre Sünd gegeben" and A2 "Der ist wieder erstanden/Und hat uns bracht das Leben." Section B is initiated in the alto (High Voice II), which articulates the concluding portion of the text: "Des wir sollen fröhlich sein, Gott loben und dank bar sein und singen Alleluia." The third and final section (a rousing setting of "Alleluia") changes the pulse from duple to triple while the tempo quickens (a common technique stemming from old mensuration notation). The tempo shifts are, of course, purely editorial.

Text and Translation

This well-known text by Martin Luther from 1524 is based on Psalm 130.

Christ lag in Todesbanden	Christ lay in death's bonds
Für unsre Sünd gegeben	Given for our sins
Der ist wieder erstanden	He has risen again
Und hat uns bracht das Leben;	And has us brought life;
Des wir sollen fröhlich sein,	For this we shall be joyful,
Gott loben und ihm dankbar sein,	God praise, and to him thankful be,
Und singen Alleluia	And sing Alleluia.

Additional References and Resources

Jacobs, Arthur, ed. *Choral Music: A Symposium*. Baltimore: Penguin Books, 1963.

Jeffers, Ron, ed. *Translations and Annotations of Choral Repertoire, Vol. II*. Corvallis, OR: earthsongs, 2000.

Snyder, Kerala J. and Gregory S. Johnston, "Schein, Johann Hermann," *Grove Music Online*. Edited by L. Macy. http://www.grovemusic.com (accessed April 26, 2006).

Stone, Kurt. "Performance Suggestions" in *Johann Hermann Schein, "Christ lag in Todesbanden."* New York: Alexander Broude, 1968.

Contributed by:

Elizabeth K. Swanson

---

1 Kurt Stone, "Performance Suggestions" in *Johann Hermann Schein, "Christ lag in Todesbanden"* (New York: Alexander Broude, 1968), 11.

Teacher Resource Guide

Down by the Riverside
arr. Roger Ames

SATB with piano
Hinshaw Music: HMC 1601
Overall: 2
Vocal: 2
Tonal/Rhythm: 2

Composer

Convinced that art is the most effective teacher, Roger Ames has in his last dozen years of composing dealt with subject matter that looks at history through a fresh lens: women's rights in *The Wife of Martin Guerre*, the Holocaust in *In Memoriam Warsaw 1943*, the abuse of the Delaware Indian Tribe in *The End of Forever*, multicultural teenage relationships in *Illusions* (commissioned by the Utah Opera) and *En Mis Palabras* (commissioned by Central City Opera, Denver), and rights for the elderly in *Paradise Hills* (Alice from Wonderland is sent to a nursing home and finds Wonderland all over again). In reaction to the atrocities of September 11, Ames is publishing a series of choral octavos under the heading *Fire* and *Iron*, works written by him and several poet collaborators dedicated to the victims of that tragedy.

He has set Anne Sexton's poetry in his Mass, *Requiem for Unbelievers*. He has also used texts from William Wordsworth's *Splendor in the Grass* and numerous poems by Edna St. Vincent Millay. One of his most fascinating projects was setting the poetry of patients at a mental institution, which was commissioned by the American Chamber Ensemble and performed all over the world, premiering at the Paris Opera.

His works have premiered at the Paris Opera, New York City Off Broadway, London Fringe, Kennedy Center, Lake George Opera, Minneapolis Opera, the Berkshires, Hartford Stage, and a number of universities. Ames's recording credits include CDs by Thomas Hampson (EMI); numerous NPR, BBC, and German and French National Radio Broadcasts; and incidental music for films in Europe and plays in both London and New York.

He is published by Hinshaw Music, GIA Publications (Evoking Sound Choral Series), Belwin Mills, E. C. Schirmer, and Vista Music, Inc.

Composition and Historical Perspective

"Down by the Riverside" is a slave song written near the end of the Civil War. The text speaks of peace, but it was also a song sung by slaves desiring their freedom. Since the end of slavery this song has been used during times of conflict in the United States and around the world, most notably during the Vietnam War. It can be used in times of sadness or as a call to action. This arrangement works very well for many different occasions. Roger Ames also arranged two other American songs ("Shenandoah" and "Pick a Bail o' Cotton"), which are published separately but make a very nice concert set.

Stylistic Considerations

This arrangement of "Down by the Riverside" employs many styles of singing. Each verse should have a different sound and attitude from the choir to highlight the different musical style and the different meaning of the text. While this arrangement does have some more intricate parts, the vocal sound should remain simple and direct for the song to communicate correctly. Although this tune is originally from the African American spiritual tradition, this arrangement does not incorporate much of that style, save perhaps the gospel choir women's sections in mm. 76–95. That being said, most of the syncopated rhythms should be softened to be more "swung." A rigid reading of the many dotted eighth note rhythms will sound very affected. This can be easily achieved in rehearsals.

Musical Elements

Roger Ames's version of "Down by the Riverside" has a collection of styles. The work begins with a solo soprano or a small group of sopranos accompanied by a repeated rolled chord in the piano. The beginning is very peaceful and effectively draws the listener into the world of the soloist. While this solo looks simple, the rhythm and notes can be surprisingly tricky, and the singer must be able to discern half steps from whole steps to negotiate it; this remains true throughout this work, as Ames often uses a descending half step as a sort of a pitch bend.

In m. 19 the choir enters under the solo; one should take care to balance the choir and soloist. If the soloist is overpowered by the choir, or add a small group of sopranos to the solo. The arranger indicates this as a possibility. Also, in m. 19, the solo line is marked "freely" with the choral parts and piano accompaniment marked *colla voce*. While the soloist should feel free to phrase as she chooses, this section should not be too drawn out or have extra notes or "riffing."

Measure 23 offers and interesting rhythmic challenge, which can either be performed exactly or interpreted as Ames's attempt to write the vocal freedom into the music. This figure repeats in the solo in m. 31 and throughout the piece. The choral accompaniment under the solo in this section should be performed in long phrases. It should also be noted that the tenor and alto parts are the same for this section; one may choose to divide all singers not performing the solo line into three parts to achieve the proper balance. Ames indicates clear dynamics, shaping, and breath points; these should all be observed.

In m. 33, the tempo of half note = 60 is established in a groove of a slow swing or shuffle. The full soprano section now intones the melody. The feel of rhythmic freedom should be maintained, but in the interest of ensemble all singers should use the exact rhythms. Careful attention should be paid to which notes are "on the beat" and which are to be performed "off the beat"; the accompanying altos, tenors, and basses should have a laid-back, "dragging" type of feel to their parts to accentuate the slow swing. As one who has performed this piece many times, it is all but guaranteed that men (and maybe your pianist) will perform a G-flat on the downbeat of m. 40 during the first rehearsal. The note is in fact G-natural; it may take separate rehearsal and consistent reminders to get this to be correct.

In m. 51 the tempo quickens again to half note = 72. The piano part now becomes more active and syncopated. The pianist should be instructed to bring out the syncopated eighth note arpeggios, as they contrast with the vocal lines' straight rhythm. After this brief section, the tempo hastens to half note = 76. The piano part becomes much more grandiose and is anchored by a pedal point in the left hand. The piece, which began subdued and serene, is now at a full *forte*. The women and men present the now very familiar melody in canon at the interval of one measure. In this verse of the song, Ames sets the words "long white robe" in several different rhythms. A choir on autopilot will read these incorrectly; take the time to ensure the singers perform these rhythms as notated. Halfway through this verse (m. 68), the men jump ahead of the women in the canon, which is now at the distance of one beat.

Mm. 73–74 mark the first instance of full four-part singing. This exclamation pushes the tempo to half note = 80, and the next verse is performed in a quasi-gospel style. The men's singing of the melody should be strong and bold but not oversung. The "hal-le-lu" part in the women should be exuberant and performed with Ames's marked articulation. It is effective for the women to *crescendo* each "lu" into the following staccato "ha." This will give the part shape and interest.

In m. 80, the pattern of the "hallelu" changes; determine the shaping by the musical structure and not the text. This verse comes to a rousing end with the extension of the final line and the most extreme vocal ranges of the piece. The chord on beat three of m. 94 is one of the most dissonant in the arrangement. Isolate the tenors and sopranos on that pitch so they have a chance to hear the color of the chord.

In the transition from mm. 96–97, I have found it effective to take the half note of the previous section and make it the new quarter note of the ending section. The piano chords and vocal texture recall the beginning of the arrangement. It is possible to use the same soloist as the beginning or to highlight another one of your singers in this section. The full choir enters again in mm. 104 and 105. The melody starts as one would predict but quickly becomes augmented to highlight the end of the piece. This begins in m. 106. This simple section is tricky because it requires all singers to be counting; the fact that it occurs on a page turn further complicates the issue. Even one errant singer with destroy the tranquility of this ending. Do not take this section for granted; give it enough rehearsal time to ensure the singers are confident.

Mm. 109–110 have a syncopated figure in the soprano line, and this subtle rhythmic shift can cause the altos, tenors or basses to miscount their whole notes in these measures. All of these slight rhythmic differences make this section a prime candidate for count-singing technique. The piece should continue to get softer to the end. Judicious use of vibrato is suggested, so the contrast between the dissonant and consonant chords can be pleasing to hear.

Form and Structure

This arrangement is in strophic verse-chorus form with some slight alterations and additions at the end of each verse.

Section	Measure	Event and Scoring
Verse 1	1–17	Soprano solo
Chorus	18–33	Soprano solo with choral accompaniment
Interlude	33–36	
Verse 2	37–51	Soprano section with choral accompaniment
Chorus	52–59	Full choir in two parts
Verse 3	60–75	Canon in two parts (no chorus follows)
Verse 4	76–95	Unison men with three-part women gospel chorus
Final chorus	96–124	Solo and full choir in augmentation

Text

I'm gonna lay down my sword and shield down by the riverside,
down by the riverside, down by the riverside.
I'm gonna lay down my sword and shield down by the riverside, down by the riverside.
I ain't gonna study war no more, I ain't a gonna study war no more? . . .

I'm gonna put on my travelin' shoes down by the riverside,
down by the riverside, down by the riverside.
I'm gonna put on my travelin' shoes down by the riverside, down by the riverside.
I ain't gonna study war no more, I ain't a gonna study war no more . . .

I'm gonna put on my long white robe down by the riverside,
down by the riverside, down by the riverside.
I'm gonna put on my long white robe down by the riverside, down by the riverside.
I ain't gonna study war no more, I ain't a gonna study war no more . . .

I'm gonna lay down my sword and shield down by the riverside,
down by the riverside, down by the riverside.
I'm gonna lay down my sword and shield down by the riverside, down by the riverside.
I ain't a gonna study war no more, I ain't a gonna study war no more . . .

Contributed by:

Matthew W. Mehaffey

Teacher Resource Guide

Famine Song
VIDA
arr. Matthew Culloton

SATB a cappella
Santa Barbara Music Publishing: SBMP 575
Overall: 2
Vocal: 2
Tonal/Rhythm: 2

Composer

Matthew Culloton (b. 1976) serves as artistic director and conductor for The Singers—Minnesota Choral Artists (www.singersmca.org), a professional forty-voice choir based in the Twin Cities. Prior to that appointment, Matthew was a member of The Dale Warland Singers, having served as artistic advisor to Dale Warland, assistant conductor, bass section leader, and music librarian. From 2000–06, Matthew was director of choral activities at Hopkins High School in Minnetonka, Minnesota. The Hopkins Concert Choir performed at the 2002 and 2004 Minnesota ACDA fall conventions and the 2005 Minnesota Music Educators Association Mid-Winter Clinic.

Matthew was presented with the 2004 Minnesota ACDA Outstanding Young Choral Conductor of the Year Award. In fall 2003, he was the recipient of the VocalEssence/ACDA of Minnesota Creative Programming Award for his work at Hopkins High School.

As a composer, Matthew has been commissioned by the Dale Warland Singers, Choral Arts Ensemble of Rochester (Minnesota), Ames Chamber Artists, Chanson, the Minnesota All-State Choirs (2005 Men's Choir), and numerous high school and collegiate choirs. His works are published by Hinshaw Music, Mark Foster Music (Shawnee), Santa Barbara Music Publishing, Kjos Music, and Odhecaton.com. Along with his twin brother Michael, he serves as coeditor of the Matthew and Michael Culloton Choral Series with Santa Barbara Music Publishing.

Matthew graduated from Concordia College in Moorhead, Minnesota, and he is a member of ACDA, Chorus America, MMEA, MENC, and the American Composers Forum.

The vocal quartet VIDA was founded in Bloomington, Indiana, in 1995, touring and recording with their unique combination of original songs and traditional songs from the Americas and Europe. The subjects of their repertoire depict the struggles and joys we share across vibrantly different cultures.

Composition and Historical Perspective

"Famine Song" is a contemporary piece of world/ethnic music. Inspired by stories of Sudanese basket weavers, this song expresses the pain and hope experienced by those in the famines of the 1980s. In the midst of hardship, a wonderful new sense of creativity emerged when women began weaving baskets as a means of survival. Central to the song is a section of improvisation over shifting chords. VIDA's recorded improvisation is written as the guide (mm. 34–45). VIDA saw the two improvising voices as the women from other cultures raised in empathy—they chose a Bulgarian-influenced vocal style.

"Famine Song" was arranged with permission of Moira Smiley and VIDA for the Hopkins High School Concert Choir after students shared VIDA's fantastic recording with Matthew Culloton. The arranger was immediately taken with the originality of this piece and excited to set it for choral ensembles. In our seemingly endless search for world and ethnic music, this song is a positive addition to the repertoire of school, community, and professional choral groups.

Technical Considerations and Musical Elements

"Famine Song" has few musical hurdles to overcome. It will be a fairly easy piece to put together with choirs of any size. The musical details that need more attention include intonation; maintaining an even, sustained tone in the choral accompaniment; unification of the word "rain" throughout the ensemble; and the improvisation passage (mm. 34–47).

My choirs have performed this piece in the printed key of E minor and the lower key of E-flat minor. Intonation seems to be better in the lower of those two keys. In experimenting with F minor I found that the opening female solo is more difficult due to the register shifts, especially in adolescent girls. Choir directors should always feel free to experiment with keys, but I suggest E minor or E-flat minor.

One of the hardest things we ask young singers to do is maintain an even, sustained sound on long notes—and this piece has a lot of them. The basses drone on E in mm. 1–18, but it is broken up with nonsense syllables (*ba da*, etc.). In mm. 20–25, the male voices sing whole note chord shifts below a moving female line, and the men need to sing the long notes with the same vocal energy as the women. Mm. 34–48 feature an improvised duet (a suggested starting point is notated), and the remainder of the choir sings whole note accompaniment. This passage must be conducted *in time*, not without measures. This will allow the choir to feel subdivisions in energy on those whole notes.

The refrain echoes the text "rain, rain, rain . . ." repeatedly. This is perhaps the hardest word I ever had to teach high school singers to pronounce. On this piece, using a rolled "r" is absolutely silly! The catch is that the long "American r" sounds terrible as well. Choirs must move quickly through the "r" as in the word "rough." The vowel sound also causes headaches. The "ai" combination must focus on the primary vowel sound, saving the vanishing "ee" sound for the absolute end of the word. Do not sing the vowel as a Latin "e" (as in "bed"). Simply focus on the primary vowel until the very end of the word when the vanishing vowel is pronounced.

The improvisation section in mm. 34–47 is the most unique aspect of this piece. It should be sung by two female voices in a lamenting style. I will address the singing manner in the next section, but it should be said that while the choir is singing very metered whole notes, the duet should not feel the constraints of meter. The choir is the metronome, and the duet moves very freely in front of them.

Stylistic Considerations

I performed "Famine Song" once on a program with pieces by Ernest Bloch, Johannes Brahms, and Sergei Rachmaninoff and some spirituals. We had to change the tone drastically when performing this piece so that it had a much lesser hint of traditional choral tone. This needs to sound like an Eastern European response to the Sudanese famines of the 1980s. The choral tone can be brightened and placed more forward than usual. A certain vocal edge of raw, untrained quality is appropriate (without negatively affecting intonation).

In the improvisation duet (mm. 34–47), the two women must try to get away from the notated lines. Those are given as a guide to those who are willing to give this section a try. Singers should experiment with quarter tones and harmonic clashes. The tone ought to be fairly pressed and very lamenting. I have asked my soloists to depict mothers who have lost their young to the starvation. Moira Smiley of VIDA had the idea that it is two empathetic people sharing the agony of the famines. Both of those get to the idea of feeling deep sorrow, and the singing must reflect a very outward presentation of that pain.

In the refrain sections ("rain . . ."), the choir can refine its sound slightly toward a traditional sound, but effort should be made to keep the piece sounding earthy, not having a concert hall tone.

Form and Structure

MEASURE	EVENT AND SCORING
1–10	Opening solo with bass pedal point
11–19	Harmonized solo with bass and soprano pedal points
20–33	Refrain 1
34–47	Improvisation duet with shifting choral chords (moving in strict time)
48–55	TTBB statement, SSAA statement
56–69	Refrain 2
70–76	Coda (based in "rain" plea)

Text

Ease my spirit, ease my soul,
Please free my hands from this barren soil.
Ease my mother, ease my child,
Earth and sky be reconciled.

Rain, rain, rain . . .

Additional References and Resources

To learn more about the improvised style of singing, see www.moirasmiley.com.

Suggested Listening

Recorded by the Hopkins High School Concert Choir conducted by Matthew Culloton, available online from Santa Barbara Music Publishing.

Contributed by:

Matthew Culloton

Teacher Resource Guide

I've Been 'Buked, Children!

arr. Rollo A. Dilworth

SATB with piano and percussion or SSA with piano and percussion (SBMP 550.1)
SATB, Santa Barbara Music Publishing: SBMP 550
SSA, Santa Barbara Music Publishing: SBMP 547
Overall: 2
Vocal: 2
Tonal/Rhythm: 3

Composer

Rollo A. Dilworth is associate professor of music and director of choral activities and music education at the North Park University School of Music in Chicago. He received his Doctor of Music degree in conducting performance at Northwestern University where he studied conducting and composition with Robert A. Harris. Additional composition teachers include Robert Ray, Pauline Oliveros, and Marta Ptaszynska.

Dilworth's choral compositions are a part of the Henry Leck Creating Artistry Choral Series with Hal Leonard Corporation and Colla Voce Music Company. He has recently published pieces with the Santa Barbara Music Publishing Company as part of the Mary Alice Stollak Choral Series. Dilworth is a contributing author for the Essential Elements for Choir and the Experiencing Choral Music textbook series, both published by the Hal Leonard Corporation/Glencoe/McGraw-Hill Publications, and for Music Express! Teachers' Magazine.

An active conductor, composer, educator, and clinician, Dilworth has taught choral music at the elementary, secondary, and university levels. His performing endeavors have taken him to Europe, Asia, Africa, and Australia.

In addition to composing music in the choral genre, his research interests are in the areas of African American music and music education curriculum and instruction.

Dilworth is an active member of the Music Educators National Conference, the National Association of Negro Musicians, the American Choral Directors Association, and Chorus America. He currently serves on the ACDA Central Division Board of Directors as the repertoire and standards chairman for multicultural and ethnic music.

Composition and Historical Perspective

In "I've Been 'Buked, Children!" Rollo Dilworth has composed an effective arrangement of the classic spiritual. An experienced piano player should be employed for the often-rhapsodic piano accompaniment, as it alternates between modern and gospel styles. The score also calls for three percussion instruments: hand drum, claves, and tambourine. The score's introduction notes:

> The sound of the hand drum represents the drums that were taken away from the slaves so that they could not use them to communicate; the sound of the claves represent the lashings and physical mistreatments that the slaves endured; the sound of the tambourine depicts [the] shackles that bound the slaves' feet to prevent an escape. The ostinato patterns found in the vocal lines, the piano accompaniment, and the percussion are all intended to capture the essence of the indigenous folk music tradition that Africans brought to America as salves.

Technical and Stylistic Considerations and Musical Elements

This piece has three verses with each verse composed in a different feel, key, and harmonic palette. The first verse is the most straightforward setting, with the melody in the soprano part, harmony in the alto part, and the ostinato mentioned above in the men's parts. The text of this verse presents the whispered chanting of ancestors who tell the story of hope for deliverance. This verse is easy to learn with the exception of a few non-diatonic leaps in the tenor and bass parts. These dissonant notes, however, are very much a part of the style and will be assimilated quickly in rehearsals.

According to arranger, the second verse "depict(s) the multiple layers of conflict created by slavery. More specifically, the music in this section attempts to characterize the African salves' resistance to the pressures of assimilation into Western Culture." He accomplishes this by using an imitative texture and a modern tonal palette that never settles (assimilates) into an absolute key center.

The third verse changes character completely and has a more triumphant, revivalist feel. In this section, the percussion parts resume their ostinato, the key of A major is clearly established, vocal parts proceed in a homophonic texture, and the piano accompaniment transitions to a quasi-gospel style. According to Rollo, this verse "symbolizes the African slaves' determination to retain their African roots while at the same [time] developing new musical expressions that typify the African American culture: the spiritual, blues, ragtime, jazz, and gospel."

To attain a performance congruent with the vision of the arranger, it is important to explain the story of each verse to your singers. Knowing this background will allow your singers to change their tone color to match the mood of the verse. For instance, the first verse could have a very warm, hopeful sound, followed by a second verse that is more questioning and perhaps more emphatic. The final verse calls for a zealous tone full of energy and conviction.

The arranger uses specific markings in regard to dynamics, tempo fluctuation, and articulation, and these should be followed carefully to ensure an accurate performance. It will be very easy for the piece to snowball into a faster tempo—try to keep the tempo under control as the arranger indicates.

Text

I've been 'buked and I've been scorned.
I've been 'buked and I've been scorned, children.
I've been 'buked and I've been scorned.
I've been talked about sho's you born.

There is trouble all over this world.
There is trouble all over this world, children.
There is trouble all over this world.

But I ain't gonna lay my 'ligion down.
But I ain't gonna lay my 'ligion down, children.
But I ain't gonna lay my 'ligion down.

Contributed by:

Matthew W. Mehaffey

Teacher Resource Guide

Lirum bililirum

Rossino Mantovano

(fl. 1505–1511)

SATB
Faber Music Ltd.: HL.50440700
Overall: 2
Vocal: 2
Tonal/Rhythm: 2

Composer

What we do know for certain is that Rossino Mantovano's composition "Lirum bililirum" has been performed by both instrumental ensembles and choirs. This piece is included in the King's Singers' Madrigal Collection and was recorded by them on the album *Madrigal History Tour*. Rossino Mantovano was born in Mantua and lived at the turn of the sixteenth century. "Lirum bililirum" is his best-known composition.

Composition and Historical Perspective

This piece is also known in its instrumental form as *Un sonar de piva in fachinesco*, which has been translated as "sound of the bagpipe," although *piva* was also used to refer to the crumhorn. "Lirum bililirum" has no translation. It is much like the use of "fa la la la la" in vocal song and is meant to imitate an instrumental sound. It was a common practice of many early madrigal composers to use vocal sound effects, especially those imitating instruments. Given the translation of the alternate title we can assume the composer aimed to imitate the sound of a crumhorn, although some contend that Mantovano intended the sound to be lute-like. The text is a routine lover's complaint based on long, unrequited love.

While many categorize "Lirum bililirum" as an Italian madrigal, it is really a *frottola*—a simple homophonic Italian song with a characteristic long-short-short rhythm. Many of these *frottoli* were issued in the first-ever printed books of music between 1504 and 1514 by the Venetian Ottavino Petrucci.

"Lirum bililirum" is written in the Bergamasque dialect from the Beragamo region of northern Italy. The published version in *The King's Singers' Madrigals, Volume 1* makes slight changes to this dialect so the normal rules of Italian pronunciation can be followed.

Technical Considerations and Musical Elements

This piece is characteristic of the Italian frottola which is a secular composition for three or four voices where the soprano predominantly carries the melody. It is also characterized by the presence of a long-short-short rhythmic figure in the refrain. In "Lirum bililirum" this rhythmic figure can be found in the opening in the upper three parts.

The refrain has a simple bass line, which provides the piece's macrobeat rhythm as well as the harmonic roots. When performed with a slight stress accent, the cross rhythms are highlighted, and the effect is quite playful. The upper three parts open with the characteristic rhythm of the *frottola* but with a triple meter feeling. This only lasts through the first two measures but the contrast with the bass line sets up the cross rhythm. The refrain contains a good amount of syncopation in the upper parts as well. If the choir remains vocally playful and light, these rhythms will really dance. If the singing is heavy, the syncopation will tend to slow down the tempo, and the section will lose its momentum.

Harmonically this section relies on a tonic pedal in the bass for the majority of the time. The only deviation from the tonic, subdominant, or dominant harmonies is a delightful subtonic chord in m. 11, which helps to propel the choir into the repeat of the refrain. The opening occurrence of the refrain also has a soaring tenor line in m. 7. The octave leap from A to A1 requires a bit of finesse and tactical use of falsetto. Encouraging the tenors to think of alto color will help here as well as using some distance imagery to keep the larynx in a stable position.

Phrasing in the opening refrain is tricky. A collective choral breath anywhere before m. 24 will disrupt the flow of the piece, which moves like the unfurling of a flag. At the end of any given phrase one or more voice parts are moving toward the next phrase to keep the momentum. This happens most notably in m. 7 with the tenors and in m. 13 with both the tenor and alto. I would, therefore, recommend employing staggered breathing until the final cadence in m. 24 before the beginning of verse 1.

The verses are typical of a strophic song with the musical material repeated exactly. Each verse begins in the dominant and contains three phrases, each of which is six measures long. The text is the driving factor in the verses, with the rhythm and phrasing of the music coming directly from the text. There should be a consistency of dynamic in these verses with each phrase following a slight rise and fall to provide momentum. The rhythmic motive of quarter note, half note, quarter note is found frequently in this section. Care should be taken not to accent the half note, as it is usually found within a word.

Stylistic Considerations

Polyphonic music of the sixteenth century is not metrical. Often the phrases are of unequal length, and text rhythm can be found in the middle of measures. Barlines lose their meaning and the first note of the measure is not stressed. Musical line is of utmost importance. In the polyphonic style, each voice is not given the same weight, and moving lines must be heard above the others. However, because this piece is a *frottola*, there is a great deal of homophonic texture with the moving lines occurring in sections throughout both the verse and the refrain. Care must be taken to balance the choir appropriately in each section.

The musical line should have forward motion and momentum throughout. Mantovano accomplishes this through seemingly never-ending phrases with single voices dovetailing from phrase to phrase. Keeping the choral sound light and flexible will allow that texture to come through.

Form and Structure

The piece consists of two sections, a refrain and a verse. Each refrain is made up of four phrases in a 4 + 3 + 3 + 3 configuration. Each verse is made up of three phrases of six measures each.

Text and Translation

Lirum bililirum, li-lirum, lirum, lirum.	Lirum bililirum, li-lirum, lirum, lirum.
Deh si soni la sordina.	Ah, sound the muted instrument.
Tu m'intendi ben, Pedrina,	You hear me well, Pedrina
Ma non già per il dovirum.	—And not just out of duty.
Lirum bililirum, li-lirum, lirum li	Lirum bililirum, li-lirum, lirum li
Deh, si soni la sordina,	Ah, sound the muted instrument.
Deh, si soni la sordina. . . .	Ah, sound the muted instrument. . . .

Suggested Listening

Madrigal History Tour, King's Singers (EMI 69837).

Contributed by:

Rae Jean Teeter

Teacher Resource Guide

Mon coeur se recommande à vous

Jean-Baptiste Weckerlin

(1821–1910)

formerly attributed to Orlando di Lasso
SATB a cappella
E. C. Schirmer Music Company: 1145
Overall: 2
Vocal: 2
Tonal/Rhythm: 2

Composer

This four-voice version of "Mon coeur se recommande à vous" for many years was erroneously attributed to Orlando di Lasso (1532–1594). It was, however, composed in the nineteenth century by French composer Jean-Baptiste Weckerlin. Because it is in the style of a Renaissance chanson, it is discussed below in those terms. Weckerlin's works are not widely known, although he composed in a variety of genres, including stage works, choral music, piano works, orchestral music, and folksong settings.

Composition and Historical Perspective

While this edition refers to the work as a madrigal, it is a chanson-like composition. The genre during the Renaissance period was greatly influenced by the Italian madrigal, especially in that the chanson is usually text-driven, with careful musical consideration for the poetry. A mixture of homophony and imitation is common, as can be seen in "Mon coeur" with the verses being homophonic while the refrain is imitative.

Technical Considerations and Musical Elements

One of the greatest challenges of "Mon coeur" for an amateur choir is the language. Depending on their level of experience with French texts, the chorus may need extensive instruction on the major principles of pronunciation and careful demonstration by the conductor or language coach. (See Additional References and Resources for suggested diction guides.) Beyond mechanics, the style of the language, with its legato syntax and phrasing should be carefully explained. French is pronounced with emphasis on vowel sounds, and, unlike English, German, or Italian, the consonants are neither prolonged nor emphasized.[1] Once the chorus is comfortable with the text, rehearsing the piece on the vowels only may prove helpful.

The barlines in this edition are helpful from the standpoint of ensemble organization, but they do not always aid the direction and "line" of each phrase or the syntax of the text. Often, the text is improperly divided by the barlines so that strong syllables often fall on weak beats or vice versa. Furthermore, there are times when pitch movement works better in triple than in duple. An example of this is the soprano part in mm. 9–15, which is divided in the following manner:

Text: Fai - | tes qu'a-dieu | vous puis-se | di - - - - | - - - - - - | - - - - - | re!
Beats: 2 1 2 3–4 1–2 3 4 1–2–3–4 1–2–3–4 1–2–3–4 1–2

To produce an inflection of the text that is more appropriate, as well as to better project the rhythmic motion of the phrase, the part can be remeasured as follows:

Text: Fai - tes | qu'a-dieu | vous puis-se | di - - - - - | - - - - | - - - - | - - - re!
Beats: 1–2 3 1 2–3 1–2 3 4 1–2–3–4 1–2–3 1–2–3 1–2–3–4

Depending on the skill level of the chorus, a great deal of creativity may be necessary to achieve success with the remeasuring. It may be difficult to dictate the changes in rehearsal, so an overhead projection with the changes may expedite the process. The singers can easily bracket duple and triple figures so that as they read the score, they can see the rhythmic scheme more clearly. If necessary, the conductor can even make his or her own partbook edition. The director may choose to measure the parts to reflect the duple/triple groupings or not at all. With the parts notated separately, each section can learn the notes in sectional rehearsals, focusing on the movement and inflection of its respective parts. While this is obviously more helpful for a work that is contrapuntal throughout, it will certainly strengthen the singers' awareness of the phrasing, especially the imitative sections (mm. 9–15 and 34–40).

Tonally, the work presents two minor problems. One, it is pitched in F major, which is notoriously difficult to tune, largely due to where the half steps in the scale are located. For example, in the first phrase, the half step from leading tone to tonic occurs several times in the tenor part, which is in a segment of the range that is often problematic, especially for young singers. Sometimes it is helpful to either raise the key or lower it by a half step. Experimentation in this manner during rehearsals can be interesting and instructional for the singers, while at the same time bringing the possibility of better performance. Changing the key is usually recommended relatively late in the preparation process.

The other tonal difficulty is the lowered seventh that appears in the refrain, again occurring in the tenor line. This alteration of the harmony appears immediately after the progression from F to E-natural has been heard in the soprano. This note can significantly affect the intonation, so it is important to carefully tune it within the harmony. The best solution is first to make the tenors aware that it is an altered harmony (encourage them to circle the note) and second to sustain the note outside the context of the rhythm with the other parts sounding along with it. This may need to be repeated over several rehearsals to reinforce aural perception.

Stylistic Considerations

"Mon coeur se recommande à vous" is an unaccompanied choral piece that imitates the style of a Renaissance chanson. It should be sung with a tone quality that is light with little vibrato. It is best performed by a small chorus, perhaps with three voices on each part. Even if used for a concert involving a large choir, the conductor may select a semi-chorus, bringing a variety of sound to the program.

Form and Structure

ABA

Section	Measure	Event and Scoring
A	1–15	Refrain; F major, sometimes with lower seventh
B	16–25	Stanza; tonality hints at D minor, but never settles
A	26–40	Refrain

Text and Translation

Mon coeur se recommande à vous,	My heart commends itself to you,
Tout plein d'ennui et de martyre;	All full of boredom and martyrdom;
Au moins en dépit des jaloux	At least despite the jealous people
Faites qu'adieu vous puisse dire!	Bid only farewell that's what may be said!

Ma bouche qui savait sourire	My mouth that knew how to smile
Et conter propos gracieux	And make gracious comments
Ne fait maintenant que maudire	Only knows now how to curse
Ceux qui m'ont banni de vos yeux.	Those who banished me from your eyes.

Text by Clément Marot (1496–1544), translated by Chris Edwards

Additional References and Resources

Allen, Sheila, et al. *Diction for Singers: A Concise Reference for English, Italian, Latin, German, French, and Spanish Pronunciation*. Dallas: Pst...Inc., 1990.

Moriarty, John. *Diction*. Boston: E. C. Schirmer Music Company, 1975.

Stolba, K. Marie. *The Development of Western Music: A History*. Dubuque, IA: Wm. C. Brown Publishers, 1990.

Suggested Listening

Di Lasso, Orlando (attr.), "Mon coeur se recommande à vous," *Madrigal Masterpieces: The Renaissance in France, Italy, and England*, The Deller Consort, Alfred Deller, Vanguard Classics OVC 2000.

Contributed by:

Russell Nelson

1 Allen, et. al, 180.

Teacher Resource Guide

Praise His Holy Name!

Keith Hampton

(b. 1957)

SATB and piano
earthsongs: S-85
Overall: 2
Vocal: 2
Tonal/Rhythm: 2

Composer

Keith Hampton is director of music ministries and organist at the Park Manor Christian Church in Chicago. He also teaches K–8 vocal music at the Chicago International Charter School. He earned a bachelor of music education degree from Westminster Choir College, a master of arts degree from Marywood University in Scranton, Pennsylvania, and a doctor of music degree in church music from Northwestern University.

In addition, he has attended the Robert Shaw Workshop for Choral Conductors sponsored by Carnegie Hall in New York. In the summers of 2003 and 2004, Hampton was chosen as one of fourteen conductors who participated in the Oregon Bach Festival Conducting Master Classes. This festival was held at the University of Oregon under the direction of Helmuth Rilling and Thomas Somerville. Hampton is very active as a conductor, organ soloist, and accompanist and is in demand as a workshop clinician. He has guest conducted numerous honors choirs across the country. As a published composer, Keith Hampton's arrangements of spirituals and gospel songs can be found at Augsburg Press, earthsongs, and Hinshaw Music.

Composition and Historical Perspective

Published in 1998 in the Anton Armstrong Choral Series (earthsongs), "Praise His Holy Name!" has become one of the most popular gospel songs performed by choirs. This score provides educators with an enjoyable and important part of the gospel/spiritual repertoire. In its first year of release "Praise His Holy Name!" was among the ten most popular choral pieces performed. As of this printing, Ernani Aguiar's "Salmo 150" is the only piece in the earthsongs catalog to sell more copies than this score.

Technical Considerations and Musical Elements

There are not too many technical difficulties in this work. The composer and the publisher notate directions very cleanly, and the ad lib passages are also laid out clearly.

The first potential problem conductors will see is that the first page of the score contains a single vocal line. The refrain is to be sung in three parts—sopranos, alto, and men. This engraving style means that all men will be singing on a treble clef line scored in the women's octave, and this is fairly high for school-age bass/baritones. Follow the score, and encourage men to use falsetto when necessary. At m. 29 the piece employs a four-part SATB voicing through the end.

Throughout the score, singers encounter many syncopated rhythms. As an example, the verse opening with men's voices (m. 15) is full of tricky syncopations. Often in the gospel tradition, rote learning will go a long way toward quicker learning. Having singers repeat these rhythms using a call-and-response teaching technique is much easier than rhythmic analysis of these difficult measures. I would add that mm. 32 and 33 can be learned very quickly by employing rote teaching. Of note is m. 21—beat four is often syncopated incorrectly. Make sure that "jah" comes directly on beat four, not with an early syncopation.

As for the piano part, there is no need for the accompanist to stray and improvise like in many published piano parts. The composer, by playing the part into Finale, notated and engraved a piano part that, when played exactly as written, sounds like improvisation. Your accompanist will most likely enjoy playing the piece, and the piano part certainly anchors the mood, style, and feel of this work.

At m. 26, all women should sing the alto line on the repeat as if it were a Bach motet—very cleanly. When the sopranos leave the alto part and go to the top line, they should maintain that same articulated style of singing. This allows the female lines to stand out from the broad, accented passage that the men sing below them.

In mm. 29–32, the keyboard/band should play one time through by themselves. Hampton suggests that a layering effect then happen on each repeat from the soprano voice down to the basses. Soloists may certainly ad lib in a call-and-response manner throughout this repeated section.

As for optional instrumentation, a Hammond organ synthesizer setting would be preferable with electric bass guitar and drum set.

Stylistic Considerations

The performance practice of spirituals and gospel music arranged for choirs is a widely debated topic. This work should be sung in the style of a praise song, and gospel music has long been sung by large choirs and small ensembles. (I would recommend any of the gospel recordings performed by Chanticleer.) The performance should be one of integrity, not one of overdone stereotypes (i.e., wide scooping from pitch to pitch, a blatant "shout" tone, etc.). In this score, Hampton is very clear with his articulations and dynamic markings, with specific attention given to accents, tenuto, and staccatos.

In *Teaching Music through Performance in Choir: Volume 1*, Anton Armstrong writes eloquently about the African American slave song. As spiritual and gospel music also springs from that tradition, his closing is relevant to this discussion:

> The final point I wish to emphasize is that this music has to be treated with great dignity. . . . It is the music of a proud and noble people; it is music that celebrates life and the power of goodness over the power of evil. . . . This music does and should serve as inspiration for all generations, for young people who understand that one can gain strength, comfort, and inspiration from this music. And for many people, this music leads to healing, to restoration of oneself fully in body, mind, spirit, and voice. (pp. 34–35)

Form and Structure

Measure	Event and Scoring
1–4	Four-measure piano introduction
5–12	Refrain
13–14	Two-measure piano interlude
15–22	Verse 1
5–12	Refrain
13–14	Two-measure interlude
15–22	Verse 2
5–12	Refrain
13–14	Two-measure piano interlude, skip to coda
23–26	(Sung three times) layered ostinato
27–28	Third ending/interlude
29–32	*Ad libitum* repeated section
33–38	Piano conclusion with chorus accompaniment

Text

Refrain:
Sing till the power of the Lord come down.
Shout Hallelujah! Praise His Holy name! (2x)

Verse 1:
Amazing grace, how sweet the sound that saved a wretch like me;
I once was lost, but now I'm found, was blind but now I see.
Jesus, Jesus, how I love Thee! Shout Hallelujah! Praise His Holy name!

Verse 2:
Must Jesus bear the cross alone and all the world go free?
No, there's a cross for ev'ryone and there's a cross for me.
Jesus, Jesus, how I love Thee! Shout Hallelujah! Praise His Holy name!

Contributed by:

Matthew Culloton

Teacher Resource Guide

Sounding Joy

Gwyneth Walker

(b. 1947)

SATB
E. C. Schirmer Music Company: 4318
Overall: 2
Vocal: 3
Tonal/Rhythm: 2

Composer

Gwyneth Walker is one of the country's most prolific composers, with a catalog of more than one hundred and fifty commissioned works for orchestra, band, chorus, and chamber ensembles. Her music is published by E. C. Schirmer (choral/vocal) and MB Music (orchestral/instrumental). Walker holds both undergraduate and advanced degrees in composition and is a graduate of Brown University and the Hartt School of Music. She is a former faculty member of the Oberlin College Conservatory, a position from which she resigned in 1982 to pursue a career as a full-time composer. She is a current resident of Vermont and the recipient of the 2000 Lifetime Achievement Award from the Vermont Arts Council. She is a cofounder and former director of the Consortium of Vermont Composers.

Composition and Historical Perspective

"Sounding Joy" was composed in 1985 for the Sounding Joy! Singers, a small chorus from Randolph, Vermont. The text of the piece is Psalm 95, and the opening section reflects the power and majestic, commanding nature of the text. The opening is reminiscent of the style of early New England hymn singing, but the second section is contemporary with its accented syncopation and final tone cluster.

Technical Considerations and Musical Elements

This is a piece of contrasts. The first section is very traditional in nature, and the second section is contemporary. The unifying factor is the rhythmic emphasis of the piece. There is an emphasis on the strong beats throughout section one, which changes to an emphasis on accented syncopation in the second section. The piece is in duple meter and in cut time with the tempo remaining consistent throughout.

The composer's editorial marking for the opening of the piece is "in rousing early New England style." Rousing is an excellent way to describe this piece in its entirety. This is a bold, celebratory, and declarative piece that is in no way subtle. The danger here is that the choral sound will be harsh and shouted. Encourage the choir members to think of the *forte* as an ***f*** for full, fat sound as opposed to forceful.

The unison should have a sense of buoyancy so that the strong beats have forward motion. Rudolph van Laban's work in the area of movement analysis is very useful here. I have used the image of pressing a beach ball into a pool of water as it has the proper weight, time, effort, and flow elements the choir needs in this passage. A partially submerged beach ball will spring back, giving the sense of forward motion through the phrase. The choir can "bounce" the beach ball as they sing to help them feel the style of the passage. Encourage strong entrances during the polyphonic sections with a constant awareness of the other sections so that each entrance is clear.

The second stanza of text is set in a more fluid way with each entrance beginning with legato eighth notes. Maintaining the tempo here is crucial, as the choir will have a tendency to revel in their eighth notes and slow down the pace. Each entrance needs to dovetail into the next so there is a feeling of flow throughout the entire section. In m. 26 the second half of the text is repeated with a piano dynamic and staccato articulation. The staccato markings should be interpreted as indications of separations so that the light texture is not disrupted by unintended accents. I have found that a movement indicative of the separation is helpful in rehearsals. Again with Laban movement analysis, I have used the image of dabbing into a pool of water. The "dab" has the proper weight and time elements to express the separation the choir needs in this passage. The choir can "dab" as they sing to help them feel the weight and separation needed here.

The second section of the piece is a bit more rhythmically complex. There is a great deal of emphasis placed on the syncopated combination of eighth rest, quarter note, eighth note, and half note. The meter is still duple, and the half note is still the pulse. The tempo does not change. I have found that emphasizing the percussive nature of the consonants in the repetitive text of "Sounding Joy" helps to keep the syncopation energetic and buoyant. Again, movement is crucial. A simple shifting of the weight from side to side with the body in a loose flowing position helps a great deal.

In m. 50 there is a layering that starts with the basses bouncing between C and G. The altos enter with an accented half note on beat two, also outlining the tonic to dominant harmony of each measure. The tenors then enter with one of the syncopated motives from the previous section. The sopranos follow with the same rhythmic motive but a more complicated arpeggiated figure. The effect of this section is remarkable. To me it recalls memories of riding a carousel as a child with the calliope music building in intensity and complexity. The difficulty in this section lies with keeping the build under control. Oversinging and rushing are real dangers. Encouraging the choir to move to macrobeats and think the subdivisions can help maintain a consistent tempo.

The final twelve measures recall the opening of the second section with some dynamic extremes. There are two breaks in the piece in the form of fermatas over rests. These should be relatively short so that you do not lose the momentum built in the previous section. The final ascending passage is marked by a dramatic *crescendo* and a final triumphant D major chord held by the women as the men continue into a C major triad. Let your choir revel in the dissonance, but caution them again not to oversing.

Stylistic Considerations

New England hymns frequently used psalms as texts. These were written in simple imitative counterpoint and often labeled as "fuguing tunes." The style of the New England hymn is straightforward and relatively unadorned and should be sung as such in a declarative way. The second section of "Sounding Joy," while it is different in rhythmic style, should keep to the vocal style established in the first section.

Form and Structure

"Sounding" Joy is based on a tune by eighteenth-century composer and Vermont resident Justin Morgan. Structurally the piece is in AB form with the opening section being a traditional setting of the original song in the style of a rousing early New England hymn. The piece opens with unison singing at the octave. This moves into a short polyphonic section, which is led by the basses and builds in both texture and dynamic intensity.

The second section is more contemporary and contains a syncopated rhythmic motive on the text "sounding joy." This motive finds its way into all voice parts in both homophonic and polyphonic texture. The piece builds throughout the second section, culminating in a triumphant final chord of mixed tonalities invoking the work of New England composer Charles Ives.

MEASURE	EVENT AND SCORING
1–9	Opening statement of theme; unison C major
10–17	Restatement of second phrase of text; staggered entrances into homophonic texture
18–26	Second stanza; staggered entrances; tenor and bass duet; soprano, alto, and bass finish
27–34	Restatement of second phrase of text; staggered entrances; *piano* dynamics; separated style; *forte* homophonic finish with bass leading into next section
34–49	Rhythmic motive treated homophonically and in call-and-response style; finishes on a secondary dominant of a minor but returns to C major
50–70	Layered entrances, bass section on staccato strong beats; tenor and soprano on syncopated motive
70–82	Restatement of m. 34 with dynamic extremes; climactic ending with grand *crescendo* and final tone cluster

Text

Come, sound His praise abroad, and hymns of glory sing:
Jehovah is the Sov'reign God, the Universal King.
He formed the deeps unknown; He gave the seas their bound;
The wat'ry worlds are all his own, and all the solid ground.
Sounding Joy! Sounding Joy!

Suggested Listening

Sounding Joy, The American Repertory Singers, Leo Nester, director (Arsis CD 105).

Contributed by:

Rae Jean Teeter

Teacher Resource Guide

The Divine Image

Joshua Shank

(b. 1980)

SATB with piano
Santa Barbara Music Publishing: SBMP 491
Overall: 2
Vocal: 2
Tonal/Rhythm: 2

Composer

Joshua Shank is an innovative young composer whose music has been widely performed by high school and professional ensembles alike. He received his undergraduate degree in vocal music education from Luther College in Decorah, Iowa, where he studied conducting with Weston Noble and Timothy Peter.

In 2002 Joshua became the youngest composer ever awarded the Raymond W. Brock Student Composition Award by the American Choral Directors Association. The winning piece, "Musica animam tangens" (written at the age of twenty), was premiered at the 2002 ACDA National Convention in New York City. His choral works are available exclusively through Santa Barbara Music Publishing.

Composition and Genre

"The Divine Image" is a flowing, legato piece using a text by English poet William Blake (1757–1827). The poem comes from Blake's famous anthology *Songs of Innocence and Experience* (1789). The piece was commissioned by the

Lutheran Church of Hope in Des Moines, Iowa, and premiered November 24, 2002.

The note in the score reads:

> The language of Blake's poem is nearly three hundred years old, but the message is eternal. The text itself is simple in structure; four words permeate the entire poem and serve as the central message: mercy, pity, peace, and love. Through those four sentiments, Blake tells us where the good in human nature lies—our compassion—and for me, paints a picture of Love as a beautiful woman clothed in peace, with pity on her face, and mercy in her heart.
>
> During the months I was writing *The Divine Image*, I had been listening to a lot of Brahms (his part songs in particular), so you might hear glimpses of him every now and then. Aside from the piano introduction (deliberately reminiscent of *Die Mainacht*), the gentle chromaticism and eventual optimism in the music were simply natural extensions of the beauty inherent in the poetry.

Technical Considerations

In an attempt to keep the vocal ranges conservative, the choral parts lie comfortably in the range of most high school singers until the dramatic climax when the choir sustains *forte/fortissimo* for three measures at a high tessitura. The rhythms do not present a significant challenge as they follow closely the prosody of the original poem, and the piano part (in D-flat throughout) is well within the grasp of an average player. The tonal language throughout is simple, economical, and easy to understand despite the many accidentals and tonal shifts shown in the score.

Stylistic Considerations

The music follows strictly the dramatic arc of the text to a quiet, meaningful conclusion with the central message of Blake's poem. Because of this, the major stylistic concern should simply be conveying the meaning of the text to the audience. There are also a few places in the score where there are tight, clustered harmonies. During these passages the choir will need to strive for clarity of pitch and tone in order to make the chords come across in the way desired.

Form and Structure

The piece is through-composed with the form strictly following that of Blake's poem: a stanza of poetry is a distinct section of music with independent musical ideas and conclusions. Because the second stanza was not set (due to gender-specific language) the piece can be analyzed in four sections:

Section	Measure	Event and Scoring
Section 1	1–7	Piano introduction
	8–23	Tenor and bass (lines one and two of poem)
	24–32	SATB (lines three and four)

Uses the rise and fall of a perfect fourth across chords is the basis for a melody. The tenors and basses sing the first two lines in unison with the sopranos and altos entering on the words "and to these virtues" to add weight to the text. Although there are many accidentals in the score, it is essentially a repeated pattern both in the choir (perfect fourth motive) and piano (similar arpeggiation).

	33–40	Piano interlude
Section 2	41–64	SATB (stanza three)

Consists of a repeated, raised-fourth motive descending by half step from a D-flat tonality to A-natural. This passage is sung in unison by the choir with a steady accompaniment figure in the piano. The dissonant chord in m. 62—although it appears difficult—is approached melodically with a pedal tone transitioning enharmonically (C-sharp/D-flat) into the next section.

Section 3	65–90	SATB (stanza four)

With a drone in the piano, the altos repeat a three-note motive on "then every man" with the rest of the choir joining the underlying harmony at four-measure intervals (bass–tenor–soprano). The choir's repeated motives *crescendo* into the text "prays to the human form divine."

Section 4	91–104	SATB (stanza five)

The final stanza of text is sung *a cappella* with a homophonic texture to underscore the message of the text. As the choir sustains the final word of the poem on a dissonant chord, the "Ubi caritas" chant is quoted in the piano part to highlight the similarities between the two texts. The piece ends quietly as the choir resolves to a held D-flat major chord.

Text

To Mercy, Pity, Peace, and Love,
All pray in their distress,
And to these virtues of delight
Return their thankfulness.

For Mercy, Pity, Peace, and Love,
Is God our Father dear:
And Mercy, Pity, Peace, and Love,
Is man, His child and care.

For Mercy has a human heart;
Pity, a human face;
And Love, the human form divine:
And Peace, the human dress.

Then every man of every clime,
That prays in his distress,
Prays to the human form divine
Love, Mercy, Pity, Peace.

And all must love the human form,
In heathen, Turk or Jew.
Where Mercy, Love, and Pity dwell
There God is dwelling too.

(*second stanza not used*)

Additional References and Resources

Web site:
Santa Barbara Music Publishing: www.sbmp.com

Suggested Listening

Santa Barbara Music Publishing, CD10, *Octavos 5*, The Überkor, Joshua Shank, conductor.

Musica Animam—Volume XVII, Susquehanna University Choir, Cyril Stretansky, conductor.

Contributed by:

Joshua Shank

Teacher Resource Guide

Three Madrigals

Emma Lou Diemer

(b. 1927)

SATB with piano
Boosey & Hawkes: OCTB-5417
Overall: 2
Vocal: 2
Tonal/Rhythm: 3

Composer

Emma Lou Diemer spent her childhood in Kansas City, Missouri, where she studied piano and organ. At the age of thirteen she became determined to pursue composition and began serious piano study at the Kansas City Conservatory with Wiktor Labunski. Diemer has earned composition degrees from the Yale School of Music (bachelor of music, 1949; master of music, 1950) and from the Eastman School of Music (PhD, 1960). She also spent time studying in Brussels on a Fulbright Scholarship.

Diemer taught in the Kansas City area and after receiving her doctorate became composer-in-residence in the Arlington, Virginia, schools under the Ford Foundation Young Composers Project. It is during this time that she composed *Three Madrigals*. Diemer currently serves as professor emeritus at the University of California–Santa Barbara. While at the University of California she has been instrumental in founding the electronic/computer music center as well as the PhD/doctor of music arts degree programs in composition.

Diemer's works span various genres and levels of difficulty. She has received numerous awards for both her instrumental and vocal music, including a Kennedy Center Friedheim Award in Orchestral Music for her

1991 piano concerto. Her works are published by Boosey & Hawkes, Carl Fischer, Oxford University Press, Arsis Press, Plymouth Music Company, Santa Barbara Music Publishing, Seesaw Music Corporation, and others.

Composition and Historical Perspective

Three Madrigals was first published in 1962 and written during the time Diemer was the composer-in-residence for the Arlington, Virginia, schools under the Ford Foundation Young Composers Project. The text is taken from Shakespeare's plays *Twelfth Night*, *Measure for Measure*, and *Much Ado about Nothing*. The set is written in the style of a Renaissance madrigal.

Technical Considerations and Musical Elements

All of these madrigals have their own unique feeling and texture that make Shakespeare's text come alive. While most high school choirs could perform these songs, they do have inherent technical difficulties that need to be considered so that rehearsals are efficient and an effective performance can be achieved.

The first madrigal ("O Mistress mine, where are you roaming?") is in triple meter and in the key of G major. It contains two verses, each treated in a similar way by the composer, with each verse modulating to the key of E-flat major and then returning to G. This movement is characterized by the use of a rhythmic motive of a quarter note followed by an eighth note. This gives the piece a lilting feel much like a Celtic folk tune.

The soprano section starts the melody at *mezzo piano*. The tune should be sung lightly with emphasis placed on a unified tone and clarity of diction. The phrase ends on the highest pitch, and care must be taken to stress the penultimate note so that the ends of the phrases do not feel chopped. The men echo the women and should match their light, clear quality. These echoed tetrachords in mm. 8–11 are spelled enharmonically at the modulation and are prone to intonation problems. Encouraging the choir to keep the opening half step very high will help the tetrachords remain in tune.

The men begin the second section of this movement with the tenors adding the harmony in thirds. Like the opening, the text must be clear and crisp. The dynamic here is stronger and the piano accompaniment is a bit heavier with lots of open fifths and octaves. The final section of the piece is a simple canon at the octave with the basses in their upper register at a piano dynamic. This is the most difficult section for young singers, as the tendency is to sing with a high, tight larynx. The men should be encouraged to begin the phrase with a yawning breath and to think of the pitches as further away rather than higher. Distance imagery helps maintain the larynx in a lower, more relaxed position and encourages more effective support from the abdominal wall.

The second movement ("Take, O take those lips away") is a slow moving, dramatic and passionate work. The setting is in C Dorian with the basses intoning a pedal through the majority of the movement. The accompaniment is ethereal and contains open interval arpeggios in treble clef to begin the movement. As the piece nears the climactic unison section in mm. 15–18, the piano moves into the bass clef but maintains the open arpeggios. The final phrase elongates the material found at the end of the first section with the piano now in the lowest registration. The final chord finds the piano moving back up into the treble clef and ending on the final incomplete G minor chord.

While this movement is the most moving and beautiful of the three, it is also the most difficult. Young singers need to be given lots of movement opportunity to feel the stretch and pull of these phrases. Images such as pulling taffy or stretching large elastic cords can be very useful in helping singers to feel the musical tension present. Caution needs to be taken on the unison climax in mm. 15–16 as young singers will want to sing too loudly at *forte* rather than at the warm but still restrained *mezzo forte* indicated.

Preparing the singers' ears for Dorian mode will help them sing the tight half step between the sixth and seventh scale degrees in tune. This is particularly important for the tenors, who sing primarily on these pitches in the opening phrase. Some warm-up activities using parallel fourths and some interval drills on half steps and whole steps will help the women with their intonation.

Movement three ("Sigh no more, ladies, sigh no more!") is a rollicking tribute to the shifting nature of men's affections. The movement is in a fast triple meter full of strong-beat accents and soaring ascending lines. Each verse of the text ends with a layering of voices toward a final open-fifth chord. As in movement one, there is playful echoing banter passed between the men and women sung in unison at the octave. Verses one and two are treated much the same way in the accompaniment. The piano accents the strong beats at the octave while the weaker divisions contain frequent dissonance. Musically this movement is not difficult. The text does have some challenges due to the quickness of the tempo and the Shakespearean English.

This is a remarkable piece that I have found successful for all levels from middle school to adult choirs. The music is expressive, unusual, and tremendously fun!

Stylistic Considerations

This piece is written in the style of Renaissance madrigals, which were originally sung for recreation by small groups of singers. *Three Madrigals* should retain that light treatment. There is no place for heavy-handed tone quality or a preponderance of vibrato. Think English boychoir rather than opera chorus.

The rhythm is very important, and the piece must dance. Encourage your choir to move as they rehearse to keep a sense of playfulness in the first and third movements. Movement two, while it has a different tempo, should still retain the style of a renaissance madrigal with minimal vibrato and an absolute clarity of high, spacious, and forward vowels.

Form and Structure

Measure	Event and Scoring
I. "O Mistress mine, where are you roaming?"	
1–11	First half of verse one; women lead, men echo four-note motive
12–20	Second half of verse one; E-flat major, men lead in thirds, women join with same third harmony
21–29	First half of verse two; G major, women lead and men echo four-note motive
30–36	Second half of verse two; E-flat major; men lead in thirds, women join with same third harmony
37–43	Final line of text; G major; men lead in unison, women echo; movement ends on a ii^7 chord
II. "Take, O take those lips away"	
1–10	Opening phrase; C Dorian; bass pedal first half; moving to G minor.
11–14	Second phrase; basses on G pedal.
15–18	Third phrase; E-flat major; men and women at the octave
19–29	Final phrase; repeat of opening in C Dorian with extended ending in parallel fourths and fifths
III. "Sigh no more, ladies, sigh no more!"	
1–8	Opening phrase; men and women in octaves E-flat major moving to G-flat major
9–15	Second phrase; men and women in octave canon; G-flat major moving to G major
16–26	Third phrase; begins with octave canon in G major moving to building open fifths in E-flat
27–32	Piano interlude; octaves in G major returning to introduction chords in E-flat
33–52	Repeat of mm. 3–22 with second verse text
53–59	Final phrase; building open fifths in E-flat; cadence in G

Text

I. "O Mistress mine, where are you roaming?"

O Mistress mine, where are you roaming?
O, stay and hear! Your true-love's coming.
That can sing both high and low.
Trip no further, pretty sweeting:
Journeys end in lovers meeting,
Every wise man's son doth know.

What is love? 'Tis not hereafter;
Present mirth hath present laughter;
What's to come is still unsure.
In delay there lies no plenty;
Then come kiss me sweet and twenty!
Youth's a stuff will not endure.

II. "Take, O take those lips away"

Take, O take those lips away,
That so sweetly were forsworn;
And those eyes, the break of day,
Lights that do mislead the morn!
But my kisses bring again,
Bring again;
Seals of love, but seal'd in vain,
Seal'd in vain!

III. "Sigh no more, ladies, sigh no more!"

Sigh no more, ladies, sigh no more;
Men were deceivers ever;
One foot in sea and one on shore,
To one thing constant never;
Then sigh not so, but let them go,
And be you blithe and bonny;
Converting all your sounds of woe
Into hey nonny, nonny.

Sing no more ditties, sing no mo'e,
Or dumps so dull and heavy;
The fraud of men was ever so,
Since summer first was leavy.
Then sigh not so, but let them go,
And be you blithe and bonny,
Converting all your sounds of woe
Into hey, nonny, nonny.

Additional References and Resources

Jordan, James, and Marilyn Shenenberger. *Ear Training Immersion Exercises for Choirs*. Chicago: GIA Publications, 2004.

Jordan, James, and Matthew Mehaffey. *Choral Ensemble Intonation*. Chicago: GIA Publications, 2001.

Contributed by:

Rae Jean Teeter

Teacher Resource Guide

Yet Gentle Will the Griffen Be
No. 3 from What Grandpa Told the Children

Francisco J. Núñez
(b. 1965)

Unison and piano
Boosey & Hawkes: M-051-46963-5
Overall: 2
Vocal: 2
Tonal/Rhythm: 4

Composer

Francisco J. Núñez is the founder and artistic director of the award-winning Young People's Chorus of New York City in residence at the 92nd Street Y. He has also served as the director of music for the Children's Aid Society in New York City for eight years. An active composer, conductor, and pianist, he conducts of the University Glee Club of New York City.

In 2001 Núñez initiated an annual broadcast concert series featuring premieres of newly commissioned works by some of the world's leading composers for treble voices. This concert series, Transient Glory, is partnered with a choral publishing series through Boosey & Hawkes and a CD with Vital Records. Núñez is a well-known figure in new music and music education, a frequent conductor for national and regional honor ensembles, and a lecturer on multicultural music and the child voice.

Núñez's compositions are inspired by Latin culture and musical idioms. Highly praised for both their consistent high quality and fusion of musical elements, many of his choral works have already found a firm place in both children's and advanced treble repertoire. His instrumental works have been programmed by leading soloists and ensembles such as Hu Hwang, the Bialystok State Orchestra, and Earnestine Rodgers Robinson. His numerous commissions include those from Disney World, the Phoenix Boys Choir, the Austin ProChorus, the Oklahoma All-State Chorus, and the Ithaca College Women's Chorale, who recently recorded all his treble choral works under the direction of Janet Galván.

Núñez studied piano with Seymour Bernstein and Sergei Edelmann and composition with Nils Vigeland, Ursula Mamlok, and Morton Gould. He holds degrees from New York University, and the University of Calgary and the artist-teacher diploma from the Choral Music Experience Institute.

Composition and Historical Perspective

"Yet Gentle Will the Griffen Be" is the third and final song from the set *What Grandpa Told the Children*, based on three texts by the American poet Vachel Lindsay. Both "Griffen" and the first piece, "What the Grey-Winged Fairy Said," come from Lindsay's collection *Twenty Poems in Which the Moon is the Principal Figure of Speech*. The middle piece, "The Sun Says His Prayers," from a separate collection of Lindsay's poems, provides a textual contrast to the outer movements. All three poems are highly visual descriptions of their subjects, and as such Núñez carefully sets the music to illustrate the action in the poems. In the case of "Griffen," which describes a fantastical monster with the head and wings of an eagle and the body of a lion, the unison melody soars above a highly independent piano accompaniment, portraying the Griffen's ominous encounter with the moon.

Poet Vachel Lindsay (1879–1931) was born in Springfield, Illinois, and was one of the first advocates of a style known as jazz poetry. He was known as the Prairie Troubadour because he traveled much of the country on foot selling his poetry. Once a well-respected and highly recognized poet on the level of his contemporaries Carl Sandburg and Edgar Lee Masters, he is virtually forgotten today. His best know poems include "The Congo," "General William Booth Enters into Heaven," and "Abraham Lincoln Walks at Midnight," all of which present complicated, political, controversial themes with a highly individualized approach to sound and rhythm. Lindsey also produced a great deal of more light-hearted verse like "Griffen" and its companion pieces that are well suited for exploration by school-aged children.

Technical Considerations and Musical Elements

"Yet Gentle Will the Griffen Be" is an exceptional and highly approachable piece in a distinctly less familiar tonality for treble choirs. While it is essential that the conductor clearly know and understand what the function of the pitch content is at any given moment, it is preferable, particularly for younger choirs, to solfege in familiar major tonalities whenever possible (for example, C Lydian solfeged in G major) to lock in clear and consistent intervallic relationships that will remain throughout the piece. Work toward complete vowel and pitch uniformity in the opening intervals in m. 4 and again in their inversions in the return at m. 40; the purity of these opening pitch ideas sets up the innocence of the poem as a whole as well as the harmonic and intervallic complexity encountered later in the piece.

When working in octatonic sections, try isolating a cell within a specific tonality; when this idea is then sequenced (e.g., mm. 46–48), have the choir sing each ascending group within its own "tonality" rather than as a series of chromatic intervals. As always, a light, pure, sound supported on the breath will allow the voices to soar easily above the piano line in tune; if the vocal line is well-supported from the beginning, it will allow the choir the flexibility to meet the wide dynamic contrasts expected in the piece and minimize any potential balance problems between the piano and the choir.

The piano accompaniment is highly independent from the vocal line and requires a pianist with some technical facility and a piano in good playing condition to be successful. The indicated tempo markings are correct; make sure that you and your pianist can maintain them (if possible, err toward the quicker side of the tempo indications). Although the vocal and piano lines ultimately mesh seamlessly, it is advisable to thin out the accompaniment during the early learning stages so that both the conductor and the choir can concentrate on developing the purity of the vocal line without the added complexity of active and extended harmonies; however, try to preserve the bass line and triadic harmony whenever possible.

"Griffen" also poses several conducting challenges that need to be thought out and practiced carefully *before* addressing the choir. There are two-against-three cross rhythms throughout the piece; while in general it is always best to go with the vocal groupings, there are instances (e.g., mm. 5–8) where it is preferable to alternate between a two and three pattern. There also are several controlled ritardandos that would benefit from a change in metric pattern. Two examples with potential solutions are the shift from a two to a three pattern in mm. 11–12 and a shift from two to a subdivided two pattern in mm. 34–35. In all instances, be sure to snap immediately back into tempo after the ritard. Pay careful and considerable attention to *all* transitions so that it is absolutely clear to the choir what the conductor intends. Lastly, give the caesura at m. 25 adequate time to build suspense before continuing on. It is a major signal in the piece that things are about to change, and rushing through it will lessen the impact of what follows.

Stylistic Considerations

While composing "Griffen," Núñez set out to create a contemporary art song for young voices that was compositionally complex and yet within the abilities of the performers and consistent with audience expectations. As such, the piece is a tour de force in text painting, from the gentle rocking of the opening melody to the wild flight of the piano lines and the raucous energy of the middle section. It is essential to remember throughout the rehearsal and performance process (despite *and* because of the technical challenges) the sheer wonderment and excitement (mixed with just a little bit of fear) of the text and to communicate those thoughts and feelings directly to the audience. The huge contrasts in dynamics, vocal color, and tempo all serve to reinforce Lindsay's text. Work diligently with the choir to capture every indicated nuance in the score, and take the time to discuss why Núñez sets the text in the manner he does.

Mm. 25–37 (the laughing and crying section) constitute the dramatic center of the piece and will need careful attention to ensure that the final result sounds natural, not stilted. Be very precise with the initial sixteenth note rhythms so they appear to be a momentary quaver in the voice. As the section continues, the choir should freely break into laughter; develop a cue so portions of the choir begin laughing while others continue to maintain the minor second trill. Ultimately, the whole choir should "devolve" into hysterical laughter that sounds completely unplanned.

The piano is a good guide for mood throughout the piece, particularly in the center section. It should sound like a slightly off-kilter circus act that the choir can use as a springboard to react to. Be certain that the laughter fades away to nothing into the transition at m. 30. Stress the initial pitch on each "cry" (mm. 34–37) so the effect is almost a sigh, much like the sigh of regaining composure after a nervous laughing fit. The C-sharp in m. 36 is a transitional pivot harmonically as well as for the text; sing lightly on the top of the pitch so that the audience's attention is on the wonderful gentleness of the transition and not on the tuning.

Choirs find that "Griffen" is a highly rewarding piece well-worth its initial challenge because it demonstrates both beauty of tone as well as deeply dramatic character, a combination that is often difficult to find, particularly in unison literature. Younger and more advanced treble groups will delight audiences with this piece. The choir will also find it satisfying because there is always something more to explore musically and dramatically; "Griffen" holds up extremely well for repeat performances.

Form and Structure

This piece makes extensive use of the interplay between the major and minor second intervals. Frequent use of Lydian mode (raised fourth), octatonic, and whole tone scales, which deprive the piece of a strong pull between tonic and dominant tonalities, give it an exotic yet wholly attainable sound in keeping with the mysterious nature of the griffen's journey. The sectional and interior divisions of the vocal and piano line frequently overlap; when this occurs, the analysis uses the vocal line to designate new material.

The piece divides unequally into five sections, which can be grouped loosely together to provide an ABA´-like structure with a coda with sections I and II constituting the initial A section, section III providing B content, and sections IV and V providing the return and a coda.

SECTION	MEASURE	EVENT AND SCORING
Section I		Twelve measures (3 + 4 + 3 + 2)
	1–7	C Lydian (F-sharp = raised fourth)
	8–12	Octatonic cell repeated and sequenced
Section II		Twelve measures [4 + 3 + 5 (2 + 3)]
	13–18	Pivot to F major (B-flat—alternatively, a shift to C Mixolydian); subsequent shift to F Lydian—modal mixture with F-sharp and B-flat
	19–24	Octatonic scale content, first in voices, then in piano; caesura at m. 25
Section III		Fifteen measures [6 (3 + 3) + 5 (2 + 3) + 4]
	25–29	Whole tone pattern to minor second trill to uncontrolled laughing
	30–39	Octatonic content
Section IV		Twelve measures [6 (2 + 2 + 2) + 3 + 4]
	40–45	Return to C Lydian
	46–48	Octatonic cell, ascending sequence
	49–52	Whole tone scale content
Section V		Eight measures (3 + 2 + 3)
	53–60	Return to C Lydian

Text

The moon? It is a griffin's egg,
Hatching to-morrow night.
And how the little boys will watch
With shouting and delight
To see him break the shell and stretch
And creep across the sky.
The boys will laugh. The little girls,
I fear, may hide and cry.
Yet gentle will the griffin be,
Most decorous and fat,
And walk up to the milky way
And lap it like a cat.

—Vachel Lindsay
from *Twenty Poems in Which the Moon Is the Principal Figure of Speech*

Please note: while Lindsay's original poem spells the mythical creature as "griffin," Núñez titled his setting with the spelling "griffen." Both spellings are acceptable.

Suggested Listening

Núñez, Francisco J. "Yet Gentle Will the Griffen Be" on *Cantan: The Treble Works of Francisco J. Núñez,* Janet Galván, Ithaca College Women's Chorale, Ithaca College, available from www.ypc.org/store/.

Contributed by:

Michael Lippert

Teacher Resource Guide

I Am His Child

Moses Hogan

(1957–2003)

SSA and piano
Alliance: AMP 0349
Overall: 2
Vocal: 2
Tonal/Rhythm: 2

Composer

Moses George Hogan was born March 13, 1957 in New Orleans, Louisiana. He studied music at the New Orleans Center for Creative Arts, Oberlin Conservatory of Music, the Juilliard School of Music, and Louisiana State University in Baton Rouge. An accomplished pianist, Hogan began focusing on choral music in 1980 when he formed his New World Ensemble, through which the Moses Hogan Chorale was formed. Recordings of his arrangements include those for the 1995 PBS documentary *The American Promise*, and performances by the Mormon Tabernacle Choir and Derek Lee Ragin are widely available. Tragically, Hogan died young on February 11, 2003.

Composition and Historical Perspective

"I Am His Child" is one of Moses Hogan's original compositions. Unlike his spiritual arrangements, it is in modern gospel style arranged for SSA choir with piano accompaniment. It is also available for SATB choir and for solo voice with piano. This SSA arrangement of the song is very useful for a choir of young girls. Both the text and the level of difficulty are perfect for young singers. The pop-like tune and harmonies are immediately appealing to a wide variety of performers and audiences alike—prevented from being saccharine or trite by the sophisticated piano part.

Technical Considerations and Musical Elements

This piece is quite easy. With an elaborate piano accompaniment, the vocal parts are homophonic when they are not unison. There is a very small amount of easy-to-learn, jazzy chromaticism and even less syncopation. Both the melody and the harmonies are singable and tuneful. The verses and the refrain are consistent throughout. Because of the simplicity of the musical elements, it would make a great vehicle for teaching vocal production early in the school year. The time you don't have to spend teaching pitches and rhythms you can spend working on developing a deeper understanding of their voices.

The syllabic text setting can easily sound "talky" or chatty and lose forward motion and legato. Ways to avoid this include:

- Hissing while audiating the parts with the accompaniment playing, creating a continuous line of music.
- Singing on a single neutral vowel with no consonant or humming parts.
- Singing the words without the consonants, changing vowels consistently and smoothly.
- Singing the words completely, but on just one pitch, connecting vowels and consonants so they feel glued to each other.
- Singing the words and music together but slowly. Imagine singing through the consonants as much as the vowels, continuously flowing from syllable to syllable with no bumps or jerking in between.

The range is quite low for most high school girls and younger trebles—probably comfortable for most, but in the ideal range of only a few and bordering on too low for some. This will make balance a challenge. The higher part, being easier to sing, will naturally be much louder than lower parts, so consider having fewer singers on the top part and more singers on the middle and bottom parts.

The unison part goes down to an A below middle C, and the highest part only goes up to a fourth-line D. It is important that even in this low/middle range girls use head voice to refine the sound. In order to encourage this:

- Ask them to sing softly at first to prevent the tone from getting heavy. They can imagine that they are excited about what that are singing but must keep it a secret.
- Play recordings during rehearsal. Though the Moses Hogan Chorale never recorded this piece, they recorded plenty of gospel music—always with a warm, rich tone, never shouty or inaccurate. Have students listen to examples like this and even write a list of words to describe the tone. They can compare the singing style of pop and

gospel singers they hear on the radio and television to the sound of these gospel singers. Discuss why it's appropriate for the style.

- Use neutral syllables like "du" and "do" to aid in creating a round, warm, heady tone.
- Emphasize that the imagination controls the voice. Let them try singing part of the piece imagining one mood and then another. Using this demonstration, explain that they can make any sound they imagine, and encourage them to learn to imagine more possibilities for their voices. Especially with adolescent girls, the transition into a tonal concept of a "woman's" voice is tricky. Finally, ask them to determine the mood of the piece and begin trying to capture that in their voices.

The marking "with feeling" opens the door for this discussion. Use images to determine a specific goal for the sound of the piece: If it were a color, what color would it be? Would the color change anywhere? Can they imagine that kind of color in their voices? If it were a landscape painting, what would be in it? Calm weather or stormy? Mountains, ocean, or prairie? Or, if they were dancers, what kind of dance would they do to this piece?

Stylistic Considerations

This piece calls for warmth of tone and rich, full vocal production. A tinny, shallow, bright sound, combined with the song's simplicity, would make for a cartoonish, superficial performance. Singers should not be encouraged to use chest voice to achieve a gospel tone—this would more likely result in a shouty, harsh pop sound. Instead, they need to sing with focused sound and perform with intent and sincerity to create the earthy color and character of gospel.

However, some scooping up to pitches and stylistic ornamentation would also be really appropriate. Not all the singers have to agree on what to add or when, but it will be at your discretion to draw the line between ornamentation and a big aural mess.

The dramatic, theatrical development of this song's style and would make it suitable for a concert closer if the sacred text is acceptable in your school.

Form and Structure

Section	Measures
Piano introduction	1–3
Verse	4–11 and 4–10 and 12
Refrain	13–21
Verse	22–28
Refrain	29–37
Verse	38–43
Coda	44–51

Text

The text is by Moses Hogan and can be very personal for young singers. The text is sacred, of course, but quite ecumenical. The refrain in particular is intensely religious. For schools where sacred music raises eyebrows, be prepared to defend your selection of this song with all the musical elements it teaches—homophonic texture, parallel harmonies, its usefulness in teaching vocal production, and so on. You may also need to discuss how singers can approach performance of a piece with a text that may not describe their own personal beliefs. Use examples from theater and secular music you're performing to illustrate.

Contributed by:

Amelia Nagoski

Teacher Resource Guide

I Once Loved a Lad

arr. Michael Neaum

SSA and piano
Theodore Presser Company: 312-41750
Overall 2
Vocal: 2
Tonal/Rhythm: 3

Composer

Michael Neaum has been the accompanist for the acclaimed choir Cantamus since 1973. Their repertoire includes many of Neaum's arrangements, which are beautifully crafted and singable by choirs of all levels. Many of these arrangements have been recorded by Cantamus, including the album *Michael Neaum's Arrangements*, produced in 1997. Neaum's arrangements are published by Theodore Presser Company, Banks Music Publications, and Oxford University Press and have been performed by choirs around the world. In addition, he has had works commissioned by many choirs, including the Newfoundland Symphony Youth Choir, which performed his arrangement of the national anthem for Her Majesty the Queen.

Neaum holds both undergraduate and graduate degrees from Birmingham University where he was a recipient of both the Barber Undergraduate and Graduate Scholarships. He has extensive international experience as an accompanist. His arrangements are widely appealing because of their striking use of texture and color and melodic interest.

Composition and Historical Perspective

"I Once Loved a Lad" is a setting of a well-known Celtic folk song for three-part women's voices with piano accompaniment. The melody is found primarily in the first soprano voice with the second soprano and alto parts providing harmony both in cannon and chordal style. There is also a section of whispered cannon, which provides for a creative texture.

This modern setting of the folk song was first published in 1997. While the melodic material remains true, the setting has a contemporary feel with its unusual phrase structure and inventive use of whispered vocal lines. The harmonies are also contemporary with an abundance of ninth chords and occasional cluster harmonies in the piano accompaniment. The piano provides a great deal of rhythmic interest and helps to color the change in mood of each verse.

Technical Considerations and Musical Elements

Like many Celtic folk songs, this piece is in the Mixolydian mode. This presents an intonation challenge to singers if they are not aurally immersed in the mode. The tuning of the seventh scale degree is problematic and must be reinforced as a whole step away from the tonic. I have found it helpful to use simple echo drills on the tonic (Sol, Ti, Re) and subtonic (Fa, La, Do) patterns in different combinations. The difficulty lies in hearing the subtonic relationship of a whole step rather than a leading tone relationship of a half step. The singing of simple rote tunes in mixolydian such as "Old Joe Clark" would also be helpful to prepare the aural skills of the choir.

This piece is in triple meter and has a nice lilting feel when taken at the andante tempo. The tempo remains consistent until the final phrase, which slows to the final piano arpeggio. Encouraging a sense of motion throughout the phrases will help the choir to sing the tune musically. I have often employed physical movements to help the choir feel the length and stretch of the music so that the melody retains a sense of forward motion.

While the pitches of the main theme are easily learned, the rhythm presents a bit of a challenge. The dotted eighth–sixteenth–eighth pattern and the sixteenth–dotted eighth–eighth pattern alternate throughout the melody. Some drill with rhythm syllables on these two patterns will go far in making the two rhythms distinct. Good emphasis on the consonants will also help the alternating rhythms to be precise and clear.

The rhythmic variety of this arrangement is enhanced by the alternating use of 6/8 and 9/8 in each phrase. The result is a phrase structure that contains two equal phrases per verse that appear aurally uneven because of the change in strong beat placement within each phrase. Each phrase alternates measure length with the result being four measures of 3 + 2 + 2 + 3. The measures are not marked with the changes, which makes it incumbent upon the conductor to be clear with his or her beat pattern. All of the phrases begin with a pickup, which contributes to the lilting, almost skipping feeling, of the piece. Rhythmically impelling the macrobeat of the pickup will help the choir spring off the beat and sing the pitches with energy, avoiding any slowing in tempo, which is a common problem in phrases beginning with an anacrusis.

Each verse has it's own treatment both harmonically and texturally. The opening of the piece is *a cappella* and full at a *mezzo forte* volume. It is a bold opening, which needs clear, bright vowels, clean intonation, and careful diction to highlight the touch of sarcasm in the text. The texture becomes increasingly thick with the voices moving in accented rhythms and interesting suspensions. The fourth verse lightens up considerably, and the second soprano and alto parts have a whispered canon in response to the soprano melody. This whispered section requires a great deal of breath and exaggerated consonants to keep the text clear. The soprano melody in the final verse is accompanied by the second soprano and alto entering at the end of the phrases and divided into three parts. These chords should be more legato in character than the previous verses with the consonants minimized and the vowels clear and unified. The verse has a gradual *decrescendo*, and the final phrase is punctuated by a whispered "hush" from the lower parts.

Stylistic Considerations

Folk music is so appealing because it is simple. Melodies are easily passed down through generations by grandmothers and grandfathers singing the songs they grew up with to their children and grandchildren. The Celtic folk music tradition is rich with varied melodies and a distinctive style of quick moving notes almost like grace notes, which make the music very rhythmic. The dotted rhythms and the sixteenth passing notes need to have a slight accent to bring them into the forefront of the melody. Encouraging the choir to sing with fluid lilting phrases will make this piece a valuable addition to your choir's repertoire.

Form and Structure

The overall form of the piece is a strophic song with five repetitions of the verse. Each verse is set with a different accompaniment and/or vocal texture.

Section	Measure	Event and Scoring
Verse 1	1–9	A *cappella*
Verse 2	10–18	Vocal parts predominantly unison, piano accompaniment alternating between chordal and arpeggiated texture
Verse 3	19–27	Thicker texture in the vocal parts and piano accompaniment

Section	Measure	Event and Scoring
Verse 4	28–39	Soprano melody, second soprano and alto in a whispered canon; piano accompaniment is lighter in the treble clef with a repeated arpeggiated figure
Verse 5	40–49	Soprano melody with chordal punctuation from soprano 2 divisi and alto; predominance of open-fifth harmonies in the accompaniment

Text

I once loved a lad, and I loved him so well
That I hated all others that spoke of him ill;
But now he's rewarded me well for my love,
For he's gone to be wed to another.

When I saw my love to the church go
With bride and bridesmaidens, they made a fine show,
And I followed on with a heart full of woe!
For he's gone to be wed to another!

When I saw my love sit down to dine,
I sat down beside him and I poured him some wine;
And I drank to the laddie that should have been mine;
But now he is wed to another.

The men in the forest, they ask it of me
How many strawberries are in the salt sea;
And I ask them back with a tear in my e'e,
How many ships sail in the forest.

So dig me a grave, and dig it so deep,
And cover it over with flowers so sweet;
And I will turn in for to take a long sleep,
And maybe, in time, I'll forget him.

Additional References and Resources

Jordan, James, and Marilyn Shenenberger. *Ear Training Immersion Exercises for Choirs*. Chicago: GIA Publications, 2004.

Jordan, James, and Matthew Mehaffey. *Choral Ensemble Intonation*. Chicago: GIA Publications, 2001.

Contributed by:

Rae Jean Teeter

Teacher Resource Guide

Ich wollt', meine Lieb'

Felix Mendelssohn

(1809–1847)

SA or TB with piano
National Music Publishers: NMP-146
Overall: 2
Vocal: 2
Tonal/Rhythm: 2

Composer

Born in Hamburg, Germany, in 1809 into a wealthy banking family, Felix Mendelssohn began taking piano lessons at the age of six and made his first public performance at the age of nine. By age thirteen he had written his first published work, a piano quartet, and by fourteen had composed twelve symphonies. Throughout adolescence he and his older sister, Fanny, also a virtuosic pianist and composer, were privileged to have their music performed by a private orchestra in their parents' Berlin garden home.

Mendelssohn, considered the greatest young musical prodigy after Mozart, would go on to compose operas, art songs, chamber works, symphonic works, and oratorios, including the monumental *St. Paul* and *Elijah*.

Also a gifted conductor, he is credited with reviving the music of J. S. Bach. At the age of twenty Mendelssohn's 1829 performance of Bach's *St. Matthew Passion* in Leipzig was particularly successful in bringing Bach's music out of relative obscurity. Mendelssohn's subsequent appointment in 1835 as conductor of the Leipzig Gewandhaus Orchestra would earn the composer international acclaim.

His declining health during the final years of his life was exacerbated by the death of his sister Fanny in May 1847. Quite depressed, he died six months later from a series of strokes. Clearly Mendelssohn's legacy is a body of music that exemplifies the tension between Classicism and Romanticism in the generation after Beethoven. Unlike many of his contemporaries, Mendelssohn's compositions were influenced by the great eighteenth-century masters: Bach for fugal technique, Handel for chord progressions and rhythm, Mozart for form and texture, and Beethoven for instrumental technique.

Composition and Historical Perspective

Completed in 1836, "Ich wollt', meine Lieb'" was first published in 1844 as part of a set of six pieces for soprano duet and piano under the title *Sechs zweistimmige Lieder,* Op. 63. Mendelssohn composed songs like "Ich wollt', meine Lieb'" as well as chamber works and orchestral pieces for private performance in his home's salon. In early nineteenth-century German society it was customary for the family along with invited guests to retire to the salon after dinner for an evening of musical entertainment.

Many solo German songs (lieder) had their first performances in such venues. Often composers would experiment with songs for two or more voices. These songs became known as partsongs. Twentieth-century choral ensembles have borrowed such German partsongs for concert performance. Brahms's *Zigeunerlieder* and *Liebeslieder Walzer,* for instance, are now standard choral repertoire even though these pieces were originally performed one person to a part.

Mendelssohn's use of the subtle and modest piano accompaniment in "Ich wollt', meine Lieb'" clearly demonstrates the influence of his teacher, the north German composer Carl Zelter. As in much of Mendelssohn's song literature, this piece is strophic with a modified last verse. Unlike with Schubert, there is little hint of drama, character, or text declamation. Instead, the beautiful melody dominates the Heinrich Heine poem, attaining the simplicity of a folk song.

Though Mendelssohn's solo and duet lieder do not rank among his most significant works, these partsongs contribute intimate and moderately easy two-part music to the treble or men's chorus repertoire.

Technical Considerations and Musical Elements

Given the horizontal nature of this piece, rehearsal with the choir should begin on the neutral syllable "doo." Careful attention to the choral tone must ensure that the tone is neither too bright nor that it falls into the throat. The majority of the work is homophonic, so the success of this piece will lie in the absolute rhythmic precision of the initial consonant while maintaining long legato phrases. Once the singers have achieved a good ensemble sound on the neutral syllable and are able to sing the harmonies absolutely in tune, move to the German text. Much attention must be given to the diction of the German so that it is sung as legato as possible. Overly enunciated pronunciation will disturb the legato.

This is an excellent piece for teaching solfege in compound meter. Because it has very few accidentals, this piece will facilitate a rather simple path to reinforcing diatonic sight-singing.

Stylistic Considerations

Because Mendelssohn composed "Ich wollt', meine Lieb'" as a soprano duet, the performance of this piece should mirror German art song style but with the simplicity of a folk song. The conductor should avoid dramatic, operatic gestures, ensuring that the piece remains an intimate chamber work. Unlike songs of Schubert or Wolf in which each line or even each word of the text is carefully declaimed through musical means, Mendelssohn paints an overall picture of the text in the music.

The first line of the poem, "I wish my pain would flow into a single word, which I'd give to the airy winds, who would carry it merrily along," is beautifully demonstrated in the airy, flowing accompaniment—not in word by word text painting. As in much of Mendelssohn's song literature, the beautiful melody of this piece overshadows the text. This should be the starting point for rehearsing. Work horizontally to achieve long, legato lines. Overly declamatory treatment of the text would be inappropriate and out of character. Instead allow the lovely harmonies to be buoyant and light as are the images depicted in the poem. The accompanist should be careful not to overpower but support the ensemble.

Form and Structure

The work is strophic with a modified third verse. The key is E major.

Text and Translation

Ich wollt', meine Lieb' ergösse *Sich all in ein einzig Wort,* *Das gäb' ich den lust'gen Winden,* *Die trügen es lustig fort.*	I wish my pain would flow Into a single word, Which I'd give to the airy winds, Who would carry it merrily along.
Sie tragen zu dir, Geliebte,	They would carry it to you, my beloved,
Das lieb-erfüllte Wort; *Du hörst es zu jeder Stunde,* *Du hörst es an jedem Ort.*	The pain-filled word; You hear it always, You hear it everywhere.

Und hast du zum nächtlichen Schlummer	And scarcely have you closed your eyes
Geschlossen die Augen kaum,	To night-time slumbers,
So wird mein Bild dich verfolgen	My image will follow you,
Bis in den tiefsten Traum.	Into your deepest dream.

Additional References and Resources

Randel, Don Michael, ed. *The Harvard Biographical Dictionary of Music.* Cambridge: The Belknap Press of Harvard University, 1996.

Sadie, Stanley, ed. *The New Grove Dictionary of Music and Musicians.* 2nd ed. New York: Grove, 2001.

Suggested Listening

The following recordings have the duet as performed by solo voices.

Felix Mendelssohn:

"Ich wollt', meine Lieb'" on *Mendelssohn: Songs and Duets*, Nathan Berg and Sophie Daneman, Hyperion CD66906.

"Ich wollt', meine Lieb'" on *Dvorak, Schumann, and Mendelssohn*, Marilyn Horne and Frederica von Stade, RCA 61681.

Contributed by:

James Bowyer

Teacher Resource Guide

J'entends le moulin
arr. Donald Patriquin

SS with piano and percussion, earthsongs: W-10
SATB, earthsongs: S-06
Overall: 2
Vocal: 2
Tonal/Rhythm: 3

Composer

Donald Patriquin was born in 1938 in Sherbrooke, Quebec. He completed all of his music studies in his native country of Canada, both at McGill in Montreal and the University of Toronto. In 1978 he began teaching theory and composition at McGill, as well as directing ensembles. In 1996 Patriquin retired from McGill and returned to eastern Quebec, where he lives and works as a composer.

As a composer, Patriquin's output includes works for a variety of ensemble sizes and make-ups, both choral and instrumental. An avid proponent of folksong repertoire, he has established a prominent reputation as an arranger of folk tunes, particularly those from French-speaking Canada. His original works, both small and large-scale, have also earned him great respect as a composer of contemporary music concerned with issues of global importance. Patriquin's choral music is published by earthsongs, A Tempo, and Canadian International Music.

Composition and Historical Perspective

"J'entends le moulin" was published in 1993 as the result of a commission by the Chorale of the Protestant School Board of Greater Montreal (now the English Montreal School Board Chorale). The work is based on the French folk tune "Mon père a fait batir maison," which is cataloged in the 1880 folk-song collection *Chanson populaires du Canada* by Ernest Gagnon.

The work was originally composed for two-part treble choir (soprano 1, soprano 2), piano, and optional percussion. Although Patriquin has arranged a version for SATB choir with the same instrumentation, this article concerns the two-part version.

Technical Considerations and Musical Elements

"J'entends le moulin" is based on a delightful melody that, like that of many folk songs, is short, encompasses a limited range, and is easily singable. The two voice parts interact with each other in two primary ways: alternating lines of verse and through counterpoint.

"J'entends le moulin" calls for four percussion instruments: triangle, finger cymbals, woodblock, and sticks. Conductor may wish to obtain trained percussionists to perform the piece, in which case at least two people would be needed. The parts are not difficult, however, and could ostensibly be performed by members of the choir with minimal coaching. During one four-measure passage (mm. 118 to the downbeat of 122) all percussion instruments are indicated, resulting in the need for more than two percussionists. At this point, if outside percussionists are used, the conductor may either omit two of the instruments from the passage or assign them to choir members. Due to the difficulty the piano part, an accomplished pianist is needed for a successful performance of the work.

For non-French speakers, the most challenging aspect of "J'entends le moulin" for singers is mastering the text at Patriquin's indicated tempo of *vif* (quarter note = 120+). At this tempo, learning the text and proper diction will take some dedicated rehearsal time, even for those who have experience singing French texts. For basic French pronunciation guidelines, there are a number of resources a director may consult, e.g., William May and Craig Tolin's *Pronunciation Guide for Choral Literature* (MENC, 1987) and Thomas Grubb's *Singing in French* (5th ed., Wadsworth, 1997). During rehearsals, it is advisable to spend considerable time rehearsing text only, beginning at a slow tempo and gradually increasing. Because of the highly rhythmic nature of the work, percussion effects may also be added before any notes are learned.

Form and Structure

Patriquin has cleverly structured the work into nine "verses" of two-line couplets. After the first verse, each successive couplet begins with the final line of the preceding verse. This textual dovetailing imbues the work with a seamless quality and, combined with recurring energetic rhythmic motives, provides a musical depiction of the millwheel. The line "J'entends le moulin, tique tique taque" is used as a quasi-refrain, occurring throughout the piece.

An interesting use of contrapuntal augmentation may be seen in verses 8 and 9 and in the final statement of the quasi-refrain at the end. This textbook example of a basic compositional technique provides an excellent teaching opportunity for a conductor of school choirs.

Text and Translation

The text for "J'entends le moulin" is somewhat typical of early folksong repertoire with its references to rural imagery associated with daily life of working-class people, e.g., the millwheel, carpentry, and cooking. While a bawdy storyline is evident in the text, the form of the poem is based around a contrived rhyming scheme, in that each line of text, aside from the first line, ends with the same rhyme.

J'entends le moulin tique tique taque.	I hear the millwheel, tique tique taque.
Mon père a fait batir maison. *L'a fait batir à trois pignons.* *Sont trois charpentiers qui la font.* *Le plus jeune c'est mon mignon.*	My father is having a house built. It is being built with three gables. There are three carpenters building it. The youngest is my darling.
Qu'apportes-tu dans ton jupon? *C'est un pâté de trois pigeons.* *Asseyons-nous et le mangeons.*	What have you in your apron? It is a three-pigeon pie. Let us sit and eat it.
En s'asseyant il fit un bond, *Qui fait trembler mer et poissons,* *Et les cailloux qui sont au fond.*	While sitting it makes a leap Which makes the sea and fish tremble, And the stones which are at the bottom.

Additional References and Resources

Jonas, Holly Higgins, ed. *In Their Own Words: Canadian Choral Conductors.* Toronto, Ontario: Dundurn Press, 2001.

Vachon, Jean-Pascal. "Patriquin, Donald." *Historica: The Canadian Encyclopedia.* Edited by James H. Marsh. http://www.thecanadianencyclopedia.com (accessed September 12, 2005).

Web sites:
Donald Patriquin: www.donaldpatriquin.com (accessed September 12, 2005)
The Canadian Music Centre: www.musiccentre.ca (accessed September 12, 2005)

Suggested Listening

Samples of many of Patriquin's works, including "J'entends le moulin," may be heard at the earthsongs Web site (http://www.earthsongsmus.com).

Contributed by:

Wayne Glass

Teacher Resource Guide

Morning Moon

Philip E. Silvey

(b. 1965)

SSA and piano
Santa Barbara Music Publishing: SBMP 406
Overall: 2
Vocal: 2
Tonal/Rhythm: 3

Composer

Philip Silvey was born and raised in the rural farmlands of west central Pennsylvania. He grew up in a large, musical family, studied piano from an early age, and actively participated in school music. He formally studied composition with William T. Allen at Houghton College and Burt Fenner and Bruce Trinkley at the Pennsylvania State University. In 1992 he began his career as a school vocal music teacher in Michigan, where he had the opportunity to prepare arrangements and original compositions for his choral students. After seven years of teaching, he returned to graduate school and studied at the University of Illinois at Urbana–Champaign, earning a doctorate in music education. He conducts the Women's Chorus and teaches undergraduate and graduate courses in music education at the University of Maryland.

Composition and Historical Perspective

The lyrical ballad "Morning Moon" grew out of the two-bar piano figure that now serves as the work's introduction. Silvey writes:

In summer 1995, I improvised this germinal motive at a piano after attending a choral reading session that inspired me to continue my own efforts to create original, innovative works. Over the course of the next year, through ongoing exploration at the piano, I developed an extended accompaniment, considered and revised melodic material through improvisatory singing, and began entertaining ideas for lyrics. On occasion, I had noticed the moon's lingering presence in the daylight while ascending the steps of my basement apartment on my way to school in the morning. Because of the unusual nature of these sightings, I thought the appearance of a visible moon in the daytime might carry some significance. This triggered the initial phrases of the poem that became the basis for the work's lyrics. Unlike many composers, I often begin a work by discovering an interesting harmonic progression at the piano and then adding melody and lyrics as they develop organically, in conjunction with the piano accompaniment. Ultimately, I decided to arrange this work for treble voices because an advanced women's ensemble I was teaching was invited to perform at a state invitational event.

Technical Considerations and Musical Elements

Although technically an SSA voicing, this piece uses a wide range of voice-part texture, from the initial use of unison to the seven-part divisi in m. 61. The need to shift smoothly between these textures poses a formidable challenge to singers, particularly ensembles that have a small number of singers. Teachers should not feel limited by the two-stave distribution of voice parts in the printed score but should assign divisi passages carefully, accounting for differing voice size and using a pyramidal approach with more or naturally stronger voices on the lower tones of the chord. Make an effort to balance the chord in m. 45 so that the dissonance created by the B-natural is present and in tune. It may be instructive to use solfege syllables to enable singers to relate the leading tone to the tonic (Ti and Do) in this chord. At least one or two first sopranos must be able to comfortably sustain a high G on a *diminuendo* to create the desired effect in the penultimate measure. For this reason, most voices should be assigned to sing the lowest notes of mm. 72 and 73. At the designated tempo, singers may find it difficult to keep the recurring C of the refrain from falling in pitch (starting in m. 17), particularly in light of the varied use of *crescendo* and *decrescendo*. A steady column of energized breath, along with the use of a brightened "ah" vowel on the word "rise" should help singers avoid this potential pitfall.

Stylistic Considerations

Although phrase marks do not appear over the vocal lines, singers should endeavor to keep all phrases seamlessly connected. The whimsical nature of the text (the speaker addresses the moon) requires an expressive, romanticized treatment. Use syllabic stress to shape motives (e.g., stressing the first syllable of the word "spherical" in m. 23 and elsewhere), but also attend to the effects of using musical stress (e.g., stressing the singer's initial F-sharp as it forms a tritone with the bass note of the accompaniment, then receding dynamically on the G that follows, highlighting the harmonic resolution while painting a more vivid aural gesture). Apply this kind of thought throughout the piece, choosing a combination of syllabic and musical stresses to optimally balance both melodic shape and text expression. Treat mm. 51–61 as a recitative, making liberal use of rubato and briefly pausing between phrases when appropriate. Consider the way an orator might perform a public reading of the poem, and use this as a basis for developing ideas for interpretive treatment.

Form and Structure

This work adheres primarily to a strophic song formula with added developments with each new verse and refrain. In the second refrain, singers should sound and feel emboldened. At the end of the contrasting section in mm. 51–61, as the tempo broadens, the work builds through its climax to m. 62, when the final refrain arrives and must be sung with fullness and conviction without weakening the sound when the singers transition into five-part divisi. The overall structure can be divided as follows:

Section	Measure	Event and Scoring
Introduction	1–4	Two phrases (2 + 2)
Verse 1	5–16	Three phrases (4 + 4 + 4)
Refrain	17–28	Three phrases (4 + 4 + 4)
Verse 2	29–40	Three phrases (4 + 4 + 4)
Refrain	41–50	Two phrases (4 + 6)
Bridge	51–61	Four phrases (2 + 2 + 2 + 5)
Refrain and coda	62–75	Four phrases (4 + 4 + 2 + 4)

Text

The original text explores the phenomenon of a moon still visible after the sun has risen. The speaker urges the moon to persist and sustains a one-sided conversation, exploring aspects of the moon's relationship to the sun. The open-ended text lends itself to various interpretations, one of which may have sacred connotations. In this interpretation, the moon serves as a type of Christ, with the sun representing God the Father. The moon manifests the sun's light, as Christ the son is a manifestation of the Father. The phrase "ever faithful witness" correlates with the Davidic covenant reiterated in Psalm 89, verse 37, "It [David's lineage] will be established forever, like the moon, the faithful witness in the sky" (New International Version). In a more general way, the moon can serve to embody a person or emotion that is unseen but ever-present, often forgotten when overshadowed by its surrounding context. It was the composer's intention to leave the text open to interpretation, allowing the singer to investigate the potential meaning of the moon, always present in earth's orbit, frequently evident at night, but occasionally appearing in the brightness of daylight.

Suggested Listening

Santa Barbara Music Publishing CD 8 – Octavos 4, performed by the Allegan High School Women Chamber Choir, conducted by the composer.

Contributed by:

Philip Silvey

Teacher Resource Guide

There Is Sweet Music Here

Mary Lynn Lightfoot
(b. 1952)

SSA
Heritage Music Press: 15/1869H
Overall: 2
Vocal: 2
Tonal/Rhythm: 2

Composer

Mary Lynn Lightfoot is the choral editor for Heritage Music Press, the educational division of the Lorenz Corporation in Dayton, Ohio. Lightfoot is active as a guest conductor and clinician throughout North America and has published nearly two hundred choral compositions, arrangements, and musicals. She is clear that her intent is to create music with integrity, to allow everyone the opportunity to explore singing with a credible text well wedded to the voices and accompaniment. As she did for eight years during her public school and private school teaching, and still does for thousands of singers and conductors through workshops, clinics, and conventions, Lightfoot allows her students to grow musically with quality simplicity. She inspires and motivates school choirs, church choirs, and professionals alike.

Lightfoot received her BME from Truman State University, formerly Northeast Missouri State University–Kirksville, where she graduated *magna cum laude* and was the recipient of the Sigma Alpha Iota Award. In additional to her responsibilities in publishing and composing, she served for two years as an assistant director for the Mid-America Youth Chorale's Concert Tour of Europe and for six years as the director of youth choirs and assistant chancel choir director at Blue Ridge Presbyterian Church, Raytown, Missouri.

Lightfoot has received an annual ASCAP award for her compositions from the ASCAP Standard Awards Panel each year since 1988. In 1994 she was the recipient of the Luther T. Spayde Award for Missouri Choral Conductor of the Year, and in 2005 she was the recipient of the prestigious Opus Award for her SSA composition "The Rhodora." She recently served as editor on the book *Hogey's Journey: A Memoir by Eph Ehly*, currently available and published by Heritage Music Press.

Composition and Historical Perspective

"There Is Sweet Music Here" is an original song with text by Alfred, Lord Tennyson (1809–1892) from *Choric Song* from *The Lotos-Eaters* (see text following). Lightfoot had long desired to set this text to music and had the opportunity to do so upon a commission from the Kansas City Alumnae Chapter of Sigma Alpha Iota in honor of the National Centennial Year of Sigma Alpha Iota. "There Is Sweet Music Here" was originally set for women's voices (SSA) and published in 2004 by Heritage Music Press. "There Is Sweet Music Here" is now available for SATB.

Lightfoot intended the piece to offer both a message to an audience as well as a personal message that the singers can look inward and find the music within each one of them. Both the audience and the individual members of the choir find music within their beings and their souls.

Technical and Stylistic Considerations and Musical Elements

"There Is Sweet Music Here" includes a rich, full text. The sense of line is very important in the piece, rather than allowing the text to become overly rhythmic. Work to allow the word stress to emerge within the sense of forward motion and melodic line. Mm. 1–5 of "There Is Sweet Music Here" begins with an ethereal swirling canon with an optional solo in m. 2 to set the tone. The gentle flowing quality continues in unison through m. 14 with the introduction of harmony in m. 13.

Be aware of the melody and accompaniment that continue through m. 19. M. 20 brings beautiful text painting with the sense of passing the line from one voice to another. Note the pedal C in the accompaniment beginning in m. 26 *con moto* with the text "Here are cool mosses deep" and the *diminuendo* through m. 35 as the text again turns inward "from the craggy ledge the poppy hangs in sleep." Mm. 35–36 bring a return of the flowing urgency of the opening with another optional solo in m. 47 setting up the final canonic "There is sweet music here" and concluding with the simply powerful harmony of "sweet, sweet music" in mm. 50–51.

In m. 14, the seconds and altos share the string-like harmonic accompaniment on "There is sweet music here." This similar bowing effect is also found beginning in m. 36. The effect in m. 13 should include more of the timbre of violins and violas as opposed to m. 36 which elicits a richer cello or bass sensation. In the descending lines of "down" mm. 22–25 (melodically down, then down/up, then down again), keep the feeling free and healthy, especially in m. 23 with the rise again. Be sure to consider a round [a] throughout each figure before moving to the [u] in the second half of the diphthong on the final eighth note. The F-natural in the sopranos in m. 23 also requires a very light and delicate openness.

Form and Structure

MEASURE	EVENT AND SCORING
1–2	Piano and optional solo introduction, ***p***, quarter note = 60
3–5	Canonic voices with *crescendo*, "There is sweet music here" to ***mf***
6–13	Unison voices and piano accompaniment, ***mp***, added text "that softer falls than petals from blown roses on the grass," *poco a poco crescendo*, gently flowing quarter note = 72 with ritard in m. 13
14–19	Soprano melody, seconds and altos accompaniment with piano, ***mp***, a tempo, *crescendo* and *diminuendo* through m. 19 ("tired, tired eyes")
20–25	Alternating voices with piano accompaniment, *crescendo*, and *diminuendo* through "Music that brings sweet sleep down from blissful skies"
26–35	Homophonic voices with piano reinforcing, *con moto*, quarter note = 80.
36–41	Return of melodic ideas in mm. 6–11 with melody and accompaniment figure in the voices this time (originally unison voices).
42–47	Return of the melody, accompaniment, and text of mm. 20–25
47–50	Return of the opening material (mm. 2–5) in B-flat (as opposed to the opening G), tempo 1
50–52	Concludes with homophonic voicing and supportive arpeggiated piano with the final text "sweet, sweet, music" into the piano soli B-flat arpeggio with *diminuendo* (m. 52).

Text

From *Choric Song* from *The Lotos-Eaters* by Alfred, Lord Tennyson (1809–1892)

> There is sweet music here that softer falls
> Than petals from blown roses on the grass,
> Or night-dews on still waters between walls
> Of shadowy granite in a gleaming pass;
>
> Music that gentler on the spirit lies,
> Than tired eyelids upon tired eyes;
> Music that brings sweet sleep down from the blissful skies.
>
> Here are cool mosses deep,
> And thro' the moss the ivies creep,
> And in the stream the long-leaved flowers weep.
> And from the craggy ledge the poppy hangs in sleep.

Additional References and Resources

Schott, Sally. *Common Times* 22, vol. 4, 20–21. SW Division ACDA, 2003.

Suggested Listening

Mary Lynn Lightfoot, "There Is Sweet Music Here," *2004 Lorenz Demo Recording*, Mark Recording CD.

Contributed by:

Jennifer Haywood

Teacher Resource Guide

Ave, maris stella

Diane Loomer

(b. 1940)

TTBB with solo baritone
Cyprus Choral Music: CP 1007
Overall: 2
Vocal: 2
Tonal/Rhythm: 2

Composer

Diane Loomer, one of Canada's best-known musicians, has achieved international recognition as a choral conductor, teacher, and musician. An honors graduate of Gustavus Adolphus College and the University of British Columbia's School of Music, she is founder and conductor of the prize-winning men's choir, Chor Leoni and cofounder and codirector of the outstanding Elektra Women's Choir. She taught on the music faculty at the University of British Columbia. Her choral compositions have been published, performed, and recorded internationally, and she frequently appears on CBC national radio as a commentator on and champion of the classical arts in Canada. With the help of her husband, Diane has established Cypress Choral Music as a thriving source of Canadian choral music and an encouragement to Canadian choral composers.

Loomer has given lectures on her work at local, national, and international meetings of choral professionals and is a much sought-after clinician throughout the world. She continues to travel around the world conducting, leading workshops, and spreading good choral cheer. Some of her numerous honors and awards include being the first woman to conduct the National

Youth Choir of Canada. She was awarded the Healey Willan Prize for outstanding service to Canadian Music and named as Vancouver's Woman of Distinction of Arts and Culture by the YWCA in 1994. In 1997 she received a Distinguished Alumni Award honoring her achievements and leadership in choral music.

She co-conducted the Women's Honor Choir at the 1999 convention of the American Choral Director's Association in Chicago and in 2000 conducted the Minnesota Collegiate Honour Choir. Both her women's and men's choirs have repeatedly won first prizes in national competitions. She is a recipient of the Order of Canada, given in recognition of her achievements in and service to music and humanity, and was also awarded the Golden Jubilee Medal in honor of the fiftieth anniversary of Queen Elizabeth's accession to the Throne. Most recently she has been appointed to the University Women's Scholar Lecture Series by the University of Victoria.

Composition and Historical Perspective

"Ave, maris stella" is a twentieth-century motet for male chorus. Its homophonic texture and stepwise motion gives the reverent feel of a hymn. The composer writes about the piece:

> In 1997 my Chor Leoni Men's Choir was planning a tour to the Maritimes and wanted to take along a song that would relate to Nova Scotian audiences. I did a little research about the history of music on the East Coast of Canada and found this beautiful Latin canticle "Ave, maris stella" ("Hail, Star of the Sea"). The song reflects the character of the Acadian settlers in Nova Scotia. Their life as fishermen with their families sustained by the sea was hard, living conditions difficult, but their faith and devotion to the Church helped sustain them. In 1630 they adopted "Ave, maris stella" as their signature hymn. This beautiful song has been sung now for over 400 years and can still be heard at church services, festivals, and gatherings.
>
> Chor Leoni sang *Ave Maris Stella* for the first time in Cheticamp, Nova Scotia, in July 1997. It was the first piece on our programme and none of us could ever have anticipated the reaction we received. As the men sang, the audience quietly arose, tears running down their cheeks. There was long silence after we had finished—and then the applause started and continued on and on until we sang it again. We'll never forget that experience, and "Ave, maris stella" continues on as one of our standards in Canadian repertoire.

Technical Considerations and Musical Elements

This piece could be used successfully with singers of all ability levels. The musical and technical intricacies are limited to a few minor issues: the baritone soloist, four-part male singing, melody recognition, an editorial mistake, and Latin text. I have listed below several solutions and considerations to each of these problems in an effort to help conductors out.

The Baritone Soloist

Although this solo is limited to less than an octave in rage the singer must be able to sing musically. The nature of the melody and its limited range require that the singer and conductor develop a musical phrase shape that will attract and hold the listeners' attention. Work with your soloist to:

- Group the solo in four-bar phrases
- Articulate each consonant aggressively (no one else has text)
- Apply dynamic contrast
- Follow the arranger's suggestion at mm. 12–13 and ritard
- Shape the text accents

Four-Part Male Singing

Before programming this piece, the ensemble director must ensure that the ensemble has the necessary skill and numbers. The director should be confident that there are an equal number of skilled singers for each part. Many high school and college male groups serve as educational ensembles where young men learn the fundamentals of music and rehearsal expectation. This piece, while not difficult, will require four equally strong voice parts to be performed well.

Melody Recognition

The melody gets passed around between the baritone and the second tenor part from mm. 17–26. It will take special effort to bring it out of the texture. Shift of a few voices to make the melody heard more clearly.

An Editorial Mistake

There is one minor editorial issue of which you need to be aware. The measures are numbered incorrectly. In the most recent printing, on page two of the bottom system, the editors have labeled m. 17 incorrectly. The measure indicators are one off from this point to the end of the piece. Because it is a thirty-one-measure piece, it is not a significant problem, but becoming aware of it now may save you some time later. Also, on page 3, m. 24 the last half note in the bass line should be a D, not an E as shown.

Latin Text

As choral directors, we deal with Latin on a regular basis. I doubt that any one of us fears teaching a piece with Latin text. However, in listening to high school choirs there are noticeable common pitfalls. Below are the most egregious and frequent mispronunciations.

Vowel	Example	Problem
e	bed	Often too bright ("ay" instead of "eh"); sometimes even introduces the diphthong "aye" (it is not "Adoramus Tayee")
i	key	Sometimes pronounced "ih" instead of "ee," especially in the phrase "in excelsis"
o	fought	Often pronounced "oh" or "ohoo" as a diphthong) instead of "aw" (it is not "Glohria")
s	sip	*Not* "z," although slightly softened when it comes between two vowels

Translations and Annotations of Choral Repertoire Volume I: Sacred Latin Texts by Ron Jeffers is a wonderful Latin text, and some of the suggestions above come from his book.

Stylistic Considerations

In performing this motet the conductor should work for a forward rich male chorus sound. If the tone is too covered, the harmony, especially in this low tessitura, can become muddy. As is the case with most male choir music, there are overtone possibilities if the choir sings pristinely in tune and with vowel unity. Work to unify the vowels from each of your singers, and pay careful attention to the third of the chord; you will be rewarded with a wonderful performance of this motet.

Form and Structure

Section	Measure	Event and Scoring
Introduction	1–3	
A section	4–13	(4 + 4 + 2) [(2 + 2) + (2 + 2)]
B section	14–17	(2 + 2)
A´ section	18–27	(4 + 4 + 2) [(2 + 2) + (2 + 2)]
B´ section	28–31	(2 + 2)

Text and Translation

The composer gives a short historical description this text: "The canticle was adopted by the Acadian settlers in Nova Scotia over three hundred and fifty years ago. Reflecting their devotion to the church and respect for the sea, it can still be heard today at their festivals and gatherings."

Ron Jeffers, in his *Translations and Annotations of Choral Repertoire, Volume I: Sacred Latin Texts*, gives a word by word translation and describes the origins of this text. I would recommend this text to every choral musician in addition to the translation given below.

Ave, maris stella,	Hail, star of the sea,
Dei Mater alma,	Loving Mother of God
Atque semper Virgo,	Ever a Virgin,
Felix caeli porta.	Happy gate of heaven!
Sumens illud "Ave,"	Receiving that "Ave"
Gabrielis ore,	From the lips of Gabriel
Funda nos in pace,	Establish us in peace,
Mutans Evae nomen.	Reversing the name of Eve.

Loomer does not use the entire hymn text, only the first two of seven verses.

Additional References and Resources

Jeffers, Ron. *Translations and Annotations of Choral Repertoire: Volume I, Sacred Latin Texts*. Corvallis, Oregon: earthsongs, 1988.

Web site:
Chor Leoni: www.chorleoni.org/lionsden/conductor.html

Contributed by:

Brandon Johnson

Teacher Resource Guide

Little Innocent Lamb

arr. Marshall Bartholomew

TTBB
G. Schirmer: 9907
Overall: 2
Vocal: 2
Tonal/Rhythm: 3

Composer

Marshall Bartholomew (1885–1978) achieved fame both as a folksong arranger and as a conductor. After four years as a student at Yale University (1903–07), he went to Berlin in 1910 to study composition and conducting. During the First World War, Bartholomew remained in Europe, where he worked to aid prisoners of war in several countries.

He returned to his alma mater in 1921 as the director of the Yale Glee Club, an all-male vocal ensemble that already had a rich tradition extending back into the previous century. Bartholomew held this position until 1953, transforming the Yale Glee Club into a nationally renowned ensemble that could perform folksong arrangements and serious classical works as well as the traditional Yale-oriented literature. In addition, Bartholomew was the founder of the International Student Music Council, which set up international choral competitions and festivals in both Europe and America in the 1930s. Some of these efforts were doomed by the tensions between nations that foreshadowed World War II. After his retirement from Yale, Bartholomew continued to guest conduct all over the world and to compose original music and arrangements for choruses.

Composition and Historical Perspective

"Little Innocent Lamb" is an example of an African American spiritual. Spirituals stem from the experience of African Americans during the two hundred-year period in which slavery existed in this country. The genre is multifaceted as a result, encompassing many different emotional states and attitudes. According to Anton Armstrong, the spiritual, which he calls the "African American slave song," had its origin in West African musical practices such as call and response structure and rhythms, which derived from the speech patterns of West African languages. These practices were then combined with European-American musical traditions to form the spiritual. Eventually, these songs from aural tradition were written down and arranged by a number of composers, including Harry Burleigh, William Dawson, and Jester Hairston, to name just a few.

Armstrong identifies five different categories of the spiritual: the religious spiritual, which provided instruction in the tenets of the Christian faith; the freedom spiritual, which was focused on deliverance from bondage; the escape spiritual, which contained coded messages encouraging escape from slavery; "shouts" or "hollers," which were another class of teaching songs; and work songs. "Little Innocent Lamb" falls into the first category of religious spiritual, although references in the verses to the "slippery shoe" of the devil and "Satan's wall" might be oblique references to slave masters and to slavery itself. In particular, the line "Jus' take one brick from Satan's wall/ Satan's wall gonna tumble an' fall" seems to be referring more to deliverance from slavery than deliverance from sin. The song was collected by Bartholomew on April 4, 1926, at Oak Grove, North Carolina, transcribed, and then arranged for TTBB voices for the Yale Glee Club.

Technical Considerations and Musical Elements

One of the most challenging aspects of this arrangement is the rapid text declamation. In any composition in which text declamation and rhythm are problematic, it is a good idea to separate text from pitches at first. A possible rehearsal method might be to chant the text in rhythm, making sure to instruct the choir members not to speak too low in their respective ranges and chant the text the way they would sing, with good breath management and phonation. Then pitches should be isolated on a neutral vowel-consonant combination such as "bim," followed by putting the text together with pitches at a slow to medium tempo for accuracy. This strategy, or a similar one, will be especially helpful to clarify the interlocking patterns between the baritone and bass parts in the refrain and between the second tenor and bass in the verses.

In each verse, Bartholomew cleverly divides the main melody between different sections of the choir. Musical interest is further enhanced through the change in rhythmic patterns in the melody from verse to verse. Make the singers aware of these different rhythmic patterns before they sing through the piece, perhaps by having them listen to the accompanist play the shifting rhythms. This will help guide their understanding of the piece, as well as save time and prevent frustration in rehearsal.

A large portion of "Little Innocent Lamb" is marked *piano* or *pianissimo*. Have the choir focus on singing these sections of the piece in an articulated and energetic manner with strict tempo. Soft does not equal slow! At the same time, the choir should be instructed how to sing louder dynamics in a healthy manner and how to shift back and forth smoothly between soft and loud dynamic levels. The director should make sure that choir members maintain solid vocal technique through the different dynamic levels of the composition. The dynamic indications, while not necessarily a component of the original folk song, capture the spirit of the words very nicely and should be diligently observed by the choir.

The placement of melodic material in the first tenor part might create balance issues between this part and others in the choir, especially if a high school choir performs the piece. Many high school tenors will have difficulty singing pitches higher than E above middle C in full voice. Ask the singers to analyze the music through gesture by having the different sections raise their hands when they have the melody or melodic material. Then, instruct the choir to listen for when various parts have the melody, being sensitive as to when the first tenors sing melodic material. Ask your first tenors to keep the tone energetic and vibrant, but allow them to move into head voice or falsetto above the staff. These techniques should help the melodic material sung by the first tenors become more prominent in the texture, and they will thank you for your efforts!

Mm. 32–47 should receive extra attention as this passage contains different pitch content from previous sections. Much of the previous music contains a good deal of repetition, and your singers may experience trouble in this part of the piece. There are some problematic intervals in m. 37 in particular, especially the tritone in the first tenor part followed by a C-sharp(sharp) and a relatively abrupt harmonic shift to the dominant. Instruct your singers, however, that this music is repeated later in the piece, which should help maintain their confidence.

Finally, the director should make the choir aware of tone quality on higher pitches in all parts of the choir. The sound must be warm and well produced, not strident or strained, at both the *forte* and *piano* dynamic levels. Using descending sirens to access the head and falsetto voices will help create this warmth of sound, as well as lead the singers to approach pitches from above, not below. Have the singers approach extreme pitches as if they were horizontally oriented notes on the piano, not "higher" or "lower" vertically.

Stylistic Considerations

Singing African American spirituals in dialect has been a touchy issue in the past, but the general consensus on the part of scholars is that it should be done to preserve the character of the compositions. The dialect indications in the score itself are a starting place, but it would be a good idea to consult sources for additional information, such as Anton Armstrong's chapter "Practical Performance Practice in the African American Slave Song" in *Teaching Music Through Performance in Choir, Volume 1*.

Phrasing can be a challenge in a heavily syllabic composition such as this one. Develop your own concept of phrasing in this piece and communicate it succinctly to your choir. One suggestion to aid phrasing in the refrain of the piece might be to ask the singers to make the word "innocent" a target for the whole phrase and effect a subtle *crescendo* toward that word. In the interlocking bass and baritone alternations, these parts should accent the first pitch so this repeated musical figure is highlighted in the texture.

Form and Structure

The form of this spiritual is essentially a refrain (A) and verse (B) alternation. The refrain and verses are organized in a call-and-response structure in which one voice part presents the "call" and the entire choir responds. An additional section, which can be labeled C, appears for the first time at m. 32. The form can be represented in letters in the following manner: ABAB′ CB′′AC.

Text

Refrain

Call:	Little Lamb, little Lamb, little innocent Lamb,
Response:	I'm a gonna serve God till I die,
Call:	Little Lamb, little Lamb, little innocent Lamb,
Response:	I'm a gonna serve God till I die.
Verse 1:	Hypocrite, hypocrite, tell you what he do, (I'm a gonna serve God till I die,) He'll talk about me, an' he'll talk about you, (I'm a gonna serve God till I die.) (*Refrain*)
Verse 2:	Debbil, he's got a slippery shoe, (I'm a gonna serve God till I die,) Now if you don't mind, he's gonna slip it on you, (I'm a gonna serve God till I die.)

Section C: 'Cause dere ain' no dyin' ober dere
In dat hebbenly lan',
'Cause there ain' no dyin' ober dere
In dat hebbenly lan',
Dere'll be joy! joy! joy!

Verse 3: Jes' take one brick from Satan's wall,
(I'm a gonna serve God till I die)
Satan's wall gonna tumble an' fall,
(I'm a gonna serve God till I die.)

(*Refrain, followed by Section* C)

Additional References and Resources

Armstrong, Anton. "Practical Performance Practice in the African American Slave Song." In *Teaching Music through Performance in Choir, Volume 1*, edited by Heather J. Buchanan and Matthew W. Mehaffey. Chicago: GIA Publications, 2005.

Curtis, Marvin V., and Lee V. Cloud. "The African-American Spiritual: Traditions and Performance Practice." *Choral Journal* 32: 4(1991), 15–22.

Suggested Listening

Marshall Bartholomew, arranger:

"Little Innocent Lamb" on *United We Sing*, Turtle Creek Chorale, Danny Ray, Turtle Creek Chorale label, B00005YCOA.

"Little Innocent Lamb" on *Jauchzet dem Herrn alle Welt*, various artists, Querstand Records 9810.

Contributed by:

Christopher Jackson

Teacher Resource Guide

Not While I'm Around

Stephen Sondheim

(b. 1930)

arr. Robert Page

TTBB

Hinshaw Music: HMC 1611

Overall: 2

Vocal: 2

Tonal/Rhythm: 3

Composer

Born in New York City in 1930, American composer Stephen Sondheim went on to become the preeminent voice of American musical theatre in the last third of the twentieth century. Sondheim graduated with honors from Williams College in 1950. In his youth he befriended Jimmy Hammerstein, son of the famous lyricist Oscar Hammerstein II; this relationship proved beneficial to Sondheim, and at the premiere of *South Pacific*, Sondheim met the famed Harold Prince, who would later direct many of Sondheim's musicals. Throughout Sondheim's development the elder Hammerstein guided the young composer through a series of assignments and passed on the gift of lyric writing to his pupil.

His big break came at the age of twenty-five when he was asked to write the lyrics for Leonard Bernstein's *West Side Story*; a few years later he penned the lyrics to Jules Styne's *Gypsy*. Finally, in 1962 Sondheim wrote both the music and lyrics for *A Funny Thing Happened on the Way to the Forum*, which opened on Broadway. He has gone on to compose many acclaimed scores, including *Company, A Little Night Music, Follies, Sweeney Todd, Merrily We Roll Along, Into the Woods*, and many others.

Composition and Historical Perspective

"Not While I'm Around" is a song from the second act of the musical *Sweeney Todd: The Demon Barber of Fleet Street*. The musical, produced in 1979, won eight Tony Awards including Best Musical and Best Score. The musical depicts life in eighteenth-century London and features a mad barber who kills his clients, Sweeney Todd, and Mrs. Lovett, his landlady who uses the carnage for her popular meat pies. This violent tale involves revenge on the part of Todd, who is looking to pay back a judge who wrongly incarcerated him in order to steal his wife and daughter. In the production, "Not While I'm Around" is sung by Tobias as he pledges to protect his new boss, Mrs. Lovett. Following the song Mrs. Lovett suspects Tobias may know of her arrangement with Todd and locks him in the bake-house. Following this song the conflict of the drama escalates, leading to the thrilling climax of the musical.

Technical Considerations and Musical Elements

This arrangement of "Not While I'm Around" consists of a beautiful melody accompanied by a simple pop-style piano part. Choirs working on line, legato, breath support, and expressivity will be well served by this piece. This is a wonderful work to program for a chorus of young men; even though the melody requires a gentle tone, the text evokes an image of strength. This piece, combined with other genres and pieces, can help you develop a positive image of singing among high school singers.

The recurring opening melodic figure is tonally easy but should be presented thoughtfully from a vocal perspective. Young singers have a tendency to set their voices for the first note they sing without considering the whole phrase at the time of breath and phonation; this approach will not be successful in this piece. It is important to teach the singers to bring their head voice down to the lower pitch rather than using the chest voice on higher pitches. This technique is required of all parts throughout. Proper execution will yield a spacious and warm sound, which will be very pleasing and comforting. For this reason, it would be wise to teach this technique in the warm-up for the day. In fact, small melodies from this piece can easily be used as stand-alone warm-up exercises; you could actually teach much of this piece by rote in the warm-up before ever opening the music.

There are a few dissonant chords in this piece, but they should not be too difficult to learn, as most of the dissonance is approached and resolved by diatonic steps. One of the most difficult chords to hear is the first entrance of the tenors and bass 2 in m. 6 and again in m. 10. The choral chord in these instances relates neither to the baritone line nor to piano part. Repetition of this attack in rehearsals will ensure that your singers find the pitch. Other sonorities like major seventh chords and third inversion dominant seventh chords occur often but are realized by well-designed voice leading. However, take time to tune the more dissonant chords by isolating them out of tempo; this technique will give your singers time to grasp the harmonic concept of the piece and will help your overall intonation. As the piece is strophic the music returns with same harmony, so time spent on the chords in the first verse will pay dividends in the second half of the piece.

Stylistic Considerations

Because "Not While I'm Around" is from the musical theatre genre, one should consider the following possibilities when preparing a performance.

- Attack long notes, particularly at the ends of phrases, with a straighter tone and warm them (add light vibrato) during the sustaining of the pitch.
- Clearly enunciate active and colorful words to give them an onomatopoeic quality (e.g., "demons," "prowling," "howlin'").
- Monitor the visual presentation of your choir during this piece. Make sure the singers' faces reflect the mood of this piece. Consider using a standing formation that will make this music seem more intimate to your audience.

Work with your singers to achieve as seamless a legato tone as possible. The disjunct quality of the melody can make this somewhat difficult to achieve. Consonants frequently disrupt legato line by completely stopping the airflow of the singer. If you sense this to be the barrier for your singers, rehearse the piece on a neutral syllable without a consonant, or, perhaps more effectively, sing the words of the piece without consonants (only the vowels of each syllable). This will force your singers to make the pure vowel more quickly to accomplish the right sound. You can also ask the singers to form consonants in a light and quick manner so they can spring from vowel to vowel. A non-legato performance of the piece will not attain the desired interpretation of the text.

Form and Structure

"Not While I'm Around" is set in a predictable strophic form. Phrase structure is equally as predictable; each verse is sixteen measures long and consists of four four-measure phrases.

Text

Nothing's gonna harm you, not while I'm around
Nothing's gonna harm you, no sir, not while I'm around
Demons are prowling everywhere nowadays
I'll send them howling . . .

It should be noted that this arrangement does not use the bridge of the original song. Also, in the musical version of the song, sung mostly by the character Tobias, Mrs. Lovett sings a few lines as well.

Additional References and Resources

Gottfried, Martin. *Sondheim*. New York: Harry N. Abrams, Inc., 1993.
Secrest, Meryle. *Stephen Sondheim: A Life*. New York: Alfred Knopf, 1998.
Zadan, Craig. *Sondheim & Co.* 2nd ed. New York: Harper & Row, 1986.

Contributed by:

Matthew W. Mehaffey

Teacher Resource Guide

Sam Was a Man

Vincent Persichetti

(1915–1987)

TB or SA or two-part mixed with piano
G. Schirmer: 9791
Overall: 2
Vocal: 2
Tonal/Rhythm: 3

Composer

A native of Philadelphia, Vincent Persichetti began his musical education at age five on piano. Over the next eleven years Persichetti would add double bass, organ, and tuba as well as theory and composition to the mix. By age sixteen he was appointed organist-choir director of a Presbyterian church, a post he would hold for twenty years.

At age twenty he simultaneously majored in conducting at the Curtis Institute and piano at the Philadelphia Conservatory while serving as head of the theory-composition department of Combs College. He earned a master's degree in 1941 and a doctorate in 1945 from the Philadelphia Conservatory as well as a conducting diploma from Curtis. While still a student, he was appointed in 1941 to chair the theory-composition department and to head the postgraduate department at the Philadelphia Conservatory. Within five years he joined the theory-composition faculty of the Juilliard School of Music.

At age twenty-five he married Dorothea; they had two children. Persichetti composed more than one hundred and fifty pieces in a multiplicity of styles and genres. The composer was diagnosed with lung cancer at age seventy-one and died at age seventy-two.

Composition and Historical Perspective

In his teaching, composing, and theoretical writing Persichetti sought to integrate many twentieth-century compositional movements into a seamless writing style. Equally adept at composing operas, symphonic works, keyboard pieces, and solo vocal literature, he drew from a wide range of expressive possibilities, demonstrating the clear influence of Béla Bartók, Paul Hindemith, Aaron Copland, and Igor Stravinsky. After 1950, however, he achieved a distinctive voice in his writing, one that has long bewildered music theorists and historians who have attempted to categorize his music or find some clear chronological pattern of development.

Persichetti himself identified two main currents in his compositions: "gritty" and "graceful." Beyond these, his large musical output may be characterized as having sparse textures, playful rhythms, and a solid twentieth-century harmonic vocabulary, including pandiatonicism, polytonality, and quartal and quintal harmonies. Gritty and graceful, with playful rhythms, and quartal/quintal harmonies, "Sam Was a Man" serves as an excellent song for gaining a glimpse into Persichetti's writing style.

Persichetti's choice of texts for his vocal works is also quite eclectic. His interest in authors included Walt Whitman, E. E. Cummings, W. H. Auden, Carl Sandburg, Emily Dickinson, Sara Teasdale, Robert Frost, and James Joyce. He also composed Mass settings and pieces based on biblical and multicultural sources. "Sam Was a Man," based on a poem by E. E. Cummings, was published alongside "Jimmie's Got a Goil" in *Two Cummings Choruses*, Op. 33.

Technical Considerations and Musical Elements

While this piece is not particularly musically difficult, a few considerations will be helpful in preparing the chorus for potential problems. Below is a list of three issues that a conductor might want to address prior to and during the preparation of this piece:

- Tuning intervals
- Constantly shifting tonal centers
- Rhythmic precision

Tuning intervals is enigmatic for most choirs. "Sam Was a Man" poses some difficulty both horizontally (melodically) and vertically (harmonically). Treating these tuning problems proactively, e.g., via vocalises fashioned to prepare the singers for potential problems within the piece, will save much rehearsal time. Because of the preponderance of quartal and quintal harmonies between the two vocal lines, create vocal warm-ups that specifically work on tuning these intervals. Try singing the major scale ascending and descending without stopping using solfege syllables or a neutral vowel. When the chorus can sing this absolutely in tune, split into two parts and sing canonically, first at the fifth, then at the fourth (then at the third and second). Sing the scale slowly enough for singers to sing in tune within their section and then with the other section. Give particular care to tuning the intervals between the two groups quite widely.

A second possible vocalise is to sing the first five notes of the major scale ascending and descending without stopping. Have the choir sing this on an open vowel such as "ah" or "aw." Once the choir can comfortably sing this in tune, split into two groups. The first group of lower voices continues to sing the original five-note line. The second group of upper voices sings the same musical line a perfect fifth higher. The two groups sing the exercise in parallel fifths, modulating up by half steps. Expect precision at the onset of each pitch and a perfectly unified vowel for all singers. These exercises get the quartal and quintal harmonies into the choir's ears—a reference point for tuning within the piece.

Expect your choir members to sing "Sam Was a Man" on solfege until comfortable. Help them identify where the constantly shifting tonal centers are, and adjust the solfege syllables accordingly. Once they have mastered the syllables and can sing all of the intervals in tune vertically (two parts together), move to a neutral syllable and then to the text.

Rhythmic precision is essential to the success of this piece. Count-singing is suggested to achieve clarity of onsets and releases. Phrases that end with a tied eighth note indicate a release on the eighth note. Phrases that end with a tied quarter note are best released on the rest following the tied quarter note. Secondly, rehearse the choir with a metronome until absolute precision is achieved. If consonants become blurred or misplaced, return to the metronome.

Stylistic Considerations

Stylistically, "Sam Was a Man" should enjoy the playful character and simplicity of an American folk song. Rhythmic vitality is essential. Ask the choir to sing this piece with the boldness characteristic of Sam himself. Success with this piece will be achieved when approached like an Appalachian ballad or sea chantey. Use a bright, clear tone with crisp consonants. Allow the "gritty" and "graceful" character to shine through.

Form and Structure

"Sam Was a Man" is through-composed and has D as its tonal center.

Additional References and Resources

Sadie, Stanley, ed. *The New Grove Dictionary of Music and Musicians*. 2nd ed. New York: Grove, 2001.

Contributed by:

James Bowyer

Level Three

Teacher Resource Guide

Ave Maria

Javier Busto

(b. 1949)

SATB with organ ad libitum
Walton Music Corp.: 8500076
Overall: 3
Vocal: 3
Tonal/Rhythm: 3

Composer

Javier Busto was born in Hondarribia in the Basque region of Spain in 1949. Though trained as a doctor, Busto is known internationally as a composer and conductor. He conducted the choir Eskifaia from 1978 to 1994. Then, in 1995, he formed a women's choir, Kanta Cantemus Korua—to whom he is as much a teacher as a conductor as all the singers are high school aged—who have recorded and performed around the world. Recipient of composition awards himself, Busto has juried composition competitions and adjudicated choir competitions in Europe and Asia.

Composition and Historical Perspective

A short, straightforward piece, "Ave Maria" is a motet for SATB choir typical of Busto's work. Composed for concert performance, it could be sung in a church setting. A *cappella* and organ (ad lib) accompaniment versions are available. There is also a women's choir arrangement. Busto's melodies are often described as simple, lovely, fluid, and cantabile, and "Ave Maria" is no exception. The vast majority of his output are short works for SATB and SSAA choirs.

Busto's "Ave Maria" is comparable to Renaissance motet settings of the same text and is especially similar to Arcadelt's because it is homophonic and mostly diatonic in major. Also Arcadelt uses the same music for "Ave Maria gratia plena" as he does for "Dominus tecum," and Busto does this on a smaller scale with the melody of the texts "Ave maria" and "gratia plena." Both composers set the phrase "Sancta Maria" with a grand, descending melody and open harmonization. Though Busto's setting contains only the faintest suggestion of polyphony and absolutely no imitation, the use of a new musical idea for each phrase of the text suggests the point-by-point imitation of Josquin Desprez's "Ave Maria." Singers could make comparisons based on their own observations of other settings, opening up a discussion of why composers make the choices they do and what choices the singers might make.

Technical Considerations and Musical Elements

This piece is completely diatonic and therefore a perfect candidate for applying sight-reading skills early in the year. Use fragments as sight-reading exercises to be done in unison before you begin teaching the piece as a whole. For sight-readers who are beyond the absolute basics, have them sight-sing two parts at a time, or even three at a time.

All parts have ranges limited to the staff. These factors make for very easy singing. The only possible challenge pitch-wise is the divisi in the altos, tenors, and basses. The divisi is mostly limited to mm. 14–22. The tenor split is high enough that altos could easily assist the first tenors, and the alto split is low enough that the tenors could join the second altos. The basses split occasionally throughout, even crossing voices in m. 16 and again in m. 19. In all these cases, putting an equal number of voices on each part will improve balance significantly. So instead of having all sopranos sing soprano and dividing the altos, divide the entire women's section into three equal parts when there are three women's parts. When the men divide, even if you add altos to the tenor line, divide the entire choir into four equal groups. Particularly in m. 27 at the "Sancta Maria," which should have a solid foundation, there should be at least as many singers on the second bass part as on the tenor part.

Beyond the moments of divisi, a few intervals have surprising twentieth century harmonization. In mm. 25–26, the second basses sing a descending minor seventh, from middle C down to D. This can be easily learned by practicing alone with the sopranos, who sustain a D in both measures. In those same measures, the first tenors sing a major second against the altos and a minor second against the second tenors. Getting their ears accustomed to this kind of sound can be accomplished by singing warm-ups and ear training exercises daily in the rehearsals before teaching these measures. In a comfortable key, have the basses sing Do, tenors and altos sing Mi, and sopranos sing Sol. As singers hold the chord, parts can take turns singing steps up and down, either returning to the original pitch or continuing to the next chord tone.

Another moment of nontraditional harmony are the parallel fourths between the first altos and sopranos in mm. 15–18. Though brief, the tuning should be ensured by practicing with just those two part without the second altos, who have the third.

Because the texture is generally thin and exposed, registration and intonation will be an important challenge, especially for the sopranos. The opening few notes, with two ascending fifths, cross over the most difficult break with a lot of [i] vowels. To prepare singers to navigate wide intervals across awkward parts of their range, have them sing relatively softly on a very pure [u] for the first several rehearsals, being sure to use the vowel's natural tendency to encourage head voice.

The few rhythmic concerns begin with tempo. The marking *adagio* might tempt a conductor to allow the piece to drag. This can easily result in a performance that is uninteresting. Try setting a pace that approaches the sound of speech, quarter note = ca. 72. Look first at m. 31, which contains the fastest rhythms and the most speech-like text setting. On a related note, Busto is careful to set the text following the natural word stresses. The rare exceptions—the syllable "te" in "tecum" in m. 12, "fructus" in m. 23 in the upper voices, and the basses' "peccatoribus" in m. 32—are opportunities for creating color and textural interest. The only other rhythmic challenge lies in the eighth note triplets in mm. 17–18 and 31–32. Because the rest of the rhythms are so straightforward, even beginning readers can count-sing; it would be helpful to count-sing the triplets.

Stylistic Considerations

The simplicity of melodic lines and clarity of the harmonies are the most distinctive stylistic features of this piece. Therefore, the vocal production must not be too heavy or contain excessive of vibrato. However, the texture is such that even a large choir could perform this piece without its sounding inappropriate. The edition published with organ accompaniment could easily be performed *a cappella*.

Form and Structure

The motet is through-composed; each textual phrase receives its own musical idea.

Measure	Event and Scoring
1–6	Organ introduction
7–14	SATB homophonic texture, *pianissimo*
8–20	Alternating SAA/TTBB statements, *mezzo forte*
21–30	SATBB, *forte*

Measure	Event and Scoring
31–34	SAT, speech-like singing with independent bass line, *pianissimo*
35–39	SATB homophonic texture, *mezzo piano*
40–43	Amen

Text and Translation

Ave Maria, gratia plena	Hail Mary, full of grace
Dominus tecum, benedicta tu	The Lord is with you, you are blessed
In mulieribus et benedictus	Among women and blessed is
Fructus ventris tui, Jesus.	The fruit of your womb, Jesus.
Sancta Maria	Holy Mary
Maria ora pro nobis,	Mary pray for us,
Nobis peccatoribus,	For us sinners,
Nunc et in hora,	Now and in the hour
Mortis nostrae.	Of our death.
Amen.	Amen.

Additional References and Resources

Edición de partituras de música coral de Javier Busto. http://www.bustovega.com (accessed April 14, 2006).

Suggested Listening

Javier Busto, "Ave Maria" on *Musika*, Kanta Cantemus Korua, AusArt Records (women's choir arrangement).

Dale Warland, "Ave Maria" on *December Stillness*, Dale Warland Singers, American Choral CD 121.

Contributed by:

Amelia Nagoski

Teacher Resource Guide

Ave Maria

Igor Stravinsky

(1882–1971)

SATB a cappella
Boosey & Hawkes: 1832
Overall: 3
Vocal: 2
Tonal/Rhythm: 4

Composer

A stylistic maverick of his generation, Russian composer Igor Fyodorovich Stravinsky explored numerous styles, including neoclassicism, experimental nationalism, and serialism. He was able to absorb diverse musical idioms and make them his own. He is considered one of the foremost influential composers of the twentieth century, and his music continues to be relevant today.

Born into an affluent and musical family, Stravinsky was taught piano by his mother and attended performances given by his father, a famous operatic bass, at the Imperial Opera in St. Petersburg. While attending law school, Igor was introduced to Nicolai Rimsky-Korsakov. After recognizing Stravinsky's musical talents, Rimsky-Korsakov served as a mentor and eventually persuaded him to shift his focus to composition. During his late twenties Stravinsky strengthened his ties with the Parisian impresario Sergei Diaghilev, and between 1910 and 1914 he was commissioned to compose the ballets that brought him fame: *Firebird*, *Petrushka*, and *The Rite of Spring*.

Stravinsky's second emigration took place in the early 1940s; he became a United States citizen in 1945. Stravinsky became influenced culturally and compositionally by New Yorker Robert Craft, who pulled Stravinsky toward

English and American literature and philosophy and helped Stravinsky develop an American perspective. *The Rake's Progress* (1951) marked the beginning of the serial phase in Stravinsky's compositional career. He remained in the United States during the final two decades of his life.

Stravinsky composed a total of fifteen works for chorus, of which *Symphony of Psalms*; *Anthem*, *"The Dove Descending"*; *Canticum sacrum*; and *Les Noces* are best known.

Composition and Historical Perspective

"Ave Maria" (1934) was originally set to Slavic text and was expanded and set to Latin text in 1949. This review addresses the later version. As one of three motets, it may be accompanied by "Credo" (1932) and "Pater Noster" (1926). All three compositions were intended for use in the Russian Orthodox Church, and all were reset to Latin text in 1949.

Technical Considerations and Musical Elements

"Ave Maria" is a tonal composition, although its tonal center shifts throughout, and we do not hear a significant cadence until the penultimate measure (E minor to A major). The motet sounds as if it begins in C major, but this tonality is soon evaded in the second measure with the first of many interjections of E minor chords. The E minor sonority appears at the end of every subphrase, giving the work an unresolved taste. The absence of D-sharp, however, undermines the centrality of E as a tonic, as also does the fluctuation of F-natural to F-sharp in the alto part (Fa and Fi).

The piece is to be performed *a cappella*, and it is practical to rehearse using solfege with C as Do. Despite the fact that there is no definitive tonal center, stopping to tune the E minor pillar chords on the final beats of mm. 2, 5, 6, 8, 11, 15, 18, 20, 23, 24, 26, 27, and 33 as well as the C^7 chords (mm. 3, 10, 12, 14, 16, 21, 23, 28, and 30) throughout will help to address possible intonation concerns.

Ranges are very limited for each vocal part. The soprano part spans no more than a perfect fifth (only up to a C5), the alto and bass each span a sixth, and the tenor part spans an octave. The limited ranges make the piece seem simple, but their purpose is to allow the choir to deliver the text with quiet, chant-like reverence. Melodic motives are repeated and slightly modified throughout with recurring E minor and C^7 chords. This type of motivic repetition delivers the text as an incantation.

Rhythmically, the piece is not unusual; however, there are some meter changes that coincide with the setting of the Latin text. Singers should be aware of the meter changes upon their first reading. To ensure rhythmic unity in early rehearsals, it may be helpful ask the singers to count-sing ("one-and two-and ti-and" or "one-and two-and"), speak the homophonic setting of the text aloud, conduct the meter changes, and step the quarter note pulse.

Stylistic Considerations

The conductor and vocalists should be aware of the importance of phrasing for this composition. Stravinsky's phrases follow the text, and no additional phrase or dynamic markings are offered. Just as with chant, each phrase should follow an arc, gradually building to a climax and then tapering to round off the phrase. One might ask the vocalists to pace each arching phrase with their breath and consider adding arm movement or some form of kinesthetic motion to aid with the gradual pacing of each phrase. If one cannot complete each phrase in one breath, the breathing should be staggered throughout the ensemble.

In addition to pacing each phrase, the conductor must be deliberate in establishing the tempo of this piece. Stravinsky was concerned with the relationship between music and time and took great care in designating tempos for his compositions. As he wrote, "The relation of tempo and meaning is a primary question of musical order, and until I am certain that I have found the right tempo, I cannot compose."[1] The tempo is not forced on the musical setting, in other words, it is demanded by it. It is suggested that the tempo of this piece must not be faster or slower than quarter note = 72.

Form and Structure

The structure for "Ave Maria" is dictated by the text which is set once from beginning to end. The whole of the work is separated into two large and nearly equal sections: eighteen measures for the first section and seventeen measures for the second. Both sections are clearly divided by the "Ave Maria" and "Sancta Maria" portions of the text. Recurring melodic motives are represented with shifting rhythmic durations and pitch orders.

Section	Measure	Event and Scoring
A		Eighteen measures
	1–6	Two phrases (3 + 3); *Ave Maria, gratia plena*
	7–11	Two phrases (2 + 3); *Dominus tecum, benedicta tu in mulieribus*
	12–18	Two phrases (4 + 3); *et benedictus fructus ventris tui Jesus*
A´		Seventeen measures
	19–24	Two phrases (3 + 3); *Sancta Maria, Mater Dei*
	25–28	One phrase (3); *ora pro nobis peccatoribus*
	29–36	Two phrases (6 + 2); *nunc et in hora mortis nostrae; Amen*

Text and Translation

Ave Maria, gratia plena:	Hail Mary, full of grace:
Dominus tecum,	The Lord be with you,
Benedicta tu in mulieribus,	Blessed are you among women,
Et benedictus fructus ventris tui, Jesus.	And blessed is the fruit of you womb, Jesus.
Sancta Maria, Mater Dei,	Holy Mary, Mother of God,
Ora pro nobis peccatoribus,	Pray for us sinners,
Nunc et in hora mortis nostrae. Amen.	Now and at the hour of our death. Amen.

Additional References and Resources

Jeffers, Ron. *Translations and Annotations of Choral Repertoire, Volume I: Sacred Latin Texts*. Corvalis, OR: earthsongs, 1988.

Suggested Listening

Igor Stravinsky, "Ave Maria" on *Igor Stravinsky Edition: Volume IX Sacred Works*, Igor Stravinsky conducts The Festival Singers of Toronto, Elmer Iseler, Chorus Master, Sony Classical SM2K 46 301.

Contributed by:

Elizabeth K. Swanson

---

1 Joseph Coroniti, *Poetry as Text in Twentieth-Century Vocal Music* (Lewiston, NY: Edwin Mellen Press, 1992), 57.

Teacher Resource Guide

Buffalo Gals

arr. Bob Chilcott

SATB with piano
Oxford University Press: 3432315
Overall: 3
Vocal: 2
Tonal/Rhythm: 3

Composer

British composer Bob Chilcott's involvement in choral music began at King's College, Cambridge, where he sang as a chorister and a choral scholar. He progressed to the King's Singers (1986–97) before turning his attention to full-time composing. He is a frequent and engaging workshop leader at choral music gatherings.

Chilcott conducted the Chorus at the Royal College of Music, London, is principal guest conductor of the BBC Singers, and has guest conducted major choruses around the world. He has conducted major concerts and festivals in Birmingham, Oberlin, New Orleans, Chapel Hill, and other U.S. cities and in the countries of Canada, Germany, Sweden, Japan, Estonia, and Latvia. He was a featured conductor at the Sixth World Symposium on Choral Music in Minneapolis, at the Europa Cantat Junior festival in Namur, Belgium, and at the ACDA National Convention in New York City (2003), to mention only a few from a continually growing list.

He occasionally teaches in the composition department of the Royal Academy of Music in London. Chilcott's recent commissions include "I Am the Song" (2001) for finalist choirs of the Let the People Sing competition for

BBC Radio Three, *Tandem* (2002) for two orchestras, and "Making Waves" (2001) for the Newfoundland Youth Symphony Choir. Bob and his wife, Polly, live with their four children in Oxfordshire, England. Bob is a fan of cricket, Grand Prix motor racing, and Alfa Romeos.

Composition and Historical Perspective

Frank Sargent and the Highland Park Highs School Lads and Lassies of Dallas Texas commissioned this arrangement of "Buffalo Gals." Cool White (John Hodges), who first published the tune as "Lubly Fan" in 1844, was among the first black-faced minstrels. He probably used a traditional tune, perhaps the English singing game song "Pray, Pretty Miss" or the German music hall song "Im Grunewald, im Grunewald ist Holzauktion," ("In the Green Forest Is a Timber Sale"), both of whose melodies are strikingly similar. However, some scholars believe the song originated around the Erie Canal with "Buffalo" referring to the city in New York, not the Western bison. Accordingly, as the song traveled its lyrics were regionalized (e.g., "Charleston Gals"). The strophic song is simply a fun song to sing, and like many songs of this type has uncomplicated and repetitive harmony and text. This setting is uniformly in F major and 4/4 time.

Technical Considerations and Musical Elements

Two patterns occur twice, reducing the amount of music to be learned. To rehearse efficiently:

- Begin with the refrain (mm. 15–28) with everyone singing the soprano line in a comfortable octave.
- Rehearse the refrain in its canonic presentation (mm. 15–19, SATB)
- Learn verse; all voices sing the melody on a neutral syllable, then with the text.
- Learn the rhythm of the SA line, mm. 21–25, chanting the text in rhythm in a high and resonant speaking voice.
- Have all choristers sing this rhythm in verse 3 to keep the tenors and basses from getting restless.
- Teach notes in mm. 21–22 with sopranos and tenors on the soprano and altos and basses on the alto line.
- Teach everyone the mm. 24–25 slack-string guitar slide on the word "chance" again soprano/tenor and alto/bass split.
- Teach the "Oh" exclamation and its sforzando.
- Learn the introductory "way-oh," then the similarly beginning soprano/alto m. 36; see Stylistic Considerations for a teaching suggestion for soprano/alto in mm. 37 and 39; jump forward to the last measure, back from that to the coda, and finally learn verse 3.

Stylistic Considerations

Notice and teach the difference among singing, a pitched speaking voice (e.g., m. 1), and the slack-string guitar-like lick (e.g., soprano and alto in m. 55). Notice markings like "with swing" and "cute." Impress on the choir the light jolliness of this piece, and encourage them to enter the spirit of the text. It certainly would be appropriate for the SA and the tenor/bass sections to interact—to flirt, really. You or they may even want to design a simple choreography, to move to a "girls and boys" arrangement, or to use a more casual arrangement of small groups suggesting a barn dance.

The tessitura will not strain singers; the accompaniment is simple. The occasional harmonic surprises (e.g., mm. 5, 24, and 51), the syncopations, the pace (quarter note = ca. 112), the texture variations, and especially the anacrusic "ohs" add spice.

Coach your accompanist, if necessary, to play lightly throughout: no work boots on the keys. Consider adding a washtub bass you and some students construct, or you could use a real contrabass. Even a high school–aged beginner could select some of the bottommost notes of the piano part and play a nice accompaniment. I would argue against using an electric bass.

Construct a warm-up exercise that uses the syncopated rhythm of the soprano/alto line in m. 37 or 39 and apply it to the music later. The exercise can cut learning time on this piece, serve as an attention-focuser for the warm-up period, and teach rhythmic flexibility. For instance:

- Singers tap a thigh: quarter notes (four of them), then eighth notes (eight), then sixteenth notes (sixteen).
- Still tapping sixteenths, add the words. You should model, speaking them accurately in rhythm with proper accents but without pitches in a medium to high speaking voice with good breath support.
- Finally, add the pitches of "Buffalo Gals," eventually in two parts at the interval of a third as in the piece to be learned (in a comfortable octave for the tenor/bass singers) using empty downbeats and proper accents. Walk this measure down and up by half steps, whole steps, or random intervals. Eliminate thigh-tapping.
- A caution: In my opinion, there is an accent missing from m. 39, beat 3, over the word "danced," which without an accent does not match the previous iteration of text and music.

Please note and teach the dynamic variations and expression markings from the first rehearsal. Without them the piece might become dull.

Form and Structure

SECTION	MEASURE	EVENT AND SCORING
Introduction	1–9	M. 1 pitched exclamation "oh" plus two-measure piano vamp; mm. 4–9 soprano/alto on neutral syllables over piano vamp
Verse 1	10–14	Tenor/bass over piano vamp
Refrain	15–20	After the pick-up "oh" exclamation as in m. 1; two-voice canon at the octave, one beat displacement over new piano pattern, ending with two-bar piano vamp
Verse 2	21–25	Tenor/bass unison with soprano/alto comment (a question) above over new piano vamp
Refrain	26–31	Same as mm. 15–20
Verse 3	32–35	SATB, essentially *a cappella*
Refrain	36–41	Soprano/alto = mm. 4–9, tenor/bass = refrain; pick-up exclamation in piano only
Verse 4	42–46	Same as mm. 21–25 with soprano/alto comment one of desire
	47–50	Same as mm. 15–18
Coda	51–55	No piano vamp between refrain and coda; tenor/bass unison refrain until last two bars; soprano/alto comment (an enthusiastic statement) on new material in two two-measure identical phrases; SATB closing slack-string guitar "uh-huh"

Text

As I was walking down the street,
A handsome girl I chanced to meet,
Oh she was fair to see.

Refrain
Oh! Buffalo Gals won't you come out tonight
And dance by the light of the moon?

I asked her, "Would you want to dance?
I thought that I would have a chance
To shake a foot with her.

Oh, I danced with the gal with a hole in her stockin'
And her hip kept a-rockin' and her toe kept a-knockin',
And we danced by the light of the moon.

I wanna make that gal my wife,
Then I'd be happy all my life,
If I had her with me.

Additional References and Resources

Nelson, Lesley. "Buffalo Gals." Popular Songs in American History Web site www.contemplator.com/folk.html (accessed May 14, 2005).

Contributed by:

Lani Johnson

Teacher Resource Guide

Domine, ad adjuvandum me festina

Giovanni Battista Martini
(1706–1784)

SATB, SATB soloists, strings, and organ
Concordia Publishing House: 97-5795
Overall: 3
Vocal: 3
Tonal/Rhythm: 3

Composer

Giovanni Battista Martini worked most of his life, from 1725 until his death, as *maestro di cappella* at Saint Francesco in his birthplace of Bologna, Italy. Though he was a Franciscan monk and later an ordained priest, Martini spent his days in Bologna composing, teaching, and writing. Martini composed in a wide variety of sacred and secular genres including oratorios, Masses, instrumental sonatas, sinfonias, and theatrical works.

His famous students included Mozart and J. C. Bach. Mozart enjoyed his teacher so much that he said of Martini, "I never cease to grieve that I am far away from that one person in the world whom I love, revere, and esteem most of all." Martini's other contributions to music include extensive correspondence to well known composers and theorists of the time; many letters have been preserved. Martini also wrote three volumes of historical books on music called *Storia della musica*, though he intended for the collection to be five volumes.

Composition and Historical Perspective

Martini's sacred motet "Domine, ad adjuvandum me festina" numbers itself among many other sacred works, including numerous masses and motets. The title page of the autographed score dates this motet as from 1729, around the time Martini was ordained a priest. "Domine, ad adjuvandum me festina" reflects the *galant* style that emerged in Italy in the early eighteenth century, which later influenced Haydn and Mozart's Classical Viennese Style. Motivic writing in the second half of the piece reveals Martini's Baroque roots.

This motet is scored for SATB choir and also features SATB soloists. The aria-like alto solo contrasts the other three solis, which are trios or duets. The accompaniment for this motet is four-part string orchestra and organ. If strings are not available, the motet can be performed with keyboard accompaniment only, using the reduction in the vocal score. A highly skilled keyboardist is required for this type of performance.

Technical Considerations and Musical Elements

"Domine, ad adjuvandum me festina" begins with a *largo* introduction. This section is legato and slight fermatas can be added at the end of m. 1 and m. 6. Special attention should be paid to the voice crossing between the alto and tenor parts in mm. 2-3 and to the contrasting rhythms in m. 6 on beats one and two.

A tempo change occurs at m. 7 to *allegro e spicco*. Conductors may find it helpful to create a proportional transition; that is, having the new tempo set twice as fast as the *largo* section. This lively section highlights periodic, homophonic writing, alternating chorus ritornellos with solo passages interrupted by instrumental interludes. Though the text is not difficult and the ranges are comfortable, learning the piece on a neutral syllable aids in capturing the proper *galant* style of the motet. The Classical-style shaping blossoms with great attention to word stress and feminine cadences. Modeling the shape of each phrase ensures success in these musical challenges. One common problem occurs on the word "festina." Text stress is easily placed on the middle syllable "sti" as it should be, but often the last syllable is emphasized as well. A harsh ending to the phrase occurs when too much emphasis is given on "na." The choir will need to learn to de-emphasize this final syllable, especially when it occurs on a feminine cadence (e.g., m. 16).

Once the text is added to properly shaped phrases, problems arise within the Latin text. For example, the "o" of "Domine" tends to be too closed, especially when sung by choirs unfamiliar with Italian Latin. Also the successive repetition of the syllable "ad" creates an elision if the choir is not instructed to put a glottal at the beginning of each "ah" sound. Lastly, the closed vowels in the word "festina" can sound pinched in the upper range of the sopranos (e.g., m. 45) if they are not prepared correctly. Singing tall vowels on the first and second syllables ("fe-sti") avoids this problem.

Balance in the choral homophonic sections is key to creating properly voiced chords. Likewise, balance between the soloists and the accompaniment is paramount. The organ plays a supportive role in maintaining balance by setting the registration at a softer dynamic under the soloists. Also the instrumental interludes overlap the solo sections, as in m. 33. The violins and violas *decrescendo* slightly in these instances to ensure that the entering soloist is heard.

The second section begins with the alto solo, which presents the beginning of the "Gloria Patri" text. This solo (mm. 55–68) is low in range and can easily be covered by the continuo and unison violins. One solution is to ask only one or two violins to play the obbligato part. The full choir reenters at m. 73 with similar periodic phrases as in section one; similar shaping and word stress should be employed. In mm. 73–81 two sets of notes are juxtaposed in this edition: one for the Latin text and one for the English text. Be careful to discuss which notes to follow with the choir as this can be confusing at first glance.

In the last section of the motet, Martini presents two distinct motives that are passed to each section and doubled by the strings and organ. Motive A is first heard in the alto part (mm. 83–84) followed by motive B in the tenor part (mm. 84–86). Articulations add life to these motives and prevent this section from being muddled, although no articulation is indicated in the score. The choir should learn these motives with articulation determined by the conductor; this articulation should be mimicked by the strings as well. Vocal modeling easily communicates the desired effect of each motive. Dynamic contrast also makes this last section interesting to the listener. The motives should be sung with the printed *forte* dynamic, while non-motive singing is set slightly softer.

This delightful final section ends with a ritard in m. 118 (though a *rallentando* is also effective) with an added fermata in m. 120. The last measure (m. 121) presents the liturgical "Alleluia" at a *largo* tempo. This final measure can be omitted depending on the performance situation.

Stylistic Considerations

Martini's motet reflects the *galant* style and should be treated as a Classical work in its homophonic sections. Considerations in this style include word stress, feminine cadences, dynamics, and articulations as discussed above. Many sources address proper performance practice in this style, as listed in the Additional References and Resources.

Despite the B minor setting of this motet, the light and jaunty affect created by Martini appears to contradict the penitent text of Psalm 70:1, a contrast often difficult to explain to young singers. By contrast, the motivic section represents the text "et in saecula saeculorum" with its long-winded phrases and repetition. This textual continuity and motivic writing reflect the

Baroque style still popular when Martini composed this motet. Martini's genius is revealed in this motet through the synthesis of both styles.

Form and Structure

This motet has three major sections with a short introduction; text and compositional textures determine this form. True to the *galant* style, periodic phrasing creates the smaller divisions of structure in this motet.

Section	Measure	Event and Scoring
Introduction		*Largo*, "Domine" text, B minor
	1–6	SATB with orchestra and organ
A		*Allegro e spicco*, Psalm text, B minor
	7–12	Instrumental interlude
	13–16	SATB with orchestra and organ
	17–24	Soprano/tenor duet with continuo
	25–27	F-sharp minor, instrumental interlude
	28–32	SATB with orchestra and organ
	33–42	Soprano, tenor, and bass trio with continuo
	43–44	Instrumental interlude
	45–50	B minor, SATB with orchestra and organ
	51–54	Instrumental interlude
B		"Gloria Patri" text
	55–68	D major; alto solo with continuo and unison violin
	69–72	Instrumental interlude
	73–82	F-sharp minor; SATB with orchestra and organ
C		"Et in saecula" text
	83–99	B minor; SATB with orchestra and organ
	100-120	SATB with orchestra and organ
	121	*Largo*, "Alleluia" text; SATB with orchestra and organ

Text and Translation

Domine, ad adjuvandum me festina —Psalm 70:1	Make haste, O God, to deliver me
Gloria Patri et Filio *Et Spiritui Sancto*	Glory be to the Father, and to the Son, And to the Holy Spirit.
Sicut erat in principio *Et nunc, et semper* *Et in saecula saeculorum. Amen.*	As it was in the beginning, Is now, and ever shall be, World without end. Amen.

Additional References and Resources

Donington, Robert. *The Interpretation of Early Music*. London: Faber and Faber, 1963.

Neumann, Frederick. *Performance Practices of the Seventeenth and Eighteenth Centuries*. New York: Schirmer Books, 1993.

Rosen, Charles. *The Classical Style*. London: Faber and Faber, 1976.

Sachs, Curt. *Rhythm and Tempo: A Study in Music History*. New York: W.W. Norton & Company, 1953.

Contributed by:

Lani Knutson

Teacher Resource Guide

Five Hebrew Love Songs

Eric Whitacre

(b. 1970)

SATB or SA chorus with piano and violin
Walton Music Corp.: 8501466, SATB;
Walton Music Corp.: 8501490, SA
Overall: 3
Vocal: 3
Tonal/Rhythm: 4

Composer

An accomplished composer, conductor, and lecturer, Eric Whitacre is one of the bright stars in contemporary concert music. Regularly commissioned and published, Whitacre has received composition awards from ASCAP, the Barlow International Composition Competition, the American Choral Directors Association, and the American Composers Forum. In 2001 he became the youngest recipient ever awarded the coveted Raymond C. Brock commission by the American Choral Directors Association; commercially he has worked with such luminaries as Barbra Streisand and Marvin Hamlisch.

Whitacre has already achieved substantial critical and popular acclaim. The American Record Guide named his first recording, *The Music of Eric Whitacre*, one of the top ten classical albums in 1997, and the Los Angeles Times praised his music as having "electric, chilling harmonies; works of unearthly beauty and imagination." His "Water Night" has become one of the most popular choral works of the last decade and is one of the top-selling choral publications in the last five years. *Ghost Train*, his first instrumental work, written at the age of twenty-three, is a genuine phenomenon; it has received thousands of performances in more than fifty countries and has been featured on forty different recordings. His music has been the subject of several recent scholarly works and doctoral dissertations, and his published works have sold well over 350,000 copies worldwide.

Composition and Historical Perspective

Five Hebrew Love Songs can best be described as twentieth century secular art song. In his opening remarks about the pieces he tells the reader that the pieces were intended to be "a set of troubadours songs for piano, violin, and soprano." They were composed with specific players and singers in mind and hold a very personal meaning to the composer.

It is likely that most or all of his work to date will be in retrospect categorized as his early style. The *Five Hebrew Love Songs* are among his earliest published compositions for choir and could be considered student compositions, as he was in the summer of his second year of study at Juilliard.

Technical Considerations and Musical Elements

This set of pieces is as straightforward and direct as it is sincere and fresh. The music transports the listener into the heart of love with a directness and unpretentiousness that is uncommon among modern art pieces. The songs stand neatly tied together with modal harmonic language, Hebrew text, and rhythmic interest.

Despite the outward simplicity of this music, an artistic performance will require some careful thought by the conductor. Issues of primary concern are:

- Which arrangement is best suited for the performance
- Hebrew text
- How well students will deal with the harmonic language
- How I can best conduct the music for students considering its rhythmic and notational complication
- The number of movements to perform

Different Arrangements

Due to the warm reception this music has received, there are several different arrangements of this work. The good news is that the choral parts are exactly the same for all of the different versions. If the conductor chooses to use a string group, the choir can use the same parts. The conductor will need to purchase the instrumental part and the score from Walton. The numbers listed below are the edition numbers.

SATB choir and string quartet: WJMS1038
SATB choir, violin, and piano: WJMS1038
SA choir and string quartet: WJMS1054
SA choir violin and piano: WJMS1054

Soprano, violin, and piano, full score: WJMS1038C
Violin part: WJMS1038C

The string parts are not overly difficult, and good high school players should be able to manage them nicely. If you choose the string quartet version you may also want to program additional music for the quartet and your choir. Any number of pieces would make a good pairing for your concert, but it will depend on the skill of the players and the rest of the music in your concert.

Wrestling with the Hebrew

It can be intimidating when approaching a piece in a less common foreign language. For many choral conductors it can be enough to cancel a wonderful piece that students will enjoy. The typical high school conductor's time is valuable, and many may feel they do not have the time to put into researching an unfamiliar language. In this instance, fear need not detour us from performing these pieces.

The Walton text is phonetic, and the only real confusion arises when we see an underscored word. For example, in m. 11 we find "<u>ch</u>aruta" with the "ch" underlined. This tells the singers to use the unvoiced velar consonant sound similar to the German word "ach" or [x] in the international phonetic alphabet (IPA).

This chart should help you approach this text with confidence.

Printed Vowel	IPA	Phonetic
e	ɛ	eh as in bed
é	ɛ	eh as in bed
i	i	eeh as in sleep
í	i	eeh as in sleep
ó	o	oh as in poor
o	o	oh as in poor
a	a	ah as in the Italian pronunciation of S<u>a</u>l<u>a</u>mi
á	a	ah as in the Italian pronunciation of S<u>a</u>l<u>a</u>mi
u	u	ooh as in two
ú	u	ooh as in two
<u>ch</u>	x	as in the German pronunciation of Ba<u>ch</u>

Modal Harmonic Language

Whitacre captures the flavor of the Hebrew language nicely by choosing Lydian and Mixolydian modal harmony. Approaching a piece in a new mode can be intimidating for students. The conductor could use these pieces as opportunities to discuss the modes and how they differ from the more common major-minor system. Two resources available from GIA Publications that may help in this regard are *Ear Training Immersion Exercises for Choir* by James Jordan and Marilyn Shenenberger and *Choral Ensemble Intonation: Method, Procedures, and Exercises* by James Jordan and Matthew Mehaffey.

If the conductor does not have sufficient time to delve into a more involved discussion, I have found that young singers will assimilate modal language quite well. Whitacre sets up each of the altered notes in the instrumental parts and clearly delineates his "sound world" before the first sung note. Although young singers may not read music as well as we might like, their ears are not as rigidly established in the major/minor system as adults are. It will be a helpful to play through the instrumental parts at to acclimate the singers' ears. Once they get the feel for the harmonic language they will be successful.

Conducting Considerations

There are a few conducting issues that need to be addressed before you step in front of your ensemble. I have listed a few of the difficulties and possible solutions for them. Remember that these are only suggestions, if you find that your ensemble responds better to another solution, go with it. These are intended to point out potential conducting problems and offer *a* solution, not *the only* solution.

Movement I. Temuná

One area for discussion is the tempo and pattern for the very slow 6/8 time of the first movement. Most high school singers tend to work more easily with the quarter note beat as opposed to setting the eighth note as the beat. This creates an inherent notational complication—it is simply impractical to beat this 6/8 in two. The singers need all six of the beats. So the conductor has a couple of gesture options available with the slow 6/8: conduct each measure with a six beat pattern or conduct each measure with two three beat patterns.

Depending on the level and ability of your singers and the amount of time you have to prepare the pieces, it may be easiest for your singers to look at two patterns of three instead of one pattern of six. It is always good to challenge your students' musicianship as well as your conducting, but I have always found that two three patterns are clearer and achieve equal results without confusion.

Movement II. Kalá Kallá

"Kalá Kallá" is by far the longest movement and poses the greatest challenge for the conductor. The piece moves between a very slow six and a very fast 6/8 and 2/4 combination. When dealing with the slow 6/8 one can apply the same comments from the first movement to this slower 6/8 section. The faster 6/8 and 2/4 combination can make it difficult to maintain a clear gesture under control. This type of section can easily turn into a wild ride for the conductor if it is not handled carefully.

In the faster sections, the conductor could conduct the 6/8 in two and the 2/4 in two or employ the concept of hyper-meter and conduct the 6/8 and 2/4 group in a larger four.

A brief explanation of hypermeter may be in order: in this instance, it means combining the two-measure music group into one conducting pattern. Instead of letting the barline dictate the pattern, the music to delineates the best conducting.

The second solution provides the most clarity and precision; it also groups the sound together in phrases. As you will see in the analysis section of this article, this music is comprised of six repeats of a two-measure musical package. If the conductor chooses to use the hypermeter it will reduce the confusion caused by repeating the two pattern at different speeds for such a long duration. Only one adjustment will need to be made at the end of each of these sections. In mm. 22–23, 46–47, 58–59, and 72–73, the composer adds a beat, so the conductor will need to adjust the pattern to 2 + 3 or a 5. This is intended to help the conductor's gesture become more meaningful and more precise.

Movement III. Lárov

This is a straightforward movement, but there are a couple of issues that the conductor will need to consider. The indicated quarter note = 108 provides the conductor two options: conduct the majority of the movement in two and subdivide mm. 8–11 or conduct the majority of the movement in six, allowing for an easier transition to the subdivision in the last measures.

Both of these options have strengths and weakness. Either would be a reasonable solution to the issues. The conductor should make a clear decision early on and practice the transition from mm. 8–11 to maintain the clarity necessary for the performing musicians.

Movement IV. Éyze shéleg!

The students will likely be uncertain when it comes to movement four, especially if they have not had much experience with twentieth-century notation. The first page of movement four looks complicated, but in reality, once explained, becomes quite manageable. The conductor will need to select a speaker for the whispered Hebrew text. Aleatoric sections are subject to slight change each time they are performed. They are determined by chance, so conductors should follow the notation with the understanding that each performance is intended to be different.

In the introduction to this movement, I have found it is helpful to conduct the opening half note. I chose a two pattern, the singers come in on the downbeat of the first measure of two, and they begin the non-metered "bongs" on the downbeat of the second measure of two, which is treated as a fermata. This allows me to count for the required five seconds before repeating the process with the altos, tenors, and basses.

After the introduction, the piece falls nicely into a four pattern until m. 18, where the alto and tenor return to the aleatoric material. It should be noted that the last measure of this movement is marked "ATTACCA," so the conductor must be ready to move directly into movement five. This is the only movement with this marking, so it can catch the singers by surprise if they are not fully prepared for the transition.

Movement V. Rakút

There is no real conducting challenge with this movement with the exception of mm. 31–32. Ensemble unity is likely to be a challenge and it may take several attempts to get this together. I would strongly recommend that the conductor model several times exactly what is intended while the gesture is in motion. This will help the students' ears coordinate what they see with what they hear.

The final two measures should be conducted exactly as the first two. Whichever conducting decisions are made in the first movement should be applied to the last two measures of the last movement.

Performance of Individual Movements

The piece is best performed as a complete set. Some of the movements would stand on their own nicely, while others need to be grouped carefully. If you want to do some of the movements but do not have the time to dedicate to the entire set, these are possible groupings.

1. "Temuná," "Kalá Kallá," and "Rakút"
2. "Temuná," "Éyze shéleg," and "Rakút"
3. "Kalá Kallá"

Stylistic Considerations

Much of Whitacre's music is most effective when each of the pitches of the chord clusters is well balanced and carefully in tune. One way to achieve this is forward vocal placement with minimal vibrato. However, *Five Hebrew Love Songs* can be extremely effective when the overall approach more simplistic. Originally these pieces were composed with the solo soprano voice in mind, specifically Hila Plitmann's voice. A warm, expressive folk quality gives these pieces the necessary color. They should be approached in a simple, unaffected manner. Freedom in the voice is most appropriate, especially in movement two. I caution against an extremist approach on both sides of choral tone. If one employs too much vibrato, the pieces lose their folk quality, which strikes at the heart of the composer's intention. With too little vibrato and the set can sound affected and sterile.

Form and Structure

SECTION	MEASURE	EVENT AND SCORING
"Temuná"	1–20	Twenty measures; C major
A	1–10	Ten measures [4 (2 +2) + 4 (2 + 2) + 2]
B	10–20	Ten measures [4 (2 +2) + 4 (2 + 2) + 2]
"Kalá Kallá"	1–76	Seventy-six measures; uses rhythmic motives from first movement; E major
A	1–8	[4 (2 +2) + 4 (2 + 2)]
B	9–25	[12 (2 x 6) + 4 (2 + 2)]
A´	26–33	[4 (2 +2) + 4 (2 + 2)]
B	34–50	[12 (2 x 6) + 4 (2 + 2)]
A´´	51–57	(2 + 2 + 2)
B´	58–76	[2 + 12 (2 x 6) + 4 (2 + 2)]
"Lárov"	1–11	Eleven measures; D major; [8 (4 x 2) + 3]
"Éyze shélig!"	1–22	Twenty-two measures; C minor into F major; Attacca into "Rakút"
Introduction	1	
A	1–7	(2 + 2 + 3)
B	8–17	[1 + 6 (2 + 2 + 2) + 3)]
Coda	18–21	Four measures
"Rakút"	1–35	Thirty-five measures; C major; final two measures are the same as mm. 1–2
A	1–17	[10 [6 (2 + 3 + 1) + 4 (2 + 2)] + 7 [4 (2+ 2) + 3 (2 + 1)]]
B	18–28	3 + 2 + 6
C	29–34	3 + 2
Coda	34–35	Two measures

Text

The text is written by Hila Plitmann, Whitacre's wife. She is the soprano for which the pieces were written. Plitmann was born and raised in Jerusalem and wrote this text to Whitacre after he requested "a few postcards in her native tongue." Plitmann is an accomplished soloist; in addition to premiering Pulitzer Prize winner David Del Tredici's *The Spider and the Fly* with The New York Philharmonic under the baton of Maestro Kurt Masur, she has performed as a featured soloist with the New York Philharmonic, the Chicago Symphony Orchestra, the Israel Philharmonic, the Orpheus Chamber Orchestra, the Cleveland Chamber Orchestra, the New Israeli Opera, and numerous other orchestras and ensembles in the U.S. and abroad.

Additional References and Resources

Web site:

Eric Whitacre: www.ericwhitacre.com/home.html

Contributed by:

Brandon Johnson

Teacher Resource Guide

Hark, I Hear the Harps Eternal

arr. Alice Parker

Warner Bros./Alfred Publishing Co.: LG 51331
SSATBB a cappella
Overall: 3
Vocal: 3
Tonal/Rhythm: 3

Composer

Alice Parker was born in Boston December 16, 1925. After graduating from Smith College and the Juilliard School of Music, she worked as an arranger for the Robert Shaw Chorale, taught at Westminster Choir College, and founded Melodious Accord, Inc. She has more than four hundred compositions and she has been commissioned by such well-known groups as Chanticleer, the Vancouver Chamber Singers, and the Atlanta Symphony, as well as by hundreds of community, school, and church choruses. She is arguably best-known for her collaborations with Shaw on folk songs, hymns, and spirituals.

Composition

This traditional shape-note hymn tune INVITATION, comes from *The Sacred Harp* and Parker arranged it in 1967 for the Robert Shaw Chorale. Shape-note singing came out of American singing schools in the eighteenth century and was designed to teach singing and note reading. Each note in the scale was assigned a syllable, Do–Re–Mi–Fa–Sol–La–Ti and each notehead was assigned a shape.

Technical Considerations and Musical Elements

The first major consideration in preparing the piece is choosing where to breathe. While the first inclination is to mark breaths in the homophonic sections and melodic parts, breaths must be chosen even more wisely for the vigorous accompanying rhythms in the musical "background." Parker marks in breaths for alto and bass parts during the first refrain, which begins at m. 9 but essentially leaves it up to the conductor for the rest of piece.

The conductor makes very specific decisions about articulations when choosing where to breathe. Look at the second refrain, which begins at m. 25, for example. The sopranos and tenors will most likely sing two-measure phrases throughout the chorus. However, the alto and bass parts offer a myriad of options. The first option could be to have them take a quarter note breath after every measure. While this may seem choppy, it gives quite a bit of clarity to these rhythmic figures and allows for a natural accent on the beginning of each measure. Another option could be to have them sing two-measure phrases. The first measure of each phrase could *crescendo* slightly into the next, thereby giving a forward impetus. Another option presents itself at the end of m. 28; instead of the altos and basses breathing, they could *crescendo* into the m. 29 without a breath and give some support to the first altos singing the head motive of the refrain.

While making breath choices, the conductor will have noticed that there are some very difficult rhythmic parts during the refrains. The piece can be difficult to read initially because it is in 3/2, so the conductor must be sure to teach these rhythms *very slowly* during the learning process. It will also be useful to have the choir write a slash mark over the beginning of each big beat (three per measure) in order for the choir to make sense of the rhythms visually. Altos will also want to highlight or trace their part with a pencil to know which notes to sing when the two alto parts cross.

The second refrain, beginning at m. 25, will certainly be the most difficult eight measures to learn. The alto and bass parts split and have different rhythms while the soprano and tenor parts echo each other for the first four measures of the refrain. These rhythms will have to be worked on at a slow pace with the quarter note as the beat for the rhythms to truly lock in. Pushing the tempo up early in the process may cause singers to learn the rhythms incorrectly. While the rhythms of this piece are quite tricky, the pitches are very straightforward and entirely diatonic.

Every section of the choir will sing the melody at some point during the piece, so it will be helpful to begin learning the piece by having the whole choir sing the soprano part for the first sixteen measures. It is at this first reading that you can impart your ideas about articulation and sound so that these concepts carry through the rest of the piece. The initial reading should be done on the syllable "do." The [d] will give the rhythmic clarity needed, and the [o] will encourage the full sound necessary for this style of music. Asking for crisp articulation from the first reading will also prevent singers from sliding into pitches and ensure that the shorter note values are heard. The conductor may also want to sing through the first few measures for the choir so they hear exactly what the articulation should be. Vocal modeling will be incredibly important throughout the learning process so that the choir is absolutely sure of the sound of correct articulation.

This a challenging piece to sing well. The ranges are not extreme, though the sopranos have to sing two short high As at the end of the piece. The alto must sing an F when they sing the head motive of the refrain at mm. 28 and 45. This is a golden opportunity to work on their head voice. Most altos should sing those notes easily if they are using head voice, but may have to get over their mental block against singing high.

Sopranos may find the melody to be a challenge to sing consistently. It starts out around F (above middle C) and dips down to a D before shooting up to high F for the refrain. This melody goes from high F to D (above middle C) over the course of two measures beginning at m. 12. Sopranos will have to be sure to sing everything in the "upper apartment" in order for it not to get heavy and out of tune on the bottom. Ask them to sing the bottom notes only as loud as they can sing them beautifully. They must keep head tone in the lower notes even if they cannot put much sound behind them. Asking them to put the heels of their hands on their foreheads and to sing into their hands is one technique that will help. You can also ask them to put their hand next to their cheek bones and then sing every note "above the hand."

It is also vital for sopranos to keep the sound in the body when they sing the head motive of the refrain. You can encourage them to stay on the breath by keeping your conducting gesture low as they ascend to the high F. You may also ask them to bend their knees as they approach the high F in order to keep their centers of gravity low.

This piece is full of vigorous articulation that must be sung correctly. Young singers will want to articulate through tension and will therefore allow their larynxes to raise higher and higher during the piece. The first step to getting them to articulate correctly is to work on a low breath. Ask them to breathe in silently to keep the larynx low during inhalation. Doing work on diaphragm activity is helpful as well. Ask them to make various consonant sounds ("k," "t," "p," "sh," and "f") while keeping their hands on the abdomen.

The choir is required to hum at m. 33. Ask singers to keep their lips lightly together and teeth apart. Singers should think of a hum as an infinitely small vowel on the outside with the space of a full sound on the inside. These hums will have to be *forte* to be heard. One more tip is to ask the basses to hum on an [n] so that the sound is truly high and forward. Young male singers can make a more resonant sound on an [n], and their parts will be heard more easily.

Diction will help the vocal production immensely. The consonant "r" happens quite often during the stanzas so the choir must be taught to omit them when they happen before another consonant. Choirs have a tendency to let "r" influence the vowel before it by making the vowel migrate toward the "r." Ask them to stay on the vowels and to keep them the same for the entire note value.

The refrain requires them to sing the word "hallelujah" correctly. Be sure to ask them to get through the "l" as quickly as possible. Have the choir speak the word "hallelujah" and flick every syllable with their fingers. This will show them how quickly they must get through the consonants. The word contains three vowel sounds: [a], [ɛ], and [u]. The [a] should be bright and resonant, much like an Italian "ah." Showing a little bit of teeth can brighten the vowel if necessary. The [ɛ] should have a very round lip position with a humped tongue (like [i]). Young singers will spread the vowel too much and will therefore sing the subsequent syllables out of tune. The final syllable of "hallelujah" should be an [a] sound and should not resemble "uh."

Stylistic Considerations

The vocal sound should be quite rich and full throughout the piece. This can be accomplished by asking singers to sing with their whole bodies. Asking them to use physical movement that reinforces a low center of gravity will be most helpful in teaching this. The only concern with getting younger singers to sing fully is that they lose the high focus in the sound. Ask them to keep the "high" (reflecting resonance and placement) and the "low" (reflecting support and depth) in the sound at all times.

Coloring the text will also help bring this piece to life. All words should be sung in a way that further conveys its meaning. The word "ringing" (m. 2) should sound like ringing. The word "glory" should sound glorious. Singers may want to circle the most important words of each stanza to reinforce that something special must be done when singing those words. These subtle shadings can help bring further fulfillment to both performer and listener.

Form and Structure

SECTION	MEASURE	EVENT AND SCORING
Stanza 1	1–8	SATB homophony
Refrain	9–16	Soprano/tenor melody, alto/bass accompany
Stanza 2	17–24	STB, soprano melody, tenor/bass accompany
Refrain	25–32	SAATBB, mild imitation between soprano/tenor; more complex rhythms in alto/bass

SECTION	MEASURE	EVENT AND SCORING
Stanza 3	33–40	SABB, baritone melody with solo soprano descant
Refrain	41–48	SAATBB, mild imitation across all parts
Refrain	49–56	Soprano/tenor melody, alto/bass accompaniment

Text

Hark, I hear the harps eternal
Ringing on the farther shore,
As I hear those swollen waters,
With their deep and solemn roar.
Hallelujah, praise the Lamb.
Hallelujah, Glory to the great I Am.

And my soul though stained with sorrow,
Fading as the light of day,
Passes swiftly o'er those waters
To the city far away.
Hallelujah, praise the Lamb.
Hallelujah, Glory to the great I Am.

Souls have crossed before me, saintly,
To that land of perfect rest;
And I hear them singing faintly
In the mansions of the blest.
Hallelujah, praise the Lamb.
Hallelujah, Glory to the great I Am.

Suggested Listening

Alice Parker, arranger, "Hark I Hear the Harps Eternal" on *Amazing Grace—American Hymns and Spirituals*, Robert Shaw Festival Singers, Robert Shaw, Telarc B000003CZ1.

Contributed by:

William Hammer

Teacher Resource Guide

If Music Be the Food of Love

David Dickau
(b. 1953)

Plymouth Music Co.: 36-20109
SATB with piano
Overall: 3
Vocal: 3
Tonal/Rhythm: 3

Composer

David Dickau is director of choral activities at Minnesota State University—Mankato. His work at the university includes conducting the Concert Choir and Chamber Singers as well as teaching conducting and composition. Dickau holds advanced degrees from Northwestern University and the University of Southern California. He is also the conductor of Magnum Chorum, a Twin Cities–based choir rooted in the choral traditions of the St. Olaf Choir. He is commissioned frequently by school and church choirs across the country.

Composition and Historical Perspective

The note on the inside cover states that this work is clearly written in a Romantic style. David Dickau calls on the choir to employ a full palette of tonal colors in response to the text by Col. Henry Heveningham—not William Shakespeare. (Shakespeare writes "If music be the food of love, play on" to begin *Twelfth Night*.) Commissioned for the 1998 Minnesota All-State Choir, Dickau dedicates this piece to his wife, Anne.

Technical Considerations and Musical Elements

"If Music Be the Food of Love" has been a popular piece in school and community choral settings because of the beauty Dickau elegantly captures. However, there are a number of difficult musical passages in this work that could easily turn a performance of this lovely work sour: *a cappella* sections vs. accompanied sections, diction, and intonation and balance.

First, the most difficult aspect of this work is that Dickau alternates between accompanied and *a cappella* singing frequently. This will be test the preparation of singers and conductors alike as these sections intertwine. Directors must be patient when tuning these *a cappella* stretches.

Subtle harmonic clashes occur, and the singers must understand their places in the harmonic structure and language of the passage. For instance, in. m. 24, the bass and tenor clash with the alto must be tuned very carefully. Encourage singers not to dwell on the dissonant chord because this risks obscuring the rhythm of the music.

Singers must also be taught the relation of the voice parts to the piano reentrances. In m. 29 the men must know that they are singing the third of the A-flat chord the piano enters on. If any slipping of pitch has occurred, the men must be taught to fix it immediately. Perhaps a more difficult transition occurs at m. 49. The choir sings a cluster chord when the piano enters on the A-flat that is not part of the sung chord. Again, choir members must know the relation of their cluster chord to the piano's entrance.

My choir struggled for some time with the idea of being expressive with the diction. They overdid some words to the detriment of the sound. For instance, "If music" should not become "If mmyyyoooosic." Choirs need to be expressive while still getting to the primary vowel sounds quickly. Another challenge all directors will face is getting the choir to understand that they usually underperform consonants. The "v" sound that occurs in "love" must be pronounced at least to a point of general understanding. Stress the importance of the teeth and lip vibration to this sound. It should never sound like "luff."

The composer has said that the octave leap for the sopranos has come up time and time again as a difficult passage to perform. To smooth out the octave, Dickau suggests a tried and true technique from barbershop singing. The first sound of the word "yet" is [i]; place this sound on the end of the low note. Don't let your singers include too much sliding from bottom to top, but use this vowel technique to smooth out that octave leap.

Though this score is primarily in four part SATB scoring, there are a few balance issues to address. The best advice I have when balancing chords is to understand your choir's capabilities. In m. 24, I made the two-note alto, tenor, and bass chord into an evenly balanced chord by placing a few tenors with the altos and a few baritones with the tenors. I felt that by spreading this chord around I could avoid having thirty-five young men attempt singing a *piano* D3.

Also, in mm. 77–80 for the women and 76–80 for the men, I evenly distributed the three-part chords so that there was an equal balance among all parts. Taking a few moments to balance these chords will make the ending work beautifully.

Though the score calls for dynamic flexibility, the scheming used by Dickau is fantastic. The music calls for beautiful open *fortes* and sensitive *pianissimos*. In some phrases, Dickau calls for a fairly wide dynamic scope (e.g., mm. 39–49), asking the choir to sing from ***pp*** to ***mf*** and beyond. These phrases can really allow you to teach your singers to sustain soft passages with a subtle, spinning energy below the long notes while also creating a warm, full sound as well.

The rhythms in the vocal parts are not complex at all. The text guides Dickau's compositional process, and he responds beautifully to this text in particular. Choirs will not struggle with the rhythm because of the natural feel of the text underlay.

This piece includes a lovely, fairly active piano part. The accompanist will need to reach octaves somewhat frequently in both hands. It also calls for some extremely sensitive playing—especially in keeping the more active passages subtle (mm. 1–17).

Stylistic Considerations

As Dickau suggests, tempos and dynamics should be somewhat flexible. Enjoy the opportunity to craft your choir's music-making potential around this fantastic text, and employ extreme patience throughout some sections, especially in mm. 46–49 and mm. 60–63.

The manner of singing must be legato throughout with attention paid to text stress and phrasing. Breath marks are given throughout the score, though I would suggest that conductors should feel free to add lifts where they would like if it enhances the sensitivity of the phrasing.

Vibrato should be minimized in the soft, *a cappella* passages (mm. 24–28, 39–48, and 53–63) because of the gentle dissonances that occur frequently. No vibrato should be used at the phrase endings in mm. 40, 43, 48, 59, and 63.

The piano part also allows for some rubato and expressive performance from your accompanist.

Form and Structure

Measure	Event and Scoring
1–4	Four-measure piano introduction
5–12	(4 + 4)
13–23	(4 + 3 + 3 + 1)
24–34	(5 + 2 + 4)
35–38	Four-measure piano interlude

MEASURE	EVENT AND SCORING (continued)
39–48	(2 + 5 + 4)
49–52	Four-measure piano interlude
53–63	(4 + 3 + 4)
64–74	Recap of opening (4 + 4 + 3)
75–80	Six-measure coda

Text

If music be the food of love,
Sing on till I am filled with joy;
For then my listening soul you move
To pleasures that can never cloy.
Your eyes, your mien, your tongue declare
That you are music ev'rywhere.

Pleasures invade both eye and ear,
So fierce the transports are, they wound,
And all my senses feasted are;
Tho' yet the treat is only sound,
Sure I must perish by your charms,
Unless you save me in your arms.

Suggested Listening

Suggested by the Composer
David Dickau:
"If Music Be the Food of Love," Youth Choral Academy Chorus of the Oregon Bach Festival, Anton Armstrong, conductor.
"If Music Be the Food of Love," Texas All-State Men's Choir, Jerry Blackstone, conductor (TTBB version).

Contributed by:

Matthew Culloton

Teacher Resource Guide

Innisfree

Gerald Custer
(b. 1953)

SSATB with piano
GIA Publications: G-7005
Overall: 3
Vocal: 3
Tonal/Rhythm: 3

Composer

Gerald Custer is a native of Baltimore and earned a bachelor's degree in conducting from Westminster Choir College and a master's degree in conducting with a minor in musicology from George Washington University. He is active as a composer, conductor, and writer for professional journals.

Composition and Historical Perspective

This piece won first place in the Seventy-Fifth Anniversary Composition Contest of Westminster Choir College and was premiered by the Westminster Choir. It is almost entirely homophonic, and the frequent text painting makes it feel like a "choral art song."

The text is by William Butler Yeats, an Irish poet, dramatist, and prose writer who is considered to be one of the greatest English-language poets of the twentieth century. He won the Nobel Prize for Literature in 1923. Yeats was involved in the Celtic Revival, a movement against the cultural influences of English rule in Ireland that sought to promote Ireland's native heritage. Yeats was deeply involved in politics in Ireland and was appointed a senator of the Irish Free State in 1922. In "The Lake Isle of Innisfree," he imagines leaving the life of the modern city to return to a small island in the west of Ireland. The belief that truths reside in the "deep heart's core" and the struggle to remain true to this core inspired his poetry.

Innisfree is a real place, an island in Lough (Gaelic for "Lake") Gill in County Sligo, the gateway to northwest Ireland. It is an area where Yeats spent many years, one he loved and knew well. Lough Gill is the final stop for the Garavogue River before it empties into the sea at Sligo Bay.

Gerald Custer writes about the words:

> I find two aspects of Yeats's poem especially intriguing. The first is the restrained simplicity and remarkable economy of its vocabulary. Although their politics were worlds apart, I suspect Yeats would have agreed with Churchill that "short words are better than long ones and old words the best of all." All but twenty of the words Yeats employs here are monosyllabic, and of these, only two—honeybee and Innisfree—use more than two syllables. The second aspect is the shift of verb tense in the final strophe of the poem. Although most of the work employs future tense ("I will arise . . . I shall have . . .") the last three lines shift into the present ("I hear . . . I stand. . . I hear"): a subtle and incredibly powerful bit of craft. The linnet [mentioned in the poem] is a small finch popular because of its melodious song that prefers to reside in areas of scrub such as gorse or blackthorn, in hawthorn hedges, or in low trees. Even if a dwelling constructed of clay and wattles was not as fashionable as one built from wood or stone, possession of enough land on which to plant nine full rows of beans and be surrounded by honeybee hives was to live a life of reasonably comfortable self-reliance.

Technical Considerations and Musical Elements

The homophony and syllabic setting of the text make a beautiful legato line absolutely essential to the communication of this piece. Learning the piece on a neutral syllable such as [nu] will assist in creating the desired articulation and vowel color for this piece. Speaking the rhythm of the text in heightened speech with allow the students to experience the correct singing space for the text and will allow the conductor to work on elongating the vowels. Be sure that they stay on the vowels as long as possible and speak through the vowels without changing their interior mouth space. This loss of interior space can happen on words that end in "l" such as "will," "shall," and "purple." When the singer anticipates the ending "l" and changes the vowel that precedes it, this causes a bending of the pitch and a loss of freedom in the sound.

The opening phrase (which repeats at m. 37) presents two challenges. First, the triplets in m. 3 need to be free and moving. Triplets can often become too metric and can be seen as a rhythmic value as opposed to a textual declamation. Second, the basses must be sure to keep the vowel tall in m. 5 (stay on the [a] of "now" for as long as possible) and sing with less weight into their high E-flat so that they can reach a true unison with the tenors. Ask for "less sound and bigger ears" on the unisons. All unisons and octaves should also be circled in order for singers to give their full attention to them.

It will be important for the choir to maintain a sense of rhythmic subdivision at m. 12 when the piano starts moving in half notes. There could be a tendency for the text and rhythm to become sluggish because of the less active piano part. Have the choir sing the text staccato to practice getting through consonants quickly. Make sure that they put ending consonants with the next word when appropriate (e.g., [na:I-nbi-nro:uz] in m. 12). The choir should then sing it legato while singing through the vowels. Another helpful rehearsal tactic is subdividing the vowels into eighth notes in mm. 17–19. Longer note values can cause vowels to "migrate" and lose pitch if the singer loses internal spaciousness or begins to move into the next vowel early. Singing a fresh vowel on each eighth note will get the choir to bring more integrity and direction to the vowel sounds.

One particularly difficult phrase of the piece begins at m. 24. This descending line finds two unison notes in m. 26–27 and ends on octave E-flats in m. 28. The tendency will be for the pitch to sink on this phrase because the sound placement is back and downward. The first step to combat this is to have the choir slowly lift both hands upward (palms up) as they sing the phrase and land on the unison. This movement must be paced correctly in order to be effective, and their arms should comfortably extended as they do this. The first word of this phrase, "drooping," presents a problem as well. Inexperienced choirs will want to sing the first syllable [dzru]. Ask them to sing the first syllable as if it were the word "dew" first and add the "r" later. This will assist in the intonation of the phrase. The choir will also benefit from singing "where" with an aspirated "h." The final section of the piece at m. 37 brings back previous musical material and issues.

The issues of free textual declamation and tapering at the ends of phrases are inherent throughout the piece. This can be rehearsed by having the choir speak the text in heightened speech (as if singing) while the accompanist plays their parts. These issues of musical freedom also require singers to be responsive to your conducting. Pick one phrase and conduct in a few different ways. It is most helpful to make each performance as believable and real as possible while refraining from extremes of tempo, dynamics, and articulation. Be as subtle in your gestures as possible when doing this to sharpen their focus and attention to your movements.

The ranges are very reasonable and should not present problems for less advanced choirs. The most difficult voice part to sing well is certainly the soprano part with its fast transitions between the lower and upper registers (e.g., mm. 3–4). The sopranos should think of the sound always staying spacious and resonant. They may not need to open as much in the front of the mouth on the lower notes but should maintain internal spaciousness. The three part divisi in the treble voices happens infrequently and only on two chords for the men; this should not be problematic. Balance issues may occur when the basses are doubled by the piano in the lower part of their range. At these points, tell the singers that they are too loud unless they can hear the bass part. It may also be helpful to liken the balance at these points to a pyramid (basses sing the loudest and sopranos the least).

Stylistic Considerations

The key that unlocks this piece is the expressive communication of the text. Colorful words such as "Innisfree," "drooping," and "glimmer" abound. It is imperative for the conductor to spend time speaking through the text, both in the rhythm of the music and also as pure poetry. Upon speaking through the text, the conductor will begin to find the music inherent in the spoken language and develop a passion for the sounds of the words themselves. This passion will certainly translate into the teaching of the text and will cause the choir to grow in their love of the poetry and music. It is useful to have the choir underline stressed syllables and circle the most colorful words.

Most of the phrases are arched, so the conductor must be careful not to overconduct the ends of phrases as it may cause an unnecessary accent on the last note of a phrase. It will be more helpful to gradually raise the plane of the last beats of the phrase in order to allow phrase endings to release naturally. Conductors will appreciate Custer's attention to detail when it comes to breath marks, dynamics, and tempo changes.

Studying the piano part will also give insight into the many color changes within the piece. Custer uses the piano in three different ways during the piece: moving eighth notes outlining arpeggios, homophonic chords in half notes, and occasional periods of tacet. The conductor must think about why these different effects are used at various times.

Form and Structure

The two-measure piano introduction sets the tone for the very reflective opening measures of the piece. The key of A-flat major is set early on, but we receive a surprise with a G-flat major chord on the downbeat of m. 16. The only imitation between voice parts for the whole piece occurs in mm. 24 and 25 between the sopranos/altos and tenors/basses. The piece is entirely homophonic besides those two measures. The running eighth notes in mm. 29–32 are particularly expressive and paint the words "There midnight's all a glimmer and noon a purple glow." The C section contains musical quotes from both the A and B sections but uses the final stanza of text.

SECTION	MEASURE
A	1–19 (2 + 5 + 4 + 4 + 4)
B	20–36 (4 + 5 + 4 + 4)
C	37–53 (5 + 4 + 4 + 4)

Text

I will arise and go now, and go to Innisfree,
And a small cabin build there, of clay and wattles made;
Nine bean rows will I have there, a hive for the honeybee,
And live alone in the bee-loud glade.

And I shall have some peace there, for peace comes dropping slow,
Dropping from the veils of the morning to where the cricket sings;
There midnight's all a glimmer, and noon a purple glow,
And evening full of the linnet's wings.

I will arise and go now, for always night and day
I hear lake water lapping with low sounds by the shore;
While I stand on the roadway, or on the pavements gray,
I hear it in the deep heart's core.

—W. B. Yeats (1865–1939)

Additional References and Resources

To view a picture of Innisfree, go to www.sligozone.net/Innisfree.jpg.

Suggested Listening

To obtain a recording of the Westminster Choir singing this piece at the 2002 American Choral Directors Association Eastern Division Convention, see: www.markcustom.com.

Contributed by:

William Hammer

Teacher Resource Guide

Ka Hia Manu

Stephen Hatfield

(b. 1956)

SATB
Boosey & Hawkes: 48004817
Overall: 3
Vocal: 3
Tonal/Rhythm: 4

Composer

Stephen Hatfield is a Canadian composer and arranger best known for his compositions based on folk music of a wide variety of cultures. Born in Surrey, British Columbia, in 1956, he strives—and consistently succeeds—in capturing both the musical elements and the spirit of the folk music that inspires him. Though a wide variety of cultures are represented in his music, each possess an intense and distinct personality. He says of his music:

> I fervently wish to present an alternative to the kind of choral literature that, to my ears anyway, never gets beyond the level of Jonathan Livingston Seagull. So much music is, however good its intentions, so trite, so bland, so milky safe. (I really don't mean to sound like a total snot about this—but I tell you, lads and lasses, I'd be embarrassed to sing a lot of the pieces I hear, and I think a lot of the singers are too.)

Composition and Historical Perspective

"Ka Hia Manu," a traditional Polynesian song, is a medley that includes adaptations of traditional chants from islands in Polynesia and Micronesia (a smaller group of islands east of Hawaii), drawing on cultural symbols native to the islands, such as birds and the legendary original inhabitant of the islands, King Hotu Matu'a.

The current style of music of the South Pacific is a combination of the native traditions and the influence of Christian missionaries, who arrived at various islands during the nineteenth century. Along with Christianity, which is now the religion of the majority of Polynesian Islanders, the missionaries brought Western church music. The monophonic hymn style is now married with the ancient modal traditions. The parts of "Ka Hia Manu" written in four-part harmony are chants that would authentically have been sung that way. Any music traditionally sung in unison is written in unison. Though it is from the other side of the world, students can discover the many similarities in texture and harmony between this music and the Western art music and folk songs they have sung or are currently rehearsing, such as the frequently homophonic texture and syllabic text setting.

Technical Considerations and Musical Elements

The first thing your singers notice about the score might be Stephen Hatfield's markings: relatively long, specific descriptions of not just the sound but also the reason behind it. For example, the first marking is "as if hearing distant voices singing a work song—muted but still marcato with every note full of physical energy." At m. 207 he writes, "lusty, festive, throw caution to the wind—full-volumed sound but without the ferocious edge." Other shorter notes include "explode!" and "roar it out!" Because these are the kinds of instructions conductors give their choirs all the time, they are helpful and should be heeded.

Some of the notation will draw attention, also. The part for the bamboo sticks, spoken rhythms, and semi-spoken sounds all have differently shaped noteheads as well as varying placement on the staff.

The text will probably be the most difficult challenge. The vowels are simple and spelled phonetically, but the text often moves so fast and is so foreign that getting clean and even articulations will take some preparation. Learn the notes on a neutral syllable and independent of the text so that it is not a concern and can be addressed on its own. It will help if the singers know the meaning of each phrase. Do warm-ups on short phrases from the piece; write longer phrases on the board first. Be sure to include gentle glottal stops, represented by apostrophes. As singers warm up on the text, remind them of its translation. Of course, begin by speaking the text in rhythm without pitch. When you begin singing the piece, start slowly and do sections with the same text together rather than in order. Sing the text staccato. Also, even after the pitches are learned, take the pitches away and sing the text in rhythm on one pitch.

Challenges presented by the pitches include a few moments of three-part divisi in the women's voices, which should be evenly balanced, dividing the women into three equal parts of which the middle voices always sing the middle part, whether it is notated as soprano 2 or alto 1. The sopranos have a surprising blue note in m. 46 (an F-natural in the basic key of G major).

Also in m. 46, the women's voices are in seconds. Teach them to maintain the dissonance and not be pushed into a unison or thirds by making sure they are sure of their pitches on their own, possibly singing their parts on solfeggio. Happily, this section repeats several times throughout the piece, so the time spent learning it will yield many successes. Another challenging section in the women's voices is mm. 117–125, in which the women sing in three-part parallel diminished chords. Practice this section two parts at a time—middle and upper voices, then middle and lower—so that they hear the minor thirds. There is a melodic surprise immediately before this harmonic challenge. The women sing in unison in mm. 101–112, and the end of the first two phrases in that section are chromatic, descending from A to A-flat to G to F. This pattern recurs mm. 182–189. Though descending half steps tend to flat, this passage moves quickly, is in unison, and is sung "with redoubled ferocity," so—though it is surprising at first—it shouldn't pose a problem.

Rhythmically, the tempo and meter changes do not occur frequently but do change suddenly. Practice transitions in isolation from the rest of the piece. In mm. 267–273, the meter changes come (and in Boosey & Hawkes edition OCTB7137 across a page turn). Meter changes should be counted, and even when sung on text, try speaking "three" on the quarter rest, which is the third beat of the 3/4 measures. Another rhythmic challenge is m. 61, in which the basses sing in "recitative" style. To encourage smoothly flowing singing, have basses sing on numbers, grouping eighth notes into sets of four. Singers should accent "one" and let the other numbers diminish in importance so that the next "one" is clearly stressed. Also, speak the words unpitched and with extreme legato.

The dynamics will also require special attention because of the sudden, drastic changes. Hatfield's detailed instructions make this easier because they create a story, giving reasons for the changes. However, the piano moments should never lose the energetic intensity of the *forte* parts. Practice staccato with a gesture like hammering a nail in small, strong strokes.

There are several options for dealing with the percussion part. Hatfield suggests that thin metal pipe can be used in place of bamboo poles. Long wooden dowels, available at home improvement stores, could also work. If your performance space has a linoleum or carpeted floor, you may wish to use wooden boxes as the surface to be struck by the poles.

The piece requires a great deal of focus and energy from the singers. High school singers will love its rhythmicity and exuberance and most days will be only too happy to sing with all the energy you want from them just because it's fun. However, the concern is to remember that without focus, all that energy and chest voice can lead to poor intonation. Remind them that listening is as important as impassioned singing and that even as they sing loud and enthusiastically they need to make sure they can hear other people singing, too. Also, in addition to having fun, they must always maintain a sense of regal dignity appropriate to the grand nature of the subject matter.

Stylistic Considerations

The sound of Polynesian choral music is distinctive and interesting. It is not far from Southern shape note singing in that it is and must be basically well sung and in tune but with a brightness of tone rare in choral singing. Field recordings, such as those available with the *Garland Encyclopedia of World Music* and released by the Smithsonian, will give you an immediate sense of the desired tone quality. Playing a recording to the choir will be enormously helpful in explaining the sound the music calls for.

Certainly, you will not want your choir to mimic a Polynesian choir's sound, but it would be a great experience for them to attempt to capture some of the spirit and impart a Polynesian impression on their audience. Luckily, young singers' voices are generally naturally bright, and many default to chest voice or a chest-rich blend. Rather than shaping a round, warm, head tone as you would for a piece of Western art music, allow the students to sing with whatever sound comes naturally. Some images you can give them include singing in the shower or around a campfire, doing karaoke, or playing clapping games like "Miss Suzie Had a Steamboat" and "Miss Mary Mack."

Let them make the sound even brighter and tinnier—even strident—without the song sounding bad or like an imitation. There may be some ugly sounds a few times in rehearsals, but humoring those days of free experimentation could well result in a much more interesting sound in performance.

Also, though this piece could be performed by a small group, a large group would be able to embody the song's intense, rowdy energy.

Form and Structure

Measure	Event and Scoring
1–23	80 bpm, women and men alternating then four-part ending
24–37	Alto melody then four-part ending twice on new text
38–43	Kaoha with "hm" in 3/4
43–60	60 bpm, four-part "Ka hia manu, Ava Moa, Hiva Oa" twice

Measure	Event and Scoring
61–62	Bass chant and transition
63–69	Four-part "Ka hia manu, Ava Moa, Hiva Oa"
70–76	138 bpm, women unison chant
77–112	Women chant with tenor/bass grunts
113–125	Three-part women
126–136	72 bpm, soprano/alto lullaby
137–149	Lullaby with tenor/bass drone
149–165	60 bpm, four-part "Ka hia manu, Ava Moa, Hiva Oa" twice
166–209	138 bpm, women unison chant with tenor/bass grunts and clapping
210–229	Women and men alternating, then four-part ending
230–238	Alto melody then four-part ending
239–266	Men and women alternate
267–273	Four-part, changing meter, slowing to the end of the phrase
274–287	160 bpm, coda

Text and Translation

Hatfield gathered together diverse texts and chants that create the narrative flow of a suite. Constructed like absolute music, the texts suggest ideas but don't tell a story on their own. Words are even deconstructed sometimes so that their sounds are more important than their meanings. The text is not written as a native speaker would write it because its source is a French transcription, but, as Hatfield says, "their very condition was part of the history of the islands."

Hitirere ake te haga irunga	The sun rises high in the skies
Kaoha!	Similar to "aloha"
Ua hitihiti mai te 'ava'e	The moon is rising
Te ariki Hotumatu'a	A refrain that announces the deeds of King Hotu Matu'a; ariki = king
Mato'utamariki Ganaia	We are the people of Gania
Tahiti vai mare'are'a	From a text lamenting the colonization of Tahiti
Ata rahi rumaruma	Emerald clouds
Ka hia manu	Many birds
Ava Moa	Sacred waterway
Hiva Oa.	Island said to have nurtured young Hotu Matu'a
Fakateni atu ai te igoa taku fenua	Praise the name of our Homeland

Ta'i no te moe vaikava noho, manu ino e.	Someone has been abducted by an evil bird
Tutuma hakangaro tangi	Weeping in grief
Aue te turue	Help us!
Tere te vaka o Hotumatu'a	There goes the boat of Hotomatu'a

Additional References and Resources

Web site:

Stephen Hatfield: http://www.stephenhatfield.com (accessed April 14, 2006)

Suggested Listening

Stephen Hatfield, "Ka Hia Manu" on *All Good People*, Amabile, Brenda Zadorsky, Amabile, 2004.

Contributed by:

Amelia Nagoski

Teacher Resource Guide

Love and Pizen (Springfield Mountain), Op. 60, No. 3

Kirke Mechem

(b. 1925)

SATB divisi with piano
G. Schirmer: 50482682
Overall: 3
Vocal: 3
Tonal/Rhythm: 4

Composer

Kansas-born Kirke Mechem studied at Stanford and Harvard Universities as well as in Vienna, Austria. He was composer-in-residence at San Francisco University and maintains a strong connection with the San Francisco Symphony, although his orchestral and operatic works have been performed throughout the world. He has been honored by, among other organizations, the United Nations, the National Gallery, the National Endowment for the Arts, the American Choral Directors Association (ACDA), the Music Educators National Conference, and the National Opera Association. Noteworthy among these is the 1995 ACDA national convention, which featured Mechem's cantata *Songs of the Slave* (about Frederick Douglass).

Composition and Historical Perspective

"Love and Pizen" is the final movement of *Choral Variations on American Folk Songs*. The work was commissioned by the Napa (California) High School Choir, Travis Rogers, conductor; the collection also includes arrangements of

"Skip to My Lou" and "Let Us Break Bread Together." In the May 2000 issue of *Choral Journal*, Richard Coffey had this to say about *Choral Variations on American Folk Songs* "one of America's most prolific and imaginative composers . . . a real stroke of genius . . . 'Skip to My Lou' is a genuine toe-tapper, guaranteed to generate wide smiles and bring down the house. 'Let Us Break Bread' is heartbreakingly beautiful . . . 'Love and Pizen' will spring to life in stunning fashion." Having read through "Love and Pizen," conductors may well wish to invest in the other two pieces in the set.

"Love and Pizen" is a setting of the tune "Springfield Mountain," which may be the first original American ballad, which were sung by minstrels to convey news among far-flung communities. It is a true story of twenty-two year old Lieutenant Timothy (or Thomas) Merrick (or Myrick) of Springfield Mountain (now Wilbraham), Massachusetts, who was about to be married but died from a rattlesnake bite on August 7, 1761.

The song was eventually included in minstrel and vaudeville shows, and somewhere along the way acquired humorous lyrics and even became a mini-drama. The melodies to which the various texts were set include the OLD HUNDRED hymn tune and a Scots jig. In nearly all cases, some nonsense syllables are interspersed (see Text for some interesting variants). These nonsense syllables usually are placed at specific places in the poetic form, and, no matter how complicated, always follow a developmental pattern akin to some children's play jingles and pig Latin.

Technical Considerations and Musical Elements

Think "banjo" when you approach this piece. Mechem mimics the banjo in the piano accompaniment and with the nonsense syllables that make up the refrain. You should use completely different vocal colors for the refrain and verses. I suggest experimenting with a bright nasal sound for the "banjo" refrains and a more resonant sound for the story proper. In community singing, where this song was perpetuated, instruments were not always available. Therefore, a tradition of vocally imitating instrument sounds developed: mouth music. The "voice banjo" refrains reflect this tradition. Recruit the pianist to your cause: ask for a very dry, light touch almost completely without pedal, but observing the written accents. Exceptions to the pedal prohibition include:

- M. 42, but only the one measure
- Mm. 45–46 and 104–105, crisply released on beat two
- Mm. 76–81, where sustained legato is specified
- Mm. 90–91, or you might try simply holding the half notes without pedal, as in mm. 82–89.
- Mm. 1–4, 26–32, 52–53, 72–73, 93–94, and 109–114 using sostenuto (center) pedal to sustain bass, but not treble notes

Authentic folk singers do not necessarily establish a regular verse–refrain–verse structure, assigning, for example, four lines to the verse and four to the refrain. Instead, some songs flow easily between two-line and four-line constructs, as suits the story. So does Mechem's setting.

The keys used tend to G major and use the third-related B-flat major and G minor. You will see 2/4, 5/8, 3/4, 6/8, 4/4, and 9/8 time signatures. The work unfolds naturally and should be relatively easy for the singers to comprehend.

Stylistic Considerations

Capitalize on the formal structure of variation and enable choir members to help create differences among the verses and thereby tell the story. Mechem starts the ensemble on this process by setting a number of soprano/alto and tenor/bass duet sections that delineate the characters in the story. It will be exhilarating to fully use the rich dynamic and articulation markings and the rhythmic patterns that sometimes emphasize and sometimes obliterate downbeats.

The syllable "i" interpolated into many final words in the verses is pronounced "eye." "Pizen" is "peye-zuhn" and "sarpint" is a broad "saar-puhnt." Precise articulation of consonants at the beginnings and ends of syllables would be silly, except where used for effect. In the refrains, for example, you could decide to explode the initial "d" in "diddle" and "dum" but not the "dd" in the middle. You could slow down and enjoy (chew on?) the "n" in "now" and the "m" in "Molly" in mm. 59–60, stopping short of lasciviousness, to emphasize the woman's appealing beauty. Opportunities for rubato are numerous, and suddenly resuming the "lively but not too fast" tempo will underscore the text's comical nature.

Form and Structure

This is a ballad, which means that a story is told from beginning to end, often with a terminal punch line—in this case the advice not to get snakebitten. The meters and keys change but not frequently and always with obvious purpose.

SECTION	MEASURE	EVENT AND SCORING
Introduction	1–4	
Refrain	5–15	Repeated after first text couplet
Verse 1	16–27	Tenor/bass on text, soprano/alto on "voice banjo"
Interlude	28–32	Same as mm. 1–4 plus a bar
Verse 2	33–43	
Refrain	44–57	
Verse 3/Refrain	58–81	
Verse 4a/Refrain	82–92	Sad
Interlude/vamp	93–95	

SECTION	MEASURE	EVENT AND SCORING
Verse 4b	96–102	
Refrain	103–108	Same as mm. 5–10, double fermata
Coda	109–120	*Molto moderato*, ending with a shout

Text

Refrain
Too diddle roo diddle diddle diddle day,
Too roo tiddledum, fling dang diddle dum.
Too diddle roo diddle diddle diddle day,
Fling dang diddle dum diddle dum, too ray.

On Springfield Mountain there did dwell
A lovely youth, I knowed him well-i-ell.
This lovely youth one day did go
Down to the meadow for to mow-i-ow.
He mowed and mowed and then did feel
A pizen sarpint bite his heel-i-eel.
They took him home to Molly dear
Which made her feel so very queer.
Now Molly had two ruby lips
With which the pizen she did sip-i-ip.
But Molly had a rotten tooth,
And so the pizen killed them both-i-oth.
Come all young girls and shed a tear
For this young man who died right here.
So all young men, this warning take:
Don't you get bit by no rattlesnake.

As enrichment, here are a few verses excerpted from other versions of the song.

Version 2:
On Springfield mountain there did dwell
A handsome youth, was known full well,
Lieutenant Merrill's only son,
A likely youth, near twenty-one.
On Friday morning he did go
Down to the meadows for to mow.
He mowed, he mowed all around the field
With a poisonous serpent at his heel.

Version 3:
(From *Vermont Folk-Tales and Ballads, Flanders*, collected from Mr. Brown, Townshend, Vermont)

On Springfield Mountain there did dwell
A lovely youth, I knew him well-i-ell.

Refrain
Tu rudy nu, tu rudy nay,
Tu rudy nu, tu rudy nay.

Each morning early, he did go
Up to the mountain for to mow-i-ow.

Version 4:
(Sung by Zona Everett; recorded in Oxley, Arkansas, August 20, 1959)
Oh, it was one eeda-lida-meeda-wida-weeda-wida-weeda-wida-weeda-wida-weeda-wida-worning,
Bright and ceeda-wida-weeda-wida-weeda-wida-weeda-wida-wear,
That Johnny went out in the meeda-wida-weeda-wida-weeda-wida-weeda-wida-weadow
For to meeda-wida-weeda-wida-wow.
Well, he had not meeda-wida-weeda-wida-weeda-wida-weeda-wida-wowed
More than halfway across the feeda-wida-weeda-wida-weeda-wida-weeda-wida-wield,
'Til along come a rattle come a sneeda-wida-weeda-wida-weeda-wida-wake,
And bit him on the heeda-wida-weeda-wida-weel.

Contributed by:

Lani Johnson

Teacher Resource Guide

Love Walked In

George Gershwin

(1898–1937)

arr. Steve Zegree

SATB
Hal Leonard: 8704361
Overall: 3
Vocal: 3
Tonal/Rhythm: 4

Composer

George Gershwin was born in New York City in 1898, the child of Russian immigrants. As a child Gershwin showed little interest in music until his family purchased their first piano in 1910. His brother, Ira, became his musical partner early on and continued to collaborate with him as his lyricist throughout his life.

In 1914 George dropped out of high school and began to work as a song-plugger for music publisher Jerome H. Remick & Co., promoting the company's catalog by singing and playing the songs for performers. In 1917 Gershwin left Remick & Co. to act as rehearsal pianist for the Broadway show *Miss 1917* by Jerome Kern and Victor Herbert and to pursue composition.

His talents as a composer were quickly noticed by the music community. In 1918 he was offered a 35 dollars per week contract for all future songs he composed. In 1919, Gershwin completed his first full Broadway score, *La La Lucille*. In 1924 Gershwin found further fame with the composition of *Rhapsody in Blue*. With this work Gershwin merged classical orchestral writing with jazz idioms. Additional concert works included Concerto in F (1925), *An American in Paris* (1928), and *Porgy and Bess* (1935).

In 1936 George signed a contract with film studio RKO. Gershwin's output during the late 1930s was dominated by songs for Hollywood movies, such as *Shall We Dance?* (1937), *A Damsel in Distress* (1937), and *The Goldwyn Follies* (1938). George Gershwin died of a brain tumor on July 11, 1937.

Arranger Stephen Zegree earned his doctor of musical arts at the University of Missouri–Kansas City, a master of music at Indiana University, and a bachelor of music at Miami University. He is chairman of jazz studies and professor of music at Western Michigan University, where he teaches piano and jazz, performs with the Western Jazz Quartet, and conducts Gold Company, an internationally recognized Jazz-show vocal ensemble. He is also active as a classical and jazz pianist, conductor, clinician, and adjudicator.

His arrangements have been published by Hal Leonard, Warner Bros., and Shawnee Press. He has produced several recordings, including *Mark Murphy Sings the Nat King Cole Songbook* on Muse Records, and has written *The Complete Guide to Teaching Vocal Jazz*, published by Heritage Music Press.

Composition and Historical Context

George Gershwin did much to further the genre of the American popular song, composing hundreds of tunes for Tin Pan Alley, the Broadway stage, and Hollywood film. He collaborated with his brother Ira on Broadway productions such as *Lady Be Good!*, *Of Thee I Sing*, and *Girl Crazy*. He and his contemporaries diversified the tonal landscape of these songs, incorporating modulations and melodic chromaticisms clearly influenced by jazz. In 1929 he claimed that "ordinary harmonies, rhythms, sequences, intervals, and so on failed to satisfy [his] ear . . . [he] would spend hour upon hour trying to change them around so they would satisfy [him]."

"Love Walked In" was the final collaboration between George and Ira Gershwin, written for the motion picture *The Goldwyn Follies* (1938).

The history of vocal jazz ensembles is obscure, as its roots reach deep into popular musical history with branches growing from jazz, blues, gospel, doo-wop, barbershop, and Broadway. However, adaptations of standards from the Great American Songbook are common. Early vocal ensembles that influenced the genre with such interpretations include the Hi-Los; the Four Freshman; the Platters; Lambert, Hendricks, and Ross; and the Lettermen. Contemporary vocal jazz ensembles of note include Manhattan Transfer, New York Voices, and Take Six.

Technical Considerations

Young singers may be challenged by finding a natural text declamation and tuning certain jazz harmonies. Here are some ideas to remedy these challenges:

Text declamation: Both the composer and I advocate that maintaining a natural line should be the priority, even if it requires altering the tempo and rhythm. To achieve natural declamation, practice reciting the text without pitch or rhythm. Then chant the text on a unison pitch with exaggerated syllabification. Finally, incorporate the pitches and experiment with the declamation until you achieve a natural line. Perhaps offering listening examples of the various interpretations of the original song will encourage a proper rhythmic style.

Intonation: The jazz harmonies in this piece, although derived from voice leading, may pose significant tuning problems. Often linear voice leading encourages horizontal listening. Help your singers to listen vertically to the rich palette of sonorities that Zegree provides by isolating challenging harmonies and building from the root up. Also, be diligent in unifying vowel color with tight harmonies by isolating the ideal vowel in one section and then adding voices.

Stylistic Considerations

Zegree arranged this simple Gershwin song with the specific sound of a vocal jazz ensemble in mind. The rich harmony in this piece requires an immaculately clear, vibrato-free tone from every section. Please be warned that straight-tone singing is a very specialized vocal method that can cause vocal damage and future problems for those students pursuing a classical technique. However, it *is* a legitimate tool required for specific styles of repertoire. Young singers can be exposed to this repertoire and style of singing, but focusing on this production exclusively may not be advisable for their vocal health.

Here are some tips for finding a healthy straight-tone sound:

1. Practice sirens to access head voice/falsetto. Have singers notice where they feel the resonance when they sing sirens (forehead, top of head).
2. Identify the feeling of a raised soft palate by yawning or sniffing an imaginary flower.
3. Find one vowel on which singers can quickly access the desired tone color. The vowel sound [u] as in "lute" is a good vowel with which to start. Then broaden the vowel spectrum by modulating to closely related vowels with the same tone.
4. Listen to professional period/jazz ensembles to help singers identify the type of tone you are seeking.

Musical Elements

MELODY

The melody of this piece is found exclusively in the soprano line. The dominant melodic feature is a repeating E-flat major arpeggio (mm. 2, 6, 10, 18, 22, and 27).

HARMONY

The harmonic language of the original song is quite simple (though it is harmonically richer than many contemporary songs). Zegree's arrangement adds harmonic vocabulary from the vocal jazz idiom, increasing the difficulty of the piece significantly. He incorporates many extended tertian chords, enharmonic spellings, and added-note harmonies. However, the basic harmonic motion remains intact, and the color pitches that Zegree adds are very much derived from smooth voice-leading principles. Therefore, though the harmonies are updated to fit the genre of vocal jazz, this piece remains quite easy to perform.

RHYTHM

Zegree's arrangement of "Love Walked In" maintains the simple, lyrical rhythm of the Gershwin song. There is one quarter note triplet to maneuver, but the rhythm otherwise simply has quarter and eighth note subdivisions of the half note pulse.

TEXTURE

The texture of the original Gershwin song is, of course, melody with accompaniment. Zegree adapts the texture for *a cappella* SATB vocal jazz ensemble, capitalizing on tight harmony and clear tone color with a homophonic and homorhythmic setting. There are several moments of additional three-part treble divisi and three-part bass divisi.

OTHER: DYNAMICS/ARTICULATION/TEMPO/RANGE

Dynamics: *piano* to *forte*

Articulation: Articulations are not marked, but I suggest you derive your decisions from the text, making every effort to affect a natural line.

Tempo: "Freely, with warm expression" is indicated and there are two rallentandos. Again, tempo decisions should be derived from text.

Range:

soprano: G3–E-flat5
alto: G3–B-flat4
tenor: E-flat3–E-flat4
bass: E-flat2–C4

Form and Structure

This is a two-stanza song with eight regular four-measure phrases and a two-measure tag. The first three phrases of each stanza are melodically very similar; however, the last phrase of stanza one acts as a transition into stanza two with a prevalent half cadence, while the last phrase of stanza two is clearly final as indicated by the perfect authentic cadence. The original song also includes a short recitative-like introduction, which is left out of this arrangement.

SECTION	MEASURE	EVENT AND SCORING
Stanza 1		
a	1–4	Phrase one establishes E-flat major key with arpeggio in m. 2
a´	5–8	Phrase two is derived from phrase one (E-flat major arpeggio)
a´´	9–12	Phrase three is derived from phrase one (E-flat major arpeggio)
b	13–16	Transition into stanza two, half cadence in E-flat major
Stanza 2		
a	17–20	Phrase one is similar to phrase one in stanza one, however there is an unexpected C major (add 2) chord and C major arpeggio in the first two measures of this phrase
a´	21–24	Phrase two is similar to phrase two in stanza one (variation on E-flat major arpeggio)
a´´	25–29	Phrase three is similar to phrase three in stanza one (octave E-flat major arpeggios in m. 26)
tag	30–31	Two repetitions of the text "when love walked in"
c	32–34	Phrase four is a perfect authentic cadential figure with slowed rhythm in E-flat major

Text

The recitative-like introduction to the original song is not included in this arrangement. The text is by Ira Gershwin.

Contributed by:

Emilie Sweet

Teacher Resource Guide

O Jesu Christ, mein Lebens Licht, BWV 118

Johann Sebastian Bach
(1685–1750)

SATB with orchestra
Carus-Verlag: 31.118/00
Overall: 3
Vocal: 4
Tonal: 3

Composer

Johann Sebastian Bach worked in Leipzig as kantor of the Thomasschule from 1723 until his death twenty-seven years later. In this position Bach worked as music teacher at the St. Thomas School, organist at the Thomaskirche, and director of both church music and civic music in Leipzig, the latter as required by the town council. As kantor, Bach was responsible for providing music (primarily of his own creation) for worship services in the four main Leipzig churches, including the Thomaskirche. By the time he moved to Leipzig, Bach was certainly no stranger to the composition of sacred music, having already worked for many years as organist and concertmeister at Weimar before his relocation to Cöthen and then to Leipzig.

The well-known, remarkable outpouring of cantatas during his first four years in Leipzig, approximately one each week at the two principal churches for use during Sunday and holiday services, attests not only to the rigorous demands of his employment but also his compositional skill, versatility, and reliability. In addition to his cantata output, Bach composed a number of other works, both secular and sacred. As town music director, Bach provided music for special occasions, such as weddings and funerals of government officials, dignitaries and other important figures. Although many remember Bach primarily for his sacred vocal works, he also composed a large number of instrumental works, including keyboard works, *concerti grossi*, and chamber music.

Composition and Historical Perspective

In the autograph score of "O Jesu Christ, meins Lebens Licht" (BWV 118), Bach used the descriptor "Motette" in the title of the work. This problematic genre assignment by the composer himself has resulted in debate over the correct classification of the work. Despite the appellation given by Bach, certain aspects of BWV 118 have led to its classification as a cantata. For example, in the first version of the Bach collected works, the *Bach-Ausgabe* of the late-nineteenth century, BWV 118 was included in the cantata series, probably due to the long-held belief that motets were predominantly unaccompanied choral works.

This line of thought is somewhat more easily understood when viewed against the eighteenth-century definition of a motet. Writers during Bach's lifetime described the motet as a polyphonic vocal work to be sung either unaccompanied (basso continuo excepted) or with instruments playing *colla parte* but not, presumably, in an obbligato or otherwise independent fashion. Further research into the motet genre and performance practice technique has revealed exceptions to the definition and thereby has laid to rest this misconception of the a cappella motet. In the *Neue Bach-Ausgabe*, BWV 118 is included in the motet volumes.

Although the compositional style of BWV 118 diverges somewhat from that of motets described by writers during Bach's lifetime, the circumstances surrounding its origin allow for its classification as a motet. Motets in Germany were used primarily in two ways: as introits in the Lutheran service and for special occasions, such as funerals. BWV 118 exists in two versions. It is believed that BWV 118 was originally composed sometime around 1736 for use during an outdoor burial service. Bach prepared a second version less than ten years later, but the occasion that warranted the new version is not known.

Technical Considerations and Musical Elements

The primary difference between the two versions of BWV 118 lies in the instrumentation. The original version is scored for SATB choir, two litui (the lituo is an archaic brass instrument), cornetto, and three trombones. Presumably because of its use at an open-air graveside service, the first version is lacking an independent basso continuo line. The second version, however, does call for basso continuo. In this version Bach retained the SATB texture and the two litui but replaced the trombones with strings (two violins and viola) and specified on the title page that winds (oboes and bassoon) may be used to double the voice parts. With a few minor exceptions, the vocal parts are the same from the first version to the second.

Both versions of BWV 118 have been used by editors as the basis for modern performing editions. In some cases, versions have been integrated into the modern editions, and in others separate versions are published. Piano-vocal scores and scholarly informed editions with full instrumentation are available. Horns are sometimes recommended as substitutions for the litui; depending on a director's resources and one's ability to prepare instrumental parts, trumpets (preferably B-flat) could also be used. Good flügelhorn players could also be recruited, and, in fact, this instrument might better replicate the mellow sound of the lituo.

If using brass instruments to perform BWV 118 in its original version, one should recruit players with a fair amount of instrumental proficiency. It is likely that Bach composed the original version with professional musicians from the Stadtpfeifer at his disposal. Therefore, while the parts are not extremely difficult to play on modern instruments, they do require players with good command of the instrument, particularly in the more chromatic, melismatic passages. To accommodate the range of the first trombone part, an alto trombone should be used. Alto trombones, while not entirely uncommon, are not played by all trombonists, and it may require a good bit of searching to find a player with the appropriate level of competency on the instrument. The other two trombone parts present no problems and can be played on standard tenor and bass trombones.

From a vocal standpoint, BWV 118 offers few technical difficulties and is appropriate for a variety of mixed choir types. The *cantus firmus* setting of the chorale tune in the soprano line is certainly manageable by adult or youth trebles. Breathing and stamina are potential problems in any work using *cantus firmus* technique. For untrained singers, breathing exercises as part of a warm-up routine may help. The chorale phrases in BWV 118, however, are not overly lengthy, and with a little coaching in proper breathing techniques most choirs should be able to handle them with little difficulty. Alternating breaths will also help in this regard. The lower three parts are more involved in typical Bach-like contrapuntal fashion, but the harmonic complexity and the associated chromaticism are minimal. Therefore, the parts may easily be taught to singers.

The text of the work should present no challenges to anyone with experience teaching singers the basics of German diction. Careful attention to musical articulations will also assist with diction. For example, advocating the typically Baroque articulation that involves clipping the first of two successive quarter notes that occur over textual elements separated by commas, allows for cleaner diction and a more transparent musical texture. As with sung English, crisp and shortened production of German consonants, especially those of a sibilant nature, will also result in improved diction.

The instrumental ritornelli before and between the chorale phrases, which incidentally employ a motive that bears a striking resemblance to the opening theme of the *St. Matthew Passion*, are beautifully lush and full of overlapping chains of suspensions and quasi-suspensions. Baroque articulations are necessary to avoid an excessively thick and lugubrious texture. This may also involve the assignment of bowings and specialized bowing techniques if using the string version.

As mentioned earlier, the first version of BWV 118 lacks an independent basso continuo line, although in the autograph score, Bach includes some figures above the bottom trombone line. Whether this means a (portable) continuo instrument was included in the first performance of the work is unclear. It does, however, leave room for a modern performance of the first version with basso continuo at the director's discretion.

Form and Structure

In a manner true to a traditional, somewhat archaic style of motet composition, Bach structures BWV 118 around a *cantus firmus* in long note values. The *cantus firmus* is the chorale tune "Ach, Gott, wie manches Herzeleid," a tune that was also used for the hymn "O Jesu Christ, meins Lebens Licht." For each of the four lines of text used in BWV 118 (e.g., the first verse of the hymn), Bach assigned the choral tune to the trebles. The lower voice parts accompany the *cantus firmus* with imitative counterpoint that uses thematic material drawn from the chorale tune.

The lituo duet is true obbligato, in that the two parts maintain an independent role during the ritornellos and in a subdued manner during the choral sections. The other instruments, however, play independently during the ritornellos and assume a primarily *colla parte* role as the choir enters.

In the section below measure numbers are taken from the score in the *Neue Bach-Ausgabe* volume (*NBA* III/i) of Bach's collected works.

Measure	Event and Scoring
1–19	Instrumental introduction
18–30	Chorale: stanza 1, line 1; *cantus firmus* in soprano
30–35	Ritornello overlaps with chorus mm. 34–35
34–44	Chorale: stanza 1, line 2; *cantus firmus* in soprano
44–51	Ritornello overlaps with chorus mm. 47–51
47–62	Chorale: stanza 1, line 3; *cantus firmus* in soprano
62–70	Ritornello overlaps with chorus mm. 69–70
69–90	Chorale: stanza 1, line 4; *cantus firmus* in soprano
2–19 (version 1)	*Da capo dal segno* (m. 2) with *fine* occurring in m. 19
2–108 (version 2)	*Dal segno* (m. 2); repeat of entire work with mm. 1–19 added at end

Text and Translation

The text for BWV 118 is the first verse of a hymn by early seventeenth-century pastor and hymn writer Martin Behm.

O Jesu Christ, meins Lebens Licht,	O Jesus Christ, light of my life,
Mein Hort, mein Trost, mein Zuversicht,	My refuge, my comfort, my hope,
Auf Erden bin ich nur ein Gast	On earth I am only a guest
Und drückt mich sehr der Sünden Last.	And the burden of my sins oppresses me.

Additional References and Resources

Butt, John, ed. *The Sacred Choral Music of J. S. Bach: A Handbook.* Brewster, MA: Paraclete, 1997.

Melamed, Daniel R. *J. S. Bach and the German Motet.* Cambridge: Cambridge University Press, 1995.

Parrot, Andrew. *The Essential Bach Choir.* Woodbridge, UK: Boydell, 2000.

Schulze, Hans-Joachim. "'O Jesu Christ, meins Lebens Licht': On the Transmission of a Bach Source and the Riddle of Its Origin." In *A Bach Tribute: Essays in Honor of William H. Scheide.* Edited by Ray Robinson and Paul Brainard. Chapel Hill, NC: Hinshaw, 1993.

Suggested Listening

Johann Sebastian Bach:

- "O Jesu Christ, meins Lebens Licht" on *Motets BWV 225-231, Cantatas BWV 50 & 118*, Monteverdi Choir and English Baroque Soloists, John Eliot Gardiner, Erato CD 2292-45979-2. (This performance of BWV 118 is also on J. E. Gardiner's *Bach Cantatas*, Archiv CD 463581.)
- "O Jesu Christ, meins Lebens Licht" on *Die Motetten*, Gächinger Kantorei and Bach-Collegium Stuttgart, Helmuth Rilling, Hänssler Classics CD 98.965.
- "O Jesu Christ, meins Lebens Licht" on *A Bach Album*, His Majesty's Consort of Voices, His Majesty's Sagbutts and Cornetts, Timothy Roberts, Hyperion CDA67247.
- "O Jesu Christ, meins Lebens Licht" on *Bach Edition: Vol. 17*, Holland Boys Choir, Netherlands Bach Collegium, Peter Jan Leusink, Brilliant Classics CD 99376.

Contributed by:

Wayne Glass

Teacher Resource Guide

O magnum mysterium

Tomás Luis de Victoria
(1548–1611)

SATB a cappella
G. Schirmer: 50305150
Overall: 3
Vocal: 3
Tonal/Rhythm: 4

Composer

Tomás Luis de Victoria was born in 1548 in Avila, Spain. As a boy he sang at the Avila Cathedral. He received a grant allowed for study in Rome at the Collegio Germanico, where he worked as *maestro di cappella* after the completion of his studies. He was ordained to the priesthood in 1575.

In 1585 he moved to Madrid and began service at the Monasterio de las Descalzas de Santa Clara as chaplain to King Philip II's sister, Empress Maria, for whom he worked almost exclusively until her death in 1603. Victoria continued in the role of chaplain for Maria's daughter, Princess Margaret. He died in 1611.

Victoria's known compositional output comprises only sacred music. The nature of his employment in the Santa Clara convent and other churches, as well as his own fervent dedication to the Roman Catholic faith, may have precluded any recourse to the composition of secular works. His extant works include twenty Masses, including two Requiems; eighteen Magnificats; two Passions; fifty-six motets; and many other sacred works, such as lamentations, hymns, and responsories.

Composition and Historical Perspective

In its original liturgical context, the plainchant "O magnum mysterium" was used as a responsory during the Christmas Matins service. Motet texts were often drawn from antiphons and responsories, although their placement within the service varied within the context of their function as musical embellishments of the liturgy.

Victoria's "O magnum mysterium" appeared in his first published volume of works, *Motecta* (Venice, 1572), a collection of thirty-three motets. It is composed for four voices (SATB).

Technical Considerations and Musical Elements

The ranges of the vocal parts of "O magnum mysterium," in its original tonal center of G Dorian, rarely exceed an octave, as indicated in the chart below.

Voice part	Range
Soprano	D4–D5
Alto	F3–A4
Tenor	C3–E4
Bass	F2–A3

(For modern choirs, the original is typically transposed up a minor third as in Hinshaw Music: HMC-960.)

At this tonal center, the alto part lies somewhat low. Depending on the maturity of voices in the choir, a director may choose to ask one or two light, lyric tenors to join the altos. Keep in mind, however, that in doing so, the director should ask the tenors not to oversing or push the top notes. The bass part also dips fairly low at times, which will be especially problematic for younger choirs. In this case, a director might choose simply to raise the pitch of the entire work if the work is not to be performed accompanied, otherwise the instrumental parts will also need to be transposed.

As with the performance of any Renaissance motet, singers should be encouraged to sing with minimal vibrato, especially at cadential points. With choirs of more mature singers, the director should ask singers to take some of the weight out of the voice and emphasize the core sound. Exercises focusing on intonation, especially those using *messa di voce* techniques, are helpful in training choirs to sing Renaissance literature.

The pronunciation of the text for "O magnum mysterium" should present no problems to anyone with experience singing in Latin. For those who need assistance with basic Latin pronunciation and diction, Ron Jeffers's book (see Additional References and Resources) is a good resource. As with most Renaissance motets in Latin, it is advisable to emphasize purity of vowels and clean, minimal production of consonants to enhance the linear nature of the music.

Stylistic Considerations

While it was long thought that the performance practice of Renaissance motets called for unaccompanied singing, this notion has been largely countered by convincing arguments toward the inclusion of instruments to double the voices. It is entirely conceivable that, based on extant evidence regarding the employment of instrumentalists in Spanish churches and cathedrals during Victoria's time, motets were played on instruments such as the organ, vihuela, and sackbut.

A recurring problem for music directors programming Renaissance music is the issue of *music ficta* (unsigned accidentals). Knowing how to alter notes in a work requires some knowledge of why and when such alterations were called for. While publishers of some modern performing editions approach the music from a scholarly and practical angle, not all rely on well-informed editorial decisions. Therefore, a choral director who plans to invest time in the preparation of Renaissance choral music would be well served by researching the concept to make appropriate decisions regarding *musica ficta*. Two resources that deal with the topic of *music ficta* are listed in the bibliography.

Form and Structure

Victoria's setting of "O magnum mysterium" can be divided into three main sections, all of which are structured around textual divisions. The first section may be subdivided into three subsections with distinct musical ideas. The form of the work may be seen in the following chart.

Section	Measure	Event and Scoring
Section 1	1–19	"O magnum mysterium et admirabile sacramentum"; canonic; paired imitation (soprano/alto and tenor/bass)
	20–28	"Ut animalia viderent Dominum natum"; SAT trio predominates; tertiary harmonies
	28–39	"Jacentem in praesepio!"; imitative; melodic quasi-inversion of opening motive
Section 2	40–52	"Beata Virgo, cujus viscera meruerunt portare Dominum Christum"; dramatic change to homophonic texture; harmonic coloring
Section 3	53–74	"Alleluia!"; half note (tactus) = dotted half note; returning to half note tactus at m. 67

Text and Translation

O magnum mysterium	O great mystery
Et admirabile sacramentum,	And wondrous sacrament,
Ut animalia viderent Dominum natum,	That animals should see the Lord's birth
Jacentem in praesepio!	Lying in a manger!
Beata Virgo,	O blessed Virgin,
Cujus viscera meruerunt	Whose womb was worthy
Portare Dominum Christum. Alleluia!	To bear the Lord Christ. Alleluia!

Suggested References and Resources

Bryant, James R. "*Musica ficta* in Renaissance Choral Music." *Choral Journal* 19 (October 1978), 20–25.

Cramer, Eugene. *Studies in the Music of Tomás Luis de Victoria*. Aldershot, UK: Ashgate, 2001.

———. *Tomás Luis de Victoria: A Guide to Research*. New York: Garland, 1998.

Jeffers, Ron. *Translations and Annotations of Choral Repertoire, Vol. I: Sacred Latin Texts*. Corvallis, OR: earthsongs, 1988.

Noone, Michael. Program notes to *Assumption Mass*. Performed by Orchestra of the Renaissance, Richard Cheetham, conductor. Glossa, GCD-921404, 2001.

Routley, Nicholas. "A Practical Guide to *Musica Ficta*." *Early Music* 13 (February 1985), 59–71.

Contributed by:

Wayne Glass

Teacher Resource Guide

O Sing Joyfully

Adrian Batten

(1591–1637)

SATB
Oxford University Press: 3502283
Overall: 3
Vocal: 2
Tonal/Rhythm: 3

Composer

Adrian Batten was born in Salisbury, England, in 1591. It is not known where he may have received his training, but by 1614 he was a lay vicar at Westminster Cathedral, where he made a career as a singer, composer, and copyist. Later, Batten became a vicar-choral at St. Paul's Cathedral, where it seems he remained until his death in 1637. According to Maurice Bevan in his article on Batten in the *New Grove Dictionary of Music and Musicians*, Batten was a "competent craftsman, writing in a style which was both devotional and restrained." His musical output, all of which is sacred vocal music, consists almost exclusively of services and anthems for the Anglican Church.

Composition and Historical Perspective

"O Sing Joyfully" is best described as a full anthem. The term "full anthem" indicates a work for full, *a cappella* chorus as opposed to the contemporaneous verse anthem for alternating soloist or soloists with instruments and full chorus. In Batten's day, verse anthems were becoming more common, while full anthems were viewed as a more conservative style. While it is impossible to place this work within Batten's career, "O Sing Joyfully" was written during the Elizabethan period (roughly 1570–1620), in which elements of Renaissance and Baroque styles were prevalent. The anthem is a setting of Psalm 84:1–4. The style alternates between homophony and brief imitations.

Technical Considerations and Musical Elements

The word "tabret," found in m. 12, will be unfamiliar to most singers. The Hebrew word, translated as the more usual "timbrel" in many versions of Psalm 81, is rendered as "tabret" in the King James Version, which was probably Batten's text source. A "tabret" is a small frame with jingles attached to the frame used in songs of praise by the Israelites.

Like so many other English works of the same time period, "O Sing Joyfully" contains instances of chromaticism and cross-relations that can be tricky for choirs unused to singing them. Examples of chromaticism include the G-flat and G-natural in the alto line in mm. 6–7 and the G-natural and G-flat found in the bass line in m. 38. The most obvious examples of cross-relations occur in m. 38 between the soprano and alto parts and in m. 39 between the alto and tenor lines. In both cases, these voice parts form a diminished octave, which can be uncomfortable for choristers unaccustomed to such jarring dissonances in Renaissance-era vocal music. It is incumbent upon the director to analyze these difficulties in straightforward terms to his or her singers and to rehearse them diligently on these passages.

Batten's works have been criticized at times for awkward text settings. The clearest example of this can be found in m. 35 in the alto part at the text "God of Jacob." Other instances of seemingly awkward word fitting were quite commonplace in the Renaissance and early Baroque Eras. Examples can be found in m. 8 in the tenor line at "God of Jacob" and mm. 41–42 in the alto at the repetition of "of Jacob." Once again, the director needs to make sure the choristers are thoroughly rehearsed on these passages.

Stylistic Considerations

Tempo

Tempo decisions need to be made based on such factors as the rate of harmonic change, note values, and text. The joyful text indicates an overall quick tempo tempered by the prevalence of quarter notes and eighth notes in the composition. The piece should be conducted in two despite any (editorial) indications to the contrary.

Dynamics and Interpretative Markings

The use of dynamics and interpretative markings should be governed primarily by changes of mood in the text. Dynamic indications that appear in any edition of "O Sing Joyfully" are completely editorial and represent one person's interpretation. Feel free to make changes to dynamics and interpretative markings in an edition that is not totally clean, but keep in mind that extreme dynamic ranges (***pp***, ***ff***), sudden shifts of dynamics, and dramatic *crescendos* and *diminuendos* would not have been a part of the musical language of the time period unless determined by textual considerations.

Musica Ficta

The practice of *musica ficta* in Renaissance vocal music can be defined as the introduction of accidentals not expressly written into the score. In Batten's day, it is believed that singers would add *ficta* extemporaneously in performance, following certain rules for treatment of dissonances within the music. In reliable editions, *musica ficta* decisions on the part of the editor are usually indicated either by the positioning of the accidental on top of the note instead of to the left or by putting the accidental in parentheses. One may certainly trust an editor's judgment concerning *musica ficta*, but it is a good idea to consult sources to augment one's understanding of this practice (see Additional References and Resources).

Musica ficta decisions are particularly problematic at the end of "O Sing Joyfully." The diminished octaves in mm. 38 and 39 are very jarring. However, it should be noted that these simultaneous cross-relations, while not common, are found in the music of Batten's English contemporaries. The rationale for preserving the diminished octaves is that the use of *ficta* avoids the melodic tritone in the soprano part in m. 38 and creates a typical Renaissance cadential formula in the tenor part in m. 39. As a result, the director should not alter these dissonances arbitrarily but allow his or her singers to experience them in all their pungent glory!

Phrasing

The music of Batten, as that of his sixteenth- and early seventeenth-century English colleagues, contained few if any barlines in the original manuscripts. Renaissance singers were used to reading unbarred music out of single-line partbooks, an experience completely foreign to most modern singers. Many editions of this music will add barlines so as not to disorient choristers accustomed to them. It is important to instruct singers to follow the natural accents of the text rather than the accents they might inadvertently make upon viewing the barlines in the music. In addition, singers should observe the principle of allowing accented syllables to *diminuendo* and unaccented syllables to *crescendo*, resulting in a fluid, lively phrasing.

Text Underlay

Text underlay issues abound in much literature from the Renaissance and can be very thorny for the modern day conductor to resolve. It is important to understand that seemingly awkward word fitting might truly be awkward or it may be an idiomatic Renaissance method of text underlay. Consult sources such as Robert Donington's *The Interpretation of Music* for more information. Careful preparation will make it less likely that the singers will be confused on text underlay and inadvertently fit the words incorrectly to the music.

Form and Structure

The form of the music generally follows the text. As a result, the music shifts back and forth between homophonic and imitative texture according to the sense of the words.

SECTION	MEASURE	EVENT AND SCORING
"O sing joyfully unto God our strength"	1–4	Declamatory, homophonic
"Make a cheerful noise unto the God of Jacob"	5–9	Loose imitations, possibly word painting representing the "cheerful noise"
"Take the song, bring hither the tabret: the merry harp with the lute"	10–14	Declamatory; homophonic
"Blow up the trumpet in the new moon"	14–17	Declamatory, homophonic; two pauses, the first on the second half note of m. 14 and the second in the form of a quarter rest in m. 15 between statements of "Blow up"
"Ev'n in the time appointed, and upon our solemn feast day"	18–28	Mixture of contrapuntally enlivened homophony and imitations
"For this was made a statute for Israel"	28–31	Declamatory homophony with some contrapuntally enlivened texture
"And a law of the God of Jacob"	32–42	Imitative texture

Text

O sing joyfully unto God our strength:
Make a cheerful noise unto the God of Jacob.
Take the song, bring hither the tabret:
The merry harp with the lute.
Blow up the trumpet in the new moon:
Ev'n in the time appointed, and upon our solemn feast day.
For this was made a statute for Israel:
And a law of the God of Jacob.

Suggested Listening

Adrian Batten:

"O Sing Joyfully" on *Beyond Chant–Mysteries of the Renaissance*, Voices of Ascension, Dennis Keene, Delos Records 3165.

"O Sing Joyfully" on *Music for a Great Cathedral*, Choir of St. Paul's Cathedral, Christopher Dearnley, Guild B000025YOR.

Contributed by:

Christopher Jackson

Teacher Resource Guide

Past Life Melodies

Sarah Hopkins

(b. 1958)

Mixed voices divisi (eleven parts)
Morton Music: MM2001
Overall: 3
Vocal: 4
Tonal/Rhythm: 3

Composer

Sarah Hopkins is an Australian composer-performer highly acclaimed for her visionary music and inspiring performances on cello, harmonic overtone singing, handbells, choir, and the celestial harmonic whirlies of her own creation. With a strong background and training in classical music, over the years she has moved into the realm of holistic music and has developed a distinct compositional voice. Her solo, ensemble, choral, and orchestral compositions demonstrate an expansive and pure musical style that resonates with the space and energy of the Australian landscape as well as the inner landscape of the human psyche.

To truly comprehend Sarah Hopkins's music, you must begin by understanding her philosophy:

> As a composer-performer, my desire is to create music which resonates with the space and energy of the Australian landscape as well as the inner landscape of the human psyche. I want my music to move and inspire people and reconnect them with the heart of Life. Compositionally I trust the power of the simple, direct, and heartfelt and am guided by my intuition. Sometimes dreams and visions inspire

> my music. Often melodies literally sing through me as was the case in "Past Life Melodies," "Two Kyries from the Winds of Heaven," "Return to Joy," and "Honour the Earth as Your Mother." I often feel like a "song catcher" and dreamweaver, creating sonic tapestries to bridge heaven and earth with the songs from my soul.

An accomplished performer, Hopkins's style of cello playing embraces many new and ancient sounds, including musical bird calls, deep earthy drones, lush heartfelt melodies, and the haunting rhythms of the didgeridoo, which she emulates on her cello. Vocally she specializes in harmonic overtone singing—a magical, otherworldly sound with its roots in Mongolia and Tibet. Hopkins also produces celestial music playing her harmonic whirlies, weaving together intricate patterns of movement and sound, music and dance.

Sarah lives in Brisbane, Queensland (Australia) and tours nationally and internationally performing her own original music, running workshops in holistic music and harmonic overtone singing, and working as an artist-in-residence. Her versatile and portable style of performance enables her to participate within a wide variety of settings, including international arts and music festivals, corporate events, folk and world music festivals, community arts centers, universities, and schools. In 2005 Hopkins was honored by having a street named after her—Sarah Hopkins Lane—and a Rural Housing Estate near Childers (Queensland) named after her composition *Childers Shining*.

Composition and Historical Perspective

"Past Life Melodies" was composed in 1991 on a commission from Graeme Morton, conductor of the St. Peter's Chorale, a sixty-voice high school choir in Brisbane, Australia. However, the skeletal framework and genesis of the music dates back to 1988, when the opening theme first "sang through" Hopkins. She describes this theme as "a melody of profound connection, known and remembered, as though it were a song from a past lifetime. It comes . . . to me at times of extreme emotion. It comes as a lament, as a means to express unspeakable emotions. It comes as a strength to transform sorrow . . . it comes as a song of liberation." In May 1990, a time when the composer was living in Darwin in Australia's far north, another melody came to her—this one very Aboriginal in feel. She interpreted it as "an old Aboriginal woman chanting deep inside me."

One of the interesting features of "Past Life Melodies" is the use of harmonic overtone singing. Harmonic overtone singing has its roots in Hoomei "throat" singing, which is indigenous to Western Mongolia, and the overtone chanting of Tantric Tibetan Buddhism. It is a vocal technique that allows singing in two voices simultaneously, first creating a steady fundamental note in the low register and then producing high harmonics or overtones (natural upper partials of the fundamental pitch being sung) by modulating the shape of the oral cavity.

"Past Life Melodies" has an approximate duration of 7:20 and can be performed by choirs of virtually any size. The largest choir to sing it to date was a choir of more than seven thousand high schools students with orchestra, didgeridoo, and harmonic whirlies in the Sydney Olympic Stadium as part of the Opening Ceremony for the 2000 Pan Pacific School Games. The smallest was a group of eleven singers: Chanticleer! Sarah has also created versions for SA divisi, treble voice and four cellos, orchestra, twelve cellos, brass ensemble, eight horns and optional didgeridoo, string orchestra, and concert band, and many of these arrangements can be performed together with choir.

To assist conductors in the preparation and teaching of this music, the printed resource booklet *Rehearsing and Performing "Past Life Melodies"* (Morton Music, MM 2008) and the companion CD *Sarah Hopkins Rehearses "Past Life Melodies"* (MM 3001) are highly recommended. This information is comprehensive and illuminating; twenty-seven separate tracks with examples of each section of the work in performance as well as suggested rehearsal warm-ups, and instruction for harmonic overtone singing. Unless you have enjoyed a workshop on this piece with the composer herself, this resource is a must have for the conductor interested in truly understanding the essence of this choral piece.

Technical Considerations and Musical Elements

The music divides into a total of eleven parts, and the composer provides suggestions for the division of parts in the preface to the score. The St. Peter's Chorale was a sixty-voice choir, so the number of voices per part reflects that particular choir's make-up. In this writer's experience, part division can be rather flexible and is best done by taking the strengths of each singer into consideration. Parts 1–3 are designated for sopranos, and I suggest using soprano 1 to capitalize on their range and color. Parts 4–7 feature doubling of soprano, alto and tenor voices, and I suggest using soprano 2 in these parts. Parts 8–11 are for basses and work well with baritones on parts 8 and 9 and basses on parts 10 and 11.

The topic of voice parts brings the placement of singers into question. While the composer gives a clear suggestion of three broad semicircles and the relationship of parts therein, you should be encouraged to explore various standing arrangements according to the needs and abilities of your choir and the performance venue. One highly successful format I repeatedly used on a Westminster Schola Cantorum tour was to place the choir in a large circle completely surrounding the audience. In some venues we were able to take the harmonic overtone singers up into balconies to sing across the room.

Successfully teaching the harmonic overtone singing requires time, and experience has shown that it is generally best to introduce the concept to your choir as a whole many weeks before you begin to teach the piece itself. It is often very surprising to see who ends up producing consistently successful overtones, and it takes singers regular practice of a few weeks to become confident with this type of singing. Exercises incorporating the harmonic overtone singing into warm-ups are very effective and give singers the opportunity to work on the technique in a familiar and comfortable environment. It also gives you time to assess their ability and success with the technique.

"Past Life Melodies" is comprised of three large sections, each contrasting in color, energy and style. To capture the colors the composer had in mind, it is important to understand that she wrote this piece for the "natural voice and its inherent qualities" as opposed to the classically trained Western choral sound that is the usual aim. "Past Life Melodies" requires your singers to explore their voices and produce resonant hums, long notes of pure sustained "sonic color," open-throated chant singing inspired by the Eastern European folk tradition, and Australian Aboriginal inspired chant, as well as the harmonic overtone singing. Throughout the score, the composer gives clues as to the emotional intent ("sing from your soul," "heart sound—full of love and warmth," and "earthy rhythmic chant full of primitive power and vigour") as well as more practical considerations ("smile to brighten the sound" and "nasal edge to the sound").

Form and Structure

SECTION	MEASURE	EVENT AND SCORING
Section 1	1–30	First chant to be sung "from your soul" and "with great breadth"; various colors/timbres used in chant; quarter note = 52
	1–8	Resonant humming; ***mf*** dynamic.
	8 (beat 4)–16	Brighter "ah" ("heart sound—full of love and warmth")
	16 (beat 4)–24	"Yeah" ("joyous and liberated"); *forte* dynamic
	25–30	Final "Yeah" is sustained at ***ff*** with introduction of pure "oo" from parts 1 and 2; transition into second chant section
Section 2	31–56	Second chant "earthy rhythmic, full of primitive power and vigour"; chant should have a nasal edge in the style of Australian Aboriginal singing; very strong sense of "innate" body movement on the quarter note pulse; conductor uses left hand cues to indicate each repetition of the chant

Section	Measure	Event and Scoring
	31–38	Chant in parts 5 and 8; part 6 joins with 3
	39–42	Chant in parts 1, 5, and 8; part 2 joins with 5
	43–46	Chant in parts 1, 2, 5, and 8; part 7 joins with 6, and part 11 joins with 9
	47–50	Chant in parts 1, 2, 5, and 8; part 4 joins with 6, and part 10 joins with 9
	51–58	Chant in parts 1, 2, 5, and 8 with gradual *diminuendo* until chant fades back into the B drone sung by parts 3, 4, 6, 7, 9, 10, and 11
Section 3	57–end	Harmonic overtone singing on B by six singers for approximately forty seconds while majority of choirs sustains the B fundamental in their own octave; composer specifies "six solo harmonic singers, each singing their own individual melodies like gold and silver threads; shape every breath-phrase you sing"; the piece concludes with a unified hum on the B fundamental and a gentle *decrescendo* over the final ten seconds.

Additional References and Resources

"Past Life Melodies" editions (Morton Music Publications): SA divisi, MM 2003; treble and four cellos, MM 2004; concert band, MM 2015; string orchestra, MM 2014; twelve cellos, MM 2017; brass ensemble, MM 2016; eight horns and optional didgeridoo, MM 2018; and orchestra, MM 2009.

A complete list of Sarah Hopkins' scores and recordings can be downloaded from the Australian Music Centre's Web site at www.amcoz.com.au/opac/name.aspx?id=3395. For the composer's Web site, go to www.sarahhopkins.com.

Suggested Listening

The following mixed-voice recordings of "Past Life Melodies" are excellent role models and capture the vocal colors the composer intended.

Sarah Hopkins Rehearses Past Life Melodies, Morton Music, CD MM-3001 (available from Musical Resources, Toledo, OH, 1-800-377-0234; www.musical-resources.com. This seventy-minute CD is a companion to *Rehearsing and Performing "Past Life Melodies"* (Morton Music MM-2008) and includes spoken commentary from the composer as she systematically rehearses "Past Life Melodies" with the St. Peter's Chorale. Inspiring performances of the full piece open and close the CD. The tempo and interpretation are excellent as the composer herself is directing the choir.

Reclaiming the Spirit—Sarah Hopkins, New World Music, Aust. NWCD777. Holistic music by Sarah Hopkins for cello, voices, harmonic overtone singing, choir, bells, harmonic whirlies, synthesizer, viola, and clarinet. Great for meditation and healing . . . "music which sounds like the very essence of the universe." (Phil Brown, *Oz Arts Magazine*)

Honour the Earth, New World Music—Sarah Hopkins, New World Music, Aust. NWCD570. Visionary music by Sarah Hopkins for choir, orchestra, didgeridoo, harmonic overtone singing, shakuhachi, cello and the celestial harmonic whirlies. "Inspiring, heartfelt music, fabulous for meditation and massage, *Honour the Earth* calls us back to the very heart of life itself where we find ourselves resplendent, humbled, and restored." (Kerry Harvey)

This Our Land, St. Peter's Chorale directed by Graeme Morton, Gemstone Music CD 1002 (available from Musical Resources, Toledo, OH, 1-800-377-0234; www.musical-resources.com).

Contributed by:

Heather J. Buchanan

Teacher Resource Guide

Sing Me to Heaven

Daniel Gawthrop

(b. 1949)

SATB a cappella
Dunstan House: DH 9601
Overall: 3
Vocal: 3
Tonal/Rhythm: 3

Composer, Composition, and Historical Perspective

Daniel Gawthrop admits that he is lucky to be one of a "rare breed" in being a full-time composer. He trained as an organist and pianist but also sang in choirs throughout his youth. Most of his compositions are for choir, and he runs his own publishing company, Dunstan House, where he publishes many of his own works. Gawthrop studied at Brigham Young University and Michigan State University and has held adjunct faculty positions at several institutions. Numerous organizations and institutions have commissioned him to write more than a hundred works, and he served as composer-in-residence to the Fairfax Symphony Orchestra for three years.

In addition to composing, Gawthrop has worked as a broadcaster, conductor, church musician, clinician, and a music critic for the *Washington Post*. Most likely his most recognized choral composition, "Sing Me to Heaven" was commissioned in 1990 by Voce, a community chamber choir based in northern Virginia. It is available in SATB, TTBB, and SSAA formats, all published by Dunstan House. More information on commissioning Daniel Gawthrop, his published works, and "Sing Me to Heaven" can be found at www.dunstanhouse.com.

Technical Considerations and Musical Elements

MELODY AND RANGE

"Sing Me to Heaven" has a beautiful and deceptively simple through-composed melody. Intervals of more than a third occur primarily (but not exclusively) in the melodic line, which is always placed in the highest sounding voice part (nearly always the soprano line). Although intervals in any voice sometimes involve a skip to an unprepared dissonance, the singers will find their lines easy to sing after they become familiar with the harmonic movement of the piece. As the contour of the melodic and accompanimental lines is determined by the harmonies, the conductor is advised to do the majority of his or her rehearsing with tutti voices. There will be instances where a particular section might need to be rehearsed briefly in one or two voices alone, but on the whole the ensemble will be able to deal with any interval or tuning issues in the context of a full rehearsal.

Gawthrop writes lines in a comfortable range for all the vocal parts. The sopranos nearly always sing between C4 and E5; one F-sharp5 occurs in m. 34, but the sopranos are divisi for that measure with the lower sopranos singing B4. When the sopranos are required to sing anything lower than C4, they are in unison with the alto line (e.g., mm. 2–4). After the opening four measures of the piece, where they sing in unison with the sopranos on an A-flat3 and B-flat3, the alto part lies between B3 and B4. The tenor part lies entirely between E3 and E4 and they sing primarily between G-sharp3 and D-sharp4. The basses sing between C-sharp3 and B3 for the first fifty measures of the piece; they sing B2 in mm. 51–58 and A2 in the penultimate measure (m. 57).

RHYTHM

The rhythmic elements of "Sing Me to Heaven" are not complex. Gawthrop begins in a 3/4 time signature, switches to 4/4 in m. 15 and returns to 3/4 at m. 45 for the remainder of the piece. The most difficult rhythmic pattern for the women is a dotted eighth-sixteenth in m. 14; the most difficult pattern for the men is one beat of triplet eighth notes occurring in m. 10. Other than these two instances, the most complex pattern to be found is the occasional dotted quarter note plus eighth note. The piece is entirely homophonic with staggered entrances coming in only mm. 38 and 45–47.

TONALITY

"Sing Me to Heaven" begins in A-flat major and moves to the enharmonic parallel G-sharp minor at m. 8. This change in tonality looks somewhat odd in the score, as the composer shifts from the key signature of four flats to one of five sharps, but the tonal shift is actually easy for the singers to comprehend and sing. Gawthrop moves into the relative major (B major) at m. 19 and remains there for the remainder of the piece.

Gawthrop describes his style of writing as being strongly determined by his choice of harmonies, and he employs a variety of lush higher tertian chords throughout "Sing Me to Heaven." Most of those chords seem natural to the ensemble's ears, but there are certain chord progressions that will take some careful tuning. The conductor will easily identify those points by locating the few accidentals notated in the score. These come at mm. 7 and 18, both of which directly precede a change in tonality as noted above, in mm. 10–12, 26–30, and the penultimate measure. After hearing these chord progressions once or twice the choir will be able to negotiate them with relative ease. Gawthrop describes these unexpected chord progressions as "the unexpected inevitable"—although they may startle the listener at first; after hearing the piece one cannot imagine the harmonies moving anywhere else.

Stylistic Considerations

Any SATB choir finds the music of "Sing Me to Heaven" beautiful and fairly easily, but a truly stunning performance requires careful attention to intonation and phrasing. The conductor should encourage the choir to sing with a minimum of vibrato throughout. This will ensure pure intonation, especially on higher tertian chords. Gawthrop asks for a true *forte* only at m. 34, so asking for less vibrato from the singers should not place much stress on the voice. The sectionalized nature of the piece allows for numerous starting and stopping points in rehearsals, but the conductor must be sure to continue through transitions and to rehearse larger sections rather than simply rehearsing phrase by phrase.

Tempo indications and dynamics are marked carefully in the score, and it is advisable to follow those indications closely. It is especially tempting to add additional ritards throughout, but the conductor must make sure that the piece has forward motion for larger sections. This being said, Gawthrop is more than open to various readings of his work. He says that he only indicates tempos and dynamics where he considers them "essential," and the interpreters of his work should feel free to put their own marks upon their performances.

Gawthrop does not indicate a ritard in m. 17; this is one point where the conductor might want to take additional time. It is also advised that the conductor not take too much time over the final ten measures of the piece. Gawthrop has already indicated "slowly" beginning at m. 49 and has built in a natural ritard in mm. 55–56 by writing a hemiola over those two measures.

Some specific breath marks are indicated, but the conductor will have to insert some additional breaths, depending on the ensemble's size. The conductor will also need to determine the length of the various fermatas and caesuras as well as indicating to the singers how they are to shape the dynamics of individual phrases.

Form and Structure

As mentioned previously, "Sing Me to Heaven" is basically through-composed. Gawthrop musically divides the text into four sections and writes fairly consistent groupings of antecedent and consequent phrases.

MEASURE	EVENT AND SCORING
1–18	Four phrases (2 × 4) + (4 + 6)
19–34	Four phrases (4 × 4)
35–44	Two phrases (3 × 6)
45–58	Three phrases (4 × 4 + 6)

Text

In my heart's sequestered chambers lie truths stripped of poet's gloss.
Words alone are vain and vacant and my heart is mute.
In response to aching silence memory summons half-heard voices,
And my soul finds primal eloquence and wraps me in song. . . .

Contributed by:

David Scholz

Teacher Resource Guide

Suite Nordestina
arr. Ronaldo Miranda

SATB a cappella
earthsongs: S-183
Overall: 3
Vocal: 3
Tonal/Rhythm: 4

Composer

Ronaldo Miranda is an award-winning Brazilian composer . He has also been a music critic and teacher. In addition to folk song settings, he has composed works for a variety of instruments, particularly guitar, including his *Sinfonia 2000*, commissioned by the Brazilian Ministry of Culture. He has also been honored for composition in France, Hungary, and Germany.

Composition and Historical Perspective

Suite Nordestina is a set of four songs arranged for SATB choir with limited divisi based on folk tunes from northeastern Brazil. The songs use musical elements representative of Brazilian folk style, particularly syncopated rhythms. Evolved through a combination of indigenous and imported Western music, the folk songs of Brazil use a standard diatonic scale. There is a little chromaticism in Miranda's arrangements, which is not traditional or expected for the songs, but Miranda's personal flavor.

The fact that Miranda calls this set a "suite" emphasizes the importance of the influence of dance. While not strictly dance music, even the slowest movement has a richly pulsating underlying rhythmicity.

Technical Considerations and Musical Elements

In all four pieces, rhythm is the primary outstanding musical element. The songs are so syncopated that they would be almost unreadable by beginning musicians. Especially since these are notations of folk songs, your best approach is to teach them by rote even if your singers could work to read the rhythms. To make rote learning easier:

- Do warm-ups with syncopated patterns from the pieces, such as sixteenth-eighth-sixteenth and dotted eighth-dotted eighth.
- For ties across beats or across measures, add a [d] on the note to which the first note is tied. For example, in "Dendê trapiá," the repeated "ta ta" pattern would sound like "ta ta-da." Take away the [d] when the singers are comfortable.
- Have students walk on the beat while they speak the rhythms and use rhythmic gestures like tapping knees or their neighbor's shoulder.

Another element all four pieces share is rich, complex, texture. Though the pieces possess a melody with accompaniment texture overall, the accompanying lines are sometimes homophonic but often polyphonic. This complexity makes the pieces harder to learn, but there are certainly ways to make it easier:

- Practice with similar lines together. For example, basses and tenors in the beginning of I. "Morena Bonita," altos and basses at m. 20 in II. "Dendê Trapiá," sopranos and altos at m. 7 in III. "Bumba Chora," and sopranos and tenors at m. 23 in IV. "Eu Vou."
- Have one part sing while the rest of the choir counts in a softly spoken tone, and then have two parts sing together while the remaining singers count.
- Have one part sing their line while another part speaks their line on text.

The first three pieces all have four-measure repeats, so if your students aren't already familiar with following repeat signs, they will be by the time they learn these pieces. Besides the elements shared in common among pieces, each has its own considerations.

In "Morena Bonita" the alto line begins some slinky chromaticism, which moves into the tenor and bass lines. Luckily, it comes in the form of descending half steps and not leaps. While they can easily flat, they are also easy to practice in warm-ups and even on solfeggio.

In "Dendê Trapiá" the most difficult challenge will be the fast-moving text, which is addressed below.

"Bumba Chora" is the only one of the four songs in a minor key. It also has the slowest-feeling tempo of the four, which may pose a problem, especially if your choir will perform the full set and must settle into it immediately following the very quick "Dendê Trapiá." Have students walk in place, stepping on the quarter note as they sing. As half the choir does that, ask the other singers to clap, tap, or pat the eighth note or even count softly.

The only pitch challenge is probably the sopranos' first pitch in the refrain. Dissonant against the altos' G-flat, the sopranos' F is surprising and a little tricky. Have sopranos practice both going in from the measure before and from the repeat alone; rehearse this with the men before adding the altos. When you put the sopranos and altos together, have them sing the three sixteenth notes leading into the dissonance and then hold the F and G-flat together several times until it is in their ears. Finally, the tenors split into two parts for the first six measures. If your men are capable, have them evenly cover three parts. If they need help singing in three parts, the tenor 1 line is high enough that altos can be added to fortify them. Replace those moved altos with a few sopranos, who otherwise would not sing at all for the first six measures.

In "Eu Vou" the male voices split again. Again try to divide the sections into three equal parts. If one part must be stronger than another, it should be the tenor line, which has part of the melody. Another special feature of this movement is the instrumental-style writing, including some nonstandard notation using triangular and X-shaped note heads and straight flags.

Stylistic Considerations

While they have been polished by Miranda, these pieces are essentially folk songs, so there is no need for your choir to work toward a particular style. Any size choir could perform these pieces, although rhythmic precision will be more difficult to achieve the larger the group is. While the pieces are certainly intended to be performed as a set, each song can also stand alone.

Form and Structure

SECTION	MEASURE	EVENT AND SCORING
I. "Morena Bonita"		
Refrain	1–4	
	1–3, 5	Refrain repeats with second ending
Verse	6–14	
II. "Dendê Trapiá"		
Refrain	1–5	
	1–4, 6	Refrain repeats with second ending
Verse 1	7–10	Verse 1 sung by sopranos
	11–13	Verse 1 sung by basses
Refrain	14–18	

Section	Measure	Event and Scoring
	14–17, 19	Refrain repeats with second ending
Verse 2	20–23	Verse 2 sung by altos
	24–26	Verse 2 sung by tenors
Refrain	27–35	Refrain twice to fermata
Coda	36–37	
III. "Bumba Chora"		
Verse	1–6	Verse 1 with tenor/bass accompaniment
Refrain	7–10	
	7–9, 11	Refrain repeats with second ending
Verse 2	12–19	STB accompaniment
Refrain	20–23	
	20–22, 24	Refrain repeats with second ending
Verse 3	25–28	Verse 3 with simple STB accompanying lines
Coda	29–30	Coda similar to refrain
IV. "Eu Vou"		
Refrain	1–8	
Verse 1	9–17	Verse 1 in bass solo with SATB "guitar strumming" accompaniment
Refrain	18–26	
	27–30	"Bem articulado"
Coda	31–42	

Text and Translation

I am lucky to live in an area where a significant minority of students speak Portuguese at home—both European and Brazilian dialects. For schools in areas like mine, the only challenge will be getting the Portuguese students to sing with a Brazilian accent. For American choirs, the language will be a hurdle.

Brazilian Portuguese sounds different from European Portuguese, and both sound very different from Spanish and all the other Romance languages (my Portuguese tour guide told me that this difference is intentional: they never wanted to be confused with Spain). Though the distinctive sound is vital to the color of the pieces, don't be intimidated by the language.

Because these are folk songs, they can be sung with a casual, slang-like pronunciation and an American accent wouldn't ruin the effect. A pronunciation guide is available through earthsongs in which the texts are "read slowly and as poetry," which does give you a sense of the colors and placement of the language but is not likely to help you (especially if you are a visual learner) with individual sounds or syllables. The IPA transcription of a native speaker's reading of the text will be helpful in deciphering individual sounds. It is simplified using only the most basic symbols so that even beginning IPA readers like your students can pronounce it. Like Spanish and Italian, [t] and [d] are dental. The most important, distinctive sounds are the brightness of every [a] (also similar to Spanish) and the nasal vowels—particularly [e], which is unique to Romance languages. If these two things are correct, the color will be close.

IPA Guide

I. "Morena Bonita"

mɔ-re-na bo-ni-ta-o ke vẽ vI
u sɔl na-sɛ-u vi-ro-u pɛn-dɛ-u
ʒa sɔl . . .

II. "Dendê Trapiá"

ko-ku dɛn-dI tra-pi-a ta-no ʒe-tʃi-njɔ dʒIm-bɔ-la
sɛ-gun-da-fɛ:I-ra fui a gra-dʒe da ka-de-ja
la vi ɛ-u a kɔ-I-za fɛ:I-a
a ba-la dIn-tru trɔ-vI-ʒa
ka-bra da-na-du-si nã-u tẽ kɔ-ra-ʒ‿ɛ-u tIn-jɔ
dʒI pɛ-ga ka-bra na fa-ka
i‿a-ma-ha sin-jo no‿ẽn-gɛ-njɔ ɔ:I . . .

III. "Bumba Chora"

ʃɔ-ra ʃɔ-ra‿o bum-ba ʃɔ-ra‿e-ɔ vo-mi‿Im-bɔ-ra
vo tɔ-kar min-ja vi-ɔ-la a nã nã nã . . .
e bum-ba ʃɔ-ra a ʒa ʃɔ-ra mɛ-o bum-ba ke ʃɔ-ra
vo-mi‿Im-bɔ-ra sɛ-gun-da-fɛ:I-ra ke vẽ
kẽ nã-u me kɔn-jɛ-si ʃɔ-ra
ki dʒi-ra kẽ mi kɛ bẽ
ʃɔ-ra tã bẽ ʒi-ra ke nĩ-gẽ ke bẽ
a-man-ja vo pra‿e-ʃkɔ-la‿a-prẽn-dI
a lɛ e‿a tɔ-ka vi-ɔ-la

IV. "Eu Vou"

ɛ-ɔ vo vɔ-se nã-u va:I

a-pan-jar ma-ka-u-ba nu ba-la-ju

ʃi-ki ʃi-ki ʃi-ki ʒa ua:I tũ (guitar sounds)

a *mu-jɛ du *pa-ja-su e‿ũ ko-lo-su

ka-ju da ka-ma ke-bro‿o pe-ʃkɔ-su

o-i pi-ze-i na maŋ-ga ɛ-ʃkɔ-nɛ-ge-I

a min-ja ho-pa e-o haʒ-ge-i

* These words are intentionally misspelled to force a non-standard, "country bumpkin" pronunciation, comparable in style and intention to "feller" instead of "fellow" in English. In this case, the [j] instead of [λ].

There is a lot of text, and some of it moves very fast. In several places, multiple vowels take place on one note—as often happens in Italian. In these cases, divide the note evenly so that each vowel has equal time. Ideally, text should be practiced almost to the point of memorization, where the sounds come easily and naturally, like habit.

Happily, earthsongs provides great word-by-word and poetic translations for all the texts. Typical of folksongs, they are not narrative. Rather, they are almost nonsensical—if you read them as poetry, your first reaction may be "what?" For example, the translation of "Morena Bonita" is "Beautiful brunette, what have you come to see?/ The sun rose, turned, but is already set . . ." So, the music tells as much of the story, portrays as much of the character as the text does.

Additional References and Resources

Web sites:

earthsongs: www.earthsongsmus.com (accessed May 30, 2006)

Ronaldo Miranda: www.ronaldomiranda.com (accessed May 20, 2006)

Suggested Listening

Ronaldo Miranda, arranger, Maria José Chevitarese, *Suite Nordestina* on *Coral Todo Tom da UFRJ–II*, Coral Todo Tom da UFRJ, Tons e Sons/ UFRJ–TS 9806.

Contributed by:

Amelia Nagoski

Teacher Resource Guide

The Battle of Jericho

arr. Moses Hogan

SATB divisi
Hal Leonard: 8703139
Overall: 3
Vocal: 4
Tonal/Rhythm: 3

Composer

Moses George Hogan was born March 13, 1957, in New Orleans, Louisiana. He studied music at the New Orleans Center for Creative Arts, Oberlin Conservatory of Music, the Juilliard School of Music, and Louisiana State University in Baton Rouge. An accomplished pianist, Hogan began focusing on choral music in 1980 when he formed his New World ensemble through which the Moses Hogan Chorale was formed. Recordings of his arrangements include those for the 1995 PBS documentary *The American Promise* and performances by the Mormon Tabernacle Choir and Derek Lee Ragin, which are widely available. Hogan died tragically young on February 11, 2003.

Composition and Historical Perspective

"The Battle of Jericho" is a spiritual arranged for SATB divisi choir—the style for which Hogan is best known. The story is of Joshua, successor of Moses, and his siege of the city of Jericho. God instructed Joshua, "Have all the soldiers circle the city, marching once around it. Do this for six days, with seven priests carrying ram's horns ahead of the ark. On the seventh day march around the city seven times and have the priests blow the horns. When they give a long blast on the ram's horns and you hear that signal, all the people shall shout aloud. The wall of the city will collapse and you will be able to make a frontal assault" (Joshua 6:2–5). The Israelites did all this and took the city.

Songs about battles have sprung up throughout history, and a battle fought with trumpets and shouting is perfect material for a song. Also, the subtext of the faith required by the formerly-enslaved, long-persecuted Israelites to trust that God would fight for them must have been deeply-felt by the slaves who first sang it. Hogan's arrangement manifests that power with strong rhythms and aggressive dynamics. The sounds of battle are reflected in the fast-moving sixteenth note patterns, crisp articulations, and even the final shout.

Technical Considerations and Musical Elements

The most important element of this composition is the driving rhythm. Each singer must have the tempo deeply internalized. You can prepare the choir with:

- Intense, soft rhythmic chanting of the text
- Rhythmically similar warm-ups
- Rhythmic movements such as marching in place and punching the air downward
- Audible motions such as foot stomping and knee slapping
- Singing softly while other parts count or maintain the beat in another audible way like saying "t" on every eighth note

All motions, like the piece, should have weight, so downward motions will be more effective.

Rhythmic challenges include a recurring pattern with a sixteenth note tied across the barline. To make this easier for singers, trying putting a [d] on beat one. They will sing "Jo-dosh-ua" at first and omit the [d] once the rhythm becomes familiar. Another challenge is the complex patterns mm. 23–25. Women sing one pattern while men sing another. The singers must be confident in their parts and be able to hear how their part lines up with the other pattern. Count-singing will help with this, as will soft chanting on text.

The dynamics must be attended to carefully. The men start *mezzo forte*, but in m. 3 they go down to *mezzo piano* while the women sing the refrain *mezzo forte*. However, at m. 13, when this same pattern returns, all parts are marked *mezzo piano*. Since Hogan was fastidious enough to lay that out, taking notice of it will allow the performance to be what he intended.

The articulations are also notated in detail. There are almost always accents on tied notes (which will also help the choir to sing them accurately). For most of the requirements of articulation, diction will be your best ally. For example, in the opening men's part, which repeats so many times in the piece, the word "battle" is staccato, which can be accomplished with a decidedly unvoiced "t" (not a "d," which would likely be the default sound).

An important pitch-related element is the bass pedal. Bass 2 has a low F for the first eighteen measures of the piece, and that must be solid. First of all, the men must be comfortable singing in the bottom of the range for a long time. During rehearsal, they will probably not be able to sing the part continuously unless they are exceptionally strong. Also, the intonation must be consistent. You can practice by:

- Using warm-ups with bass pedal
- Having the basses sing the F without text or rhythm while the upper voices sing as written
- Adding baritones singing an F the octave up in rehearsal; this gives the basses and the upper parts an even more solid foundation—more to listen to and making it easier to tune

Another challenge in pitch is the parallel motion between voices at various times. To ensure good tuning, try practicing with the voices only in fourths or fifths (without the third). For example, in the opening the bass 1 and tenor 2 lines move in parallel fourths, so isolate those two lines, giving the them a chance to tune every fourth carefully and the other parts an indication of what they need to be listening for even as they sing their own lines. This particular passage returns several times in the piece and represents a common pattern, so practicing it in one place will improve the rest of the song.

There are several glissandos. If this is a new concept to the choir, they will likely slide down too far and then have to slide back up to find the correct pitch at the end. Practice without the glissandos until they can perform it that way confidently. Then, as with all things that end up sounding free and spontaneous, it must be carefully and mathematically worked out. Different voices glissando different distances, but all must arrive at the same time, meaning that each section must move at a different speed, but each singer in the section must move at the same speed as the rest of the section. Therefore, practicing one part at a time—being sure they all start at the same time and move at the same speed—will be the most effective way to work this out.

For the glissando after the fermata in m. 33, plan how long they will hold the note, how much time they will have to glissando, and practice on one part at a time. Then put two parts that move similar distances together, e.g., bass 2 and alto 2 both start at G and glissando to C. You will have to be consistent with how much time you give singers to glissando so that it will be together. Eventually you may be able to allow yourself some freedom in taking more or less time, but that would only be the case if the choir has lived with the piece or for a long time.

Finally, in m. 21 the women sing a line that descends more than an octave, from the highest part of each section's range to near the bottom. Then in m. 34 a similar movement occurs but goes slightly back up at the end, which is even harder to keep in tune. These descending lines can't lose energy and must become lighter in order to be sung accurately. Ask the women to imagine singing a *decrescendo* as they descend but increasing the intensity of the tone and consonants. Practice this without pitch at first, and then add the notes.

Stylistic Considerations

Spirituals require a great deal of energy and emotional commitment. This piece can sound chatty and easily droop out of tune if it is not sung with total engagement. No unusual vocal technique is required—standard choral tone will be fine, though fullness will be more effective than refinement. There are several ways you can give your choir ideas of appropriate kind of sound:

- Listen to the recording of the Moses Hogan Chorale. A high school choir will never sound like them, but they can reproduce the intensity of the singing, the roundness of tone, and the clarity of the speech.
- Practice on round, neutral syllables with percussive opening consonants like "daw" and "doh," or start with an "n" to remind them to keep the sound forward and resonant while it is warm.

Form and Structure

Hogan seems to have brilliantly written the battle itself into the form of this piece.

Section	Measure	Event and Scoring
Introduction	1–2	
Refrain	3–7	First time around the city
Transition	7–8	Same as introduction
Refrain 2	3–8	Second time around the city
Verse 1	9–12	Third time
Refrain 3	13–18	Same as mm. 3–8; fourth time
Verse 2	19–22	Fifth time
Verse 3	23–26	Sixth time
Refrain 4	27–30	Seventh time
	27–28	Repeat mm. 27–28 with soprano descant (blowing of the ram's horns) and second ending in m. 31
Coda	32–34	Shout

Text

Refrain:
Joshua fit the Battle of Jericho, Jericho, Jericho.
Joshua fit the Battle of Jericho
And the walls come tumblin' down.

Talk about your king of Gideon,
Talk about our men of Saul,
But there's none like good old Joshua
At the Battle of Jericho.

Refrain

Right up to the walls of Jericho,
He marches with spear in hand.
"Go blow that ram horn!" Joshua cried
"'Cause the battle am in my hand."

Then the lamb, ram, sheep horn begin to blow
And the trumpet begins to sound.
Joshua commanded the children to shout!
And the walls come a-tumblin' down.

Suggested References and Resources

The New American Bible. Wichita, KS: Catholic Bible Publishers, 1970.

Web site:
Friends of Moses Hogan Society: www.moseshogan.com (accessed January 20, 2006)

Suggested Listening

Moses Hogan, "The Battle of Jericho" on *Moses Hogan Choral Series 2002*, Moses Hogan Chorale and Moses Hogan Singers, Moses Hogan, MGH Records.

Contributed by:

Amelia Nagoski

Teacher Resource Guide

The Silver Swan

Orlando Gibbons
(1583–1625)

SSATB
E. C. Schirmer Music Company: 397
Overall: 3
Vocal: 2
Tonal/Rhythm: 3

Composer

Orlando Gibbons was baptized in Oxford, England, in 1583. As a child Gibbons sang as a chorister at King's College, Cambridge, and attended the university in 1598 (MusB, 1606). Concurrently, from 1595–1602, Gibbons was employed as a musician with the town waits. From 1603 to his death, he was employed as a musician (singer, keyboardist) and composer at the Chapel Royal. His collection *The First Set of Madrigals and Mottets* was published in 1612. He died in *Canterbury in 1625.*

Composition and Historical Perspective

Elizabethan England's deep love of affair with Italy was expressed most ardently in the genre of the madrigal. In thirty-five short years (1590–1625), England saw the development, huge popularization, and decline of this seminal genre. The beginning of the era was marked by two major anthologies. In 1588 Nicholas Yonge collected an anthology of Italian madrigals and translated their texts into English in *Musica Transalpina*. Thomas Watson quickly followed with his collection *Italian madrigalls Englished* (1590).

Significant composers of the genre include Thomas Morley (ca. 1558–1602), Thomas Weelkes (ca. 1575–1623), John Wilbye (bapt. 1574–1638), and Orlando Gibbons. Gibbons's madrigal, "The Silver Swan" appears in *The First Set of Madrigals and Mottets, apt for Viols and Voyces, 5vv* and was published in London in 1612. Gibbons's oeuvre includes a wide variety of vocal and instrumental genres, but he is best known as a madrigalist and church music composer.

Technical Considerations

The function of historically informed performance practice is not to create museum-like replications of performances but rather to use scholarship to allow the voice of the composer to be heard in the context of its contemporary history. While it may seem overly academic or unfeasible to be attentive to much of the style practices of a bygone era, I encourage you to explore the resources available on the Internet, on recently produced CDs of reputable early music artists, and at your local library to help you assimilate some of the performances practices of the era.

Before you are able to incorporate performance practice in even the smallest dose into your choral program, it is important to understand how these pieces were performed. The ensembles that would perform madrigals in Elizabethan England were small groups of professional singers who would sing for courtly audiences. These singers were professionals, but their sound was significantly different than that of professional classical singers today. Vibrato was used sparingly as an ornament. However, they were not choral singers with a colorless, blending tone. The tone was soloistic with core in the sound. Singers of Elizabethan madrigals sang from part books with unbarred staves. This practice facilitated independence of line and faithfulness to text declamation. Lastly, this particular collection of madrigals by Gibbons employs a consort of viols to accompany the singers, with each viol doubling one vocal line or perhaps using a solo vocal line with viol accompaniment on the lower four parts.

Whether directors are able to incorporate all of these practices into the performance or make small changes to the current program, I hope you find that incorporating historically informed style practices into the performances brings out the vital and universally relevant voice of this rich music.

Musical Elements

Melody

Each of the five lines in this madrigal has lyrical melodic fragments. There is not one overarching melody that the remaining voices support. In performance, it is vital to bring out the separate strands of melody from the homophonic texture of the work. To illustrate the difference between homophonic and polyphonic textures to young singers, a common comparison is often drawn to varying weaves of fabric; polyphony is likened to a loose wool sweater weave with visible strands of yarn and homophony is likened to a tight knit with no visible weave.

Harmony

The harmonic language of this work is simple and diatonic in the key of F major, save for 5 chromatic chords used presumably to highlight the text (m. 1: G major "silver," m. 10: Cmin(maj)^7/G to G major "against the reedy shore," m. 12: E-flat major "last," m. 17: Cmin(maj)^7/G to G major "death come close mine eyes," and m. 19 E-flat major "live") . Many of these examples' harmonic text painting seem idiosyncratic to the application of this technique by Gibbons's contemporaries. It must be noted that it was the common practice of the day to write English texts to existing Italian madrigals, and although there is no evidence of this with this work, the misapplication of chromaticism to the text supports this theory.

Rhythm

The rhythm of this work, like many of this era, is derived from text stress. The barlines in this edition were not present in the original manuscripts, and though this edition is fairly faithful to the text stress, it would be possible to rebar this madrigal to highlight groupings of twos and threes that best serve the text.

Texture

"The Silver Swan" is scored for five voices (SSATB in this edition) and *colla parte* doubling by a consort of viols or other appropriate instruments (not indicated in this edition). The texture of the work is a homophonic/polyphonic hybrid, emphasizing the independence of individual musical lines within a chordal context. In the B sections of the work, there are contrapuntal entrances that blend again into homophony at the end.

Other: Dynamics/Articulation/Tempo

Though there are dynamic, articulation, and tempo markings suggested by the editor of this edition, these are not found in the original manuscript. As a rule, final musical decisions should be based on information provided in the manuscript.

Dynamic interpretation should be based on texture (e.g., a reduction from five to three voices), formal divisions (e.g., lower or raised dynamic at the literal repeat of section B at m. 14), and text (e.g., lower dynamic at text "Farewell all joys . . ."). Similarly, articulation decisions should be based on affect and melodic/harmonic context. The lines in this madrigal are lyrical and flowing; it would disrupt the line to insert additional articulation.

Tempo is never suggested by composers of this era. However, historically informed performance practice indicates that the tactus be closely related to the heartbeat (around 60 bpm). Although this edition uses common time, the tactus falls with every half note, and the work should, therefore, be conducted in two. Additionally, tempo decisions can be influenced by phrase length; if it is impossible for your singers to make it through phrases of text without a breath, the tempo may need to be increased.

Form and Structure

The form of "The Silver Swan" is ABB and resembles that of a canzonet, although truncated slightly. The canzonet is another anglicized version of an originally Italian genre, the canzonetta. Ruth I. DeFord writes in the *New Grove Dictionary of Music and Musicians* that "the styles of the canzonet and madrigal overlapped to a much greater extent in England than in Italy; some pieces called 'canzonets' are madrigalian in style, and some madrigals are based on translations of Italian canzonetta texts." There is some speculation that this form was a precursor to the seventeenth-century dal segno aria. The form is based on the poetic form; the six lines of the poem (each with ten syllables) are divided into three sections of two rhyming feet each.

Measure	Event and Scoring
1–7	Mostly homophonic texture
7–14	Contrapuntal choral entrances
14–21	Repeat of last seven measures, contrapuntal choral entrances

Text

Unknown text source, perhaps Orlando Gibbons

The silver swan, who living, had no note,
When Death approach'd, unlock'd her silent throat.
Leaning her breast against the reedy shore,
Thus sang her first and last, and sang no more:
Farewell all joys! O death, come close mine eyes!
"More Geese than Swans now live, more Fools than Wise."

Additional References and Resources

Donington, Robert. *The Interpretation of Early Music*. rev. ed. London: Faber and Faber, 1989.

Unbarred, unedited version, full score and part book edition (including *colla parte* doubling): www.musicaviva.com/ensemble/choir/inidex.tpl.

Suggested Listening

I recommend the following recording as a historically informed interpretation of Gibbons's madrigal: "The Silver Swan" on *The King's Singers Madrigal History Tour*, The King's Singers and The Consort of Musicke, EMI Classics, 1989.

Contributed by:

Emilie Sweet

Teacher Resource Guide

Três Cantos Nativos

Marcos Leite

(1953–2002)

SATB
earthsongs: S-68
Overall: 3
Vocal: 4
Tonal/Rhythm: 3

Composer

Born in 1953, Brazilian composer, pianist, conductor, and teacher Marcos Leite studied music from an early age. Along with several other choirs, he created the choral group Garganta Profundo in 1985, which produced five recordings under his direction. Also interested in theatrical productions and pedagogy, Leite served in the music production of various shows and taught at numerous festivals and workshops throughout his life, including a professorship at the Conservatório de Música Popular Brasileira de Curitiba. As a director and artist, he took a special interest in combined the elements of music and theater.

Composition and Historical Perspective

Três Cantos Nativos, composed in 1982, has its basis in the melodies of the Kraó tribe from northwestern Brazil. The translation of the text is unknown, so the composer wrote the music treating the text as a series of sounds, or phonemes. From our perspective as Americans, the piece can definitely be categorized in the somewhat ambiguous and wide-ranging multicultural genre.

Technical Considerations and Musical Elements

This set of three pieces will provide a program with a distinct sound and atmosphere. Although each *canto*, or section, could conceivably be performed separately, each section is so short as to make individual performances almost comical, and a complete performance is more desirable. The strongly rhythmic nature of the pieces in both the music and the percussiveness of the text, along with the addition of percussion instruments, spoken choral sections, improvised jungle sounds in the choir, and brief moments of notated vocal percussion will make this set a favorite among audience and ensemble members alike.

Text and Rhythm

Several challenges become evident upon perusal of the score, each with its own difficulties. Beginning with text, the conductor must spend time in familiarizing him- or herself with the proper pronunciation so as to effectively teach the choir members. The back page of the score gives a complete pronunciation guide that includes the original text, a standard English transliteration, and the IPA for the text, all given for each syllable.

Once the conductor and choir have mastered the pronunciation of the text, the rhythm of the music seems natural. The music has many sixteenth notes and rests, ties, etc., and as a result looks more difficult than it actually is. This being said, even the best singers will find the complexity of the rhythm problematic to comprehend.

Although the score presents a good teaching technique for deciphering complex rhythm notation, it might be advised that the conductor teach the rhythm by rote. For longer pieces this is not effective, but due to the brevity of each *canto* and the repetitive nature of each piece, teaching in this manner should occupy very little rehearsal time and will quickly allow the choir to experiment with other aspects of the music. Naturally, the conductor must sit down with the score and master the rhythm before attempting to introduce it to the choir. This may take some time; there are numerous sixteenth note offbeats to deal with.

Once again, the rhythm *looks* more difficult than it actually is. Begin slowly, pulsing the eighth note subdivision and gradually increasing the tempo up to performance speed. Follow the same procedure when introducing the music to the choir, and find ways to physically maintain a steady pulse, e.g., tapping one hand on their knees, stepping side-to-side on the macro pulse, etc. There are several sections that will require the women to sing one rhythm while the men maintain a different rhythmic pattern; teach each pattern separately to the entire choir, and then combine the different rhythms at a slow tempo while maintaining a steady pulse; then, gradually increase the tempo. Although there are a fair number of meter shifts, the essential macro pulse remains consistent (there are no asymmetrical meters), so the conductor should only need to point out the various meter changes to the choir, and the singers will quickly and easily feel the small adjustments in phrase length that are needed.

MELODY

Melodically the music is fairly simple and repetitive. There are almost no accidentals in any of the pieces (there is a G-natural for the women in m. 45 of the *segundo canto*, and a D-natural for the altos in the *primeiro canto*), thus the greatest melodic challenge might be in the speed with which larger intervals must be sung accurately. Except for one octave leap, there are no intervals greater than a fourth and no intervals are augmented or diminished.

TONALITY

Harmonically the entire set is based entirely in E major with the interval of a fifth from E to B present in virtually every measure. Care must be taken especially in the men's parts, to maintain proper intonation on the perfect intervals that are prevalent throughout, most notably at the beginning of the *primeiro canto,* where the men a split into three parts, singing on the root, fifth, and octave, sustaining those notes for eight measures.

The vocal ranges are also easily singable by even middle school or junior high choirs, although the sopranos are often required to sing low Bs (nearly always in unison with the altos in those instances). One low G is required of the sopranos, but the basses almost never sing below E3, and the tenor part does not rise above C-sharp4 with the exception of the *primeiro canto,* where they sustain E4 for the first eight measures. Perhaps the most difficult aspect in terms of intonation might be in the simplicity of the harmony. Care must be taken that pitch remains constant; it is possible that the ensemble might think (albeit subconsciously) that a lack of extended harmonies makes keeping their intonation *easy*.

PERFORMANCE CONSIDERATIONS

Several other techniques add to the excitement of *Três Cantos Nativos*, but they will require some rehearsal time to insure that the choir feels comfortable in performance. In the opening measures of the *primeiro canto,* the women are instructed in the score to "improvise animal sounds, percussive sounds, etc. (imitating the atmosphere of the rainforest jungle with sounds of the rain, river, wind, and forest animals)." Although the word "improvise" is used in the instructions, it is suggested that this improvisation be planned out (to an extent). Spend some time in rehearsals asking different choir members to demonstrate possible sounds, giving some of your own suggestions as a starting point for the members of the ensemble, possibly including whistling, clicking, rolling the tongue, etc. Then ask the singers to try their own sounds together and see what the result is. Ask them to choose a different sound and try them all together again. Although not specifically stated in the score, these sounds do not necessarily need to be made with the mouth. Encourage some singers to experiment with clapping, snapping, slapping thighs, etc. When you have found a combination that provides variety and interest, ask the singers to remember the sounds and to use them during performances.

The *segundo canto* (m. 26) begins with the women presenting two spoken lines of text. This text is notated under sets of nine and then ten eighth notes with percussion noteheads, with the ambiguous term ad libitum and a *forte* marking given. No indication of tempo or syllabic stress is given. It is suggested that the conductor might have the women present this text as quickly as possible with great force and energy, as the following ostinato pattern in the men's voices (continuing to the end of the *canto*) and the women's melody that begins in m. 31 is extremely rhythmic and forceful as well. The choir is asked to clap (eighth notes in the women, one clap on the downbeat of every two measures in the men) during mm. 39–46 of the *segundo canto*. The conclusion of the *treceiro canto* calls for the choir to perform mouth percussion by sucking air in through closed teeth.

The performance instructions indicate the use of conga(s) and two rattles, which are to "emphasize and improvise on the rhythms of the choir." If choir members are used as percussionists, they should be assigned to that role early enough in the rehearsal process to become entirely comfortable with the instruments they are playing. If outside instrumentalists are used, enough rehearsal time should be scheduled with them so they are familiar with the rhythm patterns involved as well as the form of the pieces (when to play, when not to play, changes in rhythms, etc.). In any case, the choir must become used enough to the percussion sounds they will hear so that the performance is a unified effort between singers and percussionists rather than simply choir with accompaniment.

Stylistic Considerations

These pieces should be performed with intense rhythm drive and a full, powerful sound in the singing (considering dynamics). There should be an element of wild emotion and abandonment of "careful" singing. Since the pieces are quite repetitive, it is of utmost importance that the choir be aware of the dynamic indications, accents, etc., and that they follow those indications.

Form and Structure

Section	Measure	Event and Scoring
"Primeiro Canto"	1–8	Introduction
	9–15	Main melodic material (canonic in women's parts)
	16–21	First ending, repeat to beginning
	21–25	Second ending

SECTION	MEASURE	EVENT AND SCORING
"Segundo Canto"	26	Spoken choral chant, ad libitum
	27–38	Three phrases (4 + 4 + 4)
	39–46	Two phrases (4 + 4), repeated
	47–48	Concluding measures, repeated
"Treceiro Canto"	50–58	Two phrases (4.5 + 4.5)
	59–65	Two phrases (2.5 + 4.5) repeat to beginning

Text

Leite explains underneath the pronunciation guide on the final page of the score that "the meaning of the text is not known; it was treated by the composer as a group of phonemes."

Contributed by:

David Scholz

Teacher Resource Guide

Ubi caritas

Maurice Duruflé

(1902–1986)

SATTBB

Durand S. A. Editions/Theodore Presser Co.: 312-41253

Overall: 3

Vocal: 3

Tonal/Rhythm: 4

Composer

Organist and composer Maurice Duruflé was born in 1902 in Louviers, France. Much of his early education was 1912–1918 when Duruflé was a choirboy at Rouen Cathedral. This cathedral strongly embraced the plainsong tradition, and its influence on Duruflé is quite evident.

The two primary teachers who influenced his compositions were Charles Tournemire (1870–1939) and Louis Vierne (1870–1937). In 1918 Duruflé began study with Tournemire and later became his assistant at Clotilde Cathedral. Tournemire set him on a steady diet of plainsong and modal harmony as he prepared for admission to the Paris Conservatoire.

In 1920 Duruflé was admitted to the Paris Conservatoire and began study with Vierne. While at the conservatoire Duruflé was recognized with many awards, including five *premier prix* in organ, harmony, fugue, accompaniment, and composition. From Vierne, Duruflé learned of structure and proportion in composition, and of the rich tradition of French Romantic organ technique. In 1927 he became Vierne's assistant at Notre Dame Cathedral.

Although it was speculated that Duruflé would succeed Vierne at Notre Dame, he was appointed organist at St. Etienne-du-Mont in 1930, where he remained for the rest of his life. While maintaining a full schedule as church and concert musician and composer, Duruflé taught at the Paris Conservatoire from 1943 to 1970 as well. Duruflé died in Paris in 1986.

Composition and Historical Perspective

Solo works and transcriptions for the organ as well as handful of very popular choral works dominate Maurice Duruflé's small compositional output. His significant large choral works include the Requiem (1947) for soloists, chorus, orchestra, and organ and the *Messe cum Jubilo* (1966) for baritone soloist, men's chorus, and orchestra. These two works are available in versions for organ accompaniment and for chamber orchestra.

His smaller choral works include the *Quatre Motets sur des Thèmes Grégoriennes* (1960) for *a cappella* chorus and "Notre Père" (1977) for unison men's chorus and organ or *a cappella* chorus. "Ubi caritas" is the first motet in Duruflé's *Four Motets on Gregorian Themes*. This set also includes "Tota pulchra es," "Tu es Petrus," and "Tantum ergo."

"Ubi caritas" is derived from antiphons to be performed on Maundy Thursday (Holy Thursday) after the ceremony of the washing of the feet. This antiphon, as well as the entire Maundy Thursday Mass, is intimately linked to the Eucharist and consequently is often performed as a communion anthem.

Technical Considerations

Young singers may be challenged by the frequent meter changes and intonation with this piece. Here are some suggestions for addressing these challenges:

Meter changes and text declamation: At first glance, a singer might be overwhelmed by the frequent meter changes in this piece. I suggest counting the metric shifts on numbers (one–and–two–and, etc.). This should be done in a legato context to correspond to the character of the text. In addition to helping young singers to quickly assimilate the rhythm and meter, highlighting the underlying eighth note pulse will help singers to be less inclined to drag tempo.

Intonation: Because of the harmonic language Duruflé uses (including extended tertian chords and sustained inverted harmonies), I suggest isolating one voice over a tonic and dominant drone; identifying where singers should be orienting themselves harmonically will help keep the pitch from wavering. I recommend rehearsing without the help of the piano as much as possible so as to avoid equal-tempered tuning.

Stylistic Considerations

Because of the chant-like nature of this work and the sophisticated harmonic language, I recommend a leaner vocal production with minimal vibrato.

Musical Elements

MELODY
The melody of "Ubi caritas" is derived from the plainchant of the same name. It is characterized by stepwise motion and few leaps.

HARMONY
The harmonic language of this work is functional yet includes many extended tertian and added-note chords. Chords are often found in inversions so as to maximize the melodic contour of individual lines. The divided tenor lines initially provide a sustained drone over a perfect fourth to support the melody and parallel countermelody.

RHYTHM/METER
Since it is derived from chant, the rhythm of this motet is quite simple, most often written in quarter and eighth notes. In the spirit of chant, the meter changes frequently to highlight the text. The eighth note remains constant throughout.

TEXTURE
The texture of this work is homophonic (melody with accompaniment) and homorhythmic. The chant-based melody is found in the divided alto sections as well as the soprano section. From mm. 1–14 and 29–39, the divisi is AATTBB. From mm. 15–28, the divisi is SATTBB. One might consider revoicing this work to include the full choir throughout.

OTHER: DYNAMICS/ARTICULATION/TEMPO/RANGE
Dynamics: *piano* to *mezzo forte*

Articulation: none indicated

Tempo: *andante sostenuto*, quarter note = 66; small slowing (*poco cedere*) indicated at section-ending cadences; more significant slowing in last four measures.

Range: soprano: B-flat3–E-flat5
alto: G3–B-flat4
tenor: D3–G4
bass: E-flat2–C4

Form and Structure

This short chant-based work is in ABA´ form. The A section uses antiphonal chant found in the divided alto section. The B section employs the full tutti choir at a fuller dynamic. The piece closes with a return to the A-section material and a final coda-like "Amen."

Section	Measure	Event and Scoring
A	1–4	Introduction of chant melody is in the first choir alto section with basses moving in simplified parallel contour at the sixth; divided tenors supply an E-flat and B-flat drone; phrase establishes the tonic key of E-flat major and moves to dominant
	5–8	Identical to mm. 1–4 with melody in the second choir alto section
	9–11	The second half of chant melody is in the first choir alto; basses trace the increasingly functional harmonic contour, while tenors fill out the harmony with a modified drone; again, this phrase moves from E-flat to B-flat, but includes a secondary dominant harmony
	12–14	Similar to mm. 9–11 with melody in the second choir alto section. The harmonic motion is altered slightly; instead of moving to the dominant, this phrase remains in E-flat major, ending with a plagal cadence
B	15–18	First tutti entrance (includes both choirs of altos and adds sopranos); chant melody found in the soprano line; introduces the new harmonic area of G minor (the relative minor of the dominant, B-flat major) and moves from G minor to C major
	19–21	Chant melody in the alto section; moves harmonically from F major to C major and includes a secondary dominant harmony at the cadence
	22–24	Chant melody continues in the alto section; phrase remains in F major and ends with a plagal cadence
	25–28	Similar to mm. 22–24, but transposed down a fifth (in B-flat major with a plagal cadence); one-measure tag at the end of this phrase, reestablishing E-flat major
A (modified)	29–32	Identical to mm. 1–4, moving from E-flat major to B-flat major

SECTION	MEASURE	EVENT AND SCORING
	33–39	Coda-like "amen" section; chant melody in the combined alto section over sustained harmony in the tenors and basses; underlying harmony oscillates between A-flat major(add 2) and F minor^7 and concludes with a plagal cadence in E-flat major

Text and Translation

Duruflé sets verse one of this antiphon; the full text is provided for your perusal.

Ubi caritas et amor,	Where charity and love are,
Deus ibi est.	God is there.
Congregavit nos in unum Christi amor.	Christ's love has gathered us into one.
Exultemus, et in ipso jucundemur.	Let us rejoice and be pleased in Him.
Timeamus et amemus Deum vivum.	Let us fear, and let us love the living God.
Et ex corde diligamus nos sincero.	And may we love each other with a sincere heart.
Ubi caritas et amor,	Where charity and love are,
Deus ibi est.	God is there.
Simul ergo cum in unum congregamur:	As we are gathered into one body,
Ne nos mente dividamur, caveamus.	Beware, lest we be divided in mind.
Cessent jurgia maligna, cessent lites.	Let evil impulses stop, let controversy cease,
Et in medio nostri sit Christus Deus.	And may Christ our God be in our midst.
Ubi caritas et amor,	Where charity and love are,
Deus ibi est.	God is there.
Simul quoque cum beatis videamus.	And may we with the saints also,
Glorianter vultum tuum, Christe Deus.	See Thy face in glory, O Christ our God:
Gaudium quod est immensum, atque probum:	The joy that is immense and good,
Saecula per infinita saeculorum. Amen.	Unto the ages through infinite ages. Amen.

Contributed by:

Emilie Sweet

Teacher Resource Guide

Venite exultemus Domino

Jan Pieterszoon Sweelinck

(1562–1621)

SSATB and basso continuo
GIA Publications: G-5930
Overall: 3
Vocal: 3
Tonal/Rhythm: 2

Composer

Jan Pieterszoon Sweelinck was born in Deventer and spent his entire professional career at the Oude Kerke in Amsterdam. Known as the "Orpheus of Amsterdam," he was a brilliant organist and improviser, and people traveled throughout Europe to hear him play two regular performances each day. Employed by the city, not the church (as was the custom of Calvinist society, which regarded the organ as a secular instrument inappropriate for liturgical use), many of the additional performance responsibilities required of similar civil organists of his era were waived so that Sweelinck could devote considerable time to his equally well-known role as teacher. Students were sent from far and wide at the expense of their city councils to study with him, and his standards became those against which all musicians were measured. Sweelinck's pupils were the founders of the famous north German organ school of the seventeenth century that culminated in the works of Johann Sebastian Bach.

Sweelinck was the last and most important composer of the Netherlanders era. He composed at least 254 secular and sacred vocal works, including 33 chansons, 19 madrigals, 39 motets, and 153 psalms, all of which were published within his lifetime; only 70 of his organ compositions survive in manuscript. The majority of Sweelinck's choral works are in French, including a monumental polyphonic setting of the Psalter written for private devotions rather than for the public Calvinist service. His choral compositions display the full complement of late Renaissance compositional devices, from homophony to canon and strict imitative counterpoint, to the use of *cantus firmus* and free composition techniques, often juxtaposed within the same piece.

Composition and Historical Perspective

"Venite exultemus Domino" is from Sweelinck's *Cantiones sacrae* (1619), a collection of thirty-seven motets on Latin texts from the Catholic liturgy dedicated to his young friend and pupil Cornelis Plemp. It is not clear if the works were written for a specific liturgical context, and their existence presents an interesting historical question about the religious life of Sweelinck, who spent his entire employ serving the needs of a predominantly Protestant society.

The motets do not make use of *cantus firmus* technique; instead, they are compact settings that display the full gamut of compositional procedures at use in choral writing of the time. They include more chromaticism and ornamental counterpoint than is typical in Sweelinck's other choral works. The motets are the only choral settings in which Sweelinck designates an instrumental accompaniment. Though the published editions of his time refer to the use of a basso continuo, modern scholars believe the more accurate designation is *basso seguente*, which simply doubles the lowest sounding vocal part. "Venite exultemus Domino" can be performed successfully in an entirely *a cappella* setting with a bass instrument doubling a combination of the bass and tenor lines or with the full realization provided by James Jordan, editor of the GIA Publications edition.

Technical Considerations and Musical Elements

This motet for five voices is an excellent choice for choirs with an abundance of female voices and fewer male voices. Be aware that the soprano 1 and 2 parts are equal and fully independent of each other with regular voice crossings. The alto and tenor lines also frequently inhabit the same pitch register with frequent crossings; depending on the ensemble, some judicious use of alto or tenor doubling of the other part may be warranted.

"Venite exultemus Domino" provides an excellent opportunity to demonstrate the principles of imitative writing and how it can be used to illustrate text. For example, the Latin word *exultemus* literally means "to jump about" or "let go," and this idea is clearly illustrated in the motif figure in the soprano line that starts the piece and is imitated throughout the section. A second motif appears in the bass voice in m. 2 and then travels through the tenor and alto lines. Because Sweelinck's typical compositional procedure is to introduce and develop imitative figures for each section of the text and then repeat the same material with a different vocal texture, all voices have the opportunity to introduce and imitate specific motives as they are introduced, as well as explore how multiple motives interact with and alter each other. Learning the piece becomes a musical scavenger hunt for the choir to find each new point of imitation.

There is frequent division into pairs or trios of voices in thirds or sixths, forming antiphonal choirs (e.g., mm. 25–45); students should know who their vocal "partners" are and be able to listen within their own section and across the choir. Rehearse related parts together separate from other voices to ensure careful tuning, and then add the other parts on a musical whisper before combining all parts on pitches. Once students are fully comfortable with their parts in sections, try rehearsing in a mixed formation. While doing so will obscure the antiphonal nature of some portions of the piece, the opportunity to sing out of the section will improve tuning and highlight the interactive nature of the imitative style.

This approach provides students with a strong sense of the motet's structure that is otherwise not immediately apparent, and in cases when the piece is performed without music, a this technique serves as a memory aid as well. The danger of imitative counterpoint, particularly in this compact of a style, is that it can easily become one continuous wave and dynamic of sound without definition unless the choir understands how the piece is constructed. Experiment with tiered dynamic contrasts to define sections, as the setting itself does not clearly identify them. Entrances and points of imitation need to take the foreground, and students must know exactly which voices are important to the texture and when it is less so and adjust their singing accordingly, independent of the conductor. Such a process also provides the audience with a better sense of the construction of the piece, as individual motives sonically rise out and fall back into the texture.

Stylistic Considerations

Music of this time period was written without barlines, and singers rarely saw any other line of music apart from their own. While barlines provide a useful way to count time, they can obscure the natural accents of text stress when they fall "off the beat." In most instances the imitative setting of the motet reinforces textual accent, and the editor has done an excellent job of pointing to the few instances when this is not the case. Care should be taken to follow the natural, chant-like groupings of twos and threes and not artificially bend the setting to barline stress.

In keeping with the text, the tempo should be relatively brisk and dancelike: a metronome marking within the range of 69–80 to the half note seems appropriate (note: early prints of this edition contain a misprint tempo marking that is considerably slower). Vocal production should emphasize a clear, light, and buoyant sound to aid tuning.

The two triple sections are idiomatic of the period, and care must be taken that the conductor keeps the macrobeat constant in the transitions (half note = dotted half going in and dotted half = half note going out) to preserve their dancelike character. Having the choir snap fingers on the offbeats can provide rhythmic continuity and a physical subdivision for singers, as well as a change of pace. Care should be taken, however, not to swing eighth notes while snapping (unless the Swingle Singers is the desired effect).

If you choose to use continuo in performance, a sustaining instrument like the organ is more historically appropriate than piano. The use of a positiv organ setting on an electronic keyboard could work well (avoid "full organ" voicings). Alternatively, you may wish to experiment with doubling the bass line alone on cello (bowed or pizzicato), bassoon, or organ.

Form and Structure

This motet is through-composed and makes extensive use of imitative counterpoint reflective of the Netherlander style. It is clearly modal with a pitch center around G with frequent use of chromaticism that has the effect of temporarily inferring a shift of pitch center and modality.

The motet can be divided sectionally according to text with abbreviated cadential formulas at the end of each main section but without clear divisions between sections. Within each section Sweelinck typically presents an imitative idea, develops it, and then repeats or varies the same procedures in an alternative voicing. Some sections divide the five voices into antiphonal choirs, while others make use of the entire five-voice texture in free imitation.

Section	Measure	Event and Scoring
Section I		Text: *Venite exultemus Domino*
	1–4	Two motivic ideas; a "jumping" motif in S1 and S2 voices; pitch, lower neighbor, and return in alto, tenor, and bass
	5–7	Homophonic triple section
	8–11	Same motivic ideas as mm. 1–4 but motives reversed in voices
	12–15	Homophonic triple section
Section II		Text: *jubilemus Deo salutari nostro*
	16–19	G pedal in bass voice; soprano 1 and soprano 2 in crossed-voice thirds dialogue with alto and tenor
	20–24	G pedal in bass voice; material in mm. 16–19 repeats without voice crossings

Section	Measure	Event and Scoring
Section III		Text: *praeoccupemus faciem eius in confessione*; treatment of text is subdivided within section
	25–29	*Praeoccupemus*: antiphonal exchange between alto, tenor, and bass and soprano voices
	29–33	*Faciem eius*: dialogue in thirds between tenor/bass and soprano 1/alto voices; soprano 2 serves as an echo voice
	34–37	*in confessione*: staggered quarter–quarter–half note entrance in all voices; direct imitation in soprano 1 and bass voices in descending motif
	38–41	Repeat of ideas in mm. 25–29, but two- and three-part is switched in voices
	41–45	Repeat of ideas in mm. 29–33, but with soprano voices in dialogue in sixths with tenor/bass
	46–51	Repeat of ideas in mm. 34–37, but imitation in all voices in ascending motif
Section IV		Text: *et in psalmis jubilemus ei*
	52–56	Full imitative subject introduced in soprano 1; entrances follow in tenor, soprano 2, bass, soprano 1, tenor, and alto voices
	57–61	Same imitative treatment at new pitch center; entrances in alto, tenor, bass, soprano 1, soprano 2 voices
Section V		Text: *Quoniam Deus magnus Dominus*
	62–65	Dotted half–quarter imitative entrances in soprano 1 and tenor; soprano 2, alto, and bass tutti entrance
	66–69	Soprano 1 and tenor reenter on *Dominus*
Section VI		Text: *et Rex magnus super omnes deos*; treatment of text is subdivided within section
	70–74	*Et Rex magnus*; ascending lines in soprano 1/soprano 2 in imitation
	75–85	*Super omnes deos*; descending motif in imitation, entrances in soprano 1, alto, soprano 2, tenor, soprano 1, and soprano 2 voices; descending, sustained bass

Text and Translation

Veníte exultémus Dómino,	Come, jump about [in the] Lord,
Jubilémus Deo salutári nostro:	Joyfully sing out [to the] God [that] saves us:
Praeoccupémus fáciem eius in confessióne	Come before his face in thanks,
Et in psalmis jubilémus ei.	And in psalms sing joyfully [to] him.
Quóniam Deus magnus Dóminus	Because God [is a] great master/Lord
Et Rex magnus super omnes deos.	And great King over all gods.

O come, let us sing to the Lord;
Let us make a joyful noise to the rock of our salvation.
Let us come into his presence with thanksgiving;
Let us make a joyful noise to him with songs of praise.
For the Lord is a great God, and a great King above all gods.
—Psalm 95:1–3

Contributed by:

Michael Lippert

Teacher Resource Guide

Verbum caro factum est

Hans Leo Hassler
(bapt. 1564–1612)

SSATTB with instruments ad libitum
GIA Publications: G-7037
Overall: 3
Vocal: 2
Tonal/Rhythm: 3

Composer

Born in Nuremburg, Hans Leo Hassler was widely regarded by contemporary audiences as one of the leading German composers of his time. He was the first notable German composer of the late Renaissance and the early Baroque to study in Italy, where his musical thinking was strongly influenced by Andrea Gabrieli (ca. 1510–1586). He later became acquainted with Giovanni Gabrieli (ca. 1554–1612), with whom he kept close contact. In addition to his success with composition, Hassler was an organist with outstanding technical prowess, which he cultivated from an early age.

After his studies with Andrea Gabrieli were truncated by the Venetian master's death in 1586, Hassler returned to Germany. There he began his musical tenure as a chamber musician in the court of Count Octavian Fugger II in Augsburg and later served as the Protestant Elector of Saxony and the Catholic Prince Fugger. Although Hassler was a self-declared Protestant, he composed not only liturgical music for Lutheran service but also Roman Catholic masses.

Hassler's training made him one of the first composers to promote freshly developing Venetian styles and vocal techniques in Germany. Hassler, and later

Heinrich Schütz (1585–1672), explored the concertato and polychoral styles, as well as a variety of other practices that they promptly incorporated into a German musical context. This cross-cultural expansion resulted in one of the most important Baroque developments outside of Italy. Hassler's vocal compositions include eight masses, ninety-six motets, fifty-two psalms, seventy chorale settings, two Magnificats, and a number of secular pieces.

Composition and Historical Perspective

"Verbum caro factum est" is one of thirty-one motets in the 1591 collection *Cantiones sacrae de festis praecipuis totius anni.* This compilation was expanded in 1597 to include thirty-eight sacred motets. In this motet, Hassler uses the Venetian-based polychoral style developed by late Renaissance and early Baroque composers who witnessed and subsequently wrote into their scores the sound delay caused by the substantial distance between choir lofts at St. Mark's Basilica in Venice. The resulting polychoral texture eventually became one of the major stylistic developments that crossed from the late Renaissance into the Baroque era.

The concertato (Italian, "concerted"), is yet another seventeenth-century style prevalent in Hassler's motet. Contrasting multifarious musical forces in a dramatic fashion, the concertato frequently allows a melody to be shared between groups of voices or instruments (most typically in alternation) and is almost always set over a basso continuo as illustrated in "Verbum caro factum est."

Technical Considerations and Musical Elements

Hassler's motet is an excellent choice for either liturgical or concert performance, as the history of its genre readily shows. The option of adding instrumental accompaniment to this motet provides a delightful addition to any service or program. The variety of instrumental possibilities suits the needs of most musical settings, although the choice of instrumental ensemble must, of course, depend on the size and quality of the performance space.

The harmonic structure of the piece as a whole is sophisticated for the time period in which it was composed. Tonal centers shift in nearly every phrase, and chromaticism persists throughout; both of these stylistic features are characteristic of Hassler's output in compositions completed after his Italian sojourn. Despite the seemingly continuous modulations, every large section cadences on an A major chord, which serves as the overall tonal center of the motet. Creating awareness of frequent tonal shifts and pivotal cadences will help to expedite the early process of score reading.

The texture throughout vacillates between polychoral interplay (usually SAA and TTB groupings) and homophonic textures with all six voices participating. The ranges do not exhibit extremes.

Stylistic Considerations

At the start of the Baroque period, the size of a typical choral ensemble grew to roughly thirty singers. Only festive occasions called for a larger choir. Thus, lucidity of performance, clear sonorities, and balance between sections must be given preference in rehearsals.

As Clifford G. Richter suggests:

> [M]uch of the so-called *a cappella* music of the sixteenth and seventeenth centuries can be enhanced by the addition of instruments to double the voices or substitute for some of them, a practice suggested by many of the composers themselves. Because of its rhythmic structure and antiphonal effects, Hassler's "Verbum caro factum est" offers a fine opportunity for the conductor to employ such doublings.
>
> In general, it is best if the doublings are restricted to instrumental families—strings, woodwinds, brasses—although mixtures of the families, if carefully chosen, can be very effective. The following suggestions may serve as a guide:

	Soprano I	**Soprano II**	**Alto**	**Tenor I**	**Tenor II**	**Bass**
1.	Violin	Violin	Viola (violin)	Viola (cello)	Cello	Double bass
2.	Oboe	Oboe	English horn	Bassoon	Bassoon	Bassoon
3.	Trumpet	Trumpet	French horn	French horn	Trombone	Trombone
4.	Oboe	Oboe	French horn	French horn	Trombone	Trombone
5.	Clarinet	Clarinet	French horn	French horn	Trombone	Double bass

Of course, these are only some of the possibilities—imagination and experimentation will allow the conductor to choose his [or her] own combinations.[1]

Parts for instruments listed above are available from Alexander Broude, Inc.

Form and Structure

Section	Measure	Text
A	1–15	"Verbum caro factum est; et habitavit in nobis"
A´	16–31	"Verbum caro factum est; et habitavit in nobis"
B	32–45	"Et vidimus gloriam ejus; gloriam quasi unigeniti a Patre"
C	46–53	"Plenum gratiae et veritatis"
C´	54–62	"Plenum gratiae et veritatis"

Text and Translation

John 1:14, paraphrase of the King James Bible

Verbum caro factum est	The word was made flesh
Et habitavit in nobis;	And dwelt among us;
Et vidimus gloriam ejus,	And we beheld his glory,
Gloriam quasi unigeniti a Patre,	Glory as of the only-begotten of the Father,
Plenum gratiae et veritatis.	Full of grace and truth.

Additional References and Resources

Blankenburg, Walter, and Vincent J. Panetta, "Hans Leo Hassler." *Grove Music Online*. Edited by L. Macy http://www.grovemusic.com (accessed April 28, 2006).

Jacobs, Arthur, ed. *Choral Music: A Symposium*. Baltimore: Penguin Books, 1963, 72–73.

Jeffers, Ron, ed. *Translations and Annotations of Choral Repertoire, Volume I: Sacred Latin Texts* (Corvallis, OR: earthsongs, 1988), 241.

Suggested Listening

Hans Leo Hassler, "Verbum caro factum est" on *A Rose in Winter*, Dale Warland Singers, Dale Warland, D'note Classics B000003YNQ.

Contributed by:

Elizabeth K. Swanson

1 Clifford G. Richter, "Performance Suggestions" in *Hans Leo Hassler*, "Verbum caro factum est" (New York: Alexander Broude, 1967), 1.

Teacher Resource Guide

Heart We Will Forget Him

James Mulholland

(b. 1935)

SSA with piano and horn
National Music Publishers: WHC 153
Overall: 3
Vocal: 3
Tonal/Rhythm: 3

Composer, Composition, and Historical Perspective

James Mulholland's earliest formal musical education began at the age of twelve when he began to study voice, piano (along with other instruments), and composition. He credits his mother for developing his love of music, as he spent his childhood years "listening to her sing beautiful songs." He graduated from high school at fifteen and then enrolled at Louisiana State University where he earned both a bachelor of music and master of music in voice and composition. After graduation he entered Indiana University, where he earned a DMA in performance and literature. He has been a professor of music theory and history at Butler University since 1964.

Mulholland is most well known for his choral compositions, which are written for a variety of ensembles (SSAA, SATB, etc.), often including obbligato instruments such as horn or oboe. There are numerous recordings that include his works; The Kansas City Chorale has produced a CD entirely dedicated to his compositions, *Words & Music: The Music of James Mulholland.*

Technical Considerations and Musical Elements

MELODY

Melodically the piece does not appear to be terribly challenging; however, there are several areas that might be problematic, at least at first reading. There are numerous instances of chromatic motion in the vocal (and horn) lines, and one of those chromatic motions, a rising half step in the melody (a hallmark of the piece), begins with an unprepared dissonance (e.g., the opening note of the horn part and the vocal line, mm. 1 and 5, respectively). Other dissonances are well prepared and are usually suspensions or ritards, oftentimes supported by the harmonic progressions of the piano accompaniment. After several readings, the individual lines are easily sung and seem entirely natural.

Make sure that the singers are able to sing their lines with confidence before adding the piano into the texture, as the vocal lines sometimes clash with the accompaniment. One of the main compositional techniques that make this piece so interesting is that the melody is constantly being added to or adjusted in some way. This might become problematic when the process of memorization begins. The lines are similar, but almost never identical.

RHYTHM

One issue that may be of concern is the frequent use of both duple and triple feel in all parts (including the horn and piano). This manifests itself in two ways: either combining the two directly on top of each other (most often with quarter note triplets in the piano and even quarter notes in the voice parts, e.g., mm. 21–32) or a switch from triplets to even quarter notes in the vocal parts (e.g., mm. 37–46). Have the singers speak the text in rhythm; they will quickly become used to the changes between triple and duple in their lines and will be able to hold their own against any conflicting rhythm in the piano. Make sure that the choir does not slow down the triplets. The conductor should be conducting two beats per measure (2/2 time signature), so the singers may have a tendency to slow down the main beat.

Of greater concern, and certainly more difficult to conduct, are the frequent rallentandos or ritards, the tempo changes between sections, and the numerous fermatas. Switching to a four pattern while conducting the ritards will aid in keeping everyone together rhythmically, and clear preparatory beats are essential when beginning new tempos. As far as fermatas are concerned, there are several ways that they might be approached, but in only two instances is a clear breath (m. 20) or caesura (m. 46) given. In all other cases the conductor must decide if a breath should occur, if the piano should clear the chord before continuing, etc. Sometimes the choice is obvious, sometimes not. The following list outlines all the fermatas with a suggestion as to how they should be treated, but each conductor is welcome to make her or his own musical choice, taking into account the ability levels of the singers and horn player, the performance venue, etc.

- M. 10 – voices, piano, and horn all hold the fermata (for a relatively short time, perhaps only the length of one additional quarter note, and then all continue without break.
- M. 20 – all parts hold the fermata, then break (either a measure break of one half note or perhaps a slightly longer, unmeasured break), then continue.
- M. 32 – all parts hold the fermata; the singers take a measured breath of a half note and continue while the piano and horn hold the chord to the downbeat of m. 33. The piano continues without clearing the chord.
- M. 36 – two fermatas are given in the piano in this measure. The singers and piano should hold the first fermata together, then the singers should clear on the next piano chord. This second fermata in the piano alone should then clear (either a measured or unmeasured break) before continuing when the singers reenter.
- M. 42 – the singers and the piano should hold the fermata; both should clear for a half note beat before the piano continues with the horn in m. 43.
- M. 46 – all parts hold the fermata, then clear together for a more extended, unmeasured break before continuing. (This is where a caesura is marked, indicating a break rather longer than a breath).
- M. 75 – all parts hold the fermata, then clear together before the piano and horn continue. This might also be a longer break for the sake of a dramatic finish.

Tonality

There are numerous higher tertian chords throughout the piece. The color notes (ninths and elevenths) occur in all parts (vocal and instrumental) but most of the coloristic effects occur in the piano accompaniment. Our modern ears are used to these harmonies, and they should not present a problem for the singers. Sudden shifts in harmony are approached mainly by step in the vocal parts, so once the singers hear the harmonic shifts, they should be able to maneuver their way without difficulty. Mm. 37–42 will be the greatest challenge for the singers.

Range and Texture

Vocal ranges are somewhat extended for the soprano 1 part; they are asked to sing from middle C to high A, and the altos are given a low G. Overall, there is a good balance between unison, two-part, and three-part singing (no additional divisi required). Even when there are three parts in the voices, rarely does the range between voices encompass more than an octave, which makes tuning and balance relatively easy.

ACCOMPANIMENT

The horn part for this piece will require a better than average player, especially considering how exposed the part is on occasion. The range is not too demanding and neither is the length of any particular line.

The piano accompaniment is not overly complex. Certain issues already discussed need to be taken into consideration (triple versus duple rhythms, higher tertian chords, etc). The main challenge is more of a physical nature than a musical one, as the pianist must be able to cover the interval of a tenth (plus additional chord tones) in both hands without rolling chords. In addition, much of the texture in mm. 62–74 is quite thick and switches registers frequently from bass to treble clef in the right hand. Also note that there are sections with numerous accidentals and one section of arpeggiated quarter note triplets (mm. 21–36).

Stylistic Considerations

Because this is a twentieth-century composition, there is no historically accurate performance practice. However, due to the neo-Romantic nature of the harmonies, melody text, etc., it is suggested that the choir sing with a rich, full tone, incorporating pure vowels and a well-supported, healthy technique. The singers must be careful not to allow the vibrato to fall beneath the pitch when singing in this manner; there should be a buoyancy to the singing, and the tone should never sound pressed or forced.

Form and Structure

SECTION	MEASURE	EVENT AND SCORING
Introduction	1–4	Horn and piano
A	5–36	
	5–20	Four phrases (4 + 4) + (4 + 4)
	21–36	Four phrases (4 + 4) + (4 + 4)
B	37–46	
	37–46	Two phrases (4 + 6)
C	47–62	
	47–54	Two phrases (4 + 4)
	55–62	Two phrases (4 + 4)
A´ and conclusion	63–79	
	63–70	Two phrases (4 + 4)
	71–74	One phrase (4)
	75–79	Two phrases (2 + 3)

Text

Heart, we will forget him. You and I, to-night.
You may forget the warmth he gave,
I will forget the light.

When you have done, pray tell me,
That I may straight begin!
Haste! lest while you're lagging,
I remember him.

—Emily Dickinson

Contributed by:

David Scholz

Teacher Resource Guide

Messe basse

Gabriel Fauré

(1845–1924)

SA, soprano solo and organ or harmonium
Broude Brothers: CR 37
Overall: 3
Tonal: 3
Tonal/Rhythm: 3

Composer

Gabriel Fauré was born in Pamiers, Ariège, France, on May 12, 1845.

In 1854 Louis Niedermeyer, a music pedagogue who knew of Fauré's musical skills, offered the nine-year-old a scholarship to the Niedermeyer School, which aimed to train organists and choirmasters. For the next eleven years Fauré studied in Paris at this institution, coming under the tutelage of Camille Saint-Saëns, among other noteworthy musicians and pedagogues of the time. Saint-Saëns became an influential figure to in Fauré's development as a composer, introducing him to composers like Franz Liszt, Robert Schumann, and Richard Wagner.

During his prolific career, he composed the much-loved *Cantique de Jean Racine* in 1865 and a year later was appointed organist of the Saint-Sauveur Church in Rennes, Brittany, before enlisting the Franco-Prussian War.

Fauré returned to Paris in 1871, and became organist at Saint-Honoré d'Eylau, assistant to Widor at Saint Sulpice, and substitute for Saint-Saëns at the Madeleine. In 1872 Fauré joined the faculty of the Niedermeyer School and five years later was named choirmaster of the Madeleine, one of the most important churches in the city.

His principal output from 1878-87 was piano pieces and songs. Choral works from this period include motets, the first and second of three versions of the *Messe basse* for female voices (1881 and 1882), and the *Messe de Requiem*, Op. 48 (1888).

In 1896 he was named chief organist at the Madeleine and professor of composition at the Conservatoire. His students included Maurice Ravel, Charles Koechlin, Louis Aubert, Jean Roger-Ducasse, Georges Enescu, Nadia Boulanger and Emile Vuillermoz. In October 1905 he succeeded Théodore Dubois as director of the Conservatoire where he created a series of significant reforms. In October 1920 he retired from the Conservatoire due to the loss of his hearing but continued to compose, completing the String Quartet in E Minor, Op. 121 (1924). He died in Paris on November 4 of the same year at the age of eighty. Fauré's compositions include song cycles, piano pieces, the lyric dramas *Prométhée* and *Pénélope*, incidental music, chamber music for string ensemble, and sacred and secular choral music.

Composition and Historical Perspective

Messe basse, or low mass, comes from a medieval tradition in which the celebrant speaks the prayers of the Mass for a congregation of limited size or even in the absence of worshippers altogether. However, sometimes this reading of the mass was done while the organist or choir provided a musical background. In this mass, the Gloria and Credo are not set, probably due to the length of the texts and the tradition of more elaborate music in these movements.

Originally the mass was entitled *Messe des pêcheurs de Villerville* (Fishermen's Mass). It was a joint composition of Fauré and his first pupil André Messager (first and second versions; the third and last is completely Fauré's).

First Version

This version was performed in 1881 by a three-part female choir with a straightforward accompaniment on the harmonium and a solo violin for the *O Salutaris* at the Church of Villerville on September 4, 1881. This version had two movements composed by Messager and three by Fauré:

1. Kyrie (Messager)
2. Gloria (Fauré)
3. Sanctus (Fauré)
4. O Salutaris (Messager)
5. Agnus Dei (Fauré)

Second Version

The second performance, September 10, 1882, was a second collaboration with Messager, who orchestrated all movements except the Agnus Dei for flute, oboe, clarinet, a double string quintet, and harmonium.

THIRD VERSION

After the previous two performances at Villerville, the Mass remained for some years in the Clercs family's archives. In 1906 Fauré signed a contract with the publisher Heugel and decided to publish the work without Messager's input. In 1907 the mass was published under the title of *Messe basse* for female voices (solos and chorus) with organ or harmonium accompaniment. The mass incorporated several changes:

1. The two movements by Messager (Kyrie and O Salutaris) were taken out.
2. The Gloria was, for the most part, eliminated, but the "Qui tollis" portion reappeared as the Benedictus with major changes from m. 10 on.
3. The Sanctus remained very much the same; however, there are six extra measures and major alterations in the text underlay.
4. Only the Agnus Dei remained unchanged.

Technical Considerations and Musical Elements

The *Messe basse* illustrates Fauré's musical style, especially that of the 1880s. His beautiful melodies, harmonic richness, modal atmosphere (without loss of tonality) whole tone sequences, and the use of chromaticism are clear signs of Fauré's compositional style.

KYRIE

One outstanding feature of Fauré's compositional style is long and melodious phrases. The conductor should study each phrase as a whole instead of as individual chords. Also, taking care to understand the harmonic language is imperative for the conductor. Phrases should be sung first on a neutral syllable, such as "no-o," to help singers experience the characteristic flow of the phrase. The conductor should ask the singers to shape each phrase from the beginning.

This Mass is filled with rapid switches of mode, as we can see in the Kyrie mm. 19–20. It is important for both the conductor and the choir to be aware of these sudden changes, saving valuable rehearsal time.

The Kyrie is in antiphonal style with alternation between the soprano solo and the unison choir (up until m. 42). The choir echoes the soloist, although not exactly. There are two independent lines with common melodic features. The choir should sing the *dolce/piano* dynamic with a tender and well-supported tone. The conductor can help to strengthen the *piano* dynamic by asking the singers to use the same breath support as when they are singing *forte*. Since plainchant influenced the composer's writing, singers should diminish the vibrato.

SANCTUS
In the ordinary Mass tradition, the Gloria and the Credo follow the Kyrie. In this particular mass, those two movements are not included. Therefore, the Sanctus follows the Kyrie, maintaining the mood of the Kyrie with the *dolce/piano* dynamic. This movement contains an "echo" feature when phrases like "Dominus Deus Sabaoth" (mm. 7–10) is repeated with mode and dynamic changes. As in the Kyrie, singers should be aware of pitch and mode changes so that when they sing they do not learn it wrong. In this movement the two parts work more together than in the Kyrie, because they sing at the same time, which brings up the challenge of lining up text. Rhythm and text precision can be aimed for by asking the choir to sing the text staccato so they and the conductor are aware of the unity of the consonants.

Long phrases as well as dynamic diversity are evident in this movement. They can be helped by the conductor's clarity in placing breath marks and specifying phrasing. At the end of the Sanctus, the sopranos sing a G5 at a *piano* dynamic, which could be challenging for inexperienced singers. The conductor should give sopranos a dynamic shape within the *piano* dynamic and ask them to sing in their head voice, or even boy-like (if it is not already sung by boys) but well-supported.

BENEDICTUS
The music of this movement was initially the Gloria, which was, for the most part, suppressed. The "Qui tollis" from the Gloria reappears as the Benedictus with changes from m. 10 onwards.

This is the only movement with compound meter. The Benedictus contains a soprano solo and an antiphonal aspect as well as the *dolce/piano* dynamics of the Kyrie. It is pretty much in two parts with the soprano solo and the unison of the choir and only divides into a three-part choir in the last two measures for the cadence.

Because of the nature of the meter and the melodic shape, it is important for the choir to have a strong sense of rhythm and pulse. The conductor should ask the choir first to learn the pitches on a neutral syllable, such as "bim," which will remove heaviness and help to shape the phrase.

As in the previous movement, phrases are long and breath marks must be clearly specified. This movement is legato and light. The breath flow and constant forward movement of breath is imperative to achieve the phrase length.

AGNUS DEI
An issue with this movement is that there are a few *a cappella* measures, and keeping the intonation on track, especially in the upper minor third leap, can be difficult. Because of this leap, the choir will have the tendency to accent the syllable "se" of "miserere." Instruct them in the right word stress by keeping a forward sound and a tall vowel shape. The long initial soprano line

can be aided by the conductor's clarity in placing breath marks and specifying phrasing.

The thicker texture presents more alto divisi than previous movements, which can be tricky since it can get heavy. Remind the alto II to keep the light feeling of the beginning. It is important that the choir is aware of natural word stresses within any rhythmic figure. Words like "pacem" or "nobis" set on two quarter notes, are tempting opportunities for double accents. In mm. 60–61, the "bis" of the word "nobis" should be noticeably softer than the first syllable.

The conductor might want to speak the text aloud and accurately stressed as a learning aid and then ask the choir to speak the text in rhythm with the phrases well shaped.

Stylistic Considerations

For the most part, *Messe basse* is governed by textural clarity and melodic lines while avoiding "violent emotions." The choir must understand the importance of a restrained use of vibrato. Attention to tempo is extremely important. The use of rubato and other alterations of tempo are avoided in French vocal music unless indicated by the composer.

Since this Mass is accompanied by harmonium, it is essential for the choir to sing with crisp and short consonants. The text will then be understood within the texture of the harmonium. The conductor is responsible for keeping a balance between harmonium and choir.

The harmonium part is rhythmically straightforward and generally doubles one of the vocal lines. However, this is not always the case, and it is important that the conductor understand the harmonic environment.

The conductor should coach the organist with his or her understanding of phrasing so both choir and organist shape phrases the same way.

Form and Structure

SECTION	MEASURE	EVENT AND SCORING
Kyrie	1–30	
	1–8	(2 + 4 + 2)
	9–18	(4 + 2 + 4)
	19–30	(7 + 5)
Christe	30–44	
	30–36	(3 + 3)
	36–44	(4 + 2 + 2)
Kyrie	45–51	(3 + 4)
Sanctus	1–15	(2 + 4 + 4 + 5)
	15–31	(3 + 4 + 2 + 4 + 4)
	32–36	(2 + 3)

SECTION	MEASURE	EVENT AND SCORING
Benedictus	1–13	(5 + 4 + 4)
	13–21	(2 + 2 + 4)
	21–33	(4 + 4 + 4) alto with tune
	33–38	(3 + 2)
Agnus Dei	1–20	(6 + 6 + 4 + 4)
	21–38	(6 + 4 + 4 + 4)
	39–45	(4 + 3)
	46–58	(5 + 4 + 4)
	59–72	(6 + 4 + 5)

Additional References and Resources

Jones, J. Barrie. "Fauré's Performance Practice." *Tempo* 151 (1984): 32–35.

Jordan, James. *Evoking Sound: The Choral Warm-Up: Method, Procedures, Planning, and Core Vocal Exercises*. Chicago: GIA Publications, 2005.

Nectoux, Jean-Michel. *Gabriel Fauré: A Musical Life*. Translated by Roger Nichols. Cambridge: Cambridge University Press, 1991.

———. *Gabriel Fauré: His Life through His Letters*. Translated by J. A. Underwood. London: Marion Boyars Publishers, 1984.

Vuillermoz, Èmile. *Gabriel Fauré*. Translated by Kenneth Schapin. Philadelphia: Chilton Book Company, 1960.

Contributed by:

Marcela Molina

Teacher Resource Guide

Niška Banja

arr. Nick Page

SSAA and piano
Boosey & Hawkes: MO51465170
Overall: 3
Vocal: 2
Tonal/Rhythm: 4

Composer

Nick Page is a composer, conductor, author, and song leader. His Powersings work to infuse the larger global community—choral music educators, music students, corporate leaders, and community members of all ages—with song. While working with the Chicago Children's Chorus in the mid-1980s, Page was inspired to seek out collaborative apprenticeships with Sweet Honey and the Rock and their primary arranger, Ysaye Maria Barnwell; Ladysmith Black Mambazo and their primary arranger, Joseph Shabalala; and The Bobs and their primary arrangers Bobby McFerrin and Richard Greene. He also studied ethnomusicology focusing on musics of the Indian and African diaspora. In 1990 Page founded the Mystic Chorale in Boston. This two-hundred member community chorus sings the music of many times and many places and fosters concert settings where the audience is considered an equal partner in creating the music.

Page earned his bachelor's degree in music education from Ithaca College and received his master's degree from Lesley College. Page has written two books, *Sing and Shine On!: The Teacher's Guide to Multicultural Song Leading* and *Music as a Way of Knowing*. His choral music is published by Boosey &

Hawkes and World Music Press. Page's commitment to honor the standard-bearers of a given musical tradition is shared in his musical performance notes included in the front matter of his compositions and arrangements and permeates the pieces themselves. In addition to his choral octavo compositions, Page has written several musicals, three of which were written for young people: *Olly Olly End Free*, *The Gimme-Gimmes*, and *Dare to Wonder*.

Composition and Historical Perspective

"Niška Banja" is a folk song of the Romani people still sung today in the Bosnian and Croatian regions. The language itself is neither Serbo nor Croation; it is the Romani dialect of the wandering peoples whose ancestry can be traced from India and Pakistan. Page first heard versions of this song in the 1960s. In 1986 he witnessed a Romani performance in Belgrade, Yugoslavia, requested "Niska Banja," and performed with the group onstage. Through this collaboration, Page learned some of the hidden meaning of the text and translation for more adult audiences. Consider an analogy to the "la la las" in madrigals—the risqué practice of kissing not necessarily one's spouse. See the translation below. Page recommends omitting this additional interpretation with younger singers but rather to focus on the innocent flirtations of the direct translation as a catalyst for the dance. The four-hand piano part was inspired by the jazz guitar styles of Pat Metheny.

Technical and Musical Considerations

The arrangement of "Niška Banja" is flexible—the piece can be performed by treble ensembles, changed men's ensembles, cambiata and changed men's ensembles, and mixed groups equally well. Movement may begin immediately with the four-hand piano introduction. All singers can begin with the melody Page indicates for either soprano or alto in m. 7, and repetitions may continue ad lib with the upper harmony, the second line marked as bass or soprano, joining when desired. Page points out the opportunity for a glissando "yelp" the second time through m. 7 on the first syllable "Nis." This yelp is so helpful to share the joy and improvisatory feel of the celebration.

The rich, layered texture of the "emka ravla," section (m. 11) again provides options for countless voicing choices and multiple repeats with layered options. Page gives suggestions in the score that can easily be adapted for choirs of all sizes and sounds. The repeated Fs here are fabulous for students working to establish confidence, and the octave leaping Cs provide a beautiful challenge for consistent healthy tone. After the piano interlude, the verses in m. 23 give soloists the experience to shine through. These two solo verses also work extremely well with small groups or even as a call and response with larger portions of the choral ensemble.

Throughout the piece, particular attention should be given to the ornamental feel of the pattern of two sixteenths followed by an eight note (m. 10, beat 2 on "va"; m. 14, beat 2 on "me"; m. 26, beat 2 on "kad" and "do"; and m. 30, beat two on "kad" and "do"). This same emphasis is drawn out in the coda in 8/8 (m. 32) in the syllables "me" and "ka." In each of these patterns, and particularly in the coda, a very bright and energetic vowel is encouraged. This adds to the improvisatory feel and maintains the intended vibrancy of the juxtaposition of the vowels and ornamental rhythm. Careful attention to intonation, through accurate pronunciation and free, healthy singing throughout, is key. Special attention to clarity, with open, bright vowels, is essential in the *a cappella* m. 32. Enjoy this and allow the fermata to grow in brightness and volume before moving to the ictus in m. 33.

Stylistic Considerations

In the early 1990s, I had the incredible opportunity to be coached by one of my own students on the Romani pronunciation of the piece. She confirmed Page's experience with the joy and flirtatious energy of the text and his assertion that the key to performance practice of this piece is the dance feel and, ideally, performing the piece with the dance movement whenever possible. The Eastern European 2 + 2 + 2 + 3 meter lends itself to the intended spirited four-step pattern with an elongated fourth step or skip. This dance finds its roots in Qawwali singing and Hindu dance.

My student also confirmed the Romani pronunciation as well as Page's correction that the second-verse pronunciation (m. 25) should be "choo-me dav-tey cha-yey." She encouraged all of us to embrace the Romani pronunciation and vibrancy of the upper, ringing, lifted soft palate space—just as Page does in workshop settings presenting "Niška Banja." This piece provides so many opportunities to take risks and expand the typical Western European sound. I have found the piece particularly useful in allowing students to experience a brighter quality and more vibrant vowels. The joy and infectious energy of the movement also bring freedom, health, and vibrancy to their singing.

Form and Structure

Measure	Event and Scoring
1–6	Piano introduction
7–10	Melody and upper harmony established with "Niška banja" text
11–14	Variation of the original melody with additional harmonies, "Emka ravla" text
15–22	Interlude with combined expansion of the introductory piano material end melodic variations

Measure	Event and Scoring
23–26; 27–30	Exact repetition of the four-measure verse with melody and harmony in two part voices, "Nislike su" as in mm. 7–10
11–30 (repeat)	With second verse in mm. 23–30, "Jek duj duj duj"
11–14 (repeat)	With the second time moving in m. 13 to the coda of m. 31
31–34	Coda begins with silent fermata, beat 9, m. 31, followed by *a cappella* voices m. 32 with rallentando and hold and concluding with m. 33 and 34; a tempo with chordal held voices and the return of the piano

Text and Translation

Niška Banja topla voda *Zanis lije ziva zgoda.*	The baths at Nis, hot water for the people of Nis, a lively event.
Emka ravla, emkame ravla, *Ando nisi name kavla.*	I will marry her, I will marry her or die, I will never let go.
Nislike su fine dame *Neseta ju nikad same.*	The women of Nis are fine ladies, They never stroll alone.
Jek duj duj duj duj de suj duj *Cumi davte caje ando muj.*	Kiss me, women, on the lips, In Nis I will never let her go!

Additional References and Resources

Page, Nick. *Music as a Way of Knowing*. York, ME: Stenhouse Publishers, 1995.

Page, Nick. *Sing and Shine On!: The Teacher's Guide to Multicultural Song Leading*. Portsmith, NH: Heinemann, 1995.

Web site:
Nick Page: www.nickmusic.com

Suggested Listening

Nick Page:
From the Nick Page Choral Catalog, choral groups, Nick Page, et. al.
Crossroads, San Francisco Girls Chorus, Sharon J. Paul, Barnett Music Productions.

Contributed by:

Jennifer Haywood

Teacher Resource Guide

What'll I Do?

Irving Berlin
(1888–1989)

arr. Kirby Shaw

SSAA a cappella
Hal Leonard: 8665999
Overall: 3
Vocal: 2
Tonal/Rhythm: 3

Composer

Irving Berlin, born Israel Baline, was born in Russia and immigrated to the United States with his parents at the age of five. His father died when Berlin was only thirteen, and he ran away from home soon after so he would not be a burden to the rest of his family. He taught himself to play piano while on the streets and had no formal musical training throughout his life; legend has it that he could play only in the key of F, and in his later years he had a piano built that would sound in any key of his choosing through a series of levers that shifted the action so the hammers would strike the necessary strings. He achieved his first landmark musical success with the publication of "Alexander's Ragtime Band" in 1911 and remained a fixture in American popular song with a string of hits in every decade that continued until the 1960s.

Berlin is unique among American popular composers in that he had three simultaneous, phenomenally successful careers—as an enduring Broadway composer, as a film scorer during the heyday of the film musical, and as a Tin Pan Alley craftsman with more hit singles than any other individual or team during the twentieth century. His fifty-four year career at the top of American song demonstrated his amazing ability to adapt to the latest trends and styles in popular culture until the advent of rock music fundamentally changed musical tastes. His popular hits include "Blue Skies," "Remember," "White Christmas," and "God Bless America," for which he won the Congressional Gold Medal. His landmark musicals, encompassing both stage and screen, include *As Thousands Cheer, This Is The Army, Top Hat, Holiday Inn, Annie Get Your Gun*, and *Call Me Madam*.

Composition and Historical Perspective

"What'll I Do?" originally appeared late in the season of the Music Box Revue of 1923 and became a fixture in the 1924 revue. The Music Box (on West 45th Street between Broadway and 8th Avenue) was built specifically by Berlin to showcase his own songs, making him the first combined producer, composer, and occasional star of the revue circuit in New York and put him in direct competition with his former employer Florenz Ziegfeld's *Follies*.

The Music Box Revues are notable not only for their string of hits, but also for serving as a working ground that allowed Berlin to make the transition from Tin Pan Alley to a viable composer of scripted stage and screen musicals. The songs produced for the revues demonstrate an evolution away from the customary ragtime rhythms of the time and toward a more lyrical style that would typify the American popular song.

"What'll I Do?" is an excellent example of Berlin's capacity to create songs that both personify and transcend the time period for which they were written. As a testament to its enduring presence in the Jazz Age, "What'll I Do?" was featured in the score of the 1974 film adaptation of *The Great Gatsby* in a Nelson Riddle arrangement (which sadly is not currently available in CD format). Artists as diverse as Judy Holliday and Nat King Cole to Bette Midler and Barbra Streisand continually reinterpret the song, and it has become a standard in the jazz repertoire.

Technical Considerations and Musical Elements

The tessitura, particularly in the alto voices (which regularly sing the G below middle C), is extremely low for the majority of high school female voices. Depending on the flexibility of the ensemble, transposition up a half or whole step may be beneficial. Regardless, care should be taken to nurture a healthy, unified sound throughout the register rather than allowing singers to dwell in "chest" voice, which is quickly apt to become pushed, out of tune, and out of keeping with the text and style of the piece.

The rising triadic pyramid in the alto 1 and soprano voices that permeates much of the arrangement presents several challenges. Using solfege to introduce this musical element will simultaneously develop good intonation and rounded, open vowel sounds. Insist on rounded vowels and a sense of the sound formed "in the head." To help reinforce this idea physically, have students place one hand on the top of the head and the other over the sternum to feel the vibrations as they sing. While students will and should feel vibrations in both places, ask them to try to minimize the amount of chest vibration and increase the amount of head vibration. Altos in particular need to feel a strong sense of low expansion of the breath to maintain the sustained low Gs, which can be reinforced with low outward movements of the arms and hands centered over the abdomen and hips.

Entrances in the pyramid also need to be rhythmically accurate and always have a sense of direction towards the end of the measure. Try count-singing or alternatively substituting an eighth note pulse of the solfege (e.g., do–do–do–do) or a neutral syllable to lock in clean rests and entrances as well as maintain forward direction in singing. If the syllable "dm" is used in performance, it should be sung with teeth separated and with as much space as possible in the mouth to allow the sound to resonate. Depending on circumstances, it may be advisable to substitute the syllable [du] or [lu]—experiment to hear which syllable works best for the ensemble. Monitor the possibility of vocal tension or fatigue created by these syllables by reminding students to sing with a relaxed and open throat. Initial "d" consonants on the accompanying figures should be dentalized to soften the attack.

Resist the temptation to mix the melodic line with the accompaniment until the accompaniment figures are fully mastered. As an alternative, encourage all sections to learn the melody separately, as this song is a significant representative of the American standard song style. This may require teaching the melody in a higher key that is manageable for the whole choir (perhaps D or C major) and then addressing specific vocal concerns in the lower key with only the voices that will ultimately carry it in performance. Insist that the chromaticism in the melody (particularly the interchange between E-natural and E-flat) is exactly in tune (not "blue") to prevent intonation problems with the accompaniment voices later. Provided the upper three parts are well rehearsed, the vocal melody, once practiced separately, should "lay in" to the overall texture with few problems.

Stylistic Considerations

This arrangement is suitable for a high school women's choir looking to highlight a strong set of lower voices, or alternatively, a small collegiate-style *a cappella* ensemble. In keeping with the *a cappella* jazz ballad style, the choir should strive to minimize vibrato to emphasize clarity and allow the clash of close harmonies in the B section to truly speak. Particularly in the B section, students should be aware of when they are singing "in the chord" and when they are providing the dissonant or color note. The solo line, whether sung by a soloist or by a small section, may introduce more vibrato into the sound, particularly at the ends of phrases and held notes.

The upper three voices need to create a sense of forward movement and rhythmic precision without seeming hurried. Generally speaking, once tempo is established in the accompaniment it should remain constant, reserving judicial use of rubato for the melodic line. Soften consonants in the diction to create a more conversational mood and legato feel, but be certain that the text remains clear to the listener. It is beneficial to listen to several representative recordings of this song (three are listed below—there are many, many more) so that students can hear the variety of idiomatic choices different artists make as well as begin the process of creating their own sense of phrasing and declamatory style.

The arranger clearly sets this arrangement in such a way as to draw attention to the long, legato line of the melody. Because of the large leaps in the melody and semi-static setting of the accompaniment, the song quickly can become a series of one- or two-measure phrases unless the conductor actively promotes the sense of a longer phrase. Kirby Shaw's rests in the melody line can serve as cues to one possible interpretation of a larger phrase structure.

Form and Structure

This piece is in standard thirty-two bar AABA song form with a brief introduction and coda. The introductory material in the upper three voices is constructed in such a way as to allow the elision of the ending of one phrase into the start of the next. Alto 2 carries the melody and text for all but the B section.

SECTION	MEASURE	EVENT AND SCORING
A		Twelve measures total
Introduction	1–4	Rising triadic pyramid in upper three voices (four measures)
	5–12	Alto 2 voice on melody, with vocal pyramid accompaniment (eight measures)
A		Twelve measures total
	11–14	Elision of ending of first phrase with next section in vocal pyramid (four measures)
	15–21	Alto 2 voice on melody, with vocal pyramid accompaniment (eight measures)
B		Thirteen measures total
	22	Four-voice transitional measure
	23–30	Four-voice, homophonic texture, melody in soprano 1

Section	Measure	Event and Scoring
A		Thirteen measures total
	31–38	Return to alto 2 melody and vocal pyramid accompaniment (eight measures)
	37–40	Elision of introductory material in vocal pyramid with lyric extension in alto 2 (four measures)
Coda	41–43	Over G pedal in alto 2 (three measures)

Additional References and Resources

Irving Berlin: An American Song. New Video (A&E Television Networks), VHS AAE-17672. 100 minutes. Also available on DVD.

Zegree, Stephen. *Complete Guide to Teaching Vocal Jazz (Including Pop and Other Show Styles)*. Dayton, OH: Heritage Music Press, 2002.

Suggested Listening

These recordings are intended as representative samples of the basic style and variety of interpretations of this song. None is of the arrangement reviewed.

Irving Berlin:

What'll I Do?" on *Irving Berlin: A Hundred Years*, Judy Holliday, et. al, Sony 40035.

"What'll I Do?" on *Puttin' On the Ritz: Capitol Sings Irving Berlin*, Nat King Cole Trio, et. al, Capitol 98477.

"What'll I Do?" on *Rosemary Clooney Sings the Music of Irving Berlin*, Rosemary Clooney, Concord 4255.

Contributed by:

Michael Lippert

Teacher Resource Guide

An die Frauen (To Women) Hob. XXVb:4

Franz Joseph Haydn

(1732–1809)

arr. Gregory Vancil

TBB
Southern Music Company: SC-245
Overall: 3
Vocal: 3
Tonal/Rhythm: 3

Composer

Joseph Haydn was the most celebrated composer of his time by the 1780s and is commonly considered the father of both the modern symphony and the string quartet. After a youth spent as a boy chorister in Vienna, Haydn found employment as a freelance musician and then as the music director for a local count. After the orchestra was disbanded, Haydn was employed by the prince of Esterhazy, enjoying decades of royal patronage. The music-loving prince of Esterhazy made great demands on the composer, resulting in the production of an enormous amount of music for orchestras, theaters, the court chapel, and for their own use in small chamber ensembles.

Upon the death of Prince Nikolaus, Haydn was free to travel and made two celebrated trips to England where several of his now best-known symphonies were performed to great acclaim. Upon his return to Vienna, Haydn composed the bulk of his large-scale works, including six grand Masses and two oratorios (inspired by concerts of Handel's music witnessed in England).

Composition and Historical Perspective

"An die Frauen" is a part song from a set of thirteen entitled *Aus des Ramlers Lyrischer Blumenlese* ("From Ramler's Lyric Anthology") written approximately between 1796 and 1799. According to biographer, G. A. Griesinger, Haydn composed these pieces "*con amore* in happy times and without commission." This set is one of the few compositions that Haydn wrote without a commission. Originally conceived as a vocal trio, this work—like others from this time period—works well with any size ensemble. The edition reviewed for this volume includes both the original German and an English text provided by the editor; either language works very well in performance.

Technical Considerations and Musical Elements

"An die Frauen" is quite melodic and follows predictable harmonic patterns, which make it rather easy for the singers to learn. In moments of more complex counterpoint, two of the three voices usually pair, with the third performing a countermelody. In composing this work Haydn made efficient use of a small amount of musical material and uses the opening melody as a basis for development throughout the piece, a technique commonly found in the Classical style.

The vocal parts, consisting of many short notes and disjunct contours, can make the musical line difficult to realize. In other words, this piece will sound choppy if the singers and conductor are not careful. For example, each voice part has all eighth notes in m. 19 and the first half of m. 20; each voice part must also execute some leaps in this instance. This musical contour, coupled with the singers' likely unfamiliarity with the German language can make this section sound extremely unmusical.

The conductor should shape this music so that it fits within Classical stylistic parameters. Analyze the phrase to locate destination points for each part. A possible solution in this case may be to shape four-note phrases that include the text "nicht Stahl, nicht Feur." A slight lift in each voice part after each iteration of "Feur," coupled with a swell of energy on "nicht Stahl, nicht" with a relaxation on "Feur," will make this section have a musical shape. For rehearsals, the conductor could ask the choir to sing only on vowels. This rehearsal technique prevents singers from clipping the notes with the consonant. It will also show the singers how quickly they must form their vowels for them to be comprehensible.

Stylistic Considerations

While the notes and rhythms of this work are easy to realize, achieving the proper style can be quite difficult. One of the hallmarks of Classical style is the feminine cadence, the ending of phrases on a weak beat, the weak part of a beat, or the weak part of a measure. "An die Frauen" is rife with feminine cadences in which the melody ends on the weak part of the beat. One need only examine the first entrance of each voice part to see its prevalence. The final word of the first bass entrance is "Hörner." Properly accented, it would be pronounced "HÖR-ner"; amateur singers, in an effort to make the final note short, will mostly likely accent the final syllable ("hör-NER"). This is exactly what one must avoid to achieve the proper style.

Luckily, Haydn's skill as a composer, combined with the idiosyncrasies of the German language, make this an easy task. First, Haydn almost always composes the note for the unaccented syllable lower in pitch than the accented syllable, creating the proper musical prosody. Additionally, in German, any unaccented syllable may be performed as a schwa; this may be accomplished by rounding of the lips, which will close the vowel and mute the syllable, creating an unaccented syllable. To further aid the un-accenting of a syllable, it is stylistically appropriate to perform a slight *crescendo* on the notes leading up to the final accented syllable of a phrase. The opening bass line is: "Natur gab Stieren Hörner"; if the singers slightly *crescendo* through "gab Stieren" on the way to "Hör" and perform a schwa on "ner," they will successfully achieve the style. There are dozens of these instances in "An die Frauen." Ensure that each one is performed in this manner. Additional rehearsal techniques such as movement and weight shift can add a kinesthetic dimension to your singers' understanding of this concept.

Feminine cadences are only part of Classical style, but diligence in performing will go a long way toward a fine performance. It should be noted that Classical music should always be performed with an air of grace and balance. You should not perform at extreme dynamics, and tempos or use overly expressive musical gestures. That being said, "An die Frauen" is a light-hearted character piece; the finer performances will find a way to relate the text to the audience in an innocent yet clear way.

While I advocate performance in the original language whenever possible, I also recognize the value of engaging an audience. "An die Frauen" is a delightfully charming and anachronistic in its chivalry/political correctness. This piece will get a good laugh from an American audience if it is performed in English. The English version in this edition is very well constructed and remains true to context of the original German.

Form and Structure

In "An die Frauen" Haydn develops a small amount of musical material into a full song. The vocal line and accompaniment are well integrated. As is typical of Classical compositions, the piece transitions from the home key (in this case, F major) to the dominant key (C major); after a short development section the original music returns to the home key.

Text and Translation

Natur gab Stieren Hörner,
Sie gab den Rosen Hufe,
Den Hasen schnelle Füsse,
Den Löwen weite Rachen,
Den Fischen gab sie Flossen,
Und Fittige den Vögeln;
Den Männern, den Männern aber Weisheit.

Den Männern! Nicht den Weibern?
Was gab sie diesen?
Schönheit, Schönheit.
Statt aller unsrer Spiesse,
Statt aller unsrer Schilde;
Denn wider Weibesschönheit besteht
Nicht Stahl, nicht Feuer.

Nature gives bulls horns,
She gives steeds hooves,
The hares have fast feet,
The lions huge jaws,
The fish have fins,
And birds have wings,
But men, men have only
wisdom.
Only men? Not women?
What do they have?
Beauty! Beauty!
Women's beauty triumphs
In spite of all of our spears,
In spite of all of our shields,
Or swords, or fire!

Additional References and Resources

Griesinger, Georg August. *Joseph Haydn: Eighteenth-Century Gentleman and Genius*. Madison: University of Wisconsin Press, 1963.

Suggested Listening

Netherlands Chamber Choir, *Haydn: Vocal Works*, Uwe Gronostay, conductor, Globe Records GL05080.

Contributed by:

Matthew W. Mehaffey

Teacher Resource Guide

Beati mortui, Op. 115, No. 1

Felix Mendelssohn

(1809–1847)

arr. Weber, M.

TTBB
Alliance: AMP 0311
Overall: 3
Vocal: 3
Tonal/Rhythm: 3

Composer

Felix Mendelssohn was an extraordinarily gifted child. He came from a distinguished Jewish family; his father was the head of a major Berlin banking firm and his grandfather was a famous Jewish philosopher. Mendelssohn's elaborate private education was organized by his mother and included a daily regime (which began at five o'clock in the morning) of music, languages, literature, drawing, and many other skills. He was a natural at everything he did, including music, and would have been successful in anything to which he turned his attention. His talents in music were also quite diverse. He was one of the finest pianists, conductors, and organists of his day. Some also say that he could have been one of the great violinists.

Mendelssohn's music was always skillful but conservative and polite in some ways. One cannot blame him for being conservative as he grew up in a home that taught him to be polite and to avoid offense. When compared to his contemporaries such as Wagner and Verdi, his Romanticism was very subdued.

His harmonic language was largely diatonic and his music clearly organized. He was the most classical and balanced of the early Romantics.

Mendelssohn's awareness of music's past was also responsible for one of the greatest musical resurrections in history; he conducted Bach's *St. Matthew Passion* on March 11, 1829. His masterpieces include the oratorio *Elijah*, *A Midsummer Night's Dream* Overture, Octet in E-flat Major for Strings, and his *Songs without Words* for piano.

Composition and Historical Perspective

"Beati mortui" is a motet from Mendelssohn's Op. 115, two sacred choruses for male choir and is based on Revelation 14:13. These were most likely completed between 1833 and 1834 during his time as music director in Düsseldorf. His duties there included conducting the choral and orchestral societies and providing the sacred music for Catholic services. Each month Mendelssohn prepared a major sacred work, and he frequently chose from the Masses of Mozart, Haydn, Cherubini, and Beethoven and from the Bach cantatas. Much of his energy, however, was devoted to reviving oratorios, including Haydn's *The Creation* and Handel's *Messiah*. This must have strengthened his will to undertake his first oratorio, *St. Paul*, in March 1834.

Technical Considerations and Musical Elements

"Beati mortui" requires a wonderfully vital and energized *piano* dynamic in addition to a long legato line. The piece is largely homophonic with some mild imitation for short stretches. When reading through the piece, ask the choir to sing mm. 1–17 on [nu] and have them switch to [di] beginning on beat three of m. 17. This will help set the color and dynamic for the next section. The singers should go back to [nu] on beat four of m. 30 and stay on that syllable for the rest of the piece. It will be helpful for the choir to sing all of the solo parts while learning the piece in order to understand the whole musical framework. Asking them not to sing the solo parts when learning the piece may cause them to disconnect musically during those solo parts in the performance.

One of the keys to making the phrases come alive is rhythmic intensity. Half notes and whole notes can become longer than written if rhythm isn't built into the early learning stages. Rehearsing the piece quietly on a neutral syllable while sounding a metronome (preferably an electronic one with subdividing capabilities) can help the choir to become aware of the rhythmic integrity needed. The stronger their sense of rhythm, the easier it will be for them to sing at an energized *piano*; this gives the director more freedom to shape phrases. It may also be helpful to have half of the choir sing staccato while the other half of the choir whispers eighth notes on [ta]. Be sure that the choir does not cheat the longer notes when singing staccato. Rehearsing staccato on the text later on will help to line up the vowels on the beat and make consonants happen faster.

This piece is particularly useful for teaching young male singers to sing beautiful Latin vowels. There are only nineteen words to teach, and much of the text repeats, so the language should not be a consideration in choosing this piece. However, there are some diction pitfalls to avoid. The first one happens in the first two words of the piece, "Beati mortui." Make sure that the singers don't inadvertently put a [j] glide between the first two syllables of "beati" (beh-ya-tee). A "w" can also happen between the last two syllables of mortui (mawr-too-wee). Other words in the piece with the same potential problems include "morientes," "deinceps," "requiescant," and "suis." This means that almost a third of the words you teach may be infected with the "w" or "y" virus! It is also important that young singers write the vowel sounds into their score either phonetically or using the international phonetic alphabet (IPA). This is especially helpful for words such as "in," "Domino," or "spiritus," where they may be inclined to sing an open [I] vowel instead of an [i]. Less experienced singers read text with an English bias. This may not necessarily lead to incorrect vowels but may cause pure vowels to be less pure than they should be.

When working on tone with male singers (especially inexperienced ones), it is often helpful for them to sing the piece up an octave to teach them to make enough interior space and to sing with more head tone. This may cause a few giggles initially but will become routine over time. Doing warm-up exercises that carry the falsetto further down in the range can also yield huge benefits if done consistently throughout the year.

The ranges in this piece are rather comfortable for all parts but the basses. In order for this piece to work, there are a few spots where the basses need to sing resonant low Fs and Gs. (There is also an optional low E in m. 16.) It is helpful to rehearse these passages with the basses on a bright [i] vowel to keep the sound high and forward. Ask them to show their two front teeth on the bottom to brighten the sound and bring more focus. Be sure that they don't start to growl and force the low notes.

One final suggestion for the piece is to try singing it up a half step. C major is a notoriously difficult key to sing in tune and singing the piece in C-sharp major will certainly alleviate some intonation problem. The voice part that may need extra guidance on the key change is the baritone, as many of their exposed passages sit on the middle C. Give them enough time before the performance to find where the new key sits in their voices so that they may sing those sections as beautifully as before.

Stylistic Considerations

A major stylistic choice that must be made is the type of Latin to be used for the piece. One could certainly make the case for German Latin, and this would present the piece in a different light. However, the conductor should make the choice early on and stay with the initial choice.

The tempo chosen depends on how subtly the choir can release the phrase endings. Many phrases end in a quarter note, which most likely would be changed to an eighth note and eighth rest. If the tempo is too fast, these phrase endings may not be as elegant as necessary. One way to help this would be to let those last notes ritard a bit so you can recover the tempo over the next few notes.

It is very important for the choir to hear the beginning few measures in comparison to the recapitulation at m. 37. You may want to ask them what is different and why Mendelssohn set it differently.

Form and Structure

The piece begins quietly and humbly and soon involves some simple imitation, which slowly builds to *forte* in m. 9. The solo quartet brings the dynamic down to *piano* in m. 13, and the tutti choir responds at *pianissimo* in mm. 15–17.

The B section begins with a brass-like proclamation from the baritones and basses. The four-part homophonic response is quite exciting and is quickly followed by a *subito piano*. The beginning motive of the fanfare is repeated at m. 25 by the four parts in unison and splits immediately into new music. The piece returns to *piano* at m. 32 with the baritones responding to the other three parts and gradually building into a fermata on a *forte* chord.

The recapitulation of A is the magic moment of the piece because Mendelssohn replaces the bass line with a C pedal and gives the baritone and second tenor line ascending stepwise motion in m. 39. This most vividly depicts the hopeful nature of the text. The piece builds from *piano* in m. 42 again, and there is a poignant B-flat in the baritone, which creates a gorgeous 4-3 suspension on the downbeat of m. 43 that resolves immediately thereafter. The solo quartet comes back at m. 45 in imitative fashion to be repeated four measures later.

Section	Measure	Event and Scoring
A	1–17	(4 + 8 + 4)
B	17–37	(3 + 2 + 4 + 2 + 3 + 7)
A´	37–45	(5 + 4)
Coda	45–56	(6 + 7)

Text and Translation

Beati mortui in Domino morientes deinceps,	Blessed are they who died in the Lord from now on,
Dicit enim spiritus, ut requiescant a laboribus suis.	The Spirit says that they may rest from their labors,
Et opera illorum sequuntur ipsos.	And their works will follow them.

Additional References and Resources

Schonberg, Harold C. *The Lives of the Great Composers.* 3rd ed. New York: W.W. Norton, 1997.

Suggested Listening

Felix Mendelssohn, "Beati Mortui" on *Sacred Motets of Mendelssohn and Brahms*, Gloria Dei Cantores, Elizabeth C. Patterson, Paraclete Records, GDCD 107.

Contributed by:

William Hammer

Teacher Resource Guide

Brothers, Sing On! (A Choral Salutation)

Edvard Grieg
(1843–1907)

arr. Howard D. McKinney

TTBB a cappella
J. Fischer & Bro./Alfred Publishing Co.: 6927-5
Overall: 3
Vocal: 3
Tonal/Rhythm: 3

Composer

Edvard Grieg is known as the greatest Norwegian composer of his time and the foremost Romantic nationalist of his country. Trained at the Leipzig Conservatory, his style was more standard in his early years, but he became increasingly nationalistic and personal in his compositions over his lifetime. Many of his compositions are based on Norwegian folk music, and the influence thereof can be seen in much of his music, including some of his piano works. However, he did not feel that his songs were as reflective of the folk tradition. On that subject he says, "Regarding my songs, I do not think that on the whole they have been greatly influenced by the folk song. In cases in which local color *had to play* an essential role, the influence is probably evident."[1]

Grieg is best known for his piano pieces, songs, and instrumental compositions. Perhaps his most popular works are the Piano Concerto in A Minor,

Op. 16 and *Peer Gynt*, Op. 23, which is incidental music for a drama by Ibsen. Despite the predominance of such genres, his choral music is quite extensive, representing a sizable portion of his output. He composed both *a cappella* works and pieces accompanied by piano or orchestra. He wrote for various voicings, including men's chorus, treble voices, and mixed voices. Many of his small-scale choral works were composed as individual pieces, and others as parts of larger sets, such as the *Album for Male Voices (Album for mannssang)*, Op. 30, which contains twelve pieces based on Norwegian folk songs.

Grieg traveled extensively on concert tours and was also very active as a conductor. His wife, Nina, was a talented singer, often giving recitals with her husband at the piano. Grieg had a wide range of acquaintances, both at home and abroad, and he corresponded with the likes of Johannes Brahms, Frederick Delius, Percy Grainger (who visited him at Troldhaugen), and Jean Sibelius, to name a few.

Composition and Historical Perspective

The work is a part-song for male voices originally composed as "Sangerhilsen" (EG 170) and is a setting of a text by Norwegian clergyman Sigvald Skavlan. ("EG" is a designation given to Grieg's works for which there is no opus number.) It sometimes appears under the title "A Greeting to the Singers." Like many of Grieg's works for male chorus, it was written for a specific occasion, in this case for the Sixth Great Song Festival in Trondheim, June 17–21, 1883.[2] There are two common misconceptions about the work, the first of which is that it is an arrangement of a folk song or some other preexisting melody. The other is that the text is traditional. On the contrary, the work is an original composition and the text is by a contemporary of Grieg's.

Technical Considerations and Musical Elements

The work contains several significant vocal challenges, the first being present in the opening measure. It begins with all the parts in unison, starting in a comfortable range for all voices. On beat four, however, there is an octave leap down to low A, which may be out of range or, at best, in an uncomfortable range for the tenors. (Melodic leaps are themselves problematic and will be discussed further below.) Here, it is important to discourage singers from attempting notes that are not suitable for their voices, not only because it is vocally unhealthy but because it will detract from the intonation and tone quality of the ensemble. When a singer attempts to phonate in a register that is unnatural to his voice, he will ultimately approximate the pitch and produce a sound that is unclear in the low registers.

If the chorus is large enough, it will prove helpful to omit the tenors (especially the first tenors) from beat four of the first measure altogether. If done carefully, it will not be noticeable, especially since the tempo is relatively fast and the text on that beat is not a stressed point of the phrase. Another helpful technique is to encourage the chorus to think in contrary motion.[3] In the case of the ascending triplet figure, if they imagine that the line descends as their voices ascend, it will help them keep their voices "grounded" instead of "skimming" the notes, avoiding the tendency for a thin, off-the-breath, or strident sound.

Leaps are a common element in the melody, often in successive thirds. The most striking moment is when the chorus sings the melody in unison. The succession of leaps begins with an octave down, followed by three upward leaps within an arpeggio of the same harmony. To further complicate the melody, the composer places this arpeggio over a triplet. As a result, the chorus must produce accurate pitches while performing a triple rhythm in an otherwise duple-dominated scheme. The tendency is for the chorus to slide through these pitches, approximating them under the assumption that as long as they arrive together on the downbeat of the next measure, all is well. In addition to voicing these sections appropriately (as discussed above) they must be carefully rehearsed at a slow tempo, allowing the pitches to settle into the singers' voices. Staccato singing may help solidify the pitches in their ears, but legato singing that is slow, deliberate, and precise is the best solution.

It will also assist singers' aural perception to hear these unison sections in a harmonic context. For example, in mm. 17–18, A major is clearly the harmonic framework of the unison phrase. If the singers are aware of this fact, they can "pre-hear" the harmonic arpeggio at the end of m. 17. Having the rehearsal accompanist reiterate A at the keyboard in octaves at a low register on each beat may further aid their understanding of this concept.

Stylistic Considerations

Once heard in the original Norwegian, it is somewhat difficult to reproduce the composer's intent as the declamation is different when sung in English. Grieg, in reference to his songs, speaks to the issue of translation in a letter to one of his colleagues:

> I refer to the matter of translations. That my songs . . . have thus far gained so little ground abroad . . . is so undoubtedly due in part to difficulties with translations. When I compose songs, my principal goal is not to write *music* but first of all to do justice to the *poet's* most secret intentions. To let the poem come to the fore as strongly as possible—that is my task. . . . But when Scandinavian poets, whose language foreigners neither understand nor sing, are maimed by the translations, both the poet and the composer suffer.[4]

The conductor may choose to take one of two approaches: 1) to articulate the notes in a manner similar to the original since the translation, aided by the articulation markings, is workable in this manner most of the time or 2) to perform the piece as a setting of an English poem and to express the character thereof as it is. Unlike some cases in which a translation into English entirely sabotages the syntax (e.g., a Bach cantata,), performance of the work in English produces a desirable outcome despite the lack of authenticity.

Language aside, the work should be performed with a robust, hearty sound. It was composed for a song festival, and part-songs of this type were commonly written for singing societies, a tradition to which this genre is so strongly connected. Although it is not a drinking song, it is similar in character. Using this imagery will help the chorus emote a kind of raucous, masculine character, giving this music the vitality needed for a successful performance.

Listening to the original "Sangerhilsen" sung in Norwegian can be an interesting point of departure in a teaching situation. This exercise could be part of a brief historical discussion on Grieg's choral music, giving the singers insight into the cultural settings for which part-songs were performed in the nineteenth century. Doing so will enrich the choristers by broadening their knowledge and experience and may increase their interest in singing Grieg's works. The original version can be heard on the Folke Bohlin recording (BIS Records) listed below.

Form and Structure

The work is strophic, with three stanzas set to the same musical material. Each stanza contains four phrases with a structure of 4 + 4 + 4 + 4. The key is A major with some chromatic movement in the voice parts. "Brothers, Sing On!" is homophonic and mostly syllabic throughout.

Text

Come and let our swelling song mount like the whirling wind,
As it meets our singing throng, so blithe of heart and mind.
Care and sorrow now be gone, brothers in song, sing on!
Brothers, sing on, sing on!

Youth is a wand'ring troubadour, sailing the singing breeze,
Wooing a maid on a distant shore, over the tossing seas;
Steering by the stars above, his vessel a song of love.
Brothers, sing on, sing on!

Errant minstrels, thus we greet you, list to our voices strong,
With glad and open hearts we meet you in our festival of song.
Care and sorrow now be gone, brothers in song, sing on!
Brothers, sing on, sing on!

Additional References and Resources

Benestad, Finn, ed. *Edvard Grieg: Letters to Colleagues and Friends*. Columbus, OH: Peer Gynt Press, 2000.

Benestad, Finn, and Dag Schjelderup-Ebbe. *Edvard Grieg: The Man and the Artist*. Lincoln: University of Nebraska Press, 1988.

Ehmann, Wilhelm, and Frauke Haasemann. *Voice Building for Choirs*. Chapel Hill, NC: Hinshaw Music, 1982.

Peed, John H. "Edvard Grieg's Music for Male Chorus: Forgotten Gems from Norway." *Choral Journal* 33, no. 9 (1993): 15–20.

Suggested Listening

Edvard Grieg:

"Brothers, Sing On!" on *Brothers, Sing On! Classics for Men's Choir*, Washington Men's Camerata, Frank Albinder, Gothic 49250.

"Sangerhilsen" on *Nordic Romance: Songs for Male-Voice Choir*, The Lund University Male-Voice Choir, Folke Bohlin, BIS Records 206.

Contributed by:

Russell Nelson

---

1 Finn Benestad, ed. *Edvard Grieg: Letters to Colleagues and Friends* (Columbus, OH: Peer Gynt Press, 2000), 226.

2 John H. Peed. "Edvard Grieg's Music for Male Chorus: Forgotten Gems from Norway." Choral Journal 33, no. 9 (1993): 15, 19.

3 Wilhelm Ehmann and Frauke Haasemann. *Voice Building for Choirs* (Chapel Hill, NC: Hinshaw Music, 1982), 38.

4 Benestad, 223.

Teacher Resource Guide

I'm A-Rollin'

arr. Paul Rardin

TTBB and piano
Santa Barbara Music Publishing: SBMP 474
Overall: 3
Vocal: 3
Tonal/Rhythm: 3

Composer

Paul Rardin is associate director of choirs at the University of Michigan where he teaches undergraduate conducting and conducts the Men's Glee Club and University Choir. He previously taught previously at Towson University in Towson, Maryland, where he served as director of choirs for twelve years.

Rardin is a graduate of Williams College and the University of Michigan, where he received a master of music in composition and doctor of musical arts in conducting. He has studied conducting with Theodore Morrison, Jerry Blackstone, and Gustav Meier and composition with Leslie Bassett, George Wilson, and Robert Suderburg. His settings of spirituals and folk songs are published by Santa Barbara Music Publishing.

Composition and Historical Perspective

"I'm A-Rollin'" is an arrangement of an African American spiritual. It was written for Jerry Blackstone and premiered by the University of Michigan Men's Glee Club in 2002 and subsequently arranged for mixed voices. It is the fifth of six published arrangements by Paul Rardin. Like much of the arranger's music, the piece draws from multiple influences—in this case, gospel (traditional triadic voicings of the upper three parts), jazz/pop (piano part), and blues (blues scale alterations).

The arranger writes:

> The piece is special to me because I learned it in the same way generations of African Americans learned it during and following slavery: through oral tradition. I was part of an enthralled audience that observed Keith Hampton (whose compositions and arrangements have established him as a premier contributor to spiritual and gospel choral music) teach the piece by rote, complete with three-part harmony, to a group of middle school students. I remember vividly two things about his teaching of the piece: a vocal resonance that was rich, warm, and deep and a half note pulse that was insistent and steady.
>
> As I grew more familiar with the piece I realized that this pulse, for me, embodied the essential common denominators of spirituals: pain and hope. The world about which we sing in this piece is indeed "unfriendly," and we should feel this half note pulse at least in part as painful footsteps in the midst of an agonizing day of labor, but we should also feel it in equal part as a reliable and steady companion, one whose familiarity empowers us to invite our brothers and sisters to "help [us] to pray."

Technical Considerations and Musical Elements

"I'm A-Rollin'" is built on compositional evolution: distinct musical ideas that are modified, enhanced, and embellished. Because the existing text and tune follow a traditional verse-chorus alternation, this embellishment takes place through varied repetition. Formally speaking, "I'm A-Rollin'" is very straightforward.

The piece's greatest challenges occur when divergence from the melody is greatest, e.g., the chorus' two "shouts," mm. 61–76 and mm. 118–124. Both sections present challenges of rhythm and intonation. The latter issue is paramount because the pianist rejoins the singers at the conclusion of these passages; this leaves no room for differing interpretations of pitch because pianists cannot retune their instrument mid-piece.

For intonation, I recommend two rehearsal techniques from colleagues that I use regularly with my own choirs:

Lip trills. If the passages in question are under pitch when the pianist rejoins, rehearse the sections using lip trills (lips buzzing together). The combination of greater breath support needed to keep the lips flapping and the brightest possible "vowel" placement will all but guarantee better intonation. Immediately after, have the choir resing the passage with text, using the same amount of breath support as with the lip trills.

"Higher" repeated notes. Where a section sings repeated notes, such as sopranos' mm. 73–74; four instances of A-natural), ask that they tune subsequent repeated notes incrementally higher than the previous one; this should counteract the human tendency to sing under pitch. Where a section sings sustained pitches, ask them to "dice" the note into shorter note values (e.g., the basses in m. 61 could rehearse on separated quarter notes: "ro-o-oll") and have each subsequent note "rise" in pitch. Return to the sustained pitch with new appreciation for intonation across time.

For rhythm, I recommend the following technique for isolating and fixing errors:

- Rehearse slowly at first. Robert Shaw's primary strategy was to rehearse slowly enough (or with few enough musical elements) that singers could not possibly internalize errors. This is particularly important for the unison/octave shout, in mm. 116–122.
- Staccato singing or "doots." Invite the choir to sing a challenging rhythmic passage (such as mm. 61–64) entirely staccato, either using the text or very short "doots." Tapping quarter notes during this exercise helps to instill rhythmic context of syncopated figures.
- "Filling" rests. Ask the choir to clap/tap on rests and/or sing "dummy" words during rests. Too often singers use the term "rest" to apply to brains as well as voices, and count much less well (or not at all) when not singing.

The pianist should play with absolute rhythmic security (the piece begs to rush otherwise) and supported tone ("lean into the keys"). The piano shares both the pain and the hope that the singers present; the repeated chords should have weight throughout—regardless of dynamic, they should feel heavy—and the left hand should always be at least an equal partner to the right.

Stylistic Considerations

Tone quality and articulation are the keys to effective performance of this piece. I prefer a tone quality that is warm, round, and rich—not "throaty," but certainly less "pingy" or bright than choirs might produce when singing Mozart.

I recommend inviting singers to strive for an "older" sound than the one they normally produce. To achieve this sound, rehearse a short (one- to two-measure) passage, and then ask the choir to sing it again numerous times with each one sounding "older" than the previous. *Sing this with the sound you had in elementary school . . . now middle school . . . now high school . . . now college . . . now professional.* In this fun (at times hilarious) exercise, students will gradually lift their soft palates and involve their oropharynx (throat area) resonators through the process, thereby rounding out and enriching the sound;

usually the "professional" choir sound is the one I choose.

For articulation, I ask choirs to sing gospel or gospel-influenced music using the following rules of thumb:

- Accent any note that is not sustained. ("When in doubt, sing it short and heavy.") This will insure that the swung eighths do not sound jazzy but equally weighted.
- Celebrate (initiate slightly under pitch, then quickly raise) the occasional important word or syllable that is sustained.

In the opening phrase, e.g., "I'm a-" and "lin'" should be accented, and "rol" should be initiated slightly under pitch and then quickly raised. This "celebrating" (my own term—think of it as the desirable equivalent of "scooping") of special notes is one hallmark of great gospel choirs and should be thought of less as a gradation of pitch than an embracing of word.

Taken together, these multiple influences—gospel, spiritual, blues, jazz, and pop—should meld together into a whole whose subtext is "striving." While the piece ends low, slow, and soft so soon after achieving high, fast, and loud—the text discouraged flashy endings—it does so with hope that our calls to our brothers and sisters will be answered until we move on to a decidedly friendlier world.

Form and Structure

Section	Measure	Event and Scoring
Introduction	1–4	Piano theme (4)
Chorus	5–15	Bass melody; piano theme bridge to chorus (7 + 4)
Chorus	16–22	Bass and tenor melody in unison (7)
Verse 1	23–33	Alto/tenor melody in unison; bass/piano theme bridge to chorus (7 + 4)
Chorus	34–40	Tenor melody with and basses in thirds (7)
Verse 2	41–49	Alto melody, tutti accompaniment; piano theme bridge to chorus (7 + 2)
Chorus	50–60	Soprano melody, tutti accompaniment; bass/tenor/piano theme bridge to shout 1 (7 + 4)
Shout 1	61–76	Shout 1: choir riffs on opening gesture of chorus and new triplet material (4 + 4 + 4 + 4)
Extended buildup	77–117	Based on chorus: bass/alto, then soprano joins, then tenor (borrowing tune from the spiritual "Roll, Jordan, Roll"), then tutti (8 + 8 + 8 + 8 + 8)

SECTION	MEASURE	EVENT AND SCORING
Shout 2	118–122	Choir riffs on triplet material in unison/octaves
Tag	123–126	

Text

I'm a-rollin' through an unfriendly world.
O brothers won't you help me to pray?
O sisters won't you help me to pray?
Won't you help me in the service of the Lord?
Roll, Jordan, roll.

Additional References and Resources

Curtis, Marvin V. "African-American Spirituals and the Gospel Music: Historical Similarities and Differences." *Choral Journal* 41 (March 2001), 9–21.

Johnson, James Weldon, and J. Rosamund Johnson. *The Books of American Negro Spirituals*. New York: Da Capo Press, Inc., 1969.

Southern, Eileen. *The Music of Black Americans*. 2nd ed. New York: W.W. Norton & Co., 1983.

Contributed by:

Paul Rardin

Teacher Resource Guide

What Shall We Do With the Drunken Sailor

arr. Alice Parker and Robert Shaw

TTBB
Warner Bros./Alfred Music Publishing Co.: LG 51053
Overall: 3
Vocal: 3
Tonal/Rhythm: 3

Composer

Born in Boston, Massachusetts, in 1925, Alice Parker began composing at age five and wrote her first orchestral piece in high school. Graduating from Smith College with a degree in performance and composition, she went on to complete her master of music at the Juilliard School. Here, she became the conducting student of Robert Shaw and Julius Herford and a composition student of Vincent Persichetti. Parker became involved with the early stages of the Robert Shaw chorale and for the next twenty years assisted Shaw on researching and arranging music for the group. Parker recounts that her editing sessions with Shaw want on for "twelve hours at a time, till the pads of my fingers hurt when I touched the keys." He would stand over her shoulder and make Xs over the unsatisfactory portions. However particular Shaw was, he is quoted as saying that "she possesses a rare and creative musical intelligence."

Shaw and Parker's combined skills of arranger and editor have left an enduring imprint on North American choral literature. Parker has been commissioned by numerous groups, from community choruses and church choruses to ensembles like Chanticleer, the Vancouver Chamber Singers, and the Atlanta Symphony. Currently Parker is conductor of Melodious Accord and continues to record, compose, and adjudicate and to inspire musicianship in her students.

Robert Shaw, born in Red Bluff, California, in 1916, became one of the United States' most successful conductors in both the choral and orchestral fields. Graduating from Pomona College in 1938, he then went on to be the first conductor to receive a Guggenheim Fellowship (1944). Shaw held teaching positions at the Juilliard School and the Berkshire Music Center from 1946–48. In 1948 he formed the Robert Shaw Chorale, which for the next twenty years would make many award-winning recordings and commission works from the likes of Béla Bartók, Darius Milhaud, Benjamin Britten, and Aaron Copland. In 1967 Shaw became the conductor of the Atlanta Symphony Orchestra and guided them from obscurity to an orchestra of great international status. After a rich life of teaching, conducting, and making music at the very highest level, Robert Shaw died January 25, 1999.

Composition and Historical Perspectives

This forcastle (pronounced "foc's'le") shanty was originally used on ships when taking a short trip. Parker/Shaw arrangement, with its quickly executed text and sharp rhythms, certainly captures the spirit of a brief dash out to sea. This English part-song is in a large theme-and-variations structure, in which all of the musical gestures stem from the opening tune. Ostinato patterns are relied upon heavily, especially in the bass; however, this enables the choir to quickly absorb the music. Imitation pervades throughout, evoking a scene of rowdy sailors. Parker and Shaw vary the texture expertly and rely on several forms of imitation juxtaposed with well balanced homophonic outcries. Besides the arrangement being dramatic, for didactic reasons, the men's section should develop excellent intonation due to the preponderance of fifths throughout the work. The work has survived because of the acute interplay between the music and the prosody of the text.

Technical Considerations and Musical Elements

Set for a four-part male chorus, the tessitura ranges from a low bass D to a tenor high A. The tonality is D Dorian and singable by many ensembles.

Shaw, in his own rehearsals, had a predilection for clean diction. The direction "articulated" is even included above the first staff of music. Specific rehearsal of mm. 17–18, 53–54, and 104–105 without pitch will help the choir articulate together. Glottal strokes should be applied to the accents in mm. 163–165 as well as having a slight "ng" active release on the last note (indicated with an accent).

If the choir is having trouble with the meters in mm. 160–165, allow for the accompanist to play while the choir chants numbers (ones and twos or ones, twos, and threes); follow this by adding pitch and finally using both text and pitch. M. 87 should not be overlooked for the same reason.

Metric modulations and tempo shifts occur in three places. Parker and Shaw indicate a ritard that sets the new tempo of m. 38 ("a little inebriated"). The conductor may engineer this ritard in various ways but might first try the following. Because the quarter note remains the same, the last quarter of m. 87 (marked with a ritard) will equal the downbeat of m. 88. Try subdividing the first three eighths of the 5/8 measure, followed by an upbeat in the new tempo of m. 88. Even a gentle hesitation on the top of the upbeat can make the last eighth note clear. It is possible to subdivide the last two eighths, but the result will be less obvious to both the choir and the conductor.

The tempo modulation at Tempo I (m. 104) will need to be frequently revisited. At m. 103, a stopped beat two followed by a small, sharp upbeat in the new tempo will clarify this somewhat difficult tempo change. If the conductor thinks "Heave him by the leg" in the new tempo, the delivery will be even more exact. The final metric modulation is simple (mm. 165–166). Here, the eighth note becomes the new quarter and then goes back to Tempo I in m. 170.

Stylistic Considerations

"Fast, hummy, articulated" are Parker and Shaw's instructions to the performer. Many choirs have creatively incorporated choreography to the work, which adds a "madrigalesque" flavor (e.g., m. 88 indicates the choir should be "a little inebriated"). Though the arrangement is hearty and jovial, the work's charm lies in producing specifically what Parker and Shaw mark in the score.

Instead of a North American pronunciation "early," strive for a more Treasure Islandesque "earlie." A British, colloquial flavor may add an extra liveliness to the performance.

Form and Structure

Section	Measure	Event and Scoring
Verse 1	1–8	***mf***; tenor 1 and 2 have text; bass 1 and 2 have accompaniment figures ("Drrm__")
Chorus 1	9–16	
Verse 2	17–24	***mp***; similar texture
Chorus 2	25–32	Tenors with bass divisi, ending on unison D
Verse 3	33–40	***mf***; imitative entrances
Chorus 3	41–48	***f***; four-part homophonic statement

Section	Measure	Event and Scoring
Bridge	49–52	***mp***; basses, "What shall we do . . ." begin ostinato that repeats through m. 68
Verse 4	53–68	***pp/mf***; canon with imitation from the tenor, alto, and soprano parts (61–68 = 53–60)
Chorus 4	69–87	***ff***; with three-measure extension; (8 + 8 + 3) metric modulation
Verse 1a	88–103	***pp***; slower tempo; bass divisi sings melody; tenors sing accompaniment
Verse 5	104–119	***f***; tempo I, similar to mm. 53–60
Chorus 5	120–127	Elided cadence; canon
Chorus (dev.)	128–142	***ff/f***; (8 + 7); chorus developed
Bridge	143–146	***mp***; elided cadence; basses, "What shall we do . . ." begin ostinato that repeats through m. 160
Chorus (frag.)	147–166	***pp/mp***; chorus fragmented (4 + 6)
Coda	166–173	***mp/pp***; (4 + 4) metric modulation/tempo I

Text

What shall we do with the drunken sailor . . .
Early in the morning?

Chorus
Way-hay, and up she rises . . .
Early in the morning.

Put him in the long boat until he's sober . . .
Early in the morning. (*repeat chorus*)

Pull out the plug and wet him all over, . . .
Early in the morning. (*repeat chorus*)

Put him in the scuppers with a hosepipe on him . . .
Early in the morning. (*repeat chorus*)

Heave him by the leg with a runnin' bowlin' . . .
Early in the morning. (*repeat chorus*)

Additional References and Resources

Mussulman, J. *Dear People . . . Robert Shaw: A Biography*. Bloomington, IN: Indiana Press, 1979.

Parker, Alice. *Choral Journal*, xxxvi/9 (1995–96), 15018 (Shaw issue).

Suggested Listening

Alice Parker/Robert Shaw, arrangers:

"What Shall We Do with the Drunken Sailor?" on *Let Your Voice Be Heard*, Cantus, CCTS 1201.

"What Shall We Do with the Drunken Sailor?" on *Folk Songs from Around the World*, Washington Men's Camerata, Thomas Beveridge, conductor, Gothic, G 49089.

"What Shall We Do with the Drunken Sailor?" on *Sea Shanties*, The Robert Shaw Chorale, Robert Shaw, conductor, RCA Victor, 44:49-1999.

Contributed by:

John Perkins

Level Four

Mixed voices:

Treble voices:

Men's voices:

Teacher Resource Guide

A Choral Flourish

Ralph Vaughan Williams

(1872–1958)

SATB divisi
Oxford University Press: 3535025
Overall: 4
Vocal: 4
Tonal/Rhythm: 4

Composer

Ralph Vaughan Williams was born in Gloucestershire, England. His family encouraged his early interest in music, and he first studied with us aunt who taught him piano. He attended preparatory school at Rottingdean, Sussex, while continuing studies in piano, organ, and violin, and eventually picking up viola. He loved the viola and longed for an orchestral career, which was discouraged by his family.

Vaughan Williams earned his MusB in 1894 and his bachelor of arts in history in 1895 from Trinity College, Cambridge and completed additional studies at the Royal Conservatory of Music. His post-bachelor's work at the Royal Conservatory of Music included study with composition teachers Parry, Wood, and Stanford. He studied with Bruch in 1897 in Berlin and with Ravel in 1908 in Paris.

Vaughan Williams was displeased with the current English compositional style and wanted to create something new. He also acknowledged the beauty of previous Elizabethan and Jacobean styles as well as the English folk song. He shared these musical interests with his friend Gustav Holst, whom he had met at the Royal Conservatory of Music in 1895. Throughout the rest of Holst's life, Vaughan Williams and Holst critiqued one another's work.

By 1910 Vaughan Williams was employed as a church organist as well as a writer, lecturer, music editor, and folksong collector. He published *On Wenlock Edge* and *Fantasia on a Theme by Thomas Tallis*, exemplifying his own compositional clarity. Throughout his lifetime, Vaughan Williams collected more than eight hundred folk songs, many in 1910. He had served as editor of *Welcome Songs* for the Purcell Society and selected tunes for *The English Hymnal* including melodies Vaughan Williams wrote himself and many folk songs.

Vaughan Williams also began serving as principal conductor with the Leith Hill Musical Festival in 1905. He had also completed two symphonies when he served in World War I with the Royal Army Medical Corps in France. He was then given the post of director of music for the First Army of the British Expeditionary Force, where he organized amateur musical opportunities among the troops.

In 1919 Vaughan Williams became a member of the teaching staff of the Royal Conservatory of Music and subsequently conducted the Bach Choir from 1920–28. Vaughan Williams encouraged his students at the Conservatory to find their own musical voices. Adrian Boult premiered the *Pastoral Symphony* and thereafter continued as a primary interpreter of Vaughan Williams's music. From this time period through the rest of his life, Vaughan Williams became increasingly in demand as a composer-conductor. From the 1930s through the 1950s, he received a number of honorary doctorates and musical prizes and also refused a number of awards that included obligations to a higher authority. His sixth symphony, often referred to as the "War Symphony," premiered in 1948 and was performed more than a hundred times in just over two years. The 1940s also brought opportunities for Vaughan Williams to write film scores.

The early 1950s brought significant changes in Vaughan Williams's life. He was now deaf, and his wife, Adeline, died in 1951 at the age of eighty after many years of serious illness. In 1953 he married a close family friend, Ursula Wood. In 1954 Vaughan Williams toured extensively in the United States, lecturing and conducting performances of his *London Symphony*. He also continued to live, work, and compose in and around London, where he completed his last two symphonies. Vaughan Williams died August 26, 1958.

Composition and Historical Perspective

"A Choral Flourish" was first performed November 3, 1956, for the twenty-first anniversary of the National Federation of Music Societies. The Royal Choral Society Bach Choir sang along with the St. Michael's Singers. The piece was conducted by Reginald Jacques.

New Grove describes the strength and significance of Vaughan William's music beautifully: "He cannot be adequately discussed in narrowly musical terms. His outlook was human and social. He never forgot that music was for people; he was interested in every situation, however humble, for which music was needed, and his feeling for genuinely popular traditions amounted to a reverence that was almost religious: the most obvious comparison is with Bartók and Kodály. . . . throughout a public life of more than sixty years, Vaughan Williams engaged in a wide range of musical activities, sometimes of a kind that many lesser composers would have considered beneath them; and at every stage in his development the extensive list of works shows different levels of composition, from the simplest occasional pieces to the most visionary personal expressions."

Technical Considerations and Musical Elements

"A Choral Flourish" is a glorious opener. It includes challenging melismatic and polyphonic sections. There are also times when voices split into further parts, creating up to six-part harmony. Tall, vibrant, in-tune Latin vowels are essential throughout, especially in the melismatic sections such as mm. 7–8 and 11–13. Clear, crisp consonants are also vital throughout, particularly on the polyphonic entrances in mm. 17–36.

"A Choral Flourish" is rarely performed or recorded. However, filled with beautifully challenging musical lines, it is well worth the time and attention to bring this piece to life in performance. Fortunately, the 1994 New York All-State Choir performance under the direction of James Jordan was recorded.

Stylistic Considerations

This celebratory occasional piece begins with a proclamatory incipit for two trumpets or organ and continues with *a cappella* choir throughout. Alternating polyphonic and melismatic settings of the psalm text celebrate Vaughan Williams's interest in the style and writings of Bach and the Baroque Era. The tonality within each melismatic figure, e.g., m. 4, should remain clear and vibrant with accurate Latin vowels and intonation. The text in the polyphonic or canonic sections, e.g., mm. 17–36, should exemplify clarity in both consonants and vowels with a particular emphasis on word stress. For example, in the soprano line m. 29 and 30, the "be" of "bene" should be stronger with the "ne" deemphasized and the "psa" of "psallite" should be stronger with the "llite" deemphasized.

Form and Structure

Measure	Event and Scoring
1–2	Two trumpets or organ incipit introduction
3–16	Homophonic and melismatic *fortissimo* proclamation "Exultate justi in Domino"

MEASURE	EVENT AND SCORING
17–36	Polyphonic and *marcato forte* "Rectos decet"
37–46	*Piano*, homophonic "Quia rectum est"
47–64	*Fortissimo* return of the opening text with canonic and melismatic elements
62–64	Dramatic allargando with a high-voiced chordal finish on "Domino"

Text and Translation

(from Psalm 32)

Exultate, Exultate, justi, Exultate,	Be joyful, be joyful, righteous ones, be joyful,
Exultate, justi, in Domino;	Be joyful, righteous ones, in God;
Rectos decet collandatio.	Praise is comely for the upright.
Confitemini Domino in cithara;	Praise God with harp.
Cantate ei canticum novum;	Sing to God a new song.
Bene psallite, bene psallite ei in vociferatione.	Sing good praises to him with courage.
Quia rectum est verbum Domini,	For the word of God is right,
Et omnia opera ejus in fede.	And all of his works are finished in truth.
Exultate, Exultate, Exultate, justi,	Be joyful, be joyful, be joyful, righteous ones,
Exultate, Exultate, Exultate,	Be joyful, be joyful, be joyful,
Exultate, justi, in Domino.	Be joyful, righteous ones, in God.

Additional References and Resources

Kennedy, Michael, ed. 2nd ed. *A Catalogue of the Works of Ralph Vaughan Williams*. New York: Oxford University Press, 1996.

Web site:
Grove Music Online: www.grovemusic.com

Suggested Listening

St. Louis Chamber Chorus, *Choral Masterpieces: Highlights from the 1993–1994 Season*, Philip Barnes, conductor, SLCC94.

Contributed by:

Elizabeth Swanson

Teacher Resource Guide

A Spotless Rose

Graeme Morton

(b. 1952)

SATB a cappella
Augsburg Fortress: 0-8006-7662-9
Overall: 4
Vocal: 4
Tonal/Rhythm: 5

Composer

Graeme Morton is one of Australia's most distinguished and versatile musicians, having received national and international recognition as a choral conductor, choral composer, music educator, organist, and church musician. He is director of choral activities at St. Peters Lutheran College in Brisbane, Australia, and currently conducts the Brisbane Chamber Choir, St. Peters Chorale, and the Lucian Singers (Christ Church Episcopal Church, St. Lucia). He is also Artistic Director of the National Youth Choir of Australia (NYCA) and was the founding conductor of The Australian Voices. In 1997 he was visiting professor at St. Olaf College, Minnesota, home of the renowned St. Olaf Choir.

His reputation as an advocate for Australian choral music is reflected in the numerous award-winning recordings and commissions he has elicited from Australian composers. In 2003 he received the Prime Minister's Medal for his contribution to music, and was also awarded a prestigious Churchill Fellowship. His own compositions are published with Augsburg Fortress (www.augsburgfortress.org), Kjos Music (www.kjos.com) and Morton Music (www.mortonmusic.com.au).

Composition and Historical Perspective

"A Spotless Rose" was written in early January 2002, just after Christmas and during the height of the Australian summer heat. That a piece with the text "amid the cold, cold winter and in dark midnight" could be conceived in a tropical climate is quite antithetical to the Northern hemisphere's Christmas experience. Dedicated to the composer's eldest daughter, Allison, and her husband, Grant, the music was a gift for the newly married couple, handed to them as they boarded the plane for the U.S., where they would be living for the next few years.

"A Spotless Rose" is closely modeled on the motet, owing to the *a cappella* setting, the sacred message of the text, and the vivid text-setting employed by the composer. Morton's music was inspired by the composition by the quintessential Herbert Howells (1892–1983) on the same text.

The American premiere was given in 2002, before the work was published by Westminster Schola Cantorum conducted by Heather J. Buchanan at Westminster Choir College of Rider University's annual Gifts of the Season: An Evening of Readings and Carols. It was also performed in the 2004 St. Olaf Christmas festival by the St. Olaf Cantorei, conducted by John Ferguson.

Technical Considerations and Musical Elements

In choosing the key of D-flat major rather than E-flat major, which was originally proposed, Graeme seeks to exploit the richer, darker palette of tone colors naturally created by the lower key center. The numerous metric shifts which occur almost every measure fit beautifully with the natural text declamation and are well suited to the vivid text-painting. For example, the eighth note groupings in twos and threes in the 9/8, 6/8, and 8/8 meters in mm. 3–6 eloquently portray the motion of the word "blowing." Similarly, the "singing" in mm. 24–27. The descending eighth note soprano line in 6/8 in m. 12 appropriately highlights the word "foreshowing" and draws attention to the intensity of the prophecy of the ancient seers.

Care must be taken with the choice of tempo: if it is too fast, the sense of ebb-and-flow motion and flexibility of the line in places likes mm. 3–6 and 24–27 is lost. Too slow and the music becomes unnecessarily labored and the musical line dies. The choice of tempo will be influenced by the size of the choir and the acoustic of the performance venue. The best tempos will give due consideration to the predominant musical elements in the phrase. Some examples are the shaping of the chordal movement in mm. 1–2 and 10–11 and the eighth note movement in mm. 3–6, 12–15, and 24–27.

The dynamics indicated in the score are all well chosen and reinforce the musical and textual elements. For example, the color of the opening ***p*** should be very pure and sweet, the ***mp*** at m. 10 should be rich with anticipation, the m. 23 ***mp*** should be warmer and more optimistic, the ***f*** in m. 45 should be expansive and full-bodied, and the final ***p*** should be stark and hollow in keeping with the "cold winter's night."

From a technical point of view, the sections with descending lines must take particular care not to flatten the pitch, e.g., sopranos in mm. 12, 35, 38, and 45. Repeated pitches must also be tuned and retuned within the context of every chord, and the chromatics must be attended to with care. Carefully balance each chord, particularly the inner voices and basses, which should not be overpowered by the soprano sound.

Breaths must be carefully placed and given specific rest values to avoid creating unnecessary "holes" in the *a cappella* choral sound. In m. 33 the basses must sustain the word "said" and elide with "is" in m. 34, while the remainder of the choir takes a quarter breath.

Stylistic Considerations

The relationship between the text declamation and the note groupings in each measure cannot be emphasized enough. Speaking the text and rhythm in heightened speech is an effective rehearsal technique for reinforcing this relationship. Shape the half notes with *messa di voce*, a subtle *crescendo* and *decrescendo* that will enhance the expressiveness of the music and keep the musical line alive on the sustained pitches.

The predominant diction requirement is to observe the rules of British English pronunciation. For example, take particular care with the word "Isaiah." It should be pronounced [*a*:I-*za*:Ia], quite unlike the American tendency to [*a*:I-ze:I-a]. Care should also be taken with the diphthong [*a*:I]. At no time should "r" be reflexive; all final "r" consonants should be crossed out to remind singers to avoid the reflexive "r" trap. When "r" is an initial consonant (e.g., "rose"), it should be flipped or lightly rolled. The "r" within a word is typically flipped (e.g., "purest," Mary," "through"). Ensure final "d" consonants are voiced with sufficient clarity (e.g., "cold," "maid"). Use the phonics of the words when possible to convey meaning, e.g. the crisp attack of the initial [k] of "cold"; the purity and color of the [i] vowel in "sweet." The word "p<u>u</u>rest" (mm. 39 and 40) requires enunciation of the diphthong [i:u]. At no time should the [a] vowel be overly dark (e.g., "dark," "a," "amid").

There will be slight tempo changes. Consider the flexibility of the eighth note movement and address the forward momentum and relaxation in conjunction with the text and harmonic motion. The *a tempo* on the last beat of m. 16 is important and sets up the forward motion needed through mm. 17–18. The tempos of the major cadential phrases, mm. 21–22 and 47–49, will be determined by a combination of the harmonic rhythm and articulation of the text at the prescribed dynamic level.

Form and Structure

"A Spotless Rose" comprises two main sections, mm. 1–22 and 23–49, following the two verse structure of the poem. Each section begins in D-flat major.

Section	Measure	Event and Scoring
Verse 1	1–22	
	1–9	Two phrases (4 + 5); D-flat major; sixteenth rest breath at end of m. 4
	10–16(beat 2)	One phrase; E-flat major; stagger breathing to sustain momentum over the seven measures of this phrase; *poco rallentando* m. 15, beat three, into "fruit"
	16(beat 3)–22	Two phrases (4 + 2); E-flat major cadencing in D-flat major; predominantly homophonic chordal movement; emphasize harmonic text relationship as you develop the tone/timbre of this section
Verse Two	26–49	
	23–33	Three phrases (4 + 2 + 5); D-flat major; sixteenth rest breaths after "singing" in mm 26, 28 (beat one) and "said" in m. 30
	34–41(beat 3)	Two phrases (4 + 4) with mm. 37 (beat three) to 39 (beat one) and mm. 39 (beat two) to 41 (beat three) two subphrases according to the text "In Mary purest Maid"
	41(beat 4)–46(beat 3)	Two phrases (2 + 3); Build the *crescendo* organically with the ascent of the soprano line to the climax in m. 45
	46(beat 4)–49	One phrase; cadences in E major

Text

Written by an anonymous sixteenth-century English author, this Christmas text eloquently conveys the mystery of the prophecy of the birth of the Christ child.

> A Spotless Rose is blowing,
> Sprung from a tender root
> Of ancient seer's foreshowing,
> Of Jesse promised fruit.
> Its fairest bud unfolds to light
> Amid the cold, cold winter,
> And in dark midnight.

The Rose which I am singing,
Whereof Isaiah said.
Is from its sweet root springing
In Mary purest Maid.
For through our God's great love and might,
The blessed Babe she bore us,
In a cold, cold winter's night.

Suggested Listening

"A Spotless Rose" appears on the CD *Time and Eternity* by the Brisbane Chamber Choir, directed by Graeme Morton, BCC-CD002, www.brisbanechamberchoir.org.

Contributed by:

Heather J. Buchanan

Teacher Resource Guide

Amor de Mi Alma

Z. Randall Stroope

(b. 1953)

SSATTBB with optional piano
Walton Music Corp.: 8501427
Overall: 4
Vocal: 4
Tonal/Rhythm: 4

Composer

Born in 1953 Z. Randall Stroope has distinguished himself as a composer, conductor, lecturer, clinician, and master teacher. A frequent all-state clinician, he has conducted annual national honor choirs at Lincoln Center and Carnegie Hall for several years and a choral festival each summer in Canterbury, England. His choirs have appeared at ACDA and MENC national conventions, and at a number of ACDA regional conventions and have taken several international tours, including trips to Australia, Japan, South Africa, Russia, and Eastern Europe.

Stroope holds a master's degree in voice performance from the University of Colorado (1977) and a doctorate in choral conducting from Arizona State University (1987). His principal composition teachers were Normand Lockwood and Cecil Effinger, both students of the legendary Nadia Boulanger.

Stroope has served as director of choral activities at the University of Nebraska at Omaha since 1987.

Composition and Historical Perspective

Published by Walton Music Corp. in 2001, "Amor de Mi Alma" ("Love of My Soul") was commissioned by the Meistersingers of Englewood, Colorado.

The poet Garcilaso de la Vega, whose text is used for this setting, is considered as one of the most important Castilian poets of all time. Born to an aristocratic family, his writings are a symbol of his somewhat tumultuous life, dealing with love and death, war and poetry. Garcilaso's date of birth is uncertain; some sources indicate it as early as 1498, others as late as 1503. Born in Toledo, Spain, Garcilaso died in Nice, France, in 1526.

Technical Considerations and Musical Elements

"Amor de Mi Alma" may be performed *a cappella* or with piano accompaniment "depending on the particular needs of the ensemble and the acoustic circumstances," as indicated in the printed score. The voicing is SSATTBB, with less weight on the tenor divisi. Balance may be an issue, especially because male voices are set mostly in the mid to low ranges. Vocal ranges are as follows:

Soprano = C4–A-flat5
Alto = A-flat3–E-flat5
Tenor = F3–G-flat4
Bass = F2–D-flat3

Extremes are only used occasionally, except for the low notes in the bass section.

With regard to texture, homophony prevails. In the larger scheme, the work could be considered as a melody with accompaniment. Counterpoint is minimal.

Stylistic Considerations

Z. Randall Stroope is a living composer, but Garcilaso de la Vega is an early Renaissance Spanish poet. There are some differences in diction between modern Spanish and Renaissance Spanish.

Recommendations:

- Always use dental (non-aspirated) "t" and dental "d" in Spanish.
- "R" must be flipped (not rolled) when located between vowels, e.g., "para quereros," "quiero," "muero," etc. It is suggested to flip the "r" also in the words where a single "r" antecedes or follows another consonant, e.g., "cortado," "escrito," "guardo."
- Vowels in Spanish do not use diphthongs: [i ε a o u].

Form and Structure

Poem and musical form are strictly related in Stroope's "Amor de Mi Alma." The three-stanza poem is organized into a clear three-part musical form (ABA´) with the following format:

Mm. 1–39: Stanza 1, Section A (thirty-nine measures)
Mm. 40–52: Stanza 2, Section B (thirteen measures)
Mm. 53–78: Stanza 3, Section A´ (twenty-six measures)

Despite several interpretive tempo changes indicated by the composer, the overall tempo (established at quarter note = ca. 60) dominates. Hence, observing the structural information provided above, one concludes that Stroope makes a conscious decision of using more compositional/performance time for the first stanza, less time for the third stanza (yet sharing thematic material), and the least time for the second stanza, with the contrasting B section.

Section A

A setting of the first stanza, Section A is mm. 1–39 (including the four-measure optional piano introduction). This section can be divided into two clear subsections, mm. 1–15 and mm. 16–39, based on textual and musical reasons. Stroope assigns a specific harmonic progression and melodic contour to each one of the three verses. Mm. 5–15 set the first two verses. Mm. 16–26 is a virtually verbatim repetition of mm. 5–15, the difference being the inclusion of a part for S on mm. 16–20. Mm. 27–39 are more complex: textually, Stroope uses mm. 27–30 to set verse 3, and mm. 30–39 to set the first words of verse 1 ("yo no nací") and the first words of the third verse of stanza 3 ("y por vos"); this works as a bridge to the B section (stanza 2) and at the same time as a textual and musical anticipation of the A´ section (stanza 3). Musically mm. 30–39 have a dual function: they provide a coda-like flavor and they prepare the arrival of the B section.

Section B

It could be argued that the entire piece is written in D-flat; however, Stroope chooses the enharmonic C-sharp (in the minor mode) for Section B. Section A concludes on a half cadence and Stroope uses an A-flat (men's sections) which later transforms into its enharmonic (G-sharp) as a transition. Men's voices maintain this dominant pedal throughout the entire Section B. The contrasting quality of this section is completed by the flowing women's voices using suggestive accidentals. In mm. 51–52 sopranos take over the G-sharp pedal (transforming back into its enharmonic A-flat), thus liberating the men's voices to start the A´ section.

SECTION A´

The last section of the piece runs from mm. 53–74 and includes a four-measure coda. Stroope brings back the music he used for Section A, which is now applied to the third stanza of the text. Mm. 67–71 are a variation of mm. 32–34. In the same way that the composer uses the first words of the last verse of the third stanza ("y por vos") to close Section A, Stroope uses the third verse of the first stanza ("por hábito del alma misma os quiero") for mm. 62–67, finishing the work with a well-coordinated text-music relationship between the opening and the closing sections.

Text and Translation

Yo no nací sino para quereros; I not was born expect for/to love you	I was born only to love you;
Mi alma os ha cortado a su medida; My soul (to) you has cut to its measure (size)	My soul has formed you to its measure;
Por hábito del alma misma os quiero. For garment/gown of the soul itself (to) you (I) want	I want you as a garment for my soul.
Escrito está en mi alma vuestro gesto; Written is on my soul your gesture (face or image)	Your very image is written on my soul;
Yo lo leo tan solo que aún de vos I it read so much alone that even of you	I admire it so often along that
Me guardo en esto. Me I keep in this	Such indescribable intimacy I hide even from you.
Quanto tengo confiesso yo deveros; Whatever I have confess I owe to you	All that I have, I confess I owe to you;
Por vos nací, por vos tengo la vida. For you I was born for you I have the life	Because of (for) you I was born, because of (for) you I live,

Y por vos é de morir y por vos muero.
And for you I will have of (to) die and for you I die — And because of (for) you I will have to (must) die and because of (for) you I die.

Notes:

- In contrast to English, Spanish allows for double negations. The first line of stanza 1 is literally translated as "I was not born except to love you," which would not make sense in English. "I was born only to love you" implies that the sole mission of the writer's life was to love the one and only love of his or her life.
- Spanish speakers use querer, literally "to want," to mean "to love" (amar). The context is what determines the correct meaning. For example, "Quiero estar contigo porque te quiero" is translated as "I want to be with you because I love you." In this poem, Garcilaso uses quereros (stanza 1, verse 1) with the clear meaning "love" and quiero (stanza 1, verse 3) with the clear meaning "want."
-

Early Spanish	Modern Spanish
quanto	*cuanto*
confiesso	*confieso*
deveros	*deberos*
é	*he*

Stroope takes this text from Garcilaso de la Vega's "Soneto V."
The complete text follows:

Escrito'stá en mi alma vuestro gesto
Y cuanto yo escribir de vos deseo:
Vos sola lo escribistes; yo lo leo
Tan solo que aun de vos me guardo en esto.

En esto estoy y estaré siempre puesto,
Que aunque no cabe en mí cuanto en vos veo,
De tanto bien lo que no entiendo creo,
Tomando ya la fe por presupuesto.
Yo no nací sino para quereros;

Mi alma os ha cortado a su medida;
Por hábito del alma misma os quiero;
Cuanto tengo confieso yo deberos;
Por vos nací, por vos tengo la vida,
Por vos he de morir, y por vos muero.

A *soneto* (sonnet) is a poetic composition of Italian origins. In the Romance languages, *sonetos* have a clear structure, following a specific meter and rhyme: fourteen verses, all eleven syllables, grouped in two quartets and two tercets. The rhyme for the quartets is always *abba abba* with the tercets either *cdc cdc* (like in this case), *cdc dcd*, or *cde cde*. Regularity and symmetry are indeed hallmarks of the Spanish sonnet. As it can be seen, Garcilaso's "Soneto V" perfectly fits this description.

Stroope chooses not to observe the poetic form for his musical setting. He makes a selection of verses, ending up with three tercets, and changes their order.

Additional References and Resources

McGee, Timothy, ed. *Singing Early Music: the Pronunciation of European Languages in the Late Middle Ages and Renaissance*. Bloomington, IN: Indiana University Press, 1996.

Contributed by:

Eduardo Garcia-Novelli

Teacher Resource Guide

An Elizabethan Spring

Stephen Chatman

(b. 1950)

SATB
Waterloo Music: 101312
Overall: 4
Vocal: 4
Tonal/Rhythm: 4

Composer

Stephen Chatman was born in Faribault, Minnesota, on February 28, 1950. He studied at Oberlin College with Hugh Wood and Walter Aschaffenburg (where he earned his bachelor of music in 1972) and completed studies with Leslie Bassett, William Bolcom, Ross Lee Finney, and Eugene Kurtz at the University of Michigan (where he earned his DMA in 1977). Chatman earned a Fulbright scholarship (1974), three BMI Student Composer Awards, and the Charles Ives Award from the American Academy and Institute of Arts and Letters. The NEA, the Canada Council, the U.S. National Endowment for the Arts, the CBC, and the Ontario Arts Council have all commissioned works from Chatman.

The University of British Columbia named Chatman their first compose-in-residence, where he remains the Composition Division's professor and head. Chatman's output before 1982 is often atonal and complex; however, he later changed his style to encompass all forms of twentieth-century compositional techniques. "It's easy to enjoy all types of music—I don't want to be pigeonholed. A composer must be true to himself" (Stephen Chatman brochure, PROCAN, Toronto, May 1989). After 1982, Chatman's works became broader, more easily accessible, and spiritual.

Sixty choral works have been published, including numerous orchestral works, such as *Crimson Dream* (1983), *Tara's Dream* (1999) and *Proud Music of the Storm* (2001–02). National to international in style elementary to virtuosic, Chatman's music encompasses piano, choral, and orchestral genres.

Composition and Historical Perspective

The University of British Columbia Singers under James Fankhauser premiered *An Elizabethan Spring* in November 1983. Waterloo Music published the set in Waterloo, Ontario, in 1985.

An Elizabeth Spring may be classified as a set of secular part songs with a madrigal-esque flavor. The text chosen for "Spring, the Sweet Spring," is merely an excerpt from Thomas Nashe's first stanza.

Technical Considerations and Musical Elements

"Spring, the Sweet Spring" employs both lively and repeated motoric elements. The first two sections introduce successive motives, building to a four-part texture. Chatman employs inversion and retrograde inversion (compare m. 1, beat two through m. 2, beat one with the tenor part in m. 3). The choir will gain familiarity with the texture after careful rehearsal of all voices on each motive. Discussion of the formal construction of motives, combined with vocalization on each motive, will strengthen the choir's aural acuity. This will, in turn, increase the rate at which the piece is learned.

Chatman also asks for a quasi-***fp*** by accenting each word followed by an immediate *decrescendo*. The choir will feel more freedom in the voice while providing a spirit of dance to the movement.

Tonally, the work is not too difficult to grasp, especially since the transitions (mm. 9 and 16) move either by half or whole step into new tonal areas. (The harmonies are quartal in a range no higher than a fifth for every given motive.) However, independence from the piano should begin soon after the choir has absorbed the material.

The final note is in a high tessitura for all parts but especially for the sopranos. Depending on their level of vocal expertise, the vowel in the word "ring" should be modified, or opened, to a more spacious "ih" (or IPA [I]) placement.

The second work "There Is a Garden in Her Face" marvelously contrasts "Spring, the Sweet Spring" with sumptuous phrases in a modal and harmonic context. Scored for optional three-part divisi, the baritone section splits in half and partially joins the tenors in the second half of m. 21. Chatman's revoicing supports the low tenor melody with a warm timbre.

Similar to the poetic structure, the piece is divided into three sections. The second stanza, starting before m. 12 (if performed SATB) reflects the "double row" stated in the text. Chatman beautifully yet simply paints a picture of two lovers walking in two-part harmony at the sixth (soprano and tenor). The alto and bass lines sustain another row at the octave. Pure elegance of text married with music exists in these ten measures.

It is interesting to note that the three endings of each verse are deceptively similar. The penultimate measure in verse one (m. 10) shares the same material as the penultimate measure in verse two (m. 25). However, the final measures of verses two and three (m. 21 and m. 26) both share the G major sonority. The choir should absolutely be asked to mark these aspects in their scores. An understanding of G major versus E-flat major is not important; the choir will begin to associate similarities and differences and will treat the known or unknown markings as reactive symbols.

"The Urchins' Dance" incorporates mixed meter (4/4 + 6/8), fast and articulated text, and a wider range of dynamic contrast. Similar to "Spring, the Sweet Spring," the work contains motoric qualities and repeated sections. These aspects provide continuity during the choir's initial reading of the work. For clarity, the conductor should vary the size of the gesture between the groups of ones and twos and ones, twos, and threes (quarters to dotted quarters). When conducting, avoid a tight, constricted gesture, which adds strain to the sound. A larger gesture for the dotted quarters will allow the choir freedom to sing.

Challenges arise when rehearsing the varying lengths of *crescendos* and their diacritic contrasts (e.g., mm. 35–42). Rehearsal of the longer *crescendos* (mm. 19–25) on a neutral syllable, before adding text, will instill the musical feeling.

The piece has a higher range than the previous two, especially for sopranos (A-flat5) and tenors (G4). Warm-ups incorporating pentatonic chord clusters will help with intonation problems. Finally, a typo should be noted; p. 10, m. 15, should be marked m. 13.

Stylistic Considerations

British diction should be applied to these English texts. Depending on the choir's skill level, the decision whether to use British diction should be made early in the rehearsal process.

"There Is a Garden in Her Face" gives an elegant repose from the outer movements, but it may also be taken out of context and used as separate programming material. Many conductors also open or close their concerts with "The Urchins' Dance." The set may be a fine choice when programming a concert of English madrigals, especially because there are so few twentieth-century English madrigal settings available.

Form and Structure

MEASURE	EVENT AND SCORING
I. "Spring, the Sweet Spring"	
1–8	
9–15	
16–20	
II. "There Is a Garden in Her Face"	
1–11	Four phrases (3 + 3 + 2 + 4)
12–21	Four phrases (2 + 3 + 2 + 3)
22–26	Two phrases (2 + 3)
III. "The Urchins' Dance"	
1–8	Two phrases (4 + 4)
9–17	Two phrases (7 + 2)
18–34	Four phrases (4 + 4 + 6 + 3)
35–46	Four phrases (2 + 4 + 4 + 2)
47–48	
49–56	Two phrases (4 + 4)

Text

I. "Spring, the Sweet Spring"
Spring, the sweet Spring,
Is the year's pleasant king;
Then blooms each thing,
Then maids dance in a ring.
—Thomas Nashe (1567–1601)

II. "There Is a Garden in Her Face"
There is a garden in her face
Where roses and white lilies grow;
A heav'nly paradise is that place,
Where-in all pleasant fruits do flow.

Those cherries fairly do enclose
Of orient pearl . . .
—Thomas Campion (1567–1620)

III. "The Urchins' Dance"
By the moon we sport and play,
With the night begins our day:
As we dance the dew doth fall;
Trip it, little urchins all.

Lightly as a little bee,
Two by two, and three by three,
Lightly as a little bee,
Two by two, and three by three,
Trip it, and about go we.
—Anonymous (ca. 1600)

Additional References and Resources

Campion, Thomas. *Campion's Works*. Edited by Vivian Percival. Oxford: Clarendon Press, 1909, 178.
MacMillan, R. "Canadian Distinctiveness Influencing Chatman Works." *Music Scene*, no. 313, 1980.
Web site:
Stephen Chatman: www.drstephenchatman.com/index.html

Suggested Listening

Stephen Chatman:
"Elizabethan Spring" on *Due North—Stephen Chatman Choral Works*, Vancouver Chamber Choir, Jon Washburn, conductor, Centrediscs, CMC 3388.
"Elizabethan Spring" on *In Concert*, Mount Royal Youth Choir, David Ferguson, conductor, Mount Royal College, MRYC-CD-001.

Contributed by:

John Perkins

Teacher Resource Guide

Cantemus!

Lajos Bárdos

(1899–1986)

SSATTB a cappella
Editio Musica Budapest: Z.8539
Overall: 4
Vocal: 3
Tonal/Rhythm: 5

Composer

Lajos Bárdos was born in Budapest, Hungary, in 1899. He was a Hungarian composer, musicologist, and conductor who, together with Zoltán Kodály, laid the foundations of 20th-century Hungarian choral music-making. Bárdos studied the violin and the viola as a boy. After a year (1918–19) at the technical university, he entered the Budapest Academy of Music, where he studied composition with Albert Siklós and then Kodály during the years 1921–25.

In 1925 he served as choral conductor and music teacher in a secondary school and a teacher training college. From 1928 to 1967 he was a professor at the Franz Liszt Academy of Music, where he reformed the curriculum to enhance the training of choral conductors, the teaching of church music history, and instruction in music theory. In 1931 he cofounded the publishing company Magyar Kórus and served as editor of the music periodical of that name. From 1934 he organized the Enekio Ifúsag (Singing Youth) movement for the music education of children and youth.

Through his work as a conductor Bárdos raised the standards of Hungarian choral singing to an international level within a few decades. He directed the

Cecilia (1926–41), the Palestrina Kórus (1929–33), the Budapesti Kórus (1941–7) and the choir of St. Mátyás, Budapest (1942–62). Bárdos was instrumental in encouraging the development of choral activity in remote areas of the country. His concert programming was pioneering in that he included choral music from before Palestrina, especially that of Josquin Desprez. He also actively promoted new music in Hungary such as Stravinsky's *Symphony of Psalms*. He won considerable acclaim during his tours abroad because of his vitality and interpretative powers. Bárdos directed his composition toward cultivating Hungarian choral life and used techniques like Renaissance polyphony and employed characteristics of Hungarian folk music. He continued in the tradition of Bartók and his teacher Kodály. His works are models of choral writing, and they deal sensitively with Hungarian prosody.

In the 1950s Bárdos began to develop his work and cultivate his reputation as a musicologist. He applied his gift for systematization to major studies of Gregorian melody, and modal and Romantic harmony and to the analysis of works by Liszt, Bartók, and Kodály. Due to his continuation and development of the work begun by Bartók and Kodály, he received the Erkel Prize (1953), the Kossuth Prize (1955), and the Bartók-Pásztory Prize (1984). He was awarded the titles Merited, and Eminent Artist of the Hungarian People's Republic in 1954 and 1970, respectively. He also received the Order of the Banner with Laurels in 1984 and the doctorate of musicology in 1985. Lajos Bárdos died in Budapest November 18, 1986.

Composition and Historical Perspective

"Cantemus!" is an excellent setting of a text by Bárdos himself. The best way to categorize this piece is as a choral song or possibly as a part-song. According to Nick Strimple's *Choral Music in the Twentieth Century*, Bárdos's programming as a conductor spanned from the Renaissance to the contemporary, and he used various techniques from most of these epochs. This piece draws specifically on techniques used by Kodály in pieces like "Jesus and the Traders," and it uses similar pantonality to Bartók's folksong arrangements.

Bárdos was primarily a choral composer, but he wrote some dramatic works and a few instrumental pieces. The bulk of his output for unaccompanied mixed choirs, but he also wrote a large number of pieces for children's voices. He was a moderately prolific composer early in his career, and he composed "Cantemus!" in 1977, after which his compositional output was sparse. The composer also published an arrangement of this work for three part women's chorus.

Technical Considerations and Musical Elements

This piece does not have a distinct tonal center but is pantonal, and it flows freely between several ecclesiastical modes. The harmonic language is mostly tertian, but it also uses added-tone chords, cluster chords, and extended tertian chords in inversion. Because the composer used a harmonic vocabulary that can sometimes be interpreted several different ways, the pitch center is at best ambiguous. The individual voice parts are not difficult, but they do incorporate challenging intervals that may require some time to get used to. The unusual harmonies, irregular resolutions, and sometimes challenging voice leading make the piece seem daunting to a choir of moderate skill; however, that is not the case after a period of well-planned, well-paced, and deliberate rehearsal. Expect a period of adjustment, and do not give up on this piece too early.

Stylistic Considerations

The composer uses an element of British notation to dictate precisely where the release of sound should be. Some phrase endings feature quarter notes tied to eighth notes, and the composer meant for the singers to place the final consonant on the eighth note or, in other words, on the beat.

Considering the frequent unison singing and unusual dissonances, the best way to approach tone in this piece is to minimize vibrato as much as possible without damaging the voice. Eastern European choirs use a much straighter choral tone, and this is probably what Bárdos had in mind when he composed the piece.

Form and Structure

The piece is divided into two larger contrasting sections that are further divided into smaller periods. The first half consists of three periods, and there are four periods in the second half. Bárdos uses an additive construction in the first half of the piece by scoring only one-third of the voices on the first statement, two-thirds of the voices for the second, and tutti choir for the third. He does not specify a difference in dynamic between the three parallel statements; therefore, he creates an effect that does not change the dynamic as much as it increases the intensity of the sound. He also uses the harmonic language to increase the intensity by raising the pitch of the last chord of each statement and increasing the dissonance as well.

The second half of the piece features four contrasting periods. The first period is harmonically and dynamically static, whereas the second period is shorter but moves further rhythmically and harmonically. In the third period, the composer increases the tension by setting off the melodic bass part against dissonant block chords in the upper parts and by intensifying the rhythmic content. The last period begins with points of imitation that also serve to heighten the tension by leaping higher with each entrance. Since the composer builds up the tension by way of rhythm, harmony, counterpoint, and dynamics, the next logical step is to bring the piece to a roaring climax by setting all the voices homophonically using the upper part of the tessitura. Bárdos avoids traditional harmonic cadential patterns and achieves the final cadence in a linear manner to end on octave D-flats.

Section	Measure	Event and Scoring
A		
	1–7	Three phrases (2 + 2 + 2)
	8–14	Three phrases (2 + 2 + 2)
	15–21	Three phrases (2 + 2 + 3)
B		
	22–28	Three phrases (2 + 2 + 2)
	29–31	Two phrases (1 + 2)
	32–40	Two phrases (4 + 5)
	41–51	Three phrases (4 + 2 + 5)

Text and Translation

Cantemus, quia cantare bonum est	Let us sing, because singing is fine
Cantemus, quia cantare iucundum est	Let us sing, because singing gives delight
Cantemus, quia cantare amantis est	Let us sing, because singing is lovely
Ergo: Cantemus!	Therefore: sing!

Contributed by:

G. Mikael Lindström

Teacher Resource Guide

Daemon irrepit callidus

György Orbán

(b. 1947)

SATB or TTBB a cappella
SATB, Hinshaw Music: HMC1537;
TTBB, Hinshaw Music: HMC1829
Overall: 4
Vocal: 3
Tonal/Rhythm: 4

Composer

György Orbán was born in 1947 in north-central Romania. From 1968 to 1973 he studied music composition and theory at the prestigious Academy of Music in the historic city of Cluj-Napoca. Following the completion of his studies and a subsequent teaching assignment at the same music academy, he moved to Hungary, Romania's neighbor to the west. Settling in Budapest, Orbán served as editor of Editio Musica Budapest from 1979 to 1990. In 1982 he began teaching theory and composition at the Franz Liszt Academy of Music in Budapest.

To date, Orbán's colorful output as a composer encompasses a variety of genres, from large symphonic works to art song. As a composer of choral music, he exhibits a predilection for sacred texts, although many of his works traverse the border between liturgical orientation and a more dramatic, almost theatrical, essence. His choral works include motets, psalm settings, oratorios, nine Masses, a Passion setting, two *Stabat Maters*, and other works.

Composition and Historical Perspective

"Daemon irrepit callidus," composed ca. 1995, is a short, unaccompanied piece for SATB choir. The work is approximately two and a half minutes long. Although the text, an example of medieval poetry in the Goliardic tradition, is concerned with the idea of worldly temptations pitted against the purity of Christian faith, Orbán's setting of the hymn can hardly be viewed as a sacred work. This is largely due to Orbán's engaging, frenzied musical portrayal of the demonic character.

Technical Considerations and Musical Elements

Orbán assigns a tempo indication of *allegro*. Metrically, the piece shifts between 4/4, 3/2, and 3/4 with the quarter note remaining constant. From the outset, a relentless pulsating eighth-note pattern with syllabic text underlay drives the piece forward. This, along with a nearly ceaselessly undulating half step motive, also assigned to an eighth note pattern, gives the work an eerie quality befitting the text.

Although "Daemon irrepit callidus" incorporates many techniques associated with contemporary music, e.g., shifting meters, chromaticism, and complicated rhythms, it is not a terribly difficult piece. The work often appears on high school all-state choir programs across the U.S.

One of the most demanding aspects of "Daemon irrepit callidus" is the textual underlay. The poem is typical of the medieval verse penned by the Goliardic poets in that a strong emphasis is placed on the metric flow of the Latin language. (Other examples of this trend may be seen in the thirteenth-century sequence "Dies irae" as well as in the poetry of *Carmina burana.*) Orbán complements this type of verse by using a predominantly syllabic text underlay with a syllable of text occurring on each eighth note, resulting in the nearly ceaseless pulsations that drive the work forward. The changing meter also serves to accommodate the metric accents of the poetry. During rehearsals, a conductor would be wise to slow the tempo and ask the choir to repeatedly speak the text in rhythm before any notes are learned.

There are rhythmic complexities in the work. For example, in verse three Orbán uses hocket technique in the upper three parts for the text "Adde mundorum milia" from mm. 31–43. Clapping the rhythms, followed by speaking the text in rhythm, will assist in learning this particular section. Orbán indicates that this section is not to be performed staccato but cantabile, which may take a fair amount of rehearsal time and energy to accomplish. Also regarding rhythm, care should be taken in mm. 11–14 to accurately distinguish between the triple and duple rhythmic figures. The *secco* indication during this section should apply to the diction as well as to the vocal quality. Short, crisp (but not hyperpronounced) consonants will help keep the rhythms clean and accurate.

The second-most challenging aspect of "Daemon irrepit callidus" is the intonation required to sustain the harmonic integrity of the work. Using a so-called gypsy scale built on G as its foundation (G–A–B-flat–C-sharp–D–E-flat–F-sharp), "Daemon" is not an atonal work. Orbán does, however, employ a fair number of chromatics to fully exploit the motivic material represented by the alternating major third and minor third vertical harmonies as well as the primary melodic motive of an undulating, ostinato-like minor second. Singing warm-up exercises that use the gypsy scale will help a choir grow accustomed to the seemingly unorthodox placement of whole steps and half steps as well as to the colorful augmented second that occurs between notes three and four in the scale. Choral exercises using the full chromatic scale will also be helpful, as segments of this scale are used in verse three of the work, including the exciting final two measures.

In mm. 15 and 27, Orbán shifts the meter from 4/4 to 3/2 and indicates a grouping of (3 x 2/4). This marking calls for the use of a macro-gesture in three, subdivided into units of two. Use of this macro-gesture will assist the tenors with the phrasing of their melody in mm. 17–20. It will also accommodate the shift from 3/2 to 3/4 in m. 31 by setting up the three pattern well before the meter shift takes place.

Form and Structure

"Daemon irrepit callidus" can be divided into three main sections, each coinciding with a verse from the poem.

SECTION	MEASURE	EVENT AND SCORING
Verse 1	1–15	(4 + 4) + (2 + 4) + 1; tune A in soprano, bass (mm. 3–4, 7–8); meter shift from 4/4 to 3/2 m. 15; (quarter note remains constant throughout work)
Verse 2	16–30	1 + (3 + 3) + 4 + (1 + 2 + 1); tune B in tenor (mm. 17–20); tune A in bass (mm. 25–26); meter shift from 3/2 to 3/4 in m. 21; from 3/4 to 4/4 m. 24; from 4/4 to 3/2 m. 27; from 3/2 to 4/4 m. 28; from 4/4 to 3/2 m. 30
Verse 3	31–48	(3 + 3) + (3 + 3) + (2 + 2) + 2 ; tune B in bass (mm. 31–36); tune A in soprano, bass (mm. 43–44); meter shift from 3/2 to 3/4 m. 31; from 3/4 to 4/4 m. 42

Text and Translation

For the text of "Daemon irrepit callidus," Orbán uses three of eight verses of a medieval hymn found in *Amor sanctus*, a collection of ancient Christian poetry first published in 1933. The hymn also appeared in a popular seventeenth-century Hungarian collection of religious songs known as the *Cantionale Catholicum.*

Daemon irrepit callidus,	The Devil expertly sneaks
Allicit cor honoribus,	Tempting the honorable heart,
Ponit fraudes inter laudes,	He places fraud amid praise,
Cantus, saltus,	Song, dance,
Quidquid amabile Daemon dat,	However friendly the Demon is,
Cor Jesu minus aestimat. . . .	It is always less than the heart of Jesus. . . .

Additional References and Resources

Gosta, Predrag, and John B. Haberlen. "The Hungarian School of Choral Composers, 1950–2000." *Choral Journal* 41 (August 2000), 29–35.

Varga, Bálint András. *Contemporary Hungarian Composers.* 5th ed. Budapest: Editio Musica Budapest, 1989.

Suggested Listening

György Orbán, "Daemon irrepit callidus" on *Forgotten Masters and Masterpieces*, Kantorei Chamber Choir, Alex Theimer, Kantorei Recordings CD.

Contributed by:

Wayne Glass

Teacher Resource Guide

Die mit Tränen säen, SWV 378
From Geistliche Chormusik, 1648

Heinrich Schütz
(1585–1672)

SSATB with optional accompaniment
GIA Publications: G-7039
Overall: 4
Vocal: 4
Tonal/Rhythm: 4

Composer

Heinrich Schütz was, arguably, the greatest German composer of the seventeenth century and he was also the first German composer to attain international stature. Schütz's father provided his children with a thorough religious and liberal education. He presumably received musical instruction from the local Kantor, Georg Weber, as well as from the organist Heinrich Colander who taught him to sing well at an early age.

In 1598 Landgraf Moritz von Hessen-Kassel stayed at one of the inns owned by Schütz's father. The Landgraf was an amateur composer, and he was impressed with Schütz's voice; thus, he asked permission to take the boy with him and teach him music at his court. Schütz's father, Christoph, resisted until 1599 when he brought his son to the court of the Landgraf.

Schütz excelled in all subjects. After his voice changed he was offered the opportunity to study with Giovanni Gabrieli. The teacher to student relationship was close, and Schütz never acknowledged anyone else as his teacher. He returned to the Landgraf Moritz's court in 1613 and was nearly convinced by his family to leave music in favor of a more secure profession. However, in

1614 the Elector Johann Georg I of Saxony made moves to acquire Schütz as his Kapellmeister. After some travel back and forth between the two courts, Schütz finally left for Dresden in 1615, where he would remain until his death.

Schütz was prolific in his output of primarily sacred music at the Electoral Court. He traveled to Denmark quite often to serve the royal court in Copenhagen, and in 1634 he received the title of Kapellmeister to King Christian IV of Denmark. Schütz wanted to retire in 1645 and spend most of his time away from the court in Dresden; however, the Elector only gave him permission to spend some time away, not to retire. Retirement became a reality when the Elector died in 1657 and the heir combined his own chapel with that of his father.

Schütz was still connected to the court but spent most of his time writing music and working on the Becker Psalter. He spent his last years in an apartment near the court where he, in a weakened physical condition, prepared for his death. For more than two hundred and fifty years after his death, he influenced the traditions of high craftsmanship and intellectual depth that marked the best of German music and musical through the example of his compositions and his teaching.

Composition and Historical Perspective

In his motets Schütz distinguishes between the traditional *stile antico*, or Palestrina-type sound without basso continuo, and the modern concerted motet with continuo. Among those collections that adhere most closely to the first type are the *Cantiones sacrae* (1625) for four voices and the *Geistliche Chormusic* (1648) for five to seven voices. Both collections were conceived mainly for *a cappella* performance, but because of pressure from his publishers Schütz added a figured bass part that acts almost always as a basso seguente. A basso seguente part is a separate keyboard part that is based on the lowest sounding note at all times.

The *Geistliche Chormusic* was dedicated to the Leipzig city council and the choir of the Thomaskirche. The preface states the didactic nature of these compositions. They could serve as model compositions, many of them (e.g., SWV 373 and SWV 381) alternating contrapuntal duple sections with effective declamatory sections in triple time or pitting duet and trio textures against each other in a quasi-concerted manner and contrasting them with tutti textures (SWV 378). Phrases with drawn-out rhythms alternate with busy syllabic writing or dance-like triple sections. Here, Schütz achieved a compelling cross-fertilization between musical techniques and text interpretation.

Schütz's main interest as a composer was in the word, its individual meaning and mimetic depiction through music. He never shied away from madrigalisms but also developed an exceptional sensitivity in expressing conceptual meaning in a broader context. He used a variety of musical means—rhythmic, melodic, harmonic, textural and structural—to manipulate a text and create specific musical effects to enhance its message, and his greatness stems partly from the integration of many of these stylistic traits.

Technical Considerations

The vocal parts of "Die mit Tränen säen" are not difficult as long as the singers are aware of the meter changes. The key signature indicates E Dorian; however, Schütz uses chromatic alterations to change of tonal center, which usually involves entire phrases or groups of phrases. All structurally important cadences pause on E major, which is a remnant of *stile antico* practice.

When considering the issue of performance tempo, bear in mind that the note values are generally longer in the first major section. The tempo should be stable from the beginning to the end of the composition. The first section contains mensuration changes, or meter changes, from *tempus imperfectum diminutum* (cut time) to *sesquialtera* (3/2) and back. These changes are daunting to someone who is not used to dealing with modern performance editions of early music. There are multiple ways to approach this change, as evidenced buy the plethora of available recordings of this piece. According to *Neue Ausgabe sämtlicher Werke*, the complete scholarly edition of Heinrich Schütz, the whole note in 2/2 should equal the dotted whole note in 3/2. However, many modern recordings (like the Herreweghe listed below) and the edition consulted for this guide relate the half note of the cut time to the dotted whole note of the 3/2. This results in a quicker tempo in the triple sections, which are meant to reflect joy.

Stylistic Considerations

Success in *stile antico* music performance depends on the "strong-weak" principle; that is, if there is a pair of a rhythmical value—phrase, measure, beat, division, or subdivision—the first entity of the pair should receive a greater emphasis than the second.

Measure lines are in the score only to aid the modern performer. It is difficult to ignore them; however, it is imperative to ignore the beat structure of the modern measure. The first beat of the measure is not necessarily a strong beat—the text governs the stress structure of the phrase. The points of imitation should be performed with identical emphasis. The performers of this time did not have scores; they had part books. Because they only saw their own parts they articulated them as they would a solo while listening to the other parts for balance and tuning.

Performers should minimize vibrato in order to make tuning easier. Singers should not have to sing completely void of vibrato, but vibratos may have to be matched closely among the singers to facilitate tuning.

Tuning can be a sensitive topic among choral musicians, but it is impossible to avoid it when dealing with early music. The individual voice parts could possibly be rehearsed separately in sectionals with an equal-tempered piano; however, rehearsals involving all parts together should be conducted without piano accompaniment. A harpsichord or a continuo organ tuned in quarter-meantone temperament may be used if readily available. The singers should adhere as closely as possible to just intonation, or tuning according to the overtone series.

Melismas, or runs of eighth notes, should receive clear articulations without compromising the tempo. Diaphragmatic articulations can be strenuous and could slow the tempo; therefore, aspirated consonants could prove effective as an alternative method of articulation. Original Baroque treatises on singing suggest this kind of articulation as accurate performance practice. However, young singers could damage their voices by adding tension when using this articulation.

The composers of this time period and of this style of music handle dissonances in a very controlled manner. The dissonances have to be prepared as consonances, remain stationary when other voices move to create dissonance, and finally it has to resolve properly according to the strict rules of counterpoint. The dissonances should not receive excessive emphasis, but they should be treated as organic parts of the phrases. Dissonances are harmonic occurrences that result from the movements of the individual parts, which do not include any melodic dissonances.

Form and Structure

As mentioned before, this motet consists of two larger sections that equally divide the text. The first section uses longer note values and emulates the aesthetic of *stile antico*. Each of the larger sections is divided into shorter periods of stratified affects. The first statement, exhibiting the doleful affect of the first line of text, commences as points of imitation; however, the imitation is abandoned almost immediately.

The mensuration change in m. 12 brings the affect of joy found in the second line of text in one single statement by the higher voices. At m. 15, the first line of text returns with the mournful affect, and it engages all of the voices as opposed to the first occurrence of this text. This more complete statement of the first line precedes a second proclamation of the second line of text in antiphonal phrases. The last period of this section uses the third line of text, which also exhibits a forlorn affect. This period starts with antiphonal stratification with the three lowest voices against the three highest voices. However, after the initial antiphonal statement, the voices proceed in individual contrapuntal manner.

The second larger section uses shorter note values, indicating the joyful affect of this entire portion of the work. The section has several shorter periods that overlap each other. There are several Renaissance cadences, but they are spoiled by one or more voices that start new phrases immediately after the cadences. The only perfect cadence is at the end of the piece. Point-of-imitation technique prevails in this half of the composition.

SECTION	MEASURE	EVENT AND SCORING
A	1–11	One phrase
	12–15	One phrase
	15–31	Two overlapping phrases
	32–44	Five overlapping phrases
	45–65	Five overlapping phrases
B	65–108	Overlapping imitative phrases

Text and Translation

Die mit Tränen säen,	They that sow in tears
Werden mit Freuden ernten.	Shall reap in joy.
Sie gehen hin und weinen	He that goes forth and weeps,
Und tragen edlen Samen	Bearing precious seed,
Und kommen mit Freuden	Shall doubtless come again with rejoicing,
Und bringen ihre Garben.	Bringing his sheaves with him.
—Psalm 126:5–6	

Additional References and Resources

Houle, George. *Meter in Music, 1600–1800*. Indianapolis: Indiana University Press, 1987.

Donington, Robert. *The Interpretation of Early Music*. London: Faber and Faber, 1963.

Suggested Listening

Heinrich Schütz:

Geistliche Chormusik, BIS 831/2, Bach Collegium Japan, Masaaki Suzuki, conductor.

Geistliche Chormusik 1648, Koch International Classics 7189, Emmanuel Music Chorus, Craig Smith, conductor.

Geistliche Chormusik/Motets, Harmonia Mundi 1007694, Collegium Vocale, Philippe Hereweghe, conductor.

Contributed by:

G. Mikael Lindström

Teacher Resource Guide

Four Pastorales

Cecil Effinger

(1914–1990)

SATB and oboe
G. Schirmer: "No Mark" (50310440), "Noon" (50310450), "Basket" (50310460), "Wood" (50310470)
Overall: 4
Vocal: 3
Tonal/Rhythm: 4

Composer and Historical Perspective

Written in 1964, *Four Pastorales* may bring together two of the greatest twentieth-century American artists most Americans have never heard of. Effinger was a prolific composition student of the esteemed Nadia Boulanger in Paris and an oboist, performing as the first oboist in the Denver Symphony Orchestra. Over his lifetime he composed seven symphonies, three complete operas, three oratorios, three cantatas, and numerous smaller works including forty-nine choral works.

Fellow Coloradan Thomas Hornsby Ferril, who had won *The Nation*'s poetry prize in 1927, would go on to win the Oscar Blumenthal Poetry Prize (1937), the Academy of American Poets Award (1939), the Ridgeley Torrence Memorial Award (1953), and the Robert Frost Award (1960). He was also named Colorado's poet laureate in 1979 and applauded for his work by Carl Sandburg and Robert Frost, yet his poems are still mysteriously absent in many compilations of American poetry.

Ferril's poetry is strongly inspired by the natural Coloradan landscapes. Effinger's music focuses more on communication of ideas and emotion than the more popular avant-garde styles of composition being practiced elsewhere in America. Effinger said, "If all a composer wants to do is confound the listener, that's an easy matter; the idea, however, is to communicate something to him." The *Four Pastorales* accomplish just that. Four tableau pictures depicting the human experience—the impact of human death ("No Mark"), the beating western Sun, the heat blur of images on the desert horizon, and the stillness of a quiet mind ("Noon"), the reclamation of a memory with intimate emotional value ("Basket"), and the discovery of love ("Wood").

Technical Considerations and Musical Elements

This set of pieces is well-known by many conductors yet is infrequently performed by high school ensembles for perhaps one main reason: the oboe solo. Before the conductor adds these pieces to the repertoire of her or his choir, it is absolutely essential that a more than decent oboist is available for the performance(s). Although the range for the oboe is not difficult, there are moments where more complex rhythmic patterns occur, and of course it is of great importance that the oboe soloist should play with impeccable intonation. Perhaps of greatest concern are the transitions between choral sections where the oboe plays entirely exposed. Since many of these sections also involve a change of tonal center for the choir, it is imperative that the choir hear those transitions from an early stage in the rehearsal process (even if the oboe part is played on the piano). Depending on the musical abilities of the oboe soloist, a fair amount of time may need to be spent outside the choral rehearsal with the oboist to determine rubato, breathing, phrasing, etc., before adding the oboe into the choral rehearsal.

Although the importance of the oboist's intonation has already been mentioned, a greater challenge in the *Pastorale* is the recurrence of *a cappella* sections. It is crucial that the choir retain the correct pitch, lest the entrances of the oboe after these sections be entirely dissonant (for instance, in a key center a half step higher than the choir). While this is always of concern in dealing with any piece that combines *a cappella* singing with sections for a solo instrument or sections that are accompanied, the *Pastorales* offer some additional challenges. There is a fair amount of unison singing in each of the pieces in this set. At first glance, especially to amateur singers, this may appear to mean these sections are easy (or at least easier). This could not be further from the truth. It is the tendency for even choirs of advanced ability to flat in pitch while singing in unison. For less experienced singers, this tendency is even stronger. A thorough understanding of the intricacies of each phrase and where it lies in the individual's tessitura will aid in retaining pitch during unison singing. This might only be attained through numerous repetitions, making sure that the conductor insists upon every interval being sung with great accuracy.

In sections where there is a homophonic texture (rather than the monophonic texture previously discussed), intonation (and as a result the pitch) is easier to maintain. However, these sections are not without their own challenges. Effinger has a tendency to use planing chords, which are never easy to tune, and many of these chords are higher tertian chords, although a better description might be to call them color chords involving, e.g., added fourths or seconds. Tuning individual chords with the "color note" removed, then adding that note back in, might be one way for the choir to better understand the harmonies involved. Mm. 44–52 of "No Mark" incorporate a series of planing open fourths and fifths that might require special attention, as the choir does not have the luxury of a more sonorous third or sixth in the chords to aid in their tuning.

In the areas of tonality and melody, the Effinger pieces will present learning opportunities that should prove valuable in developing a choral ensemble. This obviously will include certain challenges in both areas, the most obvious of which is that the composer does not write the pieces in a key signature; instead, he composes using only accidentals notated throughout the score. For instance, "Basket" is written with a preponderance of B-flats, E-flats, and A-flats, putting it strongly in the key of C minor for a large portion of the piece. However, he does (in "Basket" and the other three *Pastorales*) move freely to various key centers, sometimes without much warning or traditional chord progressions. As a result, short choral phrases that are interspersed with oboe solos will sometimes have tonal centers that appear not to have much relationship to each other at all.

Returning to the issue of color chords, it is perhaps easiest to say that Effinger composes with the issue of tonality and key structure being dependent upon the text of individual phrases. There are some sections that seem almost bitonal, (e.g., "Noon," mm. 37–41 and "Wood" mm. 43–45), although the differing cadential chords in the men's and women's parts are approached by step from the same tonality in these instances. This being said, once the singers become accustomed to reading the music with accidentals rather than key signatures and the sometimes abrupt changes in tonality, Effinger's compositional method will become more natural to their ears. The best advice here is that they will need to "live" with the works for an extended period of time. These are not pieces a conductor would want to hand out to the choir two weeks before a performance.

Rhythmically, the *Four Pastorales* are not complex. Time signature changes are not frequent, and when they do occur, Effinger remains in the new meter for an extended time period. There are several unmetered passages in "Wood" for the oboe soloist (mm. 20, 24–26), but phrase markings are given; it is suggested that these points be treated as pseudo-cadenzas for the oboe soloist that should not be conducted. Tempo instructions vary in specificity from very definitive (the beginning of "No Mark" is given the instruction of *allegro comodo*, quarter note = 104) to somewhat general (the change to 12/8 time at m. 41 of the same piece is marked with nothing more than *lento assai*. Other tempo indications include *risoluto, con moto* and *poco agitato,* to name a few. Conductors will need to decide upon their interpretations of these tempo indications as well as where to add ritards toward the ends of phrases. (Very few indications are given in the score, although their inclusion seems to be a natural choice, even without specific instruction.)

Effinger is fairly specific with dynamics throughout the scores, and his indications should be followed closely. However, there are times where the shaping of individual phrases and even whole sections is not given, and the conductor should feel free to shape the phrase or section according to his or her own wishes, perhaps with the input of the choir members. Once again, look to the text for clues on the best musical decisions.

The vocal ranges are fairly easy with a few caveats, mostly in "Wood," the final piece of the set. The basses and altos are required to sing one high E-flat (in unison with the tenors and sopranos respectively) in "Wood," m. 40, and the basses have a low F in "Basket," mm. 25–26. The tenors have a G-flat in m. 6 of "Wood" and conclude the same piece on a high F-sharp (first tenors only). There are short sections of divisi in every voice part throughout the set but never for more than two or three measures unless the singers are required to hold a concluding note of a phrase for several measures (e.g., tenors in "Noon," mm. 8–13).

Turning to the issue of text, one quickly discovers that interpreting the poetry of T. H. Ferril is perhaps the greatest challenge of all. This might be an opportunity for a conductor to bring in an expert on poetry to conduct a discussion on the meaning of the poetry of these pieces. Although a brief idea is given above as to the general theme of each poem, there is certainly room for much dialogue with regard to the more specific thoughts presented. This discussion should not be left as an afterthought until the day of the concert; rather it should be addressed almost immediately in the rehearsal process due to the complex nature of the poetry.

Stylistic Considerations

As this set of pieces was written within the past twenty-five years, specific performance practices cannot be clearly defined. However, although conductors can guide their ensembles toward their own preferences in tone, style, etc., there are several suggestions to be made regarding the overall character of individual pieces, sections, or even phrases.

"No Mark"

Experiment with a contrast between more separated declamation of the text on shorter note values (eighth notes and sixteenth notes) and a more sustained legato when there are longer note values. This should provide some interesting character changes throughout, especially in certain sections (e.g., mm. 22–33).

"NOON"
The languid lines of the upper voice should contrast with a more marked, almost spoken feel in the bass voices in mm. 1–41. Carefully map out the syllabic stress and slight *crescendos* and *decrescendos* in mm. 43–58.

"BASKET"
The sections in compound duple and triple (mm. 1–17 and 43–53) should have a light, dance-like quality. Make sure the singers do not slow down the eighth notes; these sections should drive forward rather than becoming stagnant and lugubrious. This will contrast well with the more sustained nature of the middle section in simple meter (mm. 18–41).

"WOOD"
A sustained, full tone should be used throughout this piece, but the choir can experiment with adjusting their tone to reflect various emotions, from dark and foreboding (mm. 1–11) to sad and thoughtful (mm. 12–19), more passionate (mm. 34–42), and full of wonder (mm. 52–58).

Form and Structure

Due to the shortness of many phrases, the fact that many phrases are essentially broken into many parts making actual length ambiguous, and the overlapping nature of the oboe part over the choral phrases, phrase length will in general not be notated and the pieces will be divided into more major sections.

SECTION	MEASURE	EVENT AND SCORING
"No Mark"		
Introduction	1–4	Oboe
Section 1	5–15	First choral material with oboe solo concurrent (choral material sung in octaves)
Section 2	16–33	Choir with oboe solo, first material that is homophonic
Section 3	34–40	Oboe solo (beginning in m. 33) with choral accompaniment, *meno mosso* tempo indication
Section 4	41–48	Oboe solo followed by choral interlude
Section 5	49–56	Concluding choral material with brief oboe interlude m. 52 and concluding melodic material mm. 55–56 over final choral chord

Section	Measure	Event and Scoring
"Noon"		
Section 1	1–13	Oboe with slow planing melisma in thirds in women and tenors, pseudo-chant in basses mm. 11-13
Section 2	14–25	Material from section one repeated with alterations and transposed up a step
Interlude	26–30	Oboe
Section 3	31–34	Continuation of previous material with elongation in the women's parts and elaboration of the oboe solo
Interlude	35–36	Oboe
Section 4	37–42	Planing chords in men's and women's parts joined by oboe solo mm. 40–42
Section 5	43–49	New melodic material presented in octaves by the choir
Interlude	50–53	Oboe
	54–58	Concluding choral statement
"Basket"		
Section 1	1–9	Choral material with oboe solo, oboe introduction m. 1
Section 2	10–17	Movement between triple and duple notation in the choir
Section 3	18–30	New melodic material, switch to simple duple meter from compound triple meter with slower tempo indication, oboe interlude mm. 22–23
Section 4	31–41	Conversation between choir and oboe
Section 5	42–53	Repeat of section one with extension
"Wood"		
Section 1	1–19	Choral material, no oboe
Interlude	20	Oboe interlude (unmeasured)
Section 2	21–33	Oboe interludes mm. 24–26, 30–33
Section 3	34–51	Oboe interlude mm. 46–51
Section 4	52–58	Concluding choral material

Text

These are partial texts only. Full texts can be found in *New and Selected Poems* by Thomas Hornsby Ferril (Harper and Row, New York).

"No Mark"
Corn grew where the corn was spilled
In the wreck where Casey Jones was killed,
Scrub-oak grows and sassafras
Around the shady stone you pass . . .

"Noon"
Noon is half the passion of light,
Noon is the middle prairie and the slumber,
The lull of resin weed,
The yucca languor . . .

"Basket"
Know me then.
The children out of thc shade
Have brought me a basket
Very small and woven of dry grass. . . .

"Wood"
There was a dark and awful wood
Where increments of death accrued
To ev'ry leaf and antlered head
Until it withered and was dead . . .

Suggested Listening

Fern Hill, Oregon Repertory Singers, Koch International Classics, 1998.

Contributed by:

David Scholz

Teacher Resource Guide

Four Slovak Folk Songs

Béla Bartók

(1881–1945)

Mixed chorus with piano
Boosey & Hawkes: 17658
Overall: 4
Vocal: 3
Tonal/Rhythm: 4

Composer

Hungarian ethnomusicologist, composer, and pianist Béla Bartók is considered—along with Franz Liszt—to be Hungary's greatest composer. Bártok made his living principally as a pianist and a teacher but is best remembered for his contributions as a composer and as a founding figure in twentieth-century Hungarian musical culture. His compositions are highly influenced by ethnomusicological studies of Hungarian, Slovak, and Romanian peasant music as well as Western historic figures such as Beethoven and Bach and contemporary composers Debussy, Stravinsky, and Schoenberg. Equally adept at writing for the stage, orchestra, chamber ensemble, or voice, Bartók's legacy is in synthesizing the Western classical tradition with Eastern European folk music and for increasing international interest in ethnomusicological research.

Composition and Historical Perspective

Bartók once said of his use of folk materials in his compositions:

> Many people think it is a comparatively easy task to write a composition on found folk tunes. This way of thinking is completely erroneous. To handle folk tunes is one of the most difficult tasks; equally difficult, if not more so, than to write a major original composition. If we keep in mind that borrowing a tune means being bound by its individual peculiarity, we shall understand one part of the difficulty. Another is created by the special character of [the] folk tune. We must penetrate it, feel it, and bring out its sharp contours by the appropriate setting. It must be a work of inspiration just as much as any other composition.

Four Slovak Folk Songs, composed in 1917 and published in 1924 as a set of arrangements for mixed chorus and piano, captures beautifully Bartók's genius at penetrating such folk materials. He retains the simplicity, style, and color of these folk songs while clothing them in a harmonic language that fuses Eastern and Western European sensibilities.

Technical Considerations and Musical Elements

In choral compositions in which the harmonies or melodic contours are not necessarily intuitive, it is imperative that the ensemble be carefully prepared prior to working through the piece. Such preparation exercises may take the form of vocalises or skill-building exercises at the beginning of the rehearsal. Because the rhythm and phrasing will likely pose a challenge, carefully count-sing each movement until all musical lines are fluid. It is further suggested that each movement be taught on solfege initially. Then, when all intervals are sung in tune, move to a neutral syllable such as "doo." After the chorus confidently sings the piece legato, in tune, and with appropriate phrasing on the neutral syllable, then, and only then, move to the text. How the piece is phrased will vary greatly depending on which of the four languages is selected for performance.

A second area of difficulty that will require attention is the asymmetrical meter (5/8 time) in the second movement. Keeping the eighth note steady without rushing will be solved quickly by count-singing using the metronome.

Intonation will likely pose a third difficulty. Rehearsing the piece using solfege cannot be emphasized enough. Solfege will anchor the ensemble despite constantly changing tonal centers and highly chromatic musical lines. If necessary, insist that choir members write solfege syllables into their music.

Stylistic Considerations

Stylistically, treat these pieces as folk songs. Retain their earthiness and simplicity by singing with a clear, resonant tone. Avoid overt or overly dramatic gestures that interfere with the storytelling. Keep the tempo absolutely steady, and ensure that the onset and release of each line are performed with absolute clarity. Keep the lines moving forward with the aid of an excellent pianist. Remember that each movement is essentially a dance and must retain its characteristic affect. Be sure that the choir understands the meaning of the text so they can effectively communicate its message. Each piece should provide a glimpse into Slovakian culture, history, and heritage.

Form and Structure

Each movement is through-composed and may be sung in English, German, Hungarian, or Slovak.

Text

I. "Wedding Song from Poniky"
Thus sent the mother her little daughter
Into a distant land.
Sternly she bid her: "Follow thy husband!
Never return to me!" . . .

II. "Song of the Hayharvesters from Hiadel"
Where the Alps soar so free,
Flow'ry vale bright with glee;
There to rest!
Oh! there's no Bed in the world softer! . . .

III. "Dancing Song from Medzibrod"
Food and drink's thy only pleasure
And to dance recklessly,
But to work with pin an needle
Never appeals to thee. . . .

IV. "Dancing Song from Poniky"
Bagpipe shall be playing!
Pairs in dance be swaying!
Piper play till all is spent
To our hearts' and heels' content! . . .

Additional References and Resources

Sadie, Stanley, ed. *The New Grove Dictionary of Music and Musicians*. 2nd ed. New York: Grove, 2001.

Suggested Listening

Béla Bartók, *Four Slovak Folk Songs* on *Westminster Choir at Spoleto Festival U.S.A.*, The Westminster Choir, Joseph Flummerfelt, conductor, Gothic CD49078.

Contributed by:

James Bowyer

Teacher Resource Guide

Geistliches Lied, Op. 30

Johannes Brahms

(1833–1897)

SATB with organ
GIA Publications: G-6480
Overall: 4
Vocal: 4
Tonal/Rhythm: 3

Composer

Johannes Brahms studied piano from age seven and theory and composition from thirteen. He also played the piano in bars and brothels as a child, which may have contributed to his lifelong bachelorhood. His musical ability was recognized by Robert Schumann in the *Neue Zeitschrift für Musik* and predicted that great things would come from him. In fact, Brahms soon moved in with Robert and his wife, Clara, an accomplished musician in her own right for whom Brahms always had a special affection.

Brahms's music synthesized Romantic harmony and language with Classical form and the counterpoint of the Baroque. He resisted the musical innovations of such contemporaries such as Liszt and Wagner, the leaders of the New German School. Brahms wrote a number of major works for orchestra, including four symphonies, two piano concertos, a violin concerto, a double concerto for violin and cello, and his *Ein Deutsches Requiem*. It is interesting to note that his intense study and veneration of the masters like Beethoven kept him from starting his first symphony until age forty-three. Brahms was also a prolific composer of choral music and was interested in folk music.

Composition and Historical Perspective

The German motet "Geistliches Lied" ("Spiritual Song") was composed in 1856 around the time that doctors pronounced Robert Schumann's illness as incurable. Brahms was very interested in early music at the time and was trading counterpoint exercises with friends by mail. It is, therefore, no surprise that he wrote this double canon at the interval of a ninth. It is particularly interesting that Brahms used organ, as he did not write very much music for this instrument. This piece in many ways deals with two of the same themes of his *Ein Deutsches Requiem*: fate and consolation for the sorrowful.

The text is by Paul Flemming, a seventeenth-century German poet who had a strong love for his country and for the cause of Evangelical religion.

Technical Considerations and Musical Elements

This piece is a vocally very challenging due to the long legato lines and German language. The parts are almost entirely polyphonic and will require quite a bit of musical independence from each section. The ranges are not difficult but the parts are difficult to sing.

The initial work on this piece should be done on a neutral syllable such as [nu] or [no] at no less than *mezzo forte*. These long legato lines will be more difficult to sing *piano* if the choir doesn't know how it feels in their body at a louder dynamic. The choir should also be reminded to sing each pitch accurately from the beginning. A slow, legato piece such as this is an invitation for the choir to slide (even very subtly) between notes. They can point with their index fingers on each note (at eye level in order to bring more head tone into the sound) to assist this.

Large leaps (both up and down) abound in this piece and may cause intonation problems if the choir is not taught to sing them correctly. For upward leaps, tell the choir to increase their internal vertical space and breath support *before* the leap. It is important for the vowel on the upper note not to become too open in front or else it may stick out of the texture. This is especially true for the basses in mm. 16 and 50. For downward leaps, ask the choir to show a little bit of teeth on the lower note and to keep the sound in the same upper "apartment." The internal space should not change so it may also be helpful to ask that the low note "sound higher."

These long legato lines will require the singers to connect deeply to the breath. Rehearsing on a voiced consonant (*m*, *n*, or *v*) will help as well as having the choir hiss their lines (with one steady stream of air) while the accompanist plays their parts. It will also be helpful to ask the choir to think of their inhalation as not only allowing them to gain air, but also to release the larynx back into its low position. Long phrases can cause singers to raise their larynx as they sustain the phrase. If their inhalation does not "reset" the larynx position, the piece will become tiresome to rehearse and perform.

The "Amen" section that begins at m. 53 brings its own set of challenges. This section requires an intense amount of listening from the ensemble to make sure that the intonation doesn't suffer. When teaching the word "Amen," have the choir first learn it as "Namen." This will assist in getting the "ah" to be forward and resonant and will also teach them to lower their jaws slightly when beginning the sound. When the "n" is taken away, ask them to still lower their jaws slightly as they begin the vowel in order for the vowel not to be "bumped." Placing an "h" in front of the vowel can also teach them to start it with air. The tenor line that begins at the end of m. 58 is the most difficult line. Ask them to move through both sets of tied half notes and to keep the air spinning throughout. Their high A-flat will most likely be sung in falsetto but ask that they use "reinforced falsetto" that is supported and spacious. They can imitate an owl sound on [u] at a loud dynamic to find this in their voices. The final challenge of the "Amen" section is the five measure *diminuendo*. Ask the choir questions about how they should sing the *diminuendo*. Should this be an intensification of sound or a relaxation of sound? Should this feel as if it is moving forward or backward? One vocal trick for the *diminuendo* is to keep the internal spaciousness while gradually muting the sound with the lips.

The German diction may be the most demanding part of the teaching process. Proper explanation of the schwa sound early will assist greatly in subsequent rehearsals. There are no less than fifteen schwas in this piece, so it will be worth the time! Be sure that the choir understands that the schwa is an unstressed syllable. Speaking words such as "father" or "sister" will make this concept clear. It is also crucial that the choir mute the schwa sound with their lips without dropping their jaws (and maintaining internal space). Dropping the jaw will cause the vowel to fall back in placement and lose pitch. Another important point in the teaching of diction will be sufficient closure of vowels, especially the German [e] and [o]. American speakers will tend not to focus these vowels enough, and the language will sound less stylistic. When talking about lip position or embouchure, be sure to emphasize that internal mouth spaciousness never changes (a good analogy is a "reverse megaphone"). The good news about the umlauts in this piece is that the all are "u" umlauts. It may be easiest to ask the choir to sing [u] lips with an [i] tongue.

A greater musical issue in this piece is getting the choir to stay musically connected throughout. Be sure to transmit to the choir a love for the music that precedes every major section. Younger singers may not see the importance of these sections and may therefore talk or shuffle their music. Ask the singers to feel as though they are singing along inside with the keyboardist.

Stylistic Considerations

Picking the proper tempo for this piece will be a central challenge for the conductor. Obviously, if the tempo is too fast the piece will seem trivial and unsubstantial, while a slower tempo may sound too labored and heavy. Good luck!

One vowel color issue to think about is how much [i] influence will be present in words such as "nicht" or "dich." Do you want an [i], a pure [I], or something in between? The opening line alone has three such vowel sounds. The conductor also needs to decide how much "eh" will be present in the sustained schwas that end the first three major sections of the piece (mm. 19, 36, and 52). These chords are crucial to the success of the piece but must not lose color on the schwa vowel regardless of the *diminuendo* marking.

The conductor must also think about what the return of the A section means. Is it more hopeful? Will the dynamic range be exactly the same as it is in the opening A section? How is this section of text different than the previous two sections? How will this section lead into the glorious "Amen"? Will the organ part that precedes this section take extra time in any places?

The beginning of the "Amen" section will be easier if the conductor breathes the [a] vowel with the basses and altos. Conducting m. 57 through the end of the piece will be the most rewarding challenge of the piece. It is important to make the *molto crescendo* happen so that the choir has a larger dynamic to *diminuendo* from. The *diminuendo* will be very difficult if the choir does not precede it with a true *forte*. The final *messa di voce* over m. 66 should be a very subtle and peaceful one. Even the thought of it in your conducting will probably be enough.

Form and Structure

The piece opens with an eight-measure organ introduction, which creates the musical atmosphere for the piece. The sopranos are the first to join as the choir continues in a double canon at the ninth, which is almost entirely diatonic. The organ plays a two and a half measure interlude, and the sopranos begin the middle section, which is just as imitative as the first. This section, however, is more chromatic and ends in a less harmonically stable way. However, part of the opening organ part comes back and leads us into a repeat of the A section. A remarkable "Amen" section follows that is polyphonic and creates a cascading of voices as they come to a *forte* dynamic and *diminuendo* over five measures down to *piano*. It is interesting that Brahms throws in a D-flat in the bass section for an unexpected harmonic turn. The last two measures have a plagal cadence that finally provides us harmonic rest. The only homophony in the whole piece occurs in the final measure of each section.

SECTION	MEASURE
A	1–19
B	20–36
A	37–52
Coda	53–67

Text and Translation

Laß dich nur nichts nicht dauren mit Trauren,	Let nothing ever grieve thee,
Sei stille, wie Gott es fügt, so sei vergnügt, mein Wille.	Be still (silent), as God ordains, so be content with my will.
Was willst du heute sorgen auf morgen?	Why will you be sorrowful today about tomorrow?
Der Eine steht allem für, der gibt auch dir das Deine.	The One stands for all, and will give you what is yours.
Sei nur in allem Handel ohn Wandel,	Be without change in your dealings,
Steh feste, was Gott beschleußt,	Stand firmly, whatever God decides.
Das ist und heißt das Beste.	It is and is ordered the best.
Amen.	Amen.

Additional References and Resources

Swafford, Jan. *Johannes Brahms—A Biography*. New York: Random House, 1997.

Suggested Listening

Johannes Brahms:

"Lass dich nur nichts nicht dauren" on *The Romantic Mass—Choral Works by Rheinberger and Brahms*, St. Clement's Choir, Philadelphia, Peter Richard Conte, Dorian 80137.

"Lass dich nur nichts nicht dauren" on *O magnum mysterium*, Westminster Choir, Joseph Flummerfelt, Chesky CD 83.

"Lass dich nur nichts nicht dauren" on *Johannes Brahms—Warum ist das Licht gegeben*, Kammerchor Stuttgart, Frieder Bernius, Carus-Verlag CD 83201.

Contributed by:

William Hammer

Teacher Resource Guide

I Have Had Singing

Steven Sametz

(b. 1954)

SSAATTBB
Steven Sametz Publications: SSP 0001
Overall: 4
Vocal: 4
Tonal/Rhythm: 4

Composer

Steven Sametz is the Ronald J. Ulrich Professor of Music and director of choral activities at Lehigh University. He also serves as artistic director for The Princeton Singers. After completing his undergraduate studies at Yale University, and the Hochschule für Musik und darstellende Kunst in Frankfurt, he earned a master of music and doctor of musical arts degree from the University of Wisconsin–Madison.

Sametz is active as a conductor, composer, and editor. He has received commissions from the National Endowment for the Arts, Connecticut Council for the Arts, and Santa Fe Music Festival to create new works for Chanticleer, the Dale Warland Singers, Philadelphia Singers, Pro Arte Chamber Choir, Santa Fe Desert Chorale, Connecticut Choral Artists, and the King of Thailand. His works have been performed throughout the United States and Canada.

Composition and Historical Perspective

"I Have Had Singing" was written in 1993. The text is from Ronald Blythe's *Akenfield, Portrait of an English Village*.

Technical Considerations and Musical Elements

This piece, a short vignette, represents a glimpse into the life of a villager from Akenfield, an East Anglian village located about ninety miles north of London. Though short, it is filled with nostalgia. The word "singing" recurs throughout the text; however, singers should be aware of the context for which this piece was written. It is not solely about the act of "singing." The text is an eighty-year-old man's reflection on his life; he describes a life of hardship that was nevertheless enriched by singing. As the old man lies on his deathbed, he reflects upon his life and proclaims, "I have had pleasure enough; I have had singing." Steven Sametz writes on the score, "His words eloquently speak to the importance of singing in our lives, whether we sing as amateurs or professionals."

A few technical aspects make "I Have Had Singing" somewhat challenging. The meter frequently shifts. The text, appropriately, closely follows these metric idiosyncrasies. The unpredictable meter also helps to deliver the text in a carefree, chant-like manner; however, the piece becomes more compelling if performed as if there is no meter. Count-singing during early rehearsals would help to bring awareness to the ever-changing meters and help to sustain the linear phrasing. If the singers are more advanced, they may benefit from conducting the changing meters. Aside from meter, the rhythms are not complex. The majority of the piece is homorhythmic, and the main challenge for the singers and the conductor is transitioning smoothly from common time quarter notes to triplet quarter notes in common time. These areas needs to be isolated during practice, or else the triplets may drag. Realizing that the text falls directly on beats one and three (in common time) will help avoid this potential problem.

The melodic contour occasionally exhibits large leaps—sometimes of an octave or more—which not only provide technical vocal challenges but may easily ruin the linear quality that the phrasing needs. Adding physical movement to the rehearsal, such as having vocalists smoothly step their parts while maintaining focus on low abdominal breathing, may aid this. Also, to bring awareness and direction to the phrasing, consider having the students dramatically paint the direction of the phrasing in the air with their hands and arms.

Dramatic shifts in dynamics aid in the overall concept of phrasing but range a great deal—from ***ppp*** to ***f***. The ending presents a particular challenge as the soprano line arpeggiates upward to an F-sharp while maintaining a decrescendo to ***ppp***. Each soprano must continue to spin the air forward while arpeggiating up to the final pitch. It may be beneficial to instruct the singers to lightly spin lifting circles with their hands near the low abdomen to encourage each breath to be low and each exhalation of air to be steady.

The entire piece is to be performed *a cappella*. While the harmonic language is not unusual, the intonation is challenged by the multiple leaps in individual lines. Intonation is something to be focused on during each rehearsal. Once the pitches are more or less in place, the choir may sing the piece or a portion of the piece on staccato [du]. The goal is to achieve accuracy of pitch and rhythmic cohesion as an ensemble. Once this is accomplished, the next step may be to sing the same except using "legato 'do.'" This will continue to encourage the accuracy of pitch and turn the focus to phrasing. After this step is achieved, text may be added.

The bass vocal range extends down to a low D (below the staff) twice. The vocal ranges are not otherwise extreme.

Stylistic Considerations

Ideal line and pacing of each phrase are challenging to attain with a limited number of singers. (An ensemble of less than thirty young adults will likely experience considerable difficulty with the phrasing.) The majority of the text is set homorhythmically, which also makes staggered breathing a requirement.

Form and Structure

Two large sections are separated by the use of past and present tense: the man's reflection on his life and the resolution of "I have had pleasure enough . . ."

SECTION	MEASURE	EVENT AND SCORING
1	1–10	Two phrases (4 + 6); "The singing . . . always singing"; the harmonic language is relatively straightforward with D major or G major being the predominant tonal centers throughout this section
2	11–18	Two phrases (3 + 5); "Here I lie. I have had pleasure enough, I have had singing"; a brief but dramatic two-measure shift in tempo takes place at the beginning of this section. This shift allows the listener to travel in time with the narrator to the present moment: "Here I lie"; the harmonic language takes a sudden turn in last four measures of the piece with an interesting shift to C-sharp major for the text "I have had singing, I have had singing"; it is clear that Sametz makes an unexpected transition from D major to take the listener to a new level of experiencing the text

Text

The text is from *Akenfield, Portrait of an English Village* by Ronald Blythe. Steven Sametz writes:

> In his work, *Akenfield, Portrait of an English Village*, Ronald Blythe recounts tales from the lives of people he met in the north of England—pigmen, grave diggers, fruit pickers, and the like—vanishing breeds in the face of progress. He was startled by the harshness and beauty of their lives. *I Have Had Singing* paraphrases words of a horseman, age eighty, whom Blythe pseudonymously called Fred Mitchell. His words eloquently speak to the importance of singing in our lives, whether we sing as amateurs or professionals.

Suggested Listening

Steven Sametz:

"I Have Had Singing" on *I Have Had Singing*, Chanticleer, Teldec, 1994.

"I Have Had Singing" on *I Have Had Singing*, Michael O'Neal Chamber Singers, Media Adventures, Inc., 2004.

Contributed by:

Elizabeth Swanson

Teacher Resource Guide

John the Revelator

arr. Paul Caldwell and Sean Ivory

SATB divisi with piano
earthsongs: S-155
Overall: 4
Vocal: 4
Tonal/Rhythm: 4

Composer

Paul Caldwell has worked in the field of choral music education for the past twenty years and has specialized in conducting children's choirs. He was a past director of the Chicago Children's Choir and was the founder of the North American Choral Company, which is based in Holland, Michigan.

Sean Ivory is the director of the Calvin College Campus Choir. He teaches music in the Forest Hills Public Schools and is a member of the conducting staff for the North American Choral Company.

Composition and Historical Perspective

"John the Revelator" has its origins in the blues and in gospel. Both of these genres developed around the same time (beginning in the early 1900s) and were heavily influenced by one another. Gospel music is associated with the rise of evangelical African-American sects like the Sanctified and Holiness churches in major cities around the United States. The worship services in these churches were characterized by spontaneous speeches and singing, called "testifying" or "shouting," done by members of the congregation. "Testifying" would often be accompanied by dance and would rise to an ecstatic peak during the course of the service. Beginning in the 1920s, artists who were associated with these religious sects began to record examples of early gospel music. This music was a fusion of traditional African American religious music and imagery with the blues and other popular forms. At the heart of this new genre was spontaneous improvisation fueled by religious fervor and strong emotion.

According to the historical note in the score, "John the Revelator" was first recorded in the 1920s and 1930s by two blues artists, Blind Willie Johnson and Son House, who were affiliated with the evangelical African-American sects. However, it is clear that the piece was in existence before that time, as both musicians identified it as traditional. It has since been recorded by a number of artists across the musical spectrum. Caldwell and Ivory's choral arrangement is heavily rooted both in the blues scale and in the gospel tradition. The lengthy coda sections in particular evoke the intensifying passion and ecstasy that were key to the Sanctified and Holiness church services.

Technical Considerations and Musical Elements

A cursory glance at this piece reveals that rhythm is one of the major issues in this arrangement. However, most of the rhythmic patterns in "John the Revelator" are repetitive and even ostinato-like. The first section of the piece (mm. 1–20), for example, is centered on a call-and-response structure in which only two rhythmic motives are prominent. Beginning in m. 34, the response changes to a more complex syncopated sixteenth note pattern, but this too repeats. Mm. 54–101 contain a choral ostinato based on a single rhythmic pattern. The director should point out the repetitions in rhythmic patterns to the singers early on in the rehearsal process, in order to calm their nerves as they look at the arrangement for the first time. It is imperative in this arrangement that the director separate rhythm from pitch in the first few rehearsals. The pitch content is not too difficult for much of the piece (up to m. 102), so many problematic aspects of the arrangement can be worked on by isolating rhythm.

Caldwell and Ivory are very exact about the placement of accent marks. The accents, which are placed primarily on beat one and the "and" of beat two, create a polyrhythmic effect and highlight the syncopated rhythms. The choir should be diligent about consistently performing the accents wherever they are marked. Furthermore, the ensemble should be reminded that the accents are created with a pulsation of the abdomen and an open throat rather than from the throat. A possible exercise to aid with this concept is to ask the singers to deliver forceful puffs of air just on the accent marks while the accompanist plays the piano part. This way, the singers concentrate only on the abdominal pulsations. Then ask the chorus members to sing the line, maintaining breath energy and an open throat as they perform the accents.

Problems related to consonants are more common in "John the Revelator" than those related to rhythm. Initial consonants need to be delivered crisply and strongly right on the beat in keeping with the highly rhythmic, percussive nature of the arrangement. Ending consonants can be problematic as well, particularly "s." Beginning in m. 54, the two "s" sounds in the text "Tell us: Who is writin'?" fall right before eighth rests. To avoid prolonged sibilants through the rests, the choir should be instructed to make these sounds as short as possible. Have the choir members imagine they are touching a hot plate in order to visualize what this "s" should sound like. Also, the singers need to be rehearsed to leave just the right amount of space for the eighth rests so that they do not rush through this section.

The piano part deserves special mention in "John the Revelator." The piece demands an expert accompanist who can do justice to the walking bass in octaves in the left hand and the jazzy flourishes in the right hand. Not only must the accompanist be absolutely top notch, but he or she should also be well versed in the gospel style. The accompanist plays a crucial role in this piece in communicating the proper style to the singers. The piano part also can provide difficulties for singers as well because it very rarely supports the vocal lines. A skilled choir is just as necessary as a skilled accompanist. There are several sections of the piece in which the choir sings, alternating with short interjections by the piano. It is crucial that these sections be diligently rehearsed.

The divisi sections are also challenging. There is almost constant two-part divisi in the soprano part throughout the piece, and there is even three-part divisi in the sopranos near the end of the piece. In addition, there are consistent divisi in the alto, tenor, and bass parts from m. 102 to the end of the piece. The choir should be large enough to perform the divisi comfortably.

Another challenging area involves the blue note (flatted fifth) prevalent throughout the arrangement. The B-flat (the blue note) alternates with B-natural, which can create intonation problems. This alternation is particularly evident in the bass line in mm. 4–12 of the piece. The basses have three statements of the text "O tell me who is that writin'?" in these measures, each of which functions as a "call" that is responded to by the rest of the choir. In the first two statements, the blue note (B-flat) is avoided and in the last one it is used. The director should instruct the singers to make a conscious distinction between the two pitches. A possible way to do this might be to ask the basses to give a thumbs-up sign when they sing B-natural (to think high on the pitch) and a "thumbs down" sign when they sing B-flat (to think low on the pitch).

One of the most engaging aspects of the arrangement is the creative use of body percussion. Beginning in m. 70, an indication is given in the score for the choir to add hand claps on beats two and four, which are referred to as "low" claps. These handclaps are augmented in m. 86 by "high" claps on all the eighth note offbeats, which are to be performed by a small group within the choir. In m. 101, all perform a combination pattern of claps and stomps, which provides an effective punctuation to this section of "John the Revelator." The complexity of the body percussion in the arrangement warrants extra rehearsal time. Also, the director must be prepared to ask the singers to memorize the piece in order to perform the claps and stomps successfully or to come up with an alternative solution.

The final section of the piece (m. 102 to the end) is clearly the most difficult. Caldwell and Ivory change the musical texture at this point from homophony to interlocking rhythmic patterns alternating between the women and the men. In this hocket-like texture, the men and the women finish each other's text phrases (e.g., immediately after the men sing "Well," the women sing "John," and the men continue with "just tell it in your book"). Therefore, perfect coordination and an absolutely rock-solid tempo are critical so that these text phrases are understandable. The tendency of the choir will be to rush in this section. The director should first rehearse at a slow but steady tempo, separating rhythm from pitch. Once the singers are secure, the tempo can gradually be increased to performance tempo, at which point pitches can be introduced.

Stylistic Considerations

"John the Revelator" starts out with the walking bass line in the piano, setting the style of the arrangement. Caldwell and Ivory are careful to indicate in the first measure that the eighth notes in the left hand should be performed straight and are never to be swung. Also, accents are placed on all the eighth note offbeats so that this "back beat" is prominent. The director should be diligent in observing these instructions, as they create the gospel music flavor that is an integral part of the piece.

Musical phrasing can be relegated to the back burner in a highly syllabic and rhythmic composition such as this one. It is important for the director to identify phrasing ideas and to communicate them to his or her singers. An example of where phrasing can get minimized is in the choral ostinato section of the piece (mm. 54–102). For each statement of "Tell us: Who is writin'?" the choir should "move the phrase" through the eighth rests to the important word "writin'" so the musical phrase does not become mechanical or choppy.

Form and Structure

SECTION	MEASURE	EVENT AND SCORING
Refrain	1–20	Organized in call-and-response structure
Verse 1	21–28	
Refrain	29–44	
Verse 2	45–53	
First coda	54–101	Lengthy choral ostinato with punctuations by piano
Second coda	102–118	Characterized by interlocking rhythms between women's and men's parts

Text

Refrain:
O tell me who is that writin'? (*call*)
John the Revelator, (*response*)
O tell me who is that writin'? (*call*)
John the Revelator, (*response*)
O tell me who is that writin'? (*call*)
John the Revelator, (*response*)
Writin' in the book of seven seals. (*everyone*)

O tell me what is he writin'?
'Bout the Revelation,
O tell me what is he writin'?
'Bout the Revelation,
O tell me what is he writin'?
'Bout the Revelation,
Writin' in the book of seven seals.

Verse 1:
When John looked over Calvary's hill,
Heard a rumblin' like a chariot wheel.
Tell us, John, what did you see?
I saw a beast rising from the sea!

(*Refrain*)

Verse 2:
Talk to us John! What's the good news?
The crippled can walk, the dumb are singin' the blues.
O John, in the graveyard, whadaya see?
The dead are dancin' all around me.

First coda:
Tell us: Who is writin'?
Tell us: What he's writin'?
Tell us: Why he's writin'?
Time for revelation and for jubilation.
Tell us what you're writin'
Read it to us, John!

Second coda:
Well, John, just tell it in your book, John.
John, write it down for us in that book.
Well, just tell in your precious book, John,
John, write it down in that book of seven seals.

Suggested Listening

Paul Caldwell and Sean Ivory, arrangers, "John the Revelator" on *One World, Many Voices, Vol. 3*, earthsongs CD-05.

Contributed by:

Christopher Jackson

Teacher Resource Guide

La Muerte del Angel

Astor Piazzolla

(1921–1992)

arr. Néstor Zadoff

SATB a cappella
Editorial Lagos: GCC-MP 2016
Overall: 4
Vocal: 4
Tonal/Rhythm: 5

Composer

Signaled as the "Duke Ellington of Argentina," Astor Piazzolla was born March 11, 1921, in Mar del Plata, Argentina. In 1925 the family moved to New York City, returning to Argentina eleven years later, in 1936.

While in New York, Piazzolla started to play the *bandoneón* (the quintessential tango instrument) and took piano lessons from Hungarian maestro Bela Wilda, a disciple of Sergei Rachmaninoff. Back in Argentina, he quickly became involved in the tango movement, playing *bandoneón* for Aníbal Troilo's orchestra and serving as its arranger. Troilo was the foremost *bandoneón* player of his time, and he and his orchestra offered perhaps the most prominent and sophisticated example of the traditional tango sound.

In 1941 Piazzolla becomes a composition student of Alberto Ginastera, Argentina's most celebrated classical music composer, who was only five years older than Piazzolla. After winning the Fabien Sevitzky composition contest, Piazzolla moved to Paris to study with the greatest master teacher of the time,

Nadia Boulanger, who bears the credit of helping Piazzolla to find his true compositional voice. Pessinis and Kuri write:

> What was once a choice between the sophisticated music *or* tango, now would be sophisticated music *and* tango, but in the most efficient way: to work the structure of sophisticated music with the passion of the tango.[1]

At different periods of his life, Piazzolla lived in Mar del Plata, New York,[2] Buenos Aires, Punta del Este,[3] Paris, and Rome. He became a true international composer and performer, playing solo *bandoneón* with orchestras all over the world and leading different chamber music ensembles, feeling equally at home in symphony halls and jazz festivals. He wrote feverishly, not only music for a variety of instrumental ensembles, including music for traditional solo instruments, electric guitar, and full-sized symphony orchestras, but also tango-songs, incidental music for more than thirty films, and even a chamber opera, *María de Buenos Aires* (1968). His output of more than three thousand works includes the celebrated "Concerto for Bandoneón and Orchestra."

Resisted by orthodox *tangueros* and reaching cult status with his followers, Piazzolla achieved the big dream for any aspiring composer of any time: the creation of a new style, a new sound, a new musical language. Rooted in the tango tradition but enriched by jazz elements and classical music thinking, the best way to describe Astor Piazzolla's music is that it sounds truly one of a kind.

Argentine choir director Néstor Zadoff was born in 1952. Educated at the Carlos López Buchardo National Conservatory in Buenos Aires, he earned a doctorate in musicology from the François Rabelais University in Tours, France, in 1979. A student of Antonio Russo, Erwin Leuchter, and Jean Michel Vaccaro, Zadoff has produced more than fifty published choral arrangements widely known in choral circles in Argentina and abroad, which have received several awards.

Since 1985 Zadoff has served as conductor of the National Young People's Choir of Argentina, an international award-winning ensemble in choir competitions throughout Europe and South America. The choir has made four CDs, toured Europe four times and regularly tours Argentina, and appeared as one of the international choirs for the 2001 ACDA National Convention in San Antonio, Texas.

Composition and Historical Perspective

The *tango* has its roots in suburban Buenos Aires and the Río de la Plata estuary during the late nineteenth century when the South American country was receiving an unprecedented influx of European immigration. This music, primarily used for dance, was first considered low-class by the elites but slowly gained a good reputation and entered the middle-class downtown theatres and upper-class fashionable soirees and, later, international popularity.

The *orquesta típica* consisted of violins, guitar, flute or double bass, piano, and, above all, *bandoneón*, the German-born accordion-like instrument thought to be a descendant of the organ. The diatonic variation of the instrument, preferred by tango players, has seventy-one buttons or keys (thirty-eight for the right hand and thirty-three for the left hand). The great difficulty lies in the fact that each of those seventy-one buttons produces two different sounds depending on the open or closed position of the *fuelle*, the body of the instrument. Astor Piazzolla is considered as one of the best bandoneonist of all times.

Most writers agree that the golden era of tango was 1935–1955 when a military coup ousted controversial Argentinean president Juan Domingo Perón. With the return of democracy in the 1980s, tango music and dance started a slow process of rebirth that continues to this day.

Not labeled as either *Guardia Vieja* ("Old Guard") or the "Evolutionists." Astor Piazzolla represents *Nuevo Tango*, the avant-garde front of this style of music.

There is no such thing as an original choral tango work. However, choral arrangements of tango music abound, and were first championed by the legendary chamber vocal ensemble Buenos Aires 8, which enjoyed an incredible success and popularity mainly in the 1970s and 1980s.

The influences of tango music can be found virtually all over the world, from the countless tango orchestras in Japan to the Gotan Project based in Paris to crossover recordings of classical artists like Yo-Yo Ma, Martha Argerich, Daniel Barenboim, Guidon Kremer, and Plácido Domingo.

Technical Considerations and Musical Elements

Vocal ranges:
Soprano = A3 (incidental)–G5
Alto = A3–D5
Tenor = D3 (incidental)–F4
Bass = G2–C3

The work is written in A minor with several short-lived tonal inflections. The meter is 4/4 throughout; however, as in all music by Piazzolla, internal rhythmic groupings in each measure produce a constant shifting accentuation organized mostly as 3–3–2 but also as 3–2–3 or 2–3–3.

Stylistic Considerations

Articulation and phrasing are of utmost importance in tango music: in fast passages, virtually every beat is accented and separated, many times even without any specific notation. Legato predominates in lyrical passages with occasional staccato marks to delineate phrasing. As explained above, recognizing the internal rhythmic organization of each measure is the key to a great performance: Piazzolla's style is infused with 3–3–2 and its variants, and this must be observed almost to a point of exaggeration.

Form and Structure

The music, forty-four measures long, is organized roughly in an AB~~A~~ + Coda structure (where ~~A~~ is a halved A), with the A section being relatively fast and rhythmic and the B section being the contrasting slow and lyrical section.

Section A = 1–18
Section B = 19–41
Coda = 42–44

SECTION	MEASURE	EVENT AND SCORING
Section A	1–18	Organized in period-like fashion, which instead of offering a harmonic closure concludes with a half cadence (V); melody with accompaniment with the sopranos always in charge of the main line and the basses holding a diatonic, stepwise delineated accompaniment; in the last six measures, the sopranos depart from the tonal center, eventually ending on V; basses accompany this move with a chromatic, stepwise accompaniment; in all cases, tenors and altos play a secondary role, showing only traces of delightful, counterpoint
	1–9	Two phrases (4 + 4)
	9–18	Two phrases (4 + 6)
Section B	19–41	Six phrases (4 + 4 + 4 + 4 + 4 + 3)
	19–26	Alto section melody
	27–34	Soprano section melody
	35–38	Alto section melody (first two measures); soprano section melody (last two measures)
	39–41	Soprano section melody, functioning as preparation for repeat; work comes to a dramatic closure on m. 41 on an $Am^{7(add9)}$ chord

Text

This excellent arrangement is based on an instrumental piece and uses nonsense syllables.

Additional References and Resources

Azzi, María Susana, and Simon Collier. *Astor Piazzolla: Su Vida y Su Música*. 2nd ed. Buenos Aires: El Ateneo, 2002. (Note: The first edition of this book was in English under the title *Le Grand Tango: The Life and Music of Astor Piazzolla*, New York, Oxford University Press, 2000.)

Collier, Simon. *A Round Table with Piazzolla. La Voz del Tango*. July-August 1997.

Pessinis, Jorge, and Carlos Kuri. *Astor Piazzolla: Chronology of a Revolution*. (www.piazzolla.org), 2002.

Piazzolla, Diana. *Astor*. Buenos Aires: Emecé, 1987.

Suggested Listening

This work is recorded by the National Young People's Choir of Argentina, conducted by Néstor Zadoff on *Four Centuries of Latin American Choral Music*, Buenos Aires, IRCO, 1995.

Contributed by:

Eduardo Garcia-Novelli

---

1 Jorge Pessinis and Carlos Kuri. *Astor Piazzolla: Chronology of a Revolution* (www.piazzolla.org), 2002.

2 During one of his long stays in New York, Piazzolla wrote "Adiós Nonino," arguably the composer's most celebrated score, after the news of the death of his father in 1959.

3 An exclusive beach resort in Uruguay, Piazzolla's favorite place to enjoy long periods of rest and music writing.

Teacher Resource Guide

Let Down the Bars, O Death, Op. 8, No. 2

Samuel Barber

(1910–1981)

SATB a cappella
G. Schirmer: 50301430
Overall: 4
Vocal: 3
Tonal/Rhythm: 4

Composer

Samuel Barber was born in West Chester, Pennsylvania on March 9, 1910. His father was a physician, and his mother was a fine pianist. His aunt Louise Homer was a distinguished contralto, and his uncle, Sydney Homer was a composer. Uncle Sydney was an early mentor and helped Barber to see life with a romantic inclination. Barber began studying piano at six and by age ten had composed one act of an opera.

Barber premiered his first song "Thy Will Be Done," at age thirteen. While in high school, Barber played organ at Westminster Church and assembled his own orchestra. At age fourteen he entered the Curtis School of Music as a charter member. After his early graduation from High School in 1926, he entered the Curtis School of Music and studied voice with Emilio de Gorgoza and composition with Rosario Scalero there for eight years. It was during this time that he met Giancarlo Menotti, who significantly influenced Barber's personal and professional life.

Upon graduation from The Curtis School of Music, Mary Curtis Bok became Barber's professional advocate and patron, which allowed him to compose and pursue musical ventures. One of these ventures brought him short-lived success as a baritone, and he performed on the NBC Music Guild series. Barber's only recording of himself appeared on a 1935 Victor LP, on which the young baritone premiered his own work, *Dover Beach*. After the premiers of his *Symphony in One Movement* and a performance of his Essay (No. 1) and the *Adagio for Strings*, premiered by Arturo Toscanini, Barber could earn a living by commission. The well-known opera *Vanessa* (1958) and the Piano Concerto (1962) won Barber a Pulitzer prize each.

After a long career, struggles with depression, alcoholism and writer's block clouded the end of his life. Accounts remark that Barber took comfort in writing for the solo voice. A difficult battle with cancer lasted from 1978 until his death in 1981.

Through all of his successes and failures, Barber's inherent lyricism reflected his Romantic vision of life.

Composition and Historical Perspective

The text by Emily Dickinson appears in *Complete Poems, Part Four: Time and Eternity*.

The secular motet "Let Down the Bars, O Death" (SATB), was published in 1936 and is coupled in Barber's Op. 8 with "The Virgin Martyrs" (SSAA), composed in 1935. "Let Down the Bars, O Death" premiered May 23, 1938. John Finley Williamson conducted various church choirs in Princeton, New Jersey, at the Princeton High School Auditorium. In a letter to his parents, Barber remarked: "I wrote a little chorus the other morning, quite good, it will be all right for someone's funeral." The work was played at Barber's various memorial services in 1981. This *a cappella* setting tonally reflects the flavor of Emily Dickinson's macabre poem. In *Samuel Barber: The Composer and His Music* Barbara Heyman remarks that the composition is a "precursor of the sensitivity to textual expression that would come to characterize Barber's later choral compositions."

The form is a simple ABA. Syllabic homophony pervades throughout the texture, which draws attention to harmonic progressions rather than motivic development.

The sonorities G minor, E-flat$^{(maj)(maj)7}$ and E-flat$^{(aug)}$ specifically color the opening A section (mm. 1–11). In the first four measures, the tessitura is lower, reflecting the text. The word "bleating" is emphasized in (m. 8) by the only E augmented^{7} chord in the work, which is quite striking after the preceding diatonic music. Barber makes a subtle onomatopoetic text setting by reiterating the G minor chord at the end of m. 8 into the downbeat of m. 9 on the word "repeat."

A *crescendo* elides the last measure of section A to section B, providing a sudden harmonic shift away from the initial key-related area of G minor. Barber reaches the apex of the piece, beginning in m. 5 (soprano C) to m. 11 (soprano D) to m. 12 (soprano E) with a final extension to F-natural in m. 14. Barber demonstrates his point further by traveling to the distantly related key areas of E minor, B major, and, finally, D minor (being modally, not harmonically related, to G minor) in m. 15. The dynamic level reflects this as well. Ominous, hymn-like chords result from a series of plagal cadences. Three of these cadences (mm. 15–16, 17–18, 19–20) end in with this progression: A minor–F-sharp(dim)^7–E major.

The final A´ section repeats mm. 1–6, with the exception of the augmented rhythm in mm. 26–30. It is the composer's choice, not the poets, to repeat the first two lines of text. Section A and A´ differ in dynamic level (***p–f***, and ***f–pp***), allowing the repeat of the text to have a sense of dramatic closure and balance.

Understanding the form is equally important for the singers as it is to the conductor. After purchasing the music, an analysis score should be in the hands of the singers. Ensure that your students understand the form of the work, for perceiving certain elements will remove the frustration of reading and provide a visual understanding of the score.

Technical Considerations and Musical Elements

The tonal language will take up a lot of the rehearsal time. Beat three of mm. 2 and 23 may require special attention for the sopranos and basses due to the leap down into the E-flat$^{(maj)(maj)7}$ tonality. The same applies to the basses on the downbeat of m. 8. Mm. 11–12 (G minor to E minor) will tune well if the tenor and bass sections are rehearsed together, apart from the upper voices. Time should be spent listening, on a neutral syllable, to the three previously mentioned F-sharp$^{(dim)7}$ chords, especially in m. 19 where the sopranos leap down a tritone.

Articulation of text may be a particular challenge, as the notes are long and sustained. Singers often get nervous in these situations and disturb the musical line by inserting consonants where it feels most comfortable. Active use of a metronome or an aural metronome (clapping, etc.), will ensure proper text declamation. Another popular method, which forces ending consonants to be attached to the beginning of the next word, is to rehearse the choir with staccato text and pitch. Frustrating though it may be, the choir will soon choose to be mindful of diction to avoid repeating the exercise.

Stylistic Considerations

Composition teachers Scalero and Sydney Homer, who taught nineteenth-century "romantic" ideals, had great influence on Barber's compositional style. It is difficult to know how much vibrato or how much rubato Barber would have enjoyed, but a decisive guess can be made from understanding his romantic background.

Form and Structure

A = 1–11 (7 + 4)
B = 12–21 (2 + 3) (2 +3)
A´ = 22–30 (9)

Text

Let down the bars, O Death!
The tired flocks come in
Whose bleating ceases to repeat,
Whose wandering is done.

Thine is the stillest night,
Thine the securest fold;
Too near thou art for seeking thee,
Too tender to be told.
—Emily Dickinson

Additional References and Resources

Hennessee, Don. *Samuel Barber, A Bio-Bibliography*. Greenwood Press, 1985.
Heyman, Barbara B. *Samuel Barber: The Composer and His Music*. New York: Oxford University Press, 1992.
Wentzel, Wayne. *Samuel Barber: A Guide to Research*. New York: Routledge Music Bibliographies, 2001.

Suggested Listening

Samuel Barber:
"Let Down the Bars, O Death" on *A Concert of American Music in Schönbrunn*, Vienna State Chorus, William Strickland, Vox PL 7750.
"Let Down the Bars, O Death" on *Adagio for Strings, et. al.* National Cathedral Choral Society Male Voices, Vladimir Goldschmann, Vanguard Classics, ATM 1649.
"Let Down the Bars, O Death" on *Barber and Schuman: Choral Music*, The Joyful Company of Singers, Peter Broadbent, ASV Living Era 939.
"Let Down the Bars, O Death" on *Choral and Organ Works*, The Cambridge University Chamber Choir, Timothy Brown. Guild GMCD 7145.

"Let Down the Bars, O Death" on *Music of the Protestant Episcopal Church: Music from Washington Cathedral*, Washington Cathedral Choir of Men and Boys, Paul Callaway, Vanguard VRS 1036, VSD 2021.

"Let Down the Bars, O Death" on *Shenandoah: An American Chorister, 1890–1990*, Los Angeles Chamber Singers, Peter Rutenberg, Klavier, catalog # 11052.

Contributed by:

John Perkins

Teacher Resource Guide

O magnum mysterium

Morten Lauridsen

(b. 1943)

SATB or TTBB divisi
SATB, Peer Music: 61860-121; TTBB, Peer Music: 62016-120
Overall: 4
Vocal: 4
Tonal/Rhythm: 4

Composer

Morten Lauridsen was born in Colfax, Washington, in 1943 and reared in Portland, Oregon. His teachers Ingolf Dahl and Halsey Stevens guided his compositional studies. A love of poetry attracted him to the vocal genre, and his output includes many art songs. His best-known works are his choral cycles *Les Chansons des Roses* (Rilke), *Mid-Winter Songs* (Graves), *Cuatro Canciones* (Lorca), *A Winter Come* (Moss), *Madrigali: Six "Firesongs" on Renaissance Italian Poems*, and *Lux aeterna*. Two of his most popular works are "Dirait-on" and Theodore Presser's best-selling work to date, "O magnum mysterium."

Lauridsen has been professor and chairman of the department at University of Southern California Thornton School of Music since 1990 and also became the composer-in-residence with the Los Angeles Master Chorale in 1994. Lauridsen's summers are spent on a small island off the coast of Washington in a cabin with no electricity or running water. Here he finds time to compose and space to contemplate new text settings.

Composition and Historical Perspective

The liturgical function of the text is as a responsory following the Fourth Lesson of the Nocturn of Matins for Christmas Day (Jeffers 177). Three distinct emotional affects are portrayed in the stanzas of text: 1) the mysterious dichotomy of the Son of God being born into lowliness, even among animals, 2) a reflection on the four Canticles which recognize Mary and establish Christ's sovereignty, and 3) an awe-inspired response to the scene with an additional reference to two animals. The animals appear in the first and third sections and may be compositionally represented with similar musical material. However, Lauridsen, as many other composers do (e.g., Thomás Luis de Victoria, Francis Poulenc, etc.), makes a different choice.

Only the first two stanzas are set and the "Alleluia," which closes the second stanza, is used as a coda (also briefly as a type of pedal in mm. 46–53). Lauridsen's head motive (A) is derived from the first line and brings back the opening formal elements in two other structural moments (mm. 19 and 46). The B material occurs only from mm. 38–45, leading into the rich and satisfying restatement of A. This expanded section (mm. 46–53) serves as the climax of the work. Lauridsen marks the climax by finally establishing tonic notes in the outer voices (first soprano and third bass). The outer voices, while singing the "Alleluia" text, fulfill both a harmonic and biblical expectation. The fulfillment of the harmony parallels the biblical fulfillment of Christ's birth. Notice also that the first two statements, from the first line of text, begin with an interruption after mm. 4 and 22; however, at the moment of "birth" (m. 49), the hold is removed from the last quarter and a *crescendo* propels the phrase to the downbeat where the Messiah arrives.

Technical Considerations and Musical Elements

As with many "O magnum mysterium" settings, one of the greatest challenges is engendering long lines of music with energy and clear intonation. The opening attack is crucial and problematic because of the vowel, the *piano* dynamic, and the sustained pitches. The technique for dealing with this is simple. Ask the singers to gently reiterate the vowel by placing it on the second eighth note subdivision. This method invigorates the sound and adds rhythmic integrity because of the rearticulation of the vowel. Try employing this at the beginning of every new phrase. If executed gently, the reiteration is unnoticeable to the audience.

Also vocally problematic are the wider contours in Lauridsen's melodies. For instance, in m. 13 the sopranos should be encouraged to take weight out of the lower D, avoiding a clash of intonation upon arrival. Roundness of the lips around the vowel will produce a brighter, less heavy, and more in-tune sound in the lower register.

Most singers will subconsciously listen down to the basses to help their own intonation. One of the beautiful aspects of the work creates an intonation problem. The lack of roots in the bass may confuse the singers, who instead should listen for the roots in the alto and tenor parts. (This knowledge affects the rehearsal process.) Solfege can aid the singers' ears by providing a reference to the tonic. In most situations the choir is inexperienced with solfege, and writing in the proper syllables is encouraged.

Later in the rehearsal process, staccato singing on the text, will promote correct vowel placement. (A note about the vowel [E], in "myst<u>e</u>rium": uniform tongue position between changing vowels will result in keeping this awkward syllable from spreading into a bright, undesirable "ehh," or worse, "aye" diphthong.)

The choir's awareness of melodic hierarchy greatly contributes to how successful the performance will be. In m. 46 it is obvious that the altos have the melodic line; however, the tenors' simplified contour of the opening motive (mm. 70–71) is more subtle and often ignored.

Overall, a careful rehearsal plan will save precious time and energy. The following rehearsal plan may be adopted for this work:

- Mm. 1–18 are almost identical to mm. 19–34. (In mm. 19–34 the text changes some of the rhythmic aspects, and the ending is different in m. 34.) Therefore, beginning the process with these two sections while pointing out the differences, will be very effective. Notice the difference between the *ritardando* and *poco ritardando* in mm. 4 and 22. Lauridsen expects that because m. 22 is a repeat of m. 4 the music should move forward.
- Next skip ahead to mm. 46–61 and practice the music for the first sopranos and basses. They act as outer "descant" parts while the inner parts remain similar, but not completely the same.
- Continue rehearsal from mm. 63–72. The motivic material is simply fragmented from the music of section A.
- Return to the pick-up to the last three quarters of m. 37, following through to the downbeat of m. 46. The only measure left to rehearse begins on the last quarter note of m. 61 to the first quarter note of m. 63, which is derived from mm. 35–36.

Not only will this process aid the singers in reading the work, but it is to the conductor's advantage to do so because it allows him or her to isolate musical figures and explain the various aspects of the text.

Stylistic Considerations

Because of the frequent dissonance, singers must be trained to hold exact pitch as well as have a comprehensive knowledge of where the dissonances occur.

The tempo markings are specific and should be strictly maintained. The other diacritical markings are equally important because they outline the work's structure.

Text stress in all languages and for all vocal works is important, but with this even, legato style proper declamation is essential. Lauridsen carefully sets the text and has even elongated many stressed syllables. The music may sound bland if unstressed syllables are not dramatically quieter than stressed syllables. Even though Lauridsen lengthens the vowel "te" of "mysterium" in m. 7 and drops the soprano tessitura on the unstressed consonants in m. 8. Many choirs unnaturally drive their sound into beats two and three of m. 8. Encouragement and repetition inspire an ensemble to become comfortable and confident in their efforts to achieve proper declamation.

Form and Structure

Section	Measure
A	
a	1–4 + 5–10
b	11–18
A1	
a1	18–22 + 23–27
b1	28–37
B	
c1	38–39, 40–41, 42–43, and 44–45
A2	
a2	46–49 + 50–54
b2	55–62
Coda	
fragments of a and b	63–65, 66–69, and 70–72

Text and Translation

O magnum mysterium,	O great mystery,
Et admirable sacramentum,	And wondrous sacrament,
Ut animalia viderent Dominum natum,	That animals should see the new-born Lord
Jacentem in praesepio!	Lying in their manger!

Beata Virgo, cujus viscera meruerunt	Blessed is the Virgin whose womb was worthy
Portare Dominum Christum. Alleluia!	To bear the Lord Jesus Christ. Alleluia!

Additional References and Resources

Jeffers, Ron. *Translations and Annotations of Choral Repertoire. Volume I: Sacred Latin Texts.* Corvalis, OR: earthsongs, 1988.

Strimple, Nick. *Choral Music in the Twentieth Century.* Amadeus Press. Portland, OR, 2002.

Suggested Listening

Morten Lauridsen:

- "O magnum mysterium" on *Lauridsen: Lux Aeterna.* Los Angeles Master Chorale, Paul Salamunovich, conductor, Rubenda Canis Musica #100305.
- "O magnum mysterium" on *O Magnum Mysterium*, Robert Shaw Festival Singers, Christopher Cock, conductor, Telarc #80531.
- "O magnum mysterium" on *Morten Lauridsen: O Magnum Mysterium and Other Choral Cycles*, Nordic Chamber Choir, Nicol Matt, conductor, Bayer #100305.

Contributed by:

John Perkins

Teacher Resource Guide

Sfogava con le stele

Claudio Monteverdi

(1567–1643)

SSATB
National Music Publishers: RCS 103
Overall: 4
Vocal: 4
Tonal/Rhythm: 4

Composer

Northern Italian Claudio Monteverdi helped change Western European musical style and set the stage for the Baroque period. Born in Cremona, he worked first in Mantua and later in Venice at San Marco cathedral. He composed in nearly every genre of the time. He wrote nine books of madrigals bridging late Renaissance and early Baroque techniques, operas for both the courts of Mantua and the public opera of Venice that incorporated Florentine opera reforms and heightened dramatic expression, sublime sacred works (*1610 Vespers*), and concerted works of great mastery. His was the first generation of composers to specify and write idiomatically for instruments. His theories on performance practice, tonality, counterpoint, text expression, and form, which arose from the Italian madrigal and polychoral traditions, were adopted and further developed both by contemporaries and succeeding generations of composers.

Composition and Historical Perspective

From the *Fourth Book of Madrigals* (1603), this work sets a text possibly by Ottavio Rinuccini that Giulio Caccini also set in *Le nuove musiche* (1602). Its use of *imitatio* (intentional use of another composer's material, often in tribute) and other oratorical devices may have been a response to Caccini's diatribe against the polyphonic madrigal, one of the genres for which Monteverdi is justly famous, in the preface to *Le nuove musiche*. The work exhibits an expanded vocal range that is one hallmark of works from Monteverdi's mature period.

Technical Considerations and Musical Elements

Several aspects of "Sfogava con le stele" point toward the Baroque Era: the rhetoric-based *affects*, the concept of *sprezzatura*, or a speech rhythm–influenced delivery, and *parlando*, which may be defined similarly to *sprezzatura* except that it is written by the composer not delivered by the performer. Modal/tonal facets, word painting, use of hexachordal inflection, and five-part voicing point backward, toward the Renaissance. All provide an opportunity to teach Baroque structural and performing ideas with short asides during the choir rehearsal. The conductor is left to decide upon whether to include accompaniment, to double voices with instruments, or to use *basso continuo*.

Regardless of these pedagogical windfalls and thorny performing decisions—luckily one cannot be entirely wrong as long as taste and thought are applied before rehearsals begin—some matters should be standard. Diction is one. The text is an archaic form of Italian familiar to lovers of early modern music, and it requires attention. Vowels are pure, never diphthongs or tripthongs unless several vowels follow one another. The plosives "d" and "t" should be stopped just behind the top teeth, not between upper and lower teeth as in American speech. "Ce" and "ci" are pronounced with an initial "ch" sound, while other "c" combinations use a hard "c" consonant. Similarly, "ge" and "gi" are soft ("je" and "ji"), but "ga," "go," and "gu" are hard. On the other hand, "ch" is pronounced "k" even when proceeded by an extra "c" ("zucchini"). "Sce" and "sci" sound "sh." "Ti" is pronounced "tsi" by American choirs, not "ti." A "z" in the middle of the word is "ts," but at the beginning is "z."

Double consonants "ll," "mm," and "nn" both pronounced twice. The "r" is rolled or flipped. "Gn" sounds like "ny," "gh" like "g," and "gli" more or less like "lyi." "H" is pronounced. Elisions are frequent and must be decided ahead of time. The usual practice, unless the note duration does not permit, is to blend so that "ch'adoro" becomes "kadoro." The accent is usually on the penultimate syllable, but a written accent mark alters that and should be observed. The site www.askoxford.com/languages/it/toi_italian/pronunciation is a good source for Italian pronunciation.

Above all such diction priorities is word rhythm. Perhaps *the* prevailing consideration for musicians of Monteverdi's time was to express the text well, both in composition and in performance. To work through the Italian poetry of this work, delivering each syllable like another vertical board in a picket fence would ruin the madrigal altogether. Consider the elision just mentioned, "ch'adoro." It is clear the "do" syllable receives the greatest accent, but expressing the text "whom I adore" requires more. As in English, a passionate rendering of the phrase will add a minute slice of time and an extra inflection to the "dore" syllable. Caccini called this effect *sprezzatura*, and artists of all eras recognize the concept. *Parlando*, "as spoken" (see m. 1) is a compositional technique that shook the seventeenth-century opera world.

The poem, read several times aloud in Italian, becomes a musical entity even before pitch and time values are added. Identify the climax, the important phrases or lines, and the lines that build to the climax or relax from it, and embody these decisions in your performance.

Finally, it should be mentioned that the madrigal "Sfogava con le stele" is not fully tonal. For example, the first phrase begins, using tonal nomenclature, in D minor but ends (m. 5) with a D major chord. This is perfectly understandable in the D Dorian modal system, but the minor dominant (m. 4) and plagal G major to D major (mm. 4–5) may also be viewed from a tonal point of departure. This ambivalent modal-tonal environment is typical of the time and alerts the choral director to watch intonation.

Stylistic Considerations

"Dignified passion" or "stylized ardor" encapsulates the stylistic intent of Monteverdi's madrigal. Ottavio Rinuccini (1562–1621) was an esteemed author and the first Western European opera librettist. His poem (if he indeed is the author) is literature, not a street ditty. As such, it adheres to poetic conventions, symbols, and usages of the time and presumes a lofty, ideal infatuation, not an uncontrolled or trivial one. The madrigal should not be sung as fluff.

Given the constant style changes from homophonic speech rhythm to counterpoint to melisma to imitative or quasi-polychoral snippets, the tempo should be noble. This also will allow the hexachordal inflections and instances of word painting to emerge. The assignment of dynamics will flow from the conductor's study of the piece; a monochromatic *mezzo forte* approach would not be artful.

Form and Structure

Measure	Event and Scoring
1–10	Homophonic *parlando* with plagal semi-cadences (e.g., mm. 4-5, breaks down gently at the word "dolore" beginning in m. 8); m. 2 (soprano line) contains a madrigal-style word-painted star, and the IV–I in mm. 4–5 is a gentle allusion to the sanctity of love; the C-sharp pitch in the alto (m. 9) is both a hard hexachordal inflection connoting pain and the leading tone (raised seventh scale degree) to the D major phrase end

Measure	Event and Scoring
11–20	*Parlando* (m. 11) is short-lived, as the words "fisso" and "loro" interrupt the strong downbeat, slowing the sense of motion in preparation for the next line of text; this line (mm. 15–20) picks up momentum in rising imitative motives from lament to ecstasy on a C major chord; a tutti rest punctuates
21–35	Monteverdi repeats the previous phrase *parlando* just long enough to create the sense of being on a level and then resumes the momentum of the previous poetic line through the phrase "ch'adoro," or "whom I adore," and another tutti rest (m. 25)—a sigh?—which places the lover on a high pedestal; immediately, the conditional phrase "si" ("if") begins in counterpoint, the two upper and three lower voices acting as separate choirs in dialogue
36–44	Both the beginning of this conditional phrase ("si") and the second half ("cosí," loosely "in the same way" or "so also") are stated in quarter notes; the second part (m. 37) proceeds with a written-out diminution to indicate action, in a pattern repeated in m. 39 over the word "vivi" ("living" or "animated") and imitated by the lower "choir" in mm. 41–44; this edition has a double barline and fermata at m. 44, surely editorial markings
45–60	This section consists of mm. 45–47, *parlando*, mm. 47 (anticipatory), and 48–56, which begins much as mm. 45–47 but advance the text through the word "pietosa," or "compassion," set in Renaissance fashion with counterpoint, repetition, hexachordal inflection, and one anticipatory voice; the final part of this section begins *parlando* in m. 57 and repeats the text a third time; climax of the work
60–74	"Come me fate amante" (loosely, "just as you made me love [her]") is the denouement after the cathartic climax; more reflective, contrapuntal, and peppered with one-voice musings on the final words of the poem

Text and Translation

Svogava con le stele un inferno d'amore	At the stars he was giving vent to an inferno of love
Sotto notturno ciel il suo dolore	To his ache under the night sky
E dice a fisso in loro:	And staring at them, he says:
O imagine belle de l'idol mio ch'adoro	"O beautiful images of my idol whom I adore,
Si com'a me mostrate	Just as you are showing me
Mentre cosí splendete la sua rara beltate	Her rare beauty while you sparkle so well,
Cosí mostrat'a lei	So also must you demonstrate to her
I vivi ardori miei	My living ardor
La fareste col vostr'aureo semblante	By your golden appearance
Pietosa si come fate amante.	Make her compassionate just as you make me loving."

Contributed by:

Lani Johnson

Teacher Resource Guide

Sing Ye Praises to Our King, Op. 20, No. 4

Aaron Copland

(1900–1990)

SATB a cappella
Boosey & Hawkes: OCTB 6021
Overall: 4
Vocal: 4
Tonal/Rhythm: 4

Composer

Aaron Copland was born to Jewish Lithuanian immigrants in Brooklyn on November 14, 1900. He began studying music early in his life and, at the age of twenty, moved to France, where he studied with Nadia Boulanger. When he returned, he chose to compose music with a distinctly American style, adopting jazz rhythms and harmonies as well as using folk tunes and hymns. He also composed the film scores for movie versions of the great American literary classics *Of Mice and Men* and *The Red Pony*.

Copland was blacklisted for communist activities during the McCarthy era. Later, he received many prestigious national honors, including the Presidential Medal of Freedom and a Kennedy Center Honor. A Congressional Gold Medal was awarded to Copland just a few years before his death at the end of 1990. Now his house is listed in the National Register of Historic Places and hosts an institute that provides support and education for young composers.

Copland's music ranges from large-scale ballets and symphonies to small motets. His best-known works are probably his ballets *Rodeo* and *Appalachian*

Spring, as well as *Fanfare for the Common Man* and *The Tenderland*, an opera commissioned by Rogers and Hammerstein for the thirtieth anniversary of the League of Composers. The opera takes place on a family farm in the Midwest and is the source of Copland's very popular choral pieces "The Promise of Living" and "Stomp Your Foot." He was an advocate for composers from the beginning of his career and by the end of his life was a highly influential scholar, author, and teacher.

Composition and Historical Perspective

Copland composed *Four Motets* during his study with Nadia Boulanger. They were performed several times in Europe but remained unpublished for forty years. Copland interprets the word "motet" roughly according to the Renaissance definition: a short, *a cappella*, sacred, choral piece. Though not written in imitative polyphony—in fact, most homophonic—each phrase has its own musical section in traditional point-by-point style. "Sing Ye Praises to Our King" is the fourth of the motets and contains shades of the American sound that would become Copland's signature, with open harmonies and contrary motion passing through dissonances as well as moments reminiscent of Methodist hymns and markings like "simple," which reflect a Quakerish aesthetic.

The texts are biblical in character, but there are no direct quotes from anywhere in the Bible. They appear to be Copland's own creation or interpretation of biblical language. What gives this away is the second motet, which is called "Thou, O Jehovah, Abideth Forever." The second person familiar conjugation of abide is abidest. Clearly, Copland is not precisely quoting the King James Bible but capturing its style.

Technical Considerations and Musical Elements

"Sing Ye Praises" has several elements that ease learning and make it singable by any four-part choir. The refrain repeats often enough that it represents almost half of the music—meaning less time spent learning pitches. The rhythms in cut time are simple and straightforward with only whole notes, half notes, quarter notes, and paired eighth notes. Only the coda contains a dotted quarter-eighth note pattern, so this would make an ideal piece for applying a rhythm-reading practice early in the year. Also, it stays strictly in four parts with no divisi. Finally, each line is almost strictly diatonic, so although sometimes Copland's music functions more modally than tonally, this piece presents a great opportunity to sing on solfeggio and/or to practice sight-reading. As with any piece, however, there are a few difficulties to consider.

Copland's marking "lively" leaves a lot of room for interpretation. This primarily affects tempo. While the exact tempo you take, as always, will depend upon the size of your choir, their skill level, the size and acoustic of your performance space, etc., half note = 69 is a good starting place: bright without sounding frantic. If your choir can go faster while keeping the sound seated, try half note= 72. A significantly faster tempo runs the risk of making the piece sound harried, even superficial.

Copland further notates his "lively" ideas through articulation. Whole sections have martellato markings over almost every note. Diction will be your best ally to achieve this and will also serve to keep the sound "lively." Crisp consonants and forward-placed vowels with just enough warmth to provide richness to the sound will keep it from getting weighed down, swallowed, and, as a result, sluggish. Maintaining the weight and separation of each note all the way through the sections that require this will be the most difficult task for the singers. To help them:

- Speak the text in a singing tone with exaggerated consonants.
- Sing the text on one pitch, focusing on separating notes and giving each one equal weight.
- Practice singing staccato on text and on the neutral syllables [di], [ni], [bi], and [mi].
- Use physical gestures like pointing down on each quarter note, bowing an imaginary violin, and painting short, separated strokes in the air with an imaginary brush.

While it is important to maintain the martellato articulation, it should not be done to the detriment of the line. Though each note is weighted and separated, they are not all equal. And not every phrase is equal. The texture of the piece grows and shrinks variously and so should the intensity of the line. To ensure that your choir does not sacrifice line for martellato, have them listen to the piano or one part of the choir singing or speaking while the rest of them moan or hiss the dynamic direction of the line. Do this one phrase at a time, and then have them all sing, applying that motion to their articulated singing.

There few difficulties with pitches because each section is basically diatonic. The one tricky transition is mm. 28 to 29. M. 28 is basically an E minor chord, leaping to a wide open B major chord. The problem is really that the measures leading up to that E minor chord are not definitively tonal but function modally. Rather than simply drilling the transition from one chord to the next, if you can make the choir hear the tonal function of the chord progression, it will actually be in tune every time.

Use solfeggio (or whatever ear training method the choir knows) to get the choir to settle their ears into they key of E minor in mm. 27 and 28. Now, the leap to B is just the dominant chord going into E major. Sing i–V–I chord progressions in warm-ups to get their ears used to the transition. Practice singing the noncompound version of each interval (sopranos go up a step instead of a ninth, altos up a third instead of a tenth).

Stylistic Considerations

Twentieth-century motets call for delicacy of tone and texture without sacrificing warmth or body in the tone. A light style of vocal production with the same earnest simplicity as Copland's writing will sound best.

Though the Mormon Tabernacle Choir has recorded it, "Sing Ye Praises" would ideally be performed by a smaller ensemble.

With these things in mind, this piece is ideal for an average to above-average level four-part high school choir of between twelve and forty voices.

Form and Structure

MEASURE	EVENT AND SCORING
1–4	Refrain in G major
5–10	Refrain with melismatic extension modulating into F major
11–14	Refrain ending in "Ruler" in G major
15–20	Refrain and coda
21–24	Modal STB soli verse ending in E minor
25–28	Modal SAB soli verse ending in E minor
29–32	Tutti verse in E major
33–40	Modal SAB soli verse
41–44	Tutti refrain in G (same as mm. 1–4)
45–51	Refrain with "all ye men" extension modulating into F major (parallels 5–10)
46–54	Tutti SB duet verse
55–58	Refrain ending in "Ruler"
59–65	Refrain and coda

Text

Sing ye praises, sing ye praises to our King.
O sing ye praises, sing ye praises to our King and Ruler.

Come and hear all ye men
Come and hear my praises
He doth bless all the earth
And bringeth peace and comfort.

Shout unto God all ye men.
Shout unto God all your praises.

He doth bless all the earth
And bringeth peace and comfort.

Sing ye praises, sing ye praises to our King.
O sing ye praises, sing ye praises to our King and Ruler.
Sing ye praises, sing ye praises to our King.

Additional References and Resources

Web site:
Copland House: www.coplandhouse.org (accessed February 1, 2006)

Suggested Listening

Aaron Copland:
"Sing Ye Praises" on *Barber Agnus Dei: An American Collection*, The Sixteen, Harry Christophers, Coro CD 7908.
"Sing Ye Praises" on *Copland: Old American Songs*, Mormon Tabernacle Choir, Keith Lockhart, Sony Masterworks CD 42140.

Contributed by:

Amelia Nagoski

Teacher Resource Guide

The Blue Bird

Charles Villiers Stanford

(1852–1924)

SSATB a cappella
Stainer & Bell: 664
Overall: 4
Vocal: 4
Tonal/Rhythm: 4

Composer

Charles Villiers Stanford is often associated with cathedral music due to his success in composing music for the Anglican service. His settings of the Magnificat and "Nunc dimittis" as well as his anthems and sacred motets are widely known. However, he was very prolific as a composer of secular music, including operas, symphonies, concertos, and partsongs. He was less isolated within Britain than so many of his predecessors; he studied composition in Leipzig under Carl Reinecke and was acquainted with Johannes Brahms, whose influence can be seen in much of his writing. Stanford held several prestigious posts, including professorships at the Royal College of Music and Cambridge, as well as a lengthy stint as conductor of the London Bach Choir. He is perhaps most appreciated for his influence on composers Charles Wood, Ralph Vaughan Williams, Gustav Holst, and Herbert Howells, to name a few.

Composition and Historical Perspective

Many English composers emulated the style of the madrigalists, but the part-song, unlike the madrigal, is usually harmonically conceived and is intended for a chorus of mixed as opposed to solo voices. Mendelssohn was highly influential in England, and the German counterpart to the glee club, known as the *Liedertafel*, flourished in Germany during the same time. Many of Mendelssohn's partsongs were translated into English and became extremely popular among British singing groups. As the genre developed, it became more "choral" in its textural treatment and was regarded more highly as a genre of musical substance.[1]

Technical Considerations and Musical Elements

Perhaps the most striking element of "The Blue Bird" is the sweet-sounding harmony, which serves as a tranquil and picturesque expression of the poetry. It is this same element that may pose the greatest challenge for the ensemble for two distinct reasons: 1) the close spacing of the parts, often with difficult harmonic intervals and 2) the range of the soprano, given the need for light, clear singing.

In order for the voice parts to sing in tune with each other, the chorus must always rehearse the pitches with the harmonic framework in mind. This is of particular importance in an *a cappella* partsong of this nature, as the altered harmonies and interval relationships can prove challenging. For example, in m. 10, there are two augmented fourths and one diminished seventh within the same chord. In sectional rehearsals, it is helpful to practice two sections at a time, instead of isolating each voice part as if it were an individual melody. If this does not work, a "choral play-and-sing" is an alternative method in which various parts are sounded on the piano against each section as they read and learn their part. Once each section is secure in singing their respective melodic intervals, staccato singing can then be very helpful as it forces the singers to align the notes accurately within the vertical harmony while preventing sliding, requiring them to pre-hear the notes and phonate each correctly.

The major second is a common harmonic interval in the work (the minor second appears occasionally), often moving to or from a major or minor third. This is seen repeatedly in the divisi alto parts. The whole step and half step movements needed for intervallic changes require careful listening; descending whole and half steps should be imagined as narrow while ascending ones should be imagined as wide. If the singers do not listen to each other carefully, these intervals can compromise the overall tuning of the ensemble, especially since each harmonic third in question usually defines the quality of the chord to which it belongs. Hearing the parts in relation to the overall harmony is particularly crucial here. It may be impractical at first to teach these intervals with other parts sounding, and it may be necessary to teach the alto part separately in sectionals at the beginning of the rehearsal process. However, doing so for a long period of time is not recommended, and the techniques described above should be used as soon as possible.

A further challenge in preparing the work is the slow tempo (*larghetto tranquillo*). The chorus must always be aware of the inner pulse underlying the slower overall pulse. Otherwise, the performance will lack energy, forward momentum, and direction in the phrasing. Subdividing at the eighth note for practice will help the singers develop the rhythmic energy needed to sustain the long note values. This can be done using a neutral syllable or a subdivided version of the text. If a neutral syllable is used, one that includes a lip vowel is best for this style (e.g., "doo" or "doh"). It is best to avoid tongue vowels, such as "ee," as this may produce a sound that is too bright, compromising the tone quality and tuning.

Despite Stanford's sensitive setting of the poetry, which lends itself to appropriate declamation, amateur chorus may still need coaching on the inflection and phrasing of the text. In the accompaniment, for example, there is an obvious ebb and flow between unstressed words and stressed ones (apparent in the rhythm) as the unstressed words are set to shorter note values than the stressed ones. This inflection is also evident in the harmony, wherein the shorter notes (the unstressed words) comprise chords that are in harmonic motion toward the longer notes, creating an anacrusis to words such as "lake," "blue," and "hill" in the first phrase. A very subtle *messa di voce* on each of the long notes may also bring more emphasis to the stressed words, generating forward momentum in the line.

Depending on the nature of the chorus, it may be helpful to assign the soprano part only to singers who possess a tone quality that is light and lyrical. In some cases, it may be a matter of assigning all of the sopranos who are capable of singing accurately and beautifully at a soft dynamic in the upper register, particularly in the range above the staff. This may be a group of three to five singers, the entire first soprano section, or, if the chorus is relatively small, a solo voice. All remaining sopranos could easily be assigned to first alto as this part lies in a comfortable range for them. Whether this is possible will, of course, depend upon the size, skill, and makeup of the group. In any case, the voicing of the ensemble is key to producing a beautiful and pleasing performance.

Stylistic Considerations

This music is intended for the enjoyment of the singers and listeners. Since partsongs are usually performed in intimate settings, there are no prescribed artistic guidelines to be followed beyond the obvious ones of good, healthy vocal production and sensitive expression of the text. It is certainly different in style from English sacred music, where one would likely find an all-male choir and cathedral acoustics. The partsong need not imitate any particular historical setting. Rather, it should reflect the sound and personality of the chorus by which it is currently being performed.

Form and Structure

The work is in strophic form, containing only two stanzas, each set with similar musical material. At the end, the first four measures of the piece are repeated, serving as a brief coda.

Text

The lake lay blue below the hill.
O'er it, as I looked, there flew
Across the waters, cold and still,
A bird whose wings were palest blue.

The sky above was blue at last.
The sky beneath me blue in blue.
A moment, ere the bird had passed,
It caught his image as he flew.
—Mary Coleridge

Additional References and Resources

Dibble, Jeremy. *Charles Villiers Stanford: Man and Musician*. New York: Oxford University Press, 2002.

Hillier, Paul, ed. Introduction to *English Romantic Partsongs*. Oxford and New York: Oxford University Press, 1986.

Suggested Listening

Charles Villiers Stanford:

"The Blue Bird" on *A Portrait of the Cambridge Singers*, The Cambridge Singers, John Rutter, Collegium CSCD 500.

"The Blue Bird" on *Chanticleer on the Air Live: Radio Highlights*, Chanticleer, Chanticleer Records CR 8807.

"The Blue Bird" on *English Madrigals and Songs*, Oxford Camerata, Jeremy Summerly, Naxos 8.553088.

Contributed by:

Russell Nelson

1 Paul Hiller, ed. Introduction to *English Romantic Partsongs*. (Oxford and New York: Oxford University Press, 1986).

Teacher Resource Guide

Three Whitman Settings

René Clausen

(b. 1953)

SATB
Shawnee Press
Overall: 4
Vocal: 4
Tonal/Rhythm: 4

Composer

René Clausen's compositional style seems to fall into two general categories: works appropriate for high school and church choirs and those more appropriate for college and professional choirs. He is a lifelong choral musician, and his knowledge has led to his wide success as a composer of choral music. Clausen's conducting experience with ensembles of all age levels contributes to his ability to compose successfully for such a broad and diverse choral audience. He has been the conductor of the renowned Concordia Choir in Moorhead, Minnesota, since 1986 and was the recipient of American Choral Directors Association Raymond Brock composition commission in 2003.

All of René Clausen's choral compositions and arrangements are published exclusively through Mark Foster Music Company (a division of Shawnee Press) in The René Clausen Choral Series.

Composition and Historical Perspective

René Clausen's *Three Whitman Settings* can be best categorized as a twentieth-century secular choral micro-form. It has similarities to the madrigal in its careful attention to the text and artful word painting. The texture varies as *Three*

Whitman Settings combines homophonic and imitative writing as dictated by the text. This set of pieces is among Clausen's earlier published works. It was commissioned by the Mu Xi Chapter of Phi Mu Alpha for the Stephen F. Austin State University *a cappella* choir.

Technical Considerations and Musical Elements

Soloist

Clausen uses two soloists in these pieces: alto and baritone. The alto solo will require a singer with an exceptionally good ear and the ability to sing wide leaps with confidence. This singer will need to be rhythmically independent, and the director and soloist will need to work together for a musical performance. The nature of this solo may be difficult for high school singers to perform musically, so it will fall to the director to make important decisions regarding phrasing and text accent.

The baritone solo in "Quicksand Years" will require a singer with a good ear. The solo is firmly in the baritone range and with some attention should be manageable by a good high school musician.

Extended Range

As is typical of many Clausen compositions, the range demands on the ensemble's outer voices (high soprano and low bass) are serious concern. In both the first and third movements the soprano section (or a small group) is asked to sing a high C without vibrato while they *decrescendo* to *piano*. This is an extremely difficult task for certain voice types while others voice types can do it comfortably. The director should find singers (including those in the alto section) to find voices that can comfortably negotiate this task. Although it seems improbable to find this voice type in the alto section, I have on a number of occasions. If an ensemble director does not find this specific voice type in the ensemble, these pieces should wait. Another common range issue among Clausen compositions is the very low bass 2 part. The ensemble will need a solid low D for the final chord. The low bass section will need at least three singers who can sing a low D for the final chord to balance.

Texture

These pieces will challenge your ensemble with its thick texture. The good news is that it is not in eight parts throughout, and if the director plans rehearsals carefully the difficult sections can be performed well. Sectionals will ensure that each group of singers works on the music that they find most difficult. This will maximize rehearsal time while giving your best students an opportunity to take ownership and to lead in the ensemble. Each of the eight sections will need several good musicians with leadership qualities to perform the eight-part music effectively.

When establishing a rehearsal plan for these pieces, I recommend rehearsing the four-part music together before breaking into sectionals so that students can get a feel for each of the movements. This will help the sectional leaders to lead more effectively.

Ensemble Flexibility

"Quicksand Years" presents a very specific ensemble problem. All of the singers need to work on vocal flexibility. Once the conductor has decided to program this piece, flexibility exercises should become part of the daily warm-up and voice building process. Some voices have more trouble with flexibility than others, so it may be necessary to provide several different vocal warm-ups for all of the students to improve.

If the conductor finds that singers are still not able effectively sing this movement after working extensively on the vocal exercises he or she may want to try selecting several students in each section to put a light "n" before each of the sixteenth notes. This approach was used by Robert Shaw in dealing with the long melismas in Baroque music. You will have to experiment with how many singers to add to each section. It will make a dramatic difference in clarity; however, you want to make sure that the audience does not perceive the "n," so only a few singers in each section are necessary.

Frequently Changing Meter

The conductor will need to be aware of the frequently changing meter in the first movement. The meter is dictated by the nature of the text and music, so it may take concentration and practice for the inexperienced conductor to clearly negotiate through this music. The conductor should completely ingest this music so that he or she becomes "ear driven" and not eye driven. It will be necessary to conduct in front of a mirror while audiating the choral parts, until the director can clearly conduct this section from memory. Once the music is in the conductor's ear, it will become more manageable.

Soloist and Ensemble Exchange

In both the first and second movement, the conductor must bring the choir in after a non-metered solo. If conducted poorly it can be confusing for the ensemble and will create an "oh-darn solo." There are a few rehearsal strategies I recommend for m. 1 in the first movement:

- Coach the soloist to sing without any assistance from you.
- Stand at the ready position.
- Give offbeat preparation, and breathe on what would be the last quarter note of the measure. The soloist should be coached to sing the final eighth note in time. It is essential that you establish your tempo with the nature of the beat and your breath. The altos must know the tempo to establish their sixteenth notes in the next measure.

- If you have trouble, you may need to practice with your ensemble to ensure a clean entrance.

STYLISTIC CONSIDERATIONS
This music requires careful balance between full, colorful singing and moments of pristine intonation with minimal (if not eliminated) vibrato. Ensembles will need to use multiple tone colors. A creative director could envision and implement the tone colors as they relate to the poetry.

The *forte* section of "Quicksand Years" will require the soloist's full, rich, most mature tone color. However, the precision of the sixteenth notes in the opening of the first movement and intricate tonal/modal implications throughout the third movement will require care and restraint from the singers. In general, the tone of this work should be characterized as rich, full, and mature, capturing the depth and warmth of these descriptive texts. The composer successfully paints imagery with the music, and it is the choir's obligation to the composer to enliven text through the music. Work for creativity in word painting. Experiment with different colors, and discuss these texts with your singers. When time allows, I am often impressed with students' ability to think through poetry, and I welcome their suggestions on how to make the ensemble sound more reflective of the composer's and poet's wishes.

Form and Structure

SECTION	MEASURE	EVENT AND SCORING
Movement I: "A Noiseless Patient Spider"	1–48	A minor to F-sharp major
A	1–16	[10 (4 + 4 + 2) + 6 + 2]
B	17–32	(8 + 8)
C	33–48	[8 (4 + 4) + 6 + 2]
Movement II: "Quicksand Years"		
	1–56	F-sharp minor to G major
A	1–27	Fugue
B	28–36	Homophonic; (7 + 1)
A´	37–56	Fugue
Movement III: "The Last Invocation"		
	1–46	B major to D major
A	1–16	(2 + 7 + 5 + 2)
B	16–35	(7 + 8 + 6 + 5)
C	36–46	(4 + 4 + 3)

Text

Walt Whitman (1819–1892), arguably America's most influential and innovative poet, was born into a working class family in West Hills, New York, a village near Hempstead, Long Island, May 31, 1819. He was among the first generation of Americans who were born in the newly formed United States. Whitman's father was a stern and sometimes hot-tempered man whom Whitman respected but for whom he never felt a great deal of affection. His mother, on the other hand, served throughout his life as his emotional touchstone. There was a special bond between Whitman and his mother, and the long correspondence between them records a kind of partnership in attempting to deal with the family crises that mounted over the years.

Additional References and Resources

René Clausen: www.reneclausen.com/index.html
The Walt Whitman Archive: www.whitmanarchive.org

Suggested Listening

The Choral Music of René Clausen, René Clausen, conductor, Concordia Recordings.

Contributed by:

Brandon Johnson

Teacher Resource Guide

Vorspruch from Mörike-Chorliederbuch, Op. 19

Hugo Distler
(1908–1942)

SATBB a cappella
Bärenreiter Verlag: BA 1519
Overall: 4
Vocal: 3
Tonal/Rhythm: 4

Composer

Hugo Distler was born in Nuremberg June 24, 1908. This German composer and organist was the illegitimate son of a manufacturer and a dressmaker. During his school years he learned to play the piano and had instruction in music history and theory. Distler began his studies at the Leipzig Conservatory in the conducting class with piano as his secondary subject; however, after a short time Hermann Grabner advised him to abandon these courses to take up composition and the organ.

Friendships that were to last throughout his life quickly developed between Distler and his teachers Grabner and Günther Ramin. His studies with Grabner, in particular, grew into fruitful discussion, with the teacher learning from the pupil. Furthermore, Friedrich Högner, who taught liturgical organ playing at the conservatory starting in 1929, exercised great influence on Distler. In this way he had contact with two of the leading figures in the *Orgelbewegung*, a movement directed to a return to the organ sound of the Baroque and pre-Baroque.

Grabner's instruction stemmed from Riemann's counterpoint teaching and so from the Protestant chorale; the religious and sensitive Distler avidly assimilated these various influences and rapidly developed them. Performances by the Thomanerchor under Karl Straube made him thoroughly familiar with new works and with the music of the sixteenth and seventeenth centuries. The Leipzig Bach tradition spurred him to study the work of the former Kantor. Heinrich Schütz's music stimulated and influenced Distler greatly as well.

Distler's first two works were published during his student days, but his most fruitful years began only after he became organist of the Jakobikirche, Lübeck, where he produced a quantity of vocal music, particularly in collaboration with Bruno Grusnick and his Lübecker Sing und Spielkreis. It was at this time, when he directed a children's choir and also the choristers of the Jakobikirche, that he composed most of his sacred works.

There was much hope that Protestant church music in Germany would be given more prominence once the National Socialists came to power. Distler, therefore, joined the NSDAP in 1933, together with many others; he could not have foreseen that his hopes would be unfulfilled and that party officials would make his future professional life uneasy. (He refrained from composing party-affirmative pieces or songs for official purposes.) In October 1933 Distler was appointed head of the chamber music department at the Lübeck Conservatory, and at about the same time he began teaching at the Church Music School in Spandau, Berlin. The motets of the *Geistliche Chormusik*, modelled on Schütz, are particularly profound works of the period; the *Totentanz* from this collection is the most notable expression of Distler's individual style. The year 1935 was taken up with the restoration of the Jakobikirche's organs since Distler himself controlled the collection of funds and the work, and when it was completed he published a book about the organs. Difficulties arose in increasing measure as a result of the hostility of the Nazis to church music and those who acknowledged the Church. Despite his honorable appointment to the Staatliche Hochschule für Musikerziehung und Kirchenmusik in Charlottenburg, Berlin, Distler decided in April 1937 to move to Stuttgart to teach at the Württemberg Hochschule für Musik.

In Stuttgart Distler had at first to counter state antagonism, which was resisted through the solidarity of the professors at the Hochschule. Gradually his duties increased; he assumed the direction of the Esslingen Singakademie and then began work with the Stuttgart Hochschule choir. At the same time, government pressures grew, and only the intervention of Gerhard Maasz was able to avert the denunciation of Distler's work as "degenerate art" at the music festival in Düsseldorf in 1938. His career kept advancing through the end of his life because of triumphs, such as the festival of German Choral Music in Graz in 1939. He became disillusioned when he became conscious of the implications that Nazi guiding principles and practices had on his personal agenda. Hugo

Distler committed suicide in Berlin on November 1, 1942, probably because he realized that he could not serve God and the Nazis at the same time.

Composition and Historical Perspective

Distler achieved his greatest public success when the Stuttgart Hochschule choir premiered sections from the *Mörike-Chorliederbuch* at the festival of German Choral Music in Graz in 1939; the event was regarded as the climax of the festival, but the dissemination of the work took place only after the war. Distler's *Mörike-Chorliederbuch* is now recognized as the most important German secular *a cappella* collection of the twentieth century.

Distler's work rediscovered of old forms and genres, and his highly effective word-painting evolved from the music of Schütz without imitating it. Distler's vocal music goes beyond its models in rhythmic and harmonic freedom, creating an individual style spread by choirs in Germany and abroad during the years after World War II, which in turn stimulated further creative work. The organ pieces are similarly new in principle; something of their originality came from Distler's work with Baroque organs, primarily in north Germany. In both vocal and organ works the distinctive features of Distler's style are the rhythms, which are derived from word stress precisely calculated to enhance the poetic content and its harmonic boldness within a tonal setting.

Technical Considerations and Musical Elements

Distler mostly employs uncomplicated tonal vocabulary in each voice, making part learning rather effortless. There are some challenging intervals, but most of the voice leading adheres to the commonly accepted practices of tonal music. The composer frequently shifts the tonality by chromatically altering a single voice while using straightforward harmonic language in all other voice parts. When Distler introduces the chromaticism, he approaches it almost exclusively by step, by triadic leap, or by descending fifth or ascending fourth. The singers would probably experience more rapid success with the piece if they rehearsed in sectionals to attain mastery of the part before engaging in full choral rehearsals. To a choir of moderate skill, the sudden tonal shifts may sound jarring in the first few rehearsals; however, once the novelty wears off, the piece will offer great rewards in performance.

The meter signatures offer minimal to no help in interpretation, although they may be helpful guides for initial pitch learning. When the text enters the process of interpretation the measure lines become a hindrance. The 3/8 sections derive their rhythmic contents from accurate declamation of word stress, and they actually employ hemiola most of the time to accommodate the poetic structure. The rhythm may appear daunting at first, but the singers will benefit tremendously after marking the stressed syllables, then marking the hemiola figures, and finally slowly speaking the poetry in rhythm.

Even a choir of moderate skill should be able to negotiate this piece with little difficulty provided that the conductor plans the rehearsal sequence carefully. Distler's setting opens the door to twentieth century music in a rather gentle manner.

Stylistic Considerations

Since Distler studied early music in general and the music by Schütz specifically, his music focuses on the declamation of the text; therefore, performers must accurately and precisely observe the stress structure of the poetry. Naturally, this applies to most western art music, but, as described above, the meter signatures in this piece often conflict with the text declamation. Do not be a slave to the measure line because it will ruin this work.

Performers should minimize vibrato to make tuning easier. Singers should not have to sing completely void of vibrato, but vibratos may have to be matched closely among the singers to facilitate tuning. By lessening the impact of natural oscillations in the voices, the frequent tonal shifts will become easier to hear and negotiate as well.

Form and Structure

Distler's music exhibits influences from several different styles and periods, but this piece employs a simple binary reprise form. The two A sections use the same music but present different lines of text. The B sections repeat verbatim and function as a refrain.

SECTION	MEASURE	EVENT AND SCORING
A		
	1–4	One phrase
	5–8	One phrase
	9–15	One phrase
	16–18	One phrase
B		
	19–23	One phrase
	23–38	Thirteen antiphonal statements
	38–42	Two phrases overlapping
	42–51	One phrase
A		Different text
	52–55	One phrase
	56–59	One phrase
	60–66	One phrase
	67–69	One phrase (*D.S. al fine*)
B		*Segno*
	19–23	One phrase

Section	Measure	Event and Scoring
	23–38	Thirteen antiphonal statements
	38–42	Two phrases overlapping
	42–51	One phrase (*fine*)

Text and Translation

Wer sich die Musik erkiest,	He who chooses music
Hat ein himmlisch Gut bekommen,	Has received a divine good,
Denn ihr erster Ursprung ist	For its ultimate origin is
Von dem Himmel selbst genommen,	Taken from Heaven itself
Weil die Engel insgemein	Because the angels are usually
Selbsten Musikanten sein.	Musicians themselves.
Wenn einst in der letzten Zeit	If someday on the Day of Judgment
Alle Ding' wie Rauch vergehen,	Everything vanishes like smoke,
Bleibet in der Ewigkeit	In eternity there will remain
Doch die Musik noch bestehen,	Music, which will persist,
Weil die Engel insgemein	Because the angels are usually
Selbsten Musikanten sein.	Musicians themselves.

Additional References and Resources

Lemmermann, Dirk. *Studien zum weltlichen Vokalwerk Hugo Distlers: Analytische, ästhetische und rezeptionsgeschichtliche Untersuchungen unter besonderer Berücksichtigung . . . studies. Series XXXVI, Musicology.* Frankfurt: Peter Lang, 1996.

Sievers, Angela. *Der Kompositionsstil Hugo Distlers dargestellt an Beispielen aus dem Mörike-Chorliederbuch.* Wiesbaden: Breitkopf & Härtel, 1989.

Suggested Listening

Mörike-Chorliederbuch, Op. 19, Berliner Vokalensembel, Musicaphon 56820.
Mörike-Chorliederbuch Vol. 1, Harald Nickoll, conductor, EBS 6074.

Contributed by:

G. Mikael Lindström

Teacher Resource Guide

Las Amarillas

Stephen Hatfield
(b. 1956)

SSA
Boosey & Hawkes: 48004535
Overall: 4
Vocal: 3
Tonal/Rhythm: 5

Composer

Canadian-born composer Stephen Hatfield has been a significant contributor to world music repertoire. A high school teacher, Hatfield started composing choral works to stretch a limited budget, aiming to meet the needs of singers with and without musical training. He has composed multicultural choral music for treble, men's, and mixed choirs in both sacred and secular genres. In addition, Hatfield composes for theater and is an active clinician.

Composition and Historical Perspective

Stephen Hatfield has been influenced directly or indirectly by musical cultures throughout the world. Hatfield aims to incorporate the emotional, spiritual, and tribal experiences in his compositions, relating them to their communal practices. This is evident in "Las Amarillas," where he uses the Mexican rhythm *huapango,* which is linked to the folk tradition of the east coast of Mexico and consists of alternating rhythmic patterns, and mixing duple and triple meters. The word *huapango* has two interpretations: "dance on a wooden stage" and "Panuco River," a river that goes through that region. The *huapango* rhythm contains features of *fandango Español* and is danced by men and women as a couple. *Huapango* is a traditional dance with lyric texts typically sung by two singers who alternate and frequently use falsetto. Originally, it was accompanied by two violins, harp, and an assortment of different guitars.

The poem used has references to nature. However, more than the meaning of words, the beauty of the text lies in their rhyming, which makes music itself.

Technical Considerations and Musical Elements

Rhythmic elements of world music strongly influence Hatfield's composition. He values the traditional musical style as a source of inspiration, motivation for the singers, and a means to strengthen musicianship. The significant challenge in this piece is its rhythmic complexity.

Start by teaching just the rhythm. A helpful way to deal with these rhythmic complexities is to introduce first those sections that have unified rhythm throughout the choir (homophonic sections) and those that repeat later in the piece. For example, begin teaching mm. 41–44 and then go to their repetition in m. 60 to the end. Go back to m. 45 and teach each voice (except the altos because that part changes slightly) the first couple of measures. They will then know the whole section from mm. 45–51 since it repeats if you point out the small changes toward the end of the section.

The section that follows (mm. 51–58) has all voices in unified rhythm, which can be quite easily learned. Once you achieve this, you have essentially taught mm. 41 to the end of the piece. The conductor will find that after teaching this section, learning all other rhythms is easier since mm. 41 to the end contain all the rhythmic figures used in the piece. Always encourage rhythmic precision during the learning process, especially in pieces like this where rhythm is the main concern. Once the choir has internalized the rhythm, introduce the text. A difficulty and challenge the choir might encounter while performing this piece might be the Spanish text once it is sung in rhythm and in tempo. Spanish has the five Latin vowels:

1. "a" as in "father"
2. "e" as in "day"—Be careful not to glide it as you do in English.
3. "i" as in the "y" in city
4. "o" as in yellow—Be careful not to glide it.
5. "u" as in food

Some of the vowels are accented (e.g., "á") and Hatfield generally helps with good text underlay. The word "Árboles" (m. 21) and the word "pero" (m. 48) leap up toward the syllable that should not be accented. The singers will be tempted to accent the highest pitch, so make sure they understand where the accent goes. Some consonants also have tricky features:

1. The "l" should not be as heavy and toward the back as in English; it is much more dentalized, bright, and forward.
2. The "ll" has several pronunciations throughout Spanish-speaking countries; it could either be as in the word "million" or as a "y."
3. The "r" is flipped; pronounce it as double "t" in "Betty."
4. The "rr" is always rolled.
5. The "j" is pronounced as an "h" ("hungry")
6. The "g", if it is in the middle of the word ("alegres"), is pronounced as in "sugar."
7. The "qu" is pronounced "k."
8. If "c" precedes "i" or "e," pronounce it as "s" ("pareces"). If it is in the middle of the word, as in "cinco," or followed by a "u" as in "cuatro," pronounce it as "k."
9. The "ch"is lighter than in English; never "sh."
10. The "h" is always silent.
11. The "t" is not exploded as in English and always dentalized; pronounce it with the tip of your tongue against the back of your upper teeth.

Another challenge in singing in Spanish is how some words or syllables glide from one to another. "Calandrias" (m. 14) "no han" (m. 22), "apachurra el" (m. 24), "chiquita y" (m. 29), "y asi" (m. 30), "como eres" (m. 30), and "como esta" (m. 48) are elided. Do not break them into two syllables and make sure they actually move smoothly. Isolate them, demonstrate them in rhythm, and ask the choir to repeat.

Once the conductor feels comfortable with the Spanish, he or she should introduce it to the choir and teach it with the rhythm. Teaching it away from its context will not have the same result. Unify their vowels and consonants and their rhythmic precision by asking the choir to sing staccato. When rhythm and text are accurate, introduce pitch. It is uncomplicated, full of repetitions (some ostinatos from the Treble III) and is in a comfortable vocal range. There is a portion of unison in Treble I and II. Be very careful with the subtle tempo markings like those in mm. 51, 55, and 59. They might be slightly different, but one is faster than the other. Ask the choir to gradually increase the tempo without getting heavy and careless with diction and rhythm.

The last thing to introduce is the body percussion. The choir needs to feel comfortable with pitch, text, and rhythm before adding anything else. Each part has melodic and rhythmic interest. The aim is to allow the singers to identify strongly with the parts and understand their relationship to the whole.

Stylistic Considerations

Hatfield's music provides the conductor with a lot of information. The metronome markings, body percussion instructions, articulation, and dynamics are very specific and should be followed as closely as possible. In the preface of "Las Amarillas," Hatfield points out the importance of the placement of the dotted quarter notes, which repeatedly falls to the Treble III. Since the Treble III part creates the *huapango* style, pay close attention to their tone and color and the relationship between their ostinato and the mixed meter. Follow the composer's indications on how the body percussion should be implemented closely; he is very specific. The rhythmic elements have to be precise and tight, but do not forget that this is a dance!-

Form and Structure

"Las Amarillas" is through-composed. However, the piece can be organized according to musical ideas and text as follows:

Measure	Event and Scoring
1–13	(4 + 4 + 5); introductory material
13–21	(2 + 4 + 2); lines one through four of the poem
21–29	(2 + 4 + 2); lines five and six
29–45	(2 + 4 + 2 + 3 + 5); lines 7 and 8; material from mm. 41–45; nonsense syllables ("na–na na–no") will appear at the end of the piece
45–51	(2 + 4); lines one and nine
51–59	(4 + 4); line ten
59–69	(4 + 6); nonsense syllables; extended material from mm. 41–45

Text and Translation

Volaron las amarillas calandrias de los nopales.	The yellow calandras fly form the cactus.
Ya no cantaran alegres los pájaros cardenales.	No longer will the cardinals sing happily,
A la tirana na na,	To the song na na,
A la tirana na no.	To the song na no.
Árboles de la ladera porque no han reverdecido	Because the trees on the hillside have not come back to life
Por eso calandrias cantan o las apachurra el nido.	For that the calandra will either sing or crush their nests.

A la tirana na na . . .	To the song na na . . .
Eres chiquita y bonita y así como eres te quiero	You are small and beautiful and I love you just the way you are
Pareces una rosita de las costas de Guerrero.	You are like a little rose from the coast of Guerrero.
A la tirana na na . . .	To the song na na . . .
Todos dan su despedida pero como esta ninguna	Everybody has their own farewell, but there's none like this one
Cuatro por cinco son veinte, tres por siete son veinte-uno.	Four times five is twenty, three times seven is twenty-one.
Na na na . . .	Na na na . . .

Additional References and Resources

Wall, Joan, et. al. *Diction for Singers: A Concise Reference for English, Italian, Latin, German, French, and Spanish Pronunciation.* Dallas: Pst...Inc., 1973.

Web sites:

David Rojas, "El Huapango...Sones Huastecos" www.folklorico.com (accessed September 1, 2005)

Stephen Hatfield: www.stephenhatfield.com (accessed September 1, 2005)

Contributed by:

Marcela Molina

Teacher Resource Guide

O aula nobilis

William Mathias
(1934–1992)

SSA with organ and brass
Oxford University Press: W 105
Overall: 4
Vocal: 3
Tonal/Rhythm: 4

Composer

Composer, conductor, and pianist William Mathias was born in 1934 in Whitland, Dyfed, Wales. He earned a BMus degree from the University College of Wales, Aberystwyth, in 1956. From 1959 to 1968 he acted as lecturer at the University College of North Wales, Bangor. He earned a DMus from the University of Wales in 1966. After a one-year appointment at Edinburgh University, Scotland, Mathias was named professor and head of the Music Department of the University College of North Wales, Bangor, in 1969. He remained in this position until he retired in 1987. In 1987 Mathias was awarded an honorary DMus from Westminster Choir College in Princeton, New Jersey. He died in 1992 at Menai Bridge, Anglesey, Wales.

As a house composer for Oxford University Press from 1961 to his death, Mathias's compositional output encompassed a wide variety of genres, including church music, four symphonies (one unfinished), several one-movement orchestral scenes, one opera, large scale choral-orchestral works, chamber music, and extensive repertoire for organ. "O aula nobilis" was commissioned by Westonbirt School to celebrate the opening of the Orangery by the prince and princess of Wales June 19, 1985.

Composition and Historical Context

The history of the secular motet is often overshadowed by its higher profile twin, the sacred motet. However, there is certainly precedence for Latin settings of secular texts. This practice is almost as old as the genre itself. Oftentimes these additional texts were on secular topics such as courtly love in a vernacular language or Latin.

The practice continued in diminished capacity through the Renaissance and early Baroque Periods with significant contributions by Orlando di Lasso and Jean-Baptiste Lully. Perhaps the most visible text sources in this genre are the collection of texts from *Carmina Burana* and *Catulli Carmina*. Perhaps this work's strongest tie to music history is the Latin motet celebrating student life and scholarship, "Gaudeamus igitur," whose multiple incarnations throughout the centuries has made it a classic.

Technical Considerations

In your preparation of this work, two areas that might present challenges are ensemble and balance. In terms of ensemble, clear conducting is key; providing cues and a clear ictus far outweigh phrase shaping. Also, it is important for the chorus to be vigilant in keeping a subdivided inner pulse present at all times to maintain tempo.

Mathias scores the piece relatively thinly scored, however, when the chorus is singing above the entire group (m. 74 to the end) balance issues may arise. There are two obvious solutions to this problem; have the choir sing louder or have the orchestra play softer. I would like to address the first solution from a vocal production perspective. First of all, the idea of "singing louder" is fraught with potential technical pitfalls for a young singer. Upon hearing this advice, a young singer with no professional guidance may push the sound from the throat. I prefer to word the advice differently, suggesting resonance above volume as a technique to be heard over the orchestra. There are several vocal warm-ups that will help your singers discover the bright, forward placement required:

1. Try any exercise using a bright [i] vowel. I prefer a simple ascending and descending five-note scale for this. Encourage modification to the German mixed vowel [y] in the *passagio*.
2. Once placement is established on the [i]/[y] vowel, expand to [e]/[oe] and then to other vowels as necessary.
3. The most difficult vowels for forward placement are [a], [I], and [E]. To help with these, I suggest using an exercise mixing easy and difficult vowels. Again, on a simple five-note scale, alternate [i] and [a] or other vowel combinations, bringing the resonance of the [i] vowel to the [a].

Lastly, I would recommend an exaggerated use of air for consonant production as well as absolute rhythmic precision of cutoffs and entrances to amplify the text.

Musical Elements

Melody

This work is based on a handful of motivic ideas that recur and develop throughout. These motivic cells are often harmonically conceived and based on text stress (e.g., pitch change on stressed syllable "no" of the "O aula nobilis" phrase). They resemble trumpet fanfare figures (rhythmic variation over a pedal tone followed by related scalar and/or arpeggiated pitch material.)

The melody is derived from material initially presented in the instrumental exposition. Instrumental exposition sections one and three (please refer to description of formal elements below for more structural information) are built on a motive of a pedal pitch varied with stepwise motion away and back, supporting a modal scalar figure. Section two is a variation on this with new sixteenth note rhythmic figurations.

Choral sections one and three are built on a motive of one pedal pitch with single stepwise motion away and back and based on material in the instrumental exposition (section one). Choral section two is a variation on this, and in addition includes a small section of fugue with stepwise pitch material and sixteenth note figurations derived from instrumental exposition in section two. The coda material is dominated by an arpeggiated trumpet figure derived from the pitch material in the opening.

Harmony

Large-scale harmonic motion traces the following key areas, G major, E major, E-flat major, and A-flat major (not in instrumental exposition). The song ends where it began, in G major. The harmonic motion highlights minor second relationships and, to a lesser degree, minor third and perfect fifth relationships (I–VI–flattedVI–flattedII–I).

On a more local phrase level, harmonic motion appears to be static with variation to accommodate the text. At formal pillars (e.g., the entrance of the choir in m. 24 and fugal entrances in m. 48), Mathias inserts diatonic dominant into the tonic harmonic language.

Rhythm

The rhythmic material in this work is vital and strong, recreating the sound of a Renaissance trumpet fanfare. There are several recurring rhythmic motives one might highlight in performances, including the dotted eighth-sixteenth figure first presented in m. 2 and the two sixteenths-eighth figure in m. 16. In the choral parts, I recommend the placement of tied eighth note cutoffs on the downbeat of the measure (e.g., in m. 27).

TEXTURE/ORCHESTRATION

This work is predominantly homophonic, with one small section of polyphony in mm. 48–55. It is scored for SSAA chorus, three trumpets in C, two pianos, timpani, side drum, cymbals, tambourine, and glockenspiel or chime bars. Although use of the full orchestral complement would be ideal, it may be possible to thoughtfully reduce this orchestration to what your program can support without compromising the work.

Form and Structure

This work is in a double ternary form. The key center migrates from G and back twice, once in the instrumental opening and again in the choral-orchestral body.

SECTION	MEASURE	EVENT AND SCORING
Instrumental Exposition		
	1–6	G modal; the mode of these sections resembles both the Lydian and Mixolydian church modes (a major scale with a raised fourth scale degree and a lowered seventh scale degree); instrumental introduction, melodic material A
	7–12	G modal to E modal; repeat of melodic material A with modulation
	13–18	E-flat modal; melodic material B
	19–24	G modal; recapitulation of melodic material A
Choral Section One		
	25–33	G major; first choral entrance, melodic material C, two times through the first foot of the poem
	34–41	E major; second choral entrance, melodic material D, two times through the second foot of the poem
Choral Section Two		
	42–47	E-flat major; third choral entrance, melodic material E, two times through the third foot of the poem
	48–57	A-flat major; fourth choral entrance, melodic material F, imitative entrances, three times through the fourth foot of the poem plus a fragment tag

SECTION	MEASURE	EVENT AND SCORING
Choral Section Three		
	58–70	G major; fifth choral entrance, full orchestral entrance, recapitulation of melodic material A in orchestra and C in chorus, one repetition of text from first foot of poem, then one time through foot five
	71–81	G major; sixth choral entrance, repetition of melodic material A in the orchestra, repetitive coda material in chorus, one time through complete text, then several repetitions of a phrase fragment
	82–84	G major; coda, spoken "vivat!" text and orchestral hit to conclude

Text and Translation

This is a ninth-century Pilgrim poem:

O *aula nobilis ludi et gloria,*	O noble hall and pride of the school,
Cunctarum aularum excellentissima,	Of all the halls the most outstanding,
Arte multorum hominum decora,	Adorned by the skills of many men,
Hodie cantibus virginum resona;	Echoing this day with the songs of young girls;
Salutem dicimus tibi per omnia,	We wish you well, we praise you:
Te benedicimus—salve per saecula!	Prosper from generation to generation!

Suggested Listening

There are no professional recordings of this work, however, there are several collegiate and high school performances of this piece available for purchase over the Internet, including:

Wartburg College—St. Elizabeth Chorale: www.wartburg.edu/steliz/01.html
Oriana Singers: www.clubs.psu.edu/up/orianasingers/triumphs.htm

Contributed by:

Emilie Sweet

Teacher Resource Guide

Salut au chevalier printemps, Op. 151, No. 2

Camille Saint-Saëns

(1835–1921)

SSA with piano
Roger Dean Publishing Company: 15/1649R
Overall: 4
Vocal: 4
Tonal/Rhythm: 3

Composer

With the encouragement of his mother and aunt (his father died when he was three months old), Camille Saint-Saëns began piano lessons at age three. His public debut occurred at the famous Salle Pleyel in Paris when he was only ten years old. In 1848 Saint-Saëns entered the Paris Conservatoire to study organ, singing, and composition. Later Saint-Saëns held appointments at the Church of the Madeleine as an organist and at École Niedermeyer as a professor, where he instructed the young composer Gabriel Fauré. Through out his career Saint-Saëns also wrote a great deal of commentary on contemporary music and composers. Well-traveled, Saint-Saëns made repeated trips to England, Russia, Italy, Egypt, Algeria, and the United States throughout his lifetime.

Saint-Saëns admired Richard Wagner, Robert Schumann, Franz Liszt, J. S. Bach, and W. A. Mozart and used their music as examples in his own compositions. His extensive travels also inspired him as a composer. Thus, Saint-Saëns created an eclectic compositional style, incorporating Classical Viennese, Romantic, and non-Western influences. He maintained musical characteristics important to the French by emphasizing form, balance, and clarity. Saint-Saëns composed in all nineteenth-century genres, and his works include symphonies, oratorios, motets, chamber works, and piano music.

Composition and Historical Perspective

Saint-Saëns composed many secular and sacred pieces for women's chorus, men's chorus, and mixed chorus. His best known choral works include *Oratorio de Noël*, *Messe de Requiem*, and the oratorio *The Promised Land.*

"Salut au chevalier printemps" is second in a set of three songs for three-part women's chorus called *Trois choeurs*, Op. 151. This piece sings like a French Romantic art song with its beautiful setting of a Paul Fournier poem. Composed in 1917 when Saint-Saëns's health was beginning to wane, *Trois choeurs* is one of his last secular choral sets to be composed.

Technical Considerations and Musical Elements

Saint-Saëns's homophonic setting of "Salut au Chevalier Printemps" creates an elegant piece appropriate for young and mature singers alike. His conservative harmonic style dominates the chromaticism of the piece. The slow-moving harmonic shifts are well prepared, creating smooth transitions. Many times the voices sing only a minor second apart, but this dissonance is easily negotiated within the context of the harmony and melodic line.

The first soprano part requires the most technical skill for this piece. They reach a high A once but remain in the *passaggio* throughout most of the piece. This range should not pose a problem for seasoned first sopranos, except when the dynamic level is *piano*. Large leaps are frequent, though they often outline the underlying harmony. The second soprano and alto parts lie in limited, comfortable ranges with a high F occurring only once for both parts.

The extensive French text poses the greatest challenge in this piece. Fortunately, the repeated musical ideas and easy-to-learn parts focus the singers' attention on the text. Also, the IPA translation in this edition is immensely helpful and can aid the conductor in his or her modeling of the text. Unified pronunciation must be established. To accomplish this, the text can be sung on a comfortable, repeated note at first. By doing this, singers concentrate on correct pronunciation. Later, the text can be added to the melody already learned on a neutral syllable. The subtle effect of the ending schwa (not heard in spoken French) proves to be most difficult for English speaking singers to produce correctly. Like a feminine cadence, the final syllable should be de-emphasized while the previous syllable is accented (e.g. m. 5 on the word "lim-pi-de" the emphasis is on the middle syllable).

The accompaniment for this song requires a skilled pianist because of the many chromatic passages, running octaves, and arpeggios. The accompaniment is crucial in setting up harmonic shifts and should be played with precision and expression.

Stylistic Considerations

Expression of the text, which celebrates the coming of spring, is paramount in creating an informed performance. The conductor and singers should be aware of the literal translation and emphasize key words; phrases should be shaped accordingly. Dynamics are provided by the composer to aid in this expression, but the conductor should feel free to add his or her own subtle interpretations to this effect. The tempo of quarter note = 120 requires the singer to perform the text quite quickly, yet this is a manageable rate. The slower tempo detracts from the liveliness of the text and subject matter.

Form and Structure

"Salut au chevalier printemps" can be divided into two musically identical sections: mm. 1–59 and mm. 60–115. The structure within these two sections is loosely defined by the poem's stanzas. Many of the four smaller sections begin with a similar motive (e.g., mm. 3–6).

Section	Measure	Event and Scoring
Section 1		
A	1–10	Stanza 1; F major
B	11–20	Stanza 2; E major
C	21–40	Stanza 3; E-flat major
D	41–59	Stanza 4 and 5; B-flat major
Section 2		
A	60–69	Stanza 5 and 6; F major
B	70–79	Stanza 7; E major
C	80–97	Stanza 8 and 9; E-flat major
D	98–115	Stanza 9 and 10; B-flat major
Coda	116–121	F major

Text and Translation

In this edition, the editor provides a poetic and literal translation of Paul Fournier's poem. An IPA translation is also given as a pronunciation guide in the Roger Dean edition.

L'azur est plus bleu;	The sky is more blue;
L'air est plus limpide;	The air more limpid;
Le soleil de fue,	Fiery sun,
Dans le ciel sans ride,	In a sky without ripples,
Comme un or liquide	As golden liquid
Inonde la plaine et le val profond.	Floods the plain and deep valley.

Quel et ce mystère?	What is this mystery?
C'est qu'enfin la terre,	It is the earth at last,
Des tristes frimas hier prisonnière,	Yesterday a prisoner of sad wintry weather,
De mille joyaux a paré son front.	Now a thousand joys adorn its head.
Chevalier printemps Couronné	Princely springtime crowned
De roses et de lilas blancs,	With roses and white lilies,
A nos portes closes	To our closed doors
Par les jours moroses,	By sullen days,
Tu viens d'apparatître enfin tout joyeux.	You come to prepare at last all happiness.
Ouvrons-lui bien vite,	Open the doors quickly,
Fètons sa visite	Celebrate his visit
Et que tout l'invite a goûter la paix	And invite him to taste the country
Sous nos vastes cieux.	Under the vast skies.
Voici donc l'Avril!	Here is April!
Sous bois la fauvette au tendre babil,	Under the forest the fawn with tender prattle
Comme l'alouette tout là-haut s'apprête	Like an alouette that gets ready
A te saluer de ses plus doux chants.	To greet you with the sweetest songs.
Que nous semble belle la saison nouvelle!	We will all be beautiful in this new season!
Comme un pur bijou sa grâce étincelle,	Like a pure jewel with its sparkling grace,
Quand soudain parait le joyeux printemps.	When suddenly the happy spring appears.
Printemps merveilleux!	Marvelous spring!
Sa beauté, sa grâce ravissent les yeux	His beauty, his grace ravishes our eyes
Et d'ja l'espace où maint oiseau passe	And already the space where so many birds pass
N'est plus vide et froid	Is no longer empty and cold
Comme au temps glacés.	Like the frozen weather.
Tout vit et palpite,	All is alive and beating,
Et dans l'air bien vite,	And in the forceful wind,
L'insecte léger s'envole et s'agite;	Insects lightly fly away and flutter;
Les jours malheureux sont enfin passés!	The unhappy days are finally past!

Précieux instants!	Precious moments!
Que de douces choses!	What sweet things!
Chevalier printemps!	Princely springtime!
Donne-nous les roses sur tes pas écloses,	Give us roses on your paths,
Viens nous prodiguer d'exquise senteurs.	Come lavish on us exquisite feelings.
Le printemps enivre,	The intoxicating springtime
Et qu'ill fait bon vivre	That makes all live
Alors que le rire a chassé les pleurs!	So that laughter chased away the tears!
Chantons et danson!	Sing and dance!
Jetons a la brise nos plus joyeux sons!	Throw to the wind our most joyous sounds!
Soit s'phir ou bise,	Be it of zephyrs or a kiss,
Tout souffle nous grise!	Every breath intoxicates us!
Une folle ivresse inspire nos chants.	A crazy drunkenness inspires our songs.
Que nous semble belle la saison nouvelle!	That we seem beautiful, the new season!
Comme un pur bijou sa grâce étincelle,	Like a pure jewel with its sparkling grace,
Quand soudain parait le joyeux printemps.	When suddenly the happy spring appears.

Additional References and Resources

Flynn, Timothy S. *Camille Saint-Saëns: A Guide to Research*. New York: Routledge Music Bibliographies, 2003.

Hervey, Arthur. *Saint-Saëns*. Freeport, NY: Books for Libraries Press, 1922.

Lyle, Watson. *Camille Saint-Saëns: His Life and Art*. Westport, CT: Greenwood Press Publishers, 1923.

Rees, Brian. *Camille Saint-Saëns: A Life*. London: Chatto & Windus, 1999.

Studd, Stephen. *Saint-Saëns: A Critical Biography*. London: Cygnus Arts, 1999.

Suggested Listening

Camille Saint-Saëns, "Salut au Chevalier Printemps," Op. 151, No. 2 on *Messe de Requiem*, Lugano Radio Svizzera Choir, Diego Fasolis, Chandos B0002AAP9E.

Contributed by:

Lani Knutson

Teacher Resource Guide

Al naharot Bavel

Salamone Rossi

(ca. 1570–ca. 1630)

ed. Joshua R. Jacobson

TTBB with piano or organ ad libitum
Broude Brothers: CR 24
Overall: 4
Vocal: 4
Tonal/Rhythm: 4

Composer

Salamone Rossi was most likely born in Mantua and spent his entire professional career there. A noted violinist and composer, he made significant contributions to the development of the trio sonata and chamber duet. Rossi probably worked for the Jewish theatrical troupes that were central to Mantuan theater life for Jews, Christians, and royalty alike. His ability to work for the church and the royal court was hampered by his Jewish faith, which prevented him from regular employment at the basilica and the royal choir; nevertheless, there is evidence that he was connected at least intermittently with the musically rich court of Duke Vincenzo Gonzaga. Vincenzo apparently thought highly of Rossi, as he decreed in 1606 that Rossi did not have to wear the yellow badge required for Jews, a courtesy extended by the Duke's successor, Francesco II, in 1612.

Rossi was a madrigalist whose work was frequently overshadowed by the compositions of his well-known Mantuan contemporaries, Claudio Monteverdi and Giovanni Giacomo Gastoldi. He published six books of madrigals, many with instrumental accompaniment, among the first published examples of continuo madrigals. Rossi's compositional style, described as light and sonorous and reminiscent of Luca Marenzio and early Monteverdi, remained uniform throughout the six volumes, published over the period 1600–1622. His sister was Madama Europa, a virtuoso singer and the only Jewish female professional singer of record who enjoyed crossover success between the theater and the royal court of the time. Rossi's last published work is dated 1628; he may have died during the destruction of the ghetto and the severe plague that followed the siege of Mantua by imperial troops in 1630.

Composition and Historical Perspective

"Al naharot Bavel" is from the collection *Ha-Shirim Ahser li-Shlomo (Songs of Solomon)* published by Pietro and Lorenzo Bragadini in Venice in 1622. The collection represents the first attempt to print Hebrew texts with music, a technical challenge that brought considerable difficulty given that Hebrew script is written right to left while musical notation moves left to right. The title appears to be a reference to Rossi's first name, rather than descriptive; of the thirty-three polyphonic settings of Hebrew psalms, hymns, prayers, and one wedding ode in the collection, none draws its inspiration from the Song of Solomon. Written for three to eight voices, the musical style is consistent with sacred Christian polyphonic settings of the same period, particularly the Mantuan style of Monteverdi and Gastoldi and, in some of the larger settings, the Venetian school. Some scholars also suggest that Rossi used Italian Jewish chants for some of the material. The result is a body of choral motets that, while not stylistically adventurous, represent a rare (but not unique) cultural fusion of polyphony and the Jewish tradition.

"Al naharot Bavel" is a setting of Psalm 137, the lament of the Jewish exiles in captivity. Like many settings of the similar Lamentations of Jeremiah by Rossi's Christian cohorts, it makes frequent use of cross-relationships and other expressive chromatic gestures within an expansively low, slow homophonic setting.

Technical Considerations and Musical Elements

This is an excellent work for four-part men's chorus with well-stratified and relatively narrow ranges for all four voice parts. Take time initially to place voices, considering which are best suited for each line so that the men can sing with ease and not weigh down the intonation. There are moments of supreme beauty best captured via a lighter, flexible vocal technique that allows the choir to capture both the vertical sonorities and the expansive phrase gestures. The piece is naturally somber in color, and there should not be a need to darken voices further.

Solfege in A to highlight the cross-relationships between major and minor tonality, paying special attention to the high placement of the altered third. Depending on the choir's facility with solfege, this may require the introduction of altered syllables, but the results will be worth it. Mm. 34–48 may tune better by solfeging in G and switching back to A at m. 49. If the use of altered syllables becomes a hindrance rather than an aid in specific locations, isolate the measures in a key that makes more sense, even if the solfege used is not ultimately "in the key." In any event, insist on clear, accurate tuning; approximate pitch will only slow down the piece further and most likely drop the overall ranges to the point where all vocal clarity is lost.

Take care to balance the parts vertically, as no one vocal line should predominate. One challenge of this work is to remain rhythmically precise, particularly through appoggiaturas and cadential formulas, without sounding metronomic. Always emphasize horizontal motion in each part and with the choir as a whole. Have the group gently step (either in place or around the room—insist on "musical" movement that is barely audible rather than a loud march step) the half note to give them the sense of something larger than the quarter note motion that dominates the piece. Alternatively, have them step on accented syllables only (well marked in the score) to emphasize the natural meter of the text. There will be a temptation to take choral breaths at regular intervals; stagger breathe and reserve choral breaths for the ends of major points in the music. Have the choir pull on an imaginary rope as they sing through extended phrases. The challenge here is to encourage students to pace the "pull" using the entire body (not arms alone) so that they still have rope left at the ends of phrases, rather than reaching the end of the pull in mid-phrase.

In performance, Rossi's setting should evoke the slow flow of a deep river with the bends, turns, ebb, and flow reflected through the modal twists of the music. It is also significant that in the two brief three-voice sections the text describes silence and the singers' absence from home. Because of the potential language barrier and the slow, somber mood of the piece, it is essential to actively engage the choir in the emotion of the text and allow them to explore personally how meaning is represented in the music.

Stylistic Considerations

The editor, Joshua Jacobson aptly notes that Rossi's score uses the traditional indicators canto, alto, tenor, and bass, but the vocal tessituras for all parts are well within the ranges for a moderate to advanced male chorus. Performance by mixed choir, while possible, is technically challenging due to the extremely low tessitura for the soprano and alto voices. Jacobson also suggests the use of Italianate Hebrew diction with minor alterations. The reviewed edition provides excellent and extensive editorial commentary, including a pronunciation guide.

Whenever possible, have someone fluent in Hebrew demonstrate diction and the ebb and flow of the language. This is particularly important given the slow setting and the placement of editorial barlines, both of which quickly can contribute to a plodding and arrhythmic performance without vigilant attention to text stress during rehearsals.

Performance within the service would have prohibited the use of any accompanying instrument. However, "Al naharot Bavel" most likely also was performed in non-liturgical venues, in which case doubling of the vocal lines, use of basso continuo, or a doubled bass part for color on keyboard or strings would be appropriate.

Form and Structure

This motet is through-composed and in three large sections with each section subdivided into two smaller units of irregular phrase lengths. A "resting point" of a half cadence or similar effect typically is embedded within each phrase. Care should be taken that arrival at these points does not disrupt motion toward the end of the phrase.

The four-voice texture is essentially syllabic and homophonic throughout. Melismatic passages in individual voices are brief, and suspensions appear equally in the tenor 2 and bass 1 parts at cadence points exclusively. There are brief tacets in both tenor parts in Section II, resulting in three-voice textures (tenor 2 tacet mm. 18–20; tenor 1 tacet mm. 26–33); baritone and bass sing throughout.

Section	Measure	Event and Scoring
Section I		
	1–7	"Al naharot Bavel"; phrase 1 (3 + 4)
	8–18	"Al aravim betocha"; phrase 2 (4 + 3 + 4)
Section II		
	19–26	"Eych nashir et shir"; phrase 1 (4 + 4)
	27–33	"Tidbak leshomi lechiki"; phrase 2 (3 + 4)
Section III		
	34–42	"Zechor Adonai"; phrase 1 (4 + 5)
	43–54	"Bat Bavel hasheduda"; phrase 2 [6 (2 + 4) + 6 (2 + 4)]

Text and Translation

Al naharót Bavél sham yshávnu
gam bachínu bezochréynu et Tsiyón.

By the rivers of Babylon we wept as we remembered Israel.

Al aravím betochá talínu kinorotéynu.

We hung our harps on the

	willows and chanted our lamentation.
Ki sham sheelúnu shovéynu divreyshír vetolaléynu simchá:	Our masters made us sing songs of joy, mocking us:
Lánu mishír Tsiyón.	"Sing us songs of Jerusalem."
Eych nashír et shir Adonái al admát nechár?	Who could sing the song of the Lord in a strange land?
Im eshkachéch Yerushaláyim tishkách yeminí,	I shall not forget Jerusalem, the holy city.
Tidbák leshoní lechikí im lo ezkeréychi,	Your name will remain on my tongue, or I shall be silent:
im lo aalé et Yerushaláyim al rosh simchatí.	Thy joy in my heart far above all others though thou art no more.
Zechór Adonái livnéy Edóm et yom Yerushaláyim, haomerím:	Remember, O Lord, Jerusalem's destruction and those who called
Áru, áru, ad hayesód ba.	For its burning.
Bat Bavél hashedudá, ashréy sheyeshalém lach et gemuléch shegamálte lánu.	Babylon soon will fall. Then we will be joyful.
Ashréy sheyochéz venipéts et olaláyich el hasála.	With joy he will take and then dash the evil ones' little children on a sharp rock.

Suggested Listening

Salamone Rossi:

"Al naharot Bavel" on *Salamone Rossi: The Songs of Solomon, Volume 2,* New York Baroque, Dorian 93220, men's voices.

"Al naharot Bavel" on *Salamone Rossi: Early Baroque Music*, Boston Early Music Ensemble, Zamir 910, mixed voices.

Contributed by:

Michael Lippert

Teacher Resource Guide

Manly Men

Kurt Knecht

(b. 1971)

TTBB
Walton Music Corp.: HL 08501442
Overall: 4
Vocal: 4
Tonal/Rhythm: 3

Composer

Kurt Knecht is a doctoral student in composition at the University of Nebraska–Lincoln, and holds degrees in piano performance, music theory, and composition. He has performed as a choral accompanist with Doreen Rao, Jo-Michael Scheibe, Eph Ehly, Robert Summer, and others. His solo keyboard career includes concerts with the Florida Orchestra and Smokey Robinson.

All-state chorus concerts in New York, Louisiana, Tennessee, and Kansas have featured his choral compositions, as did the Florida American Choral Directors Association at its 2004 convention. The 2005 College Music Society's Southern Chapter Conference premiered his song cycle *Three Poems by Gerald Manley Hopkins*.

Other Knecht works you may wish to consider, written in several different styles and for various voicings, are: "Michelangelo's On Beauty," "Go Tell It on the Mountain," "Rocka My Soul," and "Deus noster refugium."

Composition and Historical Perspective

"Manly Men" is a humorous romp that makes a great opener or encore for any moderately skilled men's chorus. The composition uses a variety of styles to relate the trials and tribulations of the various vocal sections of a men's chorus. Full of musical quotations and predictable punch lines, "Manly Men" is a must for any men's chorus, no matter how serious the group is. Paired with William Billings's "Down Sang the Bass," it would make a nice mini-section in a concert of small choral works.

Composer Kurt Knecht conceived the piece at a men's chorus concert while listening to "a particularly robust piece that sounded like every other robust men's chorus." A friend commented, "You should write a piece that goes 'We are men . . .'" and jokes about block chords and close harmony. . . . I just sort of tossed it off as a joke. Now it seems that I could write the Great American Symphony and only ever be known for writing 'Manly Men.'"

Technical Considerations and Musical Elements

"Manly Men" begins in 4/4 and the key of B-flat major with an introduction in classic male chorus style. The humor of the piece is immediately apparent and should be milked by the singers both vocally and physically. (If choreography is ever appropriate, this would be the time.) The introduction ends with the choir expressing their dislike of women's choirs, followed by a mocking falsetto sigh.

An oompah band in the lower voices accompanies the first tenors' take on "La donna é mobile" mm. 16–35. A solo high B-flat, intended to sound painful, finishes this section. A short transition in an inverted "Twist and Shout" style leads into the second tenors' verse in soft-shoe style (mm. 40–56). Next it's the baritones' turn. Using "The Toreador Song" from *Carmen*, the baritones proclaim their superiority and poke fun at first tenors. Finally, the basses lament that they are often relegated to walking bass lines and doo-wop introductions in a pastoral section in 3/4 time. Eventually, everyone joins to repeat the first section. The men have still more to communicate, and they carry their clear message into the coda (mm. 109–116), *molto pompousioso*, ending like a chorale with a "Thank you, God, for making me a man."

Vocal ranges of this piece are moderate, with the exception of the humorous high notes. The composer intends that these sound bad to get a laugh, so should not be much of a worry. The most difficult part of the piece lies in the key changes in the large sections. These occur in mm. 15, 38–39, 57–58, and 70. They should be isolated in rehearsals so that singers feel confident. During rehearsals, it will be tempting to stop before these chords because the section has just ended. If the conductor can discipline himself to take the transition every time, even when going back to work on the previous section, singers will feel confident in performance.

Any unaccompanied piece can be challenging. Some of the hardest notes are where voice parts perform an accompanimental role. Getting the choir away from piano support as early as possible in the rehearsal process will help.

Stylistic Considerations

"Manly Men" is campy, and that is how it should be performed. The first hint—after the title—about the nature of this work is the beginning expression marking *molto aplombioso*, which gives immediate permission to the director and the choir to interpret for effect. Please do so, even to the point of occasionally allowing a voice to crack or asking for body language to suit the text. In the preface to the score, Knecht writes, "Every nuance should be milked as much as possible in performance, with attention given to making the words clearly understood to make the most of each joke."

Form and Structure

Framed by an introduction and conclusion using the same musical material, the bulk of "Manly Men" is through-composed. Each voice part of the standard men's chorus is allotted a solo section, which quotes famous musical pieces or uses a stereotypical men's chorus genre as fodder

Text

We are men and we like to sing in big block chords and close harmony.
Our songs all sound the same, and most of them are really lame,
But though we may not always inspire, at least we're not a women's choir. Ah.
First tenors have the highest voice, for most of us it's not by choice
Singing still at twenty-three like we missed our puberty.
When our pitch turns sour we just sing a little louder.
Tight underwear's the key to singing a high "C." Ah. . . .

Suggested Listening

Kurt Knecht Web site: www.kurtknecht.com. There you may listen to a recording by the 2002 New York All State Chorus under the direction of Jo-Michael Scheibe.

Contributed by:

Lani Johnson

Teacher Resource Guide

Psalm 117

Stanley Hoffman

(b. 1959)

TTBB
Ione Press/ECS Publishing: 5754
Overall: 4
Vocal: 5
Tonal/Rhythm: 4

Composer

Composer Stanley Hoffman was born in Cleveland, Ohio, in 1959 and has resided in the Boston area since 1977. He received his musical education at the Boston Conservatory (bachelor of music), the New England Conservatory (master of music), and Brandeis University (PhD). His compositions tend to be rooted in the Jewish tradition. Although his harmonies and techniques are modern, the listener can detect a harkening back to the traditional Jewish style. Hoffman works as a singer, conductor, and editor. In addition to his large catalog of published works, most of his unpublished works are in the holdings of the International Archive of Jewish Music located in Southfield, Michigan. Hoffman publishes with Ione Press (ECS Publishing) for whom he also serves as chief editor.

Composition and Historical Perspective

"Psalm 117" is a complete motet setting of a new translation of the psalm by the composer. Interestingly enough, Psalm 117 is shortest poem in the book of Psalms, containing only two verses. The opening melody in the bass and baritone parts is reminiscent of chant and harkens back to the tradition of

Jewish psalmody. This "ancient" feel is contrasted with a highly energetic rhythm and a modern, modal tonal palette. The middle section uses an elaborate chord progression to highlight "God's goodness." This piece would make a great concert opener or introit.

Technical Considerations and Musical Elements

An amateur men's chorus should not attempt this piece, although with careful rehearsal a group of moderate ability can certainly give it a wonderful performance. As one can view below in the Form and Structure section, much of the musical material is repeated. Each section of the piece has its individual challenges. The A and A´ sections are more rhythmically challenging, while the B section is more harmonically challenging.

To succeed in the A section of this piece it is important that your singers have a clear understanding of pulse and syncopation. Notes in this section frequently are tied across barlines or into the next pulse. A choir without a secure sense of tempo and pulse will have a hard time keeping the first nine measures of this piece together. Because the tenor parts are essentially transposed bass and baritone parts, it may be helpful to begin this piece by asking all parts to sing mm. 1–6 of the baritone line. This will give them a feeling of the quality of syncopation as well as the modality. It should also be noted that the printed metronome marking is too fast for the early stage of rehearsal; in fact, it might be wise to learn this section in 4/8 with a slow eighth note receiving the pulse. This will allow your singers to organize the rhythms in a concrete manner. Once the singers can accurately perform the baritone part, have them read their own part and correct notes as needed. The baritone and tenor duet in mm. 7–9 can be quite tricky. Again, consistent tempo and awareness of the pulse are key.

The second portion of the A section (mm. 15–22) transitions from the highly rhythmic introduction into a more chordal, homophonic style. The chord progressions of this section and the following B section are quite beautiful and should be rehearsed thoroughly to achieve pristine intonation. You must have confident second tenors to perform this section well. Careful inspection of the score shows the second tenors are almost always have the "color" notes of each chord progression and engage in a twenty-first century version of a suspension chain (upon resolution of one suspension the second tenor part immediately becomes part of a new suspension). Most of these are easy to perform, but several, which are approached by leap, are difficult to hear (e.g., mm. 17 and 24).

It may be wise to rehearse mm. 14–31 several times without the second tenors to frame the harmonic context. Once the second tenors have heard the progression, it will be easier for them to perform their notes correctly. Along these lines, make sure you rehearse in a way that allows the singers to tune the chords. In other words, don't be afraid to isolate chords or to hold them longer.

This allows singers to hear where they are going and how they got there, giving them a chance to get it right. Conversely, you may also choose to sing these passages in a staccato style, which will force the singers to make an aural decision when attacking the pitch; if the chord does not tune on the staccato attack, they will have received immediate aural feedback. This technique is useful in developing alacrity in your singers. A combination of staccato and elongated rehearsal techniques will go a long way in establishing the desired intonation for this section.

Vocal concerns: The vocal ranges of this piece are quite extreme, requiring both high and low notes from all parts. When performing this piece with less developed voices, find the part that works best for each individual. Young singers attempting this piece may tend to push too much to get a more mature sound; discourage this at every possibility. Ask them to keep their vocal tone light and spacious. You can use vowel colors and intense diction to achieve the intensity required for this piece.

Stylistic Considerations

Every choir, regardless of ability, should be able to change the color of their tone within the course of any piece; this work does not offer an exception to that rule. The opening of this work requires a tone that is agile yet strong and exuberant; the choir should use crisp, fast consonants so that the vowels are able to speak on the beat. It will behoove the choir to "re-sing" the vowel in cases where the note changes but the syllable does not. (This is especially important in the A section, "Praise the Holy One.") Failure to do this will result in a muddy texture and yield a vocal tone that is too dark, pressed, and, consequently, out of tune.

The middle section must be blended and beautiful yet evoke a sense of praise. Achieve this by using pure vowels that are spacious, tall, and forward. You may find it useful to ask singers performing suspensions to brighten vowels on suspended notes. This will aid the intonation, which can be difficult at such low frequencies. The choir will probably have a tendency to drag this section as it is homophonic and very beautiful. Try to keep the tempo moving at the composer's intended speed: quarter note = 80.

Form and Structure

The form of this piece is ABA´ plus a coda

Section	Measure	Event and Scoring
A	1–22	This section is divided into two parts, which correspond to the two versicles of the first verse of the psalm
	1–14	"Praise the Holy one all nations"

SECTION	MEASURE	EVENT AND SCORING
	15–22	"Extol God all humankind"
B	22–34	Slower tempo at the beginning while intoning the second verse of Psalm 117; this section may also be divided by versicles
	22–31	"For God's goodness overpowered us"
	32–34	"And the faithfulness of the Holy One is everlasting"
A´	35–48	The opening musical material returns, this time with a "hallelujah" text; not a complete return of the A section as after an exact musical repeat of mm. 1–14 a final coda brings the piece to a thrilling end
Coda	48–52	"Hallelujah!"

Text

A setting of Psalm 117 in a new translation by the composer.

Praise the Holy all nations.
Extol God all humankind.
For God's goodness overpowered us
And the faithfulness of Holy One is everlasting.
Hallelujah!

Additional References and Resources

Web site:
Stanley M. Hoffman: http://mysite.verizon.net/stanleymhoffman/index.htm

Contributed by:

Matthew W. Mehaffey

Teacher Resource Guide

Sehnsucht

Franz Schubert

(1797–1828)

TTBBB a cappella
Santa Barbara Music Publishing: SBMP 254
Overall: 4
Vocal: 4
Tonal/Rhythm: 4

Composer

As a native Viennese, Franz Schubert was the beneficiary of the rich musical legacies of Joseph Haydn, W. A. Mozart, Christoph Gluck, Antonio Salieri, and Ludwig van Beethoven. Schubert's own legacy was in bringing the German art song, the *Lied,* to full maturity. Like Mozart he composed an enormous number of pieces during his short life. Before dying at the age of thirty-one he had composed more than six hundred songs, nine symphonies, seven choral masses, fifteen string quartets, and operas and incidental theatrical music. "I have come into the world for no other purpose than to compose," the young Schubert said of his career.

Schubert was born into a middle class Viennese family in 1797 and received his first musical instruction from his father, a schoolteacher and headmaster. His father observed his extraordinary musical gifts and enrolled him at the age of eleven to be a choirboy in the court chapel under Antonio Salieri's direction. Schubert soon earned a scholarship to attend the Imperial Seminary and trained to be a teacher. By his late teens he had returned to his father's school to teach, and, though he hated this job, he had already composed several masterpieces. The most notable was the masterful "Gretchen am Spinnrade" ("Gretchen at the Spinning Wheel"), a song Schubert wrote when he was only seventeen. During the next year he composed another 143 songs, including "The Erlkönig" ("The Erlking"), and by the age of nineteen he had composed two symphonies and a choral mass. At twenty-one Schubert left teaching to devote himself entirely to composition. Unlike Beethoven, the giant of the Viennese musical scene, Schubert did not socialize with the aristocracy and never found great financial success as a composer during his lifetime. Unable to afford his own rent, Schubert stayed with friends, living somewhat of a bohemian lifestyle among young Viennese poets and artists. These friends aided him by disseminating his music during literary evenings called Schubertiads in private homes.

It is rumored that Schubert visited Beethoven on his deathbed in 1827, but this has never been verified. He did, without doubt, serve as a torchbearer at his hero's funeral. Despite Schubert's declining health he went on to compose some of his most significant works, including the monumental song cycle *Winterreisse*. Advanced symptoms of syphilis would lead to delirium and Schubert's subsequent death in November 1828. A concert was held in his honor, and proceeds were allocated for the building of a monument at his grave on which was inscribed: "Here lies buried a rich treasure and yet more glorious hopes." Schubert, while still alive, never gained the stature or fame Beethoven achieved during his lifetime, but Schubert's "Unfinished Symphony" and the C major "Great Symphony" earned him recognition posthumously. These symphonic works, along with his many choral pieces and art songs, would secure Schubert a place as one of the most significant composers of the early nineteenth century.

Composition and Historical Perspective

In 1808 Carl Zelter assembled a small group of male poets, singers, and composers fashioned after the medieval *Meistersinger* guilds into what he called *Liedertafel* ("song-table"). The main purpose of the *Liedertafel* was to advance German music and literature. The members of the *Liedertafel* would meet for an evening meal followed by the singing of part-songs. Originality in the *Liedertafel* was encouraged, and the composer whose music was well received would be toasted and adorned with a medallion. Eventually the *Liedertafel* gained popularity, spreading to cities all across Germany. Schubert enjoyed the support and inspiration of the Viennese *Liedertafel* and would become its most celebrated composer. Not surprisingly, almost two-thirds of Schubert's part-songs and choruses are for male voices, many of which premiered at the Viennese *Liedertafel*. Songs like "Sehnsucht" were favorites at these local gatherings.

Composed in April 1819, "Sehnsucht" ("Loneliness") is a five-part setting of Mignon's song from *Wilhelm Meister* by Johann Wolfgang von Goethe (1749–1832). (Interestingly, Schubert set a female character's words for a male chorus.) As in his solo song literature, Schubert employed the poetry of the great German masters Goethe, Ruekert, Friedrich von Schiller, and others. Generations of song composers, including Robert Schumann, Hugo Wolf, and Johannes Brahms would be greatly influenced by Schubert's songwriting expertise.

Technical Considerations and Musical Elements

The three potential technical complications you might encounter when preparing "Sehnsucht" with your chorus involve intonation, rubato, and dynamic contrast.

Keeping the chorus in tune will probably pose the greatest challenge. Consider having your chorus learn the entire piece on solfege first. If necessary, ask each student to write the solfege syllables into his music. Once the chorus is able to sing the entire piece comfortably on solfege and can tune the chords vertically, move to a neutral syllable such as "doo." Go back to the solfege any time pitches are uncertain. After the choir sings the piece legato and in tune on the neutral syllable, move to the German text. Continue returning to the neutral syllable or to the solfege until legato, in-tune singing is achieved.

The use of rubato, a practice common to Romantic compositions, involves borrowing the duration from one note and giving it to another. The stretching, slowing, or acceleration of the musical line adds emotion and drama to the piece. Rubato in "Sehnsucht" can be achieved by count-singing the divided beat first on a unison pitch, then on the individual parts. When the choir can comfortably count-sing the piece at a steady tempo, move to more flexible, rubato phrasing while still counting. Insist that your choir follow your conducting gesture for subtle tempo changes. Finally, move to the text. Return to count-singing as needed if the choir fails to feel the subdivided beat or is unable to place the consonants collectively on onsets and releases.

Achieving dynamic contrast is more complicated than is generally understood. Singers often erroneously equate softer singing with a slower tempo and breathy tone and louder singing with a faster tempo and pressed tone. Take great care to ensure that regardless of dynamic level the choir does not go "off the voice" and always sings a resonant, supported tone. Instead, based on your understanding of the German text, allow the dynamic markings (*piano*, *forte*, etc.) signal coloristic changes, not necessarily always a shift in actual "decibel levels."

Stylistic Considerations

Nineteenth-century German part-songs should be approached in a manner similar to the German art song or *Lied* of the same era. Careful consideration should be given to the dynamic markings and tempos throughout, and rubato is appropriate as dictated by the poetry. Schubert's songwriting genius was in his lyricism and in his ability to capture musically the spirit of the poem.

In "Sehnsucht" Schubert uses harmony to represent the emotional changes in the text. Constant shifts from major to minor and into related keys, diminished seventh chords that resolve into surprising cadences, and labored dissonances on critical textual images demonstrate Schubert's gift at illuminating the text.

Schubert also used texture to illustrate poetic images. Moving from five voices to three in m. 5, for instance, exemplifies loneliness. The detached, halting phrases beginning in m. 22 bring to life Mignon's "failing senses" and "burning fire within." In preparing to teach this piece the conductor should work with a literal translation of Goethe's poem. Clarify word by word, chord by chord, how Schubert depicts the words through musical means. It is suggested that choir members write a literal translation into their music above the German text. The harmonic and melodic nuances in "Sehnsucht" may only be fully realized with a significant understanding of the original German. The Santa Barbara Music Publishing edition does provide an English language option, but this is a poetic translation.

Form and Structure

The song is through-composed with some recurring motivic material and begins and ends in E major.

Text and Translation

Nur wer die Sehnsucht kennt, weiss, was ich leide!	Only one who knows longing can know what I suffer.
Allein und abgetrennt aller Freude.	Alone and deprived of all joy.
Seh ich an's Firmament nach jener Seite.	I gaze on every side to the heavens above.
Ach! der mich liebt und kennt, ist in der Weite.	Ah! He who loves me and understands is far away.
Es schwindelt mir, es brennt mein Eingeweide.	I faint, I burn within.
Nur wer die Sehnsucht kennt, weiss, was ich leide!	Only one who knows longing can know what I suffer.

Additional References and Resources

Sadie, Stanley, ed. *The New Grove Dictionary of Music and Musicians.* New York: Grove, 2001.

Suggested Listening

Franz Schubert:

- "Sehnsucht" on *A Goethe Schubertiad*, The London Schubert Chorale, Hyperion CDJ33024.
- "Sehnsucht" on *Schubert: Songs for Male Chorus*, The Robert Shaw Chorale, Telarc CD-80340.
- "Sehnsucht" on *Schubert: Male Choruses*, Orphei Drangar Swedish Men's Choir, Robert Sund, conductor, BIS 1033.

Contributed by:

James Bowyer

Teacher Resource Guide

Shall I Compare Thee

Stephen Paulus

(b. 1949)

TTBB
Paulus Publications: SP 404
Overall: 4
Vocal: 3
Tonal/Rhythm: 4

Composer

Composer Stephen Paulus has been hailed as "a bright, fluent inventor with a ready lyric gift" (*The New Yorker*). His prolific output of more than two hundred works is represented in many genres, including music for orchestra, chorus, chamber ensembles, solo voice, keyboard, and opera. He has commissioned by the New York Philharmonic, Cleveland Orchestra, Atlanta Symphony Orchestra, Minnesota Orchestra, Dallas Symphony Orchestra, the Houston Symphony, and the St. Paul Chamber Orchestra, with subsequent performances coming from the orchestras of Los Angeles, Philadelphia, St. Louis, the National Symphony Orchestra, and the BBC Radio Orchestra. He has served as composer-in-residence for the orchestras of Atlanta, Minnesota, Tucson, and Annapolis, and his works have been championed by such eminent conductors as Sir Neville Marriner, Kurt Masur, Christoph von Dohanyi, Leonard Slatkin, Yoel Levi, Robert Shaw, and numerous others.

Paulus has been commissioned to write works for some of the world's great solo artists, including Thomas Hampson, Håkan Hagegård, Doc Severinsen, William Preucil, Cynthia Phelps, Evelyn Lear, Leo Kottke, and Robert McDuffie. Chamber music commissions have resulted in works for the

Chamber Music Society of Lincoln Center, Friends of Music at the Supreme Court, the Cleveland Quartet, and Arizona Friends of Chamber Music. He has been a featured guest composer at the festivals of Aspen, Santa Fe, Tanglewood, and, in the U.K., the Aldeburgh and Edinburgh Festivals.

As one of today's preeminent composers of opera, Paulus has written eight works for the dramatic stage. *The Postman Always Rings Twice* was the first American production to be presented at the Edinburgh Festival and has received nine productions to date. Commissions and performances have come from such companies as the Opera Theatre of St. Louis, Washington Opera, Boston Lyric Opera, Florida Grand Opera, Berkshire Opera Company, Minnesota Opera, and Fort Worth Opera, among others, as well as many universities and colleges.

His choral works have been performed and recorded by some of the most distinguished choruses in the United States, including the New York Concert Singers, Dale Warland Singers, Los Angeles Master Chorale, Robert Shaw Festival Singers, New Music Group of Philadelphia, Master Chorale of Washington DC, Vocal Arts Ensemble of Cincinnati, Mormon Tabernacle Choir, and dozens of other professional, community, church, and college choirs. He is one of the most frequently recorded contemporary composers with more than fifty recordings of his music.

A recipient of both Guggenheim and NEA fellowships, Paulus is also a strong advocate for the music of his colleagues. He is cofounder and a current board vice president of the highly esteemed American Composers Forum, the largest composer service organization in the world. Paulus serves on the ASCAP Board of Directors as the concert music representative, a post he has held since 1990.

Composition and Historical Perspective

"Shall I Compare Thee" can best be described as a twenty-first century English secular micro-form. With its homophonic texture, mostly stepwise voice leading, and multiple repeats, it has the feel of a secular hymn. It is similar to another of Paulus's often performed choral works: "Pilgrim's Hymn." "Shall I Compare Thee" was commissioned by the Harvard Glee Club, Jameson Marvin, conductor.

Technical Considerations and Musical Elements

The straightforward nature of this piece should provide for successful performances at the high school and college levels. Its main challenges include four-part male singing, voice leading difficulties (several leaps to dissonant chords), vocal range issues, and some moderate challenges in harmonic language. If the ensemble director dedicates rehearsal time to these problem areas, this can be a very effective concert piece.

Four-Part Male Singing
One of the first question the ensemble director must confront before programming this piece is: does the ensemble have the necessary skill and number of singers to perform this piece well? There are short bursts of five-part writing with the tenor splitting into three parts. There should be an equal number of skilled singers for each part. Many high school and college male groups serve as educational ensembles where young men learn the fundamentals of music and rehearsal expectation. This piece, while not extremely difficult, will require four to five equally strong voice sections to be performed well.

Voice-Leading Difficulties
On several occasions Paulus has voices leaping to dissonant chords. For inexperienced singers, this can be a difficult task. Point out the situation to your singers, and then go between the two chords a number of times until they feel confident. Often, in an effort to ensure that they sing the correct note, students will sing too loudly. For this type of harmony to be most effective, one will need to carefully balance the chord too. This can be a time-consuming process, but if the director is patient it can be remedied.

Issues of Vocal Range
The majority of the piece is in a moderate range. However, the tenors will need to be able to sing an A and the low basses a low D. While the high A is brief and can be negotiated with care, the low D is not optional and is sustained for several measures. It will take at least two singers with solid low D to make this effective.

Harmonic Language
The majority of this piece is firmly in E-flat major. However, the transition and key change in the coda will take some time for your students. There are eleven measures (mm. 55–66) will need to be worked on over several rehearsals. I would recommend dealing with these eleven measures separately first. Rehearse these measures slowly out of context. Once the coda is learned, work on the connecting material a number of times until all singers feel confident. Take the necessary time to make this section comfortable before putting it with the main musical material.

Stylistic Considerations

In performing this type of art piece, the conductor should take note to use a forward, rich male chorus sound. If the tone is too covered, the harmony for male voices, especially in this low tessitura, can become muddy. Balance each of the suspensions carefully, and pay particular attention to all of the ninth chords. As is the case with all male choir music there are overtone possibilities if the choir sings in tune and with vowel unity. Work to make this piece sparkle with overtones and color chords.

Form and Structure

Section	Measure	Event and Scoring
Introduction	1–6; 28–33	Six measures (3 + 3)
A	7–12; 34–54	Twenty-one measures (6 + 4 + 5 + 6)
Coda	55–66	Twelve measures [5 + 7 (2 + 5)]
Extro	67–73	Seven measures (3 + 4)

Text

Shall I compare thee to a summer's day?
Thou art more lovely and more temperate:
Rough winds do shake the darling buds of May,
And summer's lease hath all too short a date:
Sometime too hot the eye of heaven shines
And often is his gold complexion dimmed;
And every fair from fair sometimes declines,
By chance, or nature's changing course, untrimmed;
But thy eternal summer shall not fade,
Nor lose possession of that fair thou ow'st,
Nor shall Death brag thou wander'st in his shade,
When in eternal line to time thou grow'st:
So long as men can breathe, or eyes can see,
So long lives this, and this gives life to thee.
—Sonnet 18

Sonnet 18 is one on Shakespeare's best known sonnets. It is impossible to know for whom this sonnet was composed or even the date of its composition. David Bevington, in his book *The Complete Works of Shakespeare*, comments on the sonnets:

> Shakespeare seemed to have cared more about his reputation as a lyric poet than as a dramatist. He contributed to the major nondramatic genres of his day: to amatory Ovidian narrative in *Venus and Adonis*, to the Complaint in *The Rape of Lucrece*, to the philosophical poetry in "Phoenix and the Turtle." … To write poetry in this vein was more fashionable than to write plays, which one did mainly for money. (p. 1612)

Bevington gives a few textual definitions for this sonnet that will help you and your students relate to it more quickly.

LINE	WORD	SUGGESTED MEANING
4	lease	allotted time
	date	duration
5	eye	sun
7	fair from fair	beautiful thing from beauty
8	untrimmed	stripped of ornament and beauty
10	fair thou ow'st	beauty you own
12	line	i.e., of poetry
	To . . . grow'st	you become incorporated into time, engrafted upon it
14	this	i.e., this sonnet

Additional References and Resources

Bevington, David. *The Complete Works of Shakespeare.* 4th ed. New York: HarperCollins Publishers, 1992.

Web site:

Stephen Paulus: www.stephenpaulus.com

Contributed by:

Brandon Johnson

Level Five

Mixed voices:

Treble voices:

Men's voices:

Teacher Resource Guide

Dieu! qu'il la fait bon regarder From Trois Chansons de Charles d'Orleans

Claude Debussy

(1862–1918)

SATB a cappella
Durand: DF 7179 (France); Theodore Presser Company: 362-03316 (USA)
Overall: 5
Vocal: 4
Tonal/Rhythm: 5

Composer

Claude Debussy was born in St. Germain-en-Laye in 1862. One of the most important musicians of his time, his harmonic innovations had a profound influence on generations of composers. His first piano teacher was the Italian musician Jean Cerutti. Antoinette Mauté prepared Debussy for entrance to the Paris Conservatoire, to which he was admitted in 1872. His first Conservatoire teachers were Antoine Marmontel for piano and Albert Lavignac for solfege. They quickly recognized that he had a good ear and was an able sight-reader, although they thought that he had an unorthodox approach to the fundamentals of music.

In 1875–77, he won minor prizes for solfege and for piano, but, having failed to win a *premier prix* for piano, he was forced to give up the idea of a career as a virtuoso; he enrolled in Emile Durand's harmony class, then in August Bazille's accompaniment class, in which he won his only *premier prix*.

In 1880 he enrolled in Ernest Guiraud's composition class, supporting himself by working as accompanist in the singing classes of Victorine Moreau-Sainti. He was runner-up for the Prix de Rome in 1883, with his cantata *Le gladiateur*; by that time his works already included more than thirty *mélodies*, two *scènes lyriques*, choruses, a cello suite, and a symphony (scored only for piano four hands). He became accompanist for the Concordia choral society, where Charles Gounod took him under his wing. In 1884 his cantata *L'enfant prodigue* won him the Prix de Rome.

The elements from which Debussy gradually built up his personal style were, of course, many. Though he spent a dozen years at the Conservatoire, he instinctively picked up only what seemed to suit his natural bent; he explained to a journalist from the *New York Times* in 1910 that as a student he had striven to compose as he was expected to, adopting a more personal style for the works he wrote outside the Conservatoire. At the Conservatoire he acquired a knowledge of the traditional musical canon, including works by Bach, Mozart, Beethoven, Schumann, and Weber, and to this he added an acquaintance with the choral works of Handel, Liszt, and Gounod, which he accompanied for the rehearsals of the Concordia choral society, and with the earlier repertoire by Palestrina, Lassus, and Victoria, which he heard in Rome and at St. Gervais in Paris.

The Russian influence on Debussy was the most obvious one to his contemporaries. He was greatly struck by Tchaikovsky, but even more by Balakirev, Rimsky-Korsakov and Borodin. Traces of their influence can be found in his youthful *mélodies* and the Russian concerts at the 1889 Exposition in Paris. He discovered Mussorgsky later, in the 1890s. In a more general way, it may have been from the Russians that Debussy acquired his taste for ancient and oriental modes and for vivid colorations as well as a certain disdain for academic rules.

Debussy knew nearly all Wagner's works long before he went to Bayreuth, but his Wagnerism reached its peak in 1887–88. It was at the precise moment when he first turned his back on Wagner that Debussy discovered the music of East Asia at the 1889 Exposition. For him the revelation was far removed from the attraction of the exotic or the picturesque that it was for many French composers and concerned essentially the use of musical scales obeying conventions other than those of the West. He listened spellbound to the "infinite arabesque" of the Javanese gamelan with its percussion—the Western equivalent of which he likened to the "barbaric din of a fairground"—and the counterpoint "beside which Palestrina's is child's play." He was equally fascinated by the Annamite theatre, which impressed him by its economy of means: "an angry little clarinet" and a tam-tam.

Debussy's inventions bear equally on harmony, rhythm, texture, and form and might be summarized as a lifelong quest to banish blatancy of musical expression. His harmony inseparably binds modality and tonality, although

French music never lost its variety of modes. Debussy extended and revitalized their range and tonal potential, developing the explorations of Chabrier and Russian composers and the different modal languages of Asian music. According to Maurice Emmanuel, Debussy claimed in 1889–90 that "music is neither major nor minor" and repelled even against the rule of equal temperament.

Once he was famous, the composer was receptive to the ideas spread by writers in favor of a return to the classics, which led him to extol the values of a national tradition. He chose to set poems by Charles d'Orléans among others. Debussy died in Paris in 1918.

Composition and Historical Perspective

The *Trois Chansons de Charles d'Orleans* pay homage to the national traditions of France and replicate the archaic style of the Renaissance chanson. Debussy emulates the techniques of impressionist painters and adapts them to fit his musical language. Most of Debussy's music is understated for an intimate effect, and this particular piece is a perfect example of this intimacy. According to Nick Strimple, "the richly detailed *Trois Chansons de Charles d'Orleans* (1898–1908) epitomizes the fluidity of rhythm and texture so typical of French impressionism, while retaining the directness of expression associated with its sixteenth-century models."

All his life Debussy was driven to search for something innovative in musical expression. He experimented with new sonorities, progressions, cadences, and tone colors because he found the traditional harmonic vocabulary unsatisfactory. Yet he had no clear direction or purpose in his experimental efforts. In listening to the discussions of the Impressionists and Symbolists, he suddenly realized that those people were articulating what he had instinctively felt for a long time: their ideas about poetry and visual art were applicable to music as well or at least to the kind of music Debussy wanted to compose.

Technical Considerations and Musical Elements

The harmonic language is not difficult but may be challenging until the piece is rehearsed enough to become familiar. The composer uses the modal signature for F-sharp Mixolydian, which may initially sound foreign to a moderately skilled choir. The rhythms only appear complex because several different patterns appear at the same time, such as duplets against triplets. The majority of the piece is homophonic with some voice parts ornamented using sixteenth note triplets. Tertian harmony (approached in an unorthodox manner) prevails throughout the work. Debussy basically uses traditional cadence patterns modified by inverting the sonorities or using added-tone technique to create ambiguity.

Like the Impressionist painters, who stressed not new realities but new perceptions of it, Debussy explained that this music's "unexpected charm" came not so much from the chords or timbres themselves, which already existed in the vocabularies of composers such as Chopin, Liszt, Grieg, Franck, Balakirev, Borodin, and Wagner, but from their misplacement or the rigorous choice of what precedes and what follows the chord.

Debussy gives the musical line a decorative function. He avoids conventional melodies by fragmenting themes into short motives, and he uses repetitive figurations resembling those of Liszt and the Russian Five. Quickly moving passages wherein overall direction and texture are more audible than individual notes and rhythms give the effect of quasi-improvisation. At other moments in his and other Impressionist music two kinds of line interact.

Stylistic Considerations

French is not the easiest language to sing because of the multitude of new phonemes and nasal vowels. There are several excellent books to assist directors not completely comfortable coaching pronunciation, and there is an abundance of exceptional recordings for this work to serve as guides to the French text. Avoid the guttural "r" sound of spoken French in singing for the simple reason that it is difficult to teach effectively and tends to slow the tempo down.

When programming this piece, plan to address Impressionistic and Symbolist art and to establish the connections between the visual aspects of these movements to Debussy's setting of the love poem. The composer specified as precisely as possible by way of notation what he desired in performance; however, by not dealing with stylistic elements that inspired him, a concert presentation of this work may be sterile.

Debussy rebelled against the traditional values of harmony, but he also rejected the modern application of equal temperament. With this in mind, do not rehearse this piece too much with piano. Rehearse the individual parts in sectionals with piano, but try as much as possible to not use the piano in full choir rehearsals. Tune each sonority based on the overtone series to minimize the tension inherent in equal temperament.

Choral musicians love to hate the topic of vibrato. The stylistic model of choral sound should be that of the sixteenth-century French chanson. Because of the deliberately controlled dissonances, this piece requires a minimized vibrato to make them shimmer.

Form and Structure

For Debussy, form was the result of a succession of colors and rhythms or, as Dukas put it, "a series of sensations rather than the deductions of a musical thought." Because of this, it is challenging to determine the form of the piece. Based on the way the composer sets the text, there are two larger sections and a coda. Each of the large sections begins with the first two lines of the text, and the coda only states the first line. The phrases are almost independent events that explore a different rhythmic interrelationship among the parts. At the end of each phrase, the level of dissonance is vastly different. In the first section, all the phrases end on major or minor triads or minor thirds, but in the second section, the final chords of the phrases are seventh chords in some inversion.

Section	Measure	Event and Scoring
1	1–13	Six phrases (3 + 2 + 2 + 2 + 2 + 2)
2	14–25	Six phrases (2 + 3 + 2 + 2 + 3 + 2)
Coda	26–29	Two phrases (2 + 2)

Text and Translation

Dieu! qu'il la fait bon regarder	God! What a vision she is
La gracieuse bonne et belle;	One imbued with grace, true and beautiful;
Pour les gran biens que sont en elle	For all the virtues that are hers
Chascun est prest de la loüer.	Everyone is quick to praise her.
Qui se pourroit d'elle lasser?	Who could tire of her?
Tousjours sa beauté renouvelle.	Her beauty constantly renews itself.
Dieu! qu'il la fait bon regarder	God! What a vision she is
La gracieuse bonne et belle!	One imbued with grace, true and beautiful;
Par de ça, ne de là, la mer	On neither side of the ocean
Nescay dame ne damoiselle	Do I know any girl or woman
Qui soit en tous bien parfais telle.	Who is in all virtues so perfect.
C'est ung songe que d'i penser:	It's a dream even to think of her.
Dieu! qu'il la fait bon regarder!	God! What a vision she is!

Additional References and Resources

Strimple, Nick. *Choral Music in the Twentieth Century*. Portland, OR: Amadeus Press, 2002.

Suggested Listening

Fauré: Requiem, etc, PHILIPS, 438149, Monteverdi Choir and Sabine Vatin, Sir John Eliot Gardiner, conducting.

Europäische Chormusik aus fünf Jahrhunderten. EMI Classics, 7243 5 65344 2 1, Rundfunkchor Stockholm and Stockholmer Kammerchor, Eric Ericson, conducting.

Contributed by:

G. Mikael Lindström

Teacher Resource Guide

The Choir Invisible

Ron Harris

(b. 1944)

SATB divisi or TTBB divisi
SATB, Woodland Music Press/Carl Fischer, LLC: A50218
TTBB, Woodland Music Press/Carl Fischer, LLC: A50215
Overall: 5
Vocal: 4
Tonal/Rhythm: 5

Composer

Composer Ron Harris was born in 1944 and grew up in Los Angeles, California. He earned a bachelor of music education degree with a concentration in choral music from the University of California–Los Angeles in 1966. While at UCLA, Harris was mentored by renowned music educator Salli Terri and received valuable performance experience as a studio singer, recording as a soloist and ensemble member for film and television. Upon graduation, Harris enlisted in the United States Armed Forces and spent three years in the United States Army Band and Chorus in Washington, DC. While serving, Harris composed his first significant work, "One Small Step," commemorating the Apollo 11 moon landing of 1969. The Mormon Tabernacle Choir and the Philadelphia Symphony later recorded the work on Columbia Records.

After serving with the U.S. Army Band and Chorus, Harris returned to Los Angeles, where he freelanced as a professional choral singer with such groups as the Roger Wagner Chorale, the Gregg Smith Singers, and the Fred Waring Pennsylvanians. In 1976 Harris was appointed music director for Broadway legend Carol Lawrence, conducting symphony orchestras, the

Tonight Show Band, and various other studio ensembles as they traveled together. Meanwhile, Harris began to pursue composition more seriously, focusing his energies on gospel and a related genre he calls "inspirational music." He is perhaps most well-known for the work "In This Very Room."

Currently, Harris composes and manages his own publishing company, Woodland Music Press. "The Choir Invisible" was published in 1995 by Harris's company and is distributed by Carl Fischer. It is also available in a version for TTTTBBBB chorus.

Composition and Historical Context

"The Choir Invisible" was composed in the early 1990s as a gift for Ron Harris's dear friend Allen Crowell, his former commanding officer and conductor of the Westminster Singers at Westminster Choir College in Princeton, New Jersey. The work was first performed at the Plymouth Church of the Pilgrims in Brooklyn, New York, in 1995 by the Westminster Singers with Allen Crowell conducting and published that year.

Harris has several insights to share on his compositional process for the work:

> "The Choir Invisible" was one of my very first efforts at "serious" writing. I simply loved the words the very first time I read them. As the saying goes, they really resonated with me. I grew up singing in choirs, and I have many friends who did also. For them and for me, there is just something about the experience of singing in a choir that captures the best in humanity.
>
> [What I love about choral music is] the feeling of community; for one thing, everyone [works] together for a common goal. Often in a choir we reach levels of achievement that none of us individually could hope to achieve. And because so many of us are on the verge of being out of our league, there can often be a lot of kidding and teasing and other ways of releasing the tension that are really fun. Camaraderie is almost a natural by-product of singing in choirs. And sometimes, we even create art—a goal that would simply not be attainable for most of us alone. It's simply a great experience in many, many ways.
>
> With my orientation of seeing choral singing as one of the most positive and enriching experiences possible, it struck me as a truly wonderful idea to make use [of] the idea of a choir as a metaphor for the best qualities of our humanity.

Technical Considerations

Four challenges a choir may face and rehearsal remedies:

TUNING LATE TWENTIETH-CENTURY HARMONIES

- For extended tertian and added-note harmonies, reduce to a simpler triad then add color pitches.
- For parallel first inversion harmonies, practice identifying the root of the chord (i.e., by singing it louder or having the section with the root stand at the appropriate time) and tuning to the root.
- For third-related and other difficult chord changes, isolate the chords separately, audiate the change, and then execute.

TEXT DECLAMATION

This three-step process will help create natural text declamation:

- Have individual singers recite portions of the text.
- Recite the text collectively with exaggerated declamation (e.g., in-VIS-i-ble)
- Chant the text in rhythm on a unison pitch with exaggerated declamation.

FINDING TRUE LEGATO AND AVOIDING "NOTEINESS" CAUSED BY CONSTANT QUARTER NOTE PULSE

To achieve legato, have singers sing a subdivision of the pulse on a neutral syllable (sixteenth note subdivision on "loo"). Verbalize legato as a constant, uninterrupted flow of energy and air.

MAINTAINING TEMPO USING RUBATO

If singers are losing tempo, have them physicalize the pulse or a subdivision of it by tapping on the sternum with the index finger. Then open singers' ears to the inner pulse by singing with eyes closed.

Rehearse rubato by reciting text on unison pitch with appropriate acceleration or deceleration. Encourage watchful singing by liberal use of exaggeration.

Note: All of these techniques can be incorporated more generally into a warm-up period.

Stylistic Considerations

As this is a recently composed work, performance practice is only speculative. The score is a good source for most information. Dynamics, articulations, and tempo modifications are clearly indicated. Regarding the duration of phrase-ending pitches, I advise that notes followed by rests be held for the full written value as indicated in the score. Pronunciation for this text should be "high" American English, with open, round vowels. As the piece is dedicated to the Westminster Singers, one may assume that the "Westminster" sound is what Harris had in mind: a robust, colorful sound in all sections, not stripped of vibrato but with a natural, healthy production.

Musical Elements

Melody

This work is more textually and harmonically driven than melodically driven. However, when melodic moments occur the contour is often disjunct and nonlinear. For example, in the opening phrase of the work (mm. 1–3), the soprano line ascends more than an octave from a unison C, outlining an E minor arpeggio. In mm. 9 and 10, the basses take the melody as they outline a harmonic sequence of descending fourths. These melodic characteristics contribute to an expansive, sweeping effect, which helps to illustrate the philosophically challenging nature of the text. There are very few examples of melodic text painting as most descriptive words are depicted harmonically by the composer.

Harmony

For the most part, the harmonic language of this work is diatonic. However, Harris is liberal in his use of late twentieth-century vocabulary, including parallel first inversion chords, extended tertian harmonies, added notes, cluster chords, pedal tones, third relations, and quartal and quintal harmonies. He often uses these techniques to depict descriptive words in the text. One such example occurs in mm. 44–47 where the text reads, "Be the sweet presence of a good diffused and in diffusion ever more intense!" In mm. 44–45 Harris depicts "the sweet presence" in a reduced three-part treble texture by alternating between simple E minor and slightly dissonant added-note harmonies, C major (add 4) and F major (add 2). In m. 48, he departs from this to dramatically illustrate the word "intense." Without preparation, he moves from E minor (m. 46) to an F major ninth (m. 47, beat one) to a cluster chord outlining an A-flat major scale (m. 47, beat two), a whole tritone away from the E minor tonality of the preceding phrase. To energize the impact of this effect, Harris also doubles the leading-tone pitch in this A-flat tonality in the first soprano and second bass lines.

Rhythm

In this work, Harris approaches rhythm with the transcendent simplicity of a chorale. He makes a valid musical reference to the chorales of J. S. Bach with a near-constant quarter note pulse, homophonic texture, and a philosophical text. Like Bach, Harris employs these techniques to successfully make the music and its ideas accessible.

TEXTURE

"The Choir Invisible" is unaccompanied and is divided into eight vocal parts. The work is homophonic but uses imitation with reduced voicing and section solos with accompanying "oohs" to vary the textural landscape. There is a textual reason for these changes. Of the eight phrases in this work, only one is fully homophonic; "In thoughts sublime that pierce the night with stars, and with their mild persistence urge man's search for vaster issues." I believe that the composer depicts "sublime thoughts" and "vaster issues" with the textural depth of the full choir.

OTHER: DYNAMICS/ARTICULATION/TEMPO/RANGE

Dynamics: *piano* to *fortissimo*

Articulation: only tenuto indicated

Tempo: quarter note = 92, freely, some rubato indicated (most dramatic at m. 22)

Range: Soprano: C4–G-sharp5

Alto: F3–C5

Tenor: C3–F4

Bass: G2–C4 (F2 and optional C1 in bass 2)

Form and Structure

The structure of this work is tied to the text. The work can be divided into eight binary phrases of varying length, each of which corresponds to two feet of the poem. The piece is through-composed, although there is a partial return to the opening phrase in the last phrase of the work. This, of course, relates to the text as well, as both the first and last phrases use identical verbiage (phrase one: "O may I join the choir invisible"; phrase eight: "So shall I join the choir invisible").

MEASURE	EVENT AND SCORING
1–7	Homophonic opening from unison c, then staggered imitative entrances (soprano/alto then tenor/bass)
8–12	Bass section solo with accompanying "oohs," then soprano section solo with accompanying "oohs"
13–17	Homophonic opening from octave Gs, then soprano section solo with accompanying "oohs"
18–26	Only fully homophonic phrase
27–35	Homophonic opening, then staggered imitative entrances (soprano/alto then tenor/bass)
36–43	Only ternary phrase, first two divisions homophonic followed by soprano/alto duet with accompanying "oohs"
44–47	SSA section; trio then homophonic
48–56	Homophonic opening from unison C, then staggered imitative entrances (soprano/alto then tenor/bass)

Text

Ron Harris uses the opening and closing stanzas of this poem. The italicized portions are not included in the Harris setting.

O may I join the choir invisible
Of those immortal dead who live again
In minds made better by their presence; live
In pulses stirred to generosity,
In deeds of daring rectitude, in scorn
Of miserable aims that end with self,
In thoughts sublime that pierce the night like stars,
And with their mild persistence urge men's minds
To vaster issues.

So to live is heaven:
To make undying music in the world,
Breathing as beauteous order that controls
With growing sway the growing life of man.
So we inherit that sweet purity
For which we struggled, failed, and agonized
With widening retrospect that bred despair.
Rebellious flesh that would not be subdued,
A vicious parent shaming still its child,
Poor, anxious penitence is quick dissolved;
Its discords, quenched by meeting harmonies
Die in the large and charitable air;
And all our rarer, better, truer self,
That sobbed religiously in yearning song,
That watched to ease the burden of the world,
Laboriously tracing what must be,
And what may yet be better—saw rather
A worthier image for the sanctuary,
And shaped it forth before the multitude,
Divinely human, raising worship so
To higher reverence more mixed with love—
That better self shall live till human Time
Shall fold its eyelids, and the human sky
Be gathered like a scroll within the tomb
Unread forever.

This is life to come,
Which martyred men have made more glorious
For us who strive to follow.

May I reach
That purest heaven—be to other souls
The cup of strength in some great agony,
Enkindle generous ardor, feed pure love,
Beget the smiles that have no cruelty,
Be the sweet presence of a good diffused,
And in diffusion ever more intense,
So shall I join the choir invisible!
Whose music is the gladness of the world.
—George Eliot (1867)

Additional References and Resources

Harris, Ron. "The Choir Invisible." Personal e-mail (2005).

Suggested Listening

Ron Harris:
"The Choir Invisible" on *The Blue Estuaries: American Choral Music*, The Houston Chamber Choir, Robert Simpson, conductor, Zephyr Records B00005TS12.
"The Choir Invisible" on *Loving Again*, Golden Gate Men's Chorus, Joseph Jennings, conductor, www.ggmc.org, (TTTTBBBB version).

Contributed by:

Emilie Sweet

Teacher Resource Guide

Choral Hymns from the Rig Veda, Set 3

Gustav Holst

(1874–1934)

SSAA and piano or harp
E. C. Schirmer Music Company: 1.5091
Overall: 5
Vocal: 4
Tonal/Rhythm: 5

Composer

Gustav Holst was born in Cheltenham, England, the child of a German immigrant father. He studied composition in the 1890s with Charles Villiers Stanford, which makes him a part of the lineage of composers in the great English Revival stemming from the middle of the nineteenth century into the 1930s. Like many composers of his day, Holst was strongly influenced as a student by the harmonic language of Wagner, which is evident in his compositions. In 1919 he received the appointment of composition instructor at the Royal College of Music in London and was considered by his pupils to be a skilled teacher. Throughout his life, he maintained a close relationship (and friendly rivalry) with fellow English composer Ralph Vaughan Williams. Although famous for his orchestral suite *The Planets*, Holst also composed a large amount of choral music, including the four sets of *Choral Hymns from the Rig Veda*. Holst died in 1934 following a major operation for a stomach ulcer.

Composition and Historical Perspective

The *Choral Hymns from the Rig Veda* stem from Holst's interest in Hindu sacred literature, which began in 1895 when he was a student. They also relate to the interest in Eastern cultures evident in the works of Holst's older contemporaries Claude Debussy and Giacomo Puccini. Interestingly, he thought the English translations then available of the Rig Veda (the body of sacred writings central to Hindu religious beliefs) were awkward, so he learned Sanskrit himself so he could translate the works more accurately. The harmonic language of the third set for women's chorus is strongly reminiscent of that of Richard Wagner, Claude Debussy, and Gustav Mahler and of the late Romantic Era in general. All four sets were composed between 1908 and 1912.

Technical Considerations and Musical Elements

MOVEMENT I: HYMN TO THE DAWN

The first movement of this set of pieces opens with overlapping ascending vocal lines, a beautiful evocation of the rising sun. The voices continue in a polyphonic texture underpinned by a steady ostinato until m. 12. At this point, the vocal lines are in block homophony, *a cappella* except for one thirty-second note arpeggiated flourish in the accompaniment. This sixteen-measure section of music is then repeated twice more to different text each time. Holst is careful to mark that the second sopranos have the melody. Therefore, the director will need to think about vocal placement of the melody predominates.

Issues of harmony and tempo are most evident in this movement. The harmonic language in all four movements is very sophisticated and complex, including vertical sonorities formed by half step motion in the voice parts and quartal and secondal harmonies. In particular, the opening figure in the voices is difficult because the harmonies shift rapidly between the voice parts. The director should spend time devising creative vocalises for the choir that incorporate this rich harmonic language so that their ears become attuned to it. Although the tempo is not slow (quarter note = 66), the choir may have difficulty sustaining through the full value of the frequent half notes. The conductor should consider using count-singing in this movement so that the choir feels the subdivisions and sustains through the pitches with rhythmic accuracy.

The vocal lines in Movement I are mostly stepwise, but there are still some melodic challenges that the singers must overcome. Mm. 5–11 contain suspensions of different kinds, which will be tricky for the choir to hear at first. Also, there are two instances of voice crossing (mm. 6 and 11) between the first and second soprano parts. The director should make sure to allot a fair amount of rehearsal time to resolving these difficulties.

Movement II: Hymn to the Waters

This movement (marked *allegro* at dotted quarter note = 120) evokes flowing water. This image is reinforced by the rippling, arpeggiated thirty-second notes in the accompaniment that continue through most of the piece. The fast motion in the accompaniment in this movement is the reason why an extremely skilled harpist (or pianist) is necessary. The singers present the first of two main melodies in unison beginning in m. 3. The voices sing coloristic harmonies in m. 5, but otherwise repeat the same melody in unison in this first section. In m. 10, the choir presents the second main melody in unison. It contrasts the first melody with its prevalence of longer rhythmic values (quarter notes versus eighth notes). There is greater use of coloristic harmonies in the second section. In the third section of the movement, the key changes to A-flat major and both melodies are combined together, a small group singing the first melody and the main choir the second. The final section is a repeat of the first section.

One of the greatest difficulties in this movement is the shifting 21/8 and 7/4 meters (these notations appear alternatively throughout the movement). Holst notes that each measure is to be divided into two groups of four plus three beats. He creates further contrast between the two main melodies by organizing the grouping within the measures of the first melody as 4 + 3 and the grouping within the measures of the second as 3 + 4. Unless the singers are used to singing asymmetric meters, the long measures with the grouping separated by a dotted line will initially be confusing.

The director should get the singers habituated to the changes between 7/4 and 21/8. In particular, the singers will probably not sing the 21/8 (divided into triple subdivisions) with enough swing or lilt and will not perform the 7/4 (in duple subdivisions) with enough crispness. Count-singing can be effective to help the singers distinguish between the two meters. The conductor can also do much to reinforce this difference through changes in the quality in which the beat is delivered.

As with all of the movements, the singers will have some initial difficulties with the harmonic language. The shift in harmony between the first and second sections can be particularly problematic in that the first is organized primarily around D Dorian and the second around an E major. The director can save time in rehearsals by creating vocalises that accustom the singers to these shifts in key area. The shift to A-flat major in m. 17 could also be a problem, but the enharmonic notation of the chord in sharps should alleviate this to some extent.

Movement III: Hymn to Vena

This movement begins with chanting on a single pitch above broken eighth note patterns in the accompaniment. The impressionist harmonies formed in the accompaniment create the image of the mystery of the god Vena's arrival. Beginning in m. 7 the unison texture opens up into glorious four-part harmony. In m. 37 the tempo quickens with an *andante con moto* marking and accelerates to *allegro* following the text "With yearning heart, on thee we gaze, O gold wing'd messenger of mighty Gods." At m. 59, the original *adagio* marking returns, along a repetition of the choral chanting of the opening. Near the end of the movement, the tempo and the harmonic tension increase until a brilliant G major sonority is attained in m. 83 to cap off the piece.

The major difficulties in this exquisitely beautiful movement are the constant shifts of harmony and the modulations. In many cases, however, the harmonies are formed by horizontal motion by semitone. The choir should be more at ease with them once the director points this out. The change of key to B-flat major and then to C-flat major will have to be diligently rehearsed.

MOVEMENT IV: HYMN OF THE TRAVELERS

This movement is characterized by a repeating melody centered on a prominent rhythmic motive (a quarter note tied to four sixteenths) found in both the soprano and the alto parts. The melody is supported by an ostinato figure in the accompaniment reminiscent of walking. As with the second movement, difficulties may arise due to the asymmetric meter (in this case, 5/4, with shifting groups of 3 + 2 and 2 + 3) and some of the modal harmonies. However, this movement is somewhat more straightforward than the other three in terms of harmonic language.

Stylistic Considerations

MOVEMENT II

It is of critical importance that the tempo remain steady so that the sensation of flowing water is maintained. The choir will have a tendency to drag in the 21/8 meter because (for good reason) they will want to sing legato through each phrase. In the 21/8 sections the singers should be instructed instead to *diminuendo* on longer note values (quarter notes and dotted quarter notes) so that the proper buoyancy and lilt are achieved.

MOVEMENT III

The opening choral chant may have a tendency to become choppy because the singers have a repeated pitch. Also, the pitch may flat slightly for the same reason. To keep a steady pitch and a vibrant tone, the director should instruct the choir to follow the natural inflections of the words. This way, the choral chant will develop a suppleness and flexibility of phrasing.

MOVEMENT IV

As in Movement II the maintenance of tempo is crucial. One way to keep the tempo moving is to ask the singers to clip the tied sixteenths following the quarter notes in the main melody. This will make the singers aware of the exact rhythmic values in this passage and prevent them from singing too long on the tied note, which may cause the tempo to slow down.

Form and Structure

SECTION	MEASURE	EVENT AND SCORING
Movement I		Structured in three verses with interludes in the accompaniment
Movement II	3–9	Melody 1
	10–17	Melody 2
	18–25	Combination of melodies 1 and 2
	26–33	Repetition of first section
Movement III		In large ABA´ form
Movement IV		Organized in four verses (mm. 1–37) with a codetta (mm. 38–44)

Text

MOVEMENT I: HYMN TO THE DAWN

Hear our hymn, O Goddess,
Rich in wealth and wisdom,
Ever young yet ancient,
True to Law Eternal.

Wak'ner of the songbirds,
Ensign of th'Eternal,
Draw thou near O Fair One,
In thy radiant Chariot.

Bring to her your off'ring,
Humbly bow before her,
Raise your songs of welcome,
As she comes in splendour.

MOVEMENT II: HYMN TO THE WATERS

Flowing from the firmament forth to the ocean,
Healing all in earth and air, never halting.
Indra, Lord of Heav'n formed their courses,
Indra's mighty laws can never be broken.
Cleansing waters flow ye on, hasten and help us.

Lo, in the waters dwelleth One,
Knower of all in earth and sea,
Whose dread command no man may shun,
Varuna, soveran Lord is He.

Onward ye waters, onward hie,
Dance in the bright beams of the sun,
Obey the ruler of the sky who dug the path for you to run.

Movement III: Hymn to Vena

Vena comes, born of light,
He drives the many colour'd clouds onward.
Here, where the sunlight and the waters mingle
Our songs float up and caress the newborn infant.
Vena comes.

The child of cloud and mist appeareth on the ridge of the sky,
He shines on the summit of creation,
The hosts proclaim the glory of our Common Father.
Vena comes.

He hath come to the bosom of his beloved.
Smiling on him,
She heareth him in highest heav'n.
With yearning heart
On thee we gaze,
O gold wing'd messenger of mighty Gods.

Wise men see him in their libations
As the sacrifice mounts to the eternal heights,
Mingling with out solemn chant.
He stands erect in highest heav'n,
Clad in noble raiment,
Armed with shining weapons,
Hurling light to the farthest region,
Rejoicing in his radiant splendour.

Movement IV: Hymn of the Travelers

Go thou on before us, guide us on our way, Mighty One.
Make our journey pleasant, never let us stray.
Wonder-worker, hearken, come in thy splendour,
Come in thy mighty pow'r.

Trample on the wicked, all who would oppose, Mighty One.
Drive away the robber, drive away our foes,
Wonder-worker, hearken, come in thy splendour,
Come in thy mighty pow'r.

As we journey onward, songs to Thee we raise, Mighty One.
Thou didst aid our fathers, guard us all our days.
Wonder-worker, hearken, come in thy splendour,
Come in thy mighty pow'r.

Feed us and inspire us, keep us in thy care, Mighty One.
Lead us past pursuers, unto meadows fair,
Wonder-worker, hearken, come in thy splendour,
Come in thy mighty pow'r.

Suggested Listening

Gustav Holst, *Choral Hymns from the Rig Veda* (complete) from *Choral Dances from Gloriana,* the Holst Singers and Orchestra, Hilary Davan Wetton, Hyperion B00005NUPJ.

Contributed by:

Christopher Jackson

Teacher Resource Guide

Dúlamán

Michael McGlynn
(b. 1964)

TTB a cappella
Hinshaw Music: HMB232
Overall: 5
Vocal: 5
Tonal/Rhythm: 5

Composer

Irishman Michael McGlynn was born in Dublin in 1964. In 1987 he founded the Irish choir Anúna and, along with his brother John McGlynn, continues to lead and compose for that group to this day. Although the ten albums recorded by Anúna contain mostly vocal music by McGlynn, his compositional output includes many works for various instrumental groups.

An accomplished solo singer specializing in early music performance, McGlynn has also been involved in collaborative projects with such artists as Elvis Costello, country music artists Rodney Crowell and Delbert McClinton, and oboist Matthew Manning. He has also has served as musical director and composer for several musical theater productions, including Chekhov's *Three Sisters*, premiered at the Gate Theater in Dublin. Of his own music, McGlynn writes:

> My greatest source of inspiration has been in traditional and medieval music. I've always been fascinated by modality and ornamentation. The harmonic language I use is largely tonal and varies from lush vocal sounds to sparse one- and two-part pieces. Many of the pieces I've

written integrate techniques originating in folk music with contemporary techniques.

Composition and Historical Perspective

Written in 1995, Dúlamán incorporates an ancient Irish text set to newly composed music in Dúlamán. McGlynn says of the piece:

> In Ireland, the people who lived along the west coast often had to farm on stony land. One of the solutions to this problem was the spreading of seaweed on the land, which rotted, and was then used as soil. The text of "Dúlamán" would have been written as a work song that was sung, like the Waulking Songs of Scotland, with a cantor and an answer from the assembled company as they gathered the weed. Seaweed was also eaten (and still is) in Ireland, and most likely this text would have been sung in that context too.

"Dúlamán" was first performed and recorded by Anúna but has subsequently been performed and recorded by numerous groups, most famously by the American group Chanticleer, which included the piece on their album *Wondrous Love*, as well as in their *Silver Jubilee Anthology of Choral Music*, which includes a phonetic pronunciation guide as well as a line-by-line translation by the composer. A complete pronunciation guide as well as an audio file that demonstrates the text can be downloaded from the composer's Web site. Incidentally, the score itself can be downloaded as well; McGlynn publishes most of his own music on that Web site.

Technical Considerations and Musical Elements

The most challenging aspect of "Dúlamán" is arguably the pronunciation. Most American choirs are not well versed in ancient Irish, and the tempo marking of "fast and very rhythmically," dotted quarter note = 115 makes it difficult to spit out the words without a significant amount of rehearsal. It is fortunate that the piece is only two minutes long, allowing for frequent repetitions. It is suggested that the conductor spend as much time as is needed to be able to demonstrate the proper pronunciation for the choir without mistakes. Employing a call-and-response method between conductor and choir in short sections of the phrases, beginning quite slowly and gradually increasing the speed up to performance tempo, should be effective. Incorporating the rhythm of music itself during this process will aid in the eventual mastery of the piece.

Of nearly equal difficulty are the intensely rhythmic compositional aspects of the music itself. Not counting repeats, there are no fewer than forty-nine meter changes in the sixty-one measures of the piece, and in general these involve asymmetrical time signatures such as 7/8, 5/8, 10/8, and 11/8. Naturally this makes "Dúlamán" almost more difficult to conduct than it is to sing. If possible, it might be more effective to have the ensemble perform without a conductor, especially if the group is relatively small. Fortunately, there are numerous repetitions of rhythmic patterns, allowing the choir to unify the patterns. Unfortunately, the melodic material that accompanies those patterns changes several times throughout the piece, although the text remains constant. As a result, memorization might present more difficulties than imagined.

Melodically the piece is quite simple and repetitive. In addition, the ranges for the voices (tenor, baritone, and bass with tenor soloist or soloists), are easily sung by any age group and also allow for a performance by a small ensemble; "Dúlamán" could even be performed with as few as three singers (although breathing would present a serious problem as there is no divisi in the choral parts and the tenor soloist never sings concurrently with the choir). The tenor part ranges from D3 to F-sharp4, the baritone from A2 to A3, the bass from A2 to E3, and the solo from E3 to D4.

Written in D major, most of "Dúlamán" occurs in what could be considered the Dorian mode (with an emphasis on the notes E and B), although in the choral refrain a C-natural is notated to complete the phrase. A preponderance of open intervals (fifths and fourths) could possibly present tuning problems. The conductor should spend the necessary time when teaching the piece to allow for this potential problem by employing the following technique:

1. Teach each melodic line of the chorus individually.
2. Combine two parts at a time, (e.g., tenor and baritone, baritone and bass, bass and tenor) slowly enough to begin so that all intervals can be tuned correctly, both horizontally and vertically.
3. Combine all three parts, once again beginning at a slow tempo. It is also suggested that leaving out the rhythm and focusing on only the harmony might be appropriate. Try singing each note for the duration of a quarter note (at quarter note = 60), and then add in the correct rhythm, once again beginning with a reduced tempo.
4. If necessary, removing the text and singing on a neutral syllable might be appropriate for the previous steps. After correct intonation is achieved, the text can be added and step three repeated, beginning with slow, even quarter notes and then adding the correct rhythm and gradually increasing the tempo to performance speed.

Stylistic Considerations

Since "Dúlamán" was conceived in the style of a work song, special attention should be paid to the declamation of the text in an intensely rhythmic manner. It is suggested that the conductor familiarize him- or herself with the performance style by listening to various recordings.

Text and Translation

Dúlamán na binne buí, dúlamán Gaelach,	Seaweed of the yellow peaks, Gaelic seaweed.
Dúlamán na farraige, dúlamán Gaelach,	Seaweed of the ocean, Gaelic seaweed.
"A 'níon mhín ó! Sin anall na fir shuirí."	"O gentle daughter, here come the wooing men."
"A mháthair mhín ó! Cuir na roithleán go dtí mé!"	"O gentle mother, put the wheels in motion for me."
Rachaidh me chun 'lúir leis a' dúlamán Gaelach.	I would go to the tailor with the Gaelic seaweed.
"Ceannódh bróga daor'," arsa' dúlamán Gaelach.	"I would buy expensive shoes," said the Gaelic seaweed.
Bróga breátha dubha ar a' dúlamán Gaelach.	The Gaelic seaweed has beautiful black shoes.
Bairéad agus triús ar a' dúlamán Gaelach.	The Gaelic seaweed has a beret and trousers.
Tá ceann buí óir ar a' dúlamán Gaelach.	There is a yellow gold head on the Gaelic seaweed.
Tá dhá chluaid mhaol' ar a' dúlamán Maorach.	There are two blunt ears on the stately seaweed.

A complete pronunciation guide can be found on Michael McGlynn's Web site along with an audio file demonstrating pronunciation.

Suggested Listening

Michael McGlynn, "Dúlamán" on *Wondrous Love*, Chanticleer, Teldec/Warner Classics International.

Contributed by:

David Scholz

Teacher Resource Guide

Varjele, Jumala, soasta (God, Protect Us from War)

Veljo Tormis
(b. 1930)

TTBB
Boosey & Hawkes: 48016259
Overall: 5
Vocal: 5
Tonal/Rhythm: 5

Composer

Veljo Tormis is a leading Estonian composer. His works are part of a strong tradition of choral singing in Estonia. He studied organ at the Tallinn Conservatory in 1949, but the Soviet authorities terminated the class. He instead began to study composition with Villem Kapp. By the late 1960s, Tormis was a celebrated composer with choral works comprising a large part of his output. His music is often based on Estonian folk songs, though he composes in a modern style, making frequent use of varied repetition.

Composition

This work for male choir and tam-tam (a kind of suspended gong) is a setting of a portion of the Kanteletar, an important collection of Finnish folk poetry that is a companion work to the Kalevala, the Finnish national epic. The text is offered in Finnish with a Latin translation.

Historical Perspective

Estonia has a long tradition of choral singing, which can be traced back to the early days of the nineteenth-century when the German oriented church established schools in Estonia with singing as an important part of the curriculum. This led to the growth of well-trained parish choirs, small orchestras, and brass bands. More important, the suppression of political freedoms by first the Germans and then the Russians made choral singing an essential component of national identity and patriotic pride. The first Estonian song festival drew more than a thousand singers and established itself as an important social and patriotic event. The festival has been held every five years from 1869 to the present day.

The advent of the twentieth century saw the first Estonian graduates of the St. Petersburg Conservatory. In 1918 Estonia gained its independence, and in 1919 the Tallinn Conservatory was established. Estonia fell under Russian rule in the aftermath of World War II but became independent again in 1991.

Tormis is interested in modern compositional practices, though he is still strongly rooted in the choral tradition of his country and the folk singing tradition of its people. This particular work, though not based on Estonian poetry, draws a strong parallel between the nationalist spirit of the Finnish folk poetry and that of the Estonian folk song.

Technical Considerations

The work is almost entirely in 5/4, and the first half is rhythmically straightforward, built from recurring patterns of eighth notes and quarter notes. There is syncopation in the bass part in m. 41, but the real rhythmic challenge begins in m. 54 where measures of 5/8 are filled with unusual syncopated groupings of sixteenth notes. The piece is largely homophonic; where it is not, it is divided between two clearly delineated rhythmic strata.

There are no real low notes in the work, though the baritone rises to a high E-flat, and there is a high A for the first tenor. Long sections are sung at very soft dynamics, and the dynamic range of the work is enormous.

The work does not establish a clearly defined tonality and is rife with difficult chromaticism. There are many major and minor seconds sounded between the parts, though they frequently arise due to the movement of a melody line against a static pedal tone in a recurring pattern, making the chromaticism only moderately difficult for most of the piece.

At m. 70, sudden harmonic shifts pass through distant keys by way of strangely spelled major triads. The harmonic distance between the triads and the unusual spelling may pose some difficulty.

A tam-tam player is required to perform this work.

Stylistic Considerations

This is a modern work, alternating between flowing stepwise phrases and sections of rhythmic tone clusters evenly accented. The work is essentially dramatic, starting with a long, hushed opening, building to a strong climax between mm. 53–70, arriving on a section of triple *forte* at m. 70, and then receding from that dynamic for the remainder of the piece.

Musical Elements

This work does not establish a strong sense of tonality. One might argue that the piece revolves around the tonal center of A and that there is strong minor coloration, but the pedal tone throughout the entire first section is B. The note A emerges as a bass note in m. 41; the climax at m. 70 revolves around first an A major chord (misspelled) and then an E major chord, also misspelled. Low A reappears as a bass note in m. 83. Chords, when they appear, are largely clusters until m. 70, when they are almost all misspelled major triads. There is strong, sustained dissonance at many dynamic levels. There are no conventional cadences.

The texture is either homophonic or in two clearly marked rhythmic strata. The work is extremely repetitive, with frequently repeating phrase blocks in varied textures. Melodies are almost all stepwise. The meter shifts several times, though almost always to 5/4, 5/8, or 5/2.

Form and Structure

The work opens with the first line of text in the basses. A related gesture on "aa" from the tenors appears in m. 5. Both ideas appear together at m. 9. The opening bass gesture recurs, with or without the tenor "aa," through to m. 39 where the tenors sing the bass melody and the basses appropriate the textless tenor part. In m. 41 a new rhythmic idea appears in the basses, strongly accented sixteenth notes with a sense of syncopation. This continues at a very soft dynamic with the tenors singing the opening melody against the new idea in the bass parts until m. 53.

After a measure of 3/4, the rhythmic idea from the previous measures appears in all the voices, now laid over 5/8 measures. The dynamic slowly grows as rhythmic chord clusters steadily rise in pitch. After another measure of 3/4 at m. 64, the opening gesture returns in a thicker harmonization and at a very high dynamic level. The *crescendo* continues through to m. 70.

M. 70 marks the climax with the entrance of a very strong string of distantly related major triads sung on "aa." These triads are actually simply a harmonization of the opening melody, which is here in the first tenor and second bass. This pattern is repeated, with variation, for several measures as the dynamic level falls. In m. 75 the opening gesture returns again, this time against a sustained E major triad.

The work closes at a low volume with the opening melody slowly dying away and then replaced by the rhythmic motive at a very low volume and on a tone cluster with A in the bass.

Text and Translation

Kanteletar II: 323, 326

Varjele, vakainen Luoja, *Kaitse, kaunoinen Jumala*	Shelter us, Almighty God, Protect us, fair God
Kavioista vainovarsain, *Sokista sotahevosten,*	From the feud-foal's hoofs, From the cloven feet of the war horse,
Rauan valkian varasta, *Terän tuiman tutkaimesta,*	From the cutting iron, From the blunt point of the sword,
Tykin suuren suun e'estä, *Rautakirnujen kiasta,*	From the mouth of a gun, From long rifles,
Suurilta sotakeoilta, *Uron tappotanterilta,*	From wide battlefields, From grounds of manslaughter,
Varjele vahingon teiltä, *Kaitse kaikista pahoista!*	Shelter us from roads of harm, Protect us from all evil!
Varjele, vakainen Luoja, *Kaitse, kaunoinen Jumala!*	Shelter us, Almighty God, Protect us, fair God!

Suggested Listening

Cantus (Collegium), *Against the Dying of the Light*, Cantus.

Contributed by:

Thomas Cunningham

Index by Title for Teaching Music through Performance in Choir Volumes 1, 2

Index by Publisher for Teaching Music through Performance in Choir Volumes 1, 2*

*For updated publisher information, see www.TeachingMusic.org.

Index by Composer and Arranger for Teaching Music through Performance in Choir Volume 2

Index by Title for Teaching Music through Performance in Choir Volume 2

About the Editors

Heather J. Buchanan is director of choral activities at the John J. Cali School of Music at Montclair State University, New Jersey, where she conducts the 144-voice Chorale and 48-voice auditioned University Singers and teaches choral methods and Body Mapping. Prior to her position at Montclair, she was on the conducting faculty at Westminster Choir College of Rider University. A certified Andover Educator, Buchanan specializes in the teaching of Body Mapping and somatic pedagogy for musicians and is a PhD candidate with the University of New England (Australia) researching the impact of Body Mapping on student musicians. She is also a certified Johrei Reike practitioner.

Australian born, Buchanan earned a bachelor of music from the Queensland Conservatorium of Music (Australia) and a master of music degree with distinction from Westminster with a double major in choral conducting and music education. Her publications include coediting and compiling the GIA *Teaching Music through Performance in Choir* series, the Video-DVD *Evoking Sound: Body Mapping Principles and Basic Conducting Techniques*, and several GIA choral octavos coedited with Matthew Mehaffey. A vibrant musician and dynamic pedagogue, Buchanan is in demand as a guest conductor, clinician, and adjudicator in the U.S. and her native Australia. Recent performance highlights include preparing the Montclair State University Chorale for performances of Beethoven's Symphony No. 9 with the New Jersey Symphony Orchestra under the baton of Maestro Neeme Järvi, completing a ten-day Central European tour culminating in a performance at the Ferenc Liszt Zeneakadémia in Budapest, conducting the World Premiere performances of *Madison's Descent* by celebrated Irish composer Mícheál ÓSúílleabháin, conducting the inaugural Australian National Seniors' Choral Festival in Newcastle, Australia, and performing with renowned American composer Merideth Monk and Company in her first college choir collaboration, a historical first for the University Singers and Monk.

Matthew W. Mehaffey is assistant professor of music and the associate director of choral activities at the University of Minnesota, where he conducts the Concert Choir and the Men's Chorus and teaches graduate courses in choral conducting and literature. A native of Pittsburgh, Pennsylvania, he holds degrees from Bucknell University (bachelor of music in music education), Westminster Choir College (master of music in choral conducting) and the University of Arizona (DMA in choral conducting and historical musicology). He has also completed additional study in conducting in Switzerland and Canada. Mehaffey has studied conducting with Bruce Chamberlain, Joseph Flummerfelt, Volker Hempfling, James Jordan, and William Payn.

As a conductor, Mehaffey has prepared choirs for the concert hall, the opera house, and for radio and television programs. Recent engagements include collaborations with Washington National Opera, St. Paul Chamber Orchestra, Turner Network Television, Vocalessence, and Air America Radio. He remains active as a guest conductor throughout the country; he recently conducted honor choirs in Pennsylvania, Maryland, Virginia, North Dakota, and Minnesota.

In addition to his work with the *Teaching Music through Performance in Choir* series, he has coauthored the GIA Publications series *Choral Ensemble Intonation: Method, Procedures, and Exercises* with James Jordan of Westminster Choir College. This series provides conductors with an innovative method for attacking the problem of choral intonation.

He lives with his wife and daughter in downtown Minneapolis, Minnesota.